A HISTORY

OF

THE CHURCH

FROM

𝕿𝖍𝖊 𝕰𝖆𝖗𝖑𝖎𝖊𝖘𝖙 𝕬𝖌𝖊𝖘

TO

THE REFORMATION.

BY

THE REV. GEORGE WADDINGTON,

Vicar of Masham, and Prebendary of Chichester.

PUBLISHED UNDER THE SUPERINTENDENCE OF THE SOCIETY FOR THE
DIFFUSION OF USEFUL KNOWLEDGE.

SECOND EDITION, REVISED:

IN THREE VOLUMES.

VOL. II.

LONDON: BALDWIN AND CRADOCK,

PATERNOSTER-ROW.

1835.

LONDON:
Printed by W. Clowes and Sons,
Stamford Street.

CONTENTS

OF

THE SECOND VOLUME.

CHAPTER XIV.—*On the Government, Character, and Projects of the Church during the Ninth and Tenth Centuries.*

The subject divided under three heads. (I.) *On the independency of papal election.* The original law—when first violated and why—Otho the Great—Contest respecting imperial confirmation—Resolution established by Nicholas II. virtually successful—General observations. (II.) *The encroachments of the Church on the State.* Origin and progress of spiritual jurisdiction—its perpetual collision with the temporal authority—this confusion further augmented by the establishment of the feudal system—Union of ecclesiastical and civil dignities—The system of vassalage introduced the military character of the Clergy—The judgments of God exercised under ecclesiastical superintendence — The intellectual superiority of the Clergy — Property of the Church liable to spoliation by the Laity—The penance performed by Louis the Meek—The deposition of Wamba, King of the Visigoths in Spain—Differences between Charles the Bald and Louis of Bavaria—Council of Aix-la-Chapelle—Dispute between Charles and Pope Nicholas—between Charles and Adrian II.—The king protected by Hincmar of Rheims—Contest between Hincmar and Louis III., and strong expressions of the prelate—The imperial crown conferred by the Pope upon Charles the Bald—Dispute between Robert of France and Gregory V. (III.) *Usurpations of the See within the Church.* Gradual transfer of the metropolitan privileges to the See of Rome—Forgery of the false Decretals—Dispute between Pope Gregory IV. and the French Bishops—The double triumph obtained by Nicholas I. over Hincmar of Rheims—The Council of Troyes under John VIII.—henceforward the pallium was to be received from Rome—The character of Hincmar—Decrease of the system of appeal to Rome—Pope's Vicars—Exemptions of monasteries became more common towards the end of the ninth age—Two other objects of papal ambition—Reflections—The fable of the female Pope, p. 1.

CHAPTER XV.—*On the Opinions, Literature, Discipline, and External Fortunes of the Church.*

(I.) On the Eucharist. Original opinions of the Church—Doctrine of Paschasius Radbert combated by Ratramn and John Scotus—Conclusion of the Controversy—Predestination—Opinions and Persecution of Gotteschalchus—Millennarianism in the Tenth Century—its strange and general effect. (II.) Literature. Rabanus Maurus, John Scotus, Alfred—its progress among the Saracens — Spain — South of Italy— France — Rome— Pope Sylvester II. (III.) Discipline of the Church. Conduct of Charlemagne and his Successors —St. Benedict of Aniane—Institution of Canons regular—Episcopal election

a 2

—Translations of Bishops prohibited—Pope Stephen VI.—Claudius Bishop of Turin—Penitential system. (IV.) Conversion of the North of Europe—of Denmark, Sweden, Russia—of Poland and Hungary—how accomplished and to what extent—The Normans—The Turks, p. 32.

CHAPTER XVI.—*The Life of Gregory VII.*

SECTION I.

Pope Leo IX.—Early History of Hildebrand—Succession of Victor II.—of Stephen IX.—of Nicholas II.—his measure respecting Papal Election—the College of Cardinals—imperfection of that measure—subsequent and final regulation—Inconveniences of popular Suffrages—Restriction of the imperial Right of Confirmation—Homage of Robert Guiscard and the Normans—Dissensions on the death of Nicholas—Succession of Alexander II.—actual Supremacy of Hildebrand—Measures taken during that Pontificate—Alexander is succeeded by Hildebrand, under the title of Gregory VII., p. 59.

SECTION II.—THE PONTIFICATE OF GREGORY VII.

Gregory's First Council—its two objects—to prevent (1.) Marriage or Concubinage of the Clergy—(2.) Simoniacal Sale of Benefices—On the Celibacy of the Clergy—why encouraged by Popes—Leo IX.—Severity and consequence of Gregory's Edict—Original method of appointment to Benefices—Usurpations of Princes—how abused—the question of Investiture—explained—Pretext for Royal Encroachments—Original form of Consecration by the King and Crown—Right usurped by Otho—State of the Question at the Accession of Gregory—Conduct of Henry—further measures of the Pope—Indifference of Henry—Summoned before a Council at Rome—Council of Worms—Excommunication of the Emperor and Absolution of his Subjects from their Allegiance—Consequence of this Edict—Dissensions in Germany—how suspended—Henry does Penance at Canossa—restored to the Communion of the Church—again takes the field—Rodolphus declared Emperor —Gregory's Neutrality—Remarks on the course of Gregory's measure—Universality of his temporal Claims—his probable project—Considerations in excuse of his Schemes—partial admission of his Claims—Ground on which he founded them—power to bind and to loose—Means by which he supported them—Excommunication—Interdict—Legates à Latere—Alliance with Matilda—his Norman allies—German Rebels—internal Administration—Effect of his rigorous Measures of Reform—his grand scheme of Supremacy within the Church—False Decretals—Power conferred by them on the Pope—brought into action by Gregory—Appeals to the Pope—generally encouraged and practised—their pernicious Effects — Gregory's *double* Scheme of Universal Dominion—Return to Narrative—Clement III., Antipope—Death of Rodolphus — Henry twice repulsed from before Rome — finally succeeds — his Coronation by Clement—the Normans restore Gregory—he follows them to Salerno and there dies—his historical importance—his Character—Public —his grand principle in the Administration of the Church—Private—as to Morality—as to Religion, p. 67.

SECTION III.

(I.) Controversy respecting Transubstantiation — suspended in the Ninth, renewed in the Eleventh Century—Character of Berenger — Council of

Leo IX.—of Victor II. at Tours in 1054—Condemnation and Conduct of Berenger—Council of Nicholas II. repeated Retraction and Relapse of Berenger—Alexander II.—Council at Rome under Gregory VII.—Extent of the Concession then required from Berenger—further Requisition of the Bishops—a second Council assembled—Conduct of Gregory—Berenger again solemnly assents to the Catholic Doctrine, and again returns to his own—his old Age, Remorse, and Death—Remarks on his Conduct—on the Moderation of Gregory. (II.) Latin Liturgy—Gradual disuse of the Latin Language throughout Europe—Adoption of the Gothic Missal in Spain—Alfonso proposes to substitute the Roman—Decision by the Judgment of God—by Combat—by Fire—doubtful result—Final adoption of the Latin Liturgy—its introduction among the Bohemians by Gregory—Motives of the Popes—other instances of Services not performed in the Vulgar Tongue—Usage of the early Christian Church, p. 91.

PART IV.

FROM THE DEATH OF GREGORY VII. TO THAT OF BONIFACE VIII.

Chapter XVII.—*From Gregory VII. to Innocent III.*

(I.) Papal history—Urban II.—Council of Placentia—that of Clermont—their principal acts—The Crusades—their origin and possible advantage—Pascal II. —Renewed disputes with Henry—his misfortunes, private and public—his death and exhumation—Henry, his son, marches to Rome—Convention with Pascal respecting the regalia—its violation—Imprisonment of the Pope—his concessions—annulled by subsequent Council—Henry again at Rome—Death and character of Pascal—Final arrangement of the Investiture questioned by Calixtus II.—Observations—The first Lateran (ninth General) Council—Death of Calixtus—Subsequent confusion and its causes—Arnold of Brescia —his opinions, fate, and character—Adrian IV.—Frederick Barbarossa—Disputes between them, and final success of the Pope—Alexander III.—his quarrel with Frederick, and advantages—his talents and merits—Celestine III.—The differences between Rome and the Empire—The internal dissensions at Rome on papal election—National contentions between Church and State. (II.) Education and theological learning—Review of preceding ages—In Italy and France—Parochial schools—Deficiency in the material—Papyrus—Parchment—Consequent scarcity of MSS.—Invention of Paper—Three periods of Theological Literature—the characteristics of each—Gradual improvement in the eleventh century, p. 101.

Chapter XVIII.—*The Pontificate of Innocent III.*

[From 1198 to 1216.]

Prefatory facts and observations—Circumstances under which Innocent ascended the chair—Collection of Canons—Condition of the Clergy—Ecclesiastical jurisdiction—by what means extended—Innocent's four leading objects—(1.) To establish and enlarge his temporal power in the city and ecclesiastical states. Office of the Prefect—Favourable circumstances, of which Innocent avails himself—his work completed by Nicholas IV.—(2.) To establish the universal pre-eminence of papal over royal authority. His claims to the empire—His dispute with Philippe Auguste of France—he places the kingdom under interdict—submission of Philippe—His general assertions on supremacy—particular applications of them—to England and France, Navarre, Wallachia and Bulgaria, Arragon and Armenia—His contest with John of England—Interdict—the Legate Pandulph—Humiliation of the King—(3.) To extend his authority within the church. Italian clergy in England—his general success in influencing the priesthood—Power of the episcopal order—The fourth Lateran council. Canons on transubstantiation—on private confession—against all heretics—(4.) To extinguish heresy. The Petrobrussians—their author and tenets. Various other sects, how resisted. The Cathari—supposition of Mosheim and Gibbon—the more probable opinion. The Waldenses—their history and character—error of Mosheim—Peter Waldus—his persecution. The Albigeois or Albigenses—their residence and opinions—attacked by Innocent—St. Dominic—Title of inquisitor—Raymond of Toulouse—holy war preached against them—Simon de Montfort—resistance and massacre of the heretics—Continued persecution of the Albigeois—Death of Innocent—Remarks on his policy, p. 152.

CHAPTER XIX.—*The History of Monachism.*

(I.) *Origin of Monachism.* Early instance of the monastic spirit in the East—Pliny the philosopher—The Therapeutæ or Essenes—The Ascetics—their real character and origin—The earliest Christian hermits—dated from the Decian or Diocletian persecutions—Cœnobites—Pachomius and St. Anthony—originated in Ægypt—account of the monks of Ægypt—Basilius of Cæsara—his order and rule—his institution of a vow questionable—Monasteries encouraged by the fathers of the fourth and fifteenth ages—from what motives—Vow of celibacy—Restrictions of admission into monastic order—Original monks were laymen—Comparative fanaticism of the East and West—Severity of discipline in the West—motives and inducements to it—contrasted with the Oriental practice—Establishment of nunneries in the East. (II.) *Institution of Monachism in the West.* St. Athanasius—Martin of Tours—Most ancient rule of the Western monasteries—their probable paucity and poverty—Benedict of Nursia—his order, and reasonable rule, and object—Foundation of Monte Cassino—France—St. Columban—Ravages of the Lombards and Danes—Reform by Benedict of Aniane—The order of Cluni—its origin, rise, and reputation—its attachment to papacy and its prosperity—The order of Citeaux—date of its foundation—Dependent abbey of Clairvaux—St. Bernard—its progress and decline—Order of the Chartreux. (III.) *Canons regular and secular.* Order of St. Augustine—Rule of Chrodegangus—Rule of Aix-la-Chapelle—subsequent reforms. (IV.) Connexion between the monasteries and the pope—mutual services. *The Military orders.* (1.) The Knights of the Hospital—origin of their institution—their discipline and character—(2.) Knights Templars—their origin and object—(3.) The Teutonic order—its establishment and prosperity. (V.) *The Mendicant orders.* Causes of their

rise and great progress—(1.) St. Dominic—his exertions and designs—
(2.) St. Francis and his followers—compared with the Dominicans—apparent
assimilation—essential differences—disputes of the Franciscans with the popes,
and among themselves—Inquisitorial office of the Dominicans, their learning
and influence—quarrels with the Doctors of Paris—Austerity of the Franciscans—the Fratricilli—(3.) The Carmelites—their professed origin—(4.) Hermits of St. Augustine—Privileges of these four orders. (VI.) *Various establishments of Nuns.* Their usual offices and character—General remarks—The
three grand orders of the Western Church (suited to the ages in which they
severally appeared and flourished)—The Jesuits—The monastic system one
of perpetual reformation—thus alone it survived so long—its merits and advantages—The bodily labour of the monks—their charitable and hospitable
offices — real piety to be found among them—superintendence of education, and means of learning preserved by them—limits to their utility—
their frequent alliance with superstition—their early dependence on the
bishops—gradual exemption, and final subjection to the pope—Their profits
and opulence, and means of amassing it—Luther a mendicant, p. 195.

Chapter XX.—*History of the Popes, from the Death of Innocent III. to that of Boniface VIII.*

The ardour of the Popes for Crusades—its motives and policy—Honorius III.—
Frederic's vow to take the Cross, and procrastination—Gregory IX.—his
Coronation—he excommunicates the Emperor—who thus departs for Palestine
—Gregory impedes his success, and invades his dominions—their subsequent
disputes—Innocent IV.—his previous friendship with Frederic—Council of
Lyons—various charges urged against Frederic—Innocent deposes Frederic
and appoints his successor on his own papal authority—Civil war in Germany
—in Italy—death of Frederic—his character and conduct—his rigorous decree against Heretics—Observations—Other reasons alleged to justify his
disposition—this dispute compared with that between Gregory VII. and Henry
—Taxes levied by the Pope on the Clergy—Crusade against the Emperor—
Exaltation of Innocent—his visit to Italy and intrigues—his death—his qualities as a statesman—as a churchman—expression of the Sultan of Egypt—
Alexander IV.—Urban IV.—Clement IV.—Introduction of Charles d'Anjou
to the throne of Naples—Gregory X.—his piety, and other merits—Second
Council of Lyons—Vain preparations for another Crusade—Death of Gregory
—Objects of Nicholas II.—Martin IV.—Senator of Rome—Nicholas IV. dili-
gent against Heresy—Pietro di Morone or Celestine V.—circumstances of his
elevation—his previous life and habits—his singular incapacity—disaffection
among the higher clergy—his discontent and meditations—his resignation—
Boniface VIII.—his excessive ambition and insolence—on the decline of the
papal power—his temporal pretensions—Sardinia, Corsica, Scotland, Hungary
—Recognition of Albert, king of the Romans—and act of his submission—
Philip the Fair—the Gallician Church—origin of its liberties—Differences
between Boniface and Philip—Bull *Clericis Laicos*—its substance and subsequent interpretation—Affairs of the bishop of Parme—Bull *Ausculta Fili*—
burnt by Philip—Conduct of the French nobles—of the Clergy—of Boniface—
Bull *Unam Sanctam*—other violent proceedings—Moderation of Philip—fur-

ther insolence of the Pope—Philip's appeal to a General Council—William
of Nogaret—Personal assault on Boniface—his behaviour, and the circumstances of his death, p. 278.

CHAPTER XXI.

(I.) *On Louis IX. of France.* His public motives—contrasted with those of Constantine and Charlemagne—His virtues, piety, and charity—Particulars of his
civil legislation—His superstition—The original Crown of Thorns—its removal to Paris—its reception by the king—his death—His miracles and canonization—the Bull of Boniface VIII.—(II.) *On the Inquisition.* Whether
St. Louis contributed to its establishment—Origin of the Inquisition—Office
of St. Dominic and his contemporaries—Erection of a separate tribunal at
Toulouse—by Gregory IX.—The authority then vested in the Mendicants—
its unpopularity in France—Co-operation of St. Louis—Conduct of Frederic II.—of Innocent IV.—Limits to the prevalence of the Inquisition.—
(III.) *On the Gallician Liberties.* Remonstrance of the Prelates of France
respecting excommunications—firmness of Louis—his visit to the Cistercian
chapter—The supplication of the monks, and the reply of the King—Early
spirit and sense of independence in the French clergy—the Pragmatic Sanction of St. Louis—its principle—The six articles which constitute it—Consequences of the policy of Innocent III.—(IV.) *On the Crusades.* Remarks on
the character and circumstances of the first Crusade—Exertions of St. Bernard for the second Crusade—its fatal result—Excuse of that abbot—Causes
of the fall of the Latin kingdom of Jerusalem—Third, fourth, fifth, sixth, and
seventh Crusades—The eighth and ninth—St. Louis—Termination of the Crusades, and final loss of Palestine—General remarks—(1.) On the *Origin* and first
motives of religious pilgrimage—Treatment of first pilgrims by the Saracens—
Pilgrimage during the tenth and eleventh centuries—Conquest of Palestine
by the Turks—Practice of private feuds and warfare in Europe—prevalent in
the tenth century—The superstitious spirit of the same age—associated with
the military—General predisposition in favour of a Crusade—Failure of Sylvester II. and Gregory VII.—(2.) On the *Objects* of the Crusades—what they
were—what they were not—The object of the first distinguished from that of
following Crusades—Conduct and policy of the sovereigns of Europe—of the
Vatican—Gradual change in its objects.—(3.) On the *Results* of the Crusades
—Advantages produced by them—Few and partial—on government—on commerce—on general civilization—Evils occasioned—Religious wars—Immoral
influence—Corruption of church discipline—Canonical penance—Introduction of the Plenary Indulgence—its abuses—The Jubilee—Interests of the
clergy. *Note* (A.) On the collections of Papal Decretals—That of Gratian
—the Liber Sextus—Clementines, &c. *Note* (B.) On the University of
Paris—The Four Faculties—Foundation of the Sorbonne. *Note* (C.) On
certain theological writers—Rise and progress of the scholastic system of
theology—Peter the Lombard—His " Book of the Sentences"—St. Thomas
Aquinas—His history and productions—St. Bonaventura—the character of his
theology—The Realists and Nominalists, or Thomists and Scotists—The Immaculate Conception, p. 321.

HISTORY OF THE CHURCH.

CHAPTER XIV.

On the Government, Character and Projects of the Church during the Ninth and Tenth Centuries.

THAT we may avoid the confusion usually attending the compression of a long series of incidents, we shall here endeavour to distinguish the points which chiefly claim our notice, rather than follow chronologically the course of events; and though it may not be possible, nor even desirable, to prevent the occasional encroachments of subjects in some respects similar, yet in others very different, we shall not allow them to perplex our narrative. It is an obscure and melancholy region into which we now enter; but it is not altogether destitute of interest and instruction, since we can discern, through the ambiguous twilight, those misshapen masses and disorderly elements, out of which the fabric of Papal despotism presently arose, and even trace the irregular progress of that stupendous structure.

We shall best attain this end by giving a separate consideration to three subjects, which will be found to include the whole ecclesiastical policy of the ninth and tenth centuries. Other matters relating to that period, and possessing perhaps even greater general importance, will be treated in the next chapter; but at present we shall confine our inquiry to the following objects:—1. The endeavours of the popes to free their own election from imperial interference of every description, whether to nominate or confirm. II. The efforts of the Church to usurp dominion over the Western empire; and generally to advance the spiritual, as loftier and more legitimate than the highest temporal, authority. III. The exertions of the See of Rome to subdue to itself the ecclesiastical body, and thus to

establish a despotism *within* the Church.   In the two first of
these objects we may regard the Church as waging for the
most part an external warfare; the last occasioned her intestine
or domestic struggles: and the examination of them will necessarily lead to some mention of the peculiarities introduced by
the feudal system; of its influence on the manners, morals, and
property of the clergy.

Original
practice of
papal elec-
tion.

I. *On the independency of Papal election.*   The original
law and practice in this matter had passed, with some variations but little lasting alteration, through the succession both
of the Greek and barbarian sovereigns of Rome, from the time
of Constantine to that of Charlemagne; and that prince also
transmitted it unchanged to his posterity.   It was this,—that
the pope should be elected by the priests, nobles, and people of
Rome, but that he should not be consecrated without the consent of the emperor.   This arrangement was found, for above
eight centuries, to be consistent with the dignity of the Roman
Bishop; and it was not till his spiritual pride had been inflated
by temporal power, that it was discovered to be *doubly* objectionable—it was no longer to be endured, either that laymen
should interfere in the election of the pope, or the emperor in
his consecration.   Both these restraints became offensive to the
lofty principles of ecclesiastical independence; but the latter
was that which it was first attempted to remove.

Charlemagne was succeeded by his son Louis, commonly
called the Meek, a feeble and superstitious monarch; and of
these defects both Stephen V.* and Pascal I. so far availed
themselves, as to exercise the pontifical functions without awaiting his confirmation.   But when Eugene II. would have followed their example, Lothaire, who was associated in the
empire, complained of the usurpation, and resumed the imperial right.   Louis died in 840, and was succeeded on the
throne of France by Charles the Bald.

That prince reigned for thirty-seven years with scarcely
greater vigour than his predecessor; but his reign is on several
accounts important in the history of Popery, and chiefly on the

---

* Generally called Stephen IV.   See Baron. ann. 816. s. 96.

following. Two years before his death the imperial throne became vacant. Charles was ambitious to possess it : he went to Rome, accepted it at the hands of John VIII.; and then, that he might make a worthy return for this office, he released *Cession of* the see from the necessity of imperial consent to the consecra- *the impe-* *rial right.* tion of its bishop. The claims, which were derived by subse- *875, A. D.* quent popes from John's assumed donation of the empire, will be mentioned hereafter, and it will appear on how slight a ground they rested; but the interference of the emperor in papal elections was on this occasion directly and unequivocally withdrawn.

Neither the interests nor the honour of the see gained any thing by its independence. From that time (the event took place in 875) till 960, the most disgraceful confusion prevailed in the elections, and clearly proved that the restraint hereto-fore imposed by civil superintendence had been salutary; and if the emperors during that stormy period did not reclaim their former right, we should rather attribute the neglect to their weakness, than to their acknowledged cession of it. For in the *Its resump-* year 960, Otho the Great, on the invitation of John XII., re- *tion by* *Otho the* sumed the imperial authority in Italy, and exercised, as long *Great. 960,* as he lived, the most arbitrary discretion in the election, and *A. D.* even appointment, of the pontiff. He presently degraded John, and substituted in his place Leo VIII.; and under that pope (or anti-pope—for it is disputed) a Lateran council* was held in 964, which conferred on Otho and all his successors not merely the kingdom of Italy, but the regulation of the holy see and the arbitrary election of its bishops. And for the guidance of their successors, Otho left an edict, prohibiting the election of any pope without the *previous*† knowledge and consent of the emperor, which was enforced during the next eighty years by all who possessed the power to do so. But in the century following, in the year 1047, we observe that the same right was once more *conceded* to an emperor, Henry III.; and on this occasion an artful distinction was drawn by the Italians, which led, no doubt, to the ultimate independence of election : the

---

* Giannone, Stor. Nap., lib. viii., cap. vi.   † Mosheim, Cent. x., p. ii., c. ii.

privilege of nominating the pope was granted to Henry *personally**, not to the throne.

Subsequent changes.   This important advantage was followed almost immediately by another of still greater consequence. Nicholas II., under the direction of Hildebrand, found means to restore the original principle of election, modified as follows: the right of appointment was vested in the college of cardinals, with the consent of the people, and the approbation of the emperor. But the last-mentioned restriction was expressly understood to extend only to the emperor of the time being, and to such of his successors as should personally obtain the privilege. This grand measure was accomplished in a council held at Rome in 1059, fourteen years before the accession of Gregory VII.; and so the matter rested, when he took possession of the chair.

We observe from this short account, that after an interrupted struggle of two hundred and fifty years, an absolute independence of election was not yet confessedly effected. The contest had fluctuated very considerably; the first advantages were entirely on the side of the pope; in fact, at the death of Charles the Bald, the victory seemed perfectly secure: and the century which followed was so clouded by the mutual dissensions of the princes; it was marked by such positive weakness in their states, such vices in their personal character and internal administration, as to be in the highest degree favourable to the confirmation and extension of papal privileges. Why then was it that the privilege in question was not at the time extended, nor even permanently confirmed? Why was it even that the next interference of the emperor took place at the solicitation of a pope? Chiefly because the removal of imperial superintendence had thrown the election entirely into the hands of an unprincipled nobility†, an intriguing clergy, and a venal popu-

---

* He had occasion to exert it three times. See chap. xvi.

† From the deposition of the last Carlovingian king to the reign of Otho the Great, (a space of nearly fifty years,) the authority of the princes who held the imperial title was always vacillating and contested. In the mean time the city of Rome was no part of the kingdom of Italy, but depended on the imperial crown only; so that during the vacancy of the empire it recovered its independence, and thus fell under the turbulent oligarchy of its own nobles. These provided the candidates for the pontifical throne; and whosoever among them succeeded in

lace, whose united fraud and violence usually favoured the most flagitious candidate, and promoted his success by means the most shameful. And, therefore, through this lawless period we read of popes tumultuously chosen and hastily deposed; hurried from the monastery to the chair, from the chair to prison or to death. Their reigns were usually short and wasted in fruitless endeavours to prolong them; their sacred duties were forgotten or despised, and their personal characters were even more detestable than those of the princes their contemporaries. Further, we may observe, that when the Church began to recover from the delirium of the tenth century—when one great man did at length arise within it, Hildebrand, the future Gregory, his influence was immediately exerted, not only against imperial interferenee to confirm, but against popular license to elect: for he had learnt from long and late experience, that no scheme for the universal extension of papal authority could be made effective, until the popes themselves were secured from the capricious insolence of a domestic tyrant. If things had not been thus—if papal elections had been regularly and conscientiously conducted when the civil governments of Europe were at the lowest point of contentious and stupid imbecility—the era of pontifical despotism would have been anticipated by nearly three centuries, and the empire of opinion would have been more oppressive and more lasting, as the age was more deeply immersed in ignorance and barbarism.

II. We proceed to examine the encroachments of the Church

obtaining it, secured, by means of the church revenues, a great preponderance over all the others, and became as it were the chiefs of the republic. (See Sismondi, Repub. Ital. chap. iii.; to whose work we are compelled to refer the reader for the few facts which are ascertained respecting the revolutions of the Roman Government during this period.) For the further degradation of the Roman See the influence of female arts and charms was triumphantly exerted. "Jamais les femmes n'eurent autant do crédit sur aucun gouvernement que celles de Rome en obtinrent, dans le dixième siècle, sur celui de leur patrie. Or auroit dit que la beauté avoit succédé a tous les droits de l'empire." The names and scandals of Theodora and Marozia are distinguished in the ecclesiastical annals of the tenth century. In the rapid succession of popes, those most marked by disgrace or misfortune may have been Leo V., John X., John XI., John XII., Benedict VI., John XIV.; but to pursue the details of their history would be alike painful and unprofitable: for their crimes would teach us no lessons, and even their sufferings would scarcely raise our compassion.

Encroach-
ments of
ecclesiasti-
cal on civil
authority.

upon the State during the same period; and this part of our subject might again be subdivided under three heads—the general usurpations of the See of Rome on *any* temporal rights— the usurpations of national councils of bishops on the civil authorities—and the usurpations of the episcopal office on that of the secular magistrate. But, not to perplex this matter by an attempt at exceeding minuteness, we shall in this instance rather follow the course of events, and illustrate them with such

Spiritual
jurisdic-
tion.

observations as they may appear severally to demand. The first edict which permitted legal jurisdiction to the episcopal order, and supported its decisions by civil authority, sowed the seeds of that confusion, which afterwards involved and nearly obliterated the limits of temporal and spiritual power. There is scarcely any crime which an ingenious casuist might not construe into an offence against religion, and subject to ecclesiastical cognizance, in a rude and illiterate age; while, on the other hand, the best defined and most certain rights of an unarmed and dependent authority were liable to continual outrage, either from a sovereign possessing no fixed principles of government, or from a lawless aristocracy more powerful than the sovereign.

In the Eastern empire, indeed, this evil was in a great degree neutralized by the decided and unvarying supremacy of the civil power, nor was it immediately felt even in the West; at least we read little or nothing about the usurpation of the clergy, until after the death of Charlemagne. The popes, it is true, had displayed, from a very early period, great anxiety to enlarge their authority; but the efforts of Leo and even of Gregory were confined to the acquisition of some privilege from their own metropolitans, or some title or province from their rival at Constantinople. The dream of universal empire seems at no time to have warmed the imagination of those more moderate pontiffs. It is not that we may not occasionally discover both in the writings and in the conduct of the prelates of earlier days an abundance of spiritual zeal, ever ready to overflow its just bounds, and gain somewhat upon the secular empire. The latter, too, found its occasions to retort; but we may remark, that while its operations were generally violent and interrupted, those of the clergy were more systematic and continuous. In the mean time the distinction between the two parties was becoming wider, and their differences were approaching near to dissension, before, and even during, the reign of Charlemagne: howbeit, the vigorous grasp of that monarch so firmly wielded the double sceptre, that the rent which was beginning to divide it* was barely perceptible, when it fell from his hand; but scarcely had it begun to tremble with the feeble touch of Louis his son, when its ill-cemented materials exhibited a wide and irreparable incoherence.

The extraordinary change which had taken place in the institutions of the Western Empire during the two preceding, and which was progressive during the two present centuries, greatly increased both to church and state the facility of mutual encroachment. Until the permanent settlement of the northern nations generally introduced the feudal system of government, the Clergy, though enjoying great immunities and ample possessions, yet, as they lived under absolute rule, had little real, and no independent power, excepting such as indirectly accrued to them through their influence. If they had lands, no jurisdiction was necessarily annexed to them; they had no place in legislative assemblies; they had no control, as a body, in the direction of the state.

The devout spirit of the Barbarians presently increased the

---

* In the "Capitularies of Interrogations" proposed by Charlemagne, three years before his death,—" First," (he says,) "I will separate the bishops, the abbots, and the secular nobles, and speak to them in private. I will ask them why they are not willing to assist each other, whether at home or in the camp, when the interests of their country demand it? Whence come those frequent complaints which I hear, either concerning their property or the vassals which pass from the one to the other? In what the ecclesiastics impede the service of the laity, the laity that of the ecclesiastics? To what extent a bishop or abbot ought to interfere in secular affairs; or a count or other layman in ecclesiastical matters," &c. (Fleury, H. Eccl., l. xiv. sect. 51. Guizot, Hist. Mod., leçon 21.) Soon afterwards, in 826, the council of Paris, after proposing some very extravagant episcopal claims, observes, as one great obstacle to harmony, that the princes have long mixed too much in ecclesiastical matters, and that the clergy, whether through avarice or ignorance, take unbecoming interest in secular matters. Again, at the Synod of Aix-la-Chapelle (in 836) all the evils of the time are expressly attributed to the mutual encroachments of the spiritual and secular powers.

Union of
ecclesiasti-
cal and civil
dignities.

extent of their landed possessions, without withholding from them any of the rights which, according to their system, were inseparable from land; and thus they entered upon temporal jurisdiction co-extensive with their estates. By these means the Episcopal Courts became possessed of a double jurisdiction —over the Clergy and Laity of their diocese for the cognizance of crimes against the ecclesiastical law, and over the vassals of their barony as lords paramount—and these two departments they frequently so far confounded as to use the spiritual weapon of excommunication to enforce the judgments of both*. In the next place the Clergy became an order *in the state,* and thus entered into the enjoyment of privileges entirely unconnected with their religious character. Yet the necessary effect of the union of ecclesiastical with secular dignities was to blend two powers in the same person almost undistinguishably; and to confound, by indiscriminate use, the prerogatives of the bishop with those of the baron. Again, the bishops being once esta- blished as feudal lords, had great advantages in increasing their possessions, owing to the influence which necessarily devolved on them, not only from their greater virtues and knowledge, but also from the command of ecclesiastical authority. And as the vassals of the Church grew gradually to be better secured from oppression and outrage than those of the lay nobility, its pro- tection was more courted and its patrimonial domain more amply extended.

System of
vassalage.

At the first establishment of the system, vassalage to an ecclesiastic conferred exemption from military service; but, among rude and warlike nations, when the greater force was generally the better law, this privilege could not possibly be of long duration. It was withdrawn universally, at different times,

---

* This subject is treated clearly, though shortly, by Burke, in his Abridg- ment of English History. Mosheim, who ascribes the secular encroachments of the Bishops to their acquisition of secular titles, denies that such titles were conferred on them before the tenth age. Louis Thomassin (De Disciplin. Eccles. Vet. et Nova) endeavours to trace the practice to the ninth and even to the eighth century. Whatever may be the fact respecting the titles, the jurisdiction cer- tainly gained great ground during the ninth age; more, perhaps, through the superstition of the people, and the weakness of the princes, than by its own legi- timacy.

by different princes, according to their power or their necessities. The Church fiefdoms thus assumed a very different appearance, and the spirituality of the sacred character became still further corrupted ; for, as soon as the vassals became military, it was found difficult to hold them in subjection to an unarmed lord, and the Clergy were, in many instances, obliged to descend from their peaceful condition, assume the sword and helmet, and conduct their subjects into battle: in many instances they did so without any such obligation. The practice crept, without the same excuse, and of course with much less frequency, into the Greek Church. In the year 713 a Subdeacon commanded the troops of Naples; and the Admiral of the Emperor's fleet was a Deacon. But the low ecclesiastical rank which these officers held would prove, if it were necessary, that they did not take the field as feudal lords. In the West the abuse appears to have commenced soon after the admission of barbarians to the clerical order ; which, if we are to judge by names, scarcely took place before the seventh century. This direct dereliction of the pastoral character by the clergy, became the immediate means of securing their property* and increasing their power; but, notwithstanding the contempt to which the peaceful virtues are occasionally exposed among rude and military nations, it is probable that they lost thereby as much in influence as they gained in power.

Again, the strange and irrational method of Trials, which Judgments even now came generally into use, must have tended, by the of God. intermixture of superstition, to enlarge the dominion of ecclesiastical influence. The ordinary proofs by fire, by water, by hot iron, indicate some imposture, perhaps only practicable by the more informed craft of the clergy. The proofs of the Cross and the Eucharist bear more obvious marks of sacerdotal superintendence. Even the trial by duel, which seems the farthest removed from priestly interference, was preceded by

---

* In the address (already mentioned) which was presented on this subject to Charlemagne by his people, it is remarkable that the petitioners felt it necessary to offer a solemn assurance, that their motives for disarming the Clergy was not (as might, it seems, have been suspected) a design to plunder their property. We may add, that the indecent violation of the sacerdotal character is a reason which seems to have been overlooked by both parties.

some religious forms; great precautions were taken to prevent the arms from being enchanted; and in case of any injustice, a miracle was constantly expected to remedy it. The clergy disgraced themselves by upholding such abuses of their judicial authority, and they divide that disgrace with the kings and the civil magistrates of the time; but they had not the crime of introducing them. They received and executed them as they were handed down from a remote and blind antiquity; and it is but justice to add that they made frequent attempts to abolish them *.

Intellectual superiority of the Clergy.

Moreover, through the free spirit which formed the only merit of the feudal system, the affairs of the state were more or less regulated by public assemblies, and the higher ranks of the clergy found a place in these. Thus, again, were they placed in contact with the great temporal interests of their country, and invited to examine and direct them; and no doubt their feudal temporalities, as well as their spiritual influence, added weight and authority to their counsel. But, besides these, which some might overbear and others might affect to despise, their political consideration was derived from another—a more honourable and a more certain instrument of power—their intellectual superiority. The learning of the age continued still to be confined to their order†; few among the laity could even read, and therefore few were qualified for any public duty; and thus the various offices requiring any degree of literature fell necessarily into the hands of the clergy. Those who consider

* A council held at Attigni, probably in 822, under Louis the Meek, especially prohibited the Trial by the Cross; according to which, the two parties stood up before a cross, and whichever of them fell first lost his cause. Again, at the Council of Worms (in 829), these judgments were strongly discouraged. Agobard, Archbishop of Lyons, an influential prelate, had written expressly against them. The Council of Valence, held in 855, published the following canon. " Duels shall not be suffered, though authorized by custom. He who shall have slain his adversary shall be subject to the penance of homicide; he who shall have been slain, shall be deprived of the prayers and sepulture of the Church. The Emperor shall be prayed to abolish that abuse by public ordinance." See Fleury, l. xlvi., s. 48. l. xlvii., s. 30. l. xlix., s. 25.

† In many of the councils held during the ninth century, canons were enacted enjoining the Bishop to suspend a Priest for ignorance, and to promote and regulate the schools which were established for the education of the clergy.

their advance to such offices as usurpations do not sufficiently weigh the circumstances of the times ; they do not reflect that there are moral as well as physical necessities, and that a state of society is not even possible, in which the only persons at all qualified to fill the offices of the state should be the only persons excluded from them.   It is far from our intention to advocate any general departure from the spiritual character in the sacred orders; and the divines of the ninth and tenth centuries would undoubtedly have been great gainers both in virtue and in happiness, had they preserved that character pure and uncontaminated.   But it was made impossible, by the political system under which they lived, that it could be so ; and without seeking any excuse for the individual misconduct of thousands among them, we cannot avoid perceiving that their interference in temporal affairs, to a certain extent, was absolutely unavoidable—and where and by whom, in those unsettled ages, were the limits of that interference to be drawn and preserved ?

If the clergy were in many respects gainers by the imperfection of civil government, it would be partial to conceal that they were sufferers by it also.   In times of confusion (and those days were seldom tranquil) the property of the Church was the constant object of cupidity and invasion*.   On such occasions no inconsiderable portion of its revenues passed into the hands of lay impropriators, who employed curates at the

Spoliations of Church property.

---

* The councils of the ninth century abound with complaints of the spoliation of Church property by laymen, who are frequently specified ; and new Capitularies were continually enacted to prevent or allay differences betwen the Clergy and the laity.   The confusion generally prevalent is proved by the capitularies published at Quercy (in 857), by which every diocesan is exhorted to preach against pillage and violence, as well as by the Letters of Hincmar published in 859, and that of the Bishops of France to King Louis, attributed to the same prelate.   The frequency too of personal assaults on the Clergy is evinced by various regulations for their protection, and even more so, perhaps, by the slight punishment attached to such offences.   Some promulgated in France (probably in 822) ordain as follows—" the murderer of a Deacon or Priest is condemned to a penance of twelve years and a fine of 900 sous ; the murderer of a Bishop is to abstain from flesh and wine for the whole of his life, to quit the profession of arms, and abstain from marriage." Yet the confirmation of this canon was thought highly important by the episcopal order.   Fleury, l. xlvi., s. 48 ; l. xlix., s. 40.

cheapest rate*. And both Bishops and Monasteries were obliged to invest powerful lay protectors, under the name of Advocates, with considerable fiefs, as the price of their protection against depredators. But those advocates became themselves too often the spoilers, and oppressed the helpless ecclesiastics for whose defence they had been engaged.

We have thought it right, though at the risk of some repetition, to premise this general view of the relative situation of the clergy and laity during the period which we are describing; otherwise it would be difficult to form any just and impartial views, or even any very definite notions, of the real character of the events which are contained in it.

Penance of Louis the Meek.

In the civil war which took place in the year 833 between Louis the Meek† and his sons, Pope Gregory IV. presented himself in France at the camp of the rebels. The motive which he pretended was to reconcile the combatants and terminate a dissension‡ so scandalous to Christendom; and such really may have been his design. At least it is certain that his interference was a single and inconsequent act, unaccompanied by any insolence of pretension: the Pope offered his mediation, and though we may suspect his impartiality, he advanced no claim of apostolical authority to dispose of the crown. We shall, therefore, pass on from this event to one which immediately followed it, and which French historians consider as the first instance of ecclesiastical aggression on the rights of their sovereign. Louis was betrayed by his soldiers into the hands of his sons, who immediately deposed him and divided the empire amongst themselves; but fearing that he might hereafter be

* An abuse (as Mr. Hallam remarks) which has never ceased in the Church: Middle Ages, chap. vii. We take this opportunity of acknowledging various obligations to that historian.

† Charlemagne died in 814; Louis in 840, and his successor, Charles the Bald, in 877. The empire passed from Charlemagne's descendants to the German Conrad just a century after his death; and in 987 his dynasty was extinguished in France by the accession of Hugh Capet.

‡ Baron., ann. 833, s. v. Gregory held the See from 828 to 844. It was made a complaint against the Emperor by Agobard, the Archbishop of Lyons (ap. Baron., ann. 833. s. vi.), that he did not address the Pope with the due expressions of respect—since he saluted him, in a letter, *Brother* and *Papa*, indiscriminately: the paternal appellation should alone, it seems, have been adopted.

restored by popular favour, they determined to inflict upon him a still deeper and more effectual humiliation. An assembly held at Compiègne condemned him to perform public penance, and he submitted with some reluctance to the sentence. Having received a paper containing the list of his pretended crimes, and confessed his guilt, he prostrated himself on a rough mat at the foot of the altar, cast aside his baldric, his sword, and his secular vestments, and assumed the garb of a penitent. And after the Bishops had placed their hands on him, and the customary psalms and prayers had been performed, he was conducted in sackcloth to the cell assigned for his perpetual residence. It was intended by those who condemned him to this ignominy, thereby to disqualify him for every office both civil and military. But neither does it appear that such was the necessary consequence of canonical penance, unless when imposed for life*; nor could they have forgotten that eleven years previously the same monarch had already performed a public penance, for certain political offences then charged on him. It proved then, as might have been expected, that the ceremony described had no more important effect than the temporary humiliation of the royal person. Probably his popularity was increased by the show of persecution; and as soon as political circumstances changed in his favour, the Bishops immediately reconciled the penitent to the Church, and replaced him on the throne†.

This stretch of episcopal power is blamed by many Roman Catholic historians, who at the same time are careful to show that it was simply an act of penance, not of deposition, justified by the memorable submission of Theodosius to ecclesiastical discipline. Nevertheless, we cannot in justice otherwise consider it than as a daring outrage committed on the highest temporal authority, with the intention of perpetuating the

---

* The prohibition to carry arms or discharge civil offices did not extend beyond the duration of the penance. See Fleury, l. xlvii., s. 40. Baron. ann. 882. s. i.; ann. 833. s. xix.

† We read in Baronius (ann. 834, s. i.), that during the time of his deposition violent and unseasonable tempests prevailed, which instantly dispersed at his restoration.

deposition of Louis by the pretext of penance. Yet it had been surpassed in an earlier age and in a different country, by a measure of episcopal usurpation which is less generally recorded. At the twelfth Council of Toledo, in 682, the bishops undertook to decide on the succession to the crown. Vamba, king of the Visigoths, having done penance and assumed the monastic habit, formally abdicated in favour of Ervigius; on which matter the prelates pronounced as follows—" We have read this act, and think it right to give it our confirmation. Wherefore we declare that the *people is absolved from* all *obligation and oath* by which it was engaged to Vamba; and that it should recognise for its only master Ervigius, whom God has chosen, whom his predecessor has appointed, and, what is still more, whom the whole people desires*." Still we may observe that, even in this instance, the prelates did not professedly proceed to the whole length of deposition, though such was unquestionably the real nature of the measure. We may also remind the reader, that the aggressions which have been thus far mentioned were entirely the work of the episcopal order, not in any way directed or influenced by the See of Rome. It is very true that they may have prepared the way for the more extensive usurpations of Papacy, and the authority which had been insulted by provincial Bishops could scarcely hope to be long held sacred by the chief of the whole body: still the Pope had not yet found himself sufficiently powerful to engage in the enterprise.

Deposition of Vamba, King of the Visigoths, 682, A.D.

Charles the Bald.

The long reign of Charles the Bald furnishes more numerous instances of the exercise of ecclesiastical influence in affairs of state, and some of them deserve our notice. That prince and Louis of Bavaria, being desirous to dispossess their brother Lothaire of a portion of his dominions, did not presume, notwithstanding great military advantages which they had obtained over him, to proceed in their design without the sanction of the clergy. To that end they summoned a council of bishops and priests† at Aix-la-Chapelle, in the year 842, and submitted the

---

* It is the first canon of the Council, and is cited by Fleury, l. xl., s. 29.

† Baron., ann. 842. s. 1, 2, 3.

question to their consideration. The assembly condemned the crimes and incapacity of Lothaire, and declared that God had justly withdrawn his protection from him; but it would not permit his brothers to occupy his kingdom, until they had made a public vow to govern it, not after the example of Lothaire, but according to the will of God. The bishops then pronounced their final decision in these words—" Receive the kingdom by the authority of God, and govern it according to his will; we counsel, we exhort, we command you to do so." The effect of this sentence was not, indeed, the entire spoliation of Lothaire, who retained his throne to the end of his life; but certain provinces, already in the occupation of the conquerors, were immediately, and, as it would seem, permanently transferred to their sceptre, in consequence of the episcopal award.

In the year 859 Charles presented to the council of Savonières a formal complaint against Vénilo, archbishop of Sens, which breathes the lowest spirit of humiliation. " By his own election " (the King says), " and that of the other bishops, and by the will and consent and acclamation of the rest of my subjects, Vénilo, with the other bishops and archbishops, consecrated me king, according to the tradition of the Church, and anointed me to the kingdom with the holy chrism, and raised me to the throne with the diadem and sceptre. After which consecration and regal elevation I ought to have been degraded by no one *without the hearing and judgment of the bishops*, by whose ministry I was consecrated to royalty, who are called the thrones of God. In them God sits; by them he makes known his judgments; and to their paternal corrections and penal authority I was prepared to subject myself, and am now subject*." These words (as Fleury admits) are remarkable in the

---

* The original is cited by Baronius, ann. 959. s. xxvi. The bishops had a very simple process of reasoning, by which they proved their supremacy. A bishop can consecrate a king, but a king cannot consecrate a bishop: therefore a bishop is superior to a king. We might well wonder that any serious attention should ever have been paid to such undisguised nonsense, if we did not recollect what undue weight is always attached to *ceremony* in ignorant ages. There is a passage on this subject in Hincmar's Epist. xv.—" Ad Episcopos Regni," and which is worth citing—" Tanto gravius pondus est sacerdotum, quanto etiam pro ipsis regibus hominum in divino reddituri sint examine rationem: et tanto est

mouth of a king, and especially of a king of France; but the
example of his predecessor, enforced by his own misfortunes
and feebleness, may have reduced Charles to the necessity of
such degradation.   It should also be recollected that this was
the crisis of the general dissolution of government and society
into the feudal form.   But, on the other hand, can we feel
astonishment that the hierarchy took advantage of what appeared the voluntary and gratuitous prostration of royalty?
When we blame the ambition of those who accepted the offering, should we forget the weakness and pusillanimity of those
who presented it?

A year or two afterwards, Lothaire, King of Lorraine,
grandson of Louis the Meek, divorced his wife in order to
espouse his concubine.   It appears that no less than three
councils of bishops sanctioned the act of their monarch; nevertheless the repudiated queen made her appeal to Rome.   Nicholas I. was then pope, and he interfered in her favour with
his usual vehemence and perseverance: the threat of excommunication was long suspended over the king, who employed
submissive language and persisted in disobedience.   There is
some reason* to believe that the pope, towards the end of his
life, executed his menace; and if so, it may seem a strange
return for the generosity of Charlemagne to the holy see, that
the first discharge of its deadliest bolt should have been directed, within fifty years from his death, against one of his own
descendants.   But he had in some degree secured this retribution by his own imprudence; for it was his custom to engage
the bishops to pervert the ecclesiastical censures to the service
of the civil government.   The confusion between the two powers
was thus augmented; and the misapplication of the great spiri-

Pope Ni-
cholas I.

dignitas pontificum major quam regum, *quia reges in culmen regium sacrantur* a
pontificibus, pontifices autem a regibus consecrari non possunt; et tanto in hu-
manis rebus regum cura est propensior quam sacerdotum, quanto pro honore et
defensione et quiete S. Ecclesiæ et leges promulgando et *militando* a Rege regum
est iis curæ onus impositum." Vol. ii. p. 220. Oper. Hincm. edit. Paris.

* Fleury (l. li, s. 7.) collects the fact from the pope's letter to Charles, in favour
of Heltrude, widow of Count Berenger, and sister of Lothaire. But many historians are silent respecting it, and in the first intercourse between Lothaire and
Adrian II. the successor of Nicholas, we can discover no proof that the king was
then lying under the sentence.

tual weapon to the purposes of the state naturally led to the second abuse, which turned it, for Church purposes, against the state.

On the death of Lothaire, Adrian II. endeavoured to exclude Adrian II. Charles the Bald from the succession to his states, and to confer them on the emperor Louis. To effect this object he addressed one letter to the nobles of the kingdom of Lothaire, in which he exhorted them to adhere to the emperor on pain of anathema and excommunication; and a second to the subjects of Charles, in which he eulogized the emperor, and repeated the same menaces. He continued to the following purpose :—— " If any one shall oppose himself to the just pretensions of the emperor, let him know that the holy see is in favour of that prince, and that the arms which God has placed in our hands are prepared for his defence." We may consider this as the first attempt of papal ambition to regulate the successions of princes. It was unsuccessful; Charles, with the aid of Hincmar, Archbishop of Rheims, and other prelates, had already placed himself in possession of the throne, when the legates of Adrian arrived; and the subsequent efforts of the pontiff to oblige him to abdication were repelled with courage and constancy both by the king and his metropolitan.

The pope commanded Hincmar to abstain from the communion of Charles, if he should continue refractory. The archbishop (professedly in the name of his fellow-subjects) replied among other matters,—" Let the pope consider that he is not at the same time king and bishop; that his predecessors have regulated the Church, which is their concern—not the state, which is the heritage of kings; and consequently that he should neither command us to obey a king too distant to protect us against the sudden attacks of the Pagans, nor pretend to subjugate us, who are Franks. . . . . If a bishop excommunicates a Christian, contrary to rule, he only derogates from his own power; and he can deprive no one of eternal life who is not deprived of it by his sins. It is improper in a bishop to say that any man not incorrigible should be separated from the Christian name and consigned to condemnation—a man, whom Christ has redeemed with his blood and taught to lay down his life for his brethren—and that too, not on account of his crimes, but for the sake of withholding or conferring a temporal sovereignty. If then the pope is really desirous to establish concord, let him not attempt it by fomenting dissensions; for he will never persuade us that we cannot arrive at the kingdom of heaven, except by receiving the king whom he may choose to give us on earth*."

Lewis III. and Hincmar of Rheims, 880 A. D.

These events took place about the year 870; and ten years afterwards the same Hincmar was equally firm in defending the rights of the Church, when they were in opposition to the claims of the king, Louis III. That prince was desirous to intrude into the see of Beauvais an unworthy minister, and pressed his appointment by supplication and menace. Hincmar defended the original liberty of elections which had been restored by Louis the Meek, and the independence of the Church, and the following is the substance of some of his remonstrances :—"That you are the master of the elections, and of the ecclesiastical property, are assertions proceeding from hell and from the mouth of the serpent, and whispered into your ear for your own perdition†. Remember the promise which you made at your consecration, which you subscribed with your hand, and presented to God on the altar in the presence of the bishops. Reconsider it with the aid of your council, and pretend not to introduce into the Church that which the mighty emperors, your predecessors, pretended not in their time. I trust that I shall always preserve towards you the fidelity and

---

* The letter is published by Baronius (as Hincmari *furentis* Epistola) ann. 870. s. xix. Again, in an answer of Charles to an epistle of Adrian, that prince argues respecting the distinction between the temporal and the spiritual power, and also alleges the peculiar supremacy of the kings of France. To prove these and similar points, he refers not only to the archives of the Roman Church, but to the writings of St. Gelasius, St. Leo, St. Gregory, and even St. Augustine himself. (See Hist. Littéraire de la France. Fleury, l. lii., s. 8, 22.) Hincmar wrote many of that king's letters, and may probably have been the author of this.

† " Sunt qui dicunt, quia res ecclesiasticæ episcoporum in vestra sint potestate, ut cuicunque volueritis eas donetis. Quod si ita est, ille malignus spiritus perditionem vestram in aures vestras susurrat." Again—" Quod scripsistis, ut sicut semper regibus prædecessoribus vestris in omni utilitate regni proficus et devotus fui, ita vobis fidelis et devotus existam. Vos autem S. Ecclesiæ atque ejus rectoribus atque mihi servate quod illi conservaverunt," &c. Oper. Hinc. vol. ii, pp. 190, 191. Ed. Paris.

devotion which are due; I laboured much for your election; do not then return me evil for good by persuading me to abandon in my old age the holy regulations which I have followed, through the grace of God, during six and thirty years of episcopacy......." A subsequent letter by the same prelate contained even stronger expressions to the following effect:—"It is not you who have chosen me to govern the Church; but it is I and my colleagues and the rest of the faithful who have chosen you to govern the kingdom, on the condition of observing the laws. We fear not to give account of our conduct before the bishops, because we have not violated the canons. But as to you, if you change not what you have ill done, God will redress it in his own good time. The emperor Louis lived not so long as his father Charles; your grandfather Charles lived not so long as his father, nor your father* as his father; and when you are at Compiègne, where they repose, cast down your eyes and look where lies your father and where your grandfather is buried; and presume not to exalt yourself in the presence of Him who died for you and for us all, and who was raised again, and dies no more...... You will pass away speedily; but the holy Church and its ministers under Jesus Christ their chief will subsist eternally according to his promise." This vain menace of temporal retribution (for as such it was seemingly intended) was, however singularly, accomplished: Louis, in the vigour of youth, died in the following year; and the strange coincidence may have encouraged future prelates to indulge in similar predictions which proved not equally fortunate.

We have already mentioned that Charles the Bald, about fifteen years after his contest with Pope Nicholas, condescended to accept the vacant empire as the donation of John VIII. The immediate result of this act was, that the government of Italy and the imperial throne were, for some years afterwards, placed in a great measure at the disposal of the pope, who shamelessly abused his influence†. But it had a more lasting

Donation of the empire to Charles.

---

* Louis the Stammerer.
† See Mosh. cent. ix. p. ii. c. ii. Giannone, Stor. Nap. lib. viii. Introduct.

c 2

and still more pernicious consequence, in as far as it furnished
to the more powerful pontiffs of after ages one of their pretexts
for interference in the succession to the imperial throne.   The
ceremony of coronation, to which Charlemagne had consented
to submit at Rome, was their only ground for the pretension
that the empire had been transferred from the Greeks to the
Latins by papal authority; and on the same ground it was
subsequently transferred by the same agency from the French
to the Italians, from the Italians to Otho I. and the Germans.
The mere act of ministry in a customary, and, as was then
thought, a necessary solemnity, was exalted into a display of
superiority and an exercise of power; and many among the
ignorant vulgar were really led to believe that the rights of
sovereignty were conferred by the form of consecration.   But
the condescension of Charles the Bald, though conceding no
very definite privilege, nor any which could be reasonably
binding on his successors, yet furnished a pretence somewhat
more substantial than a mere ceremony*.

Observa-
tions.

On a review of this short narrative, we perceive that the
prelates of the ninth century advanced, for the first time, claims
of temporal authority; that such claims were asserted by
national assemblies of bishops even more daringly than by the
popes; and that they were so immoderate, as to be inconsistent with the necessary rights of princes, and the vigour and
stability of civil government.   We observe, moreover, that the
hierarchy, though on some particular occasions their efforts
were frustrated, had made, during the period of sixty-three
years from the death of Charlemagne to that of Charles the
Bald, very considerable strides in the advancement of their

* Some of the expressions of the pope delivered on this occasion should be
cited. " Unde nos, tantis indiciis divinitùs incumbentibus, luce clarius agnitis,
superni decreti consilium manifestè cognovimus. Et quia pridem Apostolicæ
memoriæ Decessori nostro Papæ Nicolao idipsum jam inspiratione divina revelatum fuisse comperimus, *elegimus* merito et *approbavimus* una cum annisu et voto
omnium Fratrum et Coepiscoporum nostrorum et aliorum Sanctæ Rom. Ecclesiæ
Ministrorum, amplique senatus, totiusque Rom. populi gentisque togatæ, et secundum priscam consuetudinem, solemniter ad *Imperii Romani Sceptra proveximus,*
et Augustali nomine decoravimus, ungentes eum oleo extrinsecus, ut interioris
quoque Spiritus Sancti unctionis monstraremus virtutem, &c." See Baron. ann.
876, s. 6.

power and privileges.   The immediate successor of Charles, Louis the Stammerer, was consecrated to the throne of France by the Pope; and a council of bishops assembled at Troyes about the same time (in 878), published as the first canon, "that the powers of the world should treat the bishops with every sort of respect, and that no one should presume to sit down in their presence unless by their command;" as the last, " that all those canons be observed, under pain of deposition for clerks, and privation of all dignity for laymen." The pope and the king were both present at this council, and the latter appears to have sanctioned the very bold usurpation contained in the last clause.

Soon after this period the popes became so much embarrassed by domestic inquietude and disorder, that they had little leisure to extend their conquests abroad; and thus for above a century the thunders of the Vatican murmured with extreme faintness, or altogether slept. But the principle of ecclesiastical supremacy, and the disposition to submit to it, were not extinguished in the tumults of the tenth age; and the storm, when it again broke forth, seemed even to have gained strength from the sullen repose which had preceded it. The occasion was this—Robert, King of France, had married a relative, four degrees removed, indeed, but still too near akin for the severity of canonical morality. Gregory V. in a council of Italian bishops, held at Rome in the year 998, launched a peremptory order, that the king should put away his wife, and both parties perform seven years of penance. The king resisted; but so united was the Church at that time, and so powerful, that he was presently excommunicated by his own prelates, and shunned by his nobles and people. At length, after some ineffectual struggles, he submitted to anathemas so generally respected and enforced*, and complied with both the

Dispute between Robert of France and Gregory V.

---

* Petrus Damiani, who wrote about sixty years afterwards, relates the ecclesiastical censure to have been so exactly observed, that no one would hold any communion with the king, excepting two servants who carried him the necessaries of life, and that even these burnt the vessels which he had used. But that author throws suspicion on a narrative not improbable, by adding that the fruit of the marriage was a monster which had the head and neck of a goose. See Fleury, l. lvii. s. 57.

injunctions of the pontiff. This is the third instance, of an authoritative interference on the part of the popes in the concerns of sovereigns, which we have had occasion to mention, and we may here remind the reader that two of them were on the ground of uncanonical marriages.

It is not our intention to enumerate the many trifling occasions on which the claims of the Church were brought into collision with the rights or dignity of monarchs: the instances which have been produced are the most important, and they are worthy of more particular reflection than can here be bestowed on them. But at present it must suffice to have noticed, even thus briefly, the earliest movements by which the spirit of ecclesiastical ambition pressed towards universal domination, and to have called some attention to those bold, but irregular, encroachments, which furnished to after ages precedents for wider and more systematic usurpation.

Internal usurpations of the Roman See.

III. We have already mentioned that, from a very early period, the Bishop of Rome possessed the first rank among the rulers of the Church; and if, after the Council of Chalcedon, it was disputed with him by the patriarch of Constantinople, it was at no time contested (at least after the reign of Constantine) in the western Churches. It is equally true, that his pre-eminence in rank was unattended by any sort of authority beyond the limits of his own diocese; and the sort of superintendence, which it might seem his duty to exercise over ecclesiastical affairs, was confined to the simple right of remonstrance. More than this is not asserted by moderate Catholics, nor can an impartial Protestant concede less.

Growth of the Papal power.

We have also noticed some of the steps which were taken by early popes, not only to extend the boundaries of their jurisdiction, but to establish an absolute authority within them. Their earliest success was the transfer to the holy see of the Metropolitan privileges throughout the diocese. Among these the most important were the consecration of bishops, the convocation of synods, and the ultimate decision of appeals—privileges which might obviously be applied to restrain the power and independence of the bishops. During the fifth and sixth centuries some little progress was made towards that

object. Valentinian III. made to Leo I. some concessions
which were valuable, though that pope had no means of enforcing them; but the acquisitions of Gregory the Great were
more substantial, and that most especially so was the establishment of the appellant jurisdiction of the see. A more general
subjection of Metropolitan to Papal authority was introduced
by the Council of Frankfort; and such was the relative situation of the parties on the accession of Charlemagne to the
empire. But presently afterwards, as if impatient of the tedious
progress of gradual usurpation, the spirit of papacy called into
existence, by an effort of amazing audacity, a new system of
government, and a new code of principles, which led by a single
step to the most absolute power. The False Decretals were
imposed on the credulity* of mankind, Still the moment was
not yet arrived in which it was possible to enforce all the rights
so boldly claimed on their authority; and though some ground
was gained by Pope Nicholas I., their efforts were not brought
into full operation till the pontificate of Gregory VII.

In recording some instances of the temporal interference of
the Church, we have remarked the success of episcopal, as
distinct from papal presumption, and observed the independence, as well as the force, with which the councils of bishops
acted against the secular powers. The Ninth has been peculiarly characterized as the Age of Bishops; it becomes therefore more important to examine the relation in which they
then stood, even in the moment of their highest glory, to the
power which was now spreading in every direction from Rome.
It has been mentioned that when the sons of Louis the Meek
were in revolt against their father, Pope Gregory IV. presented
himself at the camp of the rebels, and under pretence of mediation, favoured (as was thought) their party. On this occa- Gregory
sion, certain French prelates, who remained faithful to Louis, IV. and the
addressed an epistle to the pope, wherein they accused him of Bishops.
having violated the oath which he had taken to the emperor.

* Hincmar was not, indeed, blindly submissive to the Decretals; but it was
their authority that he questioned rather than their authenticity—proving that
his national (or episcopal) spirit of independence was greater than his critical
sagacity.

They denied his power to excommunicate any person, or make any disposition in their dioceses, without their permission; they boldly declared that if he came with the intention of excommunicating them, he should return himself excommunicated; and even proceeded so far as to threaten him with deposition. The pope was alarmed; but, on the assurance of his attendants that he had received power from God to superintend the affairs of all nations and the concord of all Churches, and that, with authority to judge every one, he was not himself subject to any judgment—he wrote in answer, that ecclesiastical is placed high above secular power, and that the obedience of the bishops was due to him rather than to the emperor; that he could not better discharge his oath than by restoring concord; and that none could withdraw themselves from the Church of Rome without incurring the guilt of schism. The irritation of the parties is sufficiently discovered in their letters; but their firmness was not put to trial; for the rebels obtained by treachery a temporary success, and the pope returned to Italy without either pronouncing or receiving excommunication.

Dispute between Nicholas I. and Hincmar of Rheims.
The occurrence which we shall next mention took place thirty years afterwards; and it is the more remarkable, because the two greatest ecclesiastics of that age, Nicholas I. and Hincmar of Rheims, were placed in direct opposition to each other. The circumstances were nearly the following. A bishop of Soissons, named Rothadus, incurred the displeasure of Hincmar, and after being condemned in two councils held at Soissons in 862, under the direction of the Metropolitan, was first excommunicated, and very soon afterwards deposed and imprisoned. Rothadus, on the first sentence, appealed to the see of Rome, and found a very willing and probably partial judge in Nicholas. The pope instantly despatched to Hincmar a peremptory order, either to restore Rothadus, within thirty days, or to appear at Rome in person or by legate for the determination of the difference, on pain of suspension from his ministry. In the year following, Hincmar sent Odo, bishop of Beauvais, to Rome, with the commission to request the pope's confirmation of the acts of the synod of Soissons. But Nicholas, on the contrary, rescinded its decisions, and demanded, with

repeated menaces, the immediate liberation of Rothadus, in order to the personal prosecution of his appeal at Rome. Through the interference of Charles the Bald, the prisoner was released; and after some delays, the deputies of Hincmar also appeared before the pontifical tribunal. The decision was such as all probably anticipated: all the charges against Rothadus were ascribed to the malice and perfidy of his enemy; he was ordered to resume the episcopal vestments, and a legate was sent to escort him on his return to his country and his see. It does not appear, from the particulars* of this contest, that Hincmar and the bishops who supported him went so far as to deny the right of a deposed bishop to appeal to Rome against the sentence of his Metropolitan; indeed they rested their defence on much lower ground, and thus conceded that which was most important. At any rate, the triumph of Nicholas was complete; and though the right in question was first advanced by him, and on no more solid authority than the (forged) " Decretals of the Ancient Pontiffs," he prevailed with scarcely any difficulty against the most learned canonist and the most independent ecclesiastic of those days.

We should also mention that, in 853, Hincmar had deposed a number of clerks ordained by his predecessor, whose canonical right to the see was disputed. In 866, Pope Nicholas ordered a revision of that affair; Hincmar maintained the sentence vigorously; but Nicholas, having Charles on his side, obtained once more a complete triumph, and restored the ecclesiastics to their rank in the Church. In both these disputes it would appear that the popular voice was against Hincmar.

About five years after the restoration of Rothadus, Hincmar found himself once more in contest with the holy see; and his

---

* Besides the ecclesiastical historians, see the life of Nicholas in the Breviarium Pontif. Romanor. R. P. Francisci Pagi, tome ii. That pope, in his epistle " Ad universos Galliæ Episcopos," admits, however, that the authority of the Decretals was not yet universally received in the Gallican Church. We read in the same author, that Adrian II. *commanded* the Gallican bishops to raise Actardus of Nantes to the first Metropolitan see which might be vacant; and that, in the year 871, he was raised to that of Tours, but with the addition—Rege, clero, ac populo postulantibus.

zeal on this occasion may possibly have been animated by the recollection of his former humiliation. His vigorous opposition to Adrian II., respecting the succession to the crown of Lorraine, has been already noticed; and if he failed, when he would have vindicated the independence of the Church of France from Roman superintendence, his success was even more remarkable, when he defended the rights of the throne from similar invasion.

John VIII.   The visit of John VIII. to France, during the year 878, certainly confirmed, and probably extended, the papal authority in that country. Before the council had assembled at Troyes, he obtained the consent of the king to some regulations, one of which was, that no Metropolitan should be permitted to ordain, until he had received the *pallium* or vest from Rome. During the session of the council we observe the following declaration to have been made by Hincmar himself:—" In obedience to the holy canons, I condemn those whom the holy see has condemned, and receive those whom it receives, and hold that which it holds in conformity with scripture and the canons." The bishops who were present professed the strictest unanimity with the pontiff; and the good understanding which was then, perhaps, established between the Churches of Rome and France, and which assumed the inferiority*, if not the dependence of the latter, appears to have subsisted long, with no material interruption.

Character of Hincmar.   Hincmar died a few years afterwards. He was descended from a noble family; and the early part of his life he so divided between the court and the cloister, and displayed so much

---

* The following is the substance of an address to the pope, made by the bishops at this council—the original may be found in Baronius, ann. 878, s. 17, &c.:—" We, the bishops of Gaul and Belgium, your sons, servants, and disciples, deeply suffer through the wounds which have been inflicted upon our Holy Mother, the mistress of all Churches, and unanimously repeat the sentence which you have launched against your enemies, excommunicating those whom you have excommunicated, and anathematizing those whom you have anathematized......And since we also have matter for lamentation in our own Churches, we humbly supplicate you to assist us with your authority, and promulgate an ordinance (Capitulum) to show in what manner we ought to act against the spoliators of the Church; that, being fortified by the censure of the apostolical see, we may be more powerful and confident," &c.

ability and enthusiasm in the discharge of the duties attached
to either situation, as to combine the practical penetration of
a statesman with the rigour of a zealous ecclesiastic.   He was
raised to the see of Rheims in the year 845, at the age of
thirty-nine, and filled it for nearly forty years with firmness
and vigour.   In the ninth century, when the mightiest events
were brought about by ecclesiastical guidance, he stands among
the leading characters, if, indeed, we should not rather consider him as the most eminent.   He was the great Churchman of the age : on all public occasions of weighty deliberation,
at all public ceremonies of coronation or consecration, Hincmar
is invariably to be found as the active and directing spirit.
His great knowledge of canonical law enabled him to rule the
councils of the clergy; his universal talents rendered him necessary to the state, and gave him more influence in political
affairs than any other subject : while his correspondence*
attests his close intercourse with all the leading characters of
his age.   In the management of his diocese, he was no less
careful to instruct and enlighten than strict to regulate; and
while he issued and enforced his capitularies of discipline with
the air and authority of a civil despot, he waged incessant warfare against ignorance.   It is indeed probable that he possessed
less theological learning than his less celebrated contemporary,

---

* Frodoard mentions 423 letters of Hincmar, besides many others not specified.
His most celebrated work is that " De Prædestinatione " (against Gotteschalcus.)
There are other very long and elaborate compositions, " De non trina Deitate,"
" De Divortio Lotharii et Teitburgiæ."   Then follow his " Capitula," of which
some further mention will be made in the next chapter.   Of his epistles and
tracts some of the most important are addressed to Charles the Bald, others to
Louis the Stammerer; and they contain some good political as well as moral
and religious counsels.   Others again are addressed to Nicholas, and several
relate to his dispute with his namesake and " Coepiscopus Hincmar Laudunensis."
Indeed his epistle to that prelate (consisting of 55 chapters and extending from
p. 386 to 593, vol. ii. Oper. Hinc. fol.) appears to us to be the most instructive, as
well as the most learned of his works.   It contains, besides much other matter, a
great deal of disquisition on the earlier canons and Decretals of the Church,
which is much more judicious than could have been expected in that age.   One of
his letters to Louis opens thus—" Dominatio vestra mihi mandavit, ut ad vos fes-
tinarem venire, quia mecum de *vestris* et S. Ecclesiæ et *regni* utilitatibus tractare
velletis," &c.   He was present at thirty-nine important councils, at most of which
he presided.   His history and character are very well illustrated by Guizot in his
28th Leçon de la Civil. en France.

Rabanus Maurus; but he had much more of that active energy of character so seldom associated with contemplative habits. It is also true that he was crafty, imperious, and intolerant; that he paid his sedulous devotions to the Virgin*, and was infected with other superstitions of his day.   His occasional resistance to the see of Rome has acquired for him much of his celebrity; but if Divine Providence had so disposed, that Hincmar had been bishop of Rome for as long a space as he was primate of France, he would unquestionably have exalted papal supremacy with more courage, consistency, and success than he opposed it.

Popish Usurpations.

We have observed that one of the favourite methods of papal usurpation within the Church was the encouragement of appeals to Rome.   It is indeed scarcely possible to measure the advantages which the see derived from that practice; and perhaps we do not value it too highly, when we ascribe to it chiefly a vague notion of the Pope's *omnipotence*, which seems to have made some impression among the laity during the ninth century.   Before we quit this subject, we should mention a remonstrance from the pen of Hincmar, which was addressed to the Pope under the name of Charles the Bald, and towards the end of his life. In this letter the Emperor is made to complain, that it is no longer deemed sufficient that Bishops, condemned by their Metropolitans, should cross the Alps for redress, but that every priest, who has been cannonically sentenced by his Bishop, now hurries to Rome for a repeal of the sentence.   The

Appeals to Rome.

origin of appeals to Rome is traced to the Council of Sardica; but by that authority they were properly liable to two restrictions—they were permitted to Bishops only, and were necessarily determined on the spot.   The inferior orders were amenable to their respective Bishops, who judged in conjunction with their Clergy; and the only lawful appeal from the decision was to a Provincial Council.   The second restriction had been confirmed by the Canons of the African Church; which in former days had defended its independence against the

---

* This appears from his epitaph, written by himself, in some very indifferent hexameter and pentameter verses,

aggressions of Rome, and which now furnished weapons to the
Prelates of Gaul, invaded after so long an interval by the persevering ambition of the same adversary.

Another method of papal encroachment was the appointment Pope's
of a Vicar in distant provinces, to whom the Pope delegated Vicars.
his assumed authority, and by whose acknowledgment the existence of that authority was in fact admitted.

In the year 876, John VIII. designated the Archbishop of
Sens as Primate of the Gauls and Germany, and Vicar of the
Pope for the Convocation of Councils and other ecclesiastical
affairs; and especially to promulgate the pontifical edicts, and
superintend their execution. The Bishops of France hesitated to receive the yoke so manifestly prepared for them; and
on this occasion we again observe Hincmar of Rheims defending and directing their opposition. He protested before the
assembled Council, that this attempt was contrary to the Holy
Canons; he appealed to the regulations of Nice, which subjected every province to its own Metropolitan, and confirmed
the original privileges of the Churches; he fortified the decisions of Nice by the authority of St. Leo and other Popes; he
denied that the particular jurisdiction which the Pontiff confessedly exercised over certain distant provinces (as Macedonia
and parts of Illyria) absorbed the rights of the Metropolitans;
and while he admitted that the popes had more than once
established their vicars in Gaul itself, he contended that the
office was temporary, instituted for occasional and specific purposes, such as the prevention of simony, the conversion of
unbelievers, the restoration of discipline; and that it ceased
with the particular abuses which had made it necessary *. The
weight of antiquity, which furnishes a conclusive argument in
ignorant ages, was, without question, on the side of Hincmar.
On the other hand, the pope had engaged the emperor in the
defence of his claims; and as it was one part of his policy to
coalesce with the national hierarchy whenever the rights of
princes could be assailed with advantage, so was it another to

---

* Fleury, H. E. lib. iii., s. 33. Frodoardus (in a passage cited by Baronius,
ann. 876. s. 24) admits the powerful resistance of Hincmar on this occasion.

draw the princes into his own designs against the power and
independence of their clergy.

Exemptions of Monasteries.

And here it is proper to notice another privilege, which,
though its origin may be traced to Gregory the Great, was little
exercised by the popes until the ninth, or the beginning of the
tenth age. Hitherto the monasteries, with very few exceptions,
were subject to the bishop of the diocese in which they stood,
and who in many cases had been their founders. Exemptions
from episcopal jurisdiction were now granted with some frequency, and the establishments thus privileged acknowledged a
direct dependence on the pope. He had many motives for this
policy, but that which most concerns our present subject is
the following. To secure his triumph over the liberties of the
Church, it was necessary to divide it; and his scheme of reducing the higher ranks of the clergy was greatly promoted by
a practice which curtailed their authority in a very important
branch, which transferred that authority to himself, and at the
same time created lasting jealousy and dissension between the
regular and secular orders.

Other objects of the See of Rome.

Two other objects may be mentioned, to which the ambition
of Rome was steadily and effectually directed—to establish the
principle, that bishops derived their power entirely from the
Pope; and to prevent the convocation of Councils without his
express command. Towards the accomplishment of the second,
very great though very gradual progress was made during the
ninth age by a series of usurpations, of which the earliest served
as precedents whereon to found the practice. The greater
obscurity and confusion of the tenth century were more favourable to the success of the first*; and though it is true that, even
after that time, there were to be found some bolder prelates,
both in France and Germany, who disputed these and others
among the pontifical claims, it cannot be questioned that they
had then acquired so much prevalence, and had struck so
deeply into the prejudices and habits of men, that a powerful
hand alone was wanted to call them into light and action, and
to give them the most fatal efficacy.

* See Mosheim, cent. x., p. 2, c. 2.

The preceding pages have presented to us a variety of inci- Reflections. dents hitherto nearly novel in the history of the Church, but with which experience will presently render us familiar. We have been astonished by the arrogant claims of the Episcopal Order and the extent of political power which it actually possessed, and shocked by the ill purpose to which it sometimes applied that power. But our most thoughtful attention has still been fixed upon the proceedings of the pope. We have observed him, in the first place, contending with the emperor for the independence of his own election with a great degree of success; next we have beheld him engaged in occasional contests with the most powerful sovereigns of the age, not only in those domestic concerns which might seem to give some plea for ecclesiastical interference, but about affairs strictly secular, and (in one instance) about the very succession to their thrones; and, lastly, we have noticed the movements of that more confined, but scarcely more legitimate ambition, which pretended to depress the superior ranks of the clergy, to despoil them of their privileges, and to remove them to so humble a distance from the Roman See, that the pope might seem to concentrate (if it were possible) in his own person the entire authority of the ecclesiastical order. The particular facts, by which these designs were manifested, belong, for the most part, to the ninth century; but the grand pontifical principles, if they suffered a partial suspension, yet lost none of their force and vitality during that which followed. And upon the whole it is a true and unavoidable observation, that the period, during which the mighty scheme first grew and developed itself, embraces that portion of papal history which, above all others, is most scandalously eminent for the disorders * of the See, and for the weakness and undisguised profligacy of those who occupied it †.

* This is more particularly true of the tenth century, but even the ninth was The female not exempt from the same charge. To this age belongs the popular story of the Pope. female Pope: the pontificate of Joan is recorded to have commenced on the death of Leo IV., in 855, and to have lasted for about two years. Historians agree that very great confusion prevailed at Rome respecting the election of Leo's successor, and that Benedict III. did not prevail without a severe and tumultuous struggle with a rival named Anastasius. The rule of Pope Joan is now indeed generally discredited; but the early invention of the tale, and the belief so long attached to it, attest a condition of things which made it at least possible.

† The Lives of the Popes (Liber Pontificalis) were written by Anastasius, a

CHAPTER XV.

On the Opinions, Literature, Discipline, and External Fortunes of the Church.

I. On the Eucharist—Original Opinions of the Church—Doctrine of Paschasius Radbert combated by Ratramn and John Scotus—Conclusion of the Controversy—Predestination—Opinions and Persecution of Gotteschalchus—Millennarianism in the Tenth Century—its strange and general effect. II. Literature—Rabanus Maurus, John Scotus, Alfred—its Progress among the Saracens—Spain—South of Italy—France—Rome—Pope Sylvester II. III. Discipline of the Church—Conduct of Charlemagne and his Successors—St. Benedict of Aniane. Institution of Canons regular—Episcopal election—Translations of Bishops prohibited. Pope Stephen VI.—Claudius Bishop of Turin—Penitential System. IV. Conversion of the North of Europe—of Denmark, Sweden, Russia—of Poland and Hungary—how accomplished and to what extent—The Normans—The Turks.

The particulars contained in the preceding Chapter present indeed an imperfect picture of the condition of Religion during the ninth and tenth centuries; but they are sufficient to exhibit the outlines of the visible Church, as it was gradually changing its shape and constitution, and passing through a region of disorder and darkness, from a state of contested rights and restricted authority to a situation of acknowledged might and unbounded pretension. They may also have discovered to us, in some manner, the process of the change, and certain of the less obvious means and causes through which it was accomplished: still the inquiry has been confined to the external Church; it has gone to examine a human and perishable institution—no farther: it has illustrated the outworks which man had thrown up for the protection (as he imagined) of God's fortress—nothing more. It remains, then, to complete the task, and to notice some circumstances in the history of this period unconnected with the ambitious struggles of popes and bishops.

It is observable that, during the seventh and eighth ages,

librarian, who died before 882; they reach as far as the death of Nicholas I. in 867. The lives of some other Popes, as far as 889, were added by another librarian named Wilhelmus. From 889 to 1050 (where the Collection of Cardinal d'Aragon begins) there is a suspension of pontifical biography.

religion lost much of its vigour in France and Italy, while it
took root and spread in Britain; during the ninth, it arose,
through the institutions of Charlemagne, with renovated power
in France; in the course of the tenth, its progress in Germany
made some amends for its general degradation. These fluctuations corresponded, upon the whole, with the literary revolutions of those countries. Learning was, in those days, the only
faithful ally and support of religion, and the causes which
withered the one never failed to blight the other. Indeed, as
learning was then almost wholly confined to the Clergy, it
naturally partook of a theological character; and as the season
of scholastic sophistry had not yet set in, the theology did not
so commonly obscure, it even commonly illustrated, the religion.

Religious zeal, when informed by imperfect education, and
unrestrained by a moderate and charitable temper, is rarely
unattended by religious dissension; and thus it happened, that,
while the intellectual torpor of the tenth century was little or
nothing agitated by such disputes, the ninth, which was partially
enlightened, witnessed three important controversies. The first
was that which Photius carried on with the Roman See, regarding Image-worship and other differences, transmitted from
preceding generations; and it has been already treated. The
other two respected the manner of Christ's presence at the
Eucharist, and the doctrine of Salvation by Grace; and they
shall now be noticed: it will afterwards be necessary to say a
few words on the discipline of the Church; and we shall then
observe the progress of Christianity among distant and barbarous nations, as well as the reverses which afflicted it.

Ecclesiastical controversies.

I. Mosheim* asserts, without hesitation, that it had been
hitherto the unanimous opinion of the Church, that the body
and blood of Christ were really administered to those who received the Sacrament, and that they were consequently *present*
at the administration; but that the sentiments of Christians
concerning the *nature* and manner of this presence were various
and contradictory. No council had yet determined with pre-

On the Eucharist.

* Cent. ix. p. 2, c. 3.

cision the manner in which that presence was to be understood; both reason and folly were hitherto left free in this matter; nor had any imperious mode of faith suspended the exercise of the one, or controlled the extravagance of the other. The historian's first position is laid down, perhaps, somewhat too peremptorily; for though many passages may be adduced from very ancient fathers in affirmation of the bodily presence, the obscurity or different tendency of others would rather persuade us, that even that doctrine was also left a good deal to individual judgment. The second is strictly true; and the question which had escaped the vain and intrusive curiosity of oriental theologians, was at length engendered in a convent in Gaul. In the year 831, Paschasius Radbert, a Benedictine monk, afterwards abbot of Corbie, published a treatise "concerning the Sacrament of the Body and Blood of Christ," which he presented, fifteen years afterwards, carefully revised and augmented, to Charles the Bald. The doctrine advanced by Paschasius may be expressed in the two following propositions:—First, that after the consecration of the bread and wine nothing remains of those symbols except the outward figure, under which the body and blood of Christ were really and locally present. Secondly, that the body of Christ, thus present, is the same body which was born of the Virgin, which suffered upon the cross, and was raised from the dead*. Charles appears decidedly to have disapproved of this doctrine. And it might perhaps have been expected that, after the example of so many princes, he would have summoned a council, stigmatized it as heresy, and persecuted its author. He did not do so; but, on the contrary, adopted a method of opposition worthy of a wiser prince and a more enlightened age. He commissioned two of the ablest

Paschasius
Radbert.

---

* Paschasius derived three consequences from his doctrine. 1. That Jesus Christ was immolated anew every day, in reality but in mystery. 2. That the Eucharist is both truth and figure together. 3. That it is not liable to the consequences of digestion. The first of these positions assumes a new and express creation on every occasion of the celebration of the Sacrament. The disputes arising from the third afterwards gave birth to the heresy named Stercoranism. Fleury, l. xlvii., s. 35. Semler (sec. ix., cap. iii.) is willing to deduce Paschasius' doctrine from the Monophysite Controversy, and the opinions respecting "one incarnate nature of Christ," which had still some prevalence in the East.

writers of the day, Ratramn* and Johannes Scotus †, to investigate by arguments the suspicious opinion. The composition
of the former is still extant, and has exercised the ingenuity
of the learned even in recent times; but they have not succeeded in extricating from the perplexities of his reasoning, and,
perhaps, the uncertainty of his belief, the real opinions of the
author. The work of Johannes Scotus is lost; but we learn Johannes
that his arguments were more direct, and his sentiments more Scotus.
perspicuous and consistent; he plainly declared, that the bread
and wine were no more than symbols of the absent body and
blood of Christ, and memorials of the last supper. Other
theologians engaged in the dispute, and a decided superiority,
both in number and talents ‡, was opposed to the doctrine of

---

* A monk of Corbie. His book was long received under the name of Bertram;
some have even supposed it to be the work of John Scotus on the same subject,
but clearly without reason. Dupin, Hist. Eccl., cent . ix., c. vii. Fleury, l. xlix.,
s. 52, 53. Semler, loc. cit. Ratramn proposes the subject in the following manner:—" Your Majesty inquires whether the body and blood of Jesus Christ,
which is received in the Church by the mouth of the faithful, is made in mystery,
—that is, if it contains anything secret which only appears to the eyes of faith—
or if, without any veil of mystery, the eyes of the body perceive without, that
which the view of the spirit perceives within: so that all which is made is manifestly apparent. You inquire besides, whether it is the same body which was born
of the Virgin Mary, which suffered, died, and was buried; and which, after its
resurrection, ascended to Heaven, and sat on the right hand of the Father."
Respecting the second question, the opinion of Ratramn was in direct opposition
to that of Paschasius; but, in the treatment of the first, it would be difficult certainly to pronounce on what they differed, or indeed on what they agreed. There
is moreover extant an anonymous composition, which combats the second proposition of Paschasius—first in itself, and then in its consequence—that Jesus Christ
suffers anew on every occasion that mass is celebrated. The writer acknowledges
the real presence as a necessary tenet. " Every Christian" (thus he commences)
" ought to believe and confess that the body and blood of the Lord is true flesh
and true blood; whoever denies this proves himself to be without faith.' It appears indeed true that Paschasius' second proposition gave much more general
offence than the first.

† John Scotus Erigena (i. e. John the Irishman) was a layman of great acuteness and much profane learning, and irreproachable moral character. He was
in high estimation at the court of Charles the Bald, and honoured by the personal partiality of that prince. He is described in the Hist. Litt. de la France,
to have been of " très petite taille, vif, pénétrant, et enjoué." Fleury (l. xlviii.,
s. 48) disputes the great extent of his theological acquirements, and perhaps with
justice. His book on the Eucharist was burnt about two hundred years afterwards by the hand of his disciple Berenger, on ecclesiastical compulsion.

Hincmar appears to have held the doctrine of the real presence; and it is

Paschasius—yet so opposed, that there was little unanimity among its adversaries, and no very perfect consistency even in their several writings*.

The controversy died away before the end of the ninth century, without having occasioned any great mischief, and the subject was left open to individual inquiry or neglect, as it had ever been. The intellectual lethargy of the century following was not to be disturbed by an argument demanding some acuteness, and susceptible of much sophistry; and an age of entire ignorance has at least this advantage over one of superficial learning†, that it suffers nothing from the abuse of the human understanding. But very early in the eleventh century, the dispute was again awakened: it assumed, under different circumstances and other principles, another aspect and character, and closed in a very different termination. But as this event belongs more properly to the life of Gregory VII. we shall not anticipate the triumph of that Pontiff, nor deprive his name of any ray of that ambiguous splendour which illustrates it.

II. The subject of *Predestination* and Divine Grace, which had already ‡ been controverted in France with some acuteness and, what is much better, with candour and charity, was subjected to another investigation in the ninth century. Gotteschalcus, otherwise called Fulgentius, was a native of Germany, and a monk of Orbais, in the diocese of Soissons. He was admitted to orders, during the vacancy of the See, by the Chorepiscopus—a circumstance to which the subsequent animosity of Hincmar is sometimes attributed. He possessed considerable learning, but a mind withal too prone to pursue abstruse

Opinions of Gotteschalcus.

difficult to pronounce whether or not he confined his meaning to a spiritual presence.

* The *worship* of the elements is not mentioned by any of the disputants—it was an extravagance of superstition too violent for the controversialists of the ninth century.

† As early as the conclusion of the eighth century, a heresy respecting the nature of Jesus Christ appeared in the Western Church—that of the Adoptians. It was condemned by Charlemagne in three Councils, between the years 790 and 800, and presently disappeared.

‡ In the fifth century.—See chap. xi.

and unprofitable inquiries. Early in life he consulted Lupus, Abbot of Ferrara, on the question, whether, after the resurrection, the blessed shall see God with the eyes of the body ? The Abbot concluded a reluctant reply with words to the following effect:—" I exhort you, my venerable brother, no longer to weary your spirit with such like speculations, lest through too great devotion to them, you become incapacitated for examining and teaching things more useful. Why waste so many researches on matters, which it is not yet, perhaps, expedient that we should know ? Let us rather exercise our talents in the spacious fields of Holy Writ ; let us apply entirely to that meditation, and let prayer be associated to our studies. God will not fail, in his goodness, to manifest himself in the manner which shall be best for us, though we should cease to pry into things which are placed above us." The speculations of Gotteschalcus were diverted by this judicious rebuke, but not repressed ; and the books of Scripture were still rivalled or superseded in his attention by those of Augustine. Accordingly he involved himself deeply and inextricably in the mazes of fatalism. About the year 846, he made a pilgrimage to Rome, and on his return, soon afterwards, expressed his opinions on that subject very publicly in the diocese of Verona. Information was instantly conveyed to Rabanus Maurus, Archbishop of Mayence, the most profound theologian of the age. That prelate immediately replied ; and in combating the error of a professed Augustinian, protected himself also by the authority of Augustine. Rabanus was the most profound divine in the ninth century, as Augustine was in the fifth ; but the spirit of the one age was original thought and reasoning—that of the other, blind and servile imitation : therefore Rabanus was contented to cite and explain Augustine ; and the controversy descended from lofty philosophical investigation to logical and even critical subtilty. The object in the fifth age was, to solve an abstruse and difficult question ; that in the ninth, only to penetrate the real opinions of an ancient writer.

Happy had it been for the author of the controversy if his adversary had allowed it to remain on that footing ; but the doctrine was becoming too popular, and threatened moral effects

Council of
Mayence,
848 A.D.
too pernicious* to be overlooked by the Church. Rabanus assembled a council at Mayence in 848, at which the king was present, and Gotteschalcus was summoned before it. Here he defended, in a written treatise, the doctrine of *double* predestination—that of the elect, to eternal life by the free Grace of God—that of the wicked, to everlasting damnation through their own sins. His explanations did not satisfy the council, and the tenet was rejected and condemned; but its advocate was not considered amenable to that tribunal, as he had been ordained in the diocese of Rheims: wherefore Rabanus consigned him to the final custody of Hincmar, who then held that see.

His condemnation,
The unfortunate heretic (he had now deserved that appellation) profited nothing by this change in jurisdiction. Hincmar, in the following year, caused him to be accused before the Council of Quincy sur Oise, when he was pronounced incorrigible, and deposed from the priesthood. Moreover, as the penalty of his insolence and contumacy, he was condemned to public flagellation and perpetual imprisonment. The sentence was rigidly executed, and Charles was not ashamed to countenance it by his royal presence. It is affirmed that, under the prolonged agony of severe torture, the sufferer yielded so far as to commit to the flames the texts which he had collected in defence of his opinions; and if he did so, it was human and excusable weakness†. But it is certain that he was confined

---

* In one of the letters written on this subject, Rabanus asserts that the doctrine of Gotteschalcus had already driven many to despair, and that several began to inquire—" Wherefore should I strive and labour for my salvation? In what does it profit me to be righteous, if I am not predestined to happiness? What evil may I not safely commit, if I am surely predestined to life eternal?" This natural inference, however disavowed by the more ingenious teachers of the doctrine, is very liable to be drawn by the people, even in ages much more enlightened than the ninth.

† Gotteschalcus solicited permission to maintain the truth of his doctrine in the presence of the king, the clergy, and the whole people, by passing through four barrels filled with boiling water and oil and pitch, and afterwards through a large fire. If he should come out unhurt, let the doctrine be acknowledged and received; if otherwise, let the flames take their course. Milner, whose account of this controversy should be mentioned with praise, can scarcely pardon this desire of his persecuted favourite—as if the champion of Predestination had been less liable than his neighbours to the superstitious contagion of his age. In this case,

to the walls of a convent for almost twenty* years, and that at and death. length, during the agonies of his latest moments, he was required to subscribe a formulary of faith, as the only condition of reconciliation with the Church—that he disdained to make any sacrifice, even at that moment, to that consideration, and that his corpse was deprived of Christian sepulture by the unrelenting bigotry of Hincmar.

The precise extent† of Gotteschalcus's errors is, according to the usual history of such controversies, a matter of difference, and for the usual reason,—that consequences were imputed by his adversaries which his followers disclaimed. But it is certain that his proselytes multiplied during the continuance of his imprisonment, and that some provincial councils declared

---

however, his imperfection was peculiarly excused by the more deliberate absurdity of Hincmar himself, who had so far degraded his genius as to write a serious treatise on "Trials by Cold Water." Epist. xxxix. Ad Hildegarim Episc. Meldens. " De judicio aquæ frigidæ, &c." See Hist. Litt. de la France.

* His death is usually referred to the year 866. We should observe that his sufferings did not escape the compassion of some of his contemporaries. Remy, who succeeded Amolon in the see of Lyons, wrote on the subject with some warmth. " It is an unprecedented instance of cruelty, which has filled the world with horror, that he was lacerated with stripes, as eye-witnesses attest, until he cast into the fire a memorial containing the passages from scripture and the fathers which he drew up to present to the council; while all former heretics have been convicted by words and reasons. The long and inhuman detention of that wretched man ought at least to be tempered by some consolation, so as rather to win by charity a brother for whom Jesus Christ died, than to overwhelm him with misery." —See Fleury, l. xlix. s. 5.

† Gotteschalcus appears to have propounded three leading questions to Rabanus and the other Doctors. (1.) Whether it could be said that there was any predestination to evil. (2.) Concerning the will and death of Christ for all men ; whether God has a true will to save any but those which are saved. (3.) Concerning free will. . . . . The theologians of Mayence, however, very prudently confined their attention to the first—" Whether it can be said that God predestinates the wicked to damnation ?" (Dupin, H. E., cent. ix.) About four years afterwards, Amolon, Archbishop of Lyons, in a letter addressed to Hincmar, reduced (or rather expanded) the errors to seven ; one of them being the following —" that God and the Saints *rejoice* in the fall of the reproved." (Fleury, H. E. lib. xlviii., s. 59.) This was obviously a *consequence ;* and no doubt the heretic had easy means of getting rid of it. For a full and perhaps faithful account of the whole controversy, see Hist. Litter. de la France, cent. ix., vol. iv. p. 263. It is, however, worth remarking, that the Divines on both sides alike professed to support the doctrine of the Church, as taught by the Fathers, and especially Augustine, whose authority on this question was universally admitted, while his opinion was disputed.

in his favour; and it is probable that his doctrines have been uninterruptedly perpetuated, not by sects only, but by individuals in the bosom of the Church, from that age to the present.

Millenna-
rian error. The dispute, however, did not long survive its author, and seems to have expired before the end of the ninth century; and during the concluding part of that which followed,—in the absence of political talent, of piety, of knowledge, of industry, of every virtue, and every motive which might give energy to the human character—in the suppression even of the narrow controversial spirit which enlivens the understanding, however it may sometimes pervert the principles,—a very wild and extraordinary delusion arose and spread itself, and at length so far prevailed as not only to subdue the reason, but to actuate the conduct of vast multitudes. It proceeded from the misinterpretation of a well-known passage in the Revelations *. "And he laid hold on the Dragon, that old Serpent, which is the devil and Satan, and bound him *a thousand years,* and cast him into the bottomless pit, and shut him up, and set a seal upon him, that he should deceive the nations no more till the thousand years should be fulfilled; And *after that* he must be loosed a little season." It does not appear that the earlier divines derived from this prophecy that precise expectation, respecting the moment of the world's dissolution, which now became general; nor do we learn that the people before this time much busied themselves about a matter which could not possibly affect their own generation; but about the year 960,

Bernhard of
Thuringia. as the season approached nearer, one Bernhard, a hermit of Thuringia, a person not destitute of knowledge, boldly promulgated (on the faith of a particular revelation from God) the certain assurance, that at the end of the thousandth year the fetters of Satan were to be broken; and, after the reign of Antichrist should be terminated, that the world would be consumed by sudden conflagration. There was something plausible in the doctrine, and it was peculiarly suited to the gloomy superstition of the age. The clergy adopted it without delay; the pulpits loudly resounded with it †; it was diffused in every

* Chap. xx. 2 and 3.
† Hist. Litt. de la France, x. Siècle. Mosheim (cent. x., p. 2, c. iii.) cites a

direction with astonishing rapidity, and embraced with an
ardour proportioned to the obscurity of the subject, and the
greediness of human credulity.   The belief pervaded and possessed every rank of society, not as a cold and indifferent assent,
but as a motive for the most important undertakings.   Many
are mentioned—not of the vulgar only, but nobles, princes and
even bishops—to have abandoned their friends and their families, and hastened to the shores of Palestine, in the pious persuasion that Mount Sion would be the throne of Christ, when
he should descend to judge the world ; and these, in order to
secure a more partial sentence from the God of mercy and
charity, usually made over their property, before they departed,
to some adjacent Church or Monastery.   Others, whose pecuniary means were thought, perhaps, insufficient to bribe the
justice of Heaven, devoted their personal service to the same
establishments, and resigned their very liberty to those holy
mediators, whose pleadings, they doubted not, would find favour
at the eternal judgment-seat.   Others permitted their lands to
lie waste, and their houses to decay; or, terrified by some
unusual phenomenon in the heavens, betook themselves in
hasty flight to the shelter of rocks and caverns *, as if the
temples of Nature were destined to preservation amidst the
wreck of man and his works.

The year of terror arrived, and passed away without any
extraordinary convulsion; and at present it is chiefly remarkable
as having terminated the most shameful century in the annals
of Christianity. The people returned to their homes, and
repaired their buildings, and resumed their former occupations;
and the only lasting effect of this stupendous panic was the
augmentation of the temporal prosperity of the Church†.

passage from the Apologeticum of Abbo, Abbot of Fleury—" De fine quoque
mundi coram populo sermonem in Ecclesia Parisiorum adolescentulus audivi,
quod statim finito mille onorum numero Anti-Christus adveniret, et non longo post
tempore universale judicium succederet ; cui prædicationi ex Evangeliis ac Apo-
calypsi et libro Danielis, qua potui virtute restiti, &c."

* An opportune eclipse of the sun produced this effect on the army of Otho the
Great.

† Almost all the donations which were made to the Church in this century
proceeded from this avowed motive. "Appropinquante jam mundi termino," &c.

State of learning,

The intellectual energy of Europe was in a condition of gradual decay from the fifth till the middle of the eighth century; and though the condition of the British Isles and the existence of the Venerable Bede* may seem to furnish some exception, it was then that the progress of ignorance reached its widest and darkest boundaries. This decline is **in Europe,** very commonly imputed to the despotism of the Church and the triumph of the papal principle of a blind faith and absolute submission, over the independence of reason. But this is a mistake proceeding from an imperfect knowledge of ecclesiastical history. At the period in question, the Church had not by any means attained the degree of authority necessary for that purpose: it was not yet sufficiently organized, nor even sufficiently united, to possess any power of universal tyranny. The *Romish* system was still only in its infancy; the Episcopal system, which was predominant, was full of disorder and disunion—the principle in question was certainly to be found in the archives of the Church, but the day was not yet arrived to enforce it. It came indeed into full effect in the twelfth and following ages, and not earlier than the twelfth; but learning then revived in despite of it, and grew up to overthrow it. The truth is, that the degradation of the sixth and seventh centuries are sufficiently accounted for by the political confusion, or rather anarchy, then so generally prevalent, as to make any moral excellence almost impossible, and to debase the Church in common with every other institution.

The progress of intellectual degradation was arrested by the genius of Charlemagne; and the beacon which was set up by his mighty hand shone forth even upon his degenerate descendants, some of whom lighted their torches at its embers. Thus, during the whole of the ninth century, the western world, and France especially, was animated by much literary exertion, and enlightened even by the ill-directed talents of many learned

---

"Since the end of the world is now at hand." Mosh., cent. x., p. 2, chap. iii. These monuments sufficiently attest the generality of the delusion.

The Venerable Bede. * Bede flourished in the early part of the eighth century. He brought down his Ecclesiastical History as far as 731, and appears to have died four years afterwards.

men. The name of Alcuin was not disgraced by those of his successors, Rabanus, Eginhard, Claudius, Gotteschalcus, Paschasius, Ratramn, Hincmar, and Johannes Scotus*. The theological works of the first of these were so highly esteemed, as not only to furnish materials for contemporary instruction, but also to maintain great authority in the religious discussions of the four following centuries; and the last, the friend and companion of Charles the Bald, displayed an accuracy of philosophical induction, and a freedom and boldness of original thought, which would have subjected him, in a somewhat later age, to ecclesiastical persecution. We should mention, too, that in the same age in which the genius of an Irishman instructed the court of France, the foundations of English learning were deeply fixed and substantially constructed by the wisdom and piety of Alfred. The comparative languor of Italy was excited by the disputes at that time so warmly waged between the Roman and Eastern Churches, and which served to sharpen the ingenuity, while they degraded the principles, of both.

At Constantinople, the Emperor Theophilus, and his son, Michael III., made some endeavours towards the revival of letters in the ninth age; but the scattered rays which may have illustrated the East at that time were overpowered by the pre-eminence of Photius, so that little has reached posterity excepting his celebrity. It is true that, in the century following, while the advance of learning was almost wholly suspended in Europe, and its growing power paralyzed, Constantine Porphyrogeneta made some zealous attempts to revive the industry of his country; but as his encouragement was directed rather to the imitation of ancient models than to the development of original thought, the impulse was faintly felt; and, so far from creating any strong and lasting effect, it failed to excite even the momentary energy of the Greeks.

But, during the same period, there occurred in the Eastern world a phenomenon, which is among the most remarkable in

In the East.

---

* Guizot has selected Hincmar and Johannes Scotus as the two representatives of the learning of the age—the former as the centre of the theological movement; the latter as the philosopher of his day. It is, indeed, impossible to convey any faithful notion of the literature of any age without entering into some such detail.

the history of literature, and which no penetration could possibly have foreseen. We have recounted that, in the seventh century, the companions and successors of Mahomet desolated the face of the earth with their arms, and darkened it by their ignorance; and the acts of barbarism ascribed to them, and, whether truly ascribed or not*, generally credited, attest at least their contempt for learning, and their aversion for the monuments which they are stated to have destroyed. In the eighth century, the conquerors settled with tranquillity in the countries which they had subdued, which, in most instances, they converted, and which they continued to possess and govern.

Revival of letters by the Arabs. In the ninth, under the auspices of a wise and munificent Caliph, they applied the same ardour to the pursuit of literature which had heretofore been confined to the exercise of arms. Ample schools were founded in the principal cities of Asia†, Bagdad, and Cufa, and Bassora; numerous libraries were formed with care and diligence, and men of learning and science were solicitously invited to the splendid court of Almamunis. Greece, which had civilized the Roman republic, and was destined, in a much later age, to enlighten the extremities of the West, was now called upon to turn the stream of her lore into the barren bosom of Asia: for Greece was still the only land possessing an original national literature. Her noblest productions were now translated into the ruling language of the East, and the Arabians took pleasure in pursuing the speculations, or submitting to the rules, of her philosophy. The impulse thus given to the genius and industry of Asia was communicated with inconceivable rapidity, along the shores of Egypt and Africa, to the schools of Seville and Cordova; and the shock was not felt least sensibly by those who last received it. Henceforward the genius of learning accompanied even the arms of the Saracens. They conquered Sicily; from Sicily they invaded the Southern Provinces of Italy; and, as if to complete the eccentric revolution of Grecian literature, the

---

* The burning of the Alexandrian Library by the Saracens stands on authority not much better than the similar Vandalism charged on Gregory the Great.

† Contemporary with the foundation of Oxford; and where are *they* now? The history and character of the *Turks* can answer that question.

wisdom of Pythagoras was restored to the land of its origin by the descendants of an Arabian warrior.

The adopted literature of that ingenious people, augmented by some original discoveries, passed with a more pacific progress from Spain into France, from France into Italy, even to the pontifical chair. In the year 999, Gerbert, a Frenchman, was raised to that eminence under the title of Sylvester II. This eminent person, whose talents, though peculiarly calculated for the comprehension of the abstract sciences, were not disqualified for less severe application, steadily devoted his industry, his intelligence, and his power to the acquirement, the amplification*, and the diffusion of knowledge. Among the vulgar, indeed, he obtained a formidable reputation for magical skill: but he was honoured by the wise and the great even of his own days; and of Sylvester *that* may be more justly affirmed, which a Roman Catholic writer has rather chosen to predicate of the *papal* energy of Leo IX., "that he undertook to repair the ruins of the tenth century." *Pope Sylvester II.*

III. At no former period had the Western Church suffered such complete disorganization as during the first half of the eighth century: the longer it was connected with the barbarous political system of the conquerors, the more closely it became associated with their institutions, their habits, and their persons, as they were gradually admitted to ecclesiastical dignities—the more shameful was the license, the deeper the corruption which pervaded it. The progress of the malady was restrained by Charlemagne—not with a reluctant or irresolute hand, but with the vigour which the occasion required, and which was justified by his noble designs. He repressed the disorders of the bishops; he assembled numerous councils, and he enforced the observance of their canons: thus he infused sudden energies into a body too torpid for self-reform; and he endeavoured to perpetuate the impulse by promoting education *Discipline of the Church.* *Reformed by Charlemagne.*

---

* Some ingenious inventions of Gerbert are mentioned in the Hist. Litt. de la France. His various virtues are highly extolled in the same work; and the only fault which his eulogists can find in his character is, "that he used too much flattery in making his court to the great." The grandees of the tenth century appear to have pardoned him this imperfection.

and rewarding literature. The last, in truth, was that which
gave his other measures their efficacy; for above sixty years
after his death, under the feeble sceptres of Louis and Charles,
the spirit sent forth by Charlemagne continued to animate the
Church. Very general activity and superior intelligence distinguished the Clergy, especially the higher orders; and the
frequency with which they assembled their councils, and the
important regulations which they enacted, evinced a zeal for
the restoration of ecclesiastical discipline, which was not wholly
without effect. Louis was probably sincere in his co-operation
for that purpose; but the merit of having directed, or even
vigorously stimulated, the exertions of his prelates cannot justly
be ascribed to so weak a prince.

Respecting Charles, there seems reason to suspect that he,
as well as his nobles, regarded with some jealousy the progress
of reform, and that the attempts, so numerous during his
reign, should rather be attributed to the perseverance of the
bishops, and especially of Hincmar, than to the virtue or wisdom of the secular government. In proof of this opinion
(which, if true, is not without importance) we may mention
the following circumstance. In the year 844, councils were
held at Thionville and Verneuil* for the remedy of abuses
both in Church and State; their regulations were confirmed
and amplified in the year following at Meaux, and after that
at Paris; and on this last occasion the prelates recurred with
some impatience to the exhortations which they had frequently
and ineffectually addressed to the throne, and to that neglect
they presumed to ascribe the temporal calamities which then
afflicted the country. Presently afterwards, in an assembly of
barons held at Epernay, the canons of Meaux and Paris were
taken into consideration; and while those which restricted
ecclesiastics received the king's assent, others which touched
the vices of the nobility were entirely rejected †. Nevertheless,
councils continued to meet with great frequency ‡ during this

Numerous councils in France.

---

* It appears, from one of the canons here published, that, in contempt of Charlemagne's capitulary, the military service of the bishops was already renewed—if,
indeed, it was ever wholly discontinued.

† Fleury, l. xlviii., s. 35.

‡ France was at this time the principal scene of ecclesiastical exertion. During

reign; but we must not suppose that all of them had the same grand object : some were convoked to arrange the disputes of the bishops, either among themselves or with the Pope, or with the king; others met to restrain, had it been possible, the general licentiousness of the times *; and of many it was the principal purpose to launch excommunication and anathema against the plunderers of ecclesiastical property, and to protect the persons of clerks and monks and nuns from the violence of the laity.

It is not easy either to specify any particular changes introduced into the discipline of the Church during these ages, or precisely to determine the rigour of that discipline : for such innovations are for the most part of slow and almost insensible growth; and though the canonical regulations are in themselves sufficiently explicit, their enforcement depended in each diocese on the authority or character of the bishop. If, indeed, it had been possible at once to force into full operation the

the forty-six years of Charlemagne's reign, the number of councils which met in France was thirty-five. Louis, in twenty-six years, held twenty-nine; but no less than sixty-nine were assembled during the thirty-seven years of Charles the Bald. Their frequency then gradually decreased; and in the following 110 years to the accession of Hugh Capet, we observe no more than fifty-six.

* Hincmar has a letter to Charles the Bald " De coercendis militum rapinis ;" and the general disorders of the age are vividly depicted in the prefatory exposition of the council of Mayence in 888. " Behold the magnificent edifices which the servants of God were wont to inhabit, destroyed and burnt to ashes ; the altars overthrown and trampled under foot, the most precious ornaments of the churches dispersed or consumed; the bishops, priests, and other clerks, together with laymen of every age and sex, overtaken by sword or fire, or some other manner of massacre, &c." (Baron., ann. 888, iv.) Similar calamities are even more particularly detailed by the council of Troslé in 909, attended with some charges of spiritual negligence in the bishops themselves :—" Videtis quam sit evidens furor Domini... jam vidimus depopulatas urbes, destructa vel incensa monasteria. Agri in solitudinem sunt redacti, ita ut vere dicere possimus—pervenit gladius usque ad animam."—(Baron., ann. 909, 3. ii., iii. Fleury, 1. liv., s. 2 and 44.) In 865, pope Nicholas addressed some strong pacific exhortations to the princes of France :—' Parcite gladio : humanum fundere sanguinem formidolosius exhorrescite ; cesset ira, sedentur odia, sopiantur jurgia, et omnis ex vobis simultas radicitùs evellatur.... Non in vobis vanæ gloriæ typus, non alterius usurpandi terminos ambitio, sed justitia, charitas, et concordia regnet et summum pax inter vos teneat omnino fastigium.' But such general addresses had probably little effect; and the first authoritative interference of the Church for the partial restoration of peace, and the institution of the Treuga Dei—Trêve de Dieu—took place in the first half of the eleventh century.

principles of the " False Decretals," the sudden revolution thus
occasioned would have been perceptible to the eye of the most
careless historian; but the pretensions, which they contained,
were utterly disproportioned to the power that the see then
possessed of asserting them*.   Their tacit acknowledgment led
to their *gradual* adoption; and in the patient progress of this
usurpation, every step that was gained gave fresh vigour, as
well as loftier ground, to the usurper: but in the ninth century
the French were too independent entirely to submit to the servitude intended for them, and in the tenth the popes were too
weak and contemptible effectually to impose it.   Nevertheless,
time and ignorance were steadily engaged in sanctifying the
imposture, and preparing it for more mischievous service in the
hand of Hildebrand.

Reform of Benedict of Aniane. Though we propose to defer a little longer any general
account of the monastic order, it is proper here to notice that
very powerful renovation of the system which was accomplished
about this time by Benedict of Aniane—a venerable name,
which yields to none save Benedict of Nursia, in the reverence
of monkish annalists. He was contemporary with Charlemagne
and his successor, and was called in 817 to preside at the
council assembled at Aix-la-Chapelle for the reform of monastic abuses.   The regulations which were then enacted,
though they offended the simplicity of the primitive rule by
many frivolous injunctions, were still useful in recalling to some
form of discipline the broken ranks of the regular clergy.   We
should also mention, that the institution of canons regular, by
Chrodegand, bishop of Metz, was undertaken during the same
period, and was completed under Louis the Meek in a council,
also held at Aix-la-Chapelle, in 826.

Episcopal Election. The original form of episcopal election had been habitually
violated by the barbarian kings; and if it was nominally re-
stored by Charlemagne, it still appears that he continued in
practice to profit by the usurpation of his predecessors, and to
fill up vacant sees by his own direct appointment.   Louis, how-

* Hincmar did indeed acknowledge them, but with a certain reservation—
discretè, prout sunt sequenda.—See Baronius, ann. 878, s. 26, on the authority of
Frodoardus, Histor. Rhemensis.

ever, had not been long on the throne when he published (seemingly at the parliament of Attigni in 822) a capitulary to reinstate the Church in her pristine rights. Nor was this concession merely formal; on the contrary, it was brought into immediate force, and for some time actually directed the form of election. For instance, we observe that, in the year 845, Hincmar was raised to the see of Rheims " by the clergy and people of Rheims, by the bishops of the province, with the consent of the archbishop of Sens, the bishop of Paris, and the abbot of St. Denis his superior, and with the approbation of the king;" and from several monuments of that age, and especially the letters of Hincmar* himself, we learn that, at least during the reign of Charles, the Church continued in the recovered possession of her original liberty.

The translation of bishops continued to be prohibited during the ninth century, according to the ancient canons; and though the rule might be occasionally violated by the interference of the prince, and though the pope did occasionally, though rarely, exercise that pernicious power which the decretals, false as they were, and fatal to ecclesiastical discipline, nevertheless gave him, the clergy and the people laboured to maintain the ancient and salutary practice. It appears, however, from a very strange occurrence, which is related to have passed in this age, that the bishops of Rome, however willing to exert their groundless authority elsewhere, were extremely jealous of any

Translation of Bishops.

---

* It appears that, as soon as the vacancy was declared, the king appointed from among the bishops a visitor to the vacant see, who presided at the election. The only persons eligible (or very nearly so) were the clergy of the diocese; but they were not the only electors; the monasteries and the curates, or parochial clergy, sent their deputies. Nor were the noble laymen or the citizens of the cathedral town excluded—on the principle " that all should assist in the election of one whom all were bound to obey." (See Fleury, l. xlvi., s. 47; l. xlviii. s. 38; l. liii., s. 33.) Still it would appear, even from the expression of Hincmar, in an epistle to Charles on this subject, as well as from a canon of the council of Valence held in 855, that the Church then exercised the privilege rather as an indulgence from the sovereign, than by its own original and lawful right. " The prince shall be petitioned to leave to the clergy and people the liberty of election. The bishop shall be chosen from the clergy of the cathedral or of the diocese, or at least of its immediate neighbourhood. If a clerk attached to the service of the prince is proposed, his capacity and his morals shall be rigorously examined, &c."—Council of Valence.

translation to their own see. In the year 892, Formosus was raised from the see of Porto to that of Rome; he was a prelate of great piety and considerable attainments, but he offered the first instance of the elevation of a foreign bishop to the throne of St. Peter. He held it for about four years, and died in possession of it. But scarcely were his ashes cold, when his successor, Stephen VI.,—a name which has earned peculiar distinction even among the pontifical barbarians of those days,—

Exhumation of Formosus, Bishop of Rome. summoned a council to sit in judgment on the deceased. Formosus was dragged from his grave and introduced into the midst of the assembly. He was then solemnly reinvested with the ornaments of office, and placed in the apostolical chair, and the mockery of an advocate to plead in his defence was added. Then Stephen inquired of his senseless predecessor —" Wherefore, Bishop of Porto, hast thou urged thy ambition so far as to usurp the see of Rome?" The council immediately passed the sentence of deposition; and the condemned carcase, after being stripped of the sacred vestments and brutally mutilated, was cast contemptuously into the Tiber. But the day of retribution was near at hand; for, in the order of Providence, the most revolting offences are sometimes overtaken by the swiftest calamities. Only a few weeks elapsed, and Stephen himself was seized, and driven from the see and thrown into an obscure dungeon, loaded with chains, where he was presently strangled.

Change of name on elevation to the popedom. It had been hitherto the practice of the bishop of Rome to retain on his election the name by which he had been previously known: the first exception to this rule took place in the tenth century. In 956, Octavianus, a noble Roman, was raised to the see at the age of eighteen, and expressed his determination to assume the name of John XII*. It does not appear that his boyish inclination was opposed; and it is certain that the precedent was very soon and very generally followed. Neither was the example of Formosus forgotten in succeeding elections, though it was not so commonly imitated; but before the end of this age we find that Gerbert, archbishop

---

* See Pagi. Breviar. Gest. Rom. Pont., Vit. Johan. XII.

of Ravenna, became, by a double change, Sylvester, bishop of Rome, without any offence or reproach.

Among the inferior clergy, the canonical discipline was ex- Discipline of the inferior clergy. tremely rigid : it was strictly forbidden to undertake the charge of two churches, to hold a prebend * in a monastery with a parochial cure, or even to exchange one church for another. That these regulations were sometimes, perhaps generally, enforced, appears from the earnestness with which they are pressed by Hincmar; and it is from his Synodal Statutes, even more than from the canons of councils, that we learn the practice of the Gallican Church during the ninth century: that of the Churches of Italy was probably less severe.

The following is the substance of some of his regulations :— " I have often notified to you respecting the poor who are inscribed in the books of the Church, how you ought to treat them and distribute to them a part of the tithe. I have forbidden you to receive, in return for their portion (called matricula), either present or service, in the house or elsewhere. I persist in forbidding it; since such conduct is to sell charity. I declare to you, that the priest who does so shall be deposed, and even the portion of the tithe which is given to other paupers shall be refused to him." Again,—" I learn that some among you neglect their churches and buy private property which they cultivate, and build houses there in which women reside; and that they do not bequeath their property to the Church, according to the canons, but to their relatives or others. Be informed that I shall punish with the utmost rigour of the rules those whom I shall find guilty of this abuse †." It was another of Hincmar's meritorious endeavours to restrict the

---

* A prebend then signified the dividend *afforded* to a canon for his subsistence. The prohibition was repeated in 889 by the council of Metz; which seems to prove that it was either not generally received, or imperfectly obeyed.

† Hincm. Capitula in Synod. Remensi data. Ann. 874. vol. i., p. 732. Ed. Par. These capitularies are addressed " Ad presbyteros parochiæ suæ," and contain various other injunctions—that presbyters are to learn by heart the Lord's Prayer and the Athanasian Creed—" De Exorcismis Catechumenorum."—" Omnis presbyter *thuribulum* et *incensum* habeat—ut tempore, quo Evangelium legitur, et finito offertorio, super oblationem incensum, ut in morte videlicet Redemptoris, ponat." In another place it was his object to prevent the exaction of fees for burials, &c., and generally to regulate the morality of the clergy.

abuse of private patronage, by refusing ordination to every unworthy candidate.

Claudius, Bishop of Turin.

The practice of auricular confession, which, though generally prevalent, was not universally received in the time of Charlemagne, became completely established during the two following ages. We observe, too, in the annals of those times, that the transfer * of relics from place to place was carried on with extraordinary ardour, proportioned to the sanctity attached to them, and to the wonders which they are recorded to have wrought. This superstition was, indeed, boldly assailed by one real Christian,—Claudius, bishop of Turin †, the protestant of the ninth century. "Wherefore (he indignantly exclaimed) do not the worshippers of the wood of the cross, in conformity with their new principles, adore chaplets of thorns, because Christ was crowned with thorns,—or cradles, linen, or boats,

* The travels of St. Vitus from Leucadia to Rome, from Rome to Saxony, may not perhaps deserve to be traced by us; but we may be excused for pursuing the history of a pious prelate, whose living virtues we found occasion to mention— St. Martin of Tours. About the middle of the ninth century, the approach of the Normans made it expedient to remove the venerable relics of that saint from Tours to Auxerre, where he was confided, as a temporary deposit, to the care of the bishop. During one-and-thirty years of exile, St. Martin continued to perform the most stupendous miracles; and thus he became so valuable to the bishop of Auxerre, that when restitution was demanded, that prelate at once refused it. Hereupon the archbishop of Tours prevailed upon a powerful baron, whose domains were adjacent, to avenge the perfidy and to recover the treasure by force. Thus St. Martin returned triumphantly to his native city, escorted by a band of six thousand soldiers. The story is told in the last chapter of Fleury, book liii. Again, in the year 826, two holy abbots set out from France to Rome, in order to bring away the bodies of St. Sebastian, and even of St. Gregory himself. They returned triumphant—the former had been solemnly granted to the emperor by the pope; the latter they had stolen away by a pious artifice. Their success is recorded by Eginhard, or Einhard, the contemporary biographer of Charlemagne. But the loss has never been acknowledged by the Romans, nor is it probable that they ever sustained it.

† He was a native of Spain, and died in his diocese of Turin, about the year 840. His vigorous opposition to the worship of images could not be so generally unpopular on the other side of the Alps as in Italy; yet we observe that one of his principal opponents was Jonas, a bishop of Orleans. It was another of his errors that he denied that the power of the priesthood, to bind and loose, extended beyond this world; and the last, and probably the greatest, that he asserted the term *Apostolical Father* to be properly applied, not to him who filled the chair of the apostle, but to him who discharged the duties attached to it. The works for which Claudius was particularly celebrated, were his Commentaries on Scripture, both of the Old and New Testament.

because he made use of them,—or spears, because he was pierced with that weapon? Or why do they not fall down before the image of an ass, because he rode on that animal? Christ Jesus did not command us to worship the cross, but to bear it—to renounce the world and ourselves." The *inconsistency* which the pious bishop objected to his Church was indeed, to a great extent, removed by the multiplied corruptions of after ages; but the remonstrances of the reformer roused the indignation of his contemporaries; his endeavours to distinguish the abuses from the substance of the system brought down upon him the usual reproaches of hostility and schism from the more rigid churchmen of the day; and had he lived in an age in which the secular power was subservient to their principles, he would have been variously known to posterity, as a chastised heretic, or as a blessed martyr.

During this same period the penitential system of the Church underwent a more regular organization; ecclesiastical* punishments were adjusted with more discrimination to the offence of the penitent, and greater uniformity of practice was established in the different dioceses. The liturgy received several improvements; indeed it assumed at this time the form in which it was transmitted, with very slight, if any, variation to the more splendid ages of the Roman Church. The celebration of the religious offices, their rules, and their history employed the

---

* The following passage (from Hincmar's Instructions to his Clergy) shows the extent to which the arm of the clergy then reached, as well as the manner in which it acted. "As soon as a homicide, or adultery, or perjury, *or any other public crime,* shall have been committed in his parish, the priest shall signify to the culprit to present himself before the dean and the other priests, and to submit to penance; and they shall send information to their superiors, who reside in the city, so that, in the course of a fortnight, the offender may appear before us and receive public penance with imposition of hands. The day on which the crime was committed shall be carefully noted down, as well as that on which the penance was imposed, and that on which absolution was granted. When the curates shall assemble at the calends of every month they shall confer together respecting their penitents, to inform us in what manner each performs his penance, that we may judge when he ought to be reconciled to the Church. If the criminal does not submit to the penance within the days specified, he shall be excommunicated until he does submit. And let every priest know besides, that if we learn what happens in his parish from any other quarter than himself, or late from himself, he shall himself remain for certain days excommunicated," &c. Capit. Ann. xii. Episc. nostri. p. 733.

diligence of the learned *, and received elaborate and useful illustrations. The credit of these exertions belongs indeed entirely to the theologians of the ninth century; but the works which they raised, after resisting the tempests that followed, continued to constitute an important portion of the ecclesiastical edifice.

External progress of Christianity.

IV. During the period which we have now described, while the centre and heart of Christendom were for the most part cold and corrupted, the vital stream was ceaselessly flowing towards the northern extremities of Europe. It would be an attractive, and it might be a profitable, employment to trace the feeble and sometimes ineffectual missions, which introduced our holy religion among the pagans of Denmark, Sweden, Russia, and Norway; and to observe the other circumstances which, in conjunction with their pious perseverance, finally established it there. This mighty success we may consider to have been obtained before the middle of the eleventh century : not, perhaps, that the faith of Christ was universally embraced by the lowest classes, still less was it thoroughly comprehended or practised; but it had gained such deep and general footing, as to secure its final and perfect triumph.

Denmark and Sweden.

We must be contented concisely to mention some of the leading circumstances by which this great event was accomplished. Heriold, king of Denmark, an exile and a suppliant at the court of Louis the Meek, was there prevailed upon to adopt the Christian religion. But as his conversion did not seem calculated to facilitate his restoration to his throne, Louis presented him with an estate in Friesland, for which he departed. He was accompanied to that retreat by a monk of Corbie, named Anscaire or Ansgarius, a young and fearless enthusiast, ardent for the toils of a missionary and the glory of a martyr. His first exertions were made in Denmark; presently afterwards (in 830) he advanced into Sweden; and such promise of suc-

* Amalarius, a disciple of Alcuin, clerk of the church of Metz, was, among these, the most celebrated. His corrected "Treatise on the Ecclesiastical Offices" was published, under the auspices of Louis, in the year 831 ; and it is highly valued by Roman Catholic writers as proving the very high antiquity of the greater part of the services of their Church. Fleury gives a short account of this work in l. xlvii., s. 36.

cess attended him, that Louis determined to establish an archiepiscopal see at Hamburgh, as the centre of future operations. Gregory IV. gave his consent, and bestowed the pallium, together with the dignity of pontifical legate, upon Ansgarius. Thus exalted and strengthened, he persevered in his enterprise, encouraging the exertions of others, and not sparing his own. And whatsoever degree of credit * we may find it possible to attach to the stories of supernatural assistance, continually vouchsafed both to him and his ministers, we may be assured that the character, with which he was occasionally invested, of ambassador from the emperor of the West, together with the fame of his private sanctity, gave additional efficacy to his religious labours.

The account of Ansgarius's successful expedition into Sweden (in the year 854), as it is transmitted to us from early days, contains much that is curious, and nothing that is improbable. When the bishop arrived at the capital, he communicated to the king, Olef or Olave, the object of his mission. The king replied—" I would willingly consent to your desire, but I can accord nothing until I have consulted our gods by the lot, and till I know the will of the people, who have more influence in public affairs than I have." Olef first consulted his nobles, and, after the customary probation by lot, the gods were ascertained to be favourable to the proposal. The general assembly of the people was then convoked; and the king caused a herald to proclaim the object of the imperial embassy. The people murmured loudly ; and while they were yet divided in their opinions as to the reception of the religion of Christ, an old man rose up among them and said—" King and people! listen to me. We are already acquainted with the service of that God, and he has been found of great assistance to those who

Marginal note: Mission of Ansgarius.

---

* After relating some extraordinary prodigies (l. xlix., s. 19), Fleury observes— "These miracles deserve belief, if ever there were any which did so, since they are related in the Life of St. Ansgarius by Rembert, his disciple and successor ; and if we are permitted to assert, that there is any occasion on which God might be expected to perform miracles it is doubtless in support of his infant Churches," —a religious and pious observation, to which we give our full assent. But the work of Rembert is lost, and our only accounts of Ansgarius are derived from the ancient chronicles.—See Baronius, Ann. 858, s. 14, 15, &c.; and Fleury, l. xlix., s. 21, and l. lv. s. 19.

invoke him. There are many among us who have experienced
it in perils by sea and on other occasions; why, then, should
we reject Him? Formerly there were some who travelled to
Dorstadt for the sake of embracing that religion, of which they
well knew the utility: why, then, should we now refuse that
blessing, when it is here proposed and presented to us?" The
people were convinced by this discourse, and unanimously consented to the establishment of the Christian religion, and the
residence of its ministers among them. Ansgarius died ten
years afterwards; and the footsteps which he had traced in
that rude soil were greatly defaced during the following century, though it is too much to assert that they were wholly
obliterated.

Russia, Poland and Hungary. Some exertions were made for the conversion of the Scla-
vonians about the middle of the ninth age; but that event was
not finally accomplished until the conquest of Bohemia by
Otho, in the year 950. In the same manner Basil, the emperor of the East, in conjunction with his Patriarch Ignatius,
endeavoured to introduce into the heart of Russia the knowledge of the Gospel. An archbishop was purposely ordained
and sent on that mission; and a miracle, which was performed
in the presence of the prince and his people, obtained a partial
reception for the new religion. This event occurred in 871;
but the faith made little consequent progress, and its ministers
were subjected to insult and persecution; nor are we justified
in assigning the complete conversion of that nation to a period
earlier than the end of the tenth century. In 989 Vladimer,
prince of the Russians, espoused the sister of the Emperors
Basil and Constantine, and embraced, in consequence, the
Christian belief. He lived to an extreme old age, and during
a long reign found many imitators: his faith became the rule
of their worship; and the knowledge of its principles and the
practice of its precepts were preceded, as in so many other instances, by its bare nominal * profession. About twenty years
earlier the duke of Poland, whose conversion is also attributed

* We are not to suppose that even the general profession of the faith was immediate: in fact we observe that a pious missionary of the Roman Church, named

to the influence of a Christian queen, promoted the spiritual regeneration of his subjects; and, during the first year of the following age, Stephen, king or duke of Hungary, undertook, with still greater zeal and success, the same holy enterprise.

The above facts, though so briefly stated, are sufficient to prove to us (and could we pursue them more deeply into detail the inference would be still clearer) that, in those days, the public preaching of pious individuals was extremely uncertain in its effect upon the mass of the community, unless when supported by the example or authority of chiefs and princes. Nor is this surprising; for to nations wholly uncivilized and uninstructed it is almost hopeless to address the revelations of truth, or the persuasions of reason. And accordingly we observe, that the little perceptible success, which attended those missionaries in their direct intercourse with the people, is usually ascribed to their miraculous powers, or possibly to the sanctity of their character; seldom to their arguments or their eloquence. But it would have been the greatest of all miracles had this been otherwise; the barbarians were too deeply plunged in ignorance and superstition long to listen to any admonitions which were not addressed to them by the voice of *power*. And thus, when it pleased God in due season to bring them over to his own service, it may be that He vouchsafed to them some faint and occasional manifestations of his own omnipotence; but it was certainly from amongst the powers and principalities of this world, that he selected his most efficient earthly instruments.

In the mean time, during the accomplishment of these gradual and distant conquests, the Saracens had wasted the south of Italy, and approached the very walls of the pontifical city. On the other side, for their chastisement and expulsion, a new and vigorous race presented itself, recently sent forth from the extremities of the North. And (what, besides, is a strange coin-

Remarks.

The Normans and Turks.

Bruno or Boniface, was massacred in the year 1009, with several associates, by certain Russians whom he would have converted. His ardour for martyrdom was roused by the sight of a church, dedicated at Rome to the ancient martyr Boniface.—See Petrus Damiani ap. Baron. Ann. 996, s. 33.

cidence, and deserving of more curious observation than we can
here bestow upon it) while the Norman pagans were over-
spreading some of the fairest provinces of the West with fire
and relentless desolation, the Turkish pagans of the East were
entering, even at the same moment, on their pestilential career
of conquest. The former adopted the religion of the vanquished,
and then, by the infusion of their own vigorous character, they
made some compensation to Christendom for the wrongs which
they had inflicted.   In like manner did the Turks embrace the
religion, while they overthrew the dynasty of the Arabs, who
preceded them—and not their dynasty only, but their arts,
their industry, and their genius.   And in the place of these
they substituted a savage and sullen despotism, alike destructive to the character and the faculties, since its firmest principles are founded in superstition, and bigotry is the legitimate
spirit by which it is warmed and animated.   It is, indeed,
true that the Arabian invaders had devastated many flourishing
Christian countries without justice and without mercy; but it
was no mild or insufficient retribution, which so soon subjected
them to the deadly scourge of Turkish oppression.

CHAPTER XVI.

The Life of Gregory VII.

WE shall divide this long and important chapter into three
sections. The first will contain the principal events which were
brought about by the popes who immediately preceded Gregory
and acted under his influence. The second will describe the
great ecclesiastical and political occurrences of his pontificate.
In the third we shall consider separately the controversy concerning Berenger and the general establishment of the Latin
liturgy.

Section I.

Pope Leo IX.—Early History of Hildebrand—Succession of Victor II.—of Stephen IX.—of Nicholas II.—his Measure respecting Papal Election—the College of Cardinals—imperfection of that Measure—subsequent and final Regulation—Inconveniences of popular Suffrage—Restriction of the imperial Right of Confirmation—Homage of Robert Guiscard and the Normans—Dissensions on the Death of Nicholas—Succession of Alexander II.—actual Supremacy of Hildebrand—Measures taken during that Pontificate—Alexander is succeeded by Hildebrand, under the title of Gregory VII.

GREAT hopes were entertained that the disorders of Italy and the calamities of the Church would find some respite, if not a final termination, on the accession of Leo IX. This pope (Bruno, bishop of Toul), a native of Germany and of splendid reputation, as well for learning as for piety, was appointed by the emperor Henry III. at the request of the Romans, and ascended the chair in the year 1049; and the dignity of his royal connexion confirmed the hopes which his personal virtues had excited. We are informed* that while he was proceeding through France into Italy in his pontifical vestments, he became acquainted at Cluni with a monk named Hildebrand, who prevailed upon him to lay aside those ornaments which he had prematurely assumed, to enter Rome in the dress of a pilgrim, and there to receive from the clergy and people that apostolical office, which no layman had the right to confer. The pope was struck by the talents and character of this monk, and carried him along with him to Rome.

Hildebrand was probably a native of Saona, in Tuscany, and (so at least it is generally asserted) of low origin†; yet he became early in life the disciple of Laurence, archbishop of

Pope Leo IX. 1049 A.D.

---

* Giannone, Storia di Napoli, l. ix., s. 3. Muratori, Vit. Rom. Pontif., t. iii., p. 2. The earliest authority for this story seems to be Otho Frisingensis, who flourished in the middle of the following century. Wibertus, who was Leo's archdeacon and biographer, does not mention it. However, the two facts that Hildebrand accompanied him to Rome, and that he entered that city in the habit of a pilgrim, are not disputed. See Pagi, Breviar. Vit. Leo IX.

† Both these facts are contested. In the chronicle of Hugo Flaviniacensis, it is expressly asserted that he was a Roman, born of Roman citizens; and Papenbrochius thinks it probable that he was of a noble family. Pagi (Vit. Greg. VII. s. 8.) admits that the truth cannot be clearly ascertained.

Melpha; presently he gained the notice and even the confidence of Benedict IX. and Gregory VI., and it was not till the death of the latter that he retired to the monastery of Cluni. From a retreat so little suited to his restless spirit he was finally called by Leo IX. to that vast theatre of ecclesiastical ambition, in which so extraordinary a part was destined to himself.

Leo presided over the Church for five years; his reign was distinguished by some attempts at salutary reform, especially by the famous council which he held at Rheims with that purpose (or under that pretext), in defiance of the royal authority; and also by an unsuccessful campaign against the Normans, in which he sustained a complete defeat in person*. On his death, the election of a successor was confided by the clergy of Rome to the judgment and address of Hildebrand. He selected Victor II., and obtained, by a difficult negociation †, his confirmation from the emperor. During this pontificate, he was sent into France as legate, and vigorously ‡ maintained the authority of the holy see. Victor was succeeded in 1057 by Stephen IX., and on his death, in the year following, a violent division arose among the electors. The nobles of Rome were, for the most part, united, and appear to have made a hasty and illegal choice; but several cardinals, who had no share in this transaction, assembled at Siena and chose another § candidate, who was finally confirmed and placed in possession of the

* On this occasion Hildebrand may have learnt the policy of cultivating their friendship.

† Leo Ostiensis, lib. ii., cap. 90. The emperor professed extreme reluctance to part with his counsellor and favourite.

‡ He deposed six bishops on various charges " by the authority of the Roman see." Respecting one of these it is recorded by several writers, that having been guilty of simony, he became unable to articulate the offended name of the Holy Ghost, though he could pronounce those of the Father and the Son without any difficulty. Petrus Damiani, Epist. ad Nicolaum Papam. Desiderius Abbas Cassinensis, &c. &c.

§ " Pope Stephen, by consent of the bishops, clergy, and Roman people, had ordained that at his death no successor should be chosen, except by the counsel of Hildebrand, then subdeacon of Rome. Hildebrand chose Gerandus, bishop of Florence, who took the name of Nicholas II." Hist. Litt. de la France, Vie Nich. II. See also Leo Ostiensis, lib. ii., cap. 101. Pagi, Breviar. Vit. Steph. IX.

see by the empress, the mother of Henry IV. This candidate was Nicholas II.; and the difficulties which had attended his own election probably led him, under the guidance of Hildebrand, his counsellor and patron, to that measure, which was the foundation of papal independence.

In a late chapter, we briefly mentioned what that measure was, and we shall now add a few remarks in illustration of it. *Enactment on Papal Election.* " We have thought proper to enact (says the pontiff) that upon the decease of the bishop of this Roman universal Church, the affair of the election be treated first and with most diligent consideration by the cardinal bishops; who shall afterwards call into their council the cardinal clerks; and finally require the consent of the rest of the clergy and people *." The term cardinal had hitherto been adopted with very great and indefinite latitude in all the Latin churches, and even applied to the regular orders, as well as to the secular clergy; but by this edict it was restrained to the seven bishops who presided in the city and territory of Rome, and to the twenty-eight clerks or presbyters who were the ministers of the twenty-eight Roman parishes or principal churches. These five-and-thirty persons *The college of cardinals.* constituted the college of cardinals. The previous examination of the claims of the candidates rested with the bishops, but they could not proceed to election except in conjunction with the presbyters. The rest of the clergy, the nobility, and the people were excluded from any positive share in the election, but were allowed a negative suffrage in giving or withholding their consent. It was obvious that this last provision would produce frequent disorder and confusion, and that those who had been so suddenly deprived of the most substantial part of their rights, would lose no opportunity of abusing that which remained to them. And it is probable that Hildebrand, when he counselled a measure of imperfect reform, was obliged to confine himself to what was at the moment practicable, reserving the completion of his design to some more favourable period.

And so, indeed, it proved; the nobles, the clergy, and the populace continued very frequently to disturb the elections

* Mosh. Cent. xi., p. ii., c. ii. The cardinals were to be unanimous in their choice. Hist. Litt. Franc., Vie Nich. II.

which they gradually lost the power to influence; and it was
not till the century following that Alexander III. found means
to perfect the scheme of Hildebrand, and finally purify them
from all such interference. Thenceforward the right was vested
in the college* of cardinals alone, and so it has continued to
the present time.

Popular election. No one acquainted with the frightful † disorders which were
the scandal of the Roman Church during the two preceding
centuries, and which were occasionally felt even at much earlier
periods, will affect to censure a measure which removed the
principal cause of them by subverting the system of popular
election. In defence of a custom which in principle was not
calculated for a numerous society, and which had been condemned by the experience of at least five centuries, it was vain
to plead the venerable institution of antiquity. Universal in
its origin, it had for some time been adopted in episcopal elections throughout the whole of Christendom; but as its inconveniences were multiplied by the increase of proselytes, it fell
into gradual disuse, first in the East, and afterwards in the
Western Church; and at the period which we are now describing, it was perhaps no where in full operation except at
Rome. The evils which at Rome it had so pre-eminently produced, abundantly justify the wisdom of the reformer.

Gibbon seems indeed to have considered the popes as *endeared*
to the people by the practice of popular election. But the affection of the Romans for their popes (we speak not now of those
earlier ages when all episcopal elections were popular) was
probably confined to that period which intervened between
their neglect by the Eastern emperor and the accession of
Charlemagne; and during that interval, while in danger from
the constant invasions of the Lombards, they were certainly
and strongly attached to their leader by the sense of common
peril. There are also other and more respectable reasons for
that attachment. The popes of that time were generally

---

* The college received, on that occasion, some additions for the purpose of con-
ciliating the aristocracy and the civil authorities; but the people gained little
or nothing by them.

† Giannone (Hist. Nap., l. v., c. vi.) details them with great force.

Romans by birth, and known to their subjects, as they are known to posterity, by their piety and their virtues. The ecclesiastical revenues were employed to protect the churches and convents against a barbarous and Arian foe; and the affection awakened by the merits of the popes was multiplied by their services. But to that period it seems to have been limited; and we are unable to discover any proofs of its prevalence after the eighth century.

We have also mentioned another important clause contained in the edict of Nicholas; that which reduced the imperial confirmation to a mere personal privilege, conferred, indeed, on Henry III., but liable to be withheld from his successors *. The long minority of that prince, and the weakness of his government, favoured this usurpation, and accelerated the result which Hildebrand foresaw from it—namely, total emancipation from imperial interference. In fact, the very following pontiff, Alexander II., maintained himself without the sanction, and even against the will, of the emperor; and though Gregory himself vouchsafed to defer his own consecration till Henry had ratified his election, succeeding popes did not on any occasion acknowledge such right as any longer vested in the throne, but proceeded to the exercise of their office, without awaiting even the form of confirmation from Germany. Thus we perceive that the celebrated council of 1059 was the instrument of finally accomplishing (and that at no very distant period) both the objects at which it aimed, without the power of immediately effecting either—the entire independence of papal election from the opposite restraints of popular suffrage and imperial confirmation. It is true that Hildebrand lived not to behold with his own eyes the completion of the work which he had projected; but such is commonly the fate of those who engage in comprehensive schemes of reformation, and whose measures are adapted to their permanent fulfilment.

Imperial Confirmation.

* It is important to cite the words of this edict. " Cardinales episcopi diligentissima simul consideratione tractantes mox sibi clericos cardinales adhibeant sicque reliquus clerus et populus ad consensum novæ electionis accedant. . . . Eligant autem de ipsius ecclesiæ gremio, si repertus fuerit idoneus; et si de ipsa non invenitur ex alia assumatur; salvo debito honore et reverentia dilecti filii nostri Henrici, qui impræsentiarum Rex habetur, et futurus Imperator Deo concedente speratur, *sicut jam ipsi concessimus,* et successorum illius *qui ab Apostolica Sede personaliter* hoc jus impetraverint." Pagi, Brev. Vit. Nicolai II., s. 7.

The work which they build is not for the gratification of their own vanity, or the profit of their own days—it is enough for them that the structure proceeds with some immediate advantage and great promise of future excellence—the use and enjoyment of its perfection is destined to other generations.

The South of Italy given in fief to Rome.

Another important event distinguished the pontificate of Nicholas. The Norman conquerors of the South of Italy, being harassed on the one hand by the hostility of the Greek Emperor, and by the violent incursions of the Saracens on the other, imagined that they should improve their title to their conquests, and increase their security, if they held them as a fief from the See of Rome. The pontiff readily availed himself of a concession, which implied the acknowledgment of one of the broadest principles of papal ambition. And thus he consented to receive the homage of the Normans, and solemnly to create Robert Guiscard Duke of Apulia, Calabria, and Sicily, on condition that he should observe, as a faithful vassal, inviolable allegiance, and pay an annual* tribute, in proof of his subjection to the apostolic see. The permanence of this feudal grant increases its claims on our attention ; and the kingdom of the two Sicilies, even as it now subsists, stands on that foundation. The nature of this transaction is so closely allied to that of others, which we are now approaching, that there is no difficulty in tracing it to the hand of Hildebrand.

Alexander II.

On the death of Nicholas in 1061, the dissensions which had disturbed his election were to some extent renewed. The more powerful party, under the guidance of Hildebrand, placed Alexander II. in the chair : the nobles resisted, and their opposition was encouraged by the direct support of the emperor ; whose confirmation had not been required by the new pope, and who was justly exasperated at the neglect. Nevertheless, the genius of Hildebrand triumphed over all difficulties ; and after a contest of three years Alexander was firmly established in the chair, though it was still feebly disputed with him. He occupied it for twelve years, and passed the greater portion of that time in the retirement of Lucca or

* "Accepta prius ab iis, cum sacramento, Romanæ ecclesiæ fidelitate ; censuque quotannis per juga boum singula denariis duodecim."—Leo Ostiensis, lib. iii. cap. 15. The words of the oath are cited by Baronius.

Monte Cassino—but the see lost nothing by his secession, since he intrusted its various interests and the entire direction of public affairs to the diligent zeal of Hildebrand, who had been raised by Nicholas to the dignity of Archdeacon of Rome, and who exerted there an unbounded and undisguised authority*.

Accordingly we find, during this pontificate, (1.) that various attempts were made to reform the morals of the clergy and the abuses of the Church : (2.) that the famous question concerning Investitures was first moved : (3.) that, by a constitution of Alexander, no bishop in the Catholic Church was permitted to exercise his functions, until he had received the confirmation of the holy see† : (4.) that the emperor himself was summoned to Rome, to answer to the charge of simony, and other complaints which had reached the see respecting him ‡.   Under these various heads we perceive the operation of the same master-spirit aiming steadily at the reform of the Church, at its independence, at the extension of papal authority over the episcopal order, and over the conduct and sceptre of princes.

Alexander II. died in 1073 : for four-and-twenty years Hildebrand had exercised in the Vatican an unremitting influence which had latterly grown into despotic authority—and thus far, contented with the reality of pontifical power, he had not cared to invest himself with the name and rank.   Perhaps he had thought the moment not yet arrived, in which he could occupy the office with dignity, or fill it with great advantage ; probably he was desirous to complete, under other names, the train which he had been long preparing, and to which he designed to

---

* The following contemporary verses perhaps do not much exaggerate the actual supremacy of Hildebrand :—

"Papam rite colo, sed te prostratus adoro ;
Tu facis hunc dominum—te facit ille Deum.
Vivere vis Romæ ? clarâ depromito voce,
Plus Domino Papæ, quam Domno pareo Papæ."
                                        Petr. Damiani.

† St. Marc, p. 460.   Hallam (Middle Ages, c. vii.) considers this provision to have contributed more than any other papal privilege to the maintenance of the temporal influence, as well as the ecclesiastical supremacy of Rome.

‡ See Semler, cent. xi. c. 1, and Pagi, Vit. Alexand. II. sect. 48.   This part of Mosheim's history is exceedingly hurried and imperfect.

apply the torch in his own person; it is even possible, that his severe and imperious character, by alienating popular* favour, rendered his election uncertain.   It was not, assuredly, that he valued the security of a humbler post; for, among the numerous vices with which he has been charged, the baseness of selfish timidity has never been accounted as one.   At length, on the very day of Alexander's death, Hildebrand was elected his successor by the unanimous suffrage of the cardinals, and the universal acclamation of the clergy and people; and that he might mark, at least, the beginning of his pontificate by an act of moderation, he waited for the emperor's consent before his consecration.   But it is true that he rather claimed than requested that consent, and that it was granted with the graceless reluctance of impotent jealousy.   He assumed the title of Gregory VII.; and, after twelve years of restless exertion, he left that name invested with a portentous celebrity, which attaches to no other in the annals of the Church.

Election of Gregory VII. (margin note)

SECTION II.—*The Pontificate of Gregory.*

Gregory's First Council—its two objects—to prevent (1.) Marriage or Concubinage of the Clergy—(2.) Simoniacal Sale of Benefices—On the Celibacy of the Clergy—why encouraged by Popes—Leo IX.—Severity and Consequence of Gregory's Edict—Original Method of appointment to Benefices—Usurpations of Princes—how abused—the Question of Investiture—Explained—Pretext for Royal Encroachments—Original form of Consecration by the King and Crown—Right usurped by Otho—State of the Question at the Accession of Gregory—Conduct of Henry—further measures of the Pope—Indifference of Henry—Summoned before a Council at Rome—Council of Worms—Excommunication of the Emperor and Absolution of his Subjects from their Allegiance—Consequence of this Edict—Dissensions in Germany—how suspended—Henry does Penance at Canossa—restored to the Communion of the Church—again takes the field—Rodolphus declared Emperor—Gregory's Neutrality—Remarks on the course of Gregory's Measures—Universality of his temporal Claims—

* This is Sismondi's opinion, chap. iii.; and we can readily believe that the stern virtues of Gregory were not likely to recommend him to a venal populace. Yet, when at length he did propose himself, we hear nothing of any opposition from that quarter, while the acclamations which attended his election are universally recorded.   But, after all, that severity of manner, which is known to be connected with an austere sanctity of life, is not an unpopular feature in the sacerdotal character.

his probable project—Considerations in excuse of his Schemes—partial admission of his Claims—Ground on which he founded them—power to bind and to loose—Means by which he supported them—Excommunication—Interdict—Legates à Latere—Alliance with Matilda—his Norman allies—German Rebels—internal Administration—Effect of his rigorous Measures of Reform—his grand scheme of Supremacy within the Church—False Decretals—Power conferred by them on the Pope—brought into action by Gregory—Appeals to the Pope—Generally encouraged and practised—their pernicious Effects—Gregory's *double* Scheme of Universal Dominion—Return to Narrative—Clement III. anti-Pope—Death of Rodolphus—Henry twice repulsed from before Rome—finally succeeds—his Coronation by Clement—the Normans restore Gregory—he follows them to Salerno and there dies—his historical importance—his Character—Public—his grand principle in the Administration of the Church—Private—as to Morality—as to Religion.

In the year following his advancement, Gregory assembled a numerous council at Rome, chiefly for the purpose of correcting two abuses in Church discipline and government, which appeared most to require reform. These were (1.) the marriage or concubinage of the clergy; (2.) the simoniacal sale of benefices.

(1.) Most of the early fathers were diligent in their endeavours to establish the connexion between celibacy and sanctity, and to persuade men that those who were wedded to the Church were contaminated by an earthly union. This notion was readily embraced by the laity; and many of the clergy acted upon it without reluctance, owing to the greater commendation of austerity which the practice was found to confer upon them: still, in the eastern Church, where it originated, it was never very rigidly enforced; and a council of Constantinople, (called the Council in Trullo,) held in 692, permitted, with certain limitations, the ordination of married men. These canons were never formally received in the West, where celibacy and strict continence were unrelentingly enjoined on all orders of the priesthood. With whatsoever laxity the latter injunction may have been observed, there are not many complaints of the open violation of the former, at least from the end of the sixth, until the conclusion of the ninth and the progress of the tenth century; but during this period the irregularity spread widely, and even displayed itself with undisguised confidence throughout every branch of the Roman hierarchy. The popes were

Celibacy of the Clergy.

Council in Trullo, 692 A.D.

F 2

naturally averse to this relaxation of discipline—partly from the continued prevalence of the original notion, that those were better qualified for spiritual meditations and offices, who were severed from secular interests and affections; partly from the scandal thus occasioned to the prejudices of the laity; partly from respect to established ordinances and usages; partly from attachment to a principle, which, by withdrawing the clergy from worldly connexions, bound them more closely to each other and to their head. At any rate the evil had now grown to so great a height, that it was become quite necessary either to repeal the laws so openly violated, or to enforce them. They chose the latter office, and the first who distinguished himself in the difficult enterprise was Leo IX. His immediate successors trod in his steps; but as sufficient measures were not taken (perhaps could not be taken) to carry those edicts into effect, they seem generally to have fallen to the ground without advantage, except in so far as they prepared the way for the more vigorous exertions of Gregory.

Council held at Rome, 1074 A. D. In the above-mentioned council it was ordained—" that the sacerdotal orders should abstain from marriage; and that such clerks as had already wives or concubines should immediately dismiss them, or quit the priestly office." The more difficult part remained to enforce this decree; and herein Gregory did not confine himself to the legitimate weapon of spiritual censure, but also exerted his powerful influence to arm the temporal authorities in his service. Numerous disorders were the consequence of this measure; at Milan* and in Germany the edict was openly resisted, and many ecclesiastics were found in every country, who preferred the sacrifice of their dignities and interests to the abandonment of those connexions which they held dearer than either †. The confusion

* At Milan a violent dispute on this subject had arisen between the Clergy and the Laity, under Stephen IX., in the year 1057. (Pagi, Vit. Steph. IX.) The schism continued under Nicholas II., who sent legates to compose it; but it still remained during the pontificate of Alexander. The popes took part with the Laity against the married Clergy, who were named Nicolaites.

† "Malle se sacerdotium quàm conjugium deserere." Lambert. Schaffn. in Chronico. Gregory is much censured by Mosheim and others for not having distinguished, in his sweeping decree, between the wives and the concubines of

thus created was indeed gradually tranquillized by the progress of time, by the perseverance of the pontiff, by the aid, perhaps, of the laity, by the indifference of the sovereigns—but entire obedience was not so easily restored; and though, through severe restraint, the rebellion was at length repressed, it continued in some degree to disturb the Church during the following century, and to call down the denunciations of her popes and her councils.

(2.) Another Edict of the same Council forbade in the severest terms the sale of ecclesiastical benefices; and the following circumstance made that Edict necessary.   The bishop was originally elected by the clergy and people of the diocese; but in process of time, the people, as we have already seen, were in most places excluded, and the election rested with the clergy alone.   Presently, in the anarchy which prevailed after the dissolution of the Western Empire, the wealth which flowed into the coffers of the Church, as it brought with it no proportionate security, not only tempted the rapacity of the nobles, but invited the usurpation of the sovereigns. Thus, at an early period, long antecedent to the reign of Charlemagne, the Western Princes commenced their interference in episcopal elections— first, as it would seem, by simple recommendation; then by the interposition of threats and the show of authority; lastly, by positive appointment.   The partial restoration of the right, which took place in the ninth century, under Louis the Meek and his successor, was probably confined to the Church of France and to the life of Hincmar.

Edict against Simony.

the Clergy; and with justice, since he visited the violation of canonical law with the same severity, with which he protected the eternal precepts of Christian morality.   It must be admitted, however, that as his object was the entire and immediate extirpation of what he considered a scandalous abuse, he took the only means at all likely to accomplish it.   It was in vain that the Milanese Clergy pleaded the authority of St. Ambrose and the example of the Greeks—it was well known that the former protected not those who admitted papal supremacy; and that the Council, which permitted the latter, was never acknowledged by the Roman Church.   It seems indeed probable that St. Gregory was the first Pope who rigidly enforced the practice of celibacy; but for two centuries after his time it was both the law and, to a great extent, the practice of the Church, and in the two ages which succeeded, though it had ceased to be the practice, it still continued the law.—See Bayle, Vie Greg. I.   Fleury, Discours sur l'H. E. depuis 600 jusqu'à 1100.

Their next step was to abuse the privilege which they had usurped, and the manner of abuse was alike indecent and scandalous : the spoils of their injustice were retailed to their avarice; and the most important charges and offices of the ministry were commonly and publicly sold to the highest bidder, without regard to literary qualification, or sanctity of character, or the most obvious interests of religion.   This was, in fact, the avowed corruption which Gregory sought to remedy ; and the specious object to which his exertions and those of his successors, through so many conflicts, tended, was to deprive the prince of his usurped authority in episcopal election.   A secondary design was closely attached to this, but not yet so boldly professed—to transfer that authority, if not in form, at least in substance, to the see of Rome, by conceding to it the right of confirmation.

Origin of the dispute about Investitures.   Thus much appears exceedingly simple ; but the point on which the dispute did in reality turn, and which has given the name to the contest, was one, as it might seem, of mere formality—the *Investiture* of the bishop or abbot.   We must now shortly explain this part of the question ; and we shall thus become acquainted with the circumstances which are urged in justification of the royal claims.   When the early conquerors of the West conferred territorial grants upon the Church, the individuals who came to the enjoyment of them were obliged to present themselves at court, to swear allegiance to the king, and to receive from his hands some symbol, in proof that the temporalities were placed in their possession.   The same ceremony, in fact, was imposed on the ecclesiastical as on the lay proprietor of royal fiefs ; and it was called Investiture.   Afterwards, when the princes had usurped the presentation to all valuable benefices, even to those which had not been derived from royal bounty, they introduced no distinction founded on the different sources of the revenue, but continued to subject those, whom they nominated, to the same oath of allegiance, and the same ceremony of investiture, with the laity.

In the mean time, it had been an early custom, on the consecration of a bishop, that the metropolitan, who by right performed the ceremony, should place in the hands of the prelate elect a *ring* and a *crosier*—symbols of his spiritual connexion with the Church, and of his pastoral duties. This was a form of investiture purely ecclesiastical, and the princes, even after they had usurped the presentation to benefices, did not at first venture to make use of it ; and it is said that they were finally led to do so by some artful attempts on the part of the clergy to recover their original right of election. Mosheim (in opposition to many less celebrated writers) is of opinion that Otho the Great was the first prince who ventured to present with profane hand the emblems of spiritual authority ; at least it is quite certain, that this custom had been in very general use for some time before the accession of Gregory. And thus the temporal power had gradually succeeded in a double usurpation on ecclesiastical privileges—first, in despoiling the lower clergy of their right of election—next, in encroaching upon the province of the metropolitans, and presuming to dispense in their place the symbols of a spiritual office.

As a partial palliation of the conduct of the throne, it is maintained, that the homage required from the bishop or abbot at investiture was for his temporalities only ; and in so far as these were the feudal grants of former princes, the claim was manifestly just, but no farther than this. The crown could not fairly assert any suzerainty over the vast domains and enormous extent of property, which had accrued to the Church from other quarters, before the establishment of the feudal system, and which, therefore, were not held on any feudal tenure ; nor can any sufficient plea be found for its general assumption of the disposal of benefices (to say nothing of the flagitious manner in which they were retailed), and its adoption of a form of investitute which was purely ecclesiastical.

Such, as nearly as we can collect, was the state of this question, when Gregory published his edict against Simony in the year 1074. The results of the council were communicated to the Emperor* Henry IV., who received the Legates courteously, and bestowed some unmeaning praise on the zeal of the pope

* According to the Church writers, King only. He had not yet gone through the ceremony of coronation at Rome,

for the reform of his Church. But Gregory was not to be satisfied with expressions ; and, as he intended to give general effect to his decrees, he desired permission to summon councils in Germany, by which those accused of simony might be convicted and deposed. Henry refused that permission, partly from the consciousness of his own criminality, partly because he was not really anxious for any reform which would curtail his own patronage. This opposition obliged the pope to proceed one step farther. After pressing the execution of his former ordinances in a variety of letters, addressed, with various effect or entire inefficacy, to different princes and bishops, he convoked, early in the year following, a second council at Rome and, with its assistance, he proceeded to those measures which he had proposed to accomplish by synods in Germany, and, probably, somewhat beyond them. On this occasion he not only deposed the Archbishop of Bremen and the Bishops of Strasbourg, Spires, and Bamberg, besides some Lombard Bishops, but also excommunicated five of the Imperial Court, whose ministry the prince had used in simoniacal transactions. At the same time he pronounced his formal anathema against any one who should receive the investiture of a bishopric or abbey from the hands of a layman, and also against all by whom such investiture should be performed*. Henry paid no other attention to this edict, than to repeat his former general acknowledgment of the existence of simony, and his intention, in future, to discourage it.

Henry summoned to Rome.   Some particular differences, respecting the appointment to the see of Milan and other matters, tended at this moment to exasperate the growing hostility of Gregory and Henry: it happened, too, that the latter was disturbed and weakened

* The words of the edict are : " Si quis deinceps Episcopatum vel Abbatiam de manu alicujus laicæ personæ susceperit, nullatenus inter Episcopos vel Abbates habeatur, nec ulla ei ut Episcopo vel Abbati audientia concedatur. Insuper etiam gratiam B. Petri et introitum Ecclesiæ interdicimus, quoad usque locum, quem sub crimine tam ambitionis quam inobedientiæ, quod est scelus idololatriæ, cepit, deseruerit. Similiter etiam de inferioribus Ecclesiasticis dignitatibus constituimus. Item si quis Imperatorum, Ducum, Marchionum, Comitum, vel quilibet secularium potestatum aut personarum investituram Episcopatus, vel alicujus Ecclesiasticæ dignitatis dare præsumpserit, ejusdem sententiæ vinculo se adstrictum sciat." Hugo Flaviniacensis, ap. Pag. Vit. Greg. VII, s. 26.

by civil dissensions, occasioned, in some degree, by his own dissolute and profligate rule, which, by distracting his forces, invited the aggression of his foreign enemies. It is even asserted (by Dupin) that the malcontents sent deputies to Rome to solicit the interference of the pope. Such an application is rendered probable by the fact which we now proceed to mention, and which is a certain and a memorable monument of papal extravagance. Gregory sent legates into Germany, bearing positive orders to the Emperor to present himself forthwith at Rome; since it became him to clear himself, before the Pope and his Council, from various charges which his subjects had alleged against him. These charges might possibly be confined to ecclesiastical offences, of which the Emperor had notoriously been guilty; but never, before the days of Hildebrand, had it been expressly asserted, that he was amenable for such offences to any ecclesiastical tribunal.

He treated the summons as a wanton insult, and wantonly retorted it. He collected at Worms* a council of about twenty German Bishops (some of whom were already personally embroiled with Gregory); and these prelates, after passing many censures on the conduct, election, and constitutions of Hildebrand, pronounced him unworthy of his dignity, and accordingly deposed him. Gregory was not further disturbed by such empty denunciations, than to take measures to return them much more effectually. In a full assembly of one hundred and ten bishops, he suspended from their offices the ecclesiastics who had declared against him; he then pronounced the excommunication of the emperor; and accompanied his anathema by the unqualified sentence, " that he had forfeited the kingdoms of Germany and Italy, and that his subjects were absolved from their oath of fealty†.'

Excommunicated and deposed.

---

* " Quæ legatio Regem vehementer permovit; statimque abjectis cum gravi contumelia Legatis, omnes qui in regno suo essent Episcopos et Abbates Wormetiæ Dominica Septuagesimæ convenire præcepit, tractare cum eis volens ad deponendum Romanum Pontificem, si qua sibi via, si qua ratio pateret: *in hoc cardine totam verti ratus salutem suam* et regni stabilitatem, *si is non esset Episcopus.*" Lambert. Schaffn. ad an. 1076.

† The words in which this celebrated sentence was conveyed should be recorded :—" Petre Apostolorum Princeps, etc. etc. Hac fiducia fretus pro Ecclesiæ

This assertion of control over the allegiance of subjects was hitherto without precedent in the history of the papal Church ; and it was now, for the first time, advanced to the prejudice of a monarch, whose character, though stained both by vices and weaknesses, was not wholly depraved, nor universally odious. Nevertheless, the edict of Gregory was diligently promulgated throughout Germany; nor was it idly cast into a kingdom already divided, and among a people already discontented and accustomed to rebellion. The dukes of Swabia, headed by Rodolphus, presently rose in arms; they were supported by a fresh revolt of the Saxons; and there were those even among Henry's best friends, whose fidelity was somewhat paralyzed by the anathema under which he had fallen. After a short but angry struggle, an arrangement was made greatly to his disadvantage—that the claims and wrongs of both parties should be subjected to the decision of the pope, who was invited to preside at a council at Augsbourg for that purpose; and that, in the mean time, Henry should be suspended from the royal dignity. It is not easy to decide how much of this success should be attributed to the previous animosity of the parties opposed to Henry, how much to a blind respect for the edict and authority of the pope; but the treaty, to which all consented, certainly implied an acknowledgment of the power which Gregory had assumed, and gave a sort of foundation and countenance to his future measures.

Henry does penance at Canossa.

Henry, who had little to hope from a public sentence, to be delivered in the midst of his rebellious subjects by his professed

tuæ honore et defensione, ex parte Omnipotentis Dei, Patris et Filii et Spiritus Sancti, per tuam potestatem et auctoritatem Henrico Regi, filio Henrici Imperatoris, qui contra Ecclesiam tam inaudita superbia insurrexit, totius regni Teutonicorum et Italiæ gubernacula contradico, et omnes Christianos *a vinculo juramenti* quod sibi fecere vel facient, *absolvo ;* et ut nullus ei sicut Regi serviat, interdico. Dignum est enim, ut, qui studet honorem Ecclesiæ tuæ imminuere, ipse honorem amittat quem videtur habere. Et quia Christianus contempsit obedire nec ad Dominum rediit, quem dimisit participando excommunicatis et multas iniquitates faciendo, *meaque monita, quæ pro salute sua sibi misi, te teste spernendo,* seque ab Ecclesia sua, tentans eam scindere separando, vinculo eum anathematis *vice tua* alligo, ut sciant Gentes et comprobent quia Tu es Petrus, et super tuam Petram Filius Dei vivi ædificavit Ecclesiam suam, et portæ Inferi non prævalebunt adversus eam." Paul. Bernried. cap. 75 ; Pagi, Vit. Greg. VII., s. 42,

enemy, determined to anticipate, or, if possible, to prevent his disgrace by an act of private submission to pontifical authority. For that purpose he crossed the Alps with few attendants, during the severity of an inclement winter, and proceeded to Canossa, a fortress in the neighbourhood of Parma, in which Gregory was then residing. In penitential garments, with his feet and head bare and unsheltered from the season, the emperor presented himself at the gate of the fortress, as a sinner and a suppliant. His humble request was to be admitted to the presence of the pontiff and to receive his absolution. For three dreary days, from dawn till sunset, the proudest sovereign in Europe was condemned to continue his fast and his penance before the walls, and probably under the eyes of Gregory, in solitary* and helpless humiliation. At length, on the fourth day, he was permitted to approach the person of the pontiff, and was absolved from the sentence of excommunication. Yet even this favour was not vouchsafed him unconditionally †: he was still suspended from the title and offices of royalty, and enjoined to appear at the congress of Augsbourg and abide by the decision which should then be passed upon him.

* Henry is represented to have traversed the Alps at extreme risk by unfrequented roads, as the ordinary passes were guarded by his enemies ; and Lambertus of Aschaffenbourg, a contemporary historian, describes the castle of Canossa as surrounded by a triple wall, within the second of which the emperor was admitted to his penance, while the whole of his suite remained without the exterior. See Sismondi, Hist. Rep. Ital., c. iii. Paulus Bernriedensis speaks of the *insolita papæ duritia* shown on this occasion.

† The oath which he took is given at length by Paulus Bernriedensis, Vit. Greg. VII. Sismondi designates the conduct of Gregory as "une trahison insigne," but not justly so; since it cannot be shown that the pope had bound himself by any engagement to the emperor which he did not strictly fulfil ; the latter did penance for his contumacy towards the Church, and the pope, in consequence, restored him to the communion of the Church. The council or diet to be held at Augsbourg was a measure previously arranged, to which many other eminent persons were parties ; and it was intended for the settlement of political, at least as much as of ecclesiastical differences ;—whereas the penance at Canossa was merely a particular atonement to the see of Rome, not at all connected with the general maladministration of Henry. In fact, Gregory's own words are conclusive on the question.—"Henricus, confusus et humiliatus ad me veniens, absolutionem ab excommunicatione quæsivit. Quem ego videns humiliatum, multis ab eo promissionibus acceptis de vitæ suæ emendatione, *solam ei communionem reddidi; non tamen in regno instauravi,* nec fidelitatem hominum qui sibi juraverant vel erant juraturi ut sibi servetur præcepi." &c. See Mabill., Vit. Greg. VII., c. 107. Pagi, Vit. Greg. VII., s. 43. Denina, Delle Rivol. d'Italia, lib. x., c. vi.

The pope's subsequent conduct.

Henry soon discovered that he had gained nothing by this degradation, except contempt; and after descending to the lowest humiliation which ever prince had voluntarily undergone, he found himself precisely in his former situation, with the council of Augsbourg still hanging over his head. Of an useless submission he repented vehemently; he abandoned himself to his feelings of shame and indignation, resumed his title and his functions, and prepared once more to confront his adversaries. The Saxons and Swabians immediately declared Rodolphus emperor of Germany (in 1077); Henry was supported by the Lombards in Italy; and a sanguinary war was carried on in both countries with various success and general devastation. For three years Gregory preserved the show, perhaps the substance, of neutrality; he received the deputies of both parties with equal courtesy, and seemed to wish to profit so far only by their dissensions, as to engage them to aid him in the execution of his original edicts. But in the year 1080, decided, as some say, by the misfortunes, as others assert, by the crimes* of Henry, he pronounced a second sentence of deposition, and conferred upon Rodolphus the crown of Germany†.

Extent of Gregory's temporal claims.

Thus far we have traced, without much comment, the rapid but regular progress of Gregory. The first measure, as we have seen, in his temporal usurpation (for in his earliest decrees against Church abuses he did not exceed the just limits of his authority), was to declare the emperor amenable to a papal court of judicature, and to summon him before it; the next was to deprive him of his throne and to absolve his subjects from their oath of allegiance; the last was to dispose of the empire, with absolute authority, as a fief of St. Peter. Without

* Sismondi, whose partialities are against Gregory and the Church, says respecting Henry, that "his character was generous and noble; but he abandoned himself with too little restraint to the passions of his age;" and those passions undoubtedly led him to the commission of great political offences. Private excesses may sometimes find their excuse in youth; but the vices of kings deserve less indulgence, since they usually influence the morals and happiness of their subjects. A less favourable, but probably a more correct view of the character of Henry is taken by Denina. Delle Rivoluz. d'Italia, lib. x.. c. v.

† The act and the authority for it were expressed in an hexameter verse, inscribed on the crown which Gregory sent to Rodolph—

Petra dedit Petro, Petrus diadema Rodolpho.

further examination we might at once have concluded, that claims so extravagant and irrational were merely the passionate ebullitions of a feeble spirit, irritated by personal pique or effeminate vanity. But this was not so ; the claims in question were advanced by the most vigorous and consistent character of his age, and they were pressed with a deliberate and earnest zeal which proved his conviction of their justice. They were not confined to the dominions of Henry ; they displayed themselves in every state and province of Europe. The kingdom of *France* was declared tributary to the see of Rome, and papal legates were commissioned to demand the annual payment of the tribute, by virtue of the true obedience* due to that see by every Frenchman. And the king himself (Philip I.) was reminded "that both his kingdom and his soul were under the dominion of St. Peter, who had the power to *bind* and to *loose* both in heaven and on earth." *Saxony* was pronounced to be held on feudal tenure from the apostolic chair and in subjection to it. It was pretended that the kingdom of *Spain* had been the property of the Holy See from the earliest ages of Christianity. William the Norman, after the conquest of *England*, was astonished to learn that he held that country as a fief of Rome and tributary to it. The entire feudal submission of the kingdom of *Naples* has been already mentioned. Nothing was so lofty as to daunt the ambition of Gregory, or so low as to escape it. The numerous dukes or princes of Germany, those of Hungary, of Denmark, of Russia, of Poland, of Croatia and Dalmatia, were either solicited to subject their states to the suzerainty of St. Peter, or reminded of their actual subjection. And the grand object of Gregory is probably not exaggerated by those who believe that he designed to re-establish the Western † empire on the basis of opinion, and to bind by one spiritual chain to the chair of St. Peter the political govern-

* " Per veram obedientiam."

† Thus, in effect, the Western empire of which the foundations were *really* laid at the coronation of Charlemagne, was not the temporal dominion at which *the prince* aspired, and which so soon passed away from his sceptre, but that spiritual despotism, affected by *the priest*, and which was much more extensive, as it was much more durable.

ments and ever-conflicting interests of the universal kingdom of Christ *.

Are we astonished at the magnificence, or do we laugh at the wildness of this project ? Let us first inquire by what means the mighty architect proposed to combine and consolidate his structure. Gregory seriously designed to regulate his truly Catholic empire by a council of bishops, who were to be assembled at Rome annually, with full power to decide the differences of princes both with each other and with their subjects; to examine the rights and pretensions of all parties, and to arbitrate in all the perplexed concerns of international policy. If we can, indeed, imagine that he was animated by that general spirit of philanthropy, which is ever found to burn most brightly in the noblest minds; if he really dared to hope that his project would reconcile the quarrels of the licentious princes of his day, or remedy the vices of their governments, or alleviate the misery of the people, who were suffering equally from both those causes—we may smile at the vanity of the vision, but we are bound to respect the motive which created it. Nor is it only the political degradation of Europe that we are called upon to consider, before we may pronounce sentence upon that Pontiff: we must also make great allowance for the principles of ecclesiastical supremacy, which had already taken root before his time, which had been partially acted upon, and which, to a certain extent, were acknowledged ; for the necessary confusion of temporal with spiritual authority, which the feudal

---

* Amid this multiplicity of objects, which divided without distracting the mind of Gregory, he did not allow himself to forget either the schism or calamities of the East; he even projected to remedy both by personally conducting an army against the Mahometans. This is mentioned in a letter (Lib. ii., 31) to Henry, written in 1074, in which, after some notice of his project, he asserts that forty thousand men were prepared to engage with him, and adds— " Illud enim me ad hoc opus permaximè instigat, quod Constantinopolitana ecclesia de Spiritu Sancto à nobis dissidens concordiam Apostolicæ Sedis expetit," &c. Pagi, Vit. Greg. VII., s. xx. We may observe that, among the numerous points of difference which had in latter times grown up between the two Churches, and had been exaggerated with such intemperate zeal by both, the eye of Gregory notices one only. Gregory addressed besides some hortative letters " Ad universos fideles, ' on the same subject.

system had still worse confounded, so that their limits were indiscernible, inviting both parties to mutual aggression; and for the usurpations which the crown had already made on the privileges of the Church, and the evil purposes to which it had turned them. These circumstances, when duly and impartially weighed, will lessen the astonishment, which the bare recital of Gregory's proceedings is calculated to awaken, and moderate the indignant censure with which the example of other writers might dispose us to visit them.

We are not, however, to imagine, that the Pope's extraordinary claims were universally admitted. The King of France refused the tribute demanded of him; the conqueror of England consented to the tribute (called Peter's pence), but disclaimed the allegiance. Various success attended his attempts on the other states, according to the variety of their strength or weakness, or the circumstances of their actual politics. But at the same time, the mere fact, that such claims were confidently asserted and repeated obstinately, that in many instances they were practically assented to, and very rarely repelled with vigour and intrepidity, persuaded ignorant people (and almost all were ignorant) that there was indeed some real foundation for them, and that the Holy See was, in truth, invested with some vague prescriptive right of universal control, and surrounded by mysterious, but inviolable sanctity.

We must add a few words, both respecting the grounds on which Gregory founded those claims, and the means which he employed to enforce them. As to the former, it does not appear that he openly availed himself of the grand forgery of his predecessors, or at least that he justified any of his pretensions by direct appeal to the "donation of Constantine;" unless, indeed, it were assumed that the universal rights of St. Peter over the Western Empire originated in that donation. Respecting Spain, for instance, he particularly admitted that, though that country was among the earliest of the pontifical possessions, the grant which made it so had perished among other ancient records *. In treating with those provinces which had formed

* Lib. x., epist. 28.

no part of the Western Empire, he seems to have assailed
them severally, as the circumstances of their history happened
to favour his demands. Saxony, for example, he asserts to
have been bestowed upon the Roman See by the piety of Charlemagne. Some among the smaller states were merely exhorted
to make a cession of their territories to St. Peter; by which it
was admitted that the apostle had yet obtained no rights over
them. Some of them made such cession, and thus encouraged
the arrogance of Gregory and the aggressions of future pontiffs.

Power to bind and to loose.

The power possessed by the successors of St. Peter " to bind
and to loose" was not confined by them to spiritual affairs,
however wide the extremities to which they pushed it in these
matters. It was extended also to temporal transactions, and
so far extended as to be made the plea of justification with a
Pope, whenever he presumed to loose the sacred bonds of allegiance, which connect the subject with the sovereign. It would
be difficult, perhaps, to produce a more certain index of the
character of religious knowledge, and the degradation of the
reasoning faculty, which prevailed in those days, than by exhi-
biting that much-perverted text as the single basis, on which so
monstrous a pretension rested and was upheld.

Various sources of his power.

The appalling influence of anathema and excommunication *
over a blind and superstitious people had long been known and
frequently put to trial by preceding popes; and the still more
formidable weapon of Interdict began to be valued and adopted
about the time of Gregory. Extraordinary legates†, whose
office suspended the resident vicars of the pontiff, had been
sparingly commissioned before the end of the tenth century;
they now became much more common, and fearlessly exercised
their unbounded authority in holding councils, in promulgating
canons, in deposing bishops, and issuing at discretion the

* The frequent use and abuse of excommunication by all orders of the priesthood had greatly diminished the terror and efficacy of the sentence even in much
earlier ages. We find the councils of the ninth century continually legislating
for the purpose of restoring their weight to both ecclesiastical weapons. By the
Council of Meaux (held in 845) it was especially enacted, that the *anathema* could
not be pronounced even by a bishop, unless by the consent of the archbishop and
the other bishops of the province.

† Called Legates *à latere*—sent from the side of the pope.

severest censures of the Church. But it was not concealed
from the wisdom of Gregory, that temporal authority could not
surely be advanced or permanently supported without temporal
power. Accordingly he cemented his previous alliance with
the Normans of Naples; and also (which was still more important, and proved, perhaps, the most substantial among his
temporal conquests) he prevailed upon Matilda, the daughter
and heiress of Boniface, Duke of Tuscany, to make over her
extensive territories to the apostle, and hold them on feudal
tenure from his successors. By these means the ecclesiastical
states were fortified, both on the north and south, by powerful
and obedient allies, while the disaffection of Henry's subjects
created a great military diversion in the pope's favour in Saxony
and Swabia.

Let us return for a moment to the internal administration
of the Church. We are disposed to think that the very vigorous measures which Gregory employed for what he considered
its reform were favourable, upon the whole, to the success of
his other projects. We may observe that these were of two descriptions, one of which tended to restore the discipline of the
clergy; the other to reduce the ecclesiastical orders to more
direct subjection to the Papal See. It is true that, by the
former of these, great disaffection was excited among such as
suffered by them; that is, among those who had been already
living in open disobedience to the canons of the Church : but
such, it is probable, were not the most numerous, as certainly
they were the least respectable, portion of the body. The same
severity which offended them would naturally gratify and attach
all those whose religious zeal and austere morality secured
them greater influence in the Church and deeper veneration
from the people. So that, notwithstanding the clamours of the
moment, we doubt not that the pope was substantially a gainer
by his exertions; and that (like every judicious reformer) he
extended his actual power and credit with only the partial loss
of a worthless popularity.

The second object of Gregory in his ecclesiastical government has not yet been mentioned by us. It seems to have
been no less than to destroy the independence of national

Objects of Gregory in the internal administration of the Church;

to restore discipline,

and subject all national Churches to Rome.

Churches; and to merge all such local distinctions in the body
and substance of the Church universal, whose head was at
Rome. For the effecting of this mighty scheme he used every
exertion to loosen the connexion of bishops and abbots with
their several sovereigns, and to persuade them that their allegiance was due to one master only, the successor of St. Peter.
And to that end he very readily availed himself of the materials
which he found prepared for his purpose, and which had been
transmitted to him undisputed by so many predecessors, that it
probably never occurred to him to doubt their legitimacy. The
False Decretals contained the canons which he sought; and
Gregory had the boldness at length to bring them forth from
the comparative obscurity in which they had reposed for above
two hundred and fifty years, and openly to force them into
action.

The False
Decretals.

We have mentioned the nature of those decretals: they
were a series of epistles professing to be written by the
oldest bishops of Rome, the Anacletus, Sextus the First and
Second, Fabian, Victor, Zephyrinus, Marcellus, and others*.
They recorded the primitive practice in the nomination to the
highest ecclesiastical offices, and in that and many other matters ascribed authority almost unlimited to the holy see. It is
worth while here to particularize, even at the risk of repetition,
some of the points on which they most insisted. (1.) That it
was not permitted to hold any council, without the command
or consent of the pope; a regulation which destroyed the independence of those local synods, by which the Church was for
many centuries governed. (2.) That bishops could not be de-
finitively judged, except by the pope. (3.) That the right of
episcopal translation rested with the pope alone. (4.) That not

* The first collection of canons made in the west was the work of a Roman
monk named Dionysius, who lived in the sixth century. This was followed by
many others: but that which gained the greatest celebrity was the one ascribed
to St. Isidore, Bishop of Seville; and it had great prevalence in Gaul as well as in
Spain. Guizot remarks that it was in the North and East of France that the
"False Decretals" first made their appearance, in the beginning of the ninth
century. (Hist. de la Civ. en France, Leçon 27.) The collection of decrees,
known by the name of Dictatus Hildebrandini, and falsely ascribed to Gregory
VII., is generally held to be the next forgery which disgraced the principles
and swelled the authority of the Roman Church.

only every bishop, but every priest, and not the clergy only, but every individual*, had the right of direct appeal from all other judgments to that of the pope. These rights, and such as these, had been neglected or vainly asserted by the Roman See during the long period of imbecility † which followed their forgery; but the spuriousness of their origin had never been exposed or suspected; and the simplicity of every succeeding generation added to their security, their antiquity, and their respectability.

Gregory at length undertook to give them full efficacy; and though none were ceded or overlooked by him, that which he appears most earnestly to have pressed was the pope's exclusive jurisdiction over the whole episcopal order : to this end he enforced universal appeal to Rome. Orders to attend before the pontifical court were issued to every quarter of Europe; and they generally met with obedient attention, not only from those whose principles sincerely acknowledged such spiritual supremacy, or who expected from their submission a more favourable sentence, but also from the great mass of offenders, who naturally preferred a distant and ecclesiastical tribunal to the close judicial inspection of a temporal magistrate. The good which Gregory proposed from this system could be one only, and that a very ambiguous advantage—to secure the *independence* of the Church, or, in fact, to withdraw it from the control of all secular power, and subject it to one single spiritual despot. The evils which he occasioned were numerous and of most serious magnitude—to create and nourish inextinguishable dissensions between princes and their clergy, to retard and perplex the operations of justice, and to multiply the chances of a partial or erroneous decision.

Marginal note: Appeals to Rome.

* Fleury, 4mo Disc. sur H. E. sect. v.
† Pope Nicholas I., who ruled from 858 to 867, is the principal exception to this remark: he is described by contemporary chronicles as the greatest pontiff since the days of St. Gregory—kind and lenient in his treatment of the clergy, but bold and imperious in his intercourse with kings. His conduct to Hincmar in the affair of Rothadus is at *seeming* variance with part of this eulogy; but though Nicholas was triumphant both in that dispute and in the more important difference with Lothaire, neither he nor any other pope under the Carlovingian dynasty could establish, in France at least, the claim *first* mentioned in the text. The emperors continued to convoke all councils and to confirm their canons.

Marginal note: Pope Nicholas I.

Gregory also obliged the Metropolitans to attend at Rome from all countries, in order to receive the *pallium* at his hands. This, together with the appeal system, kept that capital continually crowded with foreign prelates, with great vexation to themselves, with great detriment to their dioceses, and with no real profit to the Catholic Church. In the mean time, it is certain that mere *papal* influence gained by this system : for all authority, to be always respected, must sometimes be felt ; but unfounded and irrational authority most chiefly so.

In the prosecution of this history, we have sometimes lamented the necessity of dismissing some important event or useful speculation with less than due consideration, and especially do we lament it in this instance. But enough may possibly have *His double* been said to give the reader some insight into the DOUBLE *scheme of universal* scheme of universal dominion, to which the vast ambition of *dominion.* Gregory was directed—enough to make it evident how he projected, in the first place, to unite under the suzerain authority of St. Peter and his successors the entire *territory* of Christian Europe, so as to exert a sort of feudal jurisdiction over its princes, and nobles, and civil governors ; and, in the next place, to establish throughout the same wide extent of various and diversely constituted states one single *spiritual* monarchy, of which Rome should be the centre and sole metropolis,—a monarchy so pure and undivided, that every individual minister of that Church should look up to no other earthly sovereign than the pope. Such does indeed appear to have been the stupendous scheme of Gregory VII. We have already seen by what measures he proceeded to its execution, and we shall now trace his extraordinary career to its conclusion.

Henry advances to Rome. The election of a new emperor by the pope was very reasonably retorted by the election of a new pope by the emperor ; and Clement III. was exalted to the honour of being the rival of Gregory. But a much more sensible injury was inflicted on the fortunes of that pontiff immediately afterwards by the defeat and death of Rodolphus. That prince received a mortal wound in battle in the year 1080 ; and with him was extinguished the spirit of rebellion, or at least the hope of its success. Henry immediately turned his victorious arms against Italy; the opposition presented to him by Matilda and the Tuscans he over-came or evaded, and advanced with speed and indignation to the gates of Rome. From his dreams of universal empire—from the lofty anticipations of princes suppliant and nations prostrate in allegiance before the apostolic throne, Gregory was rudely awakened by the shouts of a hostile army pressing round the imperial city. But he woke to the tasks of constancy and courage; and so formidable a show of resistance was presented, that Henry, after desolating the neighbouring country, with-drew, without honour or advantage, to the cities of his Lombard allies.

Not deterred by this repulse, he renewed his attempt early in the spring following, and encountered the same opposition with the same result. The soldiers of Germany retired for the second time before the arms of the unwarlike Romans and the name of Gregory. But in the succeeding year (1084) the efforts of the emperor were followed by greater success. The citizens, wearied by repeated invasions, and suffering from the ravages attending them, abandoned that which now appeared the weaker cause—on this third occasion they threw open their gates to Henry and to Clement the antipope, who followed in his train. Henry placed his creature on the throne of Gregory, and the exultation of that moment may have rewarded him for the bitterness of many reverses. The measure which he next adopted should be carefully noticed, since it proves the venera-tion which was exacted even from him by the see itself, without consideration of its occupant. By an immediate act of submis-sion to the chair, which his own power had so recently be-stowed, he solicited the imperial crown from the hand of Clement, and he received it amid the faithless salutations of the Roman people. In the mean time, his victory was neither complete nor secure: from the castle of St. Angelo, Gregory surveyed in safety the partial overthrow of his fortunes, and awaited the succours from the South, with which he purposed to repair them. Robert Guiscard—whether mindful of his feudal allegiance, or jealous of the emperor's progress—was already approaching at the head of his Norman warriors; Henry and his pope retired with precipitate haste, and Gregory was tumultuously restored to his rightful dignity.

The success of the Normans was disgraced by the pillage of
a large portion of the city: this circumstance depressed still
further the declining popularity of the pope, and he had learnt
by his late experience how little he could confide in the
capricious allegiance of the Romans *. Accordingly, on the
return of Robert to his own dominions, Gregory followed him,
and retired, first to the monastery of Monte Cassino, afterwards
to Salerno. It is recorded that, on this occasion, Robert would
have profited by the weakness or the gratitude of Gregory, to
obtain from him the concession, on the part of the Church, of
some disputed feudal right of no great importance; but that
the pope resisted the solicitations of his protector in the very
centre of his camp. And no doubt his persevering and fearless
spirit was still meditating the re-occupation of his chair and the
prosecution of his mighty projects. But such anticipations
were speedily cut short, and in the year 1085, very soon after
Death of Gregory. his arrival at Salerno, he died †. He concluded a turbulent
pontificate of twelve years in misfortune, in exile, with little
honour, with few lamentations ‡; without having witnessed the
perfect accomplishment of any portion of the project which had
animated his existence, and even at the very moment when it
appeared most hopeless. He died—but he left behind him a
name which has arrested with singular force the attention of
history, which has been strangely disfigured indeed by her
capricious partiality, but which has never been overlooked, and
will never be forgotten. He did more than that—he left behind him his spirit, his example, and his principles; and they

* " Gli umori sempre diversi del popolo Romano."—*Denina, Riv. d' Ital.*,
lib. x. c. 8.

† These are Semler's words:—" Gregorius...tantis ausibus ipse immortuus est;
nulli jam parti carus aut amatus; diu omnibus, execrationibus, scommatibus,
satiris, *mendaciis-*que post mortem oneratus."—Sec. xi. c. 1.

‡ Gulielmus Apuliensis, a *poetical* eulogist of Gregory, sings, that Robert
Guiscard, who would have beheld with tearless eyes the death of his father, his
son, and his wife, was moved to weakness by that of Gregory :—

> Dux non se lacrymis audita forte coercet
> Morte viri tanti : non mors patris amplius illum
> Cogeret ad lacrymas, non filius ipse nec uxor,
> Extremos etsi casus utriusque videret.

Pagi, Vit. Greg. VII. sect. cxv.

In the mean time, both Robert and Gregory appear to have died in the same year,
and some are of opinion that Gregory was the survivor.

continued, through many successive generations, to agitate the His public
policy and influence the destinies of the whole Christian world. character.
The latest words of Gregory are recorded* to have been
these :—" I have loved justice and hated iniquity; therefore I
die in exile;"—words which seem to indicate a discontented
spirit, reluctantly bending before the decrees of Providence.
But the same complaint may also have proceeded from a sense
of pious intention and the recollection of duties conscientiously
performed. It becomes us, then, to inquire in what really consisted that justice which he loved, and that iniquity which he
hated? what were the principles which guided his public life?
what were the habits which regulated his private conversation?
The leading, perhaps the only, principle of his public life was
to reform, unite, and aggrandize the Church over which he
presided, and especially to exalt the office which he filled. He
may have been very serious and sincere in that principle—he
may even have considered that the whole of his duties were
contained in it, and that he was bound to pursue it through
every danger and difficulty, as a churchman and a pope. This
was his grand and original delusion, and here alone can we
discover any trace of narrowness and littleness. And yet there
have existed so many good men in all ages, even in the most
enlightened, who have mistaken their own form of faith for the
only true faith, and held their own particular Church to be
synonymous with the Church of Christ, that the error of
Gregory will meet with much sympathy, though it can deserve
no pardon. But when we observe the measures into which it
betrayed him, and through which he followed it with deliberate
hardihood; when we recollect the profusion of blood which
flowed through his encouragement or instigation, for the support of an ambitious and visionary project; and, more than
that, when we compare the nature of that project with the
humble, and holy, and peaceful system of Christ, whose gospel
was in the pontiff's hands, and whose blessed name was inces-

* Millot, Hist. de la France. They are given somewhat differently by Paulus
Bernriedensis :—" Ego, fratres mei dilectissimi, nullos labores meos alicujus
momenti facio, in hoc solummodo confidens, quod semper dilexi justitiam et odio
habui iniquitatem." And when his friends who were present expressed some
anxiety respecting his future condition, he stretched forth his hands to Heaven,
and said, " Illuc ascendam; et obnixis precibus Deo propitio vos committam."

santly profaned for the support of his purposes—it is then that
we are obliged to regard him with unmitigated disgust. His
endeavours to reform the morals of his clergy and the system
of his Church* will only be censured by those who prefer dis-
eases to their remedies, or who think it dangerous to apply any
remedy to ecclesiastical corruption—and over such persons the
sceptre of reason has no control. But his claims of temporal
sovereignty, his usurpation of spiritual supremacy, his lofty
bearing, and pontifical arrogance, were so widely at variance
with the spirit of that book † on which his Church was originally founded, that we must either suppose him wholly to have

* Some writers have represented Gregory as an enemy to innovation, as one of
those characters who have placed their pride in keeping the age stationary, and
perpetuating all that was transmitted to them. Had Gregory been such a man
he had been long ago forgotten. Far otherwise : he was the greatest of all innovators ; but, like Charlemagne and Peter of Russia, he marched to his object by
the road of despotism. The reforms which he projected in affairs civil, political,
and ecclesiastical, embraced every interest and reached every department of
society ; but it was by the establishment of a spiritual monarchy—a sort of papal
theocracy—that he proposed to compass them. Guizot has somewhere made
this observation : he has further attributed to Gregory two errors in the conduct
of his plan, but not (as it seems to us) with equal justice. He blames that pope
for having proclaimed his plan too pompously, menacing when he had not the
means of conquering ; and also for not having confined his attempts to what
might fairly seem practicable. Guizot appears, for the moment, to have forgotten
on what uncertain ground the papal power really rested ; how much of it was
built on mere claims, disputed, perhaps, at first, but finally established and enforced by mere impudent importunity—the very advance of such claims by one
pope was always a stepping-stone for his successors. Again, in treating of what
was practicable by Gregory, if we well consider the peculiar nature of his weapons,
hitherto untried in any great contest, and the character of the age to be moved
by them, it will seem quite impossible that he could exactly have calculated what
he could, or what he could not, accomplish. Under all circumstances, it was probable that the bolder were his claims, and the more loudly he asserted them, the
greater was his chance of some immediate success, and the broader the path that
was opened for future pontiffs. And Gregory had too extensive a genius not to
think and act also for posterity.

† The first evil consequence of associating tradition with the gospel as the
foundation of the Church was, that the former was soon considered as substantial
a part of the building as the latter. United in words, they were presently confounded in idea, and that not by the very ignorant only, but even by men, especially churchmen, who had deeply studied the subject, and most so by monks.
Gregory had received a monastic education ; and though his mind was naturally
vast and penetrating, it is not absurd to suppose that he might sincerely consider
the False Decretals (believing them to be genuine) as possessing authority *almost*
equivalent to the Bible ; at least, he might think it a fair compromise to govern
his Church by the former, and his private conduct by the latter rule.

disdained its precepts, or to have strangely* misinterpreted them.

In descending to the personal character of Gregory, we may *His personal character.* first observe, that he was superior to the spirit of intolerance which was then becoming manifest in his Church. The only doctrinal controversy in which he was engaged was that with Berenger, on transubstantiation. The pope maintained the doctrine which appears then to have been generally received in Italy and France, and he may have menaced the contumacy of the heretic. But no impartial reader can rise from the perusal of that controversy with the impression that Gregory was personally the advocate of persecution. On the contrary, his moderation has been noticed by writers† little favourable to his character, and has even led some to the very unjust inference that he was friendly to the opinion, because he spared and endured its author.

After all, it is a question whether Gregory's moderation on questions purely theological does not furnish a fair argument against his general conduct. It proves, at least, that his violence and arrogance were not merely faults of temper, showing themselves whenever there was a dispute; but feelings which, to excite them, required the stimulus of ambition. Again, in an age when reason and philosophy had little influence, moderation on theological questions naturally excites the suspicion of indifference; but if Gregory was indifferent on theological questions, and violent on matters touching the temporal

---

* In his epistles he frequently repeats the prophet's words:—" Cursed is he that doeth the work of the Lord deceitfully,"—" that keepeth back his sword from blood ;" that is, who does not execute God's commands in punishing God's enemies: hence his severity with simoniacal bishops and other ecclesiastical offenders.

† Jortin (among others) thinks that the pope was much inclined to defend Berenger—a merit which might have led that candid writer to pause before he entered into the absurd and fanatical notion that Gregory was Antichrist. Milner also holds this last opinion more confidently—a very remote point of contact between two men of very different and even opposite views, but of equal sincerity and excellence ! But (to speak without reference to either of those authors) it has been the misfortune of Gregory to excite the spleen of two descriptions of writers who agree in very few of their principles—those who abhor the Roman Catholic Church and all its supporters with vehement and unqualified hatred, and those who dislike every church and every assertor of ecclesiastical rights. The former are our religious, the latter our philosophical, historians—both are equally unjust.

aggrandizement of himself and his Church, his character had even less merit than we are disposed to assign to it.

Among the calumniators of Gregory, none are found so unjust as to deny his extraordinary talents and address, his intrepid constancy, his inflexible perseverance. And there are none among his blindest admirers who would excuse the unchristian arrogance of his ambition. His other qualities are for the most part disputed :—his moral excellence* and the depth of his private piety have been strongly asserted by some, and contested by others: for our own part, after carefully comparing the conclusions of his more moderate historians with the particular acts and general spirit of his life, we are disposed to assent to the more favourable judgment—to this extent at least, that we believe him to have possessed those austere monastic virtues, common, perhaps, in the cloister, but rare in those days either among princes† or popes. And if, indeed, in addition to those merits, he was compassionate to the poor, the defender of the oppressed, the protector of the innocent (as a very impartial

---

* His intrigue with Matilda, which is insinuated in a very childish manner by Mosheim, is expressly denied by Lambertus, a contemporary historian of good repute. Ambition was motive quite sufficient for his intimacy with that princess, and his advanced age (seventy-two) might reasonably have saved him from the imputation of any other. Besides which, there is no single fact or circumstance to authorize the suspicion; and his deep enthusiasm and intrepid zeal, and the very austerity which made him dangerous, are qualities wholly inconsistent with vulgar hypocritical profligacy. " That a widow of thirty (says Denina), also motherless, should be the declared protectress and body-guard of an old and austere pontiff, furnished a famous pretext for calumny to the concubinary clergy who were persecuted by the pope " (Rivoluz. d'Ital., l. x., c. 6); and to them we may probably ascribe this charge. In the mean time, if his own evidence is of any value in such a question, we have a letter addressed by him to the Countess (Lib. i., ep. 47), in which he exhorts her to take the sacrament frequently, and to be sedulous in devotion to the Holy Virgin—" accipe quotidie quod quotidie tibi prosit—sic vive, ut quotidie merearis accipere."

† Gregory reproved the abbot who admitted Hugo, duke of Burgundy, into his monastery, on this ground—" We have abundance of good monks, but there is a great scarcity of good princes." Those are the virtues which Gibbon calls *dangerous;* and it is in speaking of Gregory that he advances that remarkable assertion—that the vices of the clergy are less dangerous than their virtues,—a position which is seldom understood with the qualification which the author obviously intended to attach to it. The passage is illustrated by another in the sixty-ninth chapter—" The scandals of the tenth century were obliterated by the austere and more dangerous virtues of Gregory VII."

as well as accurate writer* affirms), we shall find the greater reason to lament that his private sanctity was overshadowed and darkened by his public administration.

Respecting his religious disposition, though passages may be found in his Epistles not uninspired with Christian piety, it is more probable that he sought his motives of godliness † and the aliment of his fervour in the interests of his Church, than in the lessons of his Bible. A profound canonist, a skilful theologian, a zealous churchman, he may still have been unacquainted with the feelings of a Christian, and uninformed by the spirit of the faith; and it is not impossible that even his reforms in discipline and morals, which were the best among his acts, proceeded from a narrow ecclesiastical zeal, not from the purer and holier influence of evangelical devotion.

SECTION III.

(I.) Controversy respecting Transubstantiation—suspended in the Ninth, renewed in the Eleventh Century—Character of Berenger—Council of Leo IX. —of Victor II. at Tours in 1054—Condemnation and Conduct of Berenger— Council of Nicholas II.—repeated Retractation and Relapse of Berenger—Alexander II.—Council at Rome under Gregory VII.—Extent of the Concession then required from Berenger—further Requisition of the Bishops—a Second Council assembled—Conduct of Gregory—Berenger again solemnly assents to the Catholic Doctrine, and again returns to his own—his old Age, Remorse, and Death—Remarks on his Conduct—on the Moderation of Gregory. (II.) Latin Liturgy—Gradual Disuse of the Latin Language throughout Europe— Adoption of the Gothic Missal in Spain—Alfonso proposes to substitute the Roman—Decision by the Judgment of God—by Combat—by Fire—doubtful Result—final adoption of the Latin Liturgy—its Introduction among the Bohemians by Gregory—Motives of the Popes—other Instances of Services not performed in the Vulgar Tongue—Usage of the early Christian Church.

THE age of Gregory was distinguished by a very important Opinions and conduct of Beduct of Bepugnacious in asserting the most inadmissible rights of the renger. Church, he showed no disposition to encourage the dispute in

---

* Giannone, Storia di Napoli, lib. x., c. 6. Gregory has been reproached with placing faith in the predictions of astrologers; with dealing in divinations, interpreting dreams, and exercising the magical art. Few of those who have shone with great splendour in an ignorant age have escaped the same suspicion.

† When Muratori (Vit. Rom. Pontif. in Leo IX.) speaks of him as "Adolescens .... clari ingenii, sanctæque *Religionis*," and when Giannone calls him " uomo pieno di Religione," nothing more is at all necessarily implied than Gregory's monastic sanctity would justify.

question, nor any furious zeal to extirpate the supposed error ;
and yet the error was no less than a disbelief in the mystery
afterwards called transubstantiation. We have already mentioned the promulgation of that dogma by Paschasius Radbertus : we have observed with what ardour and liberty it was both
supported and combated during the ninth century, until the
flames of the controversy, unsustained by any public edicts,
gradually and innocently expired. The arguments which had
been urged on both sides were thus left to produce their respective fruits of good or evil, according to the soil on which
they fell, and the season in which they were sown. Both these
circumstances were fearfully unfavourable to the growth of any
wholesome knowledge : for in those days reason was less per-
suasive than its abuse, and truth was less attractive than specious show ; so that religion was buried in superstitious observances. Thus it happened that, during the tenth century, the
opinion in question made a general, though silent progress ;
and, in the beginning of the eleventh, it was tacitly understood
to be the doctrine of the Roman Church*. In the year 1045,
Berenger, principal of the public school (Scholastic) at Tours,
and afterwards archdeacon† of Angers, publicly professed his
opposition to it.

Roman Catholic writers do not dispute the brilliancy of his
talents, the power of his eloquence, his skill in dialectics, and
his general erudition; they admit, too, that habits of exemplary
virtue and piety gave life and efficacy to his genius and learn-
ing‡. By these merits he acquired the veneration of the people,
and the friendship of the most distinguished ecclesiastics of his
day. But when some historians assert, that his virtues sud-

---

* In the Acts of the Council of Arras (held in 1025) the sacramental body is
expressly declared to be the same flesh, "quæ ex Virgine nata, in cruce passa, de
sepulcro levata, super cœlos exaltata, sedet in paternæ majestatis gloria. Hoc
qui audit incredulus (the decree continues) huic nec Christus natus, nec passus,
nec sepultus est, nec cum Christo partem beatæ resurrectionis obtinebit." The
same council defended the doctrine of justification by faith with almost equal zeal.

† Mosheim is guilty of a strange blunder in making him archbishop of Angers,
and of designating him throughout as a *prelate*. In fact, Angers is only an episcopal see, and Eusebius Bruno, one of Berenger's own pupils, was raised to it in
1047. Hist. Litt. de la France, Vie de Bérenger.

‡ He attained the honourable reputation (common to him with so many learned
persons) of being a magician.

denly deserted him, and were even changed into their opposite vices, at the moment when he propounded his opinion, we can only consider them as illustrating their own definition of " heresy." It is also said, that Berenger was stimulated to publish, even to invent, his doctrine by private jealousy of the learned Lanfranc ; and in truth the most splendid actions do so commonly originate in sordid motives, that this charge may possibly be true: but it is not probable, because it is at variance with the tenor of his character ; nor is it at all important, since it affects neither the truth nor the prevalence of his doctrine.

Berenger's opposition to transubstantiation became known to Leo IX., who condemned it at a council held at Rome in 1050; His opinion condemned and in the same year two other councils were summoned in by various France, at Verceil and Paris, both of which strongly anathe- councils. matized the heresy ; and, in consequence of the decree of the latter, Henry I. deprived the offender of the temporalities proceeding from his benefice. He did not attend these councils, but continued to profess and promulgate his doctrine. During the pontificate of Victor II. a council was assembled at Tours in 1055*, at which Hildebrand presided as legate of the pope. Berenger was summoned before it, and on this occasion he obeyed the summons—with the less apprehension, because he possessed the personal regard of Hildebrand. He appears to have urged little in defence of his opinion, and to have made no difficulty in subscribing on oath to the received faith of the Church, concerning the real presence of the body and blood of Jesus Christ in the eucharist. And having subscribed to this faith, he immediately returned to the propagation of his actual opinions.

He then remained undisturbed for four or five years, until Nicholas II. called upon him to justify himself before a Roman

---

* See Pagi, Vit. Victor II., s. v., where various authorities are collected, and among them the following expressions from Lanfranc addressed to Berenger:— " Denique in Concilio Turonensi, cui ipsius Victoris interfuere legati, data est tibi optio defendendi partem tuam. Quam cum defendendam suscipere non auderes, confessus coram omnibus communem ecclesiæ fidem, jurâsti te ab illa hora ita crediturum, sicut in Romano Concilio te jurasse est superius comprehensum." From this it would appear that Berenger had been present at the council of Leo, though he disregarded those assembled in France ; unless indeed the Roman council mentioned by Lanfranc be that afterwards held by Nicholas, which is more probable.

Council. He appeared there, and professed his readiness to
follow the doctrine which should seem good to that assembly.
Accordingly, a profession of faith was drawn up, which went to
the farthest extent to which the dogma has ever been carried*,
and with the same hand which signed it Berenger committed
to the flames the books containing his opposition to it.   He
then returned to France, resumed his sincere profession, and
abjured his abjuration.

Alexander II. (acting probably under his archdeacon's
counsels) contented himself with addressing to the heretic a
letter of peaceful and friendly exhortation; but as his opinion
and his contumacy now created some confusion in the Church,
Hildebrand, not long after his elevation to the chair, summoned
Berenger to Rome a second time.   For the space of nearly a
year Gregory retained him near his person, and honoured him
with his familiarity; and then, in a council in 1078, he was
contented to require his subscription to a profession, which
admitted the real presence without any change of substance;
and Berenger did not hesitate to sign it.

But this moderation did not satisfy the zeal of certain ardent
prelates, who required not only a more specific declaration of
orthodoxy, but also that the sincerity of the retractation should
be approved by the fiery trial.   Berenger is stated to have
prepared himself by prayer and fasting for submission to that
ceremony; but Gregory, though he accorded the first of their
requisitions, refused to countenance the senseless mockery of
the second.   The year following, another council assembled,
and once more Berenger in their presence solemnly renounced

* In the presence of the pope, and one hundred and thirteen bishops, Berenger
subscribed the following profession: "Ego Berengarius, indignus diaconus, &c.
. . , consentio S. R. Ecclesiæ et Ap. Sedi, et ore et corde profiteor de sacramento
Dominicæ mensæ eam fidem me tenere quam dominus et venerabilis Papa Nico-
laus et hæc sancta synodus tenendam tradidit . . scilicet panem et vinum, quæ in
altari ponuntur, post consecrationem non solum sacramentum sed etiam verum
corpus et sanguinem Domini nostri Jesu Christi esse ; et sensualiter, non solum
sacramento sed in veritate, manibus sacerdotum tractari et frangi et fidelium den-
tibus atteri; jurans per sanctam et homoousiam Trinitatem.   Eos vero qui contra
hanc fidem venerint æterno anathemate dignos esse pronuntio.   Quod si ego aliquando aliquid contra hæc sentire et prædicare præsumpsero subjaceam canonum
severitati. Lecto et perlecto *sponte* subscripsi." It is cited by Pagi in the Life of
Nicholas II., as are the second and third professions of Berenger (in 1078 and
1079) in the Life of Gregory, sect. lxx. lxxii.

his opinions, and confirmed by oath his adherence to the broadest interpretation of the Catholic faith. He was then dismissed
by the pontiff, with new proofs of his satisfaction; and no
sooner was he restored to the security of his native country,
than he renewed the profession of the doctrine which he had
never in truth abandoned. But he received little further mo-
lestation* from the ecclesiastical powers, and died in 1088, at a
very advanced age, with no other disquietude, it is said, than
those severe mental sufferings which may well have been the
consequence of his repeated and deliberate perjuries†.

Berenger was anxious for the reputation of a great Reformer, His con-
and perhaps sincerely zealous for the removal of what he con- duct and
sidered a revolting corruption—but he did not aspire to the character.
glory of martyrdom. And when he presented himself at four
successive councils, under the obligation either to defend or
retract his opinions, we cannot doubt that, as he saw the former
course to be useless as well as dangerous, he went to them
calmly prepared to debase himself by an insincere act of per-
jured humiliation. Perhaps he preserved his property, or prolonged his life for a few years, by such reiterated sin and
degradation; but, if his latest days were passed in remorse
and bitter penitence, his gain was not great, and the moments
which he added to his existence were taken away from his
happiness. His followers were not, probably, very numerous,
at least they formed a very trifling proportion to the whole
body of the church. They contained no individual of any
great eminence, nor do they appear to have existed *as a sect*
after the death of Berenger—doubtless, they were chilled by
his weakness and confounded by his frequent recantations. His
fortitude and constancy would have confirmed and multiplied
and perpetuated them. We admire his talents, we respect his
virtues, and venerate the cause in which he displayed them;

* Dupin mentions that he was summoned before a council at Bordeaux, in
1080, "where he gave an account of his faith."

† A loud and very unimportant dispute has been raised between Papists and
Protestants as to the opinions in which Berenger actually *died*. The truth appears to be that he died a penitent,—and the former attribute to the consciousness
of his heresy that remorse, which the latter much more probably ascribe to his
perjury.

but in that age the defence of that cause demanded (as it deserved) a character of sterner materials and more rigid consistency, than was that of Berenger.

Conduct of Gregory VII.

From the moderation which Gregory used towards the person of that Reformer, it has been inferred, as we have said, that he secretly favoured his opinions; and this may be so far true, that he inculcated in general terms an adherence to the words of scripture*; and discouraged any curious researches and positive decisions respecting the *manner* of Christ's presence at the Eucharist. And as a real spiritual (or intellectual†) presence was probably admitted by Berenger himself, who professed only to follow the opinions of John Scotus‡, there could remain no ground for any violent difference between the pope and the heretic. They were agreed as to the fact of the presence; and its manner, which was the only point in dispute with the one, was held to be inscrutable, or unimportant, by the other§.

General establishment of the Latin Liturgy.

II. But if we are to consider the doctrine of transubstantiation to have been effectually established, rather through the obstinate zeal of his ecclesiastics, than by the favour of Gregory, we shall have no hesitation in attributing to his personal exertions a contemporary corruption in the ceremonies of the Church. It was the will of Hildebrand that the liturgy of the Universal Church should be performed in Latin only; and having once adopted that scheme, as in every other object which he thought proper to pursue, he neglected no imaginable means to carry it into effect. The use of Latin as the vulgar tongue, which had prevailed throughout the southern provinces of Europe, gradually ceased during the course of the ninth century; and the language of the first conquerors was insensibly corrupted by the barbarous jargon of the second. Latin

* Mosheim, cent. xi.

† Hist. Litt. de la France, Vie de Bérenger.

‡ Ambrose, Jerome, and Augustine are the Fathers on whose authority Berenger chiefly rests his defence. Lanfranc, before he became Archbishop of Canterbury, was his most distinguished opponent.

§ From his letter to Matilda (Lib. i. Ep. 47.) it appears that Gregory considered the Eucharist as a sacrifice, and he even cites a passage from St. Gregory, to show that he too held it in the same light.

thus became a subject of study, and all knowledge of it was presently confined to the priesthood.   Still it seems clear that, in France as well as in Italy, the services of the church continued to be performed entirely in Latin, and even that sermons were for some time delivered in that tongue to an audience most imperfectly acquainted with it.   But in Spain, the Gothic ritual in Spain. had supplanted the Roman,—if indeed the Roman had at any time been received in Spain,—and at the middle of the eleventh century it was universally prevalent in that church.   Soon after that time, by the united influence (as is said) of Richard, the papal legate, and Constance, Queen of Leon (who had brought with her from France an attachment to the forms of her native church), Alfonso, the Sixth of Leon and First of Castile, was persuaded to propose the introduction of the Roman liturgy. The nobility and the people, and even the majority of the clergy, warmly supported the established form; and after some heats had been excited on both sides, a day was finally appointed to decide on the perfections of the rival rituals.   To this effect, recourse was had, according to the customs of those days, to the "judgments of God," and the trial to which they were first submitted was that by combat.   Two knights contended in the presence of a vast assembly, and the Gothic champion prevailed.   The king, dissatisfied with this result, subjected the rituals to a second proof, which they were qualified to sustain in their own persons—the trial by fire.   The Gothic liturgy resisted the flames, and was taken out unhurt, while the Roman yielded, and was consumed.   The triumph of the former appeared now to be complete, when it was discovered that the ashes of the latter had curled to the top of the flames, and leaped out of them.   By this strange phenomenon the scales were again turned, or at least the victory was held to be so doubtful, that the king, to preserve a show of impartiality, established the use of both liturgies.   It then became very easy, by an exclusive encouragement of the Roman, effectually, though gradually, to banish its competitor*.

* See Dr. M'Crie's History of the Progress and Suppression of the Reformation in Spain.   The contest between the liturgies began during the pontificate of Alexander II., between the years 1060 and 1068; but one of the first acts of Gregory

Bohemia.   It was one of the latest acts of Alexander II. especially to
prohibit the Bohemians from performing service in their native
Sclavonian, and to impose on them the Roman missal; and
about seven years afterwards Gregory prosecuted, as pope, the
enterprise which, as archdeacon, he had doubtless originated.
Little serious resistance appears to have been opposed to this
and similar attempts; and it may be asserted without dispute,
that before the conclusion of the eleventh century, the Latin
liturgy was almost universally received in the western churches.

Conceal-   One motive of the popes for this vexatious exertion of eccle-
ment of the siastical tyranny was fairly avowed by Gregory, in his answer
Scriptures.
to Vratislaus, Duke of Bohemia, viz.—the impolicy of making
the scriptures too public; and, in this document, it is curious
to observe with what ease, when it suited his purpose, he could
dispense (like Gregory the Great) with the authority of the
primitive church, so conclusive and venerable when it was
expedient to follow it. It was clear to his mind that it was
the will of the Omnipotent, that the scriptures should in some
places be concealed, lest they should become despicable through
publicity, or through misinterpretation generate error. The
contrary was one of many practices which the primitive church
had *dissembled,* and which were corrected by the holy fathers
in the progress of the religion*.

Another motive, undoubtedly, was the zeal for the unity of
the Church, as one body under one head; and to this end it
certainly conduced, that she should speak to all her children,

was to give his strenuous and effectual support to the Roman.   See Pagi, Vit.
Alex. II. et Greg. VII.

    * The expressions of so great a pontiff, on so important a subject, deserve
to be recorded:—"Quia Nobilitas tua postulavit, quod secundum Sclavonicam
linguam apud vos divinum celebrari annueremus officium, scias nos huic petitioni
tuæ nequaquam posse favere.   Ex hoc nempe sæpe volventibus liquet non im-
merito *Sacram Scripturam omnipotenti Deo placuisse quibusdam locis esse occultam,*
ne, si ad liquidum cunctis pateret, forte vilesceret et subjaceret despectui, aut
pravè intellecta a mediocribus in errorem induceret.   Neque enim ad excusationem
juvet, quod quidam religiosi viri hoc quod simpliciter populus quæsivit, patienter
tulerunt, seu incorrectum dimiserunt; cum *Primitiva Ecclesia multa dissimulaverit,*
quæ a sanctis Patribus, postmodum firmata Christianitate et religione crescente,
subtili examinatione correcta sunt.   Unde ne id fiat, quod a vestris imprudenter
exposcitur, auctoritate B. Petri inhibemus, atque ad honorem omnipotentis Dei
huic vanæ temeritati viribus totis resistere præcipimus."

of all nations and races, in one language only.   It was also necessary that that language should be Latin, because it thus became a chain which not only united to each other the extremities of the North and West, but also bound them in universal allegiance to a common sovereign.   But this policy, like some others of the profoundest schemes of the Vatican, was calculated on the continuation of general ignorance and the stability of principles which the slightest efforts of reason were sufficient to overturn.

We should add, however, that a similar custom prevails among certain other nations and creeds, which cannot have originated in similar motives, but is rather to be attributed to the superstitious reverence for antiquity, so common where the understanding has been little cultivated.   The Egyptians, or Jacobites, performed their service in Coptic; the Nestorians in Syriac; the Abyssinians in the Old Æthiopic; and the prayers which are offered to the God of the Mahometans are universally addressed in Arabic.   But the usage was entirely contrary to the practice* of the early Church, which permitted every variety of language in its ceremonies—a practice which received the positive confirmation of the Council of Francfort at the end of the eighth century, and which was not entirely subverted till the pontificate of Gregory and his immediate successors.

The primitive usage.

---

* " You may have observed (says Fleury) that the offices of the Church were then in the language most used in each country : that is to say—in Latin throughout all the West—in Greek through all the East, except in the remoter provinces —as in the Thebais where the Egyptian was spoken, and in Upper Syria where Syriac was used . . . The Armenians have from the beginning performed divine service in their own tongue. If the nations were of a mixed kind, there were in the church interpreters to explain what was read . . . In Palestine, St. Sabas and St. Theodosius had in their monasteries many churches, wherein the monks of different nations had their liturgies, each in his own language.''

END OF PART III.

PART IV.

FROM THE DEATH OF GREGORY VII. TO THAT OF BONIFACE VIII.

CHAPTER XVII.

From Gregory VII. to Innocent III.

(I.) Papal history—Urban II.—Council of Placentia—that of Clermont—their principal acts—The Crusades—their origin and possible advantage—Pascal II. —Renewed disputes with Henry—his misfortunes, private and public—his death and exhumation—Henry, his son, marches to Rome—Convention with Pascal respecting the regalia—its violation—Imprisonment of the Pope—his concessions—annulled by subsequent Council—Henry again at Rome—Death and character of Pascal—Final arrangement of the Investiture question by Calixtus II.—Observations—The first Lateran (ninth General) Council—Death of Calixtus—Subsequent confusion and its causes—Arnold of Brescia—his opinions, fate, and character—Adrian IV.—Frederick Barbarossa—Disputes between them, and final success of the Pope—Alexander III.—his quarrel with Frederick, and advantages—his talents and merits—Celestine III.—The differences between Rome and the Empire—The internal dissensions at Rome on papal election—National contentions between Church and State. (II.) Education and theological learning—Review of preceding ages—in Italy and France—Parochial schools—Deficiency in the material—Papyrus—Parchment—Consequent scarcity of MSS.—Invention of paper—Three periods of theological literature —the characteristics of each—Gradual improvement in the eleventh century.

THE death of Gregory did not restore either concord to the Church or repose to the Empire. The successor whom, at the solicitation of his cardinals, he nominated on his death-bed, testified a singular, but sincere, repugnance for a dignity which, being probably too feeble to sustain, he was too wise to desire. Desiderius*, Abbot of Mount Cassino, held for a short period, under the name of Victor III., a disputed rule; and on his early death in the year 1087, Urban II., a native of France, was proclaimed in his place. But Clement the Antipope was still in

* His disinclination for the dangerous honour is said to have been so great, that he was actually dragged to the church, and forcibly invested with the pontifical garments. Fleury, H. E., liv. lxiii., sect. 25 and 27. This circumstance is not mentioned by Pagi; though, on the authority of Leo Ostiensis, he bears ample testimony to Victor's reluctance.

possession of the capital, where the imperial party was triumphant; and five years of dissension * intervened before the authority of Urban was generally acknowledged. That Pope had been a monk of Clugni, and owed his preferment to the See of Ostia to the favour of Gregory ; and he continued to the end of his life to exhibit his fidelity by following, as far as his talents permitted him, the schemes which had been traced by his patron.

Urban II.   Of the numerous councils held during his pontificate two are entitled to particular attention—those of Placentia and Clermont† : in both of these he confirmed the laws and asserted the principles of Gregory, and carried his favourite claims to their full extent; for by the fifteenth canon of the latter he enacted, " that no ecclesiastic shall receive any church dignity from the hand of a layman, or pay him liege homage for it : and that no prince shall give the investiture ‡." But that council is recommended to general history by other and more important recollections. And while at Placentia the final sanction was given to the two strongest characteristics in the doctrine and in the discipline of the Roman Church—namely §, transubstan-

---

* The only remarkable act of personal hostility which these two rivals appear to have exchanged, was a satiric taunt couched on either side in a pair of very innocent hexameters. Clement, insolent in the possession of the city, wrote to his rusticating adversary as follows :—

Diceris Urbanus, cum sis projectus ab Urbe !
Vel muta nomen, vel regrediaris ad Urbem.

To this Urban replied,

Clemens nomen habes, sed Clemens non potes esse,
Tradita solvendi cum sit tibi nulla potestas.

Hist. Litt. de la France.

† Both were held in 1095—the former on March 1, the latter on November 18. At the former were present two hundred bishops, nearly four thousand of the inferior clergy, and more than thirty thousand of the laity; so that the assemblies were held in the open air. The latter appears to have been still more numerously attended. See Fleury, H. E., liv. lxiv., sect. 22. Hist. Litt. de la France.

‡ " Ne episcopus vel sacerdos regi vel alicui laico in manibus ligiam fidelitatem faciat." See Mosheim, Cent. xi, p. ii., c. ii.

§ Hist. Litt. de la France. Vie de Berenger. The question regarding the ordination of the sons of presbyters, which was warmly debated about this time, was set at rest by the Council of Clermont. It was conceded, that with dispensation from the Pope they might be admitted to Holy Orders. Pagi (Vit. Urban. II., sec. 43.) ascribes to this period the practice of administering the Eucharist to the laity under one species only, which, he adds, became more confirmed after the

tiation and the celibacy of the clergy, the Council of Clermont first sounded that blast of fanaticism which shook the whole fabric of society, from the extremities of the West even to the heart of Asia, for above two centuries.

It may seem strange that the sanguinary project of launch- Origin of ing the power of Christendom in one vast armament against the the Crusades. Mahometan conquerors of the Holy Land should first have been proposed by a Pope who was celebrated for his cultivation of the noblest arts of peace. It was Sylvester II.* with whom the scheme of a general crusade originated; but to him it may have been suggested by personal observation of the sufferings of Spain and the humiliation of the Christian name. And to any one beholding and deploring the various disorders of Europe—the fierce contentions of kings with each other, their more fatal dissensions with their subjects, the military license which everywhere prevailed and forbade all security of person or property—it might have seemed an act of comparative mercy to unite those discordant spirits even by the rudest tie, and to divert against a common foe the turbulence which engaged them in mutual destruction. The same measure was not without some justification in prudence; since the slightest caprice of a Saracen conqueror might have directed his rage against Christendom, and especially against Italy, the most attractive, the most exposed, the least defensible province—the centre of the Christian Church, and, as it were, the Palestine of the West. These and similar considerations may have recommended the same project to a much greater mind than that of Sylvester; for it was also (as has been mentioned) a favourite design of Gregory VII., who proposed personally to conduct

establishment of the kingdom of Jerusalem by the crusaders; for in that Church (he maintains) it had existed from primitive times. We may also mention in this place, that the "Office of the Holy Virgin," though perhaps not composed by Urban, was brought into more general use during his pontificate.

* It will be recollected that Sylvester, as well as Urban and his agent Peter the Hermit, was a Frenchman. So that the entire credit of the scheme, both of its invention and the bringing it into practice, belongs, such as it is, to that enthusiastic and inconsiderate people. It is a remark of Gibbon, that at the Council of Placentia, in Italy, the people wept over the calamities of the Christians of the East—while at Clermont, in France, they took up arms to avenge them.

against the infidel the universal army of Christ. It was realized by Urban II.; and his exhortations * to the Council of Clermont, being at the same time addressed to the superstitious and the military spirit, the two predominant motives of action in that age, were received with an enthusiastic acclamation of frenzy, which was mistaken for the will of God.†

Pascal II.   Urban died in 1099, and was succeeded by Pascal II. Nearly contemporaneous with the decease of Urban was that of Clement III., the antipope, who had maintained with some interruptions the possession of the capital, though unacknowledged by the great body of the Church. The imperial party was at that moment too weak to appoint a successor, and therefore Pascal entered into undisputed occupation of the chair. Pascal, as well as Gregory and Urban, had been educated in the monastery of Clugni: like the former, he was a Tuscan; like the latter, he was indebted for his early advancement to Gregory; and thus the spirit of that extraordinary man, by animating the congenial bosoms of his two disciples, continued to haunt the pontifical chair, and to regulate the councils of the Vatican, for above thirty years after his departure ‡. And if Urban prosecuted the reforms undertaken by his master, and realized one of his fondest speculations, to Pascal remained the more difficult and odious office of resuming with fresh violence the

* The Pope closed the session of the council by a sermon, which has been variously reported by different writers. Fleury gives the following sentences as a part of it, on the authority of William of Tyre, " a grave and judicious author :" —" Do you then, my dear children, arm yourselves with the zeal of God ; march to the succour of our brethren, and the Lord be with you. Turn against the enemy of the Christian name the arms which you employ in injuring each other. Redeem, by a service so agreeable to God, your pillages, conflagrations, homicides, and other mortal crimes, so as to obtain his ready pardon. We exhort you and enjoin you, for the remission of your sins, to have pity on the affliction of our brethren in Jerusalem, and to repress the insolence of the infidels, who propose to subjugate kingdoms and empires and to extinguish the name of Christ." Hist. Eccl., liv. lxiv., sect. 32. As the populace devoutly believed the Pope's assurance, that the pilgrimage would atone for the most abominable crimes, the immediate effect of the crusade might be to rid Europe of the refuse of its population; just as the certain consequence would be the encouragement of crime, when the method of atonement was always at hand.

† We shall return to this subject in the 21st Chapter.

‡ Pascal died on January 18th, 1118, after an unusually long pontificate of eighteen years, five months, and five days.

contest with the empire. He engaged in it earnestly, if not eagerly ; and as the emperor was still unprepared for submission, he prevented an attempt (perhaps an insidious attempt) at compromise, by renewing (in 1102) all former decrees against investitures ; and then commenced the conflict by the usual sentence of excommunication.

Henry IV., after surviving so many popes, was still in possession of the throne ; but his latter years had been afflicted by the rebellion, and, what might be less bitter to him, by the death of his eldest son. The affections of his subjects he never possessed nor deserved ; but we do not learn that by any domestic delinquency he had forfeited the less dissoluble allegiance of his children. And yet, scarcely had Conrad terminated his unnatural impiety by death, when—as if the anathemas of Gregory were still suspended over him—as if to accomplish the *temporal* retribution which that pontiff had denounced against the foes of St. Peter *—Henry, his other son, on learning the excommunication of his father, rose in arms against him. A scene revolting to nature and humanity was the consequence ; and even the death of the emperor, which speedily followed, does not close the story of his persecutions. His body, which was still lying under the anathema, having been inconsiderately consigned to consecrated ground, was immediately dug up, ejected from the holy precincts, and condemned to an unhallowed sepulchre † ; and there it rested for the space of five years, a revolting monument of papal power and papal malignity : at length the sentence was withdrawn, and Henry V. was permitted to make a tardy atonement to offended nature and piety.

Misfortunes and death of Henry IV.

* It will be recollected that, in his second excommunication of Henry, Gregory supplicated St. Peter to take away from that prince prosperity in war and victory over his enemies, "that all the world may know" (says he) "that thou hast power both in heaven and on earth."

† " Comprobantibus his qui aderant Archiepiscopis et Episcopis ; quia quibus vivis ecclesia non communicat, illis etiam nec mortuis communicare possit."—Urspergensis Abbas, ap. Pagi, Vit. Pascalis II. Some ascribe this act of barbarity to the German Bishops, and exculpate the Pope, except in as far as he had set them the example, by exhumating the bones of Guibert the Antipope, who had been buried at Ravenna, and casting them into the neighbouring river.

There is no proof that Pascal positively excited this monstrous rebellion, but it is well known that he countenanced and promoted it, and that too, not as a reluctant concession of virtue to interest, but with ardent and uncompromising zeal. Indeed, his interest was not engaged in this matter, but his passions merely, and the vindictive hatred for Henry IV. which he had contracted in the school of Gregory. The holy see had nothing to gain by the death or deposition of an unpopular monarch, but everything to fear from the union which would probably ensue among his subjects. For as to any prospect of gratitude from his successor—any hope that the emperor would be mindful of services conferred upon the rebel,—a Tuscan and a pope could scarcely indulge so simple an expectation. If Pascal did so, he very speedily discovered his error ; for scarcely was Henry IV. dead, when his son asserted with equal vehemence the disputed rights. The pope resisted, and both parties prepared for a second struggle.

Henry V., nothing deterred by the portentous appearance of a comet, which inspired general dismay, descended into Italy during the summer of 1110, carefully prepared for a twofold contest with the holy see; for he was not only attended by a powerful army, but also by a suite of *literary* protectors*, so that the pen might be at hand to justify the deeds of the sword. His advance was preceded by a declaration of his intention, which was " to maintain a right acquired by privilege and the custom of his predecessors from the time of Charlemagne, and preserved during three hundred years under sixty-three popes —that of presenting to bishoprics and abbeys by the ring and crosier." In reality, his object, when more fully explained, was to prevent the election of bishops without his consent, to invest the bishop elect with the regalia, to receive from him homage and the oath of allegiance. At the same time, he proposed to undergo the solemn ceremony of coronation at the hands of the pope.

* " One of them was a Scotsman named David, who had presided over the schools at Wurtemberg, and whom the king had appointed his chaplain, *à cause de sa vertu.* He wrote a relation of this expedition, but rather as a panegyrist than an historian." Fleury, liv. lxvi., s. 1, on authority of Will. Malmes., lib. v., p. 166.

By the regalia above mentioned were understood various _{Dispute be-}
grants conferred on the bishops by Charlemagne, which par-
took of the privileges of royalty, such as the power of raising
tribute, coining money, and also the possession of certain independent lands, directly derived from the crown, with some
other immunities. And it seemed natural that the successors
of Charlemagne should retain the right of confirming the
privileges which he had bestowed. This circumstance involved
the pope in great perplexity; and though it was easy to publish edicts and advance vague and exorbitant pretensions when
the emperor was distant or embarrassed, he could scarcely
hope, by such expedients, to withstand his near and armed
approach. In this difficulty, Pascal proved at least the sincerity of his professions, and his attachment to the best and
purest interests of the Church. He had the virtue to prefer
its spiritual independence to its worldly splendour, and the
courage to proclaim his preference. This better part being
chosen, he concluded a treaty with Henry, by which it was
agreed that the bishops, on the one hand, should make to
Henry a positive cession of all that belonged to the crown in
the time of Louis, Henry, and his other predecessors, on pain
of excommunication if they attempted to usurp such regalia;
and that the emperor, on the other, should resign the right of
investiture. On this arrangement the pope consented to perform the ceremony of coronation*, and Henry proceeded to
Rome for that purpose.

The circumstances which followed are told with some trifling
variations, but were probably thus:—the bishops interested in
the treaty, and especially those of Germany, who would have
been the greatest sufferers, felt the deepest repugnance to resign
so large a portion of their splendid temporalities for a remote
and invisible object, which, however it might be accessory to

* For this compact we have the authority of Petrus Diaconus (who cites a contemporary account of the transaction) confirmed by that of Urspergens. Abbas,
as follows : " Ibi Legati Apostolici cum missis Regis advenientes, promptum
esse papam ad consecrationem.... si tamen ipse sibimet annueret libertatem ecclesiarum, laicam ab illis prohibens investituram—recipiendo nihilominus ab ecclesiis Ducatus, Marchias, Comitatus, Advocatias, Moneta, Telonia, cæterorumque
Regalium quæ possident summam."—See Pagi, Vit. Pasch. II.

the honour of the Church, did not benefit their own immediate interests. Consequently, they protested with so much violence against the compromise, which seemed to them to exchange a substance for a shadow, that the pope despaired of his power to execute that condition of the treaty. In the mean time, Henry arrived at Rome : he was conducted with acclamations to the Basilica of St. Peter, where the pope, with his bishops and cardinals, was waiting to receive him. The king, according to the accustomed ceremony, prostrated himself before the pope, and kissed his feet; he then read the usual oath, and they advanced together into the church*. But here, before they proceeded to the office of consecration, a dispute broke out respecting the fulfilment of the treaty, and it was presently inflamed into an angry quarrel. Henry availed himself of the presence of his soldiers to arrest the pope with several cardinals; the Roman populace took arms and endeavoured to rescue him; a fierce and tumultuous conflict ensued, and the courts of the Vatican, and even the hallowed pavement of St. Peter, were polluted with blood: but the Germans succeeded in securing their prisoners, and carried them away to their neighbouring encampment at Viterbo. After a rigorous confinement of two months, Pascal yielded to such persuasion as a king may exercise over his captive; and then he not only performed the required ceremony, but, by a new convention, ceded unconditionally the right of investiture.

Compulsory concession of Pascal;

The presence of the emperor was demanded in Germany; Pascal returned to Rome; but he was saluted there by such a tempest of indignation as to find it necessary, in the year following, to submit the whole affair, even as it involved his own personal conduct, to a very numerous council at the Lateran. Here the pope confessed the error into which his weakness had betrayed him; and the council, with his consent, solemnly revoked and cancelled the treaty, and justified their perfidy by

revoked at a Lateran Council, 1112, A.D.

---

* This took place on Feb. 11, 1111. " Ter se invicem complexi, ter se invicem osculati sunt; et, sicut mos, Rex dexteram Pontificis tenens cum magno populi gaudio et clamore ad Portam venit Argenteam. Ibi ex libro professionem imperatoriam faciens a Pontifice designatus est Imperator, &c."—Acta Vaticana ap. Baronium.

pleading the violence which had extorted it. The immediate resentment of Henry was diverted by civil disorders; but in 1117 he marched to Rome as an avowed enemy; Pascal retired to Benevento, and sought the protection of his Norman vassals, still faithful to the chair of Gregory. The emperor presently withdrew, and Pascal returned to his see and died; and his fortunes, in many respects similar to those of his patron, were blessed with a happier termination, since he was permitted to close his eyes at Rome. His fortunes were, in some respects, similar to those of Gregory, and similar was the audacity of his pretensions; but he wanted the firmness necessary to dignify the former, and to give weight and stability to the latter; his adversity was inglorious, and his arrogance feeble and without consequence. The levity of his character disqualified him for the task he had undertaken, and its pliancy did not compensate for its want of coherence and consistency.

The question respecting investitures, after having variously agitated the kingdoms of the West for half a century, was now drawing near to its final decision. After a short interval of disputed succession*, then usual on the death of every pope, Calixtus II., archbishop of Vienna, a count of Burgundy, and a near relative of the emperor, was raised to the pontifical chair. It does not appear, however, that he sacrificed to the claims of consanguinity any portion of the rights or pretensions of his see; but he consented that the differences should be submitted for their final arrangement to a council, or diet, to be assembled at Worms for that purpose. A convention was there concluded (in September, 1122), which was reasonable and permanent: its substance was this † :—(1.) That the election of bishops and abbots, in his Teutonic kingdom, take place in its rightful form, without violence or simony, in the presence of the emperor or his legate, so that in case of a difference, his protection be given, with the advice of the metropolitan, to the juster claim‡. (2.) That the ecclesiastic elected receive his

Conclusion of the quarrels about investitures, 1122 A. D. at the Diet of Worms.

---

* Gelasius II. stands in the list of popes as having filled that interval.

† See Fleury, liv. lxvii., sect. 30.   Pagi, Vit. Callisti II., sect. xxiv. xxv.

‡ " Si qua inter partes discordia emerserit, metropolitani provincialium con-

regalia at the hand of the emperor, and do homage for them. But (3.) that in the ceremony of investiture the emperor no longer use the insignia of spiritual authority, but the *sceptre* only. A similar arrangement had previously* taken place in England between Henry I. and Pascal II.; and in France †, if the custom of investiture by the ring and crosier ever prevailed, which seems uncertain, it had been abolished about the same time.

Observations on the real results of the Convention of Worms.

The terms of this treaty, in which each party yielded what was extravagant in his claims ‡, were undoubtedly favourable to the Church. Her restitution of the " rightful form" of election deprived the emperor of an usurped privilege which had been extremely valuable and profitable to him, both in its use and its abuse. And since the popes, ever after the edict of Alexander II., had claimed as indisputable the right of *confirmation* in episcopal election—a claim which, as it was purely ecclesiastical, the emperor had not greatly cared to contest—a large portion of the influence which was ceded by the crown did in fact *devolve* on the holy see. Again, the *original* form of election was in no case positively restored, since the advantage of excluding the people, and even the body of the diocesan clergy, had been long and generally acknowledged; so that the right seems to have been invested almost immediately in the

silio vel judicio, saniori parti assensum et auxilium præbeas." So this clause is expressed in the acts of the Lateran council held in the following year.

* Probably in 1106, after a severe dispute between the pope and king during the primacy of Anselm. Hist. Litt. France, Vie Pascal. Pagi, Vit. Pascal. II.

† Guillaume de Champeau, bishop of Chalons, is related to have addressed (in 1119) the following discourse to the emperor :—" Sire, if you desire a substantial peace, you must absolutely renounce the investiture to bishoprics and abbeys. And to assure you that you will thus suffer no diminution of your royal authority, let me inform you, that when I was elected in the kingdom of France, *I received nothing from the hand of the king*, neither before nor after consecration. Nevertheless, I serve him as faithfully in virtue of the tributes and various other rights of the state which Christian kings have in ancient days given to the Church, as faithfully, I say, as your bishops in your kingdom serve you, in virtue of that investiture which has drawn such discords and anathemas on you." Fleury, H. E., liv. lxvii., sec. 3. The emperor yielded to that argument.

‡ The peace of the Church is thus celebrated by Gotfridus of Viterbo, in his Chronicle :

> Reddit Apostolico Cæsar quæcunque rogavit ;
> Pax bona conficitur; sublata Deo reparavit ;
> Jura suæ partis lætus uterque trahit.

chapters of the cathedral churches : at least it was confirmed
to them about the end of the twelfth century.

The second condition of the Convention secured to the sovereign the civil allegiance of his ecclesiastical subjects, and repressed their dangerous struggles for entire immunity from
feudal obligations.   At the same time it restored to them the
integrity of their ghostly independence, and cut off the last pretence for secular interference in matters strictly spiritual.

So easy and reasonable was the conclusion of that debate,
which, in addition to the usual calamities of international warfare, had excited subjects against their sovereign, and children
against their fathers, which had convulsed the holy Church, and
overthrown its sanctuaries, and stained its altars with blood.
However, on a calm historical survey of the circumstances of
the conflict, and of the crimes and errors which led to them, we
are little disposed to load with unmixed reprehension any individual of either party.   The *crimes,* indeed, and the passions
which produced them, were equally numerous and flagrant on
either side : on the one, were tyranny and profligacy and brutal
violence ; arrogance and obstinacy and imposture, on the other ;
pride and ambition and injustice, on both.   Yet our prejudices
naturally incline to the imperial party ; because the same or
equal vices become infinitely more detestable when they are
found under the banners of religion*.   But the *errors* were
those of the times rather than of the men, and even served, in
some degree, to palliate the crimes.   The barbarism of preceding ages, and the ignorance actually existing, had engendered
and nourished a swarm of obscure notions and active prejudices,
which infatuated the vulgar, and partially blinded even the

---

* Mosheim is disposed to throw all the reproach of this dispute on the *monastic*
education and character of Gregory and his two disciples ; and these he contrasts
with the secular virtues which high birth and society had nourished in Calixtus.
But in the first place, the whole blame was not by any means on that side, but was
very equally divided with the empire; and in the next, Pascal at least did
actually prove, by his arrangement with the English king, his disposition to end
the controversy, on the very terms finally accepted by Calixtus.   Mosheim mo-
derates with great impartiality between contending sects, and a very great merit
that is ; but when the contest is between a Pope and a German sovereign, his
feelings sometimes overpower his perfect judgment.

best and the wisest. The records of past events were little studied; indeed they were seen only by those discontinuous glimpses which perplex and deceive far more than they enlighten; and reason had lost her native force, and health, and penetration, through neglect and abuse—so that claims the most absurd were established by arguments the most senseless; and men could not rightly discern the real nature of their adversaries' pretensions, nor even the strength of their own, so as effectually to controvert the one, or rationally to maintain the other. Thus were their contests carried on in a sort of moral obscurity, which took off nothing from their positiveness and obstinacy, and permitted even additional licence to their malignity.

The first great Lateran Council, 1123, A.D.

In the following year a very numerous * assembly was held at Rome, which is acknowledged in that Church as the ninth General, and the First Lateran Council. Of the two-and-twenty canons which resulted from its labours, the greater part were in confirmation of the acts of preceding popes; and we observe that the object of several of the original enactments was to protect the property of the Church from alienation, and lay usurpations. There was one which promoted the crusading zeal both by spiritual promises and menaces. And among the most important we may consider that (the 17th) which prohibited abbots and monks from the performance of public masses, the administration of the holy chrism, and other religious services, and confided those solemn offices entirely to the secular clergy. This was an early and very public manifestation of that jealousy between the two orders of the Romish hierarchy, which in a later age displayed itself so generally as to become an efficient instrument in working its overthrow.

Popular tumults at Rome.

Calixtus died in 1124; and during the thirty years which followed, the pontifical city enjoyed scarcely any intermission from discord and convulsion. The names of Honorius and Innocent †

* About a thousand prelates were present, of whom above three hundred were bishops, and above six hundred abbots. Many pontifical councils had been previously held at the Lateran, but this was the first which obtained a place among the General Councils.

† The pontificate of Innocent II., though interrupted by frequent dissension, was the longest and the most important.

and Anaclete and Eugenius, with some others, pass by in rapid and tumultuous procession. The chair, which was generally contested, was seldom maintained to any good purpose; and one of its possessors, Lucius II., was actually murdered by the populace in an attempt to restore tranquillity.

But we must here observe, that the popular commotions of this period were not of the same description with those which we have already found occasion to notice; the question of papal election had ceased to be their sole, or even their principal, cause; the turbulence which had been occasioned by the abuse of that right and prolonged by the endeavour to reclaim it, was now founded in a deeper and much more powerful motive. A party had lately grown up in the Roman city of patriots ambitious to restore the name, and, as some might fondly deem, the glory of the ancient republic. And the first and necessary step towards the accomplishment of this scheme was the sub-version, or, at least, the entire reconstruction of the ecclesiastical system. To diminish the privileges, to reduce the revenues of the Church, to deprive the pontiff of temporal power and all civil jurisdiction, and to degrade (should we not rather say, to exalt?) his stately splendour to the homeliness of his primitive predecessors—these were the projects preparatory to the political regeneration of Rome. About the year 1135, Arnold, a native of Brescia, a disciple of the celebrated Abelard, returned to Italy from the schools of Paris, and having assumed the monastic habit, began publicly to preach and declaim against the vices of the clergy. Arnold maintained that there was no hope of salvation for prelates who held baronies, or for any clerks or monks who possessed any fixed property; that those possessions belonged to the prince, and that he alone could bestow them, and on laymen only; that the clergy ought to live on the tithes and the voluntary oblations of the people, content with a moderate and frugal sufficiency*. It is admitted by a Catholic writer †, that the pomp of the prelates, and the soft licentious life both of clerks and monks, furnished abundant materials for his denunciations; but it is complained

Remarks on their character.

Arnold of Brescia.

* Pagi, Vit. Innocent. II., sect. lxix., refers to Otho Frisingensis.
† Fleury, H. E., lib. lxviii., sect. 55.

that he exceeded the limits of truth and moderation ; and it is besides asserted, that his orthodoxy was liable to suspicion, and that he held some unsound opinions respecting the Eucharist and infant baptism.   In consequence of these various charges, Second La- he was condemned by the Second Lateran (or Tenth General) teran Council, held by Innocent II., in 1139: he immediately retired Council. 1139 A.D. from Italy, and transferred his popular declamation to Zurich, in Switzerland.

That council is stated to have been composed of about a thousand bishops; and it published thirty canons, which are collected by Baronius (ann. 1139).   They were directed for the most part against the ecclesiastical abuses of the day— against simony ; against the marriage, or concubinage, of the clergy ; against the practice of medicine by monks or canons ; and for the stricter morality of clerks and nuns.   They like- wise condemned usurious exactions and uncanonical marriages, and prohibited the possession of tithes by the laity.

Not many years after his condemnation, Arnold, encouraged by the independent spirit which was rising at Rome, boldly selected that metropolis for the scene of his two-fold exertions against papacy and despotism.   In the mean time (in the year 1154) a man of decided firmness and energy had obtained Adrian IV. possession of the chair.   Adrian IV., the only Englishman who ever attained that dignity, had raised himself from the very lowest office in society* to the throne of St. Peter; and though the arrogance which he then exhibited might entirely belong to his latest fortunes, an intrepid resolution, tempered by the most refined address, must have characterised every stage of his pro- gress; since these are qualities which offices and dignities may exercise, but can never bestow.   In the year following his elevation, one of his cardinals was dangerously wounded in some tumult, excited by the associates of Arnold.   Adrian instantly placed the city of Rome under an interdict; the churches were closed, and the divine offices for some time sus- pended, in the very heart of the Catholic Church.   The priests

* His name was Nicholas Breakspeare : going to Arles, in Provence, he was admitted in the quality of servant to the canons of St. Rufus; he presently became monk, and in the sequel abbot and general of the order.

and the people wearied the pontifical chair with supplications for a recall of the edict; but Adrian did not relent until Arnold and his associates were expelled from the city. "All the people (says Fleury) blessed God for this mercy: on the following day (Holy Thursday), they rushed from every quarter to receive the customary absolution, and a vast multitude of pilgrims was also present. Then the pope, attended by bishops and cardinals, and a numerous troop of nobles, came forth from his residence, and crossing the extent of Rome, amidst the acclamations of the people, arrived at the Lateran Palace, where he celebrated the festival of Easter."

Soon afterwards, Arnold unhappily fell into the power of Frederic Barbarossa, who was then in Italy on his advance to Rome; and the emperor, probably actuated by a common dislike to independence and innovation under every form, yielded up his prisoner to the solicitations of the pope. He was conducted to Rome, and subjected to the partial judgment of an ecclesiastical tribunal. His guilt was eagerly pronounced; the prefect of the city delivered his sentence, and he was burnt alive, "in the presence of a careless and ungrateful people." *Execution of Arnold.* But lest this same multitude, with the same capriciousness, should presently turn to adore *the martyr* and offer worship at his tomb, his ashes were contemptuously scattered over the bosom of the Tiber. His name has been the subject of splendid panegyric and scandalous calumny: with his claims to political celebrity we have no concern in this history; but in respect to his disputes with the Church, we may venture to rank Arnold of Brescia among those earnest but inconsiderate reformers, whose premature opposition to established abuses has produced little immediate result, except their own discomfiture and destruction; but whose memory has become dear, as their example has been useful, to a happier and a wiser posterity, whom we celebrate as martyrs to the best of human principles, and whose very indiscretions we account to them for zeal and virtue.

Frederic Barbarossa, whose elevation was nearly contemporaneous with that of Adrian, had also announced his intention to restrain the increasing wealth and moderate the insolence of *Frederic Barbarossa.*

the pope and his clergy ; and in 1155, he proceeded to Rome for the purposes of celebrating his coronation and commencing his reform : but he found the pontiff as firm and as powerful to resist imperial interference, as to quell domestic disorder. And so far was Adrian, on this occasion, from betraying the interests of his order, or the prerogatives of his office, that he even asserted a recent and ambiguous and singularly offensive claim—he demanded the personal service of the emperor to hold his stirrup when he mounted his horse*. A precedent for this indignity having been pointed out to him, Barbarossa, the haughtiest prince in Europe, at the head of a powerful and obedient army, submitted to an office of servitude, which he may possibly have mistaken for Christian humiliation. But, however that may be, the triumph of the see over so great a monarch proved the substantial reality of its power, and the awe which it deeply inspired into the most intrepid minds.

Some vexatious pretensions of Adrian respecting the regalia, and a gratuious insinuation that Frederic held the empire as a fief (beneficium) from Rome, served to keep alive a jealous irritation between the Church and the empire, though peace was not actually interrupted. Frederic, on the other hand, published, in 1158, an edict, of which the object was to prevent the transfer of fiefs without the knowledge and consent of the superior, or lord in whose name they were held. It was by such unauthorized transfers of feudal property that the territories of the Church had for a long period been gradually swollen, so as to spread themselves in every direction over the surface of Europe. The law in question was well calculated to check their further increase, and it seems to have been the first that was enacted for that purpose. Its obvious tendency did not escape the directors of the Church; but the opposition which it had peculiarly to expect from the Holy See was suspended by the death of Adrian and the confusion which followed it.

His law on the transfer of fiefs.

Alexander III. was immediately elected by a very large

---

* " This homage (says Gibbon) was paid by kings to archbishops, and by vassals to their lords ; and it was the nicest policy of Rome to confound the marks of filial and feudal subjection." Chap. lxix.

majority of the cardinals; but as some of the other party still Election of
Alexander
persisted in supporting a rival named Octavian*, Frederic, on III.
his own authority, summoned a General Council at Pavia to
decide on their claims.   Alexander disputed the Emperor's
right to arbitrate or at all to interfere in the schisms of the
Church †; and, as he refused to present himself at the Council,
his rival was declared to be duly elected, and the decision received the approbation of the Emperor.   But Alexander was
still sustained by the more faithful and powerful party within
the Church, and acknowledged by most of the sovereigns of
Europe; and from these supports he derived confidence sufficient to excommunicate his adversary, and to absolve his subjects from their oath of fidelity.   But Frederic did not feel the
blow; he proceeded to place his creature in possession of the
pontifical city, while Alexander adopted the resolution, so commonly followed by his successors in after ages, to seek security
in the territories of France.   He withdrew to Montpelier with He retires
his whole court, and resided in that neighbourhood for the to France,
space of three years, till circumstances enabled him to return
to Rome in 1165.   Here he was soon afterwards assailed by
Frederic in person, and though defended for some little time
by the ambiguous and venal fidelity‡ of the Romans, he was
finally obliged to escape in the disguise of a pilgrim.   He
retired to Benevento, but not till he had thundered another
anathema against Frederic; and on this occasion he not only
deprived him of the throne, but also forbade, "by the authority

* After the death of Octavian, Alexander had still to struggle successively
with three other antipopes.   The second, called by his adherents Calixtus III.,
was appointed in 1168, and abdicated in about ten years; but his party replaced
him by another puppet, whom they called Innocent III.

† Frederic had two precedents for his claim, though he might not perhaps
much regard, or even know, that circumstance.   In 408 Honorius held a Council
at Ravenna to decide the disputed election between Boniface and Eulalius, and
his decision was followed by the Church.   Afterwards the schism between Symmachus and Laurentius was terminated by Theodoric, though an Arian.   The
imperial power does not appear to have been disputed in either instance.

‡ It appears that he could secure little influence over the Roman people, "who,
pretending to wish well to both parties, were faithful to neither," until he received
a large sum of money from William, his Sicilian vassal.   Fleury, H. E., liv. lxxi.,
sec. 34. &c. &c.

of God, that he should thereafter have any force in battle, or triumph over any Christian; or that he should enjoy anywhere peace or repose, until he had given sufficient proofs of his penitence*." The denunciations contained in this frightful sentence were not, indeed, wholly accomplished; yet did it so come to pass, that Frederic was obliged to retire almost immediately from Rome by the sickness of his army; and that, in the long and destructive war which followed, he suffered such reverses as to find it expedient (in the year 1177) to sign a

but finally triumphs. disadvantageous treaty with the Pope†. The war was for the most part carried on in the North of Italy; and as it was fomented by the address and policy, rather than by the sword, of Alexander, the calm expression of his exultation was in some manner justified—"it hath pleased God (he said) to permit an old man and a priest to triumph without the use of arms over a powerful and formidable emperor‡."

From that time Alexander possessed in security the chair which he had merited by his persevering exertions, as well as by his various virtues. He immediately turned his attention to the internal condition of the Church, and his first object was to remove from his successors an evil which had so long and so dangerously afflicted himself. Accordingly he summoned (in

Third Lateran Council. 1179 A.D. 1179) a Council, commonly called the third of Lateran, and there enacted those final regulations respecting papal election which have already been mentioned; and they were so effectual, that, during the 600 following years, a double choice (as Gibbon has observed) only once disturbed the unity of the College.

Its principal canons. The third Lateran, or eleventh General Council was composed of three hundred Bishops, and published twenty-seven

---

* See Pagi, Vit. Alexandri III., sect. 66, who reasonably assigns this event to the year 1167.

† Alexander is accused, and with some justice, of having too exclusively consulted his own interests in this affair, and of having negotiated a truce only for his faithful allies, while he secured an honourable and profitable peace for himself. Denina (Rivol. d'Ital. L. xi. C. iv.) calls it a "Pace *particolare* fra Alessandro III. è Federico."

‡ Muratori, in his forty-eighth dissertation, describes Frederic as "Vir alti animi, acris ingenii, multarumque virtutum consensu ornatus."

canons for the regulation of ecclesiastical affairs. These prohibited any man from being raised to a Bishopric under thirty
years of age, or to any inferior dignity under twenty-five. They
restrained the luxury and exactions of Bishops and their trains
in the course of their visitations. They forbade any one to be
ordained without a title. They abolished all fees on the en-
thronement of Bishops and the installation of other dignitaries,
and also on sepulture, marriage and the other sacraments.
They denounced the incontinence of the clergy, and the possession of pluralities, an abuse which at that time had grown to
great excess in the Church. At the same time they protected
the clergy against the extortions of the civil magistrate—and
while they prohibited tournaments and confirmed the " Truce
of God," they excommunicated the Paterini, Cathari and other
heretics, and sanctioned the invocation of the secular power for
their extinction*.

Among the very few characters which throw an honourable Virtues of
lustre upon the dark procession of pontifical names, we may Alexander
confidently record that of Alexander III., not only from the III.
splendour of his talents, his constancy, and his success, but from
a still nobler claim which he possesses on our admiration. He
was the zealous champion of intellectual advancement, and the
determined foe of ignorance. The system of his internal administration was regulated by this principle, and he carried it
to the most generous extent. He made inquiries in foreign
countries, and especially in France, for persons eminent for
learning, that he might promote them, without regard to birth
or influence, to the highest ecclesiastical dignities. He caused
large numbers of the Italian Clergy, to whom their own country
did not supply sufficient means of instruction, to proceed to
Paris for their more liberal education ; and having learnt, that
in some places the chapters of cathedrals exacted fees from
young proficients before they licensed them to lecture publicly,
Alexander removed the abuse, and abolished every restriction
which had been arbitrarily imposed on the free advance of

* William of Tyre (De Bello Sacro, Lib. xxi.) mentions that he was present,
and, at the request of the Fathers, wrote an account of the council, extant in the
archives of Tyre.

learning. At the same time he was not so blinded by his zeal, as to consider the mere exercise of the understanding as a sufficient guarantee for moral improvement. But observing, on the contrary, with great apprehension the progress of the scholastic system of theology, and the numberless vain disputations to which it gave rise, he assembled a very large Council of Men of Letters* for the purpose of condemning that system, and discouraging its prevalence at Paris.

Celestine III.

He died in 1181 : in the course of the ten following years four pontiffs ruled and passed away, and in 1191 the chair was occupied by Celestine III., the fifth from Alexander. This prelate has deserved a place in the history of mankind by the protection which he afforded to Richard I. of England, when imprisoned on his return from the Holy Land. He died in 1198, and was succeeded by Lotharius, Count of Segni, a Cardinal Deacon, who assumed the name of Innocent III.

Observations on the dissensions of this period.

We shall conclude this account with a few of the observations which most naturally offer themselves. From the moment that the Roman See put forward its claims to temporal authority, its history presents a spectacle of contentions, varying indeed in character and in bitterness, but in their succession almost uninterrupted. The retrospect of the period of one hundred and fifteen years, of which the most memorable circumstances have now been related, presents to us a mass of angry dissensions, which may generally be distinguished into three classes : (1.) The first and most prominent of these contains such quarrels as arose in continuation of the grand debate between the popedom and the empire. It was not sufficient that the original matter of dispute was removed by the concordat of Calixtus ; the roots of animosity lay deeper than the form of an investiture, and they had branched out more widely and more vigorously during the contest which succeeded that concordat. The coronation of every new emperor was now attended by a new dispute, which usually caused immediate bloodshed, and was sometimes prolonged into obstinate warfare. Rome had

---

* Three thousand Gens de lettres are said to have been assembled on that occasion, Hist. Litt. de la France, xii siècle.

never a more formidable German adversary than Frederic Barbarossa; yet so far was he from obtaining any lasting advantage over her, that the papal pretensions appear to have gained considerably both in consistency and general credit during his reign, or, to speak more properly, during the pontificate of Alexander III. Frederic was not justified in contesting the legitimacy of that pontiff. Whatsoever general rights he might possess over the Roman church (and they were very vague and could only be temporal); whatsoever precedents he might plead for interference (and those were very remote, and not wholly applicable to the present case); the election of Alexander was unquestionably valid, according to the canons which had been enacted a century before and never repealed nor contested; and according to the practice of the See since the days of Gregory VII. Assuredly, the desire to recover an obsolete privilege, virtually ceded by the silence of intervening treaties, was excuse insufficient for that violent opposition, which did properly terminate in defeat and humiliation, as it was commenced and continued in injustice.

(2.) The contentions among the rival candidates for the pontifical chair, so scandalous and so usual in former periods, had abated nothing of their rage in the present; for though they changed their character, they lost not any part of their virulence, from the intermixture of political animosity. The short reigns of the greater number of the pontiffs, and the most trifling divisions in the college, gave frequent occasion, and some pretence, for popular interference; and this could never be exercised without excess. The regulation of Nicholas II. was not in fact of much real advantage, except as a preparatory measure to that of Alexander III.,—for it was vain to exclude from positive election an unprincipled and venal mob, as long as they retained a negative influence,—it was of no avail, as a final arrangement, to forbid their suffrage, and to require their consent,—for the turbulent expression of their disapprobation was instantly seized by the defeated candidate, as furnishing some hope for success, or, at least, some plea for perseverance. And perhaps it was not the least evil of those tumults, that they encouraged and almost invited the interference of the

emperor, so seldom offered with any friendly intention. There
was no other possible method of securing at once the justice
and decency of papal election, than by the entire exclusion of
the people—this measure was at length effected by Alexander.

(3.) Of another description again were those dissensions,
which distracted the several kingdoms of Europe by the internal division of the Church and the state—that is, by the opposition of the ecclesiastical to the civil authorities. But since in
these matters the affairs of every nation constitute histories essentially distinct from each other, and mainly influenced, in
every instance, by civil concerns; and since the detached incidents which we might produce would form independent nar-
ratives, standing, for the most part, on separate foundations, it
would be difficult, in these pages, to give them consistency, or
even coherence. We must, therefore, content ourselves with
referring to the annals of the different nations for the details
of such disputes; to those of France, for instance, for the
quarrel between Louis le Gros and the bishop of Paris, who
had the boldness to excommunicate his sovereign; and to those
of our own country for the particulars of the aggression of
William Rufus on the property of the Church, made during
the pontificate of Urban II., and of the protection perseveringly
vouchsafed to Thomas à Becket by the piety, or policy, of
Alexander III.

To those abovementioned we might reasonably add another
form of discord which was beginning obscurely to present itself,
with omens and menaces of tribulation. The voice of heresy
had been already raised in the valleys of France, and the
ministers of spiritual despotism had already bestirred themselves for its suppression. But this subject is so peculiarly
connected with the celebrity of Innocent III., that we shall
not disconnect it from his name.

Education
and theo-
logical
learning.
II. The gradual establishment of the peculiar doctrines and
practices of the Church of Rome, though occasionally influenced
by the vicissitudes of literature, is not inseparably connected
with its history, but was promoted in different ages by very
different causes. It is, indeed, remarked, that in the tenth
century the disputes respecting predestination and other subtile

questions became less common, and gave place to the final establishment of the doctrine of purgatory—a change well suited to the transition from an age (the ninth), distinguished by some efforts of intellectual inquisitiveness, into one remarkable for the general prostration of the human understanding. But, on the other hand, we find that, in the eleventh and twelfth ages, the necessity of *secret* confession was more strictly and assiduously inculcated ; yet the firmer riveting of that spiritual chain cannot certainly be attributed to any further access of darkness. In fact, the contrary was the case, since the partial revival of letters is very justly ascribed to that period. But the innovation which we have last mentioned, and to which others might be added, was probably occasioned by the disputes then prevailing between the Church and the empire, which made it necessary to extend, by every exertion, the influence of the clergy over their lay fellow-subjects. Again, the use (or rather the abuse) of indulgences in the place of canonical penance, which grew up in the twelfth age, was one of the first and most pernicious consequences of the crusades, and wholly independent of the growth and movements of literature. But notwithstanding these and many other points of disconnexion, there has ever existed a sort of general correspondence between religion and learning, most especially remarkable in those ages when the ministers of the one could alone give access to the mysteries of the other, and when the only incentive to studious application was religious zeal or ecclesiastical ambition; so that it would be as improper entirely to separate those subjects as it would be impossible, in these pages, to enter very deeply into discussion concerning the ecclesiastical literature of so many ages. We shall therefore content ourselves with striving, from time to time, to illustrate this work by such subsidiary lights, as may most obviously present themselves, so far, at least, as regards the different forms of theological learning, and the methods of theological education. At present, after a very brief review of earlier times, we shall conclude our imperfect inquiries at the end of the eleventh century.

The earliest schools established in the provinces of the Early schools.

Western empire were of civil foundation, and intended entirely
for the purposes of civil education; and so they continued
until the social system was subverted by the barbarian conquest. This revolution affected literary institutions in common
with all others; in the course of the sixth century profane
learning entirely disappeared, together with the means of ac-
quiring it; and before its conclusion, the office of instruction
had passed entirely into the hands of the clergy. The municipal schools of the empire gave place to cathedral or episcopal
establishments, which were attached, in every diocese, to the
residence of the bishop; and throughout the country elemen-
tary schools were formed in many of the monasteries, and even
in the manses of the parochial priesthood.

In Italy.   The system of education which prevailed in those of Italy,
and which was probably very general, is described by the
canon* which enjoins it:—" Let all presbyters who are appointed to parishes, according to the custom so wholesomely
established throughout all Italy, receive the younger readers
into their houses with them, and feeding them, like good
fathers, with spiritual nourishment, labour to instruct them in
preparing the Psalms, in industry of holy reading, and in the
law of the Lord." Such regulations prove, no doubt (if they
were really enforced), that the education of the clergy was not
entirely neglected: but they prove also, that education, even in
that early age, was confined to the clergy, and that it embraced
no subjects of secular erudition. It is true, indeed, that the
names of rhetoric, dialectics, and the former subjects of civil
instruction, were perpetuated in the ecclesiastical seminaries;
but those sciences were only taught as they were connected, or
might be brought into connexion, with theology, and made instrumental in the service of the Church †.

---

* Concilium Vasense Secundum (529 A.D.) The materials for the following
pages are principally taken from the Dissertations (43 and 44) of Muratori, the
Hist. Litt. de la France, two Discourses of Fleury, and the 16th Leçon of Guizot.

† The reproach addressed by Gregory the Great to St. Dizier, bishop of Vienne,
is commonly known. That prelate had ventured to deliver lessons on "Grammar"
in his cathedral schools: " It is not meet (said the Pope) that lips consecrated
to the praises of God should open to those of Jupiter." The extensive meaning
then attached to the word grammar will be mentioned presently.

But even this partial glimmering of knowledge was extinguished by the invasion of the Lombards, and the very genius of Italy seems to have been chilled and contracted by the iron grasp of the seventh century. Rome alone retained any warmth or pulsation of learning: if learning that can be called, which scarcely extended beyond a superficial acquaintance with the canons of the Church. And though there exist some monuments which appear to prove the existence of presbyteral or archipresbyteral schools in the eighth century, we need scarcely hesitate to prolong to the middle of that age the stupefaction of the preceding, and to attribute the first movement of reanimation to the touch of Charlemagne or his immediate predecessor.

While Italy was thus lifeless, some seeds from the plant of In France. knowledge, which had been blown to the western extremity of Europe, took root there, and reached a certain maturity. Accordingly, we find it recorded, that " two Irishmen, persons incomparably skilled in secular and sacred learning," had reached the shores of France, and were giving public lectures to the people*. Their fame reached the ears of Charlemagne, who immediately employed them in the education of the youth of Gaul and Italy.

Alcuin, as we have mentioned, enjoyed the honour of affording personal instruction to the emperor and presiding over his Exertions of Charlemagne. Palatine school; and Dungal, another native of Ireland†, has acquired some importance in the history of Italy by the lessons which he delivered in her schools. This eagerness of Charlemagne to avail himself of foreign talent and acquirements evinces his earnestness in the prosecution of his great project, to civilize by the path of knowledge—a project which failed, indeed, through the perversity of political circumstances and the incapacity of most of his successors, but which, if perseveringly pursued, must generally be successful, because it is

* Not gratuitously, it would seem, as literary missionaries, but for money contributed by their hearers.

† Scotus: a term which was long confined to the sister island. Muratori condescends to employ some pains to ascertain whether or not Dungal was a monk, as were his two compatriots mentioned in the text—a question deemed of some importance to the honour of the monastic order.

in unison with the natural inclinations, and energies, and prospects of the mind of man.

France profited by this conjuncture more rapidly than Italy, as she had not previously fallen quite so low in ignorance; and it would even seem that the schools, which were now instituted in that country, were open to the laity, as well as to those intended for the sacred profession, though the office of instruction remained entirely in the hands of the clergy. But it is certain, that very few were found to avail themselves of a privilege, of which they knew not the value. Among the numerous names which adorn the literary annals of France during the ninth century, there are scarcely one or two, which are not ecclesiastical. Even Germany outstripped, in the race of improvement, the languid progress of Italy ; and under a sky so splendidly prolific of taste and genius, there arose not any one character conspicuous, even in his own day, for intellectual advancement, through a space of more than four centuries*. And this extraordinary dearth of merit is not entirely to be charged on the neglect of rulers, whether temporal or spiritual. Italy shared with his other provinces the admirable institutions of Charlemagne and of some of his successors; and there are canons of Roman councils still extant, published in the ninth century, in the years 826 and 853, which directed the suspension of any among the priesthood who should be convicted of ignorance, and provided means for the instruction of the rural clergy †. But these measures, though they might possibly secure a mediocrity of theological acquirement, were insufficient to call forth any commanding spirit into the field of literature.

The tenth century did not increase the store of knowledge, nor multiply the candidates for fame either in Italy or France‡.

---

* Some may consider Pope Nicholas as an exception ; and he certainly possessed great talents, and was not devoid of canonical learning, though in both respects probably much inferior to Hincmar. But his character was essentially ecclesiastical ; it is not adorned by any recollection purely literary.

† The decree of Pope Leo IV. is cited by Muratori.

‡ The two leading literary heroes of France during this age were (1.) St. Odo, abbot of Cluni, who wrote some theological works and a Life of St. Gregory of Tours—he died in 942—and (2.) Frodoard, canon of Rheims, who composed the

In France, the depredations of the Normans during the con- Destruction of manuscripts.
clusion of the preceding age destroyed not only the leisure and
security, but even the means and food of study.   For, in their
savage incursions, those unlettered pagans directed their rage
against the monasteries, as being the principal seats of letters
and religion; the buildings were reparable, but the manuscripts
which they contained perished irretrievably.   Nor was this the
only calamity, nor even the most fatal of the injuries, which Influence of the feudal system.
obstructed the progress of learning; for it was during the same
period that the kingdom of France was broken up into small
principalities under independent hereditary vassals, who despoiled the people of the few rights and blessings which they
had possessed under a single sceptre, and whose rule permitted
the license which their example encouraged.   In the prostration of human laws, the law divine was easily forgotten, and
the hand, which was accustomed to robbery, did not long
refrain from sacrilege.   In such wild periods, the wealth and
the weakness of the clergy have always pointed them out as
the earliest victims*; and this domestic anarchy was probably
more effectual in arresting the steps of learning and civilization,
than the more transient tempests of foreign invasion. We shall
here only pause to remark, that during the struggles of this
frightful period, the defence of the tower of knowledge, as
heretofore its construction, was entrusted by Providence to ecclesiastical hands; while its walls were incessantly menaced or
violated by a lawless military aristocracy, which had closely
wrapped itself in ignorance, and was partly jealous and partly
contemptuous of every exertion to improve and enlighten mankind.

We are not surprised to observe that a condition of civil General ignorance and demoralization.
demoralization, such as then existed, should have been attended
by corruption in every rank of the clergy.   The Bishops were
negligent and immoral, and the inferior orders indulged in still

History of the Church of Rheims, and a Chronicle, extending from 919 to 966,
the year of his death.

* Most of the monasteries which escaped destruction fell into the hands of
lay abbots, who used them as residences or castles, or usually as hunting seats.
On the other hand, the foundation of Cluni, in the same age, compensated the
loss of many old, and probably corrupt, establishments.

grosser vices and more offensive indecencies*; and we may be
well assured, that the laity were still further debased by the
example of deformities, which their own turbulence had so
greatly tended to create.

Comets, and eclipses, and earthquakes were fearful prodigies
and sure prognostics of disaster, and the most penetrating
astronomers† of the day shared (or pretended to share) the
common solicitude. Enchantments, auguries, and divinations
were ardently sought after, and commanded implicit belief.
The forms of trial called "the Judgments of God," were of the
same description, and scarcely less remote from the precincts
of reason; and yet these degrading superstitions, though never
canonically received as a part of Church discipline, and even
continually combated by the more enlightened ecclesiastics,
were both respected and practised among the lower Clergy
during this and the three following ages.

Howbeit, even in the dreary records of this century we find
traces of parochial schools for the instruction of children of both
sexes‡; and we read a long list of literary worthies, whose
names have in many cases survived their works, and whose
works were chiefly remarkable for the meanness of their subjects, and the perplexed or puerile manner in which they are
treated. Yet even these are sufficient to exhibit to us the
spirit of improvement striving against the casual torrents which
threatened to wash it away; and though it unquestionably
receded during the calamitous interval between the death of
Hincmar and the end of the tenth century§, still, if we look

* In the enumeration of these by the truly Catholic compilers of the Hist. Litt.
de la France, it is mentioned, as not the lightest scandal, that "there were priests
who dared to marry publicly."

† Astrologers, we should rather say. Muratori (Dissert. 44) attributes the introduction of these vanities to the study of Arabic literature. But was that study
generally in fashion before the time of Pope Sylvester?

‡ According to the regulations of that at Toul the children were admissible at
seven years of age, and received their first lessons in the Psalms; and it was provided that the boys and girls should be taught separately. The parochial curés
appear (as in Italy) to have had the charge of such establishments.

§ About this time the establishment of some Greek commonalties took place in
Lorraine, introducing a partial knowledge of that language. And these Orientals
were there encountered by certain emigrants from Ireland—a country which appears

somewhat farther back, and confine our attention to the country about which we are best informed, we need not hesitate to pronounce that the literary condition of France was, upon the whole, more prosperous when Sylvester II. ascended the chair, than when Charlemagne mounted the throne of Rome.

As to Italy, the spell which had bound her genius during the preceding centuries seemed to be confirmed and riveted in the tenth. It is true, that some schools were yet found scattered through the towns and villages, which may have raised the character of the clergy somewhat above the degradation of the seventh and eighth centuries, to which the Lombard conquest had reduced it: but the industry of those schools appears still to have been confined to the study of grammar and some necessary knowledge of canonical law; and it is complained that the nobles, who sent their sons to them, had rather in view the episcopal dignities, for which they thus became qualified, than the spiritual fruits of religious education. It is very probable that they were attended by none of any class, excepting those intended for some branch of the ministry.

These remarks sufficiently explain to what extremely narrow limits was confined, both in respect to its character and diffusion, the learning of those ages which immediately followed the subversion of the Western Empire. From civil, it had passed under ecclesiastical superintendence; but the Church which undertook the charge was itself corrupted and barbarized by contact with the profound ignorance and rude character and institutions of the conquerors: so that the immortal models were neglected, the precepts of the ancient masters forgotten, and the whole light of literature, properly so called, extinguished. Nevertheless, we are not to suppose that the ecclesiastics of those days offered to their contemporaries no substitute for those treasures which they had not the means or the inclination to dispense. On the contrary, their productions were at some periods extremely abundant in number, and in character, *Literary productions of the dark ages.*

never to have forfeited the affections, nor to have secured the residence, of its sons. " Nationem Scotorum quibus consuetudo peregrinandi jam pæne in naturam conversa est." Walafridus Strabus (liv. ii., c. 27, de vita Sancti Galli) apud Murat. Diss. 37.

in many instances, far from unprofitable; and on this last point there is one important observation, which it is here proper to make, and which we press the more seriously, because it is not commonly urged. These writings were almost wholly confined to theological matters, and their object (however faultily it may sometimes have been pursued) was very frequently *practical*. Instructions, sermons, homilies, interpretations and illustrations of scripture, were published in great profusion, and furnished to the people the only means of intellectual instruction. It is true that they were rude and unskilfully composed; but they were addressed to rude assemblies, and were for the most* part directed to the moral improvement of those who read and heard them. Moreover, their tendency to that end, whatsoever it may have been, was at least not counteracted by any other description of literature: the great mass had one object only, and that, upon the whole, beneficial. Even the "Lives of the Saints," and other legends of those days, may have conduced, though by a different and more doubtful path, to the same purpose; for among the swarms of those compositions which were then produced, and of which so many had a tendency to mere superstition, some may be found unquestionably calculated to move the real devotion and amend the moral principles of a barbarous people. Thus was there much, even in the effusions of the most illiterate times, which must have persuaded, influenced, and profited the generation to which they were addressed: but their action was confined to their own day, to the moment of their delivery; they were not associated with any of the stable wisdom of former ages; nor were they qualified, nor were they indeed intended, to fix the attention of posterity.

Scarcity of manu-scripts.   Italy had suffered to a certain extent from calamities similar to those which suspended the progress of France, and which

---

* It is unquestionable that these writings contained a vast deal calculated to mislead—many errors of an absurd and superstitious tendency; but these evils were probably more than counterbalanced, in their immediate effect upon the people, by the expositions of sound doctrine and lessons of practical piety, which are even more abundant. We refer, as a fair example, to the passage of St. Eligius, cited in a former chapter.

were there followed by the same moral degeneracy; but these causes would scarcely have been adequate to so general an extinction, not of learning only, but almost of the curiosity and wish to learn, had they not been powerfully aided by another circumstance, which is less regarded by historians; this was no other than the extreme scarcity and dearness of manuscripts. This misfortune was not entirely, nor even mainly, attributable either to the destruction of monasteries or the indolence of monks: a more general and substantial cause existed in the absolute deficiency of the *material*. The ancients had obtained from the shores of the Nile, through easy and continual inter-course with Alexandria, sufficient supplies of papyrus to satisfy at a slight expense their literary wants; but after the conquest of Egypt by the Saracens, the communication became less fre-quent and secure, and the fabric of an implement of peace was probably discouraged by the warlike habits of the conquerors. At least it is certain that about that period the papyrus began to be disused throughout Europe, and that the monuments which remain of the seventh, eighth, and ninth centuries are invariably composed of parchment. It was not possible, when the material was so expensive, that manuscripts could multiply very rapidly, or even that the losses occasioned by decay or devastation could be repaired with any facility; and thus the libraries of the cathedrals and monasteries, to which all the treasures of former ages were at this period confided, were gradually impoverished or destroyed. The records of the time abound with complaints of this general penury of books, as well as with facts in proof of it, one of which is the following:—In the year 855, Lupus, of Ferrara, wrote from his abbey, in France, to Pope Benedict III., praying for the loan of the concluding part of St. Jerome's Commentary on Jeremiah, with a promise that it should be speedily copied and returned —"for in our regions nothing is to be found later than the Sixth Book, and we pray to recover through you that which is wanting to our own insignificance." In addition to this, he ventured to solicit the use of three books of profane writers—the Treatise of Cicero de Oratore, the Institutions of Quintilian, and Donatus's Commentary on Terence.

Muratori considers the zealous Abbot's request as unreasonable and immoderate, and we do not learn whether or not the Pope consented to grant it; but if the resources of France were really unable to supply him with the books in question, we need not distrust him when he laments the general scarcity of ancient and valuable compositions. This consideration will prevent the disdainful feeling which is almost necessarily roused, when we observe a succession of generations plunged in torpid ignorance, without an effort to extricate themselves from shame, or to let loose the human mind on its natural career of advancement: it disposes us much more nearly to compassion—especially if we reflect how frequently the energy of a vigorous and enterprising soul, secluded in the hermitage or the cloister, must have exhausted itself on the most contemptible subjects, or pined away from the mere dearth of literary sustenance. We shall find little reason to be astonished that genius itself was so seldom able to emerge out of the noisome mist, and rise into light and vigour, since its infancy was chilled by prejudices, unexcited by any wholesome exercise, and famished by the positive destitution of intellectual nourishment.

Invention of paper.

The cause of literary stagnation which we have last mentioned was removed in the eleventh century by the invention of paper*, and accordingly we find that the number of MSS. was greatly multiplied after that time†. But the fury of civil dissension was not mitigated; and under governments at the same time feeble and arbitrary, there was little encouragement for studious application, as indeed there was little honour, or even security, except in the profession of arms. And in sad truth, during the earlier years of this age, the wildest disorders were of such ordinary perpetration, misery had such universal prevalence, and injustice walked abroad so boldly and tri-

* A very interesting account of the progress of paper-making, writing, printing, &c. may be found in the Life of Caxton published by this Society.

† Still it was in the eleventh age that a Countess of Anjou is recorded to have purchased the Homilies of Haimon, at the price of 200 sheep, besides a very large payment in wheat, barley, skins, and other valuable articles. Hist. Litt. de la France, xi. siècle.

umphantly, that there were those who held the persuasion that
the millennarian prophecy *had been* already accomplished; that
Satan had shaken off his fetters at the thousandth year, and
was actually directing the evil destinies of the human race.

At the same time, let us recollect that great exertions were Exertions
made by the higher ecclesiastical orders to apply an indirect of ecclesiastics.
but very powerful remedy to these excesses, by re-establishing
the discipline of the Church. For this purpose, about eighty
councils were held in France alone during the eleventh century*.
We have already related how zealously the authority of Rome
had engaged itself in the same cause; and by a necessary re-
action, the success of every effort for the improvement of
morality was favourable to the advancement of literature. The
example of Sylvester II. might be sufficient to rouse the jealous
emulation of Italy; and Sylvester left to that country not his
example only, but the fruits of his active zeal in encouraging
the learned of his own time, and in establishing schools and
collecting libraries for the use of other generations. Some of
the Popes, his successors, followed his traces with more or less
earnestness; and among the rest, Gregory VII. added to his
extraordinary qualities the undisputed merit of promoting the
progress of education†.

The voice of controversy, which was once more heard in this Lanfranc.
century, not only created another motive for literary activity,
but proved the revival of a spirit of inquiry, inconsistent at least
with universal ignorance. The talents of Lanfranc‡, the earliest

* The zeal which was applied in the beginning of this age to the building and
restoration of churches, basilicæ, monasteries, and other holy edifices, is warmly
praised by ecclesiastical writers. " Erat enim instar ac si mundus ipse excutiendo
semet, rejecta vetustate, passim candidarum ecclesiarum vestem indueret." Gla-
brus Rodolph. apud Du Chesne, Script. Franc., lib. xiv., cap. 4, cited by Muratori.

† In a council held in 1078, he strongly pressed on all bishops the necessity of
superintending education in their respective dioceses.

‡ " Lanfrancus teneriorem ætatem in sæcularibus detrivit, sed in Scripturis
divinis animo et ævo maturavit." France was for some time the principal field
of his exertions, and Muratori supposes that Hildebrand, attracted by his celebrity, may have visited that country for the purpose of hearing him. The name
of Anselm succeeds to that of Lanfranc: that learned prelate was born at Aosta,
which then belonged to the Duke of Burgundy—so that France disputes with
Italy the honour of having produced him. He too is considered by Muratori as
having prepared the way for the scholastic system of theology.

boast of reviving Italy, were animated by the "heresy" of Berenger; and to the ingenious disputations thus occasioned it is
usual to attribute the growth of the new system of theological
science, afterwards called Scholastic.

Three cha-
racters of
theological
literature.

That is a very broad, but in many respects a correct view of
early theological literature, which distributes it into three æras.
The *first* of these comprehends the whole list of the ecclesiastical fathers—men who, though they varied exceedingly in
character, style, and even opinion, were nevertheless united by
one great principle ; for they acknowledged no other sources of
faith, and reverenced no other authority, than Scripture and
apostolical tradition.   On this foundation, they boldly applied
to the elucidation of religious subjects such reasoning and eloquence as Nature had bestowed on them : perverted, it might
be, by the peculiar prejudices of the times and countries wherein
they lived, but little restrained either by the use or abuse of
educational discipline, and wholly exempt from servile subjection to the opinions of any predecessor. The characteristics
of this age are such as we should expect from such principles
—an overflow of piety stained by superstition, exuberance of
learning without a proportionate fruit of knowledge, and sallies
of oratory, which sometimes ascended into eloquence, and
sometimes dwindled away into puerile declamation, or cold
and empty allegory.   This æra is by many extended down to
the eighth century, and considered as properly terminating
with John Damascenus; but the concluding half of the fourth
age and the beginning of the fifth was the true period of its
glory: and thence we may trace the gradual dissolution of its
distinguishing qualities into that system which was afterwards
established in its place and on its ruins.

The *second* was the æra of intellectual blindness and dependence : its most laborious works were mere collections,
quotations, and compilations; as if the minds of that generation
were stupified by gazing on the brilliant creations of their predecessors, till they mistook them for pure and inimitable perfection. St. Augustine and St. Gregory were the idols of those
abject worshippers; and if their piety was sometimes kindled
by the enthusiasm of the former, their catholic zeal and papal

prejudices were more commonly (or at least more manifestly) nourished by the principles of Gregory. The termination of this period is fixed at the middle of the eleventh century: but its character had been partially interrupted by the writers of the ninth, and most especially by John Scotus; and his style and manner, as well as his opinions, were followed and revived by Berenger.

The grand principle of the *third* æra was the exaltation of reason to its proper pre-eminence over the influence of human authority; a true and noble principle as long as reason itself can be restrained to its just province, so as neither to deviate into minute and barren sophistry, nor to break loose into those dark and interminable inquiries which God has closed against it. Unhappily it was not long before it fell into both these errors, which are, indeed, very closely connected. In the establishment and support of the scholastic theology, it so frequently descended to degrading artifice, and perplexed itself so blindly in the mazes of chicanery, as to make it doubtful whether religious truth was not more disfigured by the minute disceptations which thenceforward prevailed, than by the superstitious extravagance of the first period, or the obsequious ignorance of the second.

We shall recur to this subject hereafter. At present we need only remark, that during the latter half of the eleventh century considerable addition was made both to the copiousness of libraries and the number of schools and of students, as well in Italy as in France*; but the course of study was still generally confined to the two paths denominated the Trivium and Quadrivium. The first of these embraced grammar, rhetoric, *Objects of study.* *The Trivium and Quadrivium.*

* Schools of civil law were founded in both those countries in the eleventh century, and acquired some eminence before its conclusion. Physic, of course, had never been entirely neglected; and as we find that by a council held at Rheims, in 1131, monks were forbidden the practice either of law or medicine, we would willingly have hoped that some attention now began to be paid to the education of the laity. But the prohibition only extended to the walls of the monasteries; the practice of those professions is described to have been very lucrative, and for that reason, and through the continued ignorance of the laity, even in the century following (if we are to believe the compilers of the Hist. Littéraire), there were scarcely any who professed medicine except clerks and monks; with the addition indeed of certain Jews, who were held the most skilful practitioners.

and dialectics; and grammar was defined to be "the art of writing and speaking well*," and professed to comprehend the study of several classical as well as sacred writers. The knowledge of arithmetic, music, geometry, and astronomy swelled the pretensions of the Quadrivium.

But in real truth, the productions and language of the Greeks were wholly neglected and unknown. The science of criticism —the art of distinguishing what is graceful in style, and what is *true* in fact—was not cultivated; and both the study and composition of history were still confined to legendary chronicles†, or to the ill-digested details of contemporary narrative. Besides which, the sciences professed were for the most part imperfectly understood even by those who pretended to them; and it is moreover admitted that, as the students of those days usually affected to become acquainted with all the subjects placed before them, they generally departed without any profitable knowledge of any of them. The great mass of the people had no education whatsoever. The result was such as must necessarily follow, whenever the possession of any valuable portion of literary acquirement is confined to very few individuals: the possessors employed it to delude, at least as much as to enlighten, the people. So that those ages, deeply as they suffered from the scanty provision of useful and liberal knowledge, were scarcely less vitiated through the inequality with which that little was distributed. The small number, who had penetrated the mysteries, felt too strongly the advantage and the power conferred by exclusive initiation, to desire their more general promulgation. The more numerous class, who from a distant and hasty glimpse had caught some imperfect insight, by communicating their own obscure views and misconceptions, disseminated many fanciful, if not pernicious, errors and absurd notions. So it proved, that the lights which were thus faintly transmitted to the body of the people, were

* Hist. Lit. de la France, xii. siècle.

† The first Christian chronicler was Gregory of Tours, whom we have mentioned in the ninth chapter. His History of the Franks, which contains some faint indications of an educated mind, was not surpassed during the sixth century, nor the two which followed. Its continuation by Fredegarius is in a still inferior style.

not faint only, but sometimes false and deceitful also.   And it is a question for the decision of philosophy, whether plain and downright ignorance, with all its demoralizing consequences, be not a condition of less danger and better hope, than one of mistake and delusion.

NOTE ON ST. BERNARD.

THE life of St. Bernard connected, within a few years, the pontificate of Gregory VII. with that of Alexander III.   Born in 1091, he flourished during one of the rudest periods of papal history; and he died (in 1153) just before the era commenced of its proudest triumphs, and, perhaps, of its deepest crimes. His actions and his writings throw the best light which now remains upon that period, and even the following short account of them will not be without its use.   St. Bernard was a native of Fontaines, in Burgundy, and descended from a noble family. He entered, at the age of twenty-two, into the monastery of Citeaux, near Dijon; and so early was the display of his zeal and his talents, that only two years afterwards he was appointed to establish a religious colony at Clairvaux*, in the diocese of Langres. It grew with rapidity, and spread its scions with great luxuriance under his superintendence—so that at his decease, at no very advanced age, he was enabled to bequeath to the Church the inestimable treasure of about one hundred and sixty monasteries, founded by his own exertions. As for himself, though it seems clear that the highest ecclesiastical dignities were open, and even offered to him, his humbler ambition was contented to preside over the society which he had first created, and to influence the character of those which had proceeded from it, by his counsel, example, and authority.

The founder of many monasteries.

But the influence of St. Bernard was not confined to his monastic progeny—it displayed itself in all grand ecclesiastical transactions, in France, in Germany, in Italy; from the altars of the church it spread to courts and parliaments.   And, as it was founded on reputation, not on dignity; as it stood on no

* Or Clairval—Clara Vallis.

other ground than his wisdom and sanctity, so was it generally exerted for good purposes; and always for purposes which, according to the principles of that age, were accounted good.

On the schism which took place after the death of Honorius II.*, St. Bernard advocated the cause of the legitimate claimant, Innocent II., with great zeal and effect. During eight years of quarrel and turbulence he persevered in the struggle. His authority † unquestionably decided the king and the clergy of France. The king of England ‡ at Chartres, the emperor at Liege, are stated to have listened and yielded to his persuasions. He reconciled Genoa and Pisa to the cause of Innocent. In the latter city a council was held in 1134, in which St. Bernard was the moving and animating spirit. Nevertheless it is obvious, from the genuine piety which pervades so many of his works, that his mind was then most at home when engaged in holy offices and pious meditation. How well soever he might be qualified to preside in the assemblies,

His exertions at the Council of Pisa.

---

* In 1130. Innocent II. succeeded, and ruled thirteen years and a half. Eugenius III. was elected 1145, and reigned for eight years.

† The means by which ecclesiastical authority sometimes (and not, perhaps, very uncommonly) attained its ends in those days, are well displayed in the following anecdote of St. Bernard. The Duke of Guienne had expelled the Bishops of Poitiers and Limoges, and refused to restore them, even on the solemn and repeated injunctions of the pope and his legate. St. Bernard had exerted his influence for the same purpose, equally in vain. At length, when celebrating, on some particular occasion, the holy sacrifice, after the consecration was finished and the blessing of peace bestowed upon the people, St. Bernard placed the body of the Lord on the plate, and carrying it in his hand, with an inflamed countenance, and eyes sparkling fire, advanced towards the Duke, and uttered these thrilling words:—" Thus far we have used supplication only, and you have despised us; many servants of God, who were present in this assembly, joined their prayers with ours, and you have disregarded them: behold, this is the Son of God, who is the King and Lord of the Church which you persecute, who now advances towards you;—behold your Judge !—at whose name every knee bends in heaven, in earth, and beneath the earth. Behold the just avenger of crimes, into whose hands that very soul which animates you will some day fall. Will you disdain him also? Will you dare to scorn the Master, as you have scorned his servants ?" This tremendous appeal was successful. The Duke is related to have fallen with his face to the earth when he heard it; the prelates were restored to their sees, and the schism extinguished. See Dupin, Nouvelle Bilioth., tom. ix., ch. iv.

‡ Ernardus, Vita Sancti Bernardi. Pagi, Gest. Pontif. Roman. Vit. Innocent. II.

and rule the passions, and reconcile the interests of men, it was in the peaceful solitude of Clairvaux that his earthly affections were placed, and it was to the mercy-seat of heaven that his warmest vows and aspirations were addressed.   Through these various qualities—through his charitable devotion to the poor ; through that earnest piety which tinctured his writings with a character sometimes approaching to mysticism; through his imitation of the ancient writers, Augustine and Ambrose ; through his zeal for the unity and doctrinal purity of the Church, St. Bernard has acquired and deserved the respectable appellation of the *Last of the Fathers.* The last of theFathers.

The remaining works of St. Bernard consist of about four hundred and fifty Letters, a great number of Sermons, and some very important Tracts and Treatises.   It would not here be possible, nor any where very profitable, to present a mere analysis of compositions so numerous and various.   A great proportion of the matter is devoted to the ends of piety and charity,— to the exaltation of the soul of man,—and the inculcation of his highest duties.   On points of doctrine, the Abbot of Clairvaux was too ardently attached to his Church to venture upon any deviation from the established, or, at least, the tolerated faith. On the important subject of grace, he appears to have followed the opinion of St. Augustine.   He considered the freedom of will to be preserved by the voluntary consent which it gives to the operations of grace; that that consent is indeed brought about by grace, but that being voluntary, and without constraint, it is still free.   The necessity of this freedom he argues at great length, as indispensable to any system of retribution*. " Where there is necessity there is not liberty ; where there is not liberty, neither is there merit, nor, consequently, judgment."   (Ubi necessitas, ibi libertas non est ; ubi libertas non est, nec meritum, nec per hoc judicium.)   On the other hand, he maintained the indisputable efficacy of grace ; and in defining the limits of its operation, and reconciling its overruling influence with the necessary liberty of a responsible agent, he His doctrine.

* " Excepto sane per omnia originali peccato, quod aliam constat habere rationem."—S. Bernardi " Tractatus de Gratiâ et Libero Arbitrio."

fathomed the depths, and, perhaps, exhausted the resources of human reason.

As Lanfranc had been the champion of the Church against the heresy of Berenger; as the admirable Anselm * had maintained the better reason and sounder doctrine against the dangerous subtilties of Roscellinus †; so St. Bernard, in his turn of controversy, was confronted with the most ingenious scholastic of the age, Peter Abelard. This celebrated doctor was born in Britanny, in 1079; and while St. Bernard was shaping his character and his intellect after the rigid model of Augustine, Abelard was learning a dangerous lesson of laxity in the school of Origen. We shall not trace the various and almost opposite heresies ‡ into which he was betrayed by the obtuse subtilty of his principles; still less are we disposed to investigate the oblique paths by which he reached those conclusions. It may suffice to say, that he was charged with being at the

Peter Abelard. (margin)

Anselm. (margin) * Anselm was probably born at Aosta in 1035, and died in 1105; and though he is claimed by the Gallican Church as its noblest ornament since the fifth century, his history belongs more properly to our own. He wrote several works, against the "Greek Doctrine of the Holy Procession,"—" On the Trinity and Incarnation," against Roscellinus,—" On the Immaculate Conception,"—" On the Fall of the Devil,"—" On Freewill,"—" On Original Sin,"—" Necessity," —" Predestination,"—on which latter subjects he had drawn at the well of St. Augustine. "His obsequies (says the writer in the Histoire Littéraire de la France) were preceded, attended, and followed by some miracles; but the holy prelate had performed a vast number more during his lifetime." His Life, as given in the Histoire Littéraire, is an abridgment of that by the Monk Edmen, his pupil and panegyrist.

† During the infancy of St. Bernard.

‡ The opinions generally attributed to him are, that he considered the doctrine of the Trinity to have been known to certain ancient philosophers, and revealed to them in recompense for their virtues,—that the Son bore the same relation to the Father as the species does to the genus; as a certain power to power; as materiatum to materia; as man to animal; as a brazen seal to brass; —that he denied the Atonement, and reasoned against the murder of an innocent being as the means of appeasing God's anger;—that he consequently denied the Redemption, though he received the Incarnation as the properest method for illuminating the world with divine light and love;—that the Holy Ghost proceeded from the Father and the Son, but not from their substance; and that it was the soul of the world;—that it is not the fault, but the penalty, of original sin, which we derive from Adam;—that free will, without the help of grace, was sufficient for salvation. In addition to these and many other imputations, he was also charged before the Council of Soissons (1121) with Tritheism, and at the same time with having asserted that the Father alone was almighty.

same time an Arian, a Nestorian, and a Pelagian; and with as much justice, perhaps, as such charges were usually advanced by the Roman Catholic Church against its refractory children.

The history of the crimes and the misfortunes of Abelard is known to every one. When the abbot of Clairvaux, in the course of his official visitation, inspected the nunnery of the Paraclete, he found the establishment well conducted, and he approved of every regulation. Only, in the version of the Lord's prayer there in use, he observed these words.—" Give us this day our super-substantial (ἐπιούσιον) bread"—and he thought it insufferable that the very prayer, which the Deity had deigned to communicate to man for His own service, should be thus senselessly corrupted by the infection of Aristotle. Abelard defended his version; and hence arose the first recorded alter- cation between those celebrated theologians. The strictures of St. Bernard irritated that vain scholastic; and as it happened that a large assembly of the clergy of France was appointed to meet in the city of Sens, on some occasion deemed important *, Abelard challenged his rival to make good, in the presence of that august body, his repeated charges of heresy. St. Bernard would willingly have declined that conflict: he feared the supe- riority of an experienced polemic;—" I was but a youth †, and he a man of war from his youth. Besides, I judged it improper to commit the measures of divine faith, which rested on the foundations of eternal truth, to the petty reasonings of the schools." Howbeit, the counsel of his friends prevailed; after some hesitation he accepted the challenge, and appeared on the appointed day.

Louis VII. honoured the assembly with his presence; the nobles of his court, the leading prelates and abbots, and the most learned doctors of the kingdom were there; and the highest expectations were raised, from one end of the realm to the

Contro- versy be- tween St. Bernard and Abe- lard.

---

* For the translation of the body of some saint into the cathedral church. The assembly took place in 1140.

† The Abbot probably meant a youth *in controversy*,—for as to age, he was then forty-nine, and his adversary only two years older. Milner, whose account of this transaction has great merit, seems to have understood him literally.

other, by the rumour of this theological monomachy. The two champions were confronted. Bernard arose: " I accuse not this man ; let his own works speak against him. Here they are, and these are the propositions extracted from them. Let him say—I wrote them not ; or let him condemn them, or let him defend them against my objections." The charges were not entirely read through, when Abelard interrupted the recital, and simply interposed his *appeal to the pope.* The assembly was astonished at his hasty desertion of the field, which he had so lately sought. " Do you fear," said St. Bernard, " for your person ? You are perfectly secure; you know that nothing is intended against you ; you may answer freely, and with the assurance of a patient hearing." Abelard only replied, " I have appealed to the court of Rome ;" and retired from the assembly. " I know nothing," says Milner *, " in Bernard's history more decisively descriptive of his character, than his conduct in this whole transaction. By nature sanguine and vehement, by grace and self-knowledge modest and diffident, he seems on this occasion to have united boldness with timidity, and caution with fortitude. It was evidently in the spirit of the purest faith in God, as well as in the most charitable zeal for divine truth, that he came to the contest."

His eccle-
siastical
principles.

We shall now proceed to consider St. Bernard in another

---

* Church Hist. Cent. xii. ch. 2. This author is probably nearer to truth in his praise of Bernard, than in his censure of the " heretic." The reason of Abelard's sudden appeal to a higher court was, unquestionably, his distrust of that before which he stood : he might doubt its impartiality, or he might certainly have discovered its determined prejudice against him ; and that it was, in fact, very provident in him to appeal betimes from its decision is clearly proved by a passage in the account which certain bishops of France addressed to the pope of the proceedings at Sens. " As the arguments of the Abbot of Clairvaux ... convinced the assembled bishops that the tenets which he opposed were not only false, but heretical, they, *sparing his* (the heretic's) *person out of deference to the apostolic see,* condemned the opinions." " A loco et judice quem sibi ipse elegerat, sine læsione, sine gravamine, ut suam prolongaret iniquitatem, Sedem Apostolicam appellavit. Episcopi autem, qui propter hoc in unum convenerant, vestræ Reverentiæ deferentes nihil in personam ejus egerunt, sed tantummodo capitula librorum ejus," &c. &c. It is therefore manifest that this appeal saved him from some personal infliction. This Letter is published among the works of St. Bernard, p. 1560, edit. Lutet. (Paris) 1640. After all, it is some satisfaction to record, that Abelard died (in 1142) in quiet obscurity, in the Monastery of Cluni.

(if, indeed, it is another) character,—that of a zealous defender
of the power and prerogatives of the Church; and we shall observe how far the same principle engaged him, on the one
hand, in the support of papal authority, and in the extirpation
of heresy on the other. We willingly omit all mention of the
miracles which are so abundantly ascribed to him,' and which,
if they are not merely the fabrications of his panegyrists, are
equally discreditable to his honesty and his piety. We defer
to a future chapter any notice of the very equivocal zeal which
urged him to preach a holy war, to proclaim its predestined
success with a prophet's authority, and then to excuse the
falsification of his promises by a vulgar and contemptible sub-
terfuge. Yet were all these transactions very certain proofs of
his attachment to the principles of the Roman Catholic Church.
Of the same nature were the eulogies which he so warmly
lavished, in one of his treatises, upon the newly instituted order
of the Templars. But we pass these matters over, and proceed
directly to observe the expressions by which he characterised
the Bishop of Rome. " Let us inquire," he says, in his letter
to Pope Eugenius III.*, " yet more diligently who you are,
and what character you support for a season in the Church of
God. Who are you?—a mighty priest, the highest pontiff.
You are the first among bishops, the heir of the apostles; in
primacy Abel, in government Noah, in patriarchate Abraham,
in order Melchisedech, in dignity Aaron, in authority Moses,
in judgment Samuel, *in power Peter, in unction Christ.* You
are he to whom the keys have been delivered, to whom the
flock has been entrusted. Others, indeed, there are, who are
doorkeepers of heaven, and pastors of sheep; but you are pre-
eminently so, as you are more singularly distinguished by the
inheritance of both characters. They have their flocks assigned
to them, each one his own; to you the whole are entrusted, as
one flock to one shepherd; neither of the sheep only, but of
their pastors also; you alone are the pastor of all. Where is
my proof of this?—in the Word of God. For to which, I say,
not of bishops, but of apostles, was the universal flock so posi-

* " De Consideratione," lib. ii., c. viii.

tively entrusted ?   ' If thou lovest me, Peter, feed my sheep.'
.... Therefore, according to your canons, others are called to
a share of the duty, you to a *plenitude of power*. The power
of others is restrained by fixed limits; yours is extended even
over those who have received power over others. Are you not
able, if cause arise, to exclude a bishop from heaven, *to depose
him from his dignity*, and even to consign him over to Satan ?
These your privileges stand unassailable, both through the keys
which have been delivered, and the flock which has been confided to you," &c.   Thus the authority of St. Bernard, which
was extremely great, both in his own age and those which
immediately followed, was exerted to subject the minds of religious men to that spiritual despotism, which was already swollen
far beyond its just limits, and was threatening a still wider and
more fatal inundation.

His prin-
ciples re-
garding
Heretics.

Among the numerous discourses of St. Bernard, two* were
more especially directed against the Heretics of the day; and
the preacher declares, that he was moved to this design by
" the multitude † of those who were destroying the vine of
Christ, by the paucity of its defenders, by the difficulty of its
defence."   In the discharge of this office he inveighs against
the innovators in the usual terms of theological bitterness ; and
at the same time charges them with those flagrant violations of
morality and decency, which were so commonly imputed to
seceders from the Church, though they were, in truth, inconsistent with the first principles of civil society.   We shall not
repeat those charges, nor copy his ardent vituperations; but
there is one passage (in the sixty-sixth sermon), which possesses
some historical importance, and which exposes besides the principles of the orator.   " In respect to these Heretics, they are
neither convinced by reasons, for they understand them not;
nor corrected by authority, for they do not acknowledge it; nor
bent by persuasion, for they are wholly lost.   It is indisputable
that they prefer death to conversion.   Their end is destruction;

* Sermons " Super Cantica," lxv. et lxvi.
† In other places he acknowledges the same fact. " Et item de hæresi, quæ
clam pæne ubique serpit, apud aliquos sævit palam. Nam parvulos Ecclesiæ
passim et publice deglutire festinat," &c. &c. De Consid., lib. iii., c. i.

the last thing which awaits them is the flames. More than once the Catholics have seized some of them, and brought them to trial. Being asked their faith, and having wholly denied, as is their usage, all that was laid against them, they were examined by the *Trial of water**, and found false. And then, since further denial was impossible, as they had been convicted through the water not receiving them, they seized (as the expression is) the bit in their teeth, and began with pitiable boldness, not so much to make confession as profession of their impiety. They proclaimed it for piety ; they were ready to suffer death for it; and the spectators were not less ready to inflict the punishment. Thus it came to pass that the populace rushed upon them, and gave the heretics some fresh martyrs to their own perfidy. I approve the zeal, but I do not applaud the deed; because faith is to be the fruit of persuasion, not of force. Nevertheless, it were unquestionably better that they should be restrained by the sword,—the sword of him, I mean, who wears it not without reason,—than be permitted to seduce many others into their error; ' for he is the minister of God, a revenger to execute wrath upon him that doeth evil.'...Some wondered that the offenders went to execution not only with fortitude, but, as it seemed, with joy ; but those persons had not observed how great is the power of the Devil, not only over the bodies, but even over the hearts of men, which have once delivered themselves into his possession. ...The constancy of martyrs and the pertinacity of heretics has nothing in common; because that which operates the contempt of death in the one is piety,—in the other, mere hardheartedness."...Marcus Antoninus, in the insolence of empire and philosophy, insulted by a similar distinction the firmness of those sainted sufferers, to whom the Abbot of Clairvaux addressed, as to heavenly mediators, his daily and superstitious supplications. And now again, after another long revolution of centuries and of principles, those despised outcasts, whom St. Bernard, in the loftier pride of ecclesiastical infallibility, consigned, with no better spirit, to eternal condemnation, are

* This was one of the most popular among " the judgments of God."

revered *by us* as victims in a holy cause, the earliest martyrs of the reformation!

His exhortations to Pope Eugenius.

In the same work in which the office and prerogatives of the Pope were so highly exalted, the writer boldly exposed some of the favourite abuses of the system; and dictated, from his cell at Clairvaux, rules for its better administration, and for the guidance of the autocrat of the church. His instructions were wise, because they were virtuous, and proceeded from a true sense of spiritual duties and dignity. His general exhortations to Eugenius to cast aside the unworthy solicitude respecting secular matters, which at once embarrassed and degraded the Roman See, and to emulate the venerable patriarchs of the ancient church; to leave to kings and their ministers the jarring courts of earthly justice*, and to content himself with distributing the judgments of heaven—these lessons were conceived in the loftiest mood of ecclesiastical exaltation, and with the justest sense of ecclesiastical policy; but the venom had already sunk too deep, and the healing admonitions of the reformer failed to arrest for a moment the progress of corruption.

On the evils of appeal to Rome.

St. Bernard next addressed his censures more particularly to the practice of appeal to Rome, which was then growing into a notorious abuse. After enumerating some of the evils thus occasioned, the delay, the vexation, the positive perversion of all the purposes of justice, "How much longer," he exclaims, "will you shut your ears, whether through patience or inadvertency, against the murmur of the whole earth? How much longer will you slumber? How much longer will your attention be closed against this monstrous confusion and abuse? Appeals are made in defiance of law and equity, of rule and order. No distinction is made in place, or mode, or time, or cause, or person. They are commonly taken up with levity, frequently too with malice; that terror which ought to fall upon the wicked, is turned against the good; the honest are summoned by the

* "Quænam tibi major videtur et potestas et dignitas; dimittendi peccata, an prædia dividendi? Sed non est comparatio. Habent hæc infima et terrena judices suos et reges et principes terræ. Quid fines alios invaditis? Quid falcem vestram in alienam messem extenditis? Non quia indigni vos; sed quia indignum vobis talibus insistere, quippe potioribus occupatis." De Consid., lib. i., c. vi.

bad, that they may turn to that which is dishonest; and they tremble at the sound of your thunder. Bishops are summoned, to prevent them from dissolving unlawful marriages, or from restraining or punishing rapine and theft and sacrilege, and such like crimes. They are summoned, that they may no longer exclude from orders and benefices unworthy and infamous persons..... And yet you, who are the minister of God, pretend ignorance that that which was intended as a refuge for the oppressed has become an armoury for the oppressor; and that the parties who rush to the appeal are not those who have suffered, but those who meditate, injustice."

Another papal corruption, against which St. Bernard inveighed with equal zeal was the abuse of exemptions. " I express the concern and lamentations of the churches. They exclaim that they are maimed and dismembered. There are none, or very few, among them which do not either feel or fear this wound : Abbots are removed from the authority of their Bishops, Bishops from that of their Archbishops, Archbishops from that of their Patriarchs and Primates. Is the appearance of this good ? Is the reality justifiable ? If you prove the plenitude of your power by the frequency of its exercise, haply you have no such plenitude of justice. You hold your office, that you may preserve to all their respective gradations and orders in honour and dignity, not to grudge and curtail them." . . . If the virtuous Abbot was moved to such boldness of rebuke by the delinquencies of the eleventh century—the earliest and perhaps the most venial excesses of pontifical usurpation—with what eyes had he beheld the court of Innocent IV., or the chancery of John XXII.! with what a tempest of indignation had he visited the enormities of later and still more degenerate days—jubilees and reservations, annates and tenths and expectative graces—the long and sordid list of Mammon's machinations! The halls of Constance and Basle would have rung with his lamentation and his wrath, and Gerson* and

The abuse of exemptions.

* John Gerson was a great admirer of St. Bernard : he frequently cited his authority, and composed one discourse expressly in his honour. We always watch with anxiety, and record with respect, the expressions, in which one great man has celebrated the excellence of another ; but in Gerson's " Sermo de Sancto Bernardo " we can discover little but fanciful and mystical rhapsody.

Julian would have shrunk before the manifestation of a spirit loftier far than themselves.

But the inquisition of St. Bernard was not confined to the courts of the Vatican. It penetrated into the dwelling-places and into the bosoms of prelates and of monks. " Oh, ambition, thou cross of those who court thee! How is it that thou tormentest all, and yet art loved by all? There is no strife more bitter, no inquietude more painful than thine, and yet is there nothing more splendid than thy doings among wretched mortals! I ask, is it devotion which now wears out the apostolical threshold, or is it ambition? Does not the pontifical palace, throughout the long day, resound with *that* voice? Does not the whole machine of laws and canons work for its profit*? Does not the whole rapacity of Italy gape with insatiable greediness for its spoils? Which is there among your own spiritual † studies that has not been interrupted, or rather broken off, by it? How often has that restless and disturbing evil blighted your holy and fruitful leisure! It is in vain that the oppressed make their appeal to you, while it is through you that ambition strives to hold dominion in the Church."...
In another place‡—" The unsavoury contagion creeps through the whole Church, and the wider it spreads the more hopeless is the remedy; the more deeply it penetrates, the more fatal is the disease. . . . They are ministers of Christ, and they are servants of Antichrist. They walk abroad honoured by the blessings of the Lord, and they return the Lord no honour: thence is that meretricious splendour everywhere visible—the vestments of actors—the parade of kings; thence the gold on their reins, their saddles, and their spurs, for their spurs (calcaria) shine brighter than their altars (altaria): thence their tables splendid with dishes and cups; thence their gluttony and drunkenness—the harp, the lyre, and the pipe, larders stored with provision, and cellars overflowing with wine. . . .

* " Annon quæstibus ejus tota legum Canonumque disciplina insudat ? "

† This passage is from the Third Book of the " Consideratio." It is addressed, we should recollect, to Pope Eugenius, who had been educated in the monastery of Clairvaux.

‡ " Super Cantica, Ser. xxxiii."

For such rewards as these men wish to become, and do be-come, rectors of churches, deans, archdeacons, bishops, arch-bishops—for these dignities are not bestowed on merit, but on the thing which walks in darkness." . . . . A considerable portion of another composition * is devoted to the exposure of monastic degeneracy. " It is truly asserted and believed that the holy fathers instituted that life, and that they softened the rigour of the rule in respect to weaker brethren, to the end that more might be saved therein. But I cannot bring myself to believe that they either prescribed or permitted such a crowd of vanities and superfluities, as I now see in very many monas-teries. It is a wonder to me whence this intemperance, which I observe among monks in their feasting and revels, in their vestures and couches, in their cavalcades and the construction of their edifices, can have grown into a practice so inveterate, that where these luxuries are attended with the most exquisite and voluptuous prodigality, *there* the order is said to be best preserved, there religion is held to be most studiously culti-vated. . . . For behold ! frugality is deemed avarice; sobriety is called austerity; silence is considered as moroseness. On the other hand, laxity is termed discretion; profusion, liberality; loquacity, affability ; loud laughter, pleasantness ; delicacy and sumptuousness in raiment and horses, taste; a superfluous change of linen, cleanliness ; and then, when we assist each other in these practices, it is called charity. This is a charity indeed which destroys all charity; it is a discretion which con-founds all discretion; it is a compassion full of cruelty, since it so serves the body, as mortally to stab the soul." ... Again : " What proof or indication of humility is this, to march forth with such pomp and cavalcade, to be thronged by such an obsequious train of long-haired attendants, so that the escort of one abbot would suffice for two bishops ? I vow that I have seen an abbot with a suite of sixty horsemen and more†. To

---

* Ad Guilielmum Abbat. Apologia — An Apology to William, abbot of St. Thierry.   The *pretext* for this Apology was, to defend himself and his own re-formed order of Cistercians from the charge of calumniating the rival order, their more opulent brethren of Cluni. St. Bernard did not lose that opportunity of generally inveighing against monastic abuses.

† " Mentior," says the holy abbot, " si non vidi abbatem sexaginta equos et eo amplius in suo ducere comitatu. Dicas, si videas eos transeuntes, non patres esse

see them pass by, you would not take them for fathers of monasteries, but for lords of castles; not for directors of souls, but for princes of provinces." . . . St. Bernard then proceeds to censure the show of wealth which is exhibited *within* the monasteries *, and subsequently exposes the secret motive of such display. "Treasures are drawn towards treasures; money attracts money, and it happens that where most wealth is seen, there most is offered. When the relics are covered with gold, the eyes are struck, and the pockets opened. The beautified form of some saint is pointed out, and the richer its colours the greater is deemed its sanctity. Men run to salute it—they are invited to give, and they admire what is splendid more than they reverence what is holy. To this end circular ornaments are placed in the churches, more like wheels than crowns, and set with gems which rival the surrounding lights. We behold inventions, like trees, erected in place of candlesticks, with great expense of metal and ingenuity, also shining with brilliants as gaily as with the lights they hold. Say, whether of the two is the object in these fabrications—to awake the penitent to compunction, or the gazer to admiration? Oh vanity of vanities, and as insane as it is vain! The church is resplendent in its walls—it is destitute in its poor. It clothes its stones with gold —it leaves its children naked. The eyes of the rich are ministered to, at the expense of the indigent. The curious find wherewithal to be delighted—the starving do not find wherewith to allay their starvation†." . . .

monasteriorum, sed dominos castellorum; non rectores animarum, sed principes provinciarum."

* "Omitto oratorium immensas altitudines, immoderatas longitudines, supervacuas latitudines, sumptuosas depolitiones, curiosas depictiones, quæ dum orantium in se detorquent aspectum impediunt et affectum, et mihi quodammodo repræsentant antiquum ritum Judæorum. Sed esto—fiant hæc ad honorem Dei. Illud autem interrogo monachus monachos, quod in gentilibus gentilis arguebat— Dicite, Pontifices, in sancto quid facit *aurum?* Ego autem dico, Dicite *Pauperes!* Non enim attendo versum sed sensum— Dicite, inquam, pauperes, si tamen pauperes, in sancto quid facit aurum?"— Loc. citat. It seems probable that St. Bernard, in the interval of his theological labours, had studied the Roman satirists with pleasure, and not without advantage.

† "O vanitas vanitatum, sed non vanior quam insanior. Fulget ecclesia in parietibus, et in pauperibus eget. Suos lapides induit auro et suos filios nudos deserit. De sumptibus egenorum servitur oculis divitum. Inveniunt curiosi quo delectentur, et non inveniunt miseri quo sustententur."

Such was the abbot of Clairvaux; in profession and habits a His cha-
monk—in ecclesiastical polity at once a reformer and a bigot racter.
—in piety a Christian.   His single example (if every page in
history did not furnish others) would suffice to show that a
very great preponderance of excellence is consistent with many
pernicious errors; and that innumerable ensamples of purity
and holiness have flourished in every age, as they doubtless
still flourish, in the bosom of the Roman Catholic Church.
Because many popes were ambitious and many prelates profligate, it would be monstrous to suspect that righteousness was
nowhere to be found in that communion; it would be unreasonable to suppose that the great moral qualities, which distinguished St. Bernard, were not very common among the
obscurer members and ministers of his Church.   His genius,
indeed, was peculiarly his own.   The principles which least
became him were derived from his Church and his age; but
his charity and his godliness flowed from his religion, and thus
they found sympathy among many, respect and admiration
among all.   These were the crown of his reputation; and
while they fortified and exalted his genius, they also gave it
that commanding authority which, without them, it could never
have acquired.   From this alliance of noble qualities St. Bernard possessed a much more extensive influence than any
ecclesiastic of his time—more, perhaps, than any individual
through the mere force of personal character has at any time
possessed; nor is it hard to understand, if we duly consider the
imperfect civilization of that superstitious age, that monarchs,
and nobles, and nations should have respectfully listened to
the decisions of a monk, who gave laws from his cloister in
Burgundy to the Universal Church.

CHAPTER XVIII.

The Pontificate of Innocent III.

[From 1198 to 1216.]

Prefatory facts and observations—Circumstances under which Innocent ascended the chair—Collection of canons—Condition of the clergy—Ecclesiastical jurisdiction—by what means extended—Innocent's four leading objects—(1.) To establish and enlarge his temporal power in the city and ecclesiastical states. Office of the Prefect—Favourable circumstances, of which Innocent avails himself—his work completed by Nicholas IV.—(2.) To establish the universal pre-eminence of papal over royal authority. His claims to the empire—His dispute with Philippe Auguste of France—he places the kingdom under interdict—submission of Philippe—His general assertions on supremacy—particular applications of them—to England and France, Navarre, Wallachia and Bulgaria, Arragon and Armenia—His contest with John of England—Interdict— the Legate Pandulph--Humiliation of the king—(3.) To extend his authority within the church. Italian clergy in England—his general success in influencing the priesthood—Power of the episcopal order—The fourth Lateran council. Canons on transubstantiation—on private confession—against all heretics— (4.) To extinguish heresy. The Petrobrussians—their author and tenets. Various other sects, how resisted. The Cathari—supposition of Mosheim and Gibbon—the more probable opinion—The Waldenses—their history and character—error of Mosheim—Peter Waldus—his persecution. The Albigeois or Albigenses—their residence and opinions—attacked by Innocent—St. Dominic —title of inquisitor—Raymond of Toulouse—holy war preached against them —Simon de Montfort—resistance and massacre of the heretics—Continued persecution of the Albigeois—Death of Innocent—Remarks on his policy.

State of the Church on the accession of Innocent III. DURING the period of one hundred and thirteen years, which intervened between Gregory VII. and Innocent III., the progress of ecclesiastical power and influence was very considerable; and the latter ascended the pontifical chair unembarrassed by many of the difficulties which impeded the enterprises of the former. The principal causes of that progress may be traced, perhaps, in a few sentences. In the first place, new facilities to learning had been opened during the twelfth century, of which the clergy had availed themselves very generally, and which the laity had as generally neglected. It is true that the kind of learning then in fashion possessed for the most part, no substantial or permanent value; still it was a weapon as powerful, perhaps, for the government of the ignorant, as if its polish had been brighter, or its edge more keen ; and, as its real inefficiency was unknown, it equally answered the end of exciting a blind respect for those who had the exclusive use of it. In the next place, the discipline of the Church had undergone an important reformation, the honour of which we are bound to ascribe to the vigorous exertions of Gregory, imitated, with more advantage perhaps, by feebler successors. Three Lateran councils (the first general councils of the Western Church) were held during the twelfth century ; and the second and third of these, assembled respectively in 1139 and 1179, by Innocent II. and Alexander III., more particularly directed their attention to the extirpation of ecclesiastical abuses, to the confirmation of ancient canons, and the introduction of such others as might amend the discipline and consolidate the interests of the Church.   This object was materially advanced by the labour of a monk of Bologna, named Gratian, who published, in 1151, his celebrated Collection of Canon Laws*. And this branch of study, thus facilitated, received further encouragement from Eugenius III., who instituted the degrees of Bachelor, Licentiate, and Doctor in that science.   By the advance of learning among the sacred profession, by the greater precision and more general knowledge of the canons of the Church, and by the rigour with which they were frequently enforced, the morals of every rank of the clergy were essentially improved.   The two notorious scandals of the former age, concubinage and simony, if not effectually removed, were at least restrained within more decent limits ; and the extreme licence in some other respects, which had prevailed for about two centuries before Gregory VII., was checked and repressed. So that Innocent was called to the command of a more enlightened, a more orderly, a more moral, and therefore a more influential priesthood.

It may be true, as Mosheim asserts, that the revenues of the pope had received no considerable augmentation between the ninth century and the time of Innocent ; but those of the clergy, Ecclesiastical property.

---

* The accidental discovery of the Pandects of Justinian, in 1137, may have furnished to Gratian the notion, as it certainly supplied the model, of his work.

and especially of the monastic orders, had been swelled during the same period by the most abundant contributions. Indeed, in most countries the territorial domains of the Church were at that time spread so widely, as almost to justify the complaint that they comprehended half the surface of Europe. Nor should we omit to mention that the clergy, though in some kingdoms liable to annual donatives, and to arbitrary plunder in all, were still legally exempt from taxation, and from every regular contribution to the service of the state. From such immunity, though it was occasionally violated, and the violation usually attended with outrage, they must, nevertheless, have reaped great advantage, and especially in peaceful periods. But such partial profits have always a drawback in the jealousy which the distinction occasions, and which exposes those who enjoy it to the distrust and dislike of their fellow-subjects.

Ecclesiastical jurisdiction.

We have already observed how extensive, and, at the same time, how indefinite, were the rights of jurisdiction, which were partly conferred on the Church and partly confirmed to it by Charlemagne,—rights which were scarcely less important to the general influence of the clergy than their learning or their revenues. During the tumults of the three following centuries, they were transgressed or exceeded, as the civil or ecclesiastical portion of the state happened in any country to preponderate; but they appear to have sustained no permanent alteration, either in abridgment or increase, until the beginning of the twelfth century. About that time the ecclesiastical tribunals commenced a system of encroachment, which made great progress even before the pontificate of Innocent, and was carried by that pope and his successors to still greater excess, and seemed to threaten the entire subversion of the secular courts *. It was the first step in this usurpation to multiply the number of *persons* subject to the jurisdiction of the Church; the next, to extend almost without limit the *offences* of which it took cognizance. The first of these objects was accomplished

* "Tirate tutte le cause d'appellazione in Roma, si procurò d'ampliare la giurisdizione del Foro Episcopale, è stendere la conoscenza de' Giudici Ecclesiastici sopra più persone ed in più cause, sicchè poco rimanesse a' magistrati secolari d'impicciarsene." Giannone, Storia di Napoli, lib. xix., c. v., sect. iii.

by the indiscriminate tonsure, which we have before mentioned The ton- to have been so generally given by the bishops. This sign of sure. the clerical state did not indicate ordination or any spiritual office; but it conferred the use of the ecclesiastical habit, and with it the various privileges and immunities enjoyed by that order, without the restraint of celibacy* to which it was liable. This very numerous class, though for the most part engaged in secular professions and occupations, was subject to no other than the episcopal tribunals †; and we may remark, that all the moveable property of this body fell under the same juris- diction ‡.

Another very large class, under the denomination of "miser- abiles personæ" (persons in distress), was also exclusively subjected to the episcopal courts. It comprehended, even in the first instance, a multitude of the lowest orders; and it was presently so enlarged, as to include orphans and widows, the stranger and the poor, the pilgrim and the leper §. Again: the opportunity offered by the Crusades was not neglected in the progress of usurpation; and in this case the arm of ecclesias- tical justice extended itself not only over all who engaged in the expedition, but over those too who had bound themselves by the vow.

A great facility was also afforded for enlarging the boun- daries of ecclesiastical jurisdiction, by the want of definiteness in the nature of the offences subject to it. These were desig- nated by one name, *spiritual;* but it is clear that, in an ignorant age, that term might be so extended by an artful priesthood as to embrace every sin and almost every crime; since there are no sins ‖ and few crimes which do not indicate some disease of the soul, and touch its eternal safety.

* In this respect, those persons were placed in the condition of the priests of the Greek Church: they were allowed to marry once only, and a virgin.

† In the kingdom of Naples, under the dynasty of Anjou, this matter after- wards went so far (says Giannone), that even *concubines* of the clergy enjoyed im- munity from secular jurisdiction.

‡ " In consequenza di quella massima mal intesa, *mobilia sequuntur personam.*" —Giann. loc. cit.

§ We refer to the seventh chapter of Mr. Hallam's Middle Ages. It is a bold, and, in most respects, an accurate disquisition on papal history.

‖ " Si *peccaverit* frater tuus, dic Ecclesiæ." This seems to have been the

The general term, under which ecclesiastics contrived to comprise the greatest number of causes, was *Bad Faith;* as being unquestionably a sin, yet such, that an action could seldom occur, in which both parties were clear from the suspicion of it. Thus they claimed for their tribunals all trials on executions of contracts, because the contract was founded on oath. They also claimed to be natural interpreters and executors of all wills and testaments, as being matters peculiarly connected with the *conscience;* and thus they gradually extended the spiritual net over the entire field of civil litigation *. But they forgot that which properly belonged to them was censure, not jurisdiction ; or they affected artfully to confound the office of penal chastisement with that of penitential correction. The encroachments of the Church were aided by the negligence, as they were almost justified by the incompetence, of the lay tribunals; and they had already made considerable advances, with little apparent opposition, and acquired extensive con-

text on which ecclesiastical jurisdiction was mainly founded. It had a much better foundation in the superior intelligence and moral principles of ecclesiastics.

* Having once interfered in the matter of wills, the bishops proceeded in some countries to arrogate the power of making wills for the laity, *ad pias causas ;* and the interests of the church were advanced by that piety. Some were found who even claimed the property of all intestate persons. Again, when the interests of a clerk were involved in *connexion* with those of laymen, the decision was claimed by the ecclesiastical court. So also, when the cause was very difficult in point of reason, in case of the incompetence, negligence, or suspiciousness of the lay judge, the matter was referred to the episcopal tribunal. So likewise, under the name of *forum mixtum,* it claimed its share in all cases of bigamy, usury, sacrilege, adultery, incest, concubinage, blasphemy, sortilege, perjury, as in those of tithes and pious legacies. So in all causes arising from marriage, as being a Sacrament of the church. And lastly, there were some Roman doctors who maintained that every condemned person in every country should be sent to Rome for punishment ; seeing that Rome was the common country and metropolis of all men, that the world was Roman, and all its inhabitants citizens and subjects of Rome.—Giannone, loc. cit. The following lines were intended to comprehend the jurisdiction of the spiritual court :—

Hæreticus, Simon, fœnus, perjurus, adulter,
Pax, privilegium, violentus, sacrilegusque ;
Si vacat Imperium ; si negligit, ambigit, aut sit
Suspectus judex ; sit subdita terra, vel usus,
Rusticus et servus, peregrinus, feuda, viator.
Si quis pæniteat, miser ! omnis causaque mista—
Si denunciat Ecclesiæ quis, judicat ipsa.

We shall take a future opportunity of recurring to the subject of ecclesiastical jurisdiction.

quests in the domains of secular jurisdiction, at the time when Innocent III. took possession of the pontifical chair.

From the above circumstances, we have reason to presume that in actual authority, not less than in moral influence, the Church had acquired growth and strength since the era of Gregory VII.; and that the sacred militia, whom Innocent was appointed to command, and by whose aid he meditated and almost accomplished the destruction of the temporal authorities, then exerted a much more powerful control over every department of society, than it had ever possessed at any former period.

We shall obtain a more distinct knowledge of the designs and success of that celebrated pope, if we examine separately the principal points to which his exertions were directed, than we could gain by a chronological narrative of his pontificate. According to such a distribution, we may properly consider these objects to have been four: not, indeed, that they were thus minutely analysed in the mind of Innocent, or that his daring schemes were subject to any such classification ; but the historian who contemplates great transactions after an interval of many centuries, and a change in many principles, is bound to consider particular actions as parts of the whole mighty drama, in the respect they bear to the circumstances of the actors, and the character of the age. Thus it is that, in studying the actions of Innocent III., our observation is necessarily most directed to the following points :—His endeavours, *Projects of Innocent III.*

I. To establish the temporal power of the Holy See in the city of Rome, and in the ecclesiastical states ; and to enlarge their boundaries. II. To fix the pre-eminence of the papal over the royal authority, throughout all the kingdoms of the West, and to reduce all princes to the condition of vassalage to the Pope ; which was indeed merely a continuation of the scheme of Gregory. III. To enlarge the pontifical authority and influence within the Church. IV. and lastly, To secure the unity of the faith by the extirpation of heresy. All these were at that time becoming essential parts of the papal polity ; and almost all the important acts of Innocent may be traced to some one of them.

The tempo-
ral power
of the Pope.

I. As the policy of the Holy See becomes more and more entangled in temporal transactions; as we observe the spiritual majesty of the apostolical chair gradually degenerating into the *court* of Rome, it is fit that we employ a few sentences on the character of the people which was subject to its immediate sway; partly because we shall thus discover what sort of instruments for their secular designs the popes possessed at home, and partly that we may learn whether the great moral blessings were more abundantly diffused among the subjects of an ecclesiastical monarchy. For this purpose we shall select two very well known authorities, the one from the tenth, the other from the thirteenth century, only premising that, though the particular facts which they convey may be highly coloured, the general consent of history confirms the substance. Luitprand*, who was sent as legate from Otho the First to the Eastern Emperor, expressed in this language the sort of reputation then

Character
of the Ro-
mans.

possessed by the Roman people:—" We Lombards despise them so deeply, that for our very enemies, when most moved against them, we can find no designation more contumelious than *Roman*. In this single term, Roman, we intend to comprehend all that is base, all that is cowardly, all that is avaricious, all that is luxurious, all that is false and lying—ay, every vice that has a name." The evidence of St. Bernard on the same subject is more particular, and scarcely more honourable to the descendants of the Gracchi:—" Why should I mention the people? the people is Roman. I have no shorter, nor have I any clearer term to express my opinion of your parishioners (parœcianis.) For what is so notorious to all men and ages as the wantonness and haughtiness of the Romans? A race unaccustomed to peace, habituated to tumult—a race merciless and intractable, and to this instant scorning all subjection, when it has any means of resistance. . . Whom will you find, even in the vast extent of your city, who would have you for pope, unless for profit, or the hope of profit†?

* See Luitpr. Legatio, apud Muratori Script. Ital. vol. ii.; also Dissertat. 40 ejusd. auct.

† Eugenius III. The passage in the De Consideratione, lib. iv. cap. ii. We have purposely omitted some parts of it in the text, the following for instance :—

And it is then most that they seek to rule, when they profess to serve. They promise fidelity, to have the better means of injuring those who trust them. . . . They are men too proud to obey, too ignorant to rule, faithless to superiors, insupportable to inferiors; shameless in asking, insolent in refusing; importunate to obtain favours, restless while obtaining them, ungrateful when they have obtained them; grandiloquous and inefficient; most profuse in promise, most niggardly in performance; the smoothest flatterers, the most venomous detractors," &c. " Among such as these you are proceeding as their pastor, covered with gold and every variety of splendour. What are your sheep looking for? . . If I dared to use the expression, I should say that it is a pasture of demons rather than of sheep." . .

Many of the features in this revolting picture are common to the courts of every climate and religion—to the sycophants of every race and age. The exclusive appropriation of meanness and treachery—the monopoly of human baseness—could not truly be ascribed even to the people of Rome. But there is one among the vices imputed to them which was indeed their characteristic—restless and turbulent insubordination. Shall we consider this defect as the corruption of an ancient virtue? Certainly even a cursory review of the government (if government it can be called) under which the imperial city had struggled for above four centuries, will show that the vice,

---

" Et nunc experire paucis noverimne et ego aliquatenus mores gentis. Ante omnia sapientes sunt, ut faciant mala, bonum autem facere nesciunt. Hi invisi terræ et cœlo utrique injecere manus, impii in Deum, temerarii in sancta, seditiosi in invicem (qu. judicem?) æmuli in vicinos, inhumani in extraneos; quos neminem amantes amat nemo. Et cum timeri affectant ab omnibus, omnes timeant necesse est. Hi sunt qui subesse non sustinent," &c...... " Ita omne humile probro ducitur *inter Palatinos,* ut facilius, qui esse quam qui apparere humilis velit, invenias. Timor Domini simplicitas vocatur, ne dicam fatuitas," &c..... These Palatines seem to have been the eminent ecclesiastics resident at the Holy See. The cardinals, who formed the nucleus of the future court of Rome, though now gradually rising in dignity, were not yet, probably, in possession of any corporate prerogatives. We shall only add one more testimony, that of John of Salisbury, the contemporary and countryman of Adrian IV., against the Roman clergy :—" Provinciarum diripiunt spolia, ac si thesauros Crœsi studeant reparare. Sed recte cum iis egit Altissimus, quoniam et ipsi aliis et sæpe vilissimis hominibus dati sint in direptionem." ...

whether indigenous or not, received much encouragement and excuse from extraneous circumstances. We have already mentioned the doubtful limits of the authority respectively exercised by the patrician and the bishop under the Greek emperors. When that rule finally passed away, Charlemagne (and before him Pepin) assumed the temporal administration of Rome under the same name, patrician; and during his reign the imperial supremacy was in practice felt, as it was undisputed in right. Weaker princes, and ages almost of anarchy succeeded. Nevertheless, the supreme dominion of the emperors, which may have been partially suspended, was re-established by Otho : " their title and image were engraven on the papal coins, and their jurisdiction was marked by the sword of justice which they delivered to *the Prefect* of the city*."

On the other hand, the residence of the emperor was remote, and the communication slow and precarious. Once only, in the course perhaps of a long reign, he presented himself to his Roman subjects. The purpose of that visit was to receive his crown from the pontifical hand, and the ceremony was usually attended with tumult and bloodshed. Again—at that coronation he thrice repeated the royal oath, to maintain the liberties of Rome. The ancient fable, too, was continually inculcated, and perhaps universally believed, that Constantine had consigned the temporal sceptre to the hand of the bishop. And in those ages of superstitious darkness, the prejudices of mankind saw nothing incongruous in the double character of a sacerdotal monarch. These circumstances were on both sides unfavourable to the welfare of Rome, for while they neutralized and almost destroyed the power of the prefect, they gave no substantial foundation to that of the pope. So that in the uncertainty thus created, as to where the civil executive authority really was placed, the people were left without any efficient control. Their inclination would naturally lead them to respect most the power which was more nearly and immediately exercised. But the short reigns of most of the popes; the tumultuous scenes which commonly disgraced their elec-

---

* See Gibbon's 69th chapter.

tion, and which were prolonged so obstinately whenever there was a rival for the chair; the very circumstance, that the choice of a ruler was influenced by the rabble—all conspired to lower his dignity, and to lessen the efficacy of his temporal authority. It is true, that during the latter half of the twelfth century, after the constitution of Alexander III. (in 1179), these evils were in some degree abated. Still there were no principles of stability in the civil administration; and it is scarcely too much to assert that, from the time of Charlemagne to that of Innocent, the pontifical city had never once felt either the restraint or the blessing of a strong government.

The regulation of Alexander III. was an omen of greater improvements. But a change of more importance in the civil history of Rome was the establishment of the Senate; and this is referred, as a permanent act, to the year 1144. In the meantime, the dignity of "Prefect of the City" had gradually declined to a municipal office, filled from the families of the native nobility. Even the name was, for a short time, abolished and succeeded by that of Patrician, though it was speedily restored, together with the original ensigns of power. But at length Innocent III. broke off the last link of the imperial power. He rejected at the same time its ancient emblem; and while he absolved the prefect from all dependence of oaths or service on the German emperors, he removed the sword from his hand, and substituted a peaceful *banner* in its place.

Innocent shakes off the imperial authority.

But the tranquillity of Rome was not secured by its independence; and other changes succeeded, in the difficult attempt at self-government by a people educated almost in anarchy. In the first instance, the name and authority of the Senate was condensed in the office of a single magistrate—*the Senator;* and soon afterwards in that of two colleagues. The most jealous precautions* were taken to secure their integrity, or,

---

* According to the laws of Rome (in the fifteenth century), the senator was required to be a doctor of laws, an alien, of some place at least forty miles distant, and unconnected, to the third canonical degree, with any Roman inhabitant. The election was annual; the departure from office was attended with a severe scrutiny; nor could the same person be re-elected until after two years. The salary was 3000 florins. Gibbon, c. 70.

at least, their harmlessness. But they were still Romans; and the turbulence of the subjects seems to have been rivalled by the rapacity of the rulers. Another scheme, which had been elsewhere successful, was then applied to the disorders of Rome. In the dearth of native virtue, or at least in the despair of domestic disinterestedness and impartiality, she called to the

Subsequent changes.

helm of state a foreign governor. It was about the year 1250, that Brancaleone of Bologna was chosen senator; and, in the progress of seventy-eight years, the same office was filled and dignified by Charles of Anjou (about 1265), by Pope Martin IV. (in 1281), and lastly, by Louis of Bavaria; "and thus (says Gibbon) both the sovereigns of Rome acknowledged her liberty by accepting a municipal office in the government of their own metropolis." A government susceptible of such strange anomalies could not hope for peace or permanence. Even the secession of the popes to Avignon did not emancipate Rome from their occasional sway, and their ceaseless persecution. And thus the people were doubly sufferers—they suffered, when subject, from the weakness of an absent sceptre— they suffered, when independent, from the perpetual struggles which were made to reduce them. After seventy years of foreign residence, the pontiffs returned to their legitimate abode. But the schism, which immediately followed the restoration, still further enfeebled a grasp already trembling with the weight of the temporal sword. That inveterate turbulence, transmitted through so many ages, continued for some generations longer; and it was not until the middle of the fifteenth century, that the pontifical city became permanently subject to pontifical government.

Temporal policy of Innocent.

From this short anticipation of some future events, we return to observe the working of that powerful hand, which influenced so deeply the destinies of the Church, and which influenced them almost wholly for evil—and in no one respect more so than when it constructed the temporal fabric for the support of a power essentially spiritual, and waved before those brilliant portals the dark blood-stained edge of the material sword. Possibly the powerful mind of Innocent was seduced into those projects by the inviting circumstances of the moment. During his entire pontificate the situation of the empire was **extremely** favourable to any hostile schemes. The legitimate sovereign (afterwards Frederic II.) was a minor, and the sceptre was for some time disputed by two princes (Philip and Otho IV.), to each of whom the patronage of the Pontiff was equally important.   At a later period, after the death of Philip, the dissension was renewed, in another form, but with the same character, between Otho and Frederic; and the latter of these rivals now became as anxious to cultivate the friendship of the Pope, as heretofore the former. Innocent availed himself of these advantages to enrich and fortify the Church at the expense of all those disputants, or at least of the empire which they disputed. Accordingly, one of the earliest acts of his reign was to disarm the Prefect of all authority derived from abroad, and thus to erase the last remaining vestige of German domination. Again, the extensive donation of territory which the Princess Matilda had made to the Roman See, during the administration of Gregory VII., had been unceasingly contested by the empire; and the greater force had generally constituted the better right. Innocent, towards the end of his pontificate, was enabled so far to profit by the weakness of Frederic, as to obtain from that prince a formal confirmation of the grant; at the same time, a considerable territorial cession, made to the see by the Count of Fundi, received the same ratification.   It is proper, indeed, to ascribe the completion of this work to Nicholas IV., who ruled about seventy years afterwards. That Pope reduced under his dominion some cities, which had hitherto owned a nominal allegiance to the Emperor; and extended the states of the Church to those nearly which are their present boundaries. But to Nicholas no higher praise is due, than that he pursued with success the policy which had descended to him from his predecessors, and which had received its first impulse from Innocent; for, until his pontificate, the temporalities of the see, notwithstanding the successive donations (pretended* or real) of Constantine, and Pepin, and Charlemagne, and Louis the

* Sismondi (Repub. Ital. c. iii.) remarks that, "as the act of Pepin's donation is lost, we know not on what conditions it may have been made." He also expresses a reasonable doubt, whether this donation, though nominally confirmed by Charlemagne and Louis, was ever effectuated.

Meek, and even Matilda, formed, in fact, if not a mere field for incessant contention, at best a very precarious and unprofitable possession.

II. *On the Usurpations of Papal over Royal Authority.*—In respect to this part of the pontifical system, we have already seen that the equivocal glory of creating it is not due to Innocent; he received it from former (perhaps from better) ages, among the established duties of the apostolical office. It was sealed by the consent of many venerable pontiffs; by the authority of Gregory VII. It was congenial to the unconverted pride of the human heart—that passion, which burnt most fiercely in the breast of Innocent, and which the waters of the gospel were seldom invited to allay. His was indeed the character formed, under whatsoever ordination of Providence, to fill up the outlines so daringly traced, and to pursue the scheme which his great predecessor had bequeathed to him. The same circumstances which forwarded his other temporal projects were, as far as they extended, favourable to this. Once more he drew his strength from the divisions of the empire. He deposed Philip—Philip denied his right; but it was willingly acknowledged by the rival Otho, who did not scruple to accept (in 1209) the diadem from the pontifical hand. Only three years afterwards the Pope pronounced, in the same plenitude of power, the same sentence of anathema and deposition against Otho. With what justice could Otho dispute the power by which he had deigned to rise? The vacant throne was then conferred upon Frederic.

A purely spiritual despotism can rest on no other ground than popular prejudice—commands, which have no visible power to enforce them, will only be obeyed through a general predisposition to believe that they proceed from some still superior authority. The monarch would have derided the sentence of deposition, had it not found attention and respect among his subjects. That it should ever have acquired such general respect may indeed seem strange, and the causes, which were then sufficient for that end, could only have operated in a very blind and ignorant age. For instance, the mere ceremony of coronation by the Pope, to which the Emperors, in imitation

Ceremony of Imperial

of Charlemagne, had almost invariably submitted, would seem Coronation
performed
by the
Pope. to afford no trifling pretext for the claims of the former; since it was in those days an easy inference, that the crown, which for many generations had been habitually received from the hand of the Pope, could not legally be worn, except through such presentation; and then it followed—since there were many who zealously inculcated the consequence—that the gift conferred was in fact the *property* of the donor*, who again had power to recall his gift, and present it to some worthier candidate. At the same time we should never lose sight of that *general* veneration for the throne of St. Peter, which at that period especially overspread the prostrate nations, and overawed the reason of man; for it was, in truth, not an uncommon belief that the blessed apostle invisibly presided over the altar of his martyrdom, and guarded and sanctified with mysterious majesty the chair of his successors.

The eagerness with which the emperors generally courted the ceremony of coronation, though it was attended by circumstances very humiliating to their pride, certainly proves that there existed among their subjects a strong feeling as to its propriety, perhaps its necessity. But that which gave the greatest colour to the extreme pretensions of the See, was the readiness with which princes acknowledged them, when they found their profit in the acknowledgment. The very edicts, which they rejected with scorn when addressed to themselves, they embraced and effectuated when levelled against a rival. The right, as a *general* right, was never admitted: but the partial interests of the moment overpowered every consideration of a broader policy; and thus amid the ever-reviving jealousies and dissensions of monarchs and pretenders, the consistent perseverance of the Vatican established the most groundless claims, and accomplished the most extravagant purposes. Of course,

---

* This inference required, of course, a large share of zeal in the teacher and docility in the disciple. The Patriarch of Constantinople had possessed from the earliest ages the office of crowning the Greek emperor, without ever dreaming that he acquired any sort of interest in the crown itself by the performance of an ordinary ceremony. But ecclesiastical matters were very differently conducted in the West.

the agents for the dissemination of its principles and the instruments of its success were the ecclesiastical orders, and especially the monks; and the very general union and co-operation which at this time prevailed (more, perhaps, than at any other period, more, certainly, than at any later period) among the pope, the clergy, and the monasteries, facilitated the execution of Innocent's boldest designs.

Contest with Philippe Auguste. The first interference of that pontiff in the affairs of the French court was defended by precedents, and occasioned by an offence at all times peculiarly liable to spiritual jurisdiction. Philippe Auguste having espoused a Danish princess, named Ingelburg, or Isemburg, hastened on the very day following the nuptials to divorce her. He pretended to have discovered that they were connected by too near a degree of affinity; and after some investigation, at which two legates of Pope Celestine assisted, the marriage was declared null. Innocent, probably considering that concession as extorted from the timidity of his predecessor, lost no time in setting aside the divorce, and commanding the king to take back his bride. He refused, and an Interdict was immediately thrown on the whole kingdom. The public offices of worship were suspended; even the doors of the churches were closed; the sacrament of Christ was no longer administered*, and the rites of marriage and sepulture remained unperformed. We should here recollect, that with the mass of an ignorant people professing a corrupt form of faith, the public exercise of religion constituted, in fact, its entire substance. Deprived of that, they had no refuge in private prayer, or the consolations of internal devotion.

Nature of an Interdict. * We should mention, that even under the oppression of the severest interdict, the sacraments of Baptism, Confession, and Extreme Unction still continued to be administered. But it was attended by other prohibitions, not strictly of a religious nature, calculated to inspire gloom and fanaticism. The hair, for instance, and the beard were to be left unshaven; the use of meat was forbidden; and even the ordinary salutation was prohibited. But the suspension of sepulture, the exposure of the corpses to dogs or birds, or even their promiscuous interment in unhallowed ground, were probably in practice the most appalling parts of the sentence. From the learned treatise, " De l'Origine et du Progrès des Interdits Ecclésiastiques," by Pierre Pithou, it appears that there were *indications* of such an exercise of ecclesiastical power in very early ages; though it was not applied to any grand purpose, as a pontifical implement, until the time of Hildebrand.

To such persons the sentence of an Interdict must have fallen like an immediate edict of rejection and separation from heaven; and such in the twelfth century was the multitude of every class. Philippe Auguste was a prince of uncommon resolution and address. Nevertheless he found it expedient to bend before the tempest, and obey the pontifical mandate.

This was the earliest triumph of Innocent, and it encouraged his ambition to attempt more daring achievements. At least he did not long confine it to objects which offered any particular justification, but advanced on the broadest ground of universal interference. In a bull published in 1197, he declared, "that it was not fit that any man should be invested with authority, who did not serve and obey the Holy See." At another time he proclaimed, "that he would not endure the least contempt of himself, or of God, whose place he held on earth, but would punish every disobedience without delay, and convince the whole world that he was determined to act like a sovereign." "As the sun and the moon are placed in the firmament, the greater as the light of the day and the lesser of the night, so are there two powers in the church, the pontifical, which, as having the charge of souls, is the greater; and the royal, which is the lesser, and to which only the bodies of men are trusted." It is from his celebrated *Rescript* to the emperor of Constantinople that the above allegory is cited. This epistle respected chiefly the immunity of clerks; and as it was founded on the maxims published by Gratian, which were themselves founded on the False Decretals, so itself became in process of time a new Decretal, the groundwork, if necessary, of other still more inordinate pretensions. It was thus that the system grew. "Though I cannot judge of a fief,*" said Innocent to the kings of France and England, "yet it is my province to judge when sin is committed, and my duty to prevent all public scandals." This was indeed the loftiest and the most respectable ground on which the Papal pretensions could be placed; and if the Bishops of Rome had really been contented with

* The general cognizance of causes relating to fiefs had escaped, as it would seem, ecclesiastical usurpation.

the exercise of a beneficial authority—if they had employed the mighty power with which they found themselves invested, *only* for the reconciliation of enmities, for the concord, the morality, the most obvious interests of the human race, then, indeed, we might have forgotten the origin of that power in its blessed uses, and pardoned to the Vicar of Christ his presumptuous appellation, when we saw him engaged in doing the works of Christ, and consoling his children upon earth.

However, the interference, even of Innocent III., was not always for evil. On the strength of his delegated authority he dictated a truce to Philippe and Richard, and after some difficulties obliged both parties to submit to it. It was about the same time that he directed one of his legates to compel the observance of peace between the Kings of Castille and Portugal, if necessary, by excommunication and interdict. He moreover enjoined the King of Arragon to restore to its intrinsic value the coin which he had lately debased, thereby oppressing and defrauding his subjects. The mere wanton display of power may *not* have been his motive—some generous considerations may sometimes have influenced him. "A great mind (says Hallam), such as Innocent III. undoubtedly possessed, though prone to sacrifice every other object to ambition, can never be indifferent to the beauty of social order and the happiness of mankind."

Not contented to influence the most vigorous monarchs of the most powerful kingdoms of the age, he descended to issue his edicts to inferior princes. He sent forth instructions to the King of Navarre respecting the restoration of certain castles to Richard. He distributed the insignia of royalty to Bricislaus, Duke of Bohemia, and to the Dukes of Wallachia and Bulgaria. He conferred the crown of Arragon on Peter II. as his subject and tributary. And finally (that no race or clime might seem inaccessible to his arm), he gave a king to the Armenian nation, dwelling on the border of the Caspian Sea.

His triumph over John of England.

Yet, with all this extent of despotic sway, it was in England that his boldest pretensions were advanced, and advanced with the most surprising success. The circumstances are known to all readers. In the year 1199, Richard I. was succeeded on the throne by John, the feeblest of the human race; and that prince was presently assailed by an outrage from the Holy See, which disturbed for some years the repose and allegiance of his subjects, and the stability of his throne. On the vacancy of the see of Canterbury, the monks in chapter publicly elected to that dignity John, bishop of Norwich, who was recommended and confirmed by the king. At the same time they chose, at a private meeting, Reginald their own sub-prior*, and sent him to Rome for institution. When this matter was referred to Innocent, he immediately reversed both elections, and nominated Stephen Langton, a Roman cardinal, of English descent. The chapter listened to the spiritual, in preference to the temporal, tyrant; and the monks were in consequence expelled from their residence, and their property was confiscated. The pope proceeded with no less energy to enforce his asserted rights, and commanded the bishops of London, Worcester, and Ely, to lay the whole kingdom under an interdict. There were some prelates, however, and several inferior ecclesiastics, who hesitated to enforce this edict; and since John made no concession, Innocent issued, in the following year (1201), a bull of excommunication against the name and person of the sovereign. This sentence, still ineffectual, was followed, in 1211, by another yet more appalling. The subjects of John were absolved from their allegiance, and commanded to avoid his presence. Yet as even this measure was insufficient for his entire success, he had then recourse to the last and most dangerous among the bolts of the Vatican. He pronounced the final sentence of deposition; and having declared the vacancy of the throne, gave force to his words by conferring it upon Philippe Auguste of France. At the same time he ordered that monarch to execute the sentence.

Philippe's obedience was secured by his ambition; he was joined by the exiles of his rival's tyranny; and to ensure his success, or, more probably, to complete the consternation of John, Innocent proclaimed a crusade against the English king as against an infidel or a heretic. The armies were assembled on both sides, and hostilities were on the point of commencing,

* Pagi Brev. Pont. Rom. Vit. Innoc. III. sect. 49.

when Pandulph, the legate of the pope, presented himself at the camp at Dover. He there displayed the final demands of the pope, and the king had courage to resist no longer. The demands to which he submitted were these,—that he should resign his crown to the legate, and receive it again as a present from the Holy See; that he should declare his dominions tributary to the same see; and that he should do homage and swear fealty to Innocent, as a vassal and a feudatory. The shame of this humiliation was increased by the ceremony attending it; by the multitude of sorrowful or indignant witnesses; by the very *manner** in which the haughty prelate bore himself in his triumph. Yet, to the eye of an earnest and fervent papist, is the degradation of England's monarch, while he stood waiting, amid his nobles and his soldiers, to accept his crown from the suspended hand of Pandulph—is it, after all, a spectacle of such lofty exultation—is it a picture so flattering to his spiritual, even to his ecclesiastical pride—as the half-naked form of the imperial penitent of older days, shivering, with his scanty train of attendants, before the castle-gates of Gregory?

III. *The increase of pontifical authority within the Church.* —The description of John's humiliation, and of the steps which led to it, connects the second with the third part of this inquiry—for, in the first place, it shows the extent to which Innocent carried his claims to patronage within the Church; and in the next, it exhibits one motive of the general anxiety evinced by the see to extend that internal influence. The Interdict, which was now become the favourite instrument of papal usurpation, however formidable in name and deed, was an empty denunciation, unless enforced by the personal exertions of the bishops, and even of the inferior clergy of the kingdom subjected to it—as we, indeed, observed, that in England the sentence of Innocent failed of its full effect, through the opposition of a part of the clergy. And thus, in any project of temporal aggrandizement which a pope might undertake,

---

* Among other circumstances it is related, that Pandulph did actually keep the crown in his possession for some minutes. The annual tribute stipulated was 1000 marks.

success could never be secured unless he could command the co-operation of the very great proportion of the ecclesiastical body. It was partly for this reason that so many foreign, and especially Italian, prelates were placed, for many ages, in English sees. In Germany, too, Innocent showed the same anxiety to extend his right of appointment; by a formal capitulation with Otho IV. he obtained that of decision in disputed cases; and it is obvious to what easy abuse it was liable. In other countries he advanced the same claim, which had been so fatally disputed in England, with less resistance and equal success. His example was imitated by following pontiffs; and the facility thus acquired, of exciting rebellion amongst a restless nobility and a superstitious people, against a weak and arbitrary government, terrified the boldest monarchs, and frequently led them to sacrifice the future security of the crown to the hopes or apprehensions of the moment.

On the other hand, the very great progress made by Innocent in extending the papal influence among the priesthood, was counteracted by a measure which may have been necessitated by other causes, but which certainly was ill calculated to increase the attachment of that body. Not contented to exact from them very considerable occasional contributions, he imposed a regular tax on ecclesiastical property, and he was the first pope who ventured upon that measure. It was called the Saladin tax; and it is true that the service of *religion*,—whether in Languedoc or in Palestine, for the murder of Saracens or of heretic Christians,—was alike the pretext, and in part the motive, for those exactions. Nevertheless, they were advanced with reluctance; and the innovation was the less tolerable, as it would certainly become a precedent for future and more oppressive extortions. The Saladin tax.

It is also necessary to observe, that the collective power of the episcopal order was not so great at that time as it had been in the ninth or tenth, or even in the earlier part of the eleventh century, owing to the gradual disuse of those national synods which, in former ages, controlled the conduct of kings. But we should at the same time remark, that the authority thus lost by the hierarchy was not gained by the sovereign. It Disuse of local councils.

changed owners, indeed, but it did not pass out of the possession of the Church. It was merely transferred from one part of that body to another—from the members to the head—from the prelacy to the pope; and by him it was exercised with a restless audacity, an unity of design, and a consistent perseverance, which could not possibly have directed a long series of local and dependent councils. So that the change in the constitution of the Church, by which it became less aristocratical (if we may so apply that term) and more despotic, though it considerably altered the relative positions of the crown and the mitre, did not at all increase the preponderance of the former; on the contrary, the greater concentration of ecclesiastical authority in one instead of many hands, made it a more dangerous rival to the civil government. The advance of pontifical power was very closely connected with the improvement of discipline, and the progress of that system of uniformity, which was designed entirely to pervade and bind together the *Universal* Church.

The fourth Lateran Council, 1215 A.D. Among the most important acts of Innocent's pontificate was the convocation of the fourth Lateran Council,—the most numerous and most celebrated of the ancient assemblies of the Latin Church. This august body consisted of nearly five hundred * archbishops and bishops, besides a much greater multitude of abbots and priors, and delegates of absent prelates, and ambassadors from most of the Christian courts of the West and of the East. It met together in the November of 1215, for the professed consideration of two grand objects. The first was the recovery of the Holy Land; the second was the Reformation of the Church in faith and in discipline. Seventy canons were then dictated by Innocent, and received its obsequious confirmation. It does not appear that its deliberations (if they may so be called) were attended with any freedom of debate; and within a month † from the day of its opening, having executed its appointed office, it was dismissed.

* The numbers are, of course, variously stated; that of the archbishops at seventy-one or seventy-seven, that of the bishops generally at four hundred and twelve, that of the abbots and priors at eight hundred.

† This fact alone proves that the canons in question were not made matter of *discussion* with that numerous assembly.

Among the articles on that occasion enacted, there were several wisely constructed for the welfare of the Roman Catholic Church : they amplified the body of the canon law, and regulated in many respects the practice of ecclesiastical procedures, which is followed to this day.   But as we cannot in this work pursue such a variety of matter into its detail, we shall select only those which were the most important in substance or in consequence.

If any doubt hitherto remained in the orthodox Church respecting the *manner* in which the body and blood of Christ were present at the eucharist, it was on this occasion removed by Innocent, who unequivocally established, or rather confirmed*, that which is now, and which had then been for some time, the doctrine of Roman Catholics.   Moreover, as he well knew the efficacy of a *name* to propagate and perpetuate a dogma, and also that he might have a fixed verbal test whereby to try the opinions and obviate the evasions of heretics, he invented and stamped upon that tenet the name of " transubstantiation." *Transubstantiation.*

Another canon (the twenty-first) strictly enjoined to all the faithful of both sexes, to make, at least once in a year, a private confession of their sins, and that to their own priest or curate; and to fulfil the penance which he might impose on them.   They were at the same time prohibited from confessing to any other priest, without the special permission of their own†. They were also directed, under severe ecclesiastical penalties in case of neglect, to receive the eucharist at Easter, unless a particular dispensation should be granted them, also by their own *Sacramental confession.*

* Mosheim is probably wrong in supposing that full liberty had hitherto been left to pious persons to interpret the doctrine according to their own reason. The sense of the Church was sufficiently expressed by the councils which were held against Berenger; or had it not been so, at least the Council of Piacenza confirmed the doctrine explicitly declared on former occasions.   It only remained to Innocent to ascertain and consolidate the tenet by the term.

† The sacrament was taken immediately after confession. "This is the first canon, as far as I know," says Fleury, "which imposes the general obligation of sacramental confession.   There was then a particular reason for it, on account of the errors of the Vaudois and Albigeois touching the sacrament of penance." At the Council of Toulouse, in 1228, the confession and sacrament were enjoined *thrice* in the year; but this again was in the very focus of heresy.

priest. By this regulation, the system of auricular confession was indeed carried to very refined perfection; and there is no reason to doubt that a canon, which imparted even to the lowest of the priesthood such close and searching influence over the conscience and conduct of a superstitious generation, was speedily brought into universal operation. That in some instances, that on very many *particular* occasions, the effect of this influence has been beneficial to society; that sinful dispositions have been frequently repressed and crimes prevented by the present and immediate control of a pious minister, is not merely probable, but indisputable. But as a *system* of morality, *that* could not possibly be creative of righteous principles which held out, through bodily penance, a periodical absolution from sin,—even if the hands which administered it were always pure. But when we consider the abuse to which such a power is inevitably liable, and how greatly, too, it would increase through the abuse, we cannot fail to perceive, that it was a machine too powerful to be entrusted to the necessary infirmity, to the possible caprice or wickedness, of man.

Extinction of heresy. By the proposed reformation in the faith of the Church, nothing was in fact meant but the extirpation of heresy; and this was the first object presented to the attention of the council. After a formal exposition of faith, upon those points especially on which the existing errors were supposed to have arisen, the pope and the prelates immediately proceeded (in the third canon) to anathematize every heresy. " As soon as they are condemned (says the council), they shall be abandoned to the secular power to receive the suitable punishment. The goods of laymen shall be confiscated; those of clerks applied to the uses of their respective churches. Those who shall only be suspected of heresy, if they do not clear themselves by sufficient justification, shall be excommunicated. If they remain a year under the suspicion, they shall be treated as heretics. The secular powers shall be advised, and, if need be, constrained by censures, to make public oath that they will exile all heretics marked out by the Church. If the temporal lord, on admonition, shall neglect to free his territories from their pollution, he shall be excommunicated by the metropolitan and the other bishops of the province; and if he should not submit within a year, the pope shall be informed, to the end that he may pronounce his vassals absolved from the oath of fidelity, and expose his domain to the conquest of the catholics. These, after having expelled the heretics, shall peaceably possess and preserve it in doctrinal purity—saving the right of the liege lord, provided he offer no obstacle to the execution of this decree." . . . It is remarkable that this decree, which placed the secular authorities directly at the disposal of the spiritual, and on the penalty, not of spiritual censures only, but of subjugation and military possession, was enacted in the presence, and with the consent, of the ambassadors of several sovereigns. But this subject has already led us to the last division of the chapter, into which we shall properly enter with a general inquiry as to the forms which heresy assumed in that age, and the measures which Innocent actually adopted for its extinction.

IV. *On the Extirpation of Heresy.*—Since the termination of the controversy concerning images, nearly four hundred years had elapsed, during which the Church had been very rarely disturbed by doctrinal dissension; and amid the various vices which may have polluted, in so long a space, her principles and her discipline, she was at least free from the blackest of all her crimes, since her hands were unstained by blood.[1] The eucharistical opinion of Johannes Scotus, which had been nourished by the partial brightness of the ninth century, and overshadowed, but not oppressed, by the stupid indifference of the tenth, when revived by Berenger, disappeared in the superstition of the eleventh, without violence or outrage. Not, perhaps, because the ecclesiastics of that age were tolerant or temperate, but rather, because its advocates were not sufficiently numerous or formidable to make a general persecution necessary for its suppression. But in the dawning light of the twelfth age some new heresies were called into life, and others, which had previously lain hid, were discovered and exposed: so that the attention of men was more generally turned to the subject, and the rulers of the Church were roused from their long and harmless repose. Since it was even thus early that several of the Protestant opinions were publicly professed, and expiated by death; and since these may be traced, under a variety of forms and names, but with the same identifying character, from the beginning of the twelfth century to the Reformation, it is proper to notice the first obscure vestiges which they have left in history. In so doing, we shall first describe those sects which were founded (in the West at least) at that time; we shall then proceed to the mention of the Vaudois, to whom a still earlier existence is, with great probability, ascribed.

The Petro-
brussians.

About the year 1110, a preacher, named Pierre de Bruys, began to declaim against the corruptions of the Church, and the vices of its ministers. The principal field of his exertions was the south of France, Provence and Languedoc, and he continued, for about twenty years, to disseminate his opinions with success, and, what may seem more strange, with impunity. Those opinions may probably have contained much that was erroneous; but they are known to us only through the representations of his adversaries. In a Letter or Treatise, composed against his followers (thence called Petrobrussians), by the Venerable Abbot of Cluni *, they are charged with a variety of offences, which the writer reduces under five heads—(1.) The rejection of infant baptism. (2.) The contempt of churches and altars, as unnecessary for the service of a spiritual and omnipresent Being. (3.) The destruction of crucifixes, on the same principle, as instruments of superstition. (4.) The disparagement of the holy sacrifice of the Eucharist, in asserting that the body and blood were not really consecrated by the priests. (5.) Disbelief in the efficacy of the oblations, prayers, and good works of the living for the salvation of the dead. These errors, howsoever various in magnitude, are controverted with equal warmth, by Peter the Abbot; but that which appears to have been most dangerous to the heretic, was the third. At least we learn that, in the year 1130, the Catholic inhabitants of St. Giles's in Languedoc were roused by their priests to holy indignation against *that* sacrilege, and consigned the offender to those flames, which his own hand had so frequently fed with

* Petri Venerabilis, Lib. contra Petrobrussianos, in Biblioth. Cluniensi.

the images of Christ. He was burnt alive in a popular tumult; and this may possibly be the suffering to which St. Bernard, in a passage already cited, has made allusion. But the errors were not thus easily consumed; the list, on the contrary, was enlarged by many additional notions, proceeding, some from the piety, others from the ignorance, of his followers.

One of these *, named Henry, an Italian by birth, obtained a place in the contemporary records, and gave an appellation to a sect, from him called Henricians. This enthusiast traversed the south of France, from Lausanne to Bourdeaux, preceded by two disciples, who carried, like himself, long staves, surmounted with crosses, and were habited as penitents. His stature was lofty, his eyes were rolling and restless; his powerful voice, his rapid and uneasy gait, his naked feet and neglected apparel, attracted an attention, which was fixed by the fame of his learning and his sanctity. These qualities gave additional force to his eloquence; and as it was not uncommonly directed against the unpopular vices of the clergy, he gained many proselytes, and excited some commotions. Eugenius III. sent forth, for the suppression of this evil, a legate named Alberic; but it appears that his mission would have been attended with but little success, had he not prevailed on St. Bernard to share with him the labour and the glory of the enterprise. Henry was then in the domain of Alfonso, Count of St. Giles and Toulouse; and St. Bernard wrote † to prepare that prince for his arrival, and to signify his motives. " The churches (he said) are without people; the people without priests; the priests without honour; and Christians without Christ. The churches are no longer conceived holy, nor the sacraments sacred, nor are the festivals any more celebrated.

The Henricians.

---

* Henry is generally described as a disciple and fellow-labourer of Pierre de Bruys. The objection to this opinion, urged by Mosheim, is, that Henry was preceded in his expeditions by the figure of the cross, whereas Pierre consigned all crucifixes to the flames. Without supposing that the objection of Pierre might be to the image of the Saviour, not to the form of the cross, the objection is far from conclusive. Some account of the heresies of the twelfth century is given by Dupin, Nouv. Biblioth., Siècle 12, c. vi.

† Epistol. 240. (Lutet. Paris, 1640.) It begins, " Quanta audivimus et cognovimus mala quæ in ecclesiis Dei fecit et fecit quotidie Henricus hæreticus ! Versatur in terra vestra sub vestimentis ovium lupus rapax," &c.

Men die in their sins—souls are hurried away to the terrible tribunal—without penitence or communion ; baptism is refused to infants, who are thus precluded from salvation." He added many reproaches against Henry, whom he accused of being an apostate monk, a mendicant, a hypocrite, and a debauchee. The biographers of that Saint relate, that he was received, even in the most contaminated provinces, like an angel from heaven; and at Albi, the place most fatally infected, an immense multitude assembled to hear his preaching. The day which he skilfully selected for their conversion, was that of St. Peter. He examined in succession the various peculiarities of their belief, and showed their deviation from the Catholic faith. He then required the people to tell him which of the two they would have. They immediately declared their horror of heresy, and their joy at the prospect of returning to the bosom of the Church. " Return, then, to the Church (replied St. Bernard); and that we may the better distinguish those who are sincere, let all true penitents lift up their hands." They obeyed this injunction with one consent : and though St. Bernard, in the course of a leisurely journey from Clairvaux to Albi, had performed many extraordinary miracles, " this (as the simple chronicler reports) was the mightiest of all." Henry himself appears to have fled to Toulouse, whither the eager abbot pursued him. Thence he once more escaped, and once more St. Bernard followed, purifying the places infected by that pestilence. At length the fugitive was seized and convicted at Rheims, before Eugenius in person, and consigned to prison (in 1148), where he presently afterwards died.

Other Heretics.

About the same time it would appear that certain other sects, differing in some less important points among themselves, but united in a sort of desultory opposition to the Roman Church, had gained footing, not in France only, but in Flanders, in Germany, and even in the north of Italy. Without any formal separation from the Church, or an entire disregard of its public offices, they had their own ministers, both bishops and priests *,

---

* Milner, Cent. xii., c. iii., cites the following passage from Evervinus's Letter to St. Bernard, preserved by Mabillon, and written about 1140 :—" There have

to whom they paid a more observant deference, and whom they affirmed to be the only legitimate descendants from the apostles. The opposition of these heretics seems to have been more particularly directed against the wealth and temporal power of the Catholic clergy—but at the same time they rejected infant baptism, the intercession of saints, purgatory—and professed, in fact, to receive only those truths which were positively delivered by Christ or his apostles. They are described to have been extremely ignorant, and confined to the lowest classes. But it is at least certain, that in the principality of Toulouse, the nobility had engaged with some obstinacy in the heresy of the Paulicians—less through error than through design, and a malicious satisfaction in the humiliation of the clergy. But the same motives are not less likely to have operated, wheresoever the same or similar opinions were promulgated.

Another religious faction had at that time considerable pre- *Heresy of* valence, which, under the various names of <u>Cathari</u> (or Catha- *the Catha-* rists—Puritans), Gazari, Paterini, Paulicians or Publicans, Bul- *ri, or Pau-* *licians.* gari or Bugari*, was more particularly charged with Manichæan opinions. The origin of these heretics has been the subject of much controversy; for while some suppose their errors to have been indigenous in Europe, there are others who derive them

been lately some heretics discovered among us, near Cologne, though several have with satisfaction returned again to the Church. One of their Bishops, and his companions, openly opposed us in the assembly of the clergy and laity, in the presence of the Archbishop, and many of the nobility, defending the heresies by the words of Christ and the apostles. Finding that they made no impression, they desired that a day might be appointed for them, on which they might bring their teachers to a conference, promising to return to the Church, provided they found their masters unable to answer the arguments of their opponents; but that, otherwise, they would rather die than depart from their judgment. Upon this declaration, having been admonished to repent for three days, they were seized by the people in the excess of zeal, and burnt to death. And what is amazing, they came to the stake, and endured the pain, not only with patience, but even with joy."

* About the middle of the thirteenth century, the Emperor Frederic II. enumerated all the forms, or rather names, of heresy then most scandalous, in the opening of an edict published against them. It begins as follows :—" Catharos, Patarenos, Speromistas, Leonistas, Arnaldistas, Circumcisos, Passaginos, Josephinos, Garatenses, Albanenses, Franciscos, Beghardos, Commissos, Valdenses, Romanolos, Communellos, Varinos, Ortulenos, cum illis de Aquâ Nigrâ, et omnes hæreticos . . . damnamus," &c. See Limborch, Hist. Inquisit. lib. i. c. 12.

in a direct line from the heart of Asia. It is certain that a very powerful sect named Paulicians, and tainted, though they might affect to disclaim it, with the absurdities of Manes, spread very widely throughout the Greek provinces of Asia during the eighth century. It is equally true, that after a merciless persecution of about one hundred and fifty years, their remnant, still numerous, was permitted to settle in Bulgaria and Thrace. Thence, as is believed by Muratori, Mosheim, and Gibbon, they gradually migrated towards the West; at first, as occasions of war, or commerce, or mendicity (another name for pilgrimage) might be presented; and, latterly, in the returning ranks of the crusaders. It is asserted, that their first migration was into Italy; that so early as the middle of the eleventh century, many of their colonies were established in Sicily, in Lombardy, Insubria, and principally at Milan; that others led a wandering life in France, Germany, and other countries; and that they everywhere attracted, by their pious looks and austere demeanour, the admiration and respect of the multitude. It is moreover maintained, that these widely scattered congregations were organized in united obedience to a primate who resided on the confines of Bulgaria and Dalmatia. In confirmation of the authorities on which these opinions rest, it should be observed, that among the various forms of heresy, which were detected by the keen eyes of the early Inquisitors, there was scarcely one which escaped the *charge* of Manichæism*.

Admitting, then, that this charge was very commonly invented for the purpose of making the others more detestable, we cannot question that it was sometimes founded in truth. And while, on the one hand, we are far removed from an opinion, that would refer the origin of all the earliest Western sects to the emigrants from the East—that would consider, not only the Cathari, but the Petrobrussians, Henricians, and even the Vaudois themselves, as descendants from the family of Manes—it is equally unreasonable to contend, that his wild

---

* The first canon of Innocent's Lateran Council distinctly states the church doctrine respecting the Unity of the Deity, in opposition to that of the Two Principles—a sufficient declaration that many Manichæans were *believed* to be found among the heretics.

opinions had no existence in the West of Europe; or even to dispute their perpetuation through parties of Paulicians, who, from time to time, may have migrated into Sicily or Italy. It is indeed unquestionable that such was the case; and it is not impossible that they may have formed, even after their dispersion throughout Europe, a distinct and characteristic sect. But it would be absurd to ascribe to their influence the formation of sects, of which the leading principles were wholly distinct, if not entirely at variance with those of the Asiatics. Even in the dawn of returning knowledge, the faintest glimmerings of reason were sufficient to light the mind to the detection of papal delinquency, of the aberrations of the Church and its ministers. It required not a star from the East to indicate, even in those dark times, how distinct were the principles of' the Church from the precepts of the Gospel; or to contrast the deformities of the Clergy with the purity of their heavenly Master. Such incongruities obtrude themselves perhaps the most forcibly upon illiterate minds, and excite the deepest disgust in the simplest conscience. It is to this cause that the heresies of those early ages may most confidently be traced: they may indeed have been infected, in a greater or less degree, with some of the notions of the Paulician colonists—but that assuredly was not the source from which they flowed.

As we have been careful to distinguish the Catharists, who may have been semi-Manichæans, from the other sects of reformers who were scattered throughout Europe, so we must again consider the Vaudois or Waldenses as a separate race The Vaudois. among these latter,—that we may not fall into the error of Mosheim, who ascribes the origin of that sect to an individual named Waldus. Peter Waldus, or Waldensis, a native of Lyons, was a layman and a merchant; but, notwithstanding the avocations of a secular life, he had studied the real character of his Church with attention, followed by shame. Stung by the spectacle of so much impurity*, he abandoned his profession,

* It is said that the worship of the Host, which was first enforced about this time, was the particular superstition which awakened the indignation of Peter Waldus. If, indeed, that practice was generally established in 1160, there remained little for Innocent to add to the sanctity of the sacrament fifty-five years afterwards.

distributed his wealth among the poor, and formed an association for the diffusion of scriptural truth.   He commenced
his ministry about the year 1160.   Having previously caused
several parts of the Scriptures to be translated into the vulgar
tongue, he expounded them with great effect to an attentive
body of disciples, both in France and Lombardy. In the course
of his exertions he probably visited the valleys of Piedmont ;
and there he found a people of congenial spirits.   They were
called Vaudois or Waldenses (Men of the Valleys); and as
the preaching of Peter may probably have confirmed their
opinions, and cemented their discipline, he acquired and deserved his surname by his residence among them. At the same
time, their connexion with Peter and his real Lyonnese disciples established a notion of their identity ; and the Vaudois, in
return for the title which they had bestowed, received the
reciprocal appellation of Leonists: such, at least, appears the
most probable among many varying accounts*.

There are some who believe the Vaudois to have enjoyed
the uninterrupted integrity of the faith even from the apostolic
ages ; others suppose them to have been disciples of Claudius
of Turin, the evangelical prelate of the ninth century. At least,
it may be pronounced with great certainty, that they had been
long in existence before the visit of the Lyonnese reformer.   A
Dominican, named Rainer Saccho, who was first a member
and afterwards a persecutor of their communion, described
them, in a treatise which he wrote against them, to the following purpose : " There is no sect so dangerous as the Leonists,
for three reasons : first, it is the most ancient,—some say as
old as Sylvester, others as the apostles themselves. Secondly,
it is very generally disseminated : there is no country where it

There is no mention of it in the ancient canonical books of the Church,—those of
Alcuin, Amularius, Walfridus, and Micrologus.   There is proof, however, that it
existed in France, both at Paris and at Tours, a century at least before Innocent
III. In Germany there is also evidence of its previous existence.   But in the
Roman Church it does not appear to have been established before the pontificate
of Boniface VIII.   See Pagi, Vit. Innoc. III. ad finem.

* There are some who derive the surname of Peter from some town or hamlet
in the vicinity of Lyons; others contend that he never personally preached among
the Vaudois of Piedmont.

has not gained some footing. Thirdly, while other sects are profane and blasphemous, this retains the utmost show of piety: they live justly before men, and believe nothing respecting God which is not good; only they blaspheme against the Roman Church and the clergy, and thus gain many followers*." The author of this passage lived about the middle of the following century; and if the sect against which he was writing had really originated from the preaching of Peter some eighty years before, the Dominican would scarcely have conceded to it the claim of high and immemorial antiquity. Again, St. Bernard in one place admits, in substance, "that there is a sect, which calls itself after no man's name†, which pretends to be in the direct line of apostolical succession; and which, rustic and unlearned though it is, contends that the Church is wrong, and that itself alone is right. It must derive (he subjoins) its origin from the devil; since there is no other extraction which we can assign to it."

At the same time we must admit that the direct historical Their anti- evidence is not sufficient to prove the uncontaminated purity of quity. the Vaudois ‡. Alcuin, the tutor of Charlemagne, may have complained " that auricular confession was not practised in the churches of Languedoc and the Alps in his time;" Claudius of Turin may have presided over a reformed and Christian diocese; somewhat later (in 945), Atto, bishop of Verceil §, may have lamented " that there were *some* in his diocese who held the divine service in derision;" and lastly, at the Synod of Arras, in 1025, it may have been deplored, " that certain persons, coming from the borders of Italy, had introduced heretical doctrines,"—and such as the Waldenses, indeed, professed. It still appears that the name is not mentioned in any

---

* Bibliotheca Patrum, apud Lenfant, Guerre des Hussites, liv. ii., sect. v.

† " Quære ab illis suæ sectæ auctorem, neminem dabit. Quæ hæresis non ex hominibus habuit proprium hæresiarcham ? Manichæi Manem habuere principem et præceptorem, Sabelliani Sabellium, &c. Ita omnes ceteræ hujusmodi pestes singulæ singulos magistros homines habuisse noscuntur, a quibus originem simul duxere et nomen. Quo nomine istos titulove vocabis ? Nullo; quoniam non est ab homine illorum hæresis,....sed magis et absque dubio per immissionem et fraudem dæmoniorum," &c. Sermo super Cant. lxvi. ad init.

‡ We refer to Mr. Gilly's well-known work on this subject.

§ A city situated between Turin and Milan.

writing before the twelfth century; and there is no specific
evidence of the previous existence of the sect. Nevertheless, as
its origin was confessedly immemorial in the thirteenth century,
and as there has not, perhaps, existed in the history of heresy
any other sect, to which some origin has not been expressly
ascribed, we have just reason to infer the very high antiquity
of the Vaudois.

Many will think it more important to learn their doctrines,
than to speculate on their origin. On almost all material points,
they were those of the Reformation*. In their discipline they
endeavoured to attain the rigid simplicity of the primitive
Christians, and in that endeavour, perhaps, they exceeded it;
for while they maintained and imitated the divine institution of
the three orders in the priesthood, they also reduced their
clergy to the temporal condition of the apostles themselves;
they denied them all worldly possessions, and while they
obliged them to be poor and industrious, they compelled them
to be illiterate also.

The persecution of Peter Waldensis, and the dispersion of
his followers, occasioned, as in so many similar instances, the
dissemination of their opinions ; and, notwithstanding some
partial sufferings which were inflicted in Picardy by Philippe
Auguste, they were a numerous and flourishing sect at the
conclusion of the twelfth century. They were often confounded
in name with the Vaudois, in crime and calamity with the
Catharists and Petrobrussians, and other adversaries of papacy.
The Albi-
geois.   But of these various descriptions such as were found in
France during the pontificate of Innocent were known by the
general name of Albigeois or Albigenses. A city in Languedoc,

* Rainer, the Dominican, already cited, also divides the crimes of the Vaudois
into three classes: 1. Their blasphemies against the Church, its statutes, and its
clergy; 2. Errors touching the sacraments and the saints; 3. Detestation of all
honest customs approved by the Church; which really means, objections to the
administration, the sacraments, and the practices of the Roman Catholic Church.
Mosheim treats the subject at Cent. xii., p. ii., ch. v. Pierra d' Ailly, in a discourse composed at the Council of Constance, alleges as their principal errors, that
they refused temporalities to the priesthood, and asserted that the Church of God
only lasted till the endowment by Constantine. Then arose the Church of Rome,
—the other being extinct, except in as far as it was perpetuated in themselves.

named Albi*, which was peculiarly prolific of heresy, is usually supposed to have given a common designation to these numerous forms of error. Such, very briefly described, were the factions which distracted the Church on the accession of Innocent III. It now remains to observe the measures which he adopted to repress them. And let us first inquire to what extent he might plead the previous practice of the Church.

It appears that, at a synod held at Orleans, in the year 1017, under the reign of Robert, a number of persons, of no mean condition or character, were accused of heretical opinions. Manichæism was the frightful term employed to express their delinquency; but it is more probable that their real offence was the adoption of certain mystical notions, proceeding, indeed, from feelings of the most earnest piety, but too spiritual to be tolerated even in that age of that Church. It is said that they despised all external forms of worship, and rejected the rites, the ceremonies, and even the sacraments of the Church; that they valued none save the religion within,—the abstracted contemplation of the Deity, and the internal aspirations of the soul after things celestial. Some philosophical speculations they may also have admitted respecting God, the Trinity, and the human soul, which excited the fears of that generation†, in

Synod of Orleans.

---

* According to the Histoire Générale de Languedoc, by the Benedictine monks, the term is more accurately derived from Albigesium, the general denomination of Narbonnese Gaul in that century. See Mosh., note on Cent. xiii., p. ii., ch. v., sect. vii.

† Such, at least, is the opinion of Mosheim (Cent. xi., p. ii., ch. v.) The history of this synod of Orleans is found in Dacherius's Spicilegium Veter. Script. (tom. ii., p. 670, Edit. Paris), and the charges there alleged (besides the usual calumny of promiscuous prostitution) respect the nativity, the death, and resurrection of Christ, and impute a disbelief in the efficacy of baptism, in the change wrought by consecration in the eucharistical elements, and in the meritoriousness of prayers to martyrs and confessors. In the place of this faith they substituted " celestial food," "angelic visions," "the companionship of God,"…and when the prelate sitting in judgment on them laid down the orthodox doctrine respecting some of those points, the heretics replied, "You may tell such tales as those to men whose wisdom is of this world, and who believe the fictions of carnal men, written on the skins (membranis) of animals. But to us, who have a law inscribed on the inward man by the Holy Spirit, and who have no other wisdom than that which we have learnt from God the creator of all things, you preach superfluous vanities, deviating from real holiness. Wherefore, cease from your discourse, and do what you will with us. Already do we behold our King reigning in the heavens, who exalts us with his right hand to immortal triumphs, and to the joys which are

the same degree that they surpassed its comprehension. Accordingly, they were accused and convicted of heresy; and as they firmly persisted in their errors, and as the king had no repugnance to enforce the sentence, they were finally consigned to the flames.

Edicts of Alexander III.

In this barbarous transaction, which was rather in anticipation of the policy of later ages, than in accordance with that of the eleventh, we have found no proof of papal interference; nor, indeed, have we observed any very important pontifical edicts for the extirpation of heresy, earlier than the reign of Alexander III. That pope, in a council held at Tours in 1163, published a decree to this effect: "Whereas a damnable heresy has for some time lifted its head in the parts about Toulouse, and has already spread its infection through Gascony and other provinces, concealing itself like a serpent within its own folds; as soon as its followers shall have been discovered, let no man afford them a refuge on his estates; neither let there be any communication with them in buying or selling; so that, being deprived of the solace of human conversation, they may be compelled to return from error to wisdom *."

The same pontiff, in the third Lateran Council, held in 1179, published other edicts against the heretics, variously named Cathari, Paterini, Publicani, &c., pursuing them with anathemas, refusal of Christian sepulture, and other spiritual chastisements. But it does not appear that he invoked, on either occasion, the secular arm to his assistance. Nevertheless, without that aid, his power was sufficient to expel Peter Waldensis from his native city, and subsequently to pursue him from Dauphiny to Picardy, and thence to Germany, till he found his final resting-place among the Bohemian mountaineers, the ancestors of Huss and Jerome. The fugitive died in that country very soon afterwards.

When the torch of persecution was transmitted to Innocent†,

above." We should recollect that this account (like almost every other in which any heretical opinions are described) comes to us from the pen of an enemy.

* The original is given by Pagi, Vit. Alexandri III., sect. xlii. He continues to apply to them, according to the ordinary confusion, the name of Waldenses.

† That Innocent was very ready to take his turn in this lampadephory appears from several epistles, written to various prelates in the very first year of his pont-

the two principal seats of religious disaffection were the valleys of Piedmont and the cities of Languedoc ; with this difference, however, that the Vaudois flourished in comparative and perhaps despised security, while the latter, more particularly denominated Albigeois, were rendered more notorious, as well as more dangerous, by the protection publicly afforded them by Raymond VI., earl of Toulouse*. Against these, therefore, the pope's earnest and most assiduous efforts were directed ; and first, observing that the bishops in those provinces were deficient in true Catholic zeal for the unity of the Church, he sent, in 1198, two legates into the rebellious districts ; but rather, as it would seem, for the purpose of exploring and menacing, than of actually commencing the contest. Presently afterwards, a more numerous commission, the advance of his array, invaded the haunts of heresy, and brought argument and eloquence in support of intimidation. This body again received great additional efficiency from the accession of a Spaniard, named *Dominic,* a young ecclesiastic, remarkable for the severity of his life, the extent of his learning, the persuasiveness of his manner, and the ardour of his zeal. These qualities, and some successful services, infused a new spirit into the ranks of the orthodox. It would also appear that their exertions were no longer restricted to verbal exhortation and reproof ; but that they also aimed to animate the civil authorities in their favour, and to enforce the infliction even of capital punishment, whenever they had influence to do so. This expedition lasted six or seven years ; and, at the end of that time, the spiritual missionaries engaged in it were generally known by the title of *Inquisitors,*—a name, not indeed honourable or innocent even in its origin, but not yet associated with horror and infamy.

Persecution of the Albigeois.

ificate, in which he exhorts them to gird themselves for the work of extirpation, and to employ, if necessary, the arms of the princes and of *the people.* This last suggestion was provident. The populace might sometimes be excited to an act of outrage, when the authorities were neutral in the quarrel.

* Limborch, in the first book of his History of the Inquisition (cap. viii.), very clearly shows, both from the "Sententiæ Inquisitionis Tolositanæ," and other evidence, that the Vaudois, while they held some opinions in common with the Albigenses, had many more points of difference, in rites as well as in doctrine ; for instance, the Manichæan errors imputed to the latter are never ascribed to the Vaudois.

Still matters did not proceed with the rapidity desired by the pontiff; and then the missionaries had recourse to a new and very harmless expedient to accelerate success. They laid aside the pomp and dignity of their train and habits, discharged the unpopular parade of servants and equipage, and continued their preaching with the more imposing pretension of apostolical humility. But neither had this method the result which was hoped from it. At length, in the year 1207, Innocent at once addressed himself to the *arms* of Philippe Auguste. He easily exhorted that monarch to march into the heretical provinces, and extirpate the spiritual rebels by fire and sword.

About the same time one of his legates or inquisitors, Pierre de Castelnovo* (or Chateau-neuf), was assassinated by the populace in the states of Raymond. The act was imputed to the connivance, if not the direct instigation, of that prince†. The pope immediately launched the bolt of excommunication; and his emissaries, by his command, proceeded to those measures which introduced a new feature into the history of inter-Christian warfare. They proclaimed a general campaign of all nations against the Albigeois, and at the same time promised a general grant of indulgences and dispensations to all who should take arms in that holy cause. Having thus reduced those dissenting Christians to the same level in a religious estimation with the Turk and the Saracen, they let loose an infuriated multitude of fanatics against them; and the word "Crusade," which had hitherto signified only religious madness, was now extended to the more deliberate atrocity of sectarian persecution.

Simon de Montfort. — Several monks and some prelates were the spiritual directors of this tempest; but the military leader was Simon, Count de Montfort, "a man like Cromwell, whose intrepidity, hypocrisy,

* Some write the name Castronovo.

† Historians differ as to the probability of his guilt; also as to the fact whether the first appeal of Innocent to the court of France preceded or followed the death of his legate. On this point we incline to the former opinion. Respecting the charge against Raymond, there seems to be no clear proof on either side; it is known that he favoured the heretics, and that circumstance might occasion either the crime or the calumny. The latter is, *perhaps*, the more probable.

and ambition marked him for the hero of a holy war[*]." To irritate his ambition, the pope artfully held out to him the earldom of Toulouse, as the recompense of his exertions in the service of the Church. His hypocrisy was displayed and hardened by the seeming devotion with which he continually perpetrated the most revolting enormities, and his intrepidity was exercised by the resistance of the heretics. It would be a painful office, and of little profit, in the present prevalence of reason and of humanity, to pursue the frightful details of religious massacre[†]. It is sufficient to say, that after many conflicts and some variety of success, but no intermission of barbarity, the triumph rested with the Catholics. It was not, however, so complete as either to exterminate the rebels, or to place the promised sceptre in the hand of the persecutor. In the year 1218, Montfort was killed in battle before the walls of the city[‡] which Innocent had vainly bestowed on him.

[*] Hallam, Middle Ages. Simon de Montfort was descended, by an illegitimate branch, from Robert, King of France. He was connected on his mother's side with the Earls of Leicester.

[†] It was said in this war, when the Crusaders were on the point of storming Beziers, that some one inquired how the Catholic were to be distinguished from the heretical inhabitants in the massacre about to take place : " Kill them all (replied Arnold, a Cistercian abbot, who happened to be present)—God will know his own." " Cædite—novit Dominus qui sunt ejus." His advice appears to have been followed, and about seven thousand of all persuasions suffered.

The Life of Innocent III. apud Muratori (which is more properly the History of Montfort's wars,) mentions many instances in which small bodies of heretics chose to be burnt, rather than return to the Catholic faith.

[‡] The recorded circumstances of his death seem well to illustrate one trait at least in his character. He was at matins (on June 25) when he was informed that the enemy were in arms, and concealed in the fosse of the fortress. He instantly armed also, and hastened to church to hear mass. Mass was just begun, and he was engaged in earnest prayer, when news was brought him that the Toulousans had made a sally, and were attacking his machines—" Let me finish the mass (he replied) and see the sacrament of our redemption." Instantly afterwards another courier arrived, and said, " Hasten to the succour; our men are pressed, and can hold out no longer." " I will not stir (he answered) until I have seen my Saviour." But as soon as the priest had lifted up the Host, according to the usage, the Count, with his knees still on earth, and his hands raised to heaven, exclaimed, " Nunc dimittis," and he then added, "Let us now go and die, if necessary, for Him who has died for us." Accordingly he went forth and died. Yet, after all, it were too much to ascribe this conduct to pure hypocrisy ; much of fanaticism was undoubtedly mixed with it ; and when religious enthusiasm is united, as has too commonly happened, with religious hypocrisy, it is impossible even for the person possessed with them to distinguish their limits.

The Council of Toulouse which established the Inquisition.

The contest was continued by succeeding popes according to the principles of Innocent; and eight years after the death of Montfort, Louis VIII., King of France, was engaged to gird on the sword of persecution. Another crusade was preached, and in 1228 a system of inquisition was permanently established within the walls of Toulouse. In the same, or the following year, a council there assembled published decrees, which obliged laymen, even of the highest rank, to close their houses, cellars, forests, against the heretical fugitives, and to take all means to detect and bring them to trial; heretics voluntarily converted were compelled to wear certain crosses on their garments; those who should return to the Church, under the influence of fear, were still to suffer imprisonment at the discretion of the bishop; all children of the age of twelve or fourteen were compelled by oath, not only to abjure every heresy, but to expose and denounce any which they should detect in others; and this code of bigotry was properly completed by a strict prohibition to all laymen to possess any copies of the Scriptures*.

Still the Count, who succeeded to the sceptre and to the moderation of Raymond, manifested not sufficient ardour in the Catholic cause, and it was not till the Archbishop of the city was formally associated with him in the office of destruc-

* Some of the statutes of this Council are worth citing, as they show not only how far the system, strictly speaking inquisitorial, was carried in that early age, but also how closely the laity at that time co-operated with the clergy for the unity of the church :—" Statuimus itaque ut archiepiscopi et episcopi in singulis parochiis, tam in civitatibus quam extra, sacerdotem unum et duos vel tres laicos vel plures etiam, si opus fuerit, juramenti religione constringant, quod diligenter, fideliter et frequenter inquirant hæreticos in iisdem parochiis, domos singulas et cameras subterraneas aliqui suspicione notabiles perscrutando, et appensa seu adjuncta in iis tectis ædificia, seu quæcunque alia latibula (quæ omnia destrui præcipimus) perquirendo repererint hæreticos, credentes, fautores et receptatores seu defensores eorum, &c. . . . Solliciti etiam sint domini terrarum circa inquisitionem hæreticorum, in villis, domibus et nemoribus faciendam ; et circa hujusmodi appensa, adjuncta, seu subterranea latibula destruenda. Statuimus igitur ut quicunque in terra permittat scienter morari hæreticum .... et fuerit inde confessus et convictus, amittat in perpetuum totam suam terram, et corpus suum sit in manu domini ad faciendum inde quod debebit. Illam domum in qua fuerit inventus hæreticus diruendam decernimus ; et locus sive fundus ipse confiscetur," &c.—See Spicileg. Dacherii (vol. ii. p. 621, Edit. Paris.) under the head "Varia Galliæ Concilia."

tion, that the work was thought to proceed with becoming rapidity*. At length, in 1253, the Count entered seriously on the hateful task; and from that moment the remnant of the Albigeois were consigned, without hope or mercy, to the eager hands of the inquisitors.

Innocent did not himself live to behold the success of his measures; and the cause which is assigned for his premature death is the more remarkable†, as it arose out of the most triumphant exploit in his life. Since the humiliation of John, the crown of England had been considered by the Pope as a possession valuable to his ambition no less than to his avarice; and when, on the deposition of John, Louis of France was proclaimed, and actually proceeded to occupy the country in spite of the pontiff's determined opposition, Innocent was indignant at the affront and the injury. He preached a sermon on some public occasion, and selected for his text, " Even say thou, the sword, the sword is drawn—for the slaughter it is furbished‡.' In the course of his passionate harangue he pronounced a solemn sentence of excommunication against Louis and his followers; and immediately afterwards, as it is said, while in the act of dictating to his secretary some very harsh censures against Philippe and his kingdom, he was seized by that fatal fever,

Death of Innocent.

* We read in Matthew Paris, that about the year 1236, the Fratres Predicatores and other divines were still making great exertions for the conversion of the misbelievers. One of those preachers, named Robert, was so powerful in prostrating an adversary as to have obtained the name of Malleus Hæreticorum—the Hammer of Heretics. Nor was this only meant in a spiritual sense, " since there were many of both sexes whom, being unable to convert, he caused to be burnt to death; so that within two or three months there were about fifty persons whom he occasioned either to be burnt or buried alive.'—Matth. Paris, Henric. III., ad an. 1236. We should add, however, for the honour of pontifical humanity, that only two years afterwards the cruelties of Robert were arrested by an order from Rome, and the persecutor (who, by the way, had previously been a heretic) was himself convicted of some less equivocal offences, and imprisoned for life.

† Some writers make no mention of this circumstance, but merely assert that Innocent died rather suddenly, while on his way to reconcile some differences between the Pisans and Genoese, which impeded his grand crusading projects.— See the Chron. of Richardus de S. Germano, and of Urspergensis Abbas. ap. Pagi, Vit. Innoc. III. sect. 104. It is certain that his death took place at Perugia, on July 16, 1216, after a reign of eighteen years and six months.

‡ Ezekiel, xxi. 28.

which was ordained, perhaps, to prevent some new enterprise of warfare and desolation.

Character of Innocent.

If we would reconcile the lofty panegyrics with the violent vituperation which are alike bestowed upon the name of Innocent III., we must first distinguish his private from his public character, and next reflect how different and even opposite are the principles on which the latter has, in different ages, been judged. The very same exploits which would naturally call forth loud approbation from the Catholic historians of those days, nay, from some perhaps even at this moment, are made the subjects of severe censure by Protestant writers. This difference is less properly historical than moral. It does not respect the reality of the questionable acts ascribed to him, but only the light in which we are bound to regard them. But in respect to the private qualities of Innocent there is no ground for such diversity; and that they were great and noble is attested by most of his biographers. That he was gifted with extraordinary talents—that he was a profound canonist, and generally conversant with the learning of his time—that he was frequent in charitable offices, and generous in the distribution of his personal revenues—that his moral conduct was without reproach, and that he was sometimes not untouched by sentiments of piety, is clear from the evidence of contemporary authors and of his own writings. But great personal virtues are perfectly consistent with great public crimes; and it is a truth which leads to melancholy reflection, that some of the heaviest evils which have ever been inflicted upon churches and nations, have proceeded from the weak or even wicked policy of men of immaculate private characters.

Such was Innocent III.; charitable to the poor who surrounded his palace, steeled against the wretch who deviated from his faith—generous in the profusion of his private expenditure, avaricious in the exactions which he levied for the apostolical treasury—humane* in his mere social relations,

* Simon de Montfort killed Peter of Arragon in battle, and took his son prisoner. The widow, unable to prevail with Montfort for the release of the boy, supplicated the interference of Innocent. There is no proof that his policy was in this matter concerned on either side, so he commanded the liberation of the captive, and for once humanity had its triumph.

merciless in the execution of his ecclesiastical projects—pious
in the expressions of internal devotion, impious and blasphemous in his repeated profanation of the name of God and of
the cross of Christ.

Again: if we confine our retrospect to the public acts of this His policy.
pontiff, we observe that they bear, perhaps without any exception, the same stamp—that of a temporal and worldly policy.
Innocent subjected the civil authority of the Imperial Prefect
to his own. He extended, with great diligence, the boundaries
of the Ecclesiastical States. He found means to control a
great portion of the secular power of Europe, so that he might
hold it at his disposal; whether it was his will to overthrow a
pretender, or to depose a king, or to extinguish a heresy. For
the accomplishment of his most important objects his final and
most confident appeal was invariably made to the material
sword. Again: as if it were little to submit the consciences
of men to the dominion of the Holy See, he endeavoured to
comprehend in its grasp their property also. Heretofore the
Popes had been contented with the exercise and the rewards
of a spiritual tyranny—they had been satisfied with the obedience, the ecclesiastical fidelity, the ghostly services of their
clergy; but Innocent opened a more direct and, as he thought,
a more solid path to power. He availed himself of the pretext
of the crusades to levy pecuniary contributions, immediately on
the clergy, and, through the clergy, on the people. *This* was
the most essential change which he introduced into the system
of the church. From this epoch its history takes another, and
we need not hesitate to say, a lower character; and though
this was not instantly developed, but awaited the profligacy of
Avignon, and the vices and necessities of the Schism, to bring
it to full perfection, still it was from this crisis that the revolution must be dated; here originated that gradual substitution
of worldly objects and vulgar motives for the splendour of spiritual pretension, which led, through a succession of pitiful
disputes and sordid usurpations, to mere naked avarice and
avowed and shameless venality.

In the comparison which we might here be tempted to draw
between Innocent III. and the greatest among his predecessors,

there is perhaps no point on which the preference could be refused to Gregory. Both availed themselves of the divisions of the empire ; but the favourable circumstances which Innocent found, Gregory in a great measure created. The design of universal monarchy, which was carried so far into execution by the one, was conceived and transmitted to him by the other. With Innocent, the liberation of the Holy Sepulchre was made the excuse for pecuniary, exactions; with Gregory, it was the lofty aspiration of erring magnanimity, earnest, and attended by a determination to devote his repose and person to the cause which he deemed holy. In the treatment of heretical delinquency, the one was moderate * beyond the principles of his age and the passions of his clergy; the other urged the course and heated the rage of persecution, and by his perversion of the crusading frenzy into that channel, identified in the popular hatred dissent with infidelity, and established the law of vengeance, and multiplied the crimes of his posterity. And after all, how severely soever we may condemn the means which have created it, there is something of majesty and magnificence in the character of a spiritual despotism — an invisible power which enthrals mankind without the aid of physical force, and even in defiance of it; which humbles the mightiest sceptre, and blunts the sharpest sword by a menace or a censure ; a power mysterious and undefinable, swaying the human race by the name—the much-abused name—of religion. If we look, indeed, to its origin, it is only an empire over man's ignorance and credulity. Still it is the empire of intellect; and as such it stands on loftier ground than that worldly fabric which employed the ambition of Innocent; the mere temporal sovereignty of arms and opulence supported by corruption and massacre.

* It is true, that Gregory offered to Sweno, king of Denmark, a province occupied by heretics. But in this matter his temporal ambition was probably more interested than his ecclesiastical bigotry.

CHAPTER XIX.

The History of Monachism.

(I.) *Origin of Monachism*—Early instance of the monastic spirit in the East—Pliny the philosopher—The Therapeutæ or Essenes—The Ascetics—their real character and origin—The earliest Christian hermits—dated from the Decian or Diocletian persecutions—Cœnobites. Pachomius and St. Anthony—originated in Ægypt—account of the monks of Ægypt—Basilius of Cæsarea—his order and rule—his institution of a vow questionable—Monasteries encouraged by the fathers of the fourth and fifteenth ages—from what motives—Vow of celibacy—Restrictions of admission into monastic order—Original monks were laymen—Comparative fanaticism of the East and West—Severity of discipline in the West—motives and inducements to it—contrasted with the oriental practice—Establishment of nunneries in the East. (II.) *Institution of Monachism in the West*—St. Athanasius—Martin of Tours—Most ancient rule of the Western monasteries—their probable paucity and poverty—Benedict of Nursia—his order, and reasonable rule, and object—Foundation of Monte Cassino—France—St. Columban—Ravages of the Lombards and Danes—Reform by Benedict of Aniane—The order of Cluni—its origin, rise, and reputation—its attachment to papacy and its prosperity—the order of Citeaux—date of its foundation—Dependent abbey of Clairvaux—St. Bernard—its progress and decline—Order of the Chartreux. (III.) *Canons regular and secular*—Order of St. Augustine—Rule of Chrodegangus—Rule of Aix-la-Chapelle—subsequent reforms. (IV.) Connexion between the monasteries and the pope—mutual services. *The Military orders*—(1.) The Knights of the Hospital—origin of their institution—their discipline and character—(2.) Knights Templar—their origin and object—(3.) The Teutonic order—its establishment and prosperity. (V.) *The Mendicant orders*—causes of their rise and great progress—(1.) St. Dominic—his exertions and designs—(2.) St. Francis and his followers—compared with the Dominicans—apparent assimilation—essential differences—disputes of the Franciscans with the popes, and among themselves—Inquisitorial office of the Dominicans, their learning and influence—quarrels with the Doctors of Paris—Austerity of the Franciscans—the Fratricilli—(3.) The Carmelites — their professed origin — (4.) Hermits of St. Augustine — Privileges of these four orders. (VI.) *Various establishments of Nuns*—their usual offices and character—General remarks—The three grand orders of the Western Church (suited to the ages in which they severally appeared and flourished)—The Jesuits—The monastic system one of perpetual reformation—thus alone it survived so long—its merits and advantages—The bodily labour of the monks — their charitable and hospitable offices—real piety to be found among them—superintendence of education, and means of learning preserved by them—limits to their utility—their frequent alliance with superstition—their early dependence on the bishops—gradual exemption, and final subjection to the pope—Their profits and opulence, and means of amassing it—Luther a mendicant.

It is not through inadvertence, nor any blindness to the magnitude and importance of the subject, that a particular account

of the monastic system has been so long deferred. We have
had frequent occasion to recognize its existence and its influence on the general character of the Church; and it was
reasonable perhaps to expect some earlier notice of its origin
and progress. But as it is absolutely necessary for the correct
comprehension of ecclesiastical history, that the scheme of
monachism be understood aright; as that end could scarcely
be accomplished, unless by presenting the entire institution at
a single view; and as it is much more instructive, in the order
of historical composition, to retrace some steps, and to revisit
such periods as have been examined imperfectly, rather than
to anticipate events and ages which are remote and wholly
unexplored—for these reasons we have abstained from a partial
or premature treatment of this extensive subject. Moreover,
when we consider the successive mutations which have perpetually varied the aspect of monasticism, it will appear,
perhaps, that the present, as being the epoch of its latest
change, is the moment most proper for the delineation of the
whole structure. The latest change (we speak only of changes
preceding the Reformation) was the institution of the Mendicant Orders—an event which arose out of the ministry of St.
Dominic, and immediately followed the death of Innocent III.
This appendage completed the anomalous fabric: and while it
was so closely intermixed with the peculiar circumstances of
the age, that its nature could not have been rightly comprehended, unless described in connexion with them; it was at the
same time an innovation so essentially affecting the form and
character of monachism, that any account, not embracing it,
would have conveyed very imperfect and even erroneous notions.
Led by such considerations, we have selected the present period
for this purpose; not unmindful how little justice after all can
possibly be done to materials so ample within such moderate
limits, and almost despairing to throw any new light on a subject which has exercised the genius, and deserved—as it still
deserves—the deepest meditation both of historians and philosophers.

SECTION I.

The origin of Monachism and its progress in the East.

THE monastic spirit was alike congenial to the scenery and climate of the East, and to the peculiar character of its inhabitants. Vast solitudes of unbroken and unbounded expanse; rocks, with the most grotesque outlines, abounding in natural excavations; a dry air and an unclouded sky, afforded facilities —might we not say temptations—to a wild, unsocial, and contemplative life. The serious enthusiasm of the natives of Egypt and Asia, that combination of indolence with energy, of the calmest languor with the fiercest passion, which mark their features and their actions, disposed them to embrace with eagerness the tranquil but exciting duties of religious seclusion. And thus, even in earlier ages, before the zeal of devotion superseded all other motives to retirement, we observe, without any surprise, the mention of that practice, as indigenous and immemorial.

Pliny * the philosopher has recorded the existence of an extraordinary race, who lived on the borders of the Dead Sea, the associates of the palm-trees, and who had been perpetuated (as it was said) through thousands of ages without women and without property. Satiety and disgust with the business of life, rather than any religious feeling, are mentioned as the motives of their seclusion. Again, it is certain that the Therapeutæ or Essenes inhabited the deserts both of Egypt and of Syria as early as the days of our Saviour. They had, probably, dwelt there long before that time; and they appear to have sought to exalt the merit of their retirement by the practice of great austerities. Some Roman Catholic writers, being anxious to prove Monachism coëval with Christianity,

Therapeutæ or Essenes.

---

* Lib. v., cap. xvii. "Ab occidente Judææ litore Esseni fugitant; gens sola et in toto orbe præter cæteras mira, sine ulla fœmina, omni Venere abdicata, sine pecunia, socia palmarum. Indiem ex æquo advenarum turba renascitur, longe frequentantibus quos vita fessos ad mores eorum fortuna fluctibus agitat. Ita per sæculorum millia (incredibile dictu) gens æterna in qua nemo nascitur. Tam fœcunda illis aliorum vitæ pœnitentia est." The most important references on this subject are collected by Hospinian. Orig. Monach.—Lib. I. cap. v.

have asserted, on the authority of Eusebius *, Sozomen, and
Cassian, that the Therapeutæ were Christians, and that they
scattered the seeds of the monastic life through the populous
villages of Lower Egypt, whilst St. Marc, their founder, presided over the Church of Alexandria. But the opinion is more
probable that they were, for the most part, Jews by religion as
well as by birth, and of a much earlier origin. Nevertheless,
it may well be that such of them as became converts to the
faith, still retained their rigid eremitical life; nor can it be
doubted that the example of their severities, and the popular
respect which followed them, would excite the attention and
emulation of surrounding Christians.

The As-
cetics.

This is one of the causes to which we may attribute the very
early existence of a sect unquestionably Christian, called the
Ascetics; and these also have been erroneously confounded
with the original monks. The term Ascetic was applied by
early† Christian writers to the most rigid and zealous among
the primitive converts, whether they exhibited their fervour in
unusual assiduity in prayer and the offices of charity, or extended it to the more equivocal merits of fasting and celibacy.
But these persons did not withdraw themselves from the world;
they merely exercised with ardour, perhaps in extravagance,
the virtues which best qualified them to benefit and amend it.
Possibly, in their rigid devotion to the duties of society, they
may have shunned with aversion even its most innocent amusements. But such pious excess, which has ever marked the
best forms and ages of Christianity, was eminently useful in
its propagation, and should be sparingly censured under any
circumstances‡. It is at least manifest, that the rule of the

* Hist. Eccles., lib. ii., c. xvi. He applied to the Christians that which Philo
had written about the Jewish Essenes. Such, at least, is the opinion of Marsham, a very impartial as well as learned writer, in his Προπύλαιον to Dugdale's
Monasticon.—See Joseph. de Bell. Judaic., lib. ii. cap. vii. for a particular description of that sect.

† Bingham (Christ. Antiq. b. vii.) confirms his account of the Ascetics by
numerous and conclusive authorities.

‡ The Ascetics were of all ranks and professions. Eusebius calls them οἱ
σπουδαῖοι—" the zealous." Clemens Alexandrinus ἐκλέκτων ἐκλεκτότεροι—" the
more elect among the elect." These expressions imply nothing more than a
greater fervour (or, at least, greater pretension) of piety.

Ascetics was essentially at variance with the monastic principle; they dwelt and associated with their fellow Christians; and perhaps they might never have acquired the historical distinction of a name, had it not been that they affected a different garb, and assumed the philosophical cloak as the badge of their sect. Their origin is attributed by Mosheim* to the double doctrine of morals, which he supposes to have prevailed in the second century: so that, while vulgar Christians were contented to obey the *precepts* of the Gospel, those who aimed at higher perfection professed to be also directed by its *counsels*. This notion is unquestionably borrowed from heathen philosophy; and if it really existed to any extent among the Ascetics, it affords another proof of their connexion with the schools of Greece. But the unsettled condition of the Church in those days, and the jealousies and sufferings to which it was subjected, the general demoralization of the pagan world, the example of popular austerities in another religion, and the melancholy genius of Egypt, where Ascetism chiefly prevailed, were causes alone sufficient to have produced—as they did produce—forms of enthusiasm far less rational than any which can justly be ascribed to the Ascetics.

But about the middle of the third century, the monastic spirit exhibited itself in a much less equivocal shape; and we may observe that the purest and most legitimate character of seclusion was that, which it first assumed. Flying from the Anchorets. fury of the Decian persecution, a number of Christians took refuge in caves, in deserts, or inaccessible islets, where they exercised their proscribed religion in solitary security. Egypt and Syria, and Mesopotamia, and the wildest parts of Asia Minor, were suddenly visited by a race of exiles, in whom devotion, irritated by injustice and fed by seclusion, sometimes sank into sullen and gloomy fanaticism. These, probably, were the earliest Christian hermits or anchorets; they professed an absolute religious solitude, occasionally interrupted,

---

* The same writer (Cent. iii., p. 2., ch. ii.) seems disposed to attribute the rise of monks and hermits to the influence of the mystical theology. Yet he admits, in the same paragraph, that that method of life was very common in Egypt, Syria, India, and Mesopotamia, even before the coming of Christ.

indeed, by the pious importunity of the neighbouring inhabitants, but never broken by any regular connexion or association
with each other.   Their numbers were further increased by
the severities of Diocletian ; and still more, perhaps, by the
reverence and sympathy which the spectacle of their austere
piety excited among the vulgar.   They continued for some
time to deserve by their habits the title of solitaries : nor do
we learn that they were formed into assemblies until after the
establishment of the Church by Constantine.

Cœnobites.   The first institution of persons *living in common* for religious
purposes, and therefore called Cœnobites, is attributed to St.
Anthony, the contemporary and friend of Athanasius, and his
fellow-labourer in the same soil.   And it is obvious to remark,
that while the greater of those champions of the ancient Church
was engaged in defending the purity of the Christian faith in
the schools of Alexandria, the other was scattering in the same
soil, with the same applause and success, the seeds of a system
directly at variance with some of its best practical principles.
Another Egyptian, named Pachomius, divides with St. Anthony
the fame of this enterprise ; in as far, at least, as he immediately extended to the Upper Thebaïd the work which Anthony commenced in the Lower*.   He even ventured thus
early to enlarge upon the first scheme of religious union, and
introduced the custom, which in much later ages was so generally adopted in the Western Church, of combining several
monasteries into one society, or "congregation."   These events
took place during the first half of the fourth century ; and it is
from this epoch that we properly date the origin of the monastic system.

The multitudes who instantly embraced that manner of life,
and thronged the primitive edifices of Upper Egypt were, no
doubt, exaggerated, when calculated at nearly half the population of the country.   But it is certain that the " New Philosophy" (it was early designated by that name) was eagerly
adopted by a crowd of proselytes : nor is this wonderful, since
those, to whom its advantages were the most obvious, and its
duties the most easy, were the lowest of mankind—and since

* Histoire des Ordres Monastiques, Dissert. Prélim.

in Egypt, more than in any other land, religious novelties have
flourished from the remotest ages with peculiar fecundity.

Since the original monks of Egypt are praised by Roman
Catholic writers as the true models of monastic perfection, and
since some accounts of them remain, which may be followed
with little suspicion, it is proper to employ some additional
attention on that subject.   John Cassian, a native of Scythia,
a deacon by the ordination of St. Chrysostom, and an inmate
of the monastery of Palestine, near Bethlehem, went forth,
about the year 395, to explore the holy solitudes of Egypt, and
draw from its more perfect institutions a profitable lesson of
religious instruction; and seven years devoted to those inquiries
give weight and credit to the descriptions which he published.
The latter part of his life was passed in retirement at Marseilles; and to the two convents which he there established,
he prescribed a rule founded on the venerable practice of the
East.   According to his account, the recluses of Egypt were
divided into three principal classes: — the Anchorets, the
Cœnobites, and the Sarabaites.   The two former, whose
numbers were nearly equal, formed the respectable and genuine
portion of the profession.   The last were independent, and
were regarded as spurious and unworthy brethren.   The Anchorets occupied, either in perfect solitude or in very small
societies, the rudest and most secluded recesses of the desert.
" We are not destitute of parental consolation, (said the hermit Abraham to Cassian, who was beginning to sigh after the
more agreeable solitudes of Asia and Europe,) nor devoid of
means of easy sustenance—were we not bound by the command of our Saviour to forsake all and follow Him.   We are
able, if it seemed good, to build our cells on the banks of the
Nile, instead of bringing our water on our heads from four
miles' distance—were it not that the apostle has told us that
' every man shall receive his reward according to his labour.'
We know that in these our regions there are some secret and
pleasant places where fruits are abundant, and the beauty and
fertility of the gardens would supply our necessities with the
slightest toil—were it not that we fear ' to receive in our lifetime our good things.'   Wherefore we scorn these things and

The monks
of Egypt.

The An-
chorets.

all the pleasures of this world; and we take delight in these horrors, and prefer the wildness of this desolation before all that is fair and attractive, admitting no comparison between the luxuriance of the most exuberant soil and the bitterness of these sands*."

Cœnobites.   The establishments of the Cœnobites, which were spread from one end of the country to the other, contained, severally, from one hundred to five thousand inhabitants. In some instances, the wall which confined them inclosed also their wells and gardens, and all that was necessary for their sustenance, so as to leave no pretext even for occasional intercourse with Their discipline. a world which they had deserted for ever. The discipline to which they were subjected was rigid, but neither barbarous nor at all charged with injurious austerities. We read nothing of those chains and collars of iron, which formed a necessary part of self-devotion in the Syrian convents, nor is there any mention of sackcloth or flagellation, or any other voluntary torture. The whole severity of their practice consisted in abstemiousness; but even that was moderate; positive fasting was not encouraged, nor was it thought necessary to macerate the body in order to purify the soul. Bread and water was, indeed, the only nourishment allowed to the healthy devotee; but the bread was abundantly supplied: and those who have drawn from their infancy the sweet waters of the Nile seldom require or seek an artificial beverage. Neither was this rule enforced on all with indiscriminate rigour; but it was frequently modified according to age, or sex, or constitution.

They assembled to prayer twice in the twenty-four hours, at evening and during the night. Twelve psalms were chaunted,

---

* Cassianus, Collationes, lib. xxiv. c. 2. Such passages are illustrated by other writers of the same, or nearly the same, age. Among many others, the description of the Egyptian monks by Gregory Nazianzen (in Orat. xxi. Εἰς τὸν Μέγαν Ἀθανάσιον) is, perhaps, worth citing: Οἱ κόσμου χωρίζοντες ἑαυτοὺς, καὶ τὴν ἔρημον ἀσπαζόμενοι ζῶσι Θεῷ πάντων μᾶλλον τῶν στεφομένων τῷ σώματι. Οἱ μὲν τὸν παντῇ μοναδικὸν καὶ ἄμικτον διαθλοῦντες βίον ἑαυτοῖς μόνοις προσλαλοῦντες καὶ τῷ Θεῷ, καὶ τοῦτο μόνον κόσμον εἰδότες ὅσον ἐν τῇ ἐρημίᾳ γνωρίζουσι· οἱ δὲ νόμον ἀγάπης τῇ κοινωνίᾳ στέργοντες, ἐρημικοί τε ὁμοῦ καὶ μιγάδες, τοῖς μὲν ἄλλοις τεθνηκότες ἀνθρώποις ἀλλήλοις δὲ κόσμος ὄντες, καὶ τῇ παραβύσει τὴν ἀρετὴν θήγοντες. The same writer describes the character of a true monk with great minuteness and fervour in his XIIth Oration, (Εἰρηνικος Α, Ἐπὶ τῇ Ἑνώσει τῶν Μοναζόντων.)

(the chaunt had been taught them by an angel,) each of which was followed by a prayer; and then two lessons were read from the Scripture to those who desired to be instructed in that volume. The hearers remained sitting during the greater part of the service, with very short interruptions of genuflexion or prostration. The signal which summoned them to prayer was a simple trumpet or horn; it was sufficient to break the silence of their deserts; and the hour of their night-prayer was indicated by the declining stars, which shine in that cloudless atmosphere with perpetual lustre. The offices of their worship were undisturbed by any sound of worldly care or irreverent levity. Their devotion, like their pyramids, was simple and solid, and they lived like strangers to the flesh and its attributes, like sojourners on earth and citizens of a spiritual community*.

Four objects were comprehended in their profession—solitude, manual labour, fasting, and prayer; and we cannot forbear to observe, how large a portion of their time was devoted to the second. Indeed, so strictly was the necessity of such occupation inculcated, that the moderation of their other duties might almost appear to have been prescribed with that view. A body, debilitated by the excess of fasting or discipline, would have been disqualified for the offices of industry which were performed by the monks of Egypt. Without any possessions, and holding it alike discreditable to beg or to accept †, they earned their daily bread by their skill and diligence in making mats or baskets, as cutlers, as fullers, or as weavers—insomuch, that their houses may seem to have resembled religious manufactories, rather than places consecrated to holy purposes; and the motive of their establishment is liable to the suspicion of being, in some cases at least, worldly and political. Yet in the descriptions of their practice, *both* objects were so united, that the prayer seems to have been inseparable from the labour ‡. To

And objects.

* See Fleury's admirable Eighth Discourse.
† Cassian. Collat. xxiv. s. 11, 12, 13.
‡ " Ita ut quid ex quo pendeat haud facile possit a quopiam discerni—*i. e.* utrum propter meditationem spiritualem incessabiliter manuum opus exerceant; an propter operis jugitatem tam præclarum profectum spiritus, scientiæque lumen acquirant." Cassian. Instit. lib. ii. c. 14.

that end, the employments which they chose were easy and sedentary, so that the mind might be free to expatiate, while the hands were in exercise. At the same time, they maintained that perpetual occupation was the only effectual method to prevent distractions, and fix the soul on worthy considerations; that thus alone the tediousness of solitude, and its attendant evils, can be remedied; that the monk who works has only one demon to tempt him, while the monk unoccupied is harassed by demons innumerable *.

Sarabaites.   The Sarabaites † are described by Cassian in language of violent and almost unmitigated censure. Yet if we neglect those expressions, which become suspicious through their very rancour, and adhere only to the facts which are mentioned as characteristic of that monastic sect, it appears, that they were seceders, or at least independent, from the Cœnobitical establishments. They claimed the name of monks; but without any emulation of their pursuits, or observance of their discipline. They were not subject to the direction of elders, nor did they strive, under traditional institutions, to subject their inclinations to any fixed or legitimate rule. If they publicly renounced the world, it was either to persevere, in their own houses, in their former occupations under the false assumption of the monastic name, or building cells, and calling them monasteries, to dwell there without any abandonment of their secular interests. They laboured indeed with industry at least as sedulous, as their more regular brethren—but they laboured for their own individual profit, not for that of an instituted community‡. From this hostile account, it would appear that

* " Unde hæc est apud Ægyptum ab antiquis Patribus sancta (al. sancita) sententia—operantem Monachum dæmone uno pulsari; otiosum vero innumeris spiritibus devastari." Cassiani Instit., lib. x. c. 23. It appears from Cassian's preceding chapter, that any superfluity which the monks might have acquired was frequently employed in charitable purposes, and especially in the redemption of captives.

† The same sect, no doubt, which St. Jerome calls Remoboth, and stigmatizes as " genus deterrimum atque neglectum." Epist. xviii. ad Eustochium. De Custodia Virginitatis.

‡ Cassian. Collat. xviii. c. 7. Cassian's dislike for the Sarabaites was probably contracted in the cells of the Cœnobites, who viewed with a sort of sectarian jealousy the industry and the profits of rebels, or of rivals.

the Sarabaites, if they were spurious monks, were at least useful members of society; and the union which they established
of the religious profession with worldly occupations, seems to
have revived, or rather perpetuated, the leading principle of
ascetism.

From Egypt, the popular institution was immediately intro- St. Basil.
duced into Syria by a monk named Hilarion ; but the Syrians
appear soon to have deviated from the simplicity and moderation of their masters into a sterner practice of mortification,
and even torture. From Syria, it was transmitted to Pontus
and the shores of the Black Sea, and there it found a respectable patron, the most eminent among its primitive protectors, Basilius, Archbishop of Cæsarea.

That celebrated ecclesiastic—who was a native of Cappa-
docia, the brother of Gregory of Nyssa, and the fellow-disciple
(as is asserted) of the future apostate Julian—has given his
name to the single order, which has subsisted in the Greek
Church *, with scarcely any variation or addition, from that
period to the present moment; and it is this circumstance, as
well as his superior antiquity, which has established him as
the most venerable of the patriarchs of Monachism. His claim
to that reputation is said to consist in this—he united the
Hermits and Cœnobites already established in his diocese ; and
to his monasteries, so formed, he prescribed a rule, which was
rigidly observed by them, and imitated by others : by this bond,
he gave them a consistency and uniformity, which had hitherto
been peculiar to the institutions of Egypt †. Besides which,

* It is true that certain heretical orders, Maronites, Jacobites, Nestorians, &c.
professed to follow the rule of St. Anthony; but St. Anthony delivered, in fact,
no rule. When solicited to impose some code upon his disciples, he is recorded to
have presented to them the Bible—an eternal and universal rule. Hospin.
lib. ii. c. 4.

† It does not, however, appear, that his rule was in the first instance very generally observed. At least we find, that as much as thirty years later, Cassian
(Institut. lib. ii. c. 2.) contrasted the diversity, particularly respecting the times
and nature of the holy offices, which prevailed elsewhere, with the uniformity of
the more ancient institutions of Egypt. " In hunc modum diversis in locis di-
versum canonem agnovimus institutum, totque propemodum typos et regulas vidimus usurpatas, quot etiam monasteria cellasque conspeximus. Sunt quibus ....
Quapropter necessarium reor antiquissimam patrum proferre constitutionem quæ

he strongly recommended* the obligation of a vow, on admission to the monastic state—an obligation which, whether it were actually established by St. Basil or not, had certainly no existence before his time.   These advancements in the system were effected from the year 360 to 370; and thus the plant, which had first been nourished by Anthony and Pachomius with imperfect, but not improvident culture, grew up, within the space of twenty years, into vigorous and lasting maturity.

Conduct of the ancient Fathers.
It is a fact demanding observation, that the fathers of the ancient Church, who flourished about this period, among whom were many eloquent and learned and pious men, were favourable, without one exception, to the establishment of monasticism : for though it might be beneath the office of reason to investigate the motives of the illiterate enthusiasts who began the work, it would be improper to pass over without comment the considerate labours of the ecclesiastics who completed it. Moreover, as they were apt enough to differ on some other points, in which the interests of religion were concerned, and as they delivered, on all occasions, their particular opinions with great boldness and independence, their unanimity in the introduction of one grand innovation is, by that circumstance, still further recommended to our attention.   Yet must we hesitate to ascribe to them motives altogether unworthy.   We should be wholly mistaken if we were to attribute their conspiracy to any deep design for the establishment of priestly rule, or the increase of the wealth and authority of the Church beyond their just limits.   These evil consequences did, indeed, result from the work, and spread, with fatal influence, over the western

nunc usque per totam Egyptum a Dei famulis custoditur," &c. It is, indeed, the opinion of Hospinian (though it does not seem sufficiently founded), that St. Basil's Cœnobia were little more than theological schools, and that his rule was no other than the ordinary form of school discipline. Such, as he thinks, were the monasteries of those days. Lib. iii. c. 2. The Rule commonly ascribed to that saint may be found, in Latin, in the same place.

* Bingham, Ch. Antiq. book vii. The author of the Histoire des Ordres Monastiques expressly asserts, that as monasteries were instituted by Anthony, and congregations by Pachomius, so the three vows (of chastity, poverty, and obedience) were the introduction of St. Basil. It is, at least, certain, that the *duties* of obedience and poverty were early and very rigidly practised by the Eastern monks.

world ; but they could not be contemplated by the fathers of the fourth and fifth centuries, because they rose and grew with the growth of *papal* usurpation, of which, in those days, there was no fear nor thought. It was the alliance between papacy and monasticism which tended more, perhaps, than any other cause, to elevate and magnify, and at the same time to vitiate both. But the eye of Athanasius, or Chrysostom, or Augustine, could not possibly foresee that union, nor penetrate the various circumstances which afterwards concurred to aggrandize the Bishop of Rome. So far may we safely acquit even the most sagacious among the fathers of monachism ; and as far as the spirit of the age can be held to excuse those whom, in appearance, it carries along with it, but who, in fact, encourage and influence it, so far may the conduct of those mistaken men be excused. And perhaps we might add, in further palliation, that the general demoralization of society, over which Christian principles were still contending for predominance with the pernicious remnants of paganism, seemed to permit so little hope of righteous conduct to persons busied in the world, as almost to justify retreat and seclusion. We should, moreover, in attempting to account for this agreement, always bear in mind, that the early patrons of monasticism were, with very few exceptions, Orientals or Africans ; men of ardent temperament, and impetuous imagination ; among whom the theory of religion too frequently tended to mysticism, and its practice to mere sensible ceremony, and bodily mortification. We have no reason to believe that any worldly premium to the new philosophy was held out by the princes or nobles of those days ; nor even that the influx of oblations from the vulgar was the immediate fruit of the profession of poverty*, as was elsewhere the case

---

* Not that even the earliest monks have escaped the reproaches of the contemporary fathers. St. Jerome especially (Epist. xxxv., ad Heliodorum Monachum) notices the birth of corruption :—" Alii nummum addant nummo, et marsupium suffocantes matronarum opes venentur obsequiis ; sint ditiores Monachi, quam fuerant sæculares ; possideant opes sub Christo paupere, quas sub locuplete Diabolo non habuerant ; et suspiret eos Ecclesia divites, quos tenuit mundus ante mendicos." . . . But notwithstanding this and other particular passages, the general expressions used by those writers respecting the monastic condition, prove its general respectability.

in later times. The monasteries of the East were at no period so overgrown with opulence as those of the Roman Church; and in their origin they certainly offered no imaginable temptations to avarice or sensuality. On these and similar considerations, we may acquit the original founders of the monastic system of those odious motives, with which they have sometimes been charged: but we must censure their encouragement of popular superstition; we must condemn that rash enthusiasm, which exceeded what is written; and we must pronounce those to have been insufficient guides to religious knowledge, who, at a crisis of such infinite importance, inculcated any other rule of life, than such as tended directly, through the plain and practical precepts of the Gospel, to the general welfare of mankind.

Early form of Mona-chism. The earliest age of monachism differed in many particulars from those, which matured and perfected the system. The vow of celibacy was either not taken by the original monks, or not universally enforced; though the practice was usual, and held indicative of a higher condition of sanctity. Community of property was indeed established among them; but that property was chiefly acquired by the labour of their hands. The necessity of manual industry, which was coeval with the institution, was subsequently enforced by St. Augustine, as the best safeguard against the snares of the Tempter; and the spiritual motives to strict moral demeanour were encouraged by the absolute poverty of the individuals. Mendicity, which had an early existence in the system, was stigmatized with immediate censure. It does not appear that the primitive monks were positively prohibited by any vow from returning, if they thought fit, to the turbulence of the world; though such desertions were strongly discouraged, as early as the Council of Chalcedon, both by ecclesiastical denunciations, and perpetual exclusion from holy orders. Several restrictions were imposed with respect to admission into the monastic order. Of husbands and wives, the mutual agreement was necessary for the seclusion of either; servants were not admitted, unless with the approbation of their masters, nor children without the consent of their parents and themselves. These and other reasonable impediments to the abuse of monachism were first weakened by the superstitious improvidence of Justinian.

The original monks were, without exception, laymen; but in situations, where the only accessible place of worship was within the walls, one priest was added to the society, and he generally filled the office of Abbot or Hegoumenos.   St. Jerome* has expressly distinguished the monastic from the sacerdotal order; and Leo I., in a communication to Maximus, Bishop of Antioch, forbade monks to usurp the office of religious instruction, which was properly confined to the priests of the Lord.   It is true indeed, that very early in monastic history those establishments were considered as schools and nurseries for the ministry, and that persons were selected for ordination from among their inhabitants: but those so ordained immediately quitted the cloister, and engaged in the duties of the secular clergy; and in Greece they were distinguished by the title of Hiero-monachoi, or Holy Monks†.

There is no doubt that Orientals are naturally more prone to acts of fanaticism and ascetic austerities, than the more rational, and, at the same time, more sensual nations of Europe; and we might have expected to find the most extraordinary instances of self-inflicted torture among those who originated that practice, and whose habits and passions peculiarly prepared them for it.   It is uncertain whether this be so; for though it is true that the madness of the Stylites gained no prevalence in the Western Church, and that the Boskoi, or Grazing Monks (an Asiatic order of the fifth century, which proposed to unite the soul to the Deity, by degrading the body

Character of Oriental Monachism.

Mystics.

* Epist. V., ad Heliodorum Monachum.   "Alia Monachorum est causa; alia clericorum.   Clerici pascunt oves; ego pascor.   Illi de altario vivunt; mihi, quasi infructuosæ arbori, securis ponitur ad radicem, si munus ad altare non defero. . . .   Mihi ante Presbyterum sedere non licet," &c. . . .   Hospinian (lib. iii., c. 13), under the head " Monachi ab initio non Clerici," adduces strong reason (in spite of some contradictory decrees) to believe that they were permitted to take orders as early as the time of Pope Siricius, in 390; and that all the privileges of the secular priesthood were subsequently conferred on monastic priests, and confirmed by Gregory the Great.   Still, as they continued to be bound by their vows, they acquired the clerical, without losing the monastic character.

† The foundation of an order of Canons, attributed to St. Augustine (which will presently be mentioned), was a distinct institution.

to a condition below humanity), found no imitators in a more
inclement climate; yet their mortifications and absurdities were
rivalled, if not in the cells of the Benedictines, at least by the
Flagellants, and some other heretics of the fourteenth century;
and the discipline of the more rigid Franciscans was probably,
in the early ages of that order, as severe as human nature
could endure.   But even among the regular orders of the
Western Church, monastic austerity was carried, under particular circumstances, and in later times, to a more perfect refinement than it ever attained in the East.   It is not difficult to
account for this singularity.   A variety of motives, and a com-
plication of passions, entered into the monkish system of the
Roman Church.   Many were unquestionably actuated by
superstition, many, perhaps, by purer sentiments of piety; but
many more were impelled by personal ambition, by professional
zeal, by the jealousy of rival orders, and, above all, by the
thirst for that wealth, which so certainly followed the reputation of sanctity.   On the other hand, the unvarying constitution, and the more tranquil character of the Eastern Church,
presented fewer and feebler inducements to excessive severity.
The passion which originally founded its monasteries, warm
and earnest enthusiasm, continued still to animate and people
them; but its ardour gradually abated; and the defect was
not supplied in the same abundance, nor by the same sources,
which sprang from the rock of St. Peter.   From the earliest
period, the Head of the Eastern Church was subject to the
civil power, and he has always continued so; and thus, as he
has at no time asserted any arrogant claims of temporal authority, nor engaged in any contests with the state, he possessed
no personal or official interest in the aggrandisement of the
monastic order.   Again, the two grand political revolutions of
the Eastern and Western empires produced effects precisely
opposite on the condition of monachism in either.   The overthrow of the latter by the Pagans of the North, the early conversion of the conquerors, and the subsequent establishment of
the feudal system, became the means of enriching the monasteries, from private, as well as royal bounty, with vast territorial endowments.   Whereas the possessions of the Oriental

Church, which, through less favourable circumstances, had already been reduced to more moderate limits, were still further despoiled by the fatal triumph of the Turks.

The institution of nunneries was contemporary with that of monasteries, and is also attributed to St. Anthony; but the earliest accounts incline us to believe that it was not equally flourishing. In countries where sterility is common, and the population either scanty or fluctuating, the government would doubtless discourage the seclusion of females. We learn, too, that their houses were less carefully regulated, and their vows less strictly observed in Asia than in the West of Europe. Athens is mentioned as the nurse of several such establishments; but it was lamented that the ladies of rank and wealth were not easily prevailed upon to devote themselves to religious seclusion. Of a convent which was founded at Constantinople by the Empress Irene (in 1108), the constitutions still remain*. But the Nuns of St. Basil were more numerous and more prosperous in the West, than in the climate of their origin; and in Sicily especially, and the South of Italy, they arrived, in later ages, at considerable wealth and importance†.

The original monastic establishments of every description were subjected, without any exception, to the bishop of the diocese. The exemptions from that authority, which were afterwards introduced, through the pernicious progress of papacy, into the Western Church, had little prevalence, as, indeed, they had no strong motive, in the East.

---

* Histoire des Ordres Monastiques, (Prem. Partie, chap. xxviii.) By a regulation peculiarly oriental, it was herein ordained, that the steward, the confessor, and the two chaplains, the only males employed about the convent, should be eunuchs. We do not learn whether this precaution was usual in the nunneries of the East.

† Another class of religious females, called Virgins of the Church, had an early existence in the East. They continued to unite the discharge of their social duties with a strict profession of religious chastity—thus advancing one step beyond the *ascetism* of their forefathers.

Section II.

Institution of Monachism in the West.

It is very generally asserted*, that the monastic system was
introduced into the West by Athanasius, during his compulsory sojourn at Rome, in 341.   It is believed that he carried
in his train to the imperial city certain monks and anchorets,
representatives of the Egyptian commonwealth, whose wild
aspect and devout demeanour moved the reverence, and at the
same time roused the emulation, of the Romans.   Some monasteries were immediately founded; and many retired to lonely
places for the exercise of solitary worship.   From Rome (if the
above account be true) the monastic practice was instantly
diffused throughout Italy; and at Milan especially it obtained
a powerful support in the patronage of Ambrose.   It speedily
extended itself to France; and the labours of Martin of Tours,
which were zealously directed to its diffusion, received at least
this posthumous recompense, that nearly two thousand holy
disciples assembled to do honour to his obsequies.   The establishments, founded by Cassian at Marseilles, and in the neighbouring islands, were immediately thronged with brethren
obedient to his rule; and Honoratus, bishop of Arles, bears
testimony (about the year 430) to the existence of "religious
old men in the Isle of Lerinus, who lived in separate cells, and
represented in Gaul the Fathers of Egypt†."

---

* Baronius (ann. 328), Mabillon, and Gibbon hold this opinion; but Muratori
pretends that the first monasteries founded in Italy were erected at Milan.
Mosheim more wisely pronounces the uncertainty of the fact.

† The following are some of the passages which bear on this subject.   St.
Jerome, speaking of the time of Athanasius's visit to Rome, says (in Epist. 16, ad
Principiam Virginem), "Nulla eo tempore nobilium fœminarum noverat Romæ
propositum Monachorum, nec audebat, propter rei novitatem, ignominiosum (ut
tunc putabatur) et vile in populis nomen assumere.   Hæc (Marcella) ab Alexan-
drinis prius sacerdotibus Papaque Athanasio, et postea Petro, . . . vitam B.
Antonii adhuc tunc viventis, Monasteriorumque in Thebaide Pachumii et Virginum
ac Viduarum didicit disciplinam, nec erubuit profiteri quod Christo placere agno-
verat."   Soon afterwards, when Jerome was at Rome, " fuerunt tam crebra Virginum Monacharumque innumerabilis multitudo, ut pia frequentia serventium
Deo, quod prius ignominiæ fuerat, esset postea gloriæ." So also Augustine (De

We may here observe, that, as in the wide wilderness of the
East, a secluded rock, or an unfrequented oasis—a spot cut off
by the circumfluous Nile, or breaking the influx of the river
into the sea—as such were the places usually selected by the
original recluses, so their earliest imitators in the West, under
different circumstances of soil and climate, adhered to the
ancient preference for insular retirement.   The islands of Dalmatia *, and others scattered along the coast of the Adriatic,
were peopled with holy inhabitants.   Along the western shores
of Italy †, from Calabria, throughout the islets of the Tuscan

Morib. Eccles. c. 33), " Romæ etiam plura Monasteria cognovit, in quibus singuli
gravitate atque prudentia et divina scientia pollentes, cæteris secum habitantibus
præerant Christiana caritate, sanctitate et libertate viventibus."   And the same
Father (Confess., lib. viii. c. 6) attests, on the authority of one Pontitianus, that
there existed at Milan " Monasterium plenum bonis Fratribus, extra urbis mœnia
sub Ambrosio nutritore."   Sulp. Severus mentions the success of St. Martin to
have been so great, " ut ad exequias ejus monachorum fere duo millia convenisse
dicantur.   Specialis Martini gloria, cujus exemplo in Domini servitute stirpe tanta
fructificaverat."   .   .   .

    * Jerome, Epist. xxxv., ad Heliodorum.   " Quumque crederet quotidie aut ad
Ægypti Monasteria pergere, aut Mesopotamiæ invisere choros, aut certe insularem
Dalmatiæ solitudines occupare," &c.

    † See Marsham's Προπυλαῖον, in Dugd. Monast. Respecting the monks of the
isles of Gorgonia and Capraria, Rutilius Numatianus composed some verses (in
the year 416), which have more of elegance (says Marsham) than of Christianity.
The following are some of them :—

           Processu pelagi jam se Capraria tollit;
            Squallet lucifugis Insula plena viris.
          Ipsi se Monachos Graio cognomine dicunt,
            Quod soli nullo vivere teste volunt.
          Munera fortunæ metuunt, dum damna verentur.
            Quisquam sponte miser, ne miser esse queat ?
          Sive suas repetunt ex fato ergastula pœnas;
            Tristia seu nigro viscera felle tument.
           *   *   *   *

          Noster enim nuper Juvenis, majoribus amplis,
            Nec censu inferior, conjugiove minor,
          Impulsus furiis homines Divosque relinquit,
            Et turpem latebram credulus exul agit.
          Infelix putat illuvie cœlestia pasci,
            Seque premit cæcis sævior ipse Deis.
          Num, rogo, deterior Circæis secta venenis?
            Tunc mutabantur corpora, nunc animi.

Many other islands are mentioned as having been thus consecrated (or desecrated—as the describer might be an ecclesiastical annalist, or a pagan poet). The

Sea, the chants of monastic devotion everywhere resounded, as well as at Lerinus and the Stœchades, consecrated by the piety of Cassian. Such, in the first instance, were the favourite nurseries of the new institution. There is even reason to believe that the rocks on the southern coast of Italy furnished the seeds of monachism to the churches of Carthage; and thus was transmitted, after a revolution of half a century, to the more Western Africans, the boon which their brethren of Egypt had first presented to the Christian world.

Prevalence and character of Monachism in the West.   It is, indeed, unquestionable, that towards the end of the fourth, but especially during the fifth century, the monastic practice obtained universal prevalence, and became almost co-extensive with the belief in Christ. And on this circumstance there is one observation which it is proper to offer, which has indeed been made before, though in a somewhat different spirit, by Roman Catholic writers—that the period, which was marked by this great religious innovation, was the same in which the religion itself seemed in imminent danger, at least throughout the Western provinces, of utter extirpation. This was the very crisis, in which the pagan inundation from the North spread itself most fiercely and fatally, and while it overthrew the bulwarks of the empire, menaced, at the same time, the foundations of the Faith. That the monastic institution was designedly interposed by Providence, in order to stay that wasting calamity, and supply new means of defence to His fainting soldiers, is a vain and even a presumptuous supposition. But it would equally be unjust to assert, that establishments of pious men, associated for religious purposes, were without their use in exciting respect in the enemy and confidence in the Christian. Still less can we hesitate to believe that they were the means of relieving much individual misery; that during

island Barbara, situated above the conflux of the Rhone and the Arar, boasted to have been one of the most ancient nurseries of the Holy Institution; and Jerome, in an epistle to Heliodorus, speaks of " Insulas et totum Etruscum mare Volscorumque provinciam, et reconditos curvorum littorum sinus, in quibus monachorum consistebant Chori." . . . . See Mabillon, Pref. in Ann. Bened. Sec. i. Giannone's View of the Origin of the Monastic Life in the West (Stor. di Nap., lib. ii., cap. 8) does not appear to be marked by the accuracy and perspicuity usual to that excellent historian.

the overthrow of justice and humanity, they derived power, as well as protection, from the name of God, and from the trust which they reposed in him; that their power was generally exerted for good purposes; and that their gates were thrown open to multitudes, who, in those days of universal desolation, could hope for no other refuge.

The rule commonly professed by the original Western monasteries was unquestionably that of St. Basil; and though it was not observed with any rigid uniformity, there was probably no material variation either in constitution or discipline throughout the whole extent of Christendom, excepting such as naturally resulted from the different climate, morals, and temperament of its inhabitants. At least, there was no distinction in order or dignity: all were united by one common appellation, extending from the deserts of Pontus to the green valleys of Ireland; and the monks of those days were sufficiently separated from the rest of mankind, and sufficiently disengaged from secular pursuits, to dispense with the baser motives to which they were afterwards reduced, of partial interest and rivalry. Some wealth, indeed, began already to flow into that channel; but the still remaining prevalence of hermits, who dwelt among the mountains in unsocial and independent seclusion, very clearly proves, that the more attractive system of the Cœnobites had not hitherto attained any luxurious refinement. No large territorial endowments had yet been attached to religious houses, and their support was chiefly derived from individual charity, or superstition. And during the course of the fifth century the progression of monachism was probably more popular, and certainly more profitable, among Eastern nations, than it had yet become on this side of the Adriatic.

But in the following age a more determined character was given to that profession. A hermit named Benedict, a native of Nursia, in the diocese of Rome, instituted, about the year 529, an entirely new order, and imposed a rule, which is still extant, for its perpetual observance. . . . No permanent and popular institution has ever yet existed, however in its abuse it have set sense and reason at defiance, which has not some pretension to virtue or wisdom, and usually much of the substance

Benedict of Nursia, A.D. 529.

of both, in its origin and its infancy. It was thus with the order of St. Benedict. That celebrated rule, which in after ages enslaved the devout and demoralized the Church—which became a sign and a watchword for the satellites of papacy— was designed for purposes which, at the time of its promulgation, might seem truly Christian. Its objects were to form a monastic body, which under a milder discipline should possess a more solid establishment, and more regular manners, than such as then existed; and also to ensure for those, who should become members of it, a holy and peaceful life, so divided between prayer, and study, and labour, as to comprehend the practical duties of religious education. Such was the simple foundation, on which all the riches, and luxury, and power, and profligacy of the Benedictines have been unnaturally piled up—consequences, which were entirely unforeseen by him who founded, and by those who immediately embraced, and by those who first protected*, a pious and useful institution.

The Rule of St. Benedict.   It is proper to confirm these observations by some account of what is, perhaps, the most celebrated monument of ecclesiastical antiquity. The Rule of St. Benedict† is introduced by a quadruple division of those who professed the monastic life. The first class was composed of the Cœnobites or Regular Monks; the second, of the Anchorets or Hermits, to whom he assigns even superior perfection; the third, of the Sarabaites, whom he describes as living without any rule, either alone or in small societies, according to their inclination; the fourth, of Gyrovagi or Vagabonds, a dissolute and degraded body. His regulations for the divine offices were formed, in a great measure, on the practice already described of the Monks of Egypt‡. Two hours after midnight they were aroused to vigils, on which occasion twelve psalms were chaunted, and certain lessons from the Scriptures read or recited. At day-break the matins, a service little different from the preceding, were per-

* Gregory the Great was a zealous patron of this institution, and so approved the moderation of the rule, that he has not escaped the suspicion of being its author.

† It is given at length by Hospinian,—De Origine Monachatûs, lib. iv. cap. v.

‡ See Mabillon, Pref. in sec. ii, Annal, Benedict, and Hist. des Ord. Monast.

formed; and the intervening space, which in winter was long and tedious, was employed in learning the Psalms by heart *, or in meditating on their sense, or in some other necessary study. But besides these and the other public services, the duty of private or mental prayer was recognized in the Institutions of St. Benedict, and regulations were imposed which, while they restricted its duration, proposed to purify and spiritualize its character.

To the duty of prayer the holy legislator added those of manual labour and reading. The summer's day was so divided, that seven hours were destined to the former occupation, and two at least to the latter †. And should it so happen (he observes) that his disciples be compelled to gather their harvests with their own hands, let not that be any matter of complaint with them; since it is then that they are indeed monks, when they live by their own handy-work, as did our fathers and the apostles. During the winter-season the hours of labour were altered, but not abridged; and those of study seemed to have been somewhat increased, at least during Lent. The Sabbath was entirely devoted to reading and prayer. Those whose work was allotted at places too remote from the monastery to admit of their return to the appointed services, bent their knees on the spot and repeated their prayers at the canonical hours. The description of labour was not left to the choice of the individual, but imposed by the Superior. Thus if any possessed any trade or craft, he could not exercise it, except by permission of the Abbot. If anything were sold, the whole value was carefully appropriated to the common fund; and it was further directed, that the price should be somewhat lower than that demanded by secular artizans for the same

Manual labour and study.

---

* In England the establishment of Monachism was contemporary with that of Christianity. "Augustinus, Monasterii Regulis eruditus, instituit conversationem, quæ initio nascentis ecclesiæ fuit patribus nostris, quibus omnia erant communia —Monasterium fecit non longe a Doroverniensi Civitate," &c. Bede, lib. i., c. xxii.

† It was ordained, that if any one were unable to read or meditate, some other occupation should be imposed on him. But as Latin, the language of religious study, was at that time the vulgar tongue, at least one great impediment to religious instruction, which was so powerful in after ages, did not then exist.

objects —" to the end that God might be glorified in all things."

In respect to abstinence*, the Rule of St. Benedict ordained not any of those pernicious austerities, which were sometimes practised by his followers.   Notwithstanding the indulgence of a small quantity of wine to those whose imperfect nature might require it, it prescribed a system of rigid temperance, which among those original Cœnobites was well enforced by their poverty—but it contained no injunction to fasting or mortification.   Those vain and superstitious practices, the fruits of mingled enthusiasm and indolence, scarcely gained any prevalence in the monasteries of the West, until increasing wealth dispensed with the necessity of daily labour.   The monks slept in the same dormitory, in which a lamp was kept constantly burning, and strict silence was imposed.   Even in the day, they spake rarely ;   and every expression partaking of levity, and calculated at all to disturb the seriousness of the community—every word that was irrelevant to its objects and uses— was absolutely prohibited within the convent-walls.   The Rule makes no mention of any sort of recreation ; but it enjoins that, every evening after supper, while the brothers are still assembled, one among them shall read aloud passages from the Lives of the Saints, or some other book of edification.

As the Abbot was then chosen by the whole society without regard to any other consideration than personal merit, so in the government of the monastery he was bound to consult the senior brethren on lesser matters, and the whole body on the more important contingencies : it was ordained, however, that, after he had taken such counsel, the final decision should rest entirely with himself. ' Obedience was the vow and obligation of the others.

The form prescribed for the reception of Novices was not such as to encourage a lukewarm candidate.   In the first

---

* In this matter St. Benedict relaxed from the rigour of the Eastern observance; but he did so with reluctance, regretting the necessary imperfection of a system, which he was compelled to accommodate to the gradually decreasing vigour of the human frame.   Even Fleury (see his Eighth Discourse) does not disdain to combat this notion.

instance, he was compelled to stand four or five days before the gates, supplicating only for admission.   If he persevered, he was received first into the Chamber of Strangers—then into that of Novices.   An ancient brother* was then commissioned to examine his vocation, and explain to him how rude and diffi- cult was the path to heaven.   After a probation of two months the Rule was read to him; again, after six other months; and a third time, at the end of the year.   If he still persisted, he was received, and made profession in the Oratory before the whole community.   And we should remark, that that profession was confined to three subjects—perseverance in the monastic life; correction of moral delinquencies; and obedience. Offences committed by the brethren were punished, according to their enormity, by censure, excommunication, or corporal inflictions; expulsion was reserved for those deemed incorrigible. Nevertheless even then the gate was not closed against repent- ance; and the repudiated member was re-admitted, on the promise of amendment, even for the third time. . . .   Such in substance was the Rule of St. Benedict; and even the very faint delineation here presented may suffice to give some insight into the real character of the original monasteries.   Perhaps too it may serve to allay the bitterness, which we sometimes are too apt to entertain against the founders and advocates of the system, by showing, that though unscriptural in its prin- ciple, and pernicious in its abuse, it was yet instituted not without some wisdom and foresight; and was calculated to confer no inconsiderable blessings on those ages in which it first arose.

The monastery of Monte Cassino, which became afterwards so celebrated in papal history, was the noblest, though not perhaps the earliest, monument of St. Benedict's exertions. The moment was favourable to his undertaking; and his name and his Rule were presently adopted and obeyed throughout the greater part of Italy.   By St. Maur, his disciple and asso- ciate, an institution on the same principle was immediately †

Progress of the institu- tion.

St. Maur.

---

* All those ancient brothers were laymen.   It does not appear that even St. Benedict himself held any rank in the clergy.

† About the year 542.   It was destroyed by the Danes, but subsequently re-

introduced into France, and became the fruitful parent of
dependent establishments.   Somewhat later in the same cen-

St. Colum- tury, St. Columban propounded in Britain a rule resembling
ban.   in many respects that of St. Benedict, but surpassing it in
severity; and it was propagated with some success on the
Continent.   But it is the opinion of the most learned writers,
that the monasteries, which at first followed it, yielded after no
long interval to the higher authority and more practicable precepts of the Nursian; whose genuine institution indeed was
soon afterwards planted in the south of the island by the monk
Augustine.   At the same time the same system was spreading
northward beyond the mountains of the Rhine; and though it
may probably be true, that the " Holy Rule " (regula sancta)
was not universally received until the ninth century—until the
practice had been vitiated by many corruptions—it is evident,
that it obtained great prevalence long before that time, while
it yet retained its original integrity; and it is equally clear,
that its moral operation upon a lawless and bloodthirsty
generation could not possibly be any other than to restrain
and to humanize.

During the greater part of the seventh and the beginning of
the following age, frightful ravages were committed by the
Lombards in Italy, and by the Danes in France and Britain,
against which even the sanctity of the monastic profession
furnished very insufficient protection.   Throughout this period
of devastation, while all other laws and establishments were
overthrown, it was not probable that even those of St. Benedict
should remain inviolate.   The monastery of Monte Cassino
was destroyed about fifty years after its foundation, and the
holy spot remained desolate for almost a century and a half *.

established about the year 934, by the Bishop of Limoges.   A great number of
abbeys presently grew up under its shadow.—Histoire des Ordres Monastiques.

* See Leo Ostiensis. Chron. Cassinens, lib. i.   Gregory III. restored the monastery, and Zachary his successor granted to it (about the year 743) the privilege
of exclusive dependence on the Bishop of Rome.   But one blessing was still
wanting to secure its prosperity—and that was happily supplied by the Abbot
Desiderius in 1066.   In exploring some ruins about the edifice, he discovered the
body of St. Benedict.   It is true that a pope was soon found to pronounce the
genuineness of the relic.   N vertheless the fact was long and malevolently disputed by rival impostors.

And though the respectable fugitives found an asylum at Rome, where the discipline was perpetuated in security during that long period of persecution, others were less fortunate; and even in those which escaped destruction a more relaxed observance naturally gained ground, in the midst of universal licentiousness. Accordingly we learn, that, towards the end of the eighth century, the order of St. Benedict had so far degenerated from its pristine purity, that a thorough reform, if not an entire reconstruction, of the system was deemed necessary for the dignity and welfare of the Church.

The individual to whom this honourable office was destined was also named Benedict; he was descended from a powerful Gothic family, and a native of Aniane in the diocese of Montpellier. Born about the year 750, he devoted his early life to religious austerities, exceeding not only the practice of his brethren, but the instruction of the founder. The Rule of St. Benedict was formed, in his opinion, for invalids and novices; and he strove to regulate his discipline after the sublimer models of Basil and Pachomius. Presently he was chosen to preside over his monastery; but in disgust, as is reported, at the inadequate practice of his subjects, he retired to Aniane, and there laid the foundation of a new and more rigid institution. The people reverenced his sanctity and crowded to his cell; the native nobles assisted him in the construction of a magnificent edifice; and endowments of land were soon conferred upon the humble Reformer of Aniane. Moreover, as he enhanced the fame of his austerities by the practice of charity and universal benevolence *, his venerable name deserved the celebrity which it so rapidly acquired. His ascetic disciples were eagerly sought after by other monasteries, as models and instruments for the restoration of discipline; and as the policy of Charlemagne concurred with the general inclination to improvement, the decaying system was restored and fortified by a bold and effectual reformation.

Marginal note: Benedict of Aniane.

---

* Besides the general mention of his profuse donations to the poor, it is particularly related respecting this Benedict, that whenever an estate was made over to him, he invariably emancipated all the serfs whom he found on it. Act. SS. Benedict., tom. v.

When Benedict of Aniane undertook to establish a system, he found it prudent to relax from that extreme austerity which, as a simple monk, he had both professed and practised. As his youthful enthusiasm abated, he became gradually convinced that the rule of the Nursian hermit was as severe as the common infirmities of human nature could endure*. He was therefore contented to revive that rule, or rather to enforce its observance; and the part which he peculiarly pressed on the practice of his disciples was the obligation of manual labour. To the neglect of that essential portion of monastic discipline the successive corruptions of the system are with truth attributed; and the regulations which were adopted by Benedict were confirmed (in 817) by the council of Aix-la-Chapelle. From this epoch† we may date the renovation of the Benedictine order; and though, even in that age, it was grown, perhaps, too rich to adhere very closely to its ancient observance, yet the sons whom it nourished may, nevertheless, be accounted, without any exaggeration of their merits, among the most industrious, the most learned, and the most pious of their own generation.

It is not our intention to trace the numberless branches‡ which sprang from the stem of St. Benedict, and overshadowed

* The duty of silence was very generally enjoined in monastic institutions. In the rule of " The Brethren of the Holy Trinity," established by Innocent III., we observe for instance—" Silentium observent semper in Ecclesia sua, semper in Refectorio, semper in Dormitorio,"—and even on the most necessary occasions for conversation, the monks were instructed to speak " remissa voce, humiliter, et honeste."—See Dugdale, vol. ii. p. 830.

† It would not appear that these changes very much influenced the condition of monachism in England. The three great reformations in that system which took place in our Church were, (1.) that of Archbishop Cuthbert, in the year 747; (2.) that of Dunstan, in 965, promulgated in the council of Winchester, on which occasion the general constitution, entitled Regula Concordiæ Anglicæ Nationis, was for the first time prescribed. It was founded partly on the rule of St. Benedict, partly on ancient customs. (3.) That of Lanfranc, in 1075, authorised by the council of London, and founded on the same principle as the second. . . Mabillon, a zealous advocate and an acute critic, sufficiently shows from John the Deacon, (who wrote the Life of Gregory the Great in 875,) that the rule of St. Benedict was received in England before the second of those reformations. Our allusions to the ecclesiastical history of England are thus rare and incidental, because that Church is intended, we believe, to form the subject of a separate work.

‡ Such as the Camaldulenses, Sylvestrini, Grandimontenses, Præmonstratenses, the monks of Vallombrosa, and a multitude of others.

the surface of Europe. But there are three at least among them, which, by their frequent mention in ecclesiastical history, demand a separate notice,—the order of Cluni, the Cistercian order, and that of the Chartreux. The monastery of Corbie, also of great renown, was founded by Charlemagne for the spiritual subjugation of Saxony; but it is no other way distinguished from the regular Benedictine institutions than by its greater celebrity.

During the ninth century, the rapid incursions of the Nor- *The order* mans, and the downward progress of corruption, once more *of Cluni,* *900 A.D.* reduced the level of monastic sanctity; and a fresh impulse became necessary to restore the excellence and save the reputation of the system. The method of reformation was, on this occasion, somewhat different from that previously adopted. A separate order was established, derived, indeed, immediately from the stock of St. Benedict, yet claiming, as it were, a specific distinction and character—it was the order of Cluni. It was founded about the year 900, in the district of Mâcon, in Burgundy, by William, duke of Aquitaine; but the praise of perfecting it is rather due to the abbot, St. Odo. It commenced, as usual, by a strict imitation of ancient excellence, a rigid profession of poverty, of industry, and of piety; and it declined, according to the usual course of human institutions, through wealth, into indolence and luxury. In the space of about two centuries, it fell into obscurity; and after the name of Peter the Venerable (the contemporary of St. Bernard), no eminent ecclesiastic is mentioned as having issued from its discipline. Besides the riches which had rewarded and spoiled its original purity, another cause is mentioned as having contributed to its decline—the corruption of the simple rule of St. Benedict by the multiplication of vocal prayers, and the substitution of new offices and ceremonies for the manual labour of former days. The ill effect of that change was indeed admitted by the venerable abbot in his answer to St. Bernard.

But in the mean time, during the long period of its prosperity, the order of Cluni had reached the highest point of honourable reputation; insomuch that, during the eleventh

century, a bishop of Ostia (the future Urban II.) being
officially present at a council in Germany, suppressed in his
signature his episcopal dignity, and thought that he adopted a
prouder title when he subscribed himself " *monk of Cluni,* and
legate of Pope Gregory*." Those two names were well associated; for it was indeed within the walls of Cluni that Hildebrand fed his youthful spirit on those dreams of universal
dominion which he afterwards attempted to realize: it was
there, too, that he may have meditated those vast crusading
projects which were accomplished by Urban his disciple. But
however that may be, the cloister from which he had emerged
to change the destinies of Christendom, and the discipline
which had formed him (as some might think) to such generous
enterprises, acquired a reflected splendour from his celebrity;
and since the same institution was also praised for its zealous
and active orthodoxy and its devotion to the throne of St. Peter,
shall we wonder that it flourished far and wide in power and
opulence, and that it numbered, in the following age, above
two thousand monasteries, which followed its appointed rule
and its adopted principles? Yet is there a sorrowful reflection
which attends the spectacle of this prosperity. Through all
the parade of wealth and dignity, we penetrate the melancholy
truth, that the season of monastic virtue and monastic utility
was passing by, if, indeed, it was not already passed irrevo-
cably; and we remark how rapidly the close embrace of the
pontifical power was converting to evil the rational principles
and pious purposes of the original institution.

The Cis-
tercian
order, 1098
A.D.
Howbeit, we do not read that any flagrant immoralities had
yet disgraced the establishment of Cluni: only it had attained
a degree of sumptuous refinement very far removed from its
first profession. This degeneracy furnished a reason for the
creation of a new and rival community in its neighbourhood.
The Cistercian order was founded in 1098†, and very soon

* See Hist. Litter. de la France, Vie Urban II.
† Anno milleno, centeno, bis minus uno,
Pontifice Urbano, Francorum Rege Philippo,
Burgundis Odone duce et fundamina dante,
Sub Patre Roberto cœpit Cistercius Ordo.—Pagi, Vit. Urban II.,

received the pontifical confirmation. In its origin it success-fully contrasted its laborious poverty and much show of Chris-tian humility with the lordly opulence of Cluni; and in its progress it pursued its predecessor through the accustomed circle of austerity, wealth, and corruption. This institution was peculiarly favoured from its very foundation ; since it pos-sessed, among its earliest treasures, the virtues and celebrity of St. Bernard. One of the first of the Cistercian monks, that venerated ecclesiastic established, in 1115, the dependent abbey of Clairvaux, over which he long presided; and such was his success in propagating the Cistercian order, that he has some-times been erroneously considered as its founder. The zeal of his pupils, aided by the authority of his fame, completed the work transmitted to them; and with so much eagerness were the monasteries of the Citeaux filled and endowed, that before the year 1250 that order yielded nothing, in the number and importance of its dependencies, to its rival of Cluni. Both spread, with almost equal prevalence, over every province in Christendom; and the colonies long continued to acknowledge the supremacy of the mother monastery. But the Citeaux was less fortunate in the duration of its authority and the union of its societies. About the year 1350, some confusion grew up amongst them, arising first from their corruptions, and next from the obstruction of all endeavours to reform them. At the end of that century, they were involved in the grand schism of the Catholic Church, and thus became still further alienated from each other, till at length, about the year 1500, they broke up (first in Spain, and then in Tuscany and Lombardy) into separate and independent establishments.

St. Bruno, with a few companions, established a residence

sect. 73. The date of another celebrated institution, which we have no space to notice, has been similarly (though less artificially) recorded :—

Anno milleno, centeno, bis quoque deno
Sub Patre Norberto Præmonstratensis viget Ordo.

Norbert was archbishop of Magdeburg, and in great repute with Innocent II. The site of the monastery was præmonstrated by a vision—hence the name. The rule was that of St. Augustine; the brethren were confirmed by Calixtus II., under the designation of Canonici Regulares Exempti; and they spread to the extremities of the East and the West,—Hospin., lib, v, c, xii.

at the Chartreuse in the summer of 1084: the usual duties of labour, temperance, and prayer were enjoined with more, perhaps, than the usual severity *. But this community did not immediately rise into any great eminence; it was long governed by priors, subject to the bishop of Grenoble; and its founder died (in 1101) in a Calabrian monastery. Nearly fifty years after its foundation, its statutes were written by a prior named Guignes †, who presided over it for eighteen years. By the faithful observance of those statutes, though in its commencement far outstripped by its Cistercian competitors, it gradually rose into honourable notoriety; and at length, about the year 1178, its rule was sanctioned by the approbation of Alexander III. From this event, its existence as a separate order in the Church is properly to be dated; and henceforward it went forth from its wild and desolate birth-place, and spread its fruitful branches over the gardens and vineyards of Europe. The rise of the Chartreux gave fresh cause for emulation to their brethren of older establishment: and the rivalry thus excited and maintained by these repeated innovations, if it caused much professional jealousy, and doubtless some personal animosity, furnished the only resource by which the monastic system could have been brought to preserve even the semblance

---

* The earliest Cistercians, under Alberic, who died in 1109, affected a rigid imitation of the rule of St. Benedict. They refused all donations of Churches and altars, oblations and tithes. It appeared not (they said) that in the ancient quadripartite division the monasteries had any share—for this reason, that they had lands and cattle, whence they could live by work. They avoided cities and populous districts, but professed their willingness to accept the endowment of any remote or waste lands, or of vineyards, meadows, woods, waters (for mills and fishing), as well as horses and cattle. Their only addition to the old rule was that of lay brothers and hired servants—*frères convers laiques.*

† Fleury, H. E. l. 67, s. 58. From these statutes it appears, that from September to Easter the monks were allowed only one meal a day; that they drank no pure wine; that fish might not be purchased except for the sick; that no superfluous gold or silver was permitted at the service of the altar; that the use of medicine was discouraged; but that, to compensate for that prohibition, the monks were bled five times a year. It is proper to add, that during the same period they were permitted to shave only six times.

Some statutes of this order are given by Dugdale, Monast. vol. i. p. 951. Among them we observe a strict injunction to manual labour:—

Nunc lege, nunc ora, nunc cum fervore labora;
Sic erit hora brevis, et labor ille levis.

of its original practice. Still it should be remarked that these successive additions to the fraternity implied no contempt of the institutions of antiquity: they made no profession of novelty or of any improvement upon pristine observances; on the contrary, the more modern orders all claimed, as they respectively started into existence, the authority and the name of St. Benedict. The monk of Cluni, the Cistercian, the Carthusian, were alike Benedictines; and the more rigid the reform which they severally boasted to introduce, and the nearer their approximation to the earliest practice, the better were their pretensions founded to a legitimate descent from the Western patriarch.

The rules of the reformed orders invariably inculcated the performance of manual labour; and the neglect of that injunction invariably led to their corruption. But an alteration had been effected in the general constitution of the body, which alone precluded any faithful emulation of the immediate disciples of St. Benedict. As late as the eleventh age the monks, who were for the most part laymen, performed all the servile offices of the establishment with their own hands. But in the year 1040, St. John of Gualbert introduced into his monastery of Vallombrosa a distinction which was fatal to the integrity of the former discipline. He divided those of his obedience into two classes—lay brethren and brethren of the choir; and while the spiritual and intellectual duties of the institution were more particularly enjoined to the latter, the whole bodily labour, whether domestic or agricultural, was imposed upon their lay associates*. Thenceforward the monks (for the higher class began to appropriate that name) became entirely composed either of clerks or of persons destined for holy orders; the religious offices were celebrated and chiefly attended by them, while the servant was commanded to repeat his *pater* without suspending his work, and presented with a chaplet for the numbering of the canonical hours. A reason was advanced for this change; and had not a much stronger been afforded

Institution of lay brethren.

* In the Ordres Monastiques, p. iv. c. 18, two sorts of laymen are mentioned as living in French monasteries: (1.) such as gave themselves over as slaves to the establishment, and were called Oblats or Donnés: (2.) such as were recommended for support to monasteries of royal foundation by the king. But neither of these classes were, properly speaking, lay brethren.

by the inordinate accumulation of wealth, it might have seemed, perhaps, not unsatisfactory.   In earlier ages, Latin, the language of prayer, was also the vulgar tongue of all Western Christians; but as that grew into disuse, and became the object of study, instead of the vehicle of conversation, the greater part of the laity were unable to comprehend the offices of the Church.   Accordingly, it was deemed necessary to distinguish between the educated and the wholly illiterate brethren; and in pursuance of the principle which then prevailed, of confining all learning to the sacred profession, the former were raised to the enjoyment of leisure and authority, the latter condemned to ignorance and servitude.   This distinction, being earlier than the foundation of the Cistercian, Carthusian, and all subsequent orders, was admitted at once into their original constitution; and therefore, however closely they might affect to imitate the most ancient models, there existed, from the very commencement, one essential peculiarity in which they deviated from it.

Papal exemptions. According to the oldest practice, every monastery was governed by an abbot, chosen by the monks from their own body, and ordained and instituted by the bishop of the diocess. To the superintending authority of the same the abbot was also subject; and thus abuses and contentions were readily repressed by the presence of a resident inspector.   But when, in the progress of papal usurpation, those establishments were *exempted* from episcopal jurisdiction, and placed under the exclusive regulation of the Vatican, the facilities for corruption were multiplied; and a number of evils were created which escaped the observation or correction of a distant and indulgent master. At the same time, the effect of this connexion was to infuse an entirely new spirit into the monastic system.   Avarice, and especially ambition, took the place of those pious motives which certainly predominated in earlier days.   The inmates of the cloister were associated in the grand schemes of the pontifical policy; they became its necessary and most obsequious instruments; they were exalted by its success,—they were stained by its vices: and the successive reformations, which professed to renovate the declining fabric, were only vain

attempts to restore its ancient character. They could at best
only expect to repair its outward front, and replace the symbols of its former sanctity; the spirit, by which it had been
really blessed and consecrated, was already departed from it.

Great complaints respecting monastic corruption were
uttered both at the Council of Paris in 1812, and the fourth of
Lateran, which met three years afterwards. But, though some
vigorous attempts were, on both those occasions, made to repress it, the counteracting causes were too powerful; and the
evil continued to extend and become more poisonous during
the times which followed. It is singular that, at the second of
those councils, it was proclaimed as a great evil in the system,
that new orders were too commonly established, and the forms
of monasticism multiplied with a dangerous fertility; and
therefore, " lest their too great diversity should introduce confusion into the Church," it was enacted that their future creation should be discouraged. This is considered by some
Catholic writers to have been a provident regulation; since the
jealousy among the rival congregations had by this time degenerated from pious emulation (if it ever possessed that character) into a mere conflict of evil passions. But whatever may
have been the policy of the statute, it was at least treated in the
observance with such peculiar contempt, that the institution of
the Mendicants, the boldest of all the innovations in the annals
of monachism, took place almost immediately afterwards.

SECTION III.

Canons Regular and Secular.

THE order of monks was originally so widely distinct from
that of clerks, that there were seldom found more than one or
two ecclesiastics in any ancient convent. But presently, in the
growing prevalence of the monastic life, persons ordained, or
destined to the sacred profession, formed societies on similar
principles; and as they were bound, though with less severity,
by certain fixed canons, they were called, in process of time,

Canonici*. The bishop of the diocese was their abbot and president. It is recorded that St. Augustine set the example of living with his clergy in one society, with community of property, according to the canons of the Church; but he prescribed to them no vow, nor any other statutes for their observance, except such instructions as are found in his 109th Epistle †. Nevertheless, above a hundred and fifty religious congregations have in succeeding ages professed his rule and claimed his parentage, and assumed, with such slight pretensions, the authority of his venerable name. The true origin of the order is a subject of much uncertainty. Onuphrius, in his letter to Platina, asserts that it was instituted by Gelasius at Rome, about 495‡, and that it passed hence into other Churches; and Dugdale appears to acquiesce in this opinion. It is, moreover, certain, that Chrodegangus, Bishop of Metz, prescribed a rule, about the year 750, to the canons of his own reformation; and that he made some efforts, though not perhaps very effectually, to extend it more widely. Still some are not persuaded that societies of clerks were subject to one specified form of discipline, till the Council of Aix-la-Chapelle §, under the direction of Louis le Debonnaire, confirmed and completed the previous enactments of Mayence (in 813), and imposed on them one general and perpetual rule.

The plausible principle on which the order of canons was

---

* The term Canon originally included not only all professors of the monastic life, but the very Hierodules and inferior officers of the Church. Mosheim (on the authority of Le Bœuf, Mémoires sur l'Histoire d'Auxerre, vol. i. p. 174) asserts that it became peculiar to clerical monks (Fratres Dominici) soon after the middle of the eighth century. But we should rather collect from the " Histoire des Ordres Monastiques," that the distinction was not generally established till the eleventh age.

† It should be observed, that this epistle, which is cited by ecclesiastical writers as containing instructions for an institution of Canons, was in fact addressed to a convent of refractory nuns, who had quarrelled with their Abbess, and exhibited some unbecoming violence in the dispute.

‡ See Dugdale, De Canonorum Ordinis Origine. There may be found the Rule which St. Augustine is *said* to have prescribed.

§ The rule here published was borrowed, in many particulars, from that of St. Benedict; but the order still retained the name and banners of St. Augustine.—Hist. des Ordres Monastiques.

founded, to withdraw from the contagion of the world those who had peculiarly devoted themselves to the service of God, was found insufficient to preserve them from degeneracy. A division was early introduced (in Germany, according to Trithemius, and in the year 977), by which the reformed were separated from the unreformed members of the community, in name as well as in deed. The former, from their return to the original rule, assumed the appellation of Canons-Regular; the latter, who adhered to the abuse, were termed, in contradistinction, Canons-Secular; and this sort of schism extended to other countries, and became permanent in many.

The discipline of the regular canons was more seriously enforced by Nicholas II. in the year 1059; and about eighty years later, Innocent II. subjected them to the additional obligation of a vow; for they seem hitherto to have been exempt from such profession. Nevertheless, in the course of the two following centuries, they once more relapsed into such abandoned licentiousness, as to require an entire reconstruction from Benedict XII. After that period, they rose into more consideration than in their earlier history they appear to have attained.

There were besides some other orders, both military and mendicant, which professed the rule, or rather the name, of St. Augustine—the Hospitallers, for instance, the Teutonic Knights, and the Hermits of St. Augustine. But they will be mentioned under those heads where we have thought it more convenient to place them, than to follow in this matter the perplexed method of the " Historian of the Monastic Orders."

SECTION IV.

On the Military Orders.

WE have thus shortly mentioned the three grand religious Orders, which have been diversified by so many names and rules, and regenerated by so many reforms; which began in austerity, and yet fell into the most shameless debauchery; which arose in piety, and passed into wicked and lying super-

stition; which originated in poverty, and finally fattened on
the credulity of the faithful, so as to spread their solid territorial acquisitions from one end of Christendom to the other.
Founded on the genuine monastic principle of devout seclusion,
so venerable to the ignorant and the vulgar, they presently
surpassed the secular clergy in the reputation of sanctity, and
in popular influence.   Thus were they soon recommended to
the Bishop of Rome ; and in his ambition to exalt himself
above his brother prelates, he discovered an efficient and willing instrument in the regular establishments.   At an early
period, he granted them protection, and patronage, and property, with the means of augmenting it : presently, he accorded
to certain monasteries exemption from the episcopal authority ;
and in process of time he extended that privilege to almost all.
Thus he gradually constituted himself sole visitor, legislator,
and guardian of the numberless religious institutions which
covered the Christian world.   The monks repaid these services
by the most implicit obedience—for obedience was that of their
three vows which they continued to respect the longest—and to
their aid and influence may generally be ascribed the triumphs
of the pontiff in his disputes with the secular clergy.   In his
contests with the State they were not less necessary to his
cause ; for, as his success in those struggles usually depended
on the divisions which he was enabled to sow among the subjects of his enemy, and the strength of the party which he
could thus create, so the monks, in every nation in Europe,
were his most powerful agents for that purpose.   And thus,
when we consider the victory, which the spiritual sometimes
obtained over the temporal power, as a mere triumph of opinion
over arms and physical force, we do indeed, at the bottom, consider it rightly ; but our surprise at the result is much diminished, when we reflect how extensive a control over men's
minds was everywhere possessed by the religious orders,—how
fearlessly and unsparingly they exercised that control, and
with what persevering zeal it was directed to the support and
aggrandizement of papal power.

The Benedictines and Augustinians were the standing army
of the Vatican, and they fought in spiritual battles with con-

stancy and success for nearly six centuries.   The first addition
which was made to them was that of the military orders; and
this proceeded not from any sense of the insufficiency of the
veteran establishment, nor from any distrust in them, but from
circumstances wholly independent of those or any such causes.
They arose in the agitation of the crusades, and they were
nourished by the sort of spirit which first created those expeditions, and then caught from them some additional fury.

The union of the military with the ecclesiastical character
was become common, in spite of repeated prohibitions, among
all ranks of the clergy.   It was exercised by the vices of the
feudal system; which had given them wealth in enviable profusion, but which provided by no sufficient laws or strength of
government for the protection of that which it had bestowed—
so that force was necessary to defend what had been lavished
by superstition.   The warlike habits which ecclesiastics seem
really to have first acquired in the defence of their property,
were presently carried forth by them into distant and offensive
campaigns, and exhibited in voluntary feats of arms, to which
loyalty did not oblige them, and for which loyalty itself furnished a very insufficient pretext.   But these general excesses
did not give birth to any distinct order professing to unite religious vows with the exercise of arms; and even the first of
those, which did afterwards make such profession, was in its
origin a pacific and charitable institution.

This was the Order of St. John of Jerusalem, or the Knights *Knights of the Hospital.*
of the Hospital.   About the year 1050, at the wish of some
merchants of Amalfi trading with Syria, a Latin Church had
been erected at Jerusalem, to which a hospital was presently
added, with a chapel dedicated to the Baptist.   When Godfrey
de Bouillon took the city in 1099, he endowed the hospital : it
then assumed the form of a new religious order, and immediately received confirmation from Rome, with a rule for its
observance*.   The revenues were soon found to exceed the
necessities of the establishment; and it was then that the grand

* The rule of the Hospitallers (as confirmed by Boniface) may be found in
Dugdale's Monasticon, vol. ii. p. 493.

master changed its principle and design by the infusion of the military character.

The Knights of the Hospital were distinguished by three gradations. The first in dignity were the noble and military; the second were ecclesiastical, superintending the original objects of the institution; the third consisted of the " Serving Brethren," whose duties also were chiefly military. To the ordinary vows of poverty, chastity, and obedience, they added the obligations of charity, fasting, and penitence : and, whatsoever laxity they may have admitted in the observance of them, they unquestionably derived from that profession some real virtues which were not shared by the fanatics who surrounded them; and they softened the savage features of religious warfare with some faint shades of unwonted humanity. So long as their residence was Jerusalem, they retained the peaceful name of Hospitallers; but they were subsequently better known by the successive appellations of Knights of Rhodes and of Malta. Faithful at least to one of the objects of their institution, they valiantly defended the outworks of Christendom against the progress of the invading Mussulman, and never sullied their arms by the massacre of Pagans or heretics.

Knights Templars.

The Knights Templars received their name from their residence in the immediate neighbourhood of the Temple at Jerusalem. The foundations of this order were laid in the year 1118; and the rule to which it was afterwards subjected was from the pen of St. Bernard. This institution, both in its original purpose and prescribed duties, was exclusively military. —To extend the boundaries of Christendom, to preserve the internal tranquillity of Palestine, to secure the public roads from robbers and outlaws *, to protect the devout on their pilgrimage to the holy places—such were the peculiar offices of the Templar. They were discharged with fearlessness and

---

* An order, with a somewhat similar object, was founded in France about the year 1233, called the Order of the Glorious Virgin Mary. It was confined to young men of family, who associated themselves, under the title of Les Frères Joyeux, for the defence of the injured, and the preservation of public tranquillity. They took vows of obedience and *conjugal* chastity, and solemnly pledged themselves to the protection of widows and orphans.

rewarded by renown.   Renown was followed by the most abundant opulence.   Corruption came in its train; and on their final expulsion from Palestine, they carried back with them to Europe much of the wild unbridled license, which had been familiar to them in the East.   But their unhappy fate, as it is connected with one of the most important periods in papal history, must be reserved for more particular mention in its proper place.

The Teutonic, or German Order, had its origin again in the offices of charity.   During the siege of Acre, a hospital was erected for the reception of the sick and wounded.   This establishment survived the occasion which created it; and, to confirm its character and its permanency, it obtained a rule (in 1192) from Celestine III., and a place among the "Orders Hospitable and Military."   On the termination of the Crusades, those knights returned to Germany*, where they enjoyed considerable possessions; and soon afterwards, by a deviation from the purpose of their institution, which might seem slight perhaps in a superstitious age, they turned their consecrated arms to the *conversion* of Prussia.

The Teutonic Order.

That country, and the contiguous Pomerania, had hitherto resisted the peaceful exertions of successive missionaries, and continued to worship the rude deities, and follow the barbarous manners of antiquity.   But where the language of persuasion had been employed in vain, the disciplined valour of the Teutonic Knights prevailed: it was recompensed by the conquest of two rich provinces; and the faith which was inflicted upon the vanquished in the rage of massacre, was perpetuated under the deliberate oppression of military government.   This event took place about the year 1230; but in another generation, when the memory of its introduction was effaced, the religion really took root and flourished, by the sure and legitimate authority of its excellence and its truth.   After that celebrated

---

* In the treaty between the empire and the popedom in 1230, we find that the interests of the three military orders were expressly stipulated for by the pope; and also, that certain places were held in sequestration by Herman, Master of the Teutonic Order, until the emperor should have fulfilled his part of the engagement. Fleury, i. 79. s. 64.

exploit, the Teutonic Order continued to subsist in great estimation with the Church; and this patronage was repaid with
persevering fidelity, until at length, when they perceived the
grand consummation approaching, the holy knights generally
deserted that tottering fortress, and arrayed their rebellious
host under the banners of Luther.

Section V.

The Mendicant, or Preaching Orders.

UNTIL the end of the twelfth century the exertions of the Popes
were almost entirely confined to the establishment of their own
supremacy in the Church, and of their temporal authority over
the State; and, through the faithful subservience of the two
ancient orders, they had obtained surprising success in both
undertakings. But the increasing light of the eleventh and
twelfth ages, and the increasing deformities of the Church,
brought into existence a number of heresies, occasioning dissensions, such as had not divided Christians since the Arian
controversy. These moreover presented themselves not with
one form, and one front, and one neck, but were scattered
under a multitude of denominations, throughout all provinces,
and among all ranks. The secular clergy, relaxed by habitual
indolence and occasional immoralities, rather gave cause to
this disaffection than subdued it; and the regular orders,
become sluggish from wealth and indulgence, wanted the
activity, perhaps the zeal, which was required of them. To
detect the latent error, to pursue it into its secret holds, to
drag it forth and consign it to the minister of temporal vengeance, was an office beyond the energy of their luxuriousness;
still less did they possess the talents and the learning to con-
fute and confound it. Wherefore, as the experience of some
centuries had now proved, that the existing orders, how often
soever and completely reformed and reproduced, had an immediate tendency to subside again into degeneracy and decay,
it seemed expedient to introduce some entirely different organization into the imperfect system.

The first notion of the new institution * was given by that St. Do-
body of ecclesiastics who were commissioned by Innocent III. minic.
to convert the Albigeois; and among these the most distinguished was St. Dominic. That favourite champion of the
Roman Church, the falsely-reputed inventor of inquisitorial
torture, was a Spaniard of a noble family and of the order of
Canons-Regular. In his spiritual campaigns (it were well had
they been no more than spiritual) against the heretics of Languedoc, he became eminent by an eloquence which always
inflamed and sometimes persuaded; and having felt the power
of that faculty, which through the space of thirteen centuries
had so rarely revisited the Roman empire, he became desirous
to establish a fraternity devoted to its exercise. His project
was not discouraged by Innocent III.; but that pontiff hesitated to give the formal sanction necessary to constitute a new
order: since the Council of Lateran, acting according to his
discretion, had pronounced it generally expedient to reform
existing institutions, rather than to augment their number.
But immediately after the death of that pope, Dominic was
established in the privileges of a " Founder," by the bull of
Honorius III. †

Contemporary with St. Dominic was his great compeer in St. Francis.
ecclesiastical celebrity, the father of the rival institution.
St. Francis was a native of Asisi in Umbria, without rank,
without letters, but of an ardent and enthusiastic temperament.
It is asserted—perhaps untruly—that his earlier age was consumed in profligacy, from which he was awakened by an opportune sickness, occasioned by his vices; and that his fears

* Hospinian's Sixth Book comprehends a quantity of valuable matter on the
subject of the Mendicants; and chapters iv. v. and vi. should particularly be
consulted. The author is laborious and learned, but not impartial. In the zeal
of the Protestant he has forgotten the moderation of the historian, and (might
we not sometimes add ?) the charity of the Christian.

† Fleury asserts, that the Frères Prêcheurs at first were not so much a new
order, as a new congregation of the Canons-Regular; since it was only at a
Chapter General held in 1220, that St. Dominic and his disciples embraced entire
poverty and mendicity. This may be so—but at any rate their original condition
was so extremely transient and destitute of all effects and characteristics, as to be
wholly insignificant in history.

suddenly impelled him into the opposite extreme of superstitious * austerity.   It is certain, that, as he inculcated by his
preaching, so he recommended by his example, the utmost
rigour of the primitive monastic principle,—" that there was
no safe path to heaven, unless by the destitution of all earthly
possessions." Popularity was the first reward of his humiliation :
he was soon followed by a crowd of imitators ; and the motive,
which probably was pure fanaticism in himself, might be want,
or vanity, or even avarice †, in his disciples.   Howbeit they
readily acquired an extensive reputation for sanctity ; and in
the year 1210 the formal protection of Innocent was vouchsafed
to the new order.

Character-
istics of the
Dominican
and Fran-
ciscan
Orders.

It appears probable that the foundation of the Franciscan
Order was laid in poverty only—not merely unaccompanied by
any obligation of a missionary or predicatory character, but
likewise free from the vow of mendicity.   St. Francis himself,
in the " Testament " which he left for the instruction of his
followers, enjoined manual labour in preference to beggary ;
though he permitted them, in case of great distress, to have
recourse to the table of the Lord, begging alms from door to
door‡.   It should be mentioned, too, that he at the same time

* The story of the Stigmata, or wounds of Christ, miraculously impressed upon
his body, is known to all.   The text on which this imposture was founded (for it
pleaded a text) was Epist. Gelat. end.   " From henceforth let no man trouble me ;
for I bear in my body the marks of the Lord Jesus." We read in Semler, ann.
1222, that a rustic, who made the same experiment on human credulity at about
the same time, was imprisoned for life—felicius cessit Francisco, sec. xiii. cap. iii.

† Giannone, an impartial writer, thus begins a section (lib. xix. cap. v. sec. v.)
entitled " Monaci e Beni Temporali."   " Henceforward we shall place together
the subjects of ' Monks' and 'Temporalities ; ' since, as we have already observed, that he who pronounces ' Monachism' (Religione) pronounces ' Riches,'
so the monks were now become incomparably more expert in the acquisition of
wealth than all the other ecclesiastics ; and the monasteries in these days reaped
profits to which those made by the Churches bore no proportion—so that the
expressions ' New Orders' and ' New Riches,' became, properly speaking,
synonymous.   And this was the more monstrous, because it was in despite of
their foundation in mendicity (whence they had the name of Mendicants) that
their acquisitions and treasures were enormous."—Polit. Eccles. del decimo terzo
secolo.

‡ Fleury, Dissertat. 8me.   St. Francis designated his disciples by the name
Fraterculi—Little Brothers ; and this became, in different languages, Fratricelli,
Fratres Minores, Frères Mineurs, Friars Minors.

prohibited them from applying to the pope for any privilege whatever. But the sophistical and contentious spirit of the age precluded that simplicity. And their founder was scarcely consigned to the grave, when his disciples obtained from Gregory IX.* a bull, which released them from the observance of his Testament, and placed an arbitrary interpretation on many particulars of his rule. It was thus that the necessity of labour was superseded, and honour and sanctity were preposterously attached to the profession of mendicity.

Here then we observe the first point of distinction in the first constitution of the two orders. The Dominicans were, in their earliest character, a society of itinerant preachers—this was the whole of their profession—they were not bound, as it would seem, by any vow of poverty. But after a short space, when their founder had possibly observed that the Franciscans prospered well under that vow—that without possessing any thing they abounded with many things†—he thought it desirable to imitate such profitable self-denial: accordingly, he also imposed upon his disciples the obligation of poverty.

Again: when the Franciscans discovered that no little influence accrued to their rivals from the office of public preaching, they also betook themselves to that practice; and, perhaps, with almost equal success. Thus it came to pass, that, after a very few years, two orders, essentially different in their original, were very nearly assimilated in character, and even in profession, and entered upon the same career with almost the same objects and the same principles.

Nevertheless, in the features of their policy and the character of their ecclesiastical influence, they continued to be distinguished Their contentions.

* This pope was at the same time a great patron of the rival order. In 1231 he wrote a letter to the Archbishop of Sorrento, in order to introduce the Dominicans to his patronage, in these terms:—"Dilectos Filios Fratres Ordinis Predicatorum velut novos Vinitores suæ vineæ suscitavit; qui, non sua sed quæ sunt Jesu Christi quærentes, tam contra profligandas hæreses, quam pestes alias mortiferas extirpandas se dedicârunt evangelizationi Verbi Dei, in abjectione voluntariæ paupertatis." The passage is cited by Giannone.

† We read, in the "Histoire des Ordres Monastiques," of Franciscan monasteries of very early foundation—residences inconsistent with the perpetual practice of beggary. But those mansions were probably the first profits of the trade, the first-fruits of the violation of the vow.

by many important diversities. The whole course of their history is more or less strongly marked by these. And if many of them were occasioned (as is unquestionably true) by the passionate jealousy which they bore to each other, and which they displayed upon all occasions, to the great scandal and injury of the Church, it is equally certain, that the difference in their first constitution ever contributed to cause a difference in their destinies. The original vow and rule of St. Francis was at no time perfectly erased from the memory of his followers. Attempts were soon made to revive it in its native austerity; and thus, in addition to the general contention with the rival order, the most violent intestine dissensions were introduced into the family of that saint, which terminated in permanent alienation and schism.

Again: another evil was brought upon the Church by these disputes—sharpened as they also were by the scholastic subtleties which in those days perverted reason. The authority of the Pope interposed to set them at rest, but his interference produced the opposite effect *: it not only increased the animosity of both parties, but also raised up a powerful branch of the fraternity in avowed opposition to the pontifical supremacy. In the controversy in which these "indocile" brethren engaged during the fourteenth age, against John XXII., they proceeded so far in rebellious audacity as formally to pass the sentence of heresy upon the Vicar of Christ, and to abet the efforts of Lewis of Bavaria to depose him! Such (as Fleury has observed) was the termination of their humility—the deposition of a pope! Owing to these internal contests, it has even been made a question with some, whether the institution of the Mendicants has not contributed, upon the whole, to the decline, rather than the advancement of the papal interests. But there is not sufficient reason for such a doubt. The wound which the Roman See may have received from the passionate insubordination of a faction of one of those orders, bears no comparison with the benefits which it has derived from the faithful assi-

* The good and simple pope, St. Celestine, sanctioned the division among the Franciscans by establishing the congregation of the " Poor Hermits."

duity, the learning, the zeal, and the uncompromising devotedness of the other.

If the Dominicans surpassed the rival order in obedience to their common master, they also afforded a better example of internal harmony and discipline. Indeed, as they adhered very closely to the original object of their institution, the destruction of heresy, there was little reason why they should dispute with each other, and the strongest motive for concord with the Holy See. The destruction of heresy they were willing (as we have observed), in the first instance, to accomplish by the sword of the Spirit; but, whether through the natural impatience of bigotry, or because the wisest among them began to suspect the weakness of their own cause, the futility of their sophistry, and the falsehood of their positions, after a very short attempt they abandoned *that* method of conversion, and betook themselves to the material weapon. The secular arm was summoned to their aid, and it became in process of time their favourite, if not their only, instrument.

Nevertheless those are in error who attribute the foundation of the Inquisition, as a fixed and permanent tribunal, to the hand of St. Dominic. It may seem indeed to have been the necessary consequence of his labours, the result to which his principles infallibly tended; and it is true that the administration of its offices was principally delegated to his order. But it was not anywhere formally established until ten or twelve years after his death*. In the mean time, the Dominicans, already trained to the chase, and heated by the scent of blood, eagerly executed the trust which was assigned to them. Over the whole surface of the western world they spread themselves in fierce and keen pursuit; and the distant kingdoms of Spain and Poland were presently afflicted with the same deadly visitation. Rome was the centre of persecution; the heart, to which the circulating poison continually returned—and whence it derived, as it flowed onward, a fresh and perennial supply of virulence and malignity.

The Dominicans, soon after their institution, seem to have

---

* The origin of the Inquisition will be described in Chapter xxi.

Dispute of
the Domin-
icans with
the Uni-
versity of
Paris. appropriated most of the learning then so sparingly distributed among the monastic orders. They applied themselves chiefly to the science of controversy, and soon became very formidable in that field—the more so, since they employed the resources of scholastic ingenuity in the defence of the papal government. The means and the end harmonized well; the prejudices of the age were to a great extent favourable to both; the exertions of reviving reason were perpetually baffled, and her friends discomfited and overthrown. We shall briefly notice one signal campaign of the Dominicans—that which they carried on for above thirty years against the University of Paris. That body, which was already the most eminent in Europe, thought it expedient, in the year 1228, to confine the Dominicans, in common with all other religious orders, to the possession of one of its theological classes, while those Mendicants warmly asserted their claim to two. Many violent contentions arose from this difference, and continued till the year 1255, with no decisive result: the matter was then referred to the wisdom of Pope Alexander IV. It is not difficult to anticipate the response of the Vatican. The University received an unqualified injunction to throw open to the Dominicans, not two classes only, but as many chairs and dignities as it might seem good to them to occupy. For four years the refractory doctors resisted the execution of the sentence with a boldness worthy of a better age and a happier result. At length, terrified by the repeated menaces of the pontiff, they submitted. Nevertheless, the struggle had not been without its benefit. During the course of a protracted controversy, subjects had been handled of higher and more general importance, than the right of lecturing in the schools of Paris. While the discipline and principles of the Mendicants were examined and assailed, the power which upheld them did not escape from public reprehension. The possibility of error *even in the Church itself* was openly maintained; and the spirit of learning, which had hitherto ministered to ecclesiastical oppression, was at length aroused against it. The first efforts of the best principles are generally baffled and disappointed; but the example which they leave does not perish; it only waits till the concurrence

of happier circumstances may bring the season for more successful imitation.

In the conduct of this dispute, as both parties became equally heated, the limits of reason were exceeded, with almost equal temerity, by both. Among many laborious productions, perhaps the most celebrated was that published by Guilliaume de St. Amour, a powerful champion of the University, "Concerning the Perils of the Latter Times." The peculiarity which has recommended it to our notice is this. It was founded on the belief that the passage of St Paul relating to "the perilous times which were to come in the last days," was fulfilled by the establishment of the Mendicants ! . . . Every age has affixed its own interpretation to that text, and all have been successively deceived; and this might teach us some caution in wresting the mysterious oracles of God from their eternal destination to serve the partial views—to aid the transient, and perhaps passionate, purposes of the moment. Yet is there an undue value almost indissolubly attached, even by the calmest minds, to passing occurrences: however trivial and fugitive their character, they are magnified by close inspection, so as to exceed the mightiest events farther removed in time; and it is this, our almost insuperable inability to reduce present occurrences to their real dimensions—to place them at a distance, and examine them side by side along with the transactions of former days—to consider them, in short, disinterestedly and *historically*—it is this cause which has begotten, and which still begets, many foolish opinions in minds not destitute of reason; and which, among other fruits, has so frequently reproduced, and in so many shapes, the pitiable enthusiasm of the Millennarians.

Though both Dominicans and Franciscans professed to be at the same time mendicants and preachers, yet, in some sort of conformity with their original rules, the former continued to retain more of the predicatory, the latter more of the mendicant, character. These last were consequently less distinguished by their literary contests, than by those which they waged against each other, respecting the just interpretation of the rule of their founder. In all other monastic institutions, the

Dissensions among the Franciscans.

possession of property was forbidden to individuals, but permitted to the community; whereas the more rigid injunction of St. Francis denied every description of fixed revenues, even to the Societies of his followers.   There were many among those who wished for a relaxation of this rule; and they obtained it without difficulty, both from Gregory IX. and Innocent IV. But another party, who called themselves the Spirituals, insisted on a strict adhesion to the original institution; they even refused to share the glorious title of Franciscan with those who had abandoned it.   This feeling displayed itself with particular vehemence in the year 1247, when John of Parma, a rigid spiritualist, was chosen general of the order.   But the more worldly brethren still adhered to their mitigated discipline; and their perseverance, which was favoured, perhaps, by the secret wishes of many of the opposite party, received the steady and zealous concurrence of the Holy See.   For whatsoever value the popes might attach to the voluntary poverty of their myrmidons,—to the respect which it excited, and the spontaneous generosity which so abundantly relieved it,—they no doubt considered, that it was more important to the permanent interests of the Church to encourage the increase of her fixed and solid and perpetual possessions.

The success of the Dominicans and Franciscans encouraged the profession of beggary; and the face of Christendom was suddenly darkened by a swarm of holy mendicants, in such manner that, about the year 1272, Gregory X. endeavoured to arrest the overgrowing evil.   To this end, he suppressed a great multitude of those authorised vagrants, and distributed the remainder, still very numerous, into four societies—the Dominicans, the Franciscans, the Carmelites, and the hermits of St. Augustine.

The Carmelites.   The order of the Carmelites was, in its origin, oriental and eremitical.   John Phocas, a monk of Patmos, who visited the holy places in 1185, thus concludes the narrative of his pilgrimage:—" On Mount Carmel is the cavern of Elias, where a large monastery once stood, as the remains of buildings attest; but it has been ruined by time and hostile incursions. Some years ago, a hoary-headed monk, who was also a priest, came from Calabria, and established himself in this place, by the revelation of the prophet Elias. He made a little inclosure in the ruins of the monastery, and constructed there a tower and a small church, and assembled about ten brothers, with whom he still inhabits that holy place*." Such appears to be the earliest authentic record of the foundation of the Carmelites. About the year 1209, Albert, patriarch of Jerusalem, gave them a rule. It consisted of sixteen articles, which contain nothing original, and are merely sufficient to prove the ignorance, the abstinence, and the poverty of the original brothers. The institution was not, however, legitimately introduced into the grand monastic family till the year 1226, when it received the sanction of Honorius III. Twelve years afterwards, it was raised from among the regular orders to the more valuable privileges and profits of mendicity; and we observe that the severe rule of its infancy was *interpreted* and mitigated soon afterwards by Innocent IV. Accordingly, it became venerable and popular, and was embraced with the accustomed eagerness in every country in Europe.

A great number of individuals were still found scattered throughout the Western Church, who cherished the name, though they might dispense with the severer duties, of hermits; and they professed a variety of rules by which their several independent societies were governed. Innocent IV. expressed his desire to unite them into one order, and it was executed by his successor. Alexander IV., the better to withdraw them from their seclusion, and engage them in the functions of the ecclesiastical hierarchy †, formed them into a single congregation under one rule and one general, and associated them by the same title of "hermits of St. Augustine." We may observe, however, that as they were the most modern, so they were the least considerable of the mendicant institutions. *[margin: Hermits of St. Augustine.]*

To these four orders the pontiffs granted the exclusive indulgence of travelling through all countries, of conversing with persons of all ranks, and instructing, wheresoever they sojourned,

* We cite the passage from Fleury, lib. lxxvi., sec. 55.
† Giannone, Stor. Nap., lib. xix., cap. v., sec. 5.

246   A HISTORY OF THE CHURCH.   [CH. XIX.

the young and the ignorant. This commission was presently extended to preaching in the churches and administering the holy sacraments. And so great veneration did they excite by the sanctity of their appearance, the austerity of their life, and the authoritative humility of their manners, that the people rushed in multitudes to listen to their eloquence, and to crave their benediction. And thus the spirit of sacerdotal despotism which had been chilled through the indecency or negligence of the secular clergy, and the luxurious languor of the regular establishments, was for a season revived and restored to an authority, in its extent more ample, and in its exercise far more unsparing, than it had possessed at any preceding period.

Early merits and degeneracy of the Mendicants. In their early years, the two great nurseries of the Dominicans were Paris and Bologna. In those cities, Jourdain, the general of the order, and successor of its founder, alternately passed the season of Lent; and thence he sent forth his emissaries through the South and the West. Among the first converts to the discipline of St. Dominic were many distinguished by rank and dignity, many eminent ecclesiastics, many learned doctors, both in law and theology, and many young students of noble parentage. Nor is it hard to believe those accounts which praise the rigour of their moral excellence and the general subjection of their carnal appetites to the control of the spirit. The very enthusiasm which at first inflamed them for the purity and beauty of their institution was inconsistent with hypocritical pretensions to piety; it tended, too, somewhat to prolong the exercise of those virtues whence it drew its origin. And thus, if their literary exertions were really stimulated by the highest motives—the glory of God and the salvation of the faithful—they may well have surpassed the languid labours of the old ecclesiastics, which were so commonly directed to mere vulgar and temporal objects. Accordingly, as the Mendicants rose, the ancient orders and the secular clergy fell into disrepute and contempt; and the chairs and the pulpits which they had so long filled were, in a great measure, usurped by more zealous, more laborious, and more popular competitors.

But these conquests were not obtained or preserved without

many violent and obstinate contests*. Both regulars and
seculars defended their ancient privileges with an ardour which
seemed to supply the want of strength.   Their disputes with
each other were for the season laid aside; they united with
equal earnestness against the invader of their common interests; and the rancour thus occasioned, and shared in some
degree, even by the most obscure individuals of both parties,
was far from favourable either to the purity of religion, or to
the honour of the Church: insomuch, that some Roman
Catholic writers have expressed a reasonable doubt whether
the interests of their Church would not have been more effectually consulted by a thorough reformation of the two classes
already consecrated to religion, than by the establishment of a
new order. It is certainly true, that no cause has more scan-
dalized the name of Christ, in every age of his faith, than the
bitter dissensions of his ministers. Their very immoralities
have scarcely been more poisonous in their influence on the
people, than the spectacle of their jealousy and rancour. And
thus, if the ancient zeal and piety could have been revived by
ordinary regulations among the ecclesiastics of the thirteenth
century—had it been possible to infuse into the decrepit the
vigour of the young, into the pampered the virtue of the poor,
—such had, indeed, been the safer method of regeneration. It
appears, however, very questionable whether the popes had
power to accomplish so substantial a reformation in the Church,
even had they been seriously bent on it. It is perfectly certain
that they were not so disposed. The interests of papacy were

---

* The grand dispute in England between the clergy and the Mendicants, in
which the archbishop of Armagh was so prominent, took place about 1357.
The great complaint at that time was, that the latter had seduced all the young
men at the University to confess to them, to enter their order, and to remain
there. And the prelate mentions the remarkable fact, that through the suspicions thus infused into families, the number of students at Oxford had been
reduced during his time from thirty thousand to six thousand. It was made
another matter of reproach on the Mendicants, that they had bought up all the
books, and collected in every convent a large and fine library. The field of contest was transferred to the pontifical court (then at Avignon); the Mendicants
were triumphant, and the archbishop's mission appears to have had no result.
And about the same time two considerable princes, Peter, infant of Aragon, and
Charles, count of Alençon, became members respectively of the Franciscan and
Dominican orders.

now becoming widely different from the interests of the Church, and their policy (though they might not themselves be conscious of the distinction) was steadily directed to the former. With *that* view, the institution of the Mendicants was eminently useful, as it communicated a sort of ubiquity to the pontifical chair. Moreover, the scandals which it occasioned were, in some measure, compensated by the energy to which the old establishments were reluctantly awakened, and which had been more honourable to themselves, and more useful to religion, had it been excited by a less equivocal motive.

One essential characteristic of the Mendicants was the want of any permanent residence; and thus their influence over the people, though at seasons vast and overruling, could not be deeply fixed, or very durable. Again, since they professed absolute poverty, they could scarcely exercise any fearless control over those on whose favour and charity they were dependent for their daily subsistence : so that their popular authority was destitute of those substantial supports which their opponents derived from the possession of opulent establishments, and rested wholly on their talents and virtues. As long as their zeal and their eloquence far surpassed those of the ancient ecclesiastics—as long as the sanctity of their moral practice was beyond reproach or suspicion—so long they deserved and maintained the superiority of their influence. But though the impression thus produced will generally last somewhat longer than the excellence which produces it, still the solid foundation of their power decayed with the decay of their original qualities ; and the wealth which they at length substituted in the place of these reduced them at best to the level of their rivals.

And no long time elapsed from their origin before the reproach of corruption was commonly and justly cast upon them*.

* The evidence of Matthew Paris, an established Benedictine of St. Alban's, may be somewhat coloured by professional jealousy, but nevertheless it is substantially true. In his Henry III., anno 1246, he mentions how, from being preachers, they became confessors, and usurped the other offices of the ordinary. In the same place, he publishes a celebrated bull of Gregory IX. in their favour, and strongly describes the insolence which they derived from it. " Ecclesiarum rectores . . procaciter alloquentes, indulta sibi talia privilegia in propatulo

General complaints arose respecting the multitude of pretexts which they invented for the extortion of money; respecting the vagabond habits, the idleness, and importunity of many among them. It was particularly asserted that, having insinuated themselves into the confidence of families, they took under their special charge the management of wills, and constructed them to their own advantage. They became perpetual attendants on the death-bed of the rich. Moreover, they engaged with intriguing activity in the political transactions of the day, and were entrusted with the conduct of difficult negotiations. The cabinets of princes were not too lofty for their ambition, the secrets of domestic life were not beneath their avarice. Again, it offended the reason of many, that holy persons, professing profound humility and perfect poverty, should appear in the character of magistrates, having apparitors and familiars at their disposal, and all the treasures and all the tortures of the Inquisition. They thus became rich, indeed, and they became powerful; but there were those who did not fail to contrast the contempt of worldly glory, which illustrated the birth of their order, with the pomp which they afterwards assumed

demonstrantes, erecta cervice ea exigentes recitari," &c. . .   He then relates the manner in which they supplanted the clergy in the affections of the people. " Esne professus? Etiam. A quo? A sacerdote meo. Et quis ille idiota? Nunquam theologiam audivit; nunquam in decretis vigilavit; nunquam unam quæstionem didicit enodare. Cæci sunt et duces cæcorum. Ad nos accedite, qui novimus lepram a lepra distinguere . . .   Multi igitur, *præcipue nobiles et nobilium uxores*, spretis propriis sacerdotibus, prædicatoribus confitebantur . . unde non mediocriter viluit ordinariorum dignitas." Matthew Paris then goes on to show the immorality thus introduced; since the people did not feel for the Mendicants any of that awe which their own priests had been accustomed to inspire, and therefore repeated their sins with less scruple. The same author (ad ann. 1235) repeats the complaints of the insolence of the Mendicants, and of the extensive footing which they had already usurped upon the domains of the old establishments.   In another place (ann. 1247) he describes them as the pope's beadles and tax-gatherers. " Utpote fratres minores et predicatores (ut credimus invitos) jam suos fecit Dominus Papa, non sine ordinis eorum læsione et scandalo teloniarios et bedellos." These passages were written within half a century from the foundation of the order. The evidence of the great Franciscan, Buonaventura, and of Thierri d'Apolde, both writers of the same age, is also adduced by Fleury, to prove the early corruption of the Mendicants. Bzovius (ann. 1304, sec. vii.) publishes a long decree of Benedict XI., still further augmenting the privileges of the Mendicants, and exempting them from certain episcopal restraints.

so willingly; and to remark, that through the abandonment of every possession, they possessed everything, and were more opulent in their poverty than the most opulent *. . . Such reflections were obvious to the most illiterate ; and they gradually diminished a popularity which was ill compensated by riches. Howbeit, amid the decline in their reputation and the degeneracy of their principles, from the one grand rule of their ecclesiastical policy they never deviated—they persevered, without any important interruption, in their faithful ministry to the Vatican. But from the time that they parted with their original characteristics, their agency became less useful; and the extravagance with which they sometimes exalted the pretensions of the see, began, in later ages, to excite some disgust among its more moderate and reasonable supporters.

Section VI.

The Establishment of Nuns.

THAT there existed, even in the Antenicene Church, virgins, who made profession of religious chastity, and dedicated themselves to the service of Christ, is clear from the writings of Tertullian, Cyprian, and Eusebius †. But there is no sufficient reason to believe that they were formed into societies ; still less that they constituted any order or congregation. They exer-

* Pietr. delle Vigne (i. Epist. 37). Fleury, lib. lxxxii., sec. 7. The Capucines, a branch of reformed Franciscans, did not arise till the beginning of the sixteenth century. Their progress, which was contemporary with that of the Lutherans and the Jesuits, is also described as extremely rapid.

† Vit. Constant. lib. iv., Tertullian, lib. ad Uxorem. Cyprian (lib. i. epist. xi. ad Pomponianum, De Virginibus) reproaches in very severe language certain consecrated virgins, who had fallen under the suspicion of incontinence,—" Quid Christus Dominus et Judex noster, cum, virginem suam sibi dicatam et sanctitati suæ destinatam jacere cum altero cernit, quàm indignatur et irascitur !" Again: " Quod si in fide se Christo dedicaverunt pudicè et castè sine ulla fabula perseverent. . . Si autem perseverare nolunt vel non possunt, melius est nubant, quam in ignem delictis suis cadant." Again, (lib. v. epist. viii.) he speaks of " Membra Christo dicata et in æternum continentiæ honorem pudica virtute devota." See also his " Tractatus de Disciplina et Habitu Virginum." These passages show, at the same time, that there were in that age virgins dedicated to religion, and they were not bound by any irrevocable vow.

cised individually their self-imposed duties and devotions ; and found their practice to be consistent, like the Ascetæ, among whom they may properly be classed, with the ordinary occupations of society.

The origin of Communities of female recluses was probably coeval with that of monasteries, and the produce of the same soil. The glory of the institution is commonly ascribed to St. Syncletica, the descendant of a Macedonian family settled in Alexandria, and the contemporary of St. Anthony. It is at least certain, that many such establishments were founded in Egypt before the middle of the fourth century ; and that they were propagated throughout Syria, Pontus, and Greece, by the same means and at the same time with those of the Holy Brothers, though not, as it would seem, in the same abundance. It appears, however, that they gradually penetrated into every province where the name of Christ was known ; they were found among the Armenians, Mingrelians, Georgians, Meronites, and others ; and finally formed an important and not incongruous appendage to the Oriental Church.

A noble Roman lady, named Marcella, is celebrated as the instrument chosen by Providence to introduce the pious institution into the West. In emulation of the models of Egypt, she assembled several virgins and widows in a community consecrated to holy purposes ; and her example found so many imitators, that the Fathers of the next generation, St. Ambrose *, St. Jerome, and St. Augustine, bear sufficient testimony to the prevalence of the institution in their time. It is true that, at least as late as the year 400, many devout virgins (Virgines Devotæ) still preserved their domestic relations and adhered to the more secular practice of the Antenicene Church ;

---

* Lib. i. de Virginibus ad Marcelliam. The testimony of St. Jerome, respecting Marcella, has been already cited.   St. Augustine (De Moribus Ecclesiæ, c. 33) says, in speaking of the monastic establishments both at Milan and Rome :—" Jejunia prorsus incredibilia, non in viris tantum, sed etiam in fœminis ; quibus item, multis viduis et virginibus simul habitantibus et lana ac tela victum quæritantibus, præsunt singulæ gravissimæ probatissimæque non tantum in instituendis componendisque moribus, sed etiam instruendis mentibus peritæ et paratæ." See Marsham's Προπύλαιον to Dugdale, and Hospinianus de Orig. Monach., lib. iii. c. xi., et seq.

and it is possible that those devotees were never wholly extinct in any age. But the Associations for the same end gradually embraced most of those with whom religious zeal was the leading motive; and their sanctity was recommended to popular reverence, as it may also have been exalted and fortified, by the discipline and the vow which restrained them.

The rules, to which the convents of Nuns* were subject, were formed for the most part upon those which bound the monks. Like the monks, they lived from common funds, and used a common dormitory, table, and wardrobe; the same religious services exercised their piety; habitual temperance and occasional fasting were enjoined with the same severity. Manual labour was no less rigidly enforced; but instead of the agricultural toils imposed upon their " Brethren," to them were committed the easier tasks of the needle or the distaff. By duties so numerous, by occupations admitting so great variety, they beguiled the tediousness of the day †, and the dullness of monastic seclusion.

---

* The words Nonnus, Nonna, are said to be of Egyptian origin. The latter is used by St. Jerome, Epist. ad Eustochium Virginem. Benedict of Nursia (Regul. 63) gives it the interpretation of paternal reverence, and ordains, that "Juniores monachi priores suos *nonnos* vocent; quod intelligitur paterna reverentia." The terms Monialis and Sanctimonialis are usually derived from Μονος. Hospin. Orig. Monach , lib. i. c. i.

† The two following passages from St. Jerome deserve to be cited, since they show as well what were the vanities, as what were the duties, of the earliest Nuns:—"Vestis tua nec sit satis munda, nec sordida, nullaque diversitate notabilis; ne ad te obviam prætereuntium turba consistat et digito monstreris. . . . Plures . . hoc ipso cupiunt placere quod placere contemnunt, et mirum in modum laus, dum vitatur, appetitur . . . Ne cogitatio tacita subrepat, ut, quia in auratis vestibus placere desiisti, placere coneris in sordidis; et quando in conventum fratrum veneris vel sororum, humilis (al. humi) sedeas; scabello te causeris indignam; vocem ex industria, quasi confectam jejuniis; non tenuis, et deficientis mutuata gressum humeris innitaris alterius. Sunt quippe nonnullæ exterminantes (extenuantes?) facies, ut appareant hominibus jejunantes; quæ statim ut aliquem viderint ingemiscunt, demittunt supercilium, et operta facie vix unum oculum liberant (al. librant) ad videndum. Vestis pulla, cingulum sacceum et sordidis manibus pedibusque; venter solus, quia videri non potest, æstuat cibo. Aliæ virili habitu, veste mutata, erubescunt esse quod natæ sunt; *crinem amputant* et impudenter erigunt facies eunuchinas. Sunt quæ ciliciis vestiuntur et cucullis fabrefactis; ut ad infantiam redeant, imitantur noctuas et bubones. . Hæc omnia argumenta sunt Diaboli."—Hieron.(Epist. xviii.) ad Eustoch. Virginem. Again, (Epist. to Demetrias, De Servanda Virginit.) " Præter Psalmorum et Orationis

It appears probable, as is warmly argued by Hospinian [*], Vow of
Chastity. that, in the very early ages, the virgins who were dedicated to religious purposes could enter without any scandal into the state of marriage.   But we should recollect that, at that time, the monastic condition, properly speaking, did not exist.   Immediately after its institution, we find the authority of St. Basil loudly declared against such a departure from the more perfect purity; that patriarch of monasticism does not hesitate to pronounce the marriage of a nun to be incest, prostitution, and adultery (incestus, stupri scelus, et adulterium); and Ambrose and Augustine exacted the same sacred obedience to the irrevocable vow.   By the Council of Chalcedon, nuns who married were made liable, together with their husbands, to the sentence of excommunication; yet in such manner, that penance might be imposed, if they reverently requested it, and communion restored in consequence of that penance, after a long interval proportioned to the offence. This canon was generally received in the West.   But in the year 407, Innocent I. closed the outlet of penance, and left no loop-hole of forgiveness open to those who had violated their vow.   Subsequent ages increased, rather than mitigated, this rigour; and imprisonment, and tortures, and death, were finally held out as the punishments of monastic incontinence.   The resource of penance was still reserved by Innocent[†] for inconstant novices—those who mar-

---

ordinem, qui tibi hora tertia, sexta, nona, ad vesperem, media nocte, et mane semper est exercendus, statue quot horis Sanctam Scripturam ediscere debeas, quanto tempore legere, non ad laborem, sed ad delectationem ac instructionem animæ. Cumque hæc finieris spatia . . . habeto lanam semper in manibus, vel staminis pollice fila deducito, vel ad torquenda subtegmina in alveolis fusa vertantur; aliarumque neta aut in globum collige, aut tenenda (nenda?) compone. Quæ texta sunt inspice : quæ errata reprehende: quæ facienda constitue. Si tantis operum varietatibus occupata fueris, nunquam dies tibi longi erunt." Similar instructions are delivered in Epist. 86, ad Eustochium Epitaph. Paulæ Matris. And St. Augustine (De Morib. Ecclesiæ. cap. 31) mentions that the garments manufactured by the nuns were given to the monks in exchange for food. " Lanificio corpus exercent et sustentant; vestesque ipsas fratribus tradunt, ab iis invicem quod victui opus est resumentes." The Tonsure was not originally imposed, though it appears to have been an Egyptian custom.

* Lib. iii. c. xii.

† Hospin. Orig. Monach. lib. iii. c. ult.

ried, after having avowed the intention of chastity, but without having yet taken the veil.

The Veil.   The ceremony of consecration and the imposition of the veil was of origin earlier even than the time of St. Ambrose *; and it appears that it might then be performed by a priest, no less than by a bishop. The words † pronounced on this occasion were prescribed by the Fourth Council of Carthage; but they varied, or were entirely changed, in subsequent times. The age at which the novice might be consecrated was equally variable, and seems to have been left, at least in early times, to the discretion of the prelate. An age as advanced as sixty years, appears at first to have been usual; but St. Ambrose gives reasons for permitting the veil to be sooner assumed; and the age of twenty-five was afterwards (generally, though by no means universally) established as the earliest at which the recluse was permitted to place the indelible seal upon her resolution.

Benedictine Nuns.   The first period, or, if we may so call it, the *antiquity* of Monachism, was terminated in the Western Church by the epoch of St. Benedict; and it is generally recorded, that while that hermit was inventing his new institution for the brothers of his obedience, his sister Scholastica was raising the standard ‡, round which the holy virgins might collect with greater regularity and discipline. It would appear, however, that the rule of her disciples was rather given in restoration of the original observance, than on any new principle of religious seclusion. The alternations of industry and prayer; abstinence, silence, obedience, chastity, were ordained, as in the primitive establish-

* We must not however be misled by the title of Tertullian's work (De Virginibus Velandis) to ascribe to that practice so high an antiquity. The object of that book is only to show, that all virgins, as well as matrons, ought, in their attendance on divine worship, to be veiled. It has no reference to any particular condition of life.

† They were these—" Aspice, filia, et intuere; et obliviscere populum tuum et domum patris tui, ut concupiscat Rex decorem tuum."

‡ Mabillon (Pref. Hist. Benedict.) asserts this Scholastica to have been the founder of regular nunneries in the West; and calls her " Virginum Benedictinarum Ducem, Magistram et Antesignanam."

ments ; and the first Benedictine nuns were in fact rather reformed nuns of St. Basil, than a distinct order. . . Howbeit,
they acquired reputation and flourished so rapidly, that in the
pontificate of Gregory the Great, Rome contained (according to the assertion* of that pope) three thousand "hand-
maids of God," (Ancillæ Dei,) who followed the Benedictine
rule. And so boldly did they afterwards rise in rank and
power, that about the year 813 it became necessary to repress
the pretended right of the Abbesses to consecrate and ordain,
and perform other sacerdotal functions†.

The establishment of female recluses followed very closely Canon-
the numerous diversities of the monastic scheme, and imitated esses.
the names of the male institutions, where they could not adopt
their practice or even their profession. An order of Canonesses-
Regular was founded, or at least presented with a rule, by the
Council of Aix-la-Chapelle, in 813. And we read, in later
times, of a community of noble young ladies, who were associated under a very easy discipline, and unrestrained by any
vow of celibacy, under the title of Canonesses-Secular. But
these last pretenders to religious seclusion were, on more
than one occasion, discountenanced by the authorities of the
Church.

An imitation of the Military Orders might, at first sight, Nuns of
seem still more repugnant to the feelings and duties of holy the hospi-
virgins. But, in respect at least to the oldest of those orders, it tal.
was in fact far otherwise. That community originated (as has
already been mentioned) in an office of gratuitous humanity;
—to entertain the stranger, and to tend the sick, were the
earliest offices of the Knight of the Hospital. By him, indeed,
those humbler tasks may afterwards have been forgotten in the
character of the soldier of the Cross; but the "Nuns of the
Hospital‡" adhered to the earliest and the noblest object of

* Lib. vi. Epist. xxiii. See Hospinian, Orig. Monach. lib. iv. c. xvi. The ceremony of consecration, by the bishop, is here given at great length.

† At the Council of Beconfeld in Kent, abbesses subscribed their signatures,
no less than Abbots and other Ecclesiastics. This is recorded to have been the
first instance of such assumption of equality.

‡ A long account of these "Religieuses Hospitalières," together with the for-
malities of reception into the order, may be found in the Hist. des Ordres Monas-

the institution.   Their foundation was contemporary with that
of the Chevaliers; and in after times they extended their
establishments, and perhaps their charities, into every part
of Europe.

The calamities of the Crusades were followed and alleviated
by another institution, in which charitable females immediately
took a share, and of which the purpose was not less worthy of
its religious profession.   A multitude of Christian captives had
been thrown by the vicissitudes of war into the power of the
Saracens; and for their redemption, the order of the " Nuns of
the Holy Trinity " was established very early in the thirteenth
century.   It survived the occasion which gave it birth, and
flourished widely, under the patronage of certain pious prin-
cesses*, especially in Spain.

Nuns of
St. Dom-
inic.

The foundation of several nunneries divided with his other
ecclesiastical duties the busy zeal of St. Dominic.   And though
we cannot discover that the essential characteristics of his order,
preaching and mendicity, were in practice communicated to the
holy sisters who bore his name, yet the name was sufficient to
procure for them wealth and popularity; and they probably
were not surpassed in either of those respects by any other
order†.   St. Catharine of Sienna, a vehement devotee, professed especially to reverence the virtues and imitate the discipline of St. Dominic; and she may properly be accounted
among his most genuine disciples, since she interposed to
smooth the political difficulties of her country, and to influence,
by her reason and authority, the most momentous concerns of

tiques, trois. partie, chap. xiv. We may remark that their " Habits de Cérémonie
de Chœur," indicate wealth, if not vanity. The "Religieuse Chevalière de l'Ordre
de St. Jaques de l'Epèe" was a Spanish invention of a much later age.   This
order seems to have originated at Salamanca.

  * Hist. Ordres Monast. partie II. chap. xlix.

  † The historian " Des Ordres Monastiques" asserts, that when he wrote (about
1715), there were in Italy more than one hundred and thirty nunneries of that
order, about forty-five in France, fifteen in Portugal, and forty in Germany, in
spite of the devastations of the heretics. The order which bears the name of St.
Catherine was probably not founded by herself (though Hospinian asserts otherwise), and it is variously assigned to the year 1372—or 1455—a diversity which
some attempt to reconcile.   We shall have occasion to make further mention of
this celebrated devotee in a following chapter.

the Church.   Among the female Mendicants, the latest institutions was that of the Carmelites.   They appear to have been founded about 1452, by virtue of a bull of Nicholas V.; and nearly a century afterwards, they were reformed by the celebrated St. Theresa, a native of Castille.

We shall not trace the endless catalogue, nor enumerate the various names, under which the same or very similar institutions perpetually re-appeared.   Among those of somewhat earlier times, that of St. Brigida, a Princess of Sweden, is most renowned.   It was an establishment for the reception of both sexes—though separated in residence—under the superintendence of an Abbess; and its Rule * was confirmed by Urban V. about the year 1360.   Though manual labour was strictly enjoined, the royal hand which founded the community appears, at the same time, to have blessed it with ample endowments.   Of the more modern orders, there is also one The Ursuwhich may seem to require our notice—that of the Ursulines. lines. Its origin is ascribed† to Angela di Brescia, about the year 1537, though the saint from whom it received its name, Ursula Benincasa, a native of Naples, was born ten years afterwards. Its character was peculiar, and recalls our attention to the primitive form of ascetic devotion.   The duties of those holy sisters were the purest within the circle of human benevolence —to minister to the sick, to relieve the poor, to console the miserable, to pray with the penitent.   These charitable offices they undertook to execute without the bond of any community, without the obligation of any monastic vow, without any separation from society, any renouncement of their domestic duties and virtues.   And so admirably were those offices, in millions of instances, performed, that, had all other female orders been really as useless and as vicious, as they are sometimes falsely described to be, the virtues of the Ursulines had alone been sufficient to redeem the monastic name.

---

* This Rule occupies eight folio pages in Hospinian, lib. vi. cap. 39.   It professed to proceed from the immediate dictation of Christ.

† Hist. des Ordres Monast. Suite de la trois. partie, chap. xiv. et xx.   The historian enumerates and describes thirteen congregations of Ursulines, established for the most part in France and in Italy.

But it is very far from true that these other orders were either commonly dissolute or generally useless. Occasional scandals have engendered universal calumnies. To recite the mere names* of those most lately founded is sufficient to show that their professed objects were almost always excellent; and it would be as injurious to human nature, as it is contrary to historical evidence, to suppose that those objects were instantly abandoned, and made merely a cover for the opposite vices. In the more secular institutions of the other sex there was greater space for the operation of evil passions. In those polluted cloisters, the seeds of avarice were commonly nourished by the practice of profitable deceptions, and the prospect of opulent benefices. The holiest contemplations were interrupted by the voice of ambition inviting the most austere recluse to dignity and power—to abbacies, to prelacies; to the councils of kings, to that predominant apostolical eminence, whence kings and their councils were insulted and overthrown. But into the cell of the female devotee those passions at least can seldom have intruded, because they had no object there†. Without insisting upon any natural predisposition to piety and

* Such were the Religieuses Hospitalières de la Charité de Notre Dame, De Notre Dame du Refuge, De N. D. de la Misericorde, &c. Orphan asylums were numerous, as "the Congregations of St. Joseph." Many were founded for the maintenance and education of poor girls; many for the sick; many for the penitent. In a description of the plague, in 1347, Fleury (Hist. Eccles. liv. xcv. s. 45) bears the following accidental testimony to female charity :—"Plusieurs Prêtres timides abandonnoient leurs troupeaux et en laissoient les soins à des Religieux plus hardis. Les Religieuses servoient les malades sans crainte, avec leur charité et leur humanité ordinaire. Plusieurs entre elles moururent, mais on les renouvelloit souvent."

† Some remarks have been suggested to us on this passage, which we recommend to the reader's consideration—premising, however, that the position in the text only affirms the moral superiority of nuns to monks, on the ground that *some* of the passions on which the habits of the latter were formed had no object to rouse them in the former.

I cannot help thinking (says an ingenious friend) that the argument implied in the words "passions which had no object there," is fallacious. Many passions, if not all, will *find* objects, natural or unnatural. The danger of wandering, in the absence of express revelation, from that knowledge of the will of God, which may be collected from induction, is as pernicious to morals, as the *à priori* reasoning is to science. An institution preventing women from becoming wives and mothers was immoral (considering the natural evidence of their propensities) in the same sense in which the opposition to the philosophy of Galileo was unreasonable.

benevolence, we may be well assured that the precincts of the convent were very fruitful in the exercise of both; and whatsoever judgment we may finally form respecting the character of that influence, which monachism has exercised through so many ages on so many forms of society, we may pronounce without hesitation the general purity and usefulness of the Female Orders.

Voltaire, in his Chapter on the Religious Orders, after eulogizing the charities of the female institutions in the noblest spirit of philanthropy, has remarked that "those who have separated themselves from the Church of Rome have but faintly imitated that generous virtue." The taunt is undeserved. We did not lay aside our charities, when we dispensed with our vows; we did not languish in the practice, when we rejected the profession; the religious motive acts not less powerfully, because the *name* is less commonly put forward; and in as far at least as the tender sex is concerned, there is not a district in our cities, nor a village in our provinces, which does not profit by the unpretending, unavowed, enlightened benevolence of Protestant Ursulines.

We shall now conclude a chapter—already disproportionate to the dimensions of this work, but far too contracted for the immensity of the subject—by a few obvious and almost necessary observations.

Without recurring to the less definite shape which monachism General assumed in the West during the fourth and fifth ages, we may observa- tions. observe, that the three distinctive characters which it afterwards adopted were well suited to the several periods in which they successively rose and flourished. First in origin were the Regular Benedictine* Cœnobites; and they reigned without any rivals over the consciences of the faithful for above six centuries.—Those were centuries of the deepest ignorance and superstition which the history of Europe exhibits. That Order imitated the Oriental enthusiasm in which the whole system

---

* We do not here intend to distinguish between monks and canons, because both were Cœnobites, and possessed the same general characteristics, widely removed from the principles both of the Military and the Mendicant Orders—still less between the Original and Reformed Benedictines.

originated; it likewise inculcated moral severity, and exercised, in a greater or less degree, both useful industry and virtuous benevolence. As it thus grew in reputation and temporal grandeur, it extended and multiplied its demands upon human credulity. The most extravagant spiritual claims were recommended by a great parade, and by some reality, of devotion. Spacious and imposing edifices, whence the chaunt of holy voices was heard unceasingly to proceed in solemn prayer, by night and by day—some practice of charitable offices—great superiority in manner and education—the possession, almost exclusive, of the learning of the age—these advantages prepared an uninstructed people to receive with blindness any form of superstition, which their ghostly directors might think proper to impose on them, and gave efficacy to deception and imposture. And thus it proved, that, when superstition had once taken root in the soil of ignorance, it was nourished through so many ages by a much less proportion of moral and religious excellence, and scarcely more of knowledge, than had been necessary to plant it there. The most inactive among the forms of monachism was found sufficient to hold the human mind, as long as it was uninformed and unexcited, in servile subjugation.

The next which rose were the Military Orders,—and of these it is sufficient to remark, that they formed no regular part of the Church system, but were the casual consequence of the Crusades. They were instituted to assail the external enemies of the faith; they were continued to repel their invasions, and defend the outworks of Christendom; but they did not very long survive the circumstances which created and sustained them. Indeed, the profession of arms in the name of Christ was so palpable a mockery of the true spirit of his religion, that its permanence was scarcely consistent with the fundamental principles of Christian society. An extraordinary occurrence could alone have given it existence, but it could not possibly give it perpetuity.

As corruption increased within the Church, and ignorance diminished without it, heresy began to spread widely, and the voice of reason found many listeners. And then it was that a band of active and intelligent emissaries was required for the maintenance of the established ecclesiastical system. For this purpose the talents of the Dominicans were more especially serviceable. But since a large measure of superstition still infected the lower orders, and none were wholly free from it, the abstinent and ragged devotion of the Franciscans was also not without its use, in exciting veneration towards themselves, and towards the Church, whose missionaries they were. Besides, the original Mendicants denounced, with courage and vehemence, the vices and the violences of the great. Their close connexion with the papal or Guelphic interests placed them in opposition to the imperial domination, and thus made them, in their political mediations, the advocates of liberal and popular principles. But, above all, they were careful to provide themselves with that powerful weapon, which, from the days of St. Augustine to those of the Crusades, had entirely rested, and which had been very partially employed afterwards. True eloquence, indeed, is not commonly attainable; but they possessed and perpetually exercised that fluency of passionate declamation, which produced on the people all the effects of eloquence. It had even some advantages over the more chastised effusions of antiquity*. It derived its authority from the oracles of God; the moral obligations which it urged were more directly subservient to human happiness; and its particular application in the mouth of the Mendicants was very commonly to a benevolent object,—to negotiate treaties, to reconcile party animosities, to stay the calamities of public or private warfare. Accordingly, the records of the thirteenth and following centuries abound with proofs of its efficacy and its influence in political, no less than in ecclesiastical, transactions. It has moreover been mentioned, that the Mendicants availed themselves with great address of the peculiar learning†

* A comparison in favour of the Mendicants is ingeniously drawn by Denina, lib. xii., cap. vi.

† Giannone even asserts, that the merit to which the Mendicants were chiefly indebted for the favour of the popes, was their success in substituting the scholastic for the dogmatic theology, and the study of antiquity and history, so as to occupy the minds of the learned with abstract and useless questions and disputes and so many *contrasti* and *raggiri*, that no one not conversant with that art could

of that age, and acquired uncommon dexterity in the perversion of reason. Conversant, more than any others, with the metaphysical subtilties of the schools, they well knew how, at the same time, to indulge the sophistical and the superstitious spirit of the age, and, by indulging, to nourish both. Thus they combined, for the defence of papacy, the abuse of reason with the abuse of religion; and their genius and their industry, by pandering to the existing prejudices, prolonged the servitude and degradation of the human mind.

A Roman Catholic writer has observed, with a demonstration of pious gratitude, that the same God who raised up St. Athanasius against the Arians, and St. Augustine against the Pelagians, and St. Dominic and St. Francis against the Albigenses, deigned, in a later and still more perilous age, to call forth the spirit of Loyola against the Lutheran and Calvinistic apostates. And it may be, that at the moment when Luther was writing his book against monastic vows, the Spaniard was composing his "Spiritual Exercises" for the restoration of other orders and the establishment of his own. It is only necessary for us to observe, that the defensive system of the Roman Church was completed by the institution of the Jesuits, though somewhat too late for its perfect preservation. And we may add, in pursuance of our other observations, that that order was as justly accommodated to the increasing intelligence of the sixteenth century, as were the Benedictines to the darkness of absolute ignorance, and the Mendicants to the twilight of reason. But each, in their turn of pernicious operation, though they enjoyed their appointed range and season of influence, were too feeble to prevent the revival, to arrest the growth, or to crush the maturity of truth and religious knowledge.

Successive reformations of the monastic system.
If we regard the monastic system in another point of view, we shall perceive it to consist in a continual succession of reformations. The foundation of every institution was laid, as it

confront them with any hope of success. It was indeed by such a method of reasoning that the pretensions of Rome were best defended; and the Mendicants were bound to defend them, since all their exemptions, and much of their property, flowed *directly* from Rome; for the pope not uncommonly gave them convents belonging to other Orders.

rose out of the corruption of its predecessor, in poverty, in the most rigid morality, in the duties of religion, of education, of charity.   The practice first, and next the show, of these qualities, led, in every instance, to wealth ; and wealth was surely followed, first, by the relaxation of discipline—next, by the contempt of decency.   Then followed the necessity of reform ; and the same system was regenerated under another, or perhaps under the same name, and passed through the same deteriorating process to a second corruption.   Again,—the Reformed Order was re-reformed and re-regenerated, and again it fell into decay and dissolution.   The history of the monastic orders, when pursued into the details of the several establish-ments, presents to us an unvarying picture of vigour, prosperity, dissension, followed by new statutes, and a stricter rule.   A system, of which the foundations were not placed either in Scripture or in reason, was necessarily liable to perpetual change ; nor was it capable of any other condition of existence, than one of continual decay and reproduction.

If we reflect for an instant on the outlines of Western Mona-chism, we observe, that the Rule of Benedict of Nursia had already fallen into great degradation, when it was revived by Benedict of Aniane.   The system then flourished with extra-ordinary vigour ; but for so short a period, that when, about the year 900, the Reformed Order of Cluni was established, its founders deserved the glory of restoring the ancient discipline ; and that event is justly considered as marking an important epoch in monastic history.   Again, within two other centuries, we observe the younger and more rigid Cistertians censuring the secular pride and luxurious relaxation of their rivals.   In the next age, it was proposed to heal the disorders, or at least to supply the deficiencies, of the old system, by the super-addition of the Mendicants, models of primitive and apostolical austerity *.   But even the very slight notice which we have

---

* This was, indeed, to seek safety in the opposite extreme, and by the *entire* renunciation of all temporalities to exceed the severity of St. Benedict ; but the disease at that time demanded a violent remedy.   The choice for such an Order lay between bodily labour and mendicity—the latter was preferred, as being, in name, more humiliating, and also more consistent with intellectual attainments, and the grand spiritual offices of instructing the vulgar, converting heretics, &c.

been able to bestow on the history of the Franciscans has
proved how very early they fell into disorders, succeeded,
though not repaired, by reformation. Even the institution of
St. Dominic was very far from securing the purity of his
children ; indeed, it was at no distant period from their foundation that a part of them assumed the distinctive appellation
of Reformed Dominicans. (Dominicani Riformati.) By this
process of continual change and restoration, the monastic
system maintained an influence, varying extremely in degree,
but never wholly suspended, over the nations of the West for
eleven hundred years. That it did so may well surprise us, if
we consider only the principles of its first foundation, and the
monstrous and avowed abuses which at various periods infected
it. But on the other hand, it was sustained by an infusion of
much real piety and of many unquestioned virtues ; and it was
prolonged from time to time by a series of judicious and season-
able alterations, such as are able to give permanence even to a
feeble and mischievous establishment, and without which there
is no security even for the wisest and the most excellent.

Still this last cause had alone been insufficient. It is not
possible, that any policy of Church government could have
upheld the system so long and so triumphantly, if it had not
possessed something not only plausible in its principle, and
respectable in its profession, but also practical and profitable
in its influence on society. It would be ungrateful and unjust
to disparage the benefits which it has really conferred on
former ages, and of which the consequences may have reached
our own.

Advan-
tages pro-
duced by
monachism We may comprehend all the useful merits which have ever
been claimed for monachism, with any shadow of reason, under
four heads. (1.) The earliest monks lived by the labour of
their hands ; and the large tracts of waste land with which
their houses were endowed, were brought into cultivation by
their personal exertions. Even in the eighth and ninth centuries, when they became for the most part clerks, their estates
continued to bear marks of more careful superintendence ; their
serfs and dependents were more numerous and more prosperous ;
cities grew up under their economy ; provinces were fertilized,

Industry of
its early
professors.

forests and marshes were peopled under their administration. Nor is there any reason to question, what is generally admitted, that the vassals of the monasteries were raised at least some degrees nearer to domestic comfort and civilization, than those of the adjacent baronies.

(2.) The earliest monasteries were very commonly conse- *Their situation in respect to the lower orders.* crated to the discharge of important moral and social, as well as religious duties. That of hospitality, or the entertainment of travellers and pilgrims, was certainly practised with great fidelity; and in ages and countries in which inns and caravanseras* were yet unknown, and even the personal safety of the stranger was ill secured by law, it was usefully and benevolently instituted that his reception and protection should, in some manner, be associated with the offices of religion. The worldly authority of religion is never more profitably employed than in supplying the defects of police, of government, and civilization. And thus it proved, that during the five or six centuries of confusion and barbarism, which followed the subversion of the Western empire, the monastic system became a powerful instrument in correcting the vices of society and alleviating their pressure on the lower orders.

The earliest donations with which the Church was enriched, were for the most part the genuine unconditional fruits of superstition. But in somewhat later times, when it was discovered that the property of the Church was liable not only to spoliation by laymen, but to abuse by churchmen, the profusion of the pious admitted the admixture of human motives, and was less than formerly directed to the support of the clergy, more to that of the poor and miserable. Accordingly, among the ecclesiastical records of the eighth and ninth centuries, no less than of those which followed, we find many monuments †,

* Muratori shows that the use of inns, as places of *reception* for strangers, was as late as the eleventh or twelfth century. He throws great light on the nature of the earliest Christian establishments for that purpose, in Dissertations 37 and 56.

† Among those produced by Muratori are some bearing the dates 718, 721, 757, 759, 764, 790, 812, 825, 847, &c. A charter given to the monks of Modena, in 996, contains these words:—" Et domum Hospitalem habeant, ubi *secundum morem* hospites de decimis laborum suorum recipiant." Some assert, that

which prove the general application of a part (and in some few cases the greater part) of the revenues of certain monasteries to the use of the sick, the poor, and the traveller. A particular building* appropriated to these purposes was attached to many monasteries, and was an essential part of the establishment. Thus these religious institutions became the channel through which the benevolence of the wealthy was communicated to the lower classes. And though the charity which seemed to acquire sanctity by passing through that medium may sometimes have been diminished or perverted, there can be no doubt that much of it reached its destination, even in the worst ages of the Church. In seasons of general strife and anarchy, the contributions of the pious found their best hope of security and usefulness in monastic hands; and if the sacred deposit was sometimes violated by the treacherous avarice of those to whom it was confided, a much greater portion was unquestionably applied to its intended purpose, the alleviation of disease and misery.

In the Eastern Church, the introduction of every variety† of charitable establishment immediately followed the reception of the Gospel. It was the work of Christian principles and of Christian men, and was closely, though not inseparably, connected with the monastic institution. Two of the greatest patrons of that system, St. Basil and St. Chrysostom, were

before the middle of the eighth century, there was no monastery in the West which had not an hospital attached to it; and we have remarked that in later ages, *that* was, in at least one instance, the very foundation on which a new order was established. We might add, that such was the origin of the Ordre du Saint Esprit at Montpelier; and we observe that in 1198, Innocent III. rebuilt an hospital, which had been founded at Rome, in 715, by a Saxon king for the use of Saxon pilgrims.

* Some of these, called Matriculæ, seem to have corresponded very nearly with our poor-houses. The Domus Hospitalis was nearly synonymous: a church was usually founded with them. We have an instance of one of these built by Ansaldus at Lucca, in 784, on the condition " that every week, twelve poor and strangers should be admitted to the table of the Church." There are abundant records of such establishments; but some of them were, in process of time, seized and appropriated by the lay-rector. See Muratori, Dissert. 37.

† This is proved by the mere use of the terms Xenodochia, Gerontocomia, Nosocomia, Orphanotrophia, Brephotrophia, Ptochotrophia, so familiar to the writers of those ages.

likewise the founders of hospitals (Nosocomia): places of entertainment for strangers (Xenodochia) were early attached to several churches, and deacons appointed to discharge their duties. But the monasteries of the East were at no period so enriched by charitable deposits, as those of the Latin Church: for the monks in those countries never obtained influence so despotic over a more enlightened people; and a more settled form of civil government secured the wealthy against the rapine to which they were continually liable under the feudal anarchy.

But it was not merely in respect to their temporal necessities that the people, and especially the lower orders, were benefited by those establishments. Many blessings were at the same time conferred by their religious character; many afflictions were consoled, many hopes suggested, many sins prevented, by the exertions of pious monks. Those brothers, though exalted as a community, were not individually removed above the condition of the peasants, and they had commonly the same origin; so that the intercourse was close and searching, and its advantages frequently reciprocal. There are many spiritual wounds, which are most effectually probed and healed by a pastor, whose condition, whose associations and understanding, are not much elevated above those of the penitent. A more perfect confidence, a deeper sympathy, is then excited, than when the parties are widely separated in rank or intellect. This advantage the monks in general possessed over the secular clergy in the Roman Church; and to this we may partly attribute the superiority of their influence. That this influence was often abused, we know too well; nor can there be any doubt that the intercourse which led to it has been sometimes injurious. But during the better ages of monachism, it is unquestionable that the blessings of that religious connexion between the monks and the poor were greatly predominant.

It is the boast of St. Bernard that those who had embraced the monastic condition lived with greater purity than other men; that they fell less frequently and rose more quickly; that they walked with greater prudence; were more constantly refreshed with the spiritual dew of heaven; rested with less danger; died with greater hope. And far as the monastic practice has generally fallen below its profession, we doubt not that in the earlier ages, and especially in the infancy of their several institutions, their inmates surpassed all other classes of society, not excepting the secular clergy, in the exercise of moral and religious offices. Devoted to the relief of the poor and the service of the sick and the stranger, they were so placed, that even the imperfect discharge of their charitable duties conferred no scanty benefits on an uncivilized generation. Among the millions who have entered religious houses, under the most solemn vows of virtue and piety, there must have been multitudes whose mere innocence made at least some amends to society for their seclusion from its cares and temptations; there were certainly many, whose acquirements and indisputable excellence threw out a light and example to their contemporaries; and some there were, and not a few, whose eminent qualities were directed, as steadily as the spirit of their age allowed them, to the honour and improvement of their Church—to alleviate private affliction and mitigate the general barbarism.

Superintendence of education.

(3.) From the earliest period, in the Eastern as well as in the Roman Church, the duties of education were entrusted to the monks. In process of time they became, in the latter Church, nearly confined to them, and they continued so at least as late as the eleventh century. Monastic schools were established by St. Benedict; they were inseparably attached to his institutions, and spread, with the progress of his order, over the kingdoms of the West; and they were open to children of the earliest age *. It would seem that, in the eighth

---

* This was peculiar to the order of St. Benedict. Hist. Litt. de la France, Siècle xii., p. 11. See also Mabillon, Etudes Monastiques, p. 1, ch. xi. The same writer (ch. xv.) enumerates several among the early Christian heroes,— Gregory Nazianzen, Chrysostom, Epiphanius, Jerome, &c.—who studied for a greater or less time in monasteries. St. Basil, in the first instance, established a school in his monastery for the reading of holy (as distinguished from profane) history, and appointed rewards for superior merit. "Nunquam de manu et oculis recedat liber," says St. Jerome; and it is from the same monastic student that we have received that much contemned precept, " ne ad scribendum cito prosilias. Multo tempore prius disce quod doceas."

century, the cathedral or episcopal academies* were first established; and these afterwards became the most distinguished for the rank and eminence of their scholars. They were conducted, under the superintendence of the bishop, by the canons of the cathedral. And here we need only repeat a former observation, that if the office of instruction was confined to the clergy, so also were its benefits, for many ages, to those intended for the ministry. So that the advantages which those establishments really conferred on the body of society were neither immediate nor certain; while the power of the clergy, being unduly exaggerated by the exclusive possession of learning, was thereby placed upon a principle absolutely at variance with the highest earthly interests of man.

(4.) This subject naturally leads us to our last consideration —the extent and character of the literature, whether sacred or profane, which was protected and nourished in the monastic establishments. On the first matter, Roman Catholic writers do not hesitate to ascribe the very preservation of the pure doctrine of the Church to the refuge which it found within those fortresses—though it may seem doubtful whether that doctrine might not have been preserved with equal purity through ages too ignorant for controversy or cavil, by the fidelity of the secular clergy. At any rate, this praise can scarcely be granted to the monks without some qualification. For if it be true that, during the Arian controversy, they were the most zealous defenders of the Nicene faith, it is not less certain that the principles of Origen and the mystical† interpretation of Scripture gained great footing among them, and that not merely in the East; nor should the support which they persevered in affording to the cause of the images during that long and angry controversy, be forgotten in any estimate which we may endeavour to form of their pretensions to doctrinal or ecclesiastical purity. It is indeed unquestionable

Preservation of MSS.

---

* See Mosh., vol. ii., p. 55.

† This is said to have been, in the first instance, occasioned by the substitution of mental prayer for manual labour. From the excesses of mysticism proceeded the errors of the Beghards and Beguines, and other enthusiasts of the thirteenth and fourteenth centuries: they strove after absolute perfection, and they fell into fanaticism.

that the externals of religion, so valuable to the Latin Church, its offices,* and ceremonies, were enriched and dignified by the monks and canons. They acquired an imposing splendour from the number engaged in their performance and the resources of their several communities. But passing over these equivocal merits, we may mention one great and truly incalculable service which those establishments conferred on future ages, though they neglected to derive much advantage from it themselves. They preserved, through dangerous and turbulent periods, ancient copies of the inspired writings, and of the most valuable commentaries made on them in the earliest times. And those were among the most profitable moments of monastic leisure, which were employed in multiplying the sacred manuscripts †.

Though religious houses were intended to be the depositaries of virtue and piety ‡, not of letters, yet letters were, to a certain extent, encouraged there, as subsidiary to the grand object of the institution. It is shown, indeed, by the learned author § of the " Monastic Studies," that the earliest monks entirely

* Fleury, Discours, depuis 800...1100. Muratori, Dissertat. 56. The monks gained great advantages by the introduction of chaunts into the service; and this was imitated, in the ninth century, by the cathedral clergy. Some rivalry ensued between these ecclesiastics, and thus, " cœpit frequentius agi et augustius procedere divina Res." Some "modulation of prayers and praises" they had indeed used from the earliest ages, but not with that plenitude and majesty, which the chorus of monks and canons afterwards introduced. The organ appears to have come into use about the year 826.

† The great increase of MSS. during the eleventh century is to be ascribed to this monastic leisure, and could scarcely be effected otherwise. And this was the first step, after the devastation of the four preceding ages, towards the revival of ancient, and the creation of modern, learning. In the twelfth age we find St. Bernard inculcating the duties of writing and copying as the best substitute for labour.

‡ "The words of St. Peter, ' We have left all to follow Thee,' are those," as St. Bernard observed, " which have founded cloisters and peopled deserts."

§ Mabillon (Etudes Monastiques, p. 1) proves the prevalence of literary industry, in the monastic life, by direct historical evidence; by the multitude of learned ecclesiastics who emerged from them; by their libraries; by express reference to the rule of St. Benedict. To the neglect of study he attributes the decline of the several Orders, and observes, that reform was commonly attended by its restoration; that academies or colleges were invariably connected with the Benedictine establishments; and that both popes and councils perpetually inculcated the duty of study.

renounced profane literature, and confined their diligence to theological works and contemplations: the authority and example of St. Jerome confirmed that preference. But in later times, and especially when the practice of manual labour fell into disuse, the limits of their studious industry were enlarged, and they gradually embraced some department of profane science, as well as of classical lore. The compilation of Decretals led to the study of canon law; the discovery of the Digest directed attention to civil legislation. The art of medicine presented a spacious field, which was made attractive, first, perhaps, by its salutary and charitable uses, afterwards by the gain * which followed it. The monastic establishments furnished the leisure and the best existing instruments for all those pursuits ; and after the eighth or ninth age, they were distinguished by some efforts after knowledge, not fruitless of beneficial effects and even of useful discoveries.

Again, many of the most precious monuments of profane antiquity owe their preservation to the sanctity of the monasteries, or to the zeal of their defenders. All these might have perished, as many, notwithstanding, did perish, had there not existed, during the long and barbarous anarchy of the Western Empire, certain communities, associated in the name of religion for peaceful, if not pious purposes, whose interests were opposed to the progress of disorder and rapine, and whose holy profession secured them some respect from a lawless, but superstitious, people. The diligence which was employed in transcribing those valuable models, while it promoted their circulation, could scarcely fail to infuse some taste or energy into the dullest mind ; and it certainly appears, that during the eighth and ninth, and especially the eleventh ages, most † of the

---

* A council held at Rheims, under Innocent II. in 1131, published a canon, prohibiting monks and canons-regular to study civil law or medicine; and the injunction was repeated by the Lateran Council in 1139. These occupations were on this occasion expressly ascribed to avarice. And we may remark, that the prohibition was confined to the monks—the secular clergy, in the entire ignorance of the laity, were permitted to practise both law and physic.

† Bede, Alcuin, Willibrod, &c. were monks ; and most of the popes and cardinals of the eleventh century rose from the ranks of the regular clergy. See Hist. Litt. de la France, Siècle xi.

characters, who acquired any ecclesiastical celebrity, proceeded
from the discipline of the cloister.

Having thus intended to give a general view of the advantages which the monastic system has conferred on society, we
cannot fail to observe, that they are for the most part confined
to ages of ignorance or turbulence; that they were almost proportionate to the debasement of the people, and to the weakness
or wickedness of the civil government. The former of those
evils was somewhat alleviated, the latter was partially obviated,
by the monastic institutions. Herein is comprehended the
sum and substance of their utility. In a civilized nation, under
a just and enlightened rule, it is their necessary effect to ob-
struct industry and retard improvement. But, on the other
hand, if we consider them in reference to the times in which
they rose and began to flourish,—if we compare the habits, the
morals, the intelligence of the monks with those of their secular
contemporaries,—shall we not immediately admit, that in bad
ages they were probably the best men; that they were the most
useful members of a disjointed community; that their vicious
principles were less vicious than the general principles of
society; that they were in advance of the civilization of their
day? If so—and to us it appears indisputable—let us be cautious how we cast unqualified censure upon a body of religious
persons, who formed, for the space of five or six centuries, the
most respectable portion of the Christian world.

Supersti-
tious ten-
dency.
At the same time, we ought not to forget, that even in those
times to which their utility was confined, it was continually
obstructed both by the original defects of their system, and its
consequent corruptions. Almost from their first establishment,
in the East no less than in the West, we find them the faithful
defenders, if not parents, of superstitious abuse. The adoration
of saints, the miraculous qualities of relics, and the homage
due to them, and, above all, the sanctity and worship of images,
have been inculcated with peculiar zeal by the monks of every
order, in every age of the Church. Again, as they ever have
been the patrons of religious abuse, so have they inflexibly
opposed any *general* attempt at church reform. Reforms, indeed, in their particular establishments have been incessant.

Such, again, as touched the discipline of the secular clergy have sometimes found support in the jealousy of the regular orders. But any exertion, tending to the restoration of pure Christianity, has ever found its fiercest opponents in the cloister; and through such opposition many unscriptural practices have been perpetuated both in the Eastern and Western Churches. Of course it is not intended to ascribe to them all the corruptions of religion; indeed, we have already traced the origin of many of these to a period preceding the creation of monachism. The " vices of the clergy" are acknowledged in ecclesiastical records long before the prevalence of monastic influence ; and it seems probable even that the traffic in indulgences, finally so scandalous to the Mendicants, was begun by the bishops *. But all existing abuses were carefully nourished and fostered by the hands of monks ; and the execution of miracles and other popular impostures was conducted with peculiar ingenuity and success by the inmates of the monastery †. And we may add, that the lucrative system of Purgatory was most zealously supported, as indeed the wealth which flowed from it was distributed for the most part among those establishments.

In early ages the monks were the subjects, and, as it were, the army of the bishops; they maintained *their* rights, they fought their battles, and profited by their protection. In the East this mutual relation long subsisted; and as the original monasteries were expressly subjected, by the Council of Chalcedon, to the bishop of the diocese, and as many were indebted for their foundation to episcopal munificence and piety, the claims were just, and the connexion natural. But in the Roman Church it was violated almost by the first movements of papal ambition. In the year 601, Gregory the Great ‡ (him-

---

* See Mosheim, vol. ii. p. 420. We may remark, that the same author sometimes distinguishes the regular canons as more exempt from the vices which he so indiscriminately objects to the other monastic orders.

† The Carthusians are stigmatized by monastic writers for inferiority in that power, if not for the entire destitution of it. The consequence is, that having performed few or no miracles, they boast very few names in the calendar of the saints. See Hospinian, lib. v. cap. vii.

‡ Giannone, Stor. Nap, lib. iv, cap. xii. Mosheim, seemingly overlooking this

self for some time the inmate of a monastery) held a Council,
in which were passed many regulations favourable to what the
monks considered their independence. They were permitted
to choose their own abbot ; and the bishop was precluded not
only from all interference in their temporalities, and all exercise of jurisdiction over them, but even from the celebration of
the divine offices in their churches. From this event (if from
any single event) we may probably date the undue aggrandizement of the monastic order, and its increasing influence on
civil as well as ecclesiastical politics. But in independence it
only so far gained, as to exchange a near for a distant master
—a petty tyrant, it might be, for an imperious but partial
despot. One evil effect of this change was presently felt,—the
removal of the bishop's immediate superintendence facilitated
the progress of abuse and licentiousness *. The eighth and
ninth ages were, in truth, the most triumphant era of monasticism †. Whatsoever learning then existed was confined, or
nearly so, to the convents; and not only did nobles and kings
contest with each other the honour of endowing them, but there
were many who took refuge there in their own persons from
the miseries and dangers of a turbulent world. By such secession they conferred the security which they courted ; and additional sanctity seemed to surround the buildings which were
dignified by the retreat of great, perhaps even of good, men.

Absolute exemptions from episcopal authority were for some
time rare. The first instance was probably that of Monte
Cassino, which might be excused by its vicinity to Rome. But

Exemp-
tions from
Episcopal
authority.

circumstance, is disposed to attribute the growing alliance of the popes and
monks in the eleventh century to the oppression and rapacity of princes and
bishops. (Cent. xi. p. 2, chap. ii.) Doubtless there were instances of this; but
the principle of the alliance was of much earlier origin.

* One of Charlemagne's Capitularies prohibited abbots and abbesses from
keeping fools, buffoons, and jugglers, for their amusement. But this implied no
particular censure on the monastic orders, since we observe the same prohibition
to be extended to bishops.

† Giannone, lib. v. cap. vi. The same have also been considered as the grand
periods of episcopal authority. Both may be true. For the monasteries, though
in some cases, and to a certain extent, independent of the bishops, were not yet
placed in rivalry with them; but they probably made common cause, whenever
the general interests of the Church were concerned.

the example, though sparingly imitated, was by no means lost on following times; and after the pontificate of Gregory VII., the abbots began universally to claim the immediate protection of St. Peter; and his successors were seldom slow to accord it. In process of time, entire congregations of monasteries (the Clunian, for instance, and the Cistertian) were included in a single exemption; so afterwards were the Mendicant Orders; and finally the whole monastic body acknowledged no other dependence than on the pope * alone. The abuse was at length pushed so far, that even a private clerk might obtain —of course by purchase—exemption from the control of his bishop. Undoubtedly, during the eleventh, twelfth, and thirteenth centuries, the Holy See derived great power from the sort of separate hierarchy thus established; and for the two following ages, when ambition became less its ruling spirit, and avarice more so, such exemptions became the means of abundantly gratifying the favourite passion. But in the excess to which they were then carried, they shook the foundation of papal power, by inflaming the jealousy and disunion of the regular and secular clergy; and thus they mainly tended to promote, in due season, the rise of the Reformation, and to facilitate its progress.

At the same time, if the popes were long supported and aggrandized through their close connexion with the monastic Orders, so were they very sedulous to return the favour, and to enrich those Orders, sometimes at the expense of the secular clergy, but more usually by contributions from the laity. In earlier ages, the profusion of kings and nobles abundantly satiated the avarice of every department of the church; but when this spirit gradually expired, and new orders were still everywhere starting up, professing poverty, and clamorous for

Monastic Wealth, Purgatory, Indulgences, &c.

---

* The papal right to grant these exemptions does not seem to have been disputed. Yet it rested on no better foundation than a confused notion, confirmed and augmented by the Decretals, that there were *no* limits to that authority. We should observe, that even in the East there were also instances of the direct dependence of monasteries on the Patriarch; but they were rare, and probably in faint imitation of the practice of the West.

wealth, it became necessary to open new resources for their nourishment. These were easily discovered in the fruitfulness of superstition. Purgatory presently assumed a more definite shape; and it was no difficult office for the priests, who created it, to conduct its administration and economy. Their power over the concerns of that state was believed on the same authority which had established its existence. This grand invention, with the devices of masses, indulgences, &c., which flowed from it, extended its influence from the highest even to the lowest classes of the people; so that through these means every condition of society became tributary to the church. The monks enjoyed a very great share in the profits of this imposture. During the tenth and eleventh centuries, the reputation to which they had already risen was so much augmented by the foundation and name of Cluni, that some are disposed to date their triumph over the secular clergy from this period[*];—it is certain that the attention of churchmen was from this time more anxiously directed to their temporalities [†] than heretofore. . . After the institution of the Mendicants, the lucrative[‡] departments of the profession were chiefly committed to their superintendence; and it was especially through their heedless abuse of favours, as heedlessly lavished on them by a succession of necessitous popes, and most so through the public and confessed venality of indulgences, that the deformities of the papal system became generally acknowledged and execrated.

[*] It is probable that they far surpassed the secular clergy of this time in austerity and even in real piety of life, which was not, indeed, any very difficult triumph. It is certain that they now began to apply not only to study, but to business, which the seculars almost equally neglected. Hence the succession of five monks, who, during the eleventh age, governed the Church for fifty years; and to whom Mosheim, in his unqualified hatred for everything monastic, attributes almost all its sins.

[†] Giannone (Stor. Nap. lib. vii., cap. v.) remarks, that censures and excommunications—those spiritual weapons which hitherto had been usually employed for the correction of sin—were from this period chiefly directed against persons who plundered or alienated the property of the Church.

[‡] It is worthy of remark that the French, in pursuance of their constant determination to preserve themselves from pure papacy, strongly discouraged the acquisition of property in France by the Mendicants, fairly objecting to them their unequivocal vow of poverty.

These were the scandals which, more than any of its pretensions and impostures, awakened the indignation of mankind. And thus it came to pass, in the fulness of time, that out of the bosom of that very order which had been most instrumental in supporting papal power, and corrupting the very corruptions of religion, the voice of Providence was pleased to call forth the great restorer of his holy Church. While the Benedictines were reposing in their luxurious edifices—while the Mendicants were openly prostituting for gold the offices and pretended solaces of religion, the progress of knowledge and the increase of impurity prepared the field of triumph for the Saxon reformer.

CHAPTER XX.

History of the Popes, from the Death of Innocent III. to that of Boniface VIII.

The ardour of the Popes for Crusades—its motives and policy—Honorius III.—Frederic's vow to take the Cross, and procrastination—Gregory IX.—his Coronation—he excommunicates the Emperor—who thus departs for Palestine—Gregory impedes his success, and invades his dominions—their subsequent disputes—Innocent IV.—his previous friendship with Frederic—Council of Lyons—various charges urged against Frederic—Innocent deposes Frederic and appoints his successor on his own papal authority—Civil war in Germany—in Italy—death of Frederic—his character and conduct—his rigorous decree against Heretics—Observations—Other reasons alleged to justify his deposition—this dispute compared with that between Gregory VII. and Henry—Taxes levied by the Pope on the Clergy—Crusade against the Emperor—Exaltation of Innocent—his visit to Italy and intrigues—his death—his qualities as a statesman—as a churchman—expression of the Sultan of Egypt—Alexander IV.—Urban IV.—Clement IV.—Introduction of Charles d'Anjou to the throne of Naples—Gregory X.—his piety, and other merits—Second Council of Lyons—Vain preparations for another Crusade—Death of Gregory—Objects of Nicholas II.—Martin IV.—Senator of Rome—Nicholas IV. diligent against Heresy—Pietro di Morone or Celestine V.—circumstances of his elevation—his previous life and habits—his singular incapacity—disaffection among the higher clergy—his discontent and meditations—his resignation—Boniface VIII.—his excessive ambition and insolence—on the decline of the papal power—his temporal pretensions—Sardinia, Corsica, Scotland, Hungary—Recognition of Albert, king of the Romans—and act of his submission—Philip the Fair—the Gallican Church—origin of its liberties—Differences between Boniface and Philip—Bull *Clericis Laicos*—its substance and subsequent interpretation—Affairs of the bishop of Parmiers—Bull *Ausculta Fili*—burnt by Philip—Conduct of the French nobles—of the Clergy—of Boniface—Bull *Unam Sanctam*—other violent proceedings—Moderation of Philip—further insolence of the Pope—Philip's appeal to a General Council—William of Nogaret—Personal assault on Boniface—his behaviour, and the circumstances of his death.

THE Church of Rome had now so habitually stained herself with blood, as to be callous to the common feelings of nature, and insensible to the miseries of mankind. For more than a century, she had employed her power in promoting the destruction of human life by the most senseless expeditions; and as the ruinousness and vanity of the Crusades became more manifest, she seemed to redouble her exertions to renew and perpetuate them : for she thrived by contributions levied for this purpose, and by the property which was thus thrown under ecclesiastical protection; and she gathered strength through the weakness of monarchs and the superstition of their subjects. Again, after Innocent had succeeded in committing an additional outrage upon humanity and reason, by converting the machine which had been intended against the enemies of Christ, into an engine of domestic persecution and torture, it became more than ever the interest of the pope to keep alive a spirit which might so easily be made to deviate into arbitrary channels. And thus the zeal for crusades, which inflamed the breast of Innocent, passed, without any diminution, into those of his successors. Moreover, it is well known how earnestly the holy see supported the interests of Frederic II. against Otho IV., as long as the former was the weaker party, and how zealously it began to raise enemies against him as soon as he became powerful; while the industry with which it renewed and prolonged the contests between the Guelphs and the Ghibelines—contests which lacerated the vitals of Italy—furnishes melancholy proof that its interests were even at this time associated with every principle that is subversive of peace and baneful to society; and that it pursued those interests with callous, persevering, uncompromising obduracy.

Innocent III. was succeeded by Honorius III., a native of Rome, who for four years had been governor of Palermo under Frederic II.; but the remembrance of that connexion was easily thrown off, as soon as he rose from the condition of a subject to that of a rival. Frederic had made a solemn vow to Innocent, to engage without loss of time in a new crusade; and on his coronation at Rome, in 1220, he renewed that promise with still greater solemnity to Honorius. In the year following, instead of proceeding on his expedition, he appears to have appointed, on his own authority, to some vacant see,— in virtue, as he maintained, of his royal right,—in violation, as the pope asserted, of the liberties of the Church. During the time consumed in this dispute, Damietta fell into the power of the Mahometans. In the year 1223, at a council held at Terentino, in Campania, the emperor renewed his oath to

Honorius III.

depart, and that within the space of two years; and to give
earnest of his sincerity, he espoused the daughter of John of
Brienne, king of Jerusalem. In the year following, that he
might atone to the Church for his continued delay, and evince
to her the sincerity of his affection, he published some savage
constitutions against heretics, which we shall presently notice.
At the same time, in a long letter to the pope, he complained
of the general indifference to the cause of the crusades, which
then unfortunately prevailed throughout Europe*. Some disputes with the Lombards formed the next excuse for his delay;
and in 1227 Honorius died, still pressing the departure of the
monarch, and still pressing it in vain.

Accession
of Gregory
IX.

Gregory IX., who was nephew of Innocent III., was immediately raised to the pontifical chair with loud and unanimous
acclamation. On the day of his coronation he proceeded to
St. Peter's, accompanied by several prelates, and assumed the
pallium according to custom; and after having said mass, he
marched to the palace of the Lateran, covered with gold and
jewels. On Easter Day, he celebrated mass solemnly at Sta.
Maria Maggiore, and returned with a crown on his head. On
Monday, having said mass at St. Peter's, he returned wearing
two crowns, mounted on a horse richly caparisoned, and surrounded by cardinals clothed in purple, and a numerous
clergy †. The streets were spread with tapestry, inlaid with
gold and silver, the noblest productions of Egypt and the most
brilliant colours of India, and perfumed with various aromatic

* See Fleury, Hist. Eccl., l. 78, sect. 66, where a part of the letter is quoted.
The actual restitution of the territories of the Countess Matilda to the Roman
see is by some ascribed to this pontificate. Raynaldus (ann. 1221, Num. 29)
asserts, that the imperial diploma existed in the Liber Censuum of the Vatican
library—apud Pagi. Vit. Honor. III., Sect. xxxi.

† This description is very faintly copied from a life of Gregory IX., cited by
Odoricus Raynaldus; the following is a specimen: " Divinis missarum officiis
reverenter expletis duplici diademate coronatus sub fulgoris specie in Cherubini
transfiguratur aspectum, inter purpuratam venerabilium Cardinalium, Clericorum,
et Prælatorum comititivam innumeram, insignibus papalibus præcedentibus, equo
in phaleris pretiosis evectus, per almæ Urbis miranda mœnia Pater Urbis et Orbis
deducitur admirandus. Hinc cantica concrepant, etc. etc." See Pagi, Vit.
Gregor. IX., s. iii. Fleury, l. 79, s. 31. There seems no reason to believe that
these demonstrations of joy or ebullitions of adulation exceeded the customary
parade of the thirteenth century.

odours. The people chaunted aloud *Kyrie eleison*, and their songs of joy were accompanied by the sound of trumpets. The judges and the officers shone in gilded habits and caps of silk. The Greeks and the Jews celebrated the praises of the pope, each in his own language; a countless multitude marched before him, carrying palms and flowers; and the senators and prefect of Rome were on foot at his side, holding his bridle— and thus was he conducted to the palace of the Lateran.

The first and immediate act of a pontificate so gorgeously undertaken, was to urge the renewal of the Crusades, both by persuasion and menace, at the various courts of Europe. The forces of Frederic were already collected at Otranto, and, if we are to believe some writers*, the emperor did actually embark, and proceed on his destination as far as the narrow sea between the Morea and Crete, when a dangerous indisposition obliged him to return. It is at least certain that he once more deferred the moment of his final departure. The pope was infuriated; he treated the story of illness as an empty pretence, and without waiting or asking for excuse or explanation, instantly excommunicated the emperor. This took place on the 29th of September, within six months from his elevation to the see; and the sword of discord, which was drawn on that day, had no secure or lasting interval of rest until the deposition, or rather the death of Frederic.

The emperor wrote several papers in his justification, and among them a letter to Henry III. of England, containing much severe and just reproach against the Roman Church. "The Roman Church, (such was the substance of his upbraiding) so burns with avarice, that, as the ecclesiastical revenues do not content it, it is not ashamed to despoil sove-

Letter of the emperor Frederic II.

* See Giannone, l. xvi., c. 6. " Sigonio seguitò la fede di Matteo Paris, il quale (ad ann. 1227, p. 286) scrisse: Animo nimis consternati in iisdem navibus quibus venerant plusquam 40 armatorum millia sunt reversi." But this passage more probably relates to the numerous pilgrims who had actually sailed to the Holy Land for the purpose of meeting Frederic, and who immediately returned on not finding him there. Fleury makes no mention of his having put to sea at all on this occasion; but Bzovius asserts—" per triduum in mare provectus cursum convertit ac se neque maris jactationem neque incommodam valetudinem pati posse asseruit." Ann. Eccles. ad ann. 1227.

reign princes and make them tributary. You have a very touching example in your father king John; you have that also of the Count of Toulouse, and so many other princes whose kingdoms it holds under interdict, until it has reduced them to similar servitude. I speak not of the simonies, the unheard-of exactions, which it exercises over the clergy, the manifest or cloaked usuries with which it infects the whole world. In the mean time, these insatiable leeches use honied discourses, saying that the court of Rome is the Church, our mother and nurse, while it is our stepmother and the source of every evil. It is known by its fruits. It sends on every side legates, with power to punish, to suspend, to excommunicate; not to diffuse the word of God, but to amass money, and reap that which they have not sown*. And so they pillage churches, monasteries, and other places of religion, which our fathers have founded for the support of pilgrims and the poor. And now these Romans, without nobility and without valour, inflated by nothing but their literature, aspire to kingdoms and empires. The Church was founded on poverty and simplicity, and no one can give it other foundation than that which Jesus Christ has fixed." At the same time, the emperor continued to prepare for immediate departure, in spite of the sentence which hung over him. The pope assembled a numerous council, and thundered forth a second excommunication; and in the spring following, without making any humiliation, or obtaining any repeal of the anathema under which he lay, Frederic set sail for the Holy Land.

Frederic II. in Palestine.

If there had been a shadow of sincerity in Gregory's professed enthusiasm for the liberation of Palestine,—if he had loved the name and birth-place of Christ with half the ardour with which he clung to his own papal and personal dignity, he would not have pursued the departed emperor with his perverse

* In 1229, Gregory IX. levied an exaction of tenths in England with so much severity, that even the standing crops were anticipated, and the bishops obliged to sell their property, or borrow money at a high interest, in order to answer the demand. " Erat Papa tot et tantis involutus debitis, ut unde bellicam, quam susceperat, expeditionem sustineret, penitus ignorabat." Matth. Paris, anno citato. Mention is made of the continual, though secret, maledictions with which the pope was pursued.

malevolence, he would not have prostituted the ecclesiastical censures, to thwart his projects and blast his hopes. Yet he did so—his mendicant emissaries were despatched to the patriarch and the military orders of Jerusalem, informing them of the sentence under which Frederic was placed, and forbidding them to act, or to communicate with him. At the same time, provoked, as some assert *, by a previous aggression from Frederic's lieutenant, he invaded with all his forces the Apulian dominions of the emperor. Under these adverse circumstances, Frederic made a hasty, but not inglorious †, treaty with the Saracens, and instantly returned to the defence of his own kingdom—a measure which became the more necessary, since the pope had issued a third excommunication, releasing his subjects from their oath of allegiance‡. We do not profess, in this peaceful narrative, to describe the details of military adventures, or to trace the perplexed and faithless politics of Italy. We must be contented to add, that some successes of the emperor led to a hollow and fruitless reconciliation; that this again broke out (in the year 1238) into open war, which lasted till the death of the pope, three years afterwards. The period of nominal peace had been disturbed by the constant complaints and recriminations § of both parties. The perusal of those papers is sufficient to convince us, that if both had some, the pope had the greater, share of blame. And while the style which the prelate assumes is that of an offended and injured protector and patron, the language of the emperor, though never abject, frequently descends to the borders of querulousness and humility.

* Fleury, l. 79, s. 43. Giannone, l. 16, c. 6.
† The possession of the City and of the Holy Sepulchre was secured to the Christians, while the Temple (now the Mosque of Omar), which had already been desecrated to the Mahometan worship, was left in the possession of the Saracens. A fair arrangement, which was misrepresented by the pope and most ecclesiastical writers, and restored to history by Gibbon and Sismondi. Rep. Ital., chap. 15.
‡ The plea which he gave was "because no one should observe fidelity to a man who is opposed to God and his saints, and tramples upon his commandments." A new maxim (as Fleury simply observes), and one which seems to authorize revolt.
§ These disputes are related at great length by Fleury, liv. 81, sect. 32, &c.

The cause of Frederic gained nothing by the death of Gregory, since he was succeeded by Innocent IV.* This extraordinary person (Sinibaldo Fieschi, a Genoese) had been distinguished as cardinal by his attachment to the person, if not to the cause, of the emperor; and on his election to the pontificate, the people of Italy indulged the fond and natural expectation, that the dissensions which blighted their happiness would at length be composed. Not so Frederic: for he was familiar with the soul of Innocent, and had read his insolent and implacable character. To his friends, who proffered their congratulations, he replied, that there was cause for sorrow rather than joy, since he had exchanged a cardinal, who was his dearest friend, for a pope, who would be his bitterest enemy †. And so, indeed, it proved. On the occasion of an early and amicable conference, Innocent refused to withdraw his predecessor's excommunication, until Frederic should restore all that he was charged with having plundered from the Church. The meeting had no result; and Innocent presently repaired to France, and summoned a very numerous council at Lyons.

As soon as the members were assembled ‡ (in 1245) Innocent, taking his throne, with Baldwin, emperor of the East, on his right hand, began the proceedings, by conferring the use of the *red* bonnet on his cardinals §—to the end that they might never forget, in the use of that colour, that their blood was at all times due to the service of the Church. At the same time he adorned them with other emblems of dignity, in imitation of regal pomp and state, and in scorn (it was thought) of a favourite expression of Frederic, that a Christian prelate ought to emulate the meekness and poverty of the disciples of Christ. He then opened his discourse respecting the defence of the Holy Land, and of other states at that time endangered

---

* On June 24, 1243. Celestine IV., in fact, intervened, but died on the sixteenth day after his election; and during 1242 the see was vacant.

† See Giannone, Stor. di Nap., lib. xvii., c. 3, and various authorities collected by Sismondi, Rep. Ital., ch. xvi.

‡ See Giannone, lib. xvii., cap. 3. Sismondi, Rep. Ital., ch. xvi.

§ Bzov. Ann. Eccles., ad ann. 1245. Giannone, loc. cit. Pagi. vit. Inn. IV., sec. xxxi., investigates the question whether this dignity was conferred at that time, or two years later.

by the Tartar invasion, and concluded with some general reproaches on the character and conduct of Frederic,—that he had persecuted the pontiffs and other ministers of the Church of God ; exiled and plundered the bishops ; imprisoned the clergy, and even put many to a cruel death, with other similar charges. The same were repeated on the next day of meeting, and supported and exaggerated by the suspicious testimony of two partial and intemperate prelates. On both occasions they were boldly repelled by the emperor's ambassador, Taddeo di Suessa. After the delay of a fortnight, occasioned by an unfounded expectation of Frederic's appearance in person, the council assembled for the third time ; and then, after premising some constitutions respecting the Holy Land, Innocent, "to the astonishment and horror of all who heard him," pronounced the final and fatal sentence against Frederic. He declared that prince deprived of the imperial crown, with all its honours and privileges, and of all his other states ; he released his subjects from their oath ; he even forbade their further obedience, on pain of excommunication, and commanded the electors to the empire to choose a successor. He presently recommended to that dignity Henry, landgrave of Thuringia. For the kingdom of Sicily, he took upon himself, "with the counsel of the cardinals, his brethren," to provide a sovereign.

Frederic was at Turin when he received the news of this proceeding. He turned to the barons, who surrounded him, and, with deep indignation, addressed them,—"The pontiff has deprived me of the imperial crown—let us see if it be so." He then ordered the crown to be brought to him, and placed it on his head, saying, "that neither pope nor council had the power to take it from him." Most of the princes of Europe were, indeed, of the same opinion, and continued to acknowledge him to the end of his life. And we may remark, that the usurpation of Innocent was in one respect marked with peculiar audacity,—he did not even plead the approbation of the Holy Council, but contented himself with proclaiming that the sentence had been pronounced *in its presence* [*].

Deposition of Frederic.

---

[*] "Sacro præsente Concilio." Bzovius (Ann. Eccles., ad ann. 1445) gives the precious document entire, prefaced, of course, with unqualified eulogy. Pagi,

It should here be mentioned, that, besides the affair of Frederic, the first General Council of Lyons professed three grand objects. (1.) To assist the Latin emperor of Constantinople against the Greeks. (2.) To aid the emperor of Germany against the Tartars. (3.) To rescue the Holy Land from the Saracens. For the attainment of the *first* of these objects, the pope ordained a contribution of half the revenues of all benefices on which the incumbents were not actually resident (a wholesome distinction), placing a still higher impost on the largest; also of a tenth of the revenues of the Church of Rome. For the *second*, he exhorted the inhabitants to dig ditches and build castles. For the *third*, he commanded the priests, and others in the Christian army, to offer up continual prayers, moving the crusaders to repentance and virtue. Besides which he promised a twentieth part of the revenues of benefices for three years, and a tenth of those of the pope and his cardinals. He likewise encouraged all who had the care of souls to influence the faithful to make donations by testament and otherwise. The decree touching the levies of money displeased many prelates, who openly opposed it, declaring that the court of Rome now perpetually despoiled them under that pretext.

The edict against Frederic found willing obedience from the superstition or the turbulence of the German barons. Henry was supported by numerous partisans, and waged a prosperous warfare against Conrad, the son of Frederic; and on his early death, William, count of Holland, was substituted by the pope as a candidate for the throne. Innocent's genius and activity suggested to him the most refined arts to insure success, and his principles permitted him to adopt the most iniquitous. He even departed so far from the observance of humanity, and the most sacred feelings of nature, as to employ his intrigues to seduce Conrad from the service of his father, into rebellious and parricidal allegiance to the Church. That virtuous prince, rejecting, with firmness, the impious proposition, replied, that he would defend the side he had chosen to the last breath of

however, (Vit. Inn. IV., sec. xx.) argues that the approbation of the Council was implied in its proceedings, if not actually expressed in the title of the sentence.

life*; and neither the pope nor the Church gained even a temporary advantage by an attempt which covers them with eternal infamy.

The same industrious hostility which had kindled rebellion among the German princes, was exerted with no less effect among the contentious states of Italy. The Guelphic interests were everywhere strengthened by the energy of Innocent; and the utmost efforts of Frederic were insufficient to restore tranquillity to Germany, or even to obtain any important triumphs over his Italian enemies. He died in Apulia, in the year 1250; and though he had never formally renounced the title of emperor, his deposition was virtually accomplished by the edict of Innocent, since the rest of his life was spent in uninterrupted confusion and alarm, in the midst of battle, and sedition, and treason, without any enjoyment of the repose of royalty, and with a very limited possession either of its dignity or authority. The character of Frederic has been vilified by Guelphic writers, and probably too highly exalted by the opposite faction. In the conduct of affairs purely temporal, he is celebrated for justice, magnificence, generosity, as well as for the patronage of arts and literature. Familiar with the use of many languages, and himself an author, he exhibited that disposition to cultivate science, and nourish every branch of knowledge, which is so seldom associated with great vices. In regard to his long and complicated contentions with the Church, it is unquestionably true that he violated, without any known necessity, certain solemn obligations respecting the time of commencing his Crusade. His reluctance to engage at all in such sanguinary and fruitless enterprises may be acknowledged and justified; but his repeated breach of faith gave some reason to the Holy See for suspecting his subsequent promises. It is also true that he exiled some bishops, and imprisoned others, and even proceeded to greater extremities against some individuals of the inferior orders of the clergy; and also that he levied contributions and imposts on all classes of his ecclesiastical subjects†. But those

His death and character.

---

* Giannone, Stor. Nap., lib. xvii., ch. 4.

† Hence (says Giannone) probably arose the report, that he had commonly proclaimed his intention of reducing the clergy to primitive poverty; "so that

who felt his rigour may probably have deserved it by moral or political misconduct; and it was just and legal * that the clergy should contribute some proportion to the support of the state. It may seem strange that, while his adversaries heap upon him the bitterest charges of impiety and blasphemy †, his friends persist in asserting the unalterable fidelity and affection which he bore to his mother-church, the protectress of his infancy; that he was ever eager to advocate her cause, and promote her interests. In support of this singular pretension, it is advanced, that he was the inflexible and implacable

His consti- extirpator of heresy. This fact, though urged by his admirers,
tutions
against he- is not disputed by his enemies. It is faithfully recorded, that
resy.
at an early period (1224) he published three constitutions, which aggravated the guilt and punishments of heresy even beyond those of treason, and placed the temporal authorities at the disposal of the ecclesiastical inquisitors ‡. "Those (he ordained) who have been arrested for heresy, and who, being moved by the fear of death, are desirous to return to the Church, shall be condemned to the penance of perpetual imprisonment. The judges shall be bound to seize the heretics discarded by the inquisitors of the Holy See, or by others zealous for the Catholic faith, and to confine them closely until their execution, according to the sentence of the Church. . . . We also condemn to

Matthew Paris, who, before Frederic's deposition, had always adhered to his party, as soon as he understood that such were his common expressions, as he was himself abbot of Monte Albano (St. Alban's), in England, and wealthy and well beneficed, was displeased with such a proposition, and so began to change his style, and to write against him, in a manner different from his former." Stor. di Nap., lib. xvii., c. 4.

* Giannone proves that such had been the invariable custom, at least in the southern provinces of the empire of Frederic.

† One of these is the celebrated expression respecting the Three Impostors, then commonly attributed to Frederic, though solemnly and publicly denied by him. Another is a tale, recorded by certain monks, that, when they requested him to spare their crop of wheat, Frederic commanded his soldiers "to desist, and to respect those ears of corn, since some day the grains which they contained might become so many Christs." Giannone, loc. cit., on authority of Simon Hanh. Hist. Germ. in Frederico II.

‡ Several authors assert that, in virtue of a promise made to Innocent III., he established a permanent inquisition in Sicily in the year 1213. Stor. di Nap. loc. cit. This, however, is scarcely probable, for the inquisition was not at that time permanently established even at Toulouse.

death those who, having abjured to save their life, shall return into error. We deprive heretics, and all who abet them, of all benefit of appeal; and it is our will that heresy be entirely banished from the whole extent of our empire. And as the crime which assails God is greater than that of treason, we ordain that the children of heretics, to the second generation, be deprived of all temporal benefits and all public offices, unless they come forward and denounce their parents*."

Such were the measures by which an independent, and powerful, and (for those days) an enlightened monarch evinced his affection for the Church of Rome! Such were the favours by which he courted her friendship, and sought to merit her gratitude! by feeding her fiercest passion—by sanctioning the most fatal of all her evil principles. It is true that Frederic may thus have established some claims on the sympathy of the furious zealots of his time; but his indulgence to those churchmen was no deed of friendship to the Church. To protect and foster the vices of a system is to prevent its permanence, and poison its prosperity; and if ever, during his long reign, he appeared as the real friend of Rome, it was at the time when he least professed that name—at the time when he exposed her abuses, and proclaimed her shame, and called upon her to repent and amend. And assuredly, when he lent his obsequious sword to swell the catalogue of her crimes, he was already preparing for his latter years the tempest which disturbed and tormented them; nor did it happen without the spirit of God, that his calamities were inflicted by that same hand whose darkest atrocities had been approved and directed by himself.

It is strange, too, that among the four reasons by which the Pope justified his sentence of deposition, it was one, that Frederic had rendered himself *guilty of heresy*, by his contempt of pontifical censures, and his unholy alliance with the Saracens. Thus, then, did that prince, according to the strict letter of his own constitutions, become liable, on his condemnation by the Church, to the monstrous penalties contained in them.

* These constitutions are found among the letters of Pietro delle Vigne, chancellor of the emperor, which shows, says Fleury, who was their author. Hist. Eccl., lib. lxxviii., sec. lxv.

Another*, perhaps a more plausible reason, was this,—that he had been deficient in that fidelity which he owed to the Pope, as his vassal for the kingdom of Sicily; for that claim, however absurd in origin and principle, had been previously asserted and acknowledged. But, in truth, when we compare the character and causes of this second conflict between the Church and the Empire with those which marked the contest of Henry with Gregory VII. and his successors, we find it much more difficult to discover what was the specific and tangible ground of quarrel. In the former instance there existed one grand and definite object, for which both parties perseveringly struggled: in the latter, many vague complaints and indeterminate offences were advanced and retorted; but no single great principle was avowedly contested, nor was any one additional right or privilege acquired or confirmed to the Church by its final triumph. Only the power and influence of Rome were made more manifest; and other nations were taught to tremble at the omnipotence of the double sword.

This leads us to remark another distinction,—that, in the contest with Henry, it was, in reality, the *Church* of Rome which rose in opposition to the empire—the spiritual, or, at least, the ecclesiastical, interests of the See were those most consulted and most prominent in the debate. In that with Frederic, it was rather from the *Court* of Rome that the spirit and motives of policy proceeded. In the former case, the material sword was introduced as secondary and subsidiary to the spiritual; but in the latter, if the contrary was not actually the case†, at least the two weapons were so dexterously substituted and interchanged for each other—the one was so continually presented under the holy semblance of the other—as to show

* See Sismondi, Rep. Ital., ch. xvi.

† In the year 1251, Christianus, (or Conrad,) Archbishop of Mentz, was actually deposed by Innocent, for reluctance to use arms in defence of the Church. "He said, that the works of war did not become the sacerdotal character; but that he was ever willing to use the sword of the spirit, which was the word of God. The scriptures had commanded him to put his sword in the sheath." . . Of this offence (and no other charge is mentioned) he was accused by the king and certain of the laity before the Pope, and was immediately degraded from his see. Pagi, Innoc. IV., sec. xlvii.

the proficiency which the See had latterly made in the art of deluding the human race.

Again—the avarice or the necessities of Rome compelled her, during these disputes, to a measure which, however expedient at the moment, was finally very injurious to her—that of levying taxes rigidly and generally upon the clergy. It was not in England only (though there most successfully*) that Gregory IX. exacted from all ranks of ecclesiastics the tenth of their moveables immediately on his breach with the emperor; and every one recollects with what repugnance his second requisition (in 1240) was admitted by our clerical forefathers. From the moment that the Pope was found so infatuated as to publish a *Crusade*† against a Catholic emperor, and to feed his own temporal ambition by despoiling his faithful Catholic clergy, the minds of all reasonable laymen were startled and revolted by the former outrage, while the hearts of the clergy,

* The pages of Matthew Paris abound with instances of pontifical rapacity and insolence. See *ad annos* 1244, 1245, 1246, 1247, 1250, 1252, &c. . . Sometimes a legate à latere was the instrument; sometimes the Mendicants acted as tax-gatherers; and even Ireland did not escape their visitations. In 1247, the complaints both of the French and English clergy assumed a formidable shape for that age. The lasting effect was, that the former devotion to Rome was turned into "execrabile odium et maledictiones occultas." For all both saw and felt that the Pope was insatiable in his extortions, to their great loss and impoverishment; and there were many who began to question whether he had really received from heaven the power of St. Peter to bind and to loose, seeing how very unlike he was to that apostle. "Resolutum est igitur os iniqua loquentium, &c." . . . and this as well in France as in England.

† The same indulgences were promised to those who armed against the emperor as against the sultan; and the apostolic preachers, under Innocent at least, even pointed out the former as the easier and broader road to salvation. Sismondi, Rep. Ital., chap. xvi. Fleury, Hist. Eccl., lib. lxxxiii., sec. xxxiii. The nobility of France, and the queen Blanche, were highly offended by this measure of Innocent, during the Crusade of St. Louis. "The Pope (they complained) is preaching a new Crusade against Christians for the extension of his own dominions, and forgets the king, our master, who is suffering so much for the faith." "Let the Pope (the queen replied) keep those who go into his service; and let them depart, never to return." The nobles also reprimanded the Mendicants who had preached this Crusade. "We build for you churches and houses: we receive, nourish, and entertain you. What good does the Pope for you? He fatigues and torments you; he makes you his tax-gatherers, and renders you hateful to your benefactors." They excused themselves on the plea of the obedience due to him. . . . Here we discover the elements of the Gallican Liberties.

being touched by the injustice of the latter, began gradually to close against so rapacious a protector.

When Innocent received the news of the death of Frederic his exultation broke forth without restraint or moderation ;— " Let the heavens rejoice, and let the earth be in festivity ; for the thunder and the tempest with which a powerful God has so long threatened your heads, are changed by the death of that man into refreshing breezes and fertilizing dews†." It was thus that he addressed the clergy of Sicily, while, at the same time, he prepared to reduce that province, together with the kingdom of Naples, under his own immediate government, and attach it in perpetuity to the dominions of the Church. In pursuance of this project, he quitted Lyons, his constant residence* during the uncertainties of the war, and visited, in a sort of triumphal procession, the Guelphic cities of Italy. He was everywhere received with an enthusiasm which he had not merited by any regard for any interests except his own ; and he is even supposed somewhat to have chilled the misplaced gratitude of his allies by the unexpected assertion of some spiritual pretensions over themselves. In Sicily, and the south of Italy, he succeeded in creating a powerful party ; but it was overthrown by the arms of Conrad and Manfred, the sons of Frederic. Foiled by force, the Pope had recourse to intrigue ; and he began to treat successively with the kings of England and France, with a view to bestow the crown of the Sicilies on a branch either of the one family or the other. In the mean time, the death of

---

* In a similar spirit of Christian forgiveness, the same Pope is related to have expressed his exultation at the death of Grostete, bishop of Lincoln. " I rejoice, and let every true son of the Church rejoice with me—that my great enemy is removed!" Assuredly that admirable prelate had gone very far in disaffection, not hesitating to denounce Innocent, almost with his dying breath, as Antichrist; " For by what other name are we to designate that power, which labours to destroy the souls that Christ came to save ? "

† On the departure of the Pope from Lyons, the Cardinal Hugo made a valedictory address to all the population of both sexes ; and it contained the following sentence :—" Amici, magnam fecimus, postquam in hanc Urbem venimus, utilitatem et eleemosynam. Quando enim primo huc venimus, tria vel quattuor protibula invenimus. Sed nunc recedentes unum solum relinquimus. Verum ipsum durat continuatum ab orientali parte civitatis usque ad occidentalem." This is related as fact by Matthew Paris, ann. 1251.

Conrad revived in him the expiring hope of uniting it to his own. Ambition resumed her sway; and he broke off the imperfect negotiations. The kingdom of Naples was again thronged with his emissaries; seditions were in every quarter excited in his favour; and even Manfred himself, in the belief that resistance would be vain, advanced to the frontiers to offer his submission, and deigned to lead by the bridle the horse of the pontiff as he crossed the Garigliano.

This event, which seemed to secure to the court of Rome the throne of Naples and Sicily, and thus to extend its dominions beyond any limits which it had at any time reached, or, till lately, aspired to, took place in the summer of 1254. The duration of this unnatural prosperity was even shorter than could have been predicted by the most penetrating statesman; for before the conclusion of the very same year, Manfred had again possessed himself of the keys of the kingdom. But Innocent did not live to witness this second reverse;—he had already expired * at Naples, in mature old age, and in the confident persuasion that he had achieved the dearest object of his ambition, and that he died the most powerful prince who had ever filled the throne of St. Peter.

During a pontificate of eleven years and five months, he had displayed all the qualities which consummate an artful poli- His Character.

---

* Soon after Innocent's death, (of which the exact day, it is proper to remark, is disputed, Pagi, Inn. IV., sec. lxv.) a cardinal had the following vision. He saw a noble matron, on whose brow the word *Ecclesia* was written, present her petition at the Judgment-seat, saying, Justissime Judex, justè judica. She then brought forward these charges against Innocent IV. (1.) At the foundation of the Church, Thou didst give it liberties proceeding from Thyself; but he has made it the vilest of slaves (ancillam vilissimam). (2.) It was founded to benefit the souls of the miserable;—he has made it a table of money-gatherers. (3.) It was founded in Faith, Justice, and Truth;—but he has staggered Faith, destroyed Justice, and clouded Truth. " Justum ergo judicium redde mihi." Then the Lord said to him, Go and receive thy reward according to thy merits. And thus he was carried away. The cardinal then woke, through the terror of this sentence, and shouted so loud, as to excite the suspicion of insanity. "Ista visio (continues Matthew Paris) (nescitur si fantastica) multos perterruit; et utinam cum effectu castigans emendavit." That it was generally propagated, and perhaps believed at the time, is sufficient to prove to us (if we needed indirect proof) what was the sort of reputation which Innocent IV. possessed among his contemporaries.

tician, and which disgrace a bishop and a Christian. As a statesman, he designed daringly, he negotiated skilfully, he intrigued successfully; he perfectly comprehended the means at his disposal, and adapted them so closely to his purposes, that his reign presented a series of those triumphs * which are usually designated glorious. As a churchman, he bade defiance to the best principles of his religion ; he set at nought the common feelings of humanity. The spiritual guide to eternal life, he had no fixed motive of action, except vulgar temporal ambition. " The servant of the servants of God," he rejected with scorn the humiliation of Frederic †, and spurned a suppliant emperor who had been his friend. And lastly, when the infant son of Conrad was presented to his tutelary protection by a dying father, the prayer was haughtily refused ; and " the father of all Christians, and the protector of all orphans," hastened to usurp the hereditary rights of a Christian child and orphan. These circumstances duly considered, with every allowance for times and prejudices, seem, indeed, almost to justify the expression of the sultan of Egypt, in his answer to a letter of Innocent—the taunt of a Mussulman addressed to Christ's vicar upon earth ;—" We have received your epistle, and listened to your envoy : he has spoken to us of Jesus Christ—whom we know better than you know, *and whom we honour more than you honour him* ‡."

Alexander IV.   Alexander IV. succeeded to the chair, to the passions, and to the projects of Innocent; and it was the leading object of

* We should mention, however, that the fall of Frederic is not wholly attributable to Innocent's influence. A very strong republican and anti-imperial spirit previously prevailed in many, especially the northern, cities of Italy, which the Pope could not have created, though he very well knew how to avail himself of it. Another remark we may here make,—that Innocent was much more successful in fomenting seditions, and making parties in foreign states, than in securing the subordination of his own capital. There were few cities in Italy where he had less influence than at Rome, which may account for his continual absence from it. See Sismondi, Rep. Ital., chap. xviii. Matthew Paris, Hist. Angliæ, ann. 1254.

† Sismondi, Rep. Ital., chap. xvii.

‡ " De quo Christo plus scimus quam vos sciatis, et magnificamus eum plusquam vos magnificatis." Bzov., Ann. Eccles., ad ann. 1264. Matthew Paris, Hist. ad ann. eundem. The letter is a very sensible composition, and deals very directly with the subjects on which it treats.

his reign of six years to maintain or recover the temporal possession of the kingdom of Manfred. But he possessed neither the firmness of character nor the various talents necessary for success. The machine, which had not always moved obediently even to the hand of Innocent, seemed to lose, in his feebler grasp, all the elasticity of its action; and it became evident, before the end of his pontificate, that the sceptre of Naples and Sicily was not destined to a bishop of Rome. At the same time, Alexander was celebrated for the exercise of some of those virtues which were not found in his predecessor—for earnestness of piety, or, at least, for assiduity in prayer, and the strict observance of Church regulations*. The favours which he bestowed upon the Mendicant orders will prove his zeal, indeed, rather than the wisdom of his policy. But the crusade which he preached, from whatsoever motive, against the tyrant Eccelino, was almost justified by the crimes of that miscreant; for though a war proclaimed "in the name of God" is, in most instances, only wickedness cloaked by blasphemy, yet we may view it with some indulgence, when it is directed against the convicted enemy of mankind.

For the seven following years (from 1261 to 1268) the chair was occupied by two Frenchmen, Urban IV. and Clement IV., who have obtained an eminent place in civil as well as ecclesiastical history, by the introduction of Charles of Anjou to the throne of Naples. Whether from personal hostility to the actual occupant of that throne, or from ecclesiastical rancour against the son of Frederic, or from a political determination to cut off all connexion between the south of Italy and the empire, or from all these causes united, the Holy See, by whomsoever administered, did not remit or relax its exertions for the expulsion of Manfred. The negotiations with the court of France, which Innocent IV. had commenced and interrupted, were renewed and concluded by Urban IV.; and during the following reign of Clement, the crusade against a legitimate and virtuous

Urban IV. and Clement IV.

---

* Alexander IV. is thus characterised by Matthew Paris:—"Satis benignus et bene religiosus; assiduus in orationibus, in abstinentia strenuus, sed sibilis adulantium seducibilis, et pravis avarorum suggestionibus inclinitivus." Pagi is very much offended by the qualification of the praise.

monarch was completed with the most sanguinary success. The brother of St. Louis supported his usurpation by the same merciless sword which had achieved it ; and the historians of Italy still recount, with tears of indignation, the more than usual horrors of the French invasion.

But however strong this pope's nationality may have been, it did not cause him to forget his papal interests. The conditions which he exacted from Charles, on investing him with the crown of Naples, contained most of the claims then in dispute between kings and popes, such as the unqualified appointment to vacant sees, the exclusive care of the temporalities during vacancy, and even the abolition of all pretensions rising from the regalia*.

Ecclesiastical writers likewise inform us that *commendams* to benefices, and the distinction between simple benefices, and those with cure of souls, were the introduction of this age ; and that the jurisdiction, privileges, and immunities of the clergy were thus extended as far as possible. Pluralities were strictly prohibited, and commonly enjoyed. On the other hand, ecclesiastics were compelled to contribute, not only to the real or pretended necessities of the church, but frequently, under one pretext or other, to the exigencies of the state.

On the death of Clement, the See was vacant, through the disunion of the cardinals, for about three years. At length, in 1272, an Italian, a native of Piacenza, was elected, and Gregory X. assumed the name of Gregory X.—" a person (says Fleury †) of little learning, but of great experience in secular affairs, and more given to the distribution of alms, than the amassing of riches." He was in the Holy Land at the time of his appointment ; and as he returned with a keen and recent impression of its sufferings, and with an enthusiasm freshly kindled by that spectacle, the first act of his pontificate was directed to

* See Giannone, Stor. di Nap., lib. xix., cap. v. In a Bull, dated in 1266, he declared that the disposition of all benefices rightfully belonged to the pope. The claims of the princes were supported by a decree of the Council of Lyons. See Dupin, Siècle xiii., sec. x.

† Hist. Eccl., lib. lxxxvi. sec. xvii.

the revival of the crusading ardour; and the same continued to the end of his life to be the favourite object of his exertions. He was successful, because he was sincere. Those, who cared not for his reasoning, listened to his disinterested supplications; those who were not inflamed by his enthusiasm, still respected and loved it. It was no longer against a Christian sectarian, or a Catholic Emperor and his persecuted race, that the monarchs of Europe were called upon to arm; it was no longer for the peculiar aggrandizement of the court or Church of Rome, that the father of Christians summoned them to battle; they had already learnt to distinguish between the interests of the Vatican and the honour of Christ; and the magic which a spiritual pope had so long exercised over the human mind lost much of its fascination and power, as soon as he degenerated into a temporal prince.

But Gregory X. had higher and less ambiguous claims on the gratitude of Christendom than any zeal for the deliverance of Palestine could possibly give him. He laboured to compose the dissensions of his distracted country; to heal the wounds which had been so wantonly inflicted by the selfish ambition of his predecessors. He interposed impartially, and therefore not vainly, to reconcile the opposite factions of Guelphs and Ghibellines*; and exhibited to them the new and venerable spectacle of a pacific pope. He interposed too in the affairs of

* Leonardus Aretinus (Histor. Florent. lib. iii. p. 48, edit. Argent. 1610) bears ample testimony to the sanctity and pacific character of Gregory, and details the circumstances of his attempt to reconcile parties at Florence. The following is given as part of his address to the citizens:—" Quæ est igitur hæc tam præpotens causa? Quod Guelphus est (inquit) aut Gibellinus—nomina ne ipsis quidem qui illa proferunt nota!—Ea nimirum causa est cur cives necantur, domus incenduntur, evertitur patria, sititur proximi sanguis. Oh puerilem stultitiam! oh amentiam non ferendam! Gibellinus est—at Christianus, at civis, at proximus at consanguineus. Ergo hæc tot et tam valida conjunctionis nomina Gibellino succumbent? Et id unum atque inane nomen (nam quid significet nemo intelligit) plus valebit ad odium, quam ista omnia tam præclara et tam solida et expressa ad caritatem, &c." These sentiments (the historian adds) were grateful to the multitude, but displeased the aristocracy. The Pope was then obliged to lay the city under an interdict; and his admirable intentions involved him in an obstinate contest with the nobles. But any doubts which might still remain respecting his sanctity were removed (as Leonardus gravely asserts) by the numerous miracles performed at his tomb.

the empire ; but it was again for the purpose of terminating a division which threatened the peace of Germany; and he proved the sincerity of his intention by confirming the election of Rodolph, who had secured and deserved the affections of his people. Another project, on which he was bent with like earnestness, had the same respectable character,—the reconciliation of the Greek and Latin Churches ; and in this difficult affair he also obtained a complete (though very transient) success, by the concessions of the Emperor Michael, and the temporary or nominal submission of his Church.

The Second Council of Lyons, 1274, A.D.

It was at the second Council of Lyons that the deputies of the East presented their faithless homage to the Roman pontiff. But that prelate had two other, and, perhaps, dearer objects in the summoning of that vast assembly *. The one was to complete the preparations for this long-projected Crusade: the other was worthier of his wisdom, and even of his piety— to reform the obnoxious abuses of his Church. In the course of the six sessions of the council, thirty-one constitutions were enacted for the better administration of the Church, and they did honour at least to the intentions of those who promulgated them. Some eight or ten of these related to the election of bishops ; several others to cures and benefices, to the discipline or temporalities of the Church. Another (the 21st) was levelled against the unlimited growth of Mendicant orders; disbanding all which had not formally received the papal confirmation, and discouraging the foundation of others. But that, among the acts of this assembly, which was at the time the most celebrated, and perhaps in effect the most permanent, was the law which regulated the method of papal election, by severe restraints imposed upon the conclave †. It was then enacted,

* Five hundred bishops, seventy mitred abbots, and a thousand inferior clergy and theologians composed this Council, assembled in 1274. The legates of Michael the Greek Emperor, and of the King of the Tartars, were present. Also the ambassadors of France, Germany, England, Sicily, &c., and one Prince, James of Arragon. Pagi, Greg. X., s. xxv.

† Pagi, Vit. Greg. X. sect. xli. Fleury, liv. lxxxvi., sect. xlv. It was quite obvious that, as men and cardinals are constituted, these regulations could not be enforced rigorously. But with some modifications they subsist even to this moment.

that the cardinals should be lodged in one chamber, without any separation of wall or curtain, or any issue—that the chamber should be so closed on every side, as to leave no possibility of entrance or exit. " No one shall approach them or address them privately, unless with the consent of all present, and on the business of the election. The conclave (properly the name of the chamber) shall have one window, through which necessary food may be admitted, without there being space for the human body to enter. And if (which God forbid) in three days after their entrance they shall not yet have come to a decision, for the fifteen following days they shall be contented with a single dish, as well for dinner as for supper. But after these fifteen days they shall have no other nourishment than bread, wine and water, until the election shall be made. During the election, they shall receive nothing from the apostolical chamber, nor any other revenues of the Roman Church."

The expedition to Palestine gave promise of the most favourable issue. The emperor Rodolph had engaged to conduct it; Philip the Hardy, king of France, Edward of England, James of Arragon, and Charles of Sicily, had pledged their faith to attend it; supplies had been secured by the universal imposition of a tax on ecclesiastical property; and the following year was devoted to the necessary preparations. At the termination of that year (in January, 1276), before one galley had departed, or perhaps one soldier embarked, the pope himself fell sick and died. From that moment (says Sismondi) the kings, into whom he had inspired his enthusiasm, renounced their chivalrous projects; the Greeks returned to their schisms, and the Catholics, divided afresh, turned against each other those arms, which they had consecrated to the deliverance of Palestine.

The short reigns of Innocent V., Adrian V., and John XXI. were not distinguished by any memorable event. Nicholas III., a Roman of the family of the Ursini, succeeded in 1277, and devoted himself with great prudence and success, not so much to enlarge the temporal edifice of his Church, as to secure the foundations on which it stood. For that purpose, he resumed some negotiations, commenced by Gregory X. at Lyons, with

Intended Crusade, and death of Gregory.

Nicholas III.

Rodolph, king of the Romans, and brought them to so fortunate a termination, that that prince finally satisfied all the
donations of preceding emperors, and recognized the cities of
the ecclesiastical states as being absolutely independent of himself, and owing their entire allegiance to the pope. Nicholas
had another object of jealousy in the increasing power of
Charles, king of Sicily, and he had the address* to engage
that prince to resign two very important dignities, which he
had probably acquired through the subservience of Clement IV.
One was the office of imperial vicar-general in Tuscany; the
other was that of senator of Rome. We have already had
occasion to mention the inefficacy of the pope's civil authority
in his own capital; and this had lately been subjected even to
additional insult by the frequent appointment of foreigners to
the highest offices. Pope Nicholas published a constitution
to prevent the recurrence of this evil, and to limit the time of
possession to one year.

It is worth remarking, that in defence of his temporal sovereignty, as well over the states, as over the city, of Rome, he
appealed to the immoveable foundations on which he conceived
them to rest. In favour of the first, he pleaded the donations
of Louis the Meek, and the confirmations of Otho I. and St.
Henry †; in favour of the second, the " Donation of Constantine;" and he maintained, that the temporal power of the pope
and his cardinals was absolutely necessary for the free exercise
of their spiritual functions. He reigned only two years and
nine months: he is commonly described as possessing many
good qualities; and we read of no other serious charge against
him than that he heaped upon his greedy relatives and connexions the most splendid benefices of the church with unme-
rited and shameless prodigality.

Martin IV.   The king of Sicily was successful in procuring the election
of a Frenchman, Martin IV., who is chiefly remarkable in

---

* The art with which he played off the emperor and king of Sicily against
each other, until he obtained all that he required from both, was worthy of the
most refined ages of papal diplomacy. See Sismondi, Rep. Ital., chap. xxii.,
ann. 1277, 1278.

† Fleury, liv. lxxxvii., sect. xv. and xvi. Rain. ann. 1278, s. 57 and 74.

history for his entire subservience to the interests of his patron. In violation of both the clauses of the constitution of Nicholas, he accepted the office of senator, and held it for life. As this was the first instance of such condescension on the part of St. Peter's successors, it has not escaped the notice of the historian. And if, indeed, the claims on the temporal sovereignty of Rome, which they had asserted for above two centuries, had been well founded, it would have been a strange and unprecedented degradation for a sovereign prince to exercise a simple magistracy in his own city *. But Martin was probably less disposed to examine the remote and general question of right than to avail himself of the substantial power thus firmly vested in his own person.

He enjoyed his dignity for a very short time, though sufficient to make him witness of the " Sicilian Vespers" and the misfortunes of his countrymen. He was buried in the church of St. Lawrence, and many sick were healed at his tomb, in the presence of vast numbers of the clergy and laity, according to the evidence of a contemporary author, who affirms that those miracles still continued while he was writing, six weeks after the decease of the pontiff †. The mention of these impostures is so common, even in the pages of the most enlightened Catholic historians, that we are not justified in passing them over in entire silence. In fact, they formed so essential a part of the Roman Catholic system, that we should do injustice to its whole character if we were not occasionally to notice them.

Martin was succeeded by a noble Roman, Honorius IV.; Nicholas and he by another native of the Roman states, Nicholas IV., IV. who was elected in 1288. The claims of this pope on historical notice are confined to some diligent but almost hopeless exer-

* Sismondi (chap. xxii.) asserts that he immediately transferred his dignity to Charles, following Jordanus apud Raynaldum, and other authorities. The words of the appointment sufficiently express the extent of the power conferred. " Nobiles viri . . Electores ordinati . . . domino Martino Papæ IV. unanimiter et concorditer transtulerunt et plenarie commiserunt regimen senatus Urbis, ejusque territorii et districtus toto tempore vitæ suæ: et dederunt sibi plenam et liberam potestatem regendi toto tempore Urbem . . . per se, vel per alium, vel per alios, et eligendi senatorem, vel senatores," &c. &c.

† Fleury, liv. lxxxviii., sect. xvii. Both Martin and his predecessor were extremely attached to the Franciscan order.

tions to excite the princes of Europe to another crusade; and
to some as zealous, and as fruitless, efforts for the extirpation
of heresy.   In 1288 he stimulated his mendicant emissaries
to peculiar diligence both in Italy and Provence, and put in
practice a somewhat singular method for securing the orthodoxy of his people*.   He obliged the converted heretic to be
bound in a pecuniary recognizance against relapse, and to find
sufficient securities for payment.   Avarice was scarcely become
even yet the ruling passion of the Vatican: but since the sway
of Innocent III., it had been rapidly gaining ground; and the
edict of Nicholas gives fearful indications of its progress.   In
the year following, an ordinance was published at Venice, for
the purpose of facilitating the operations of the inquisition;
and it was approved and confirmed by the pontiff.

Nicholas died soon afterwards; and the history of his successor is distinguished by so many strange circumstances from
the ordinary annals of papal biography, that it may afford
relief as well as advantage to unfold its particulars.   Through
the disunion of the cardinals, the see had already been vacant
for seven-and-twenty months, and no progress seemed yet to
have been made towards the decision.   They were still assembled in conclave, and still without any prospect of immediate accommodation, when, on some day in the beginning of
July, 1294, one of their number was prevented from attending
the deliberation by the sudden and violent death of his brother.
By this casual occurrence, the thoughts of the venerable society
were directed to man's mortality; and their reflections assumed
a serious and solemn character.   At length, returning to the
subject before them, the bishop of Tusculum asked with vehemence, " Why then delay we so long to give a head to the
Church? whence this division among us?" To which Cardinal
Latino added, " It has been revealed to a holy man, that unless we hasten to the election of a pope, in less than four
months the anger of God will burst upon us." Hereupon,
Benedict Gaietano (the same who was afterwards Boniface

Election of
Pietro di
Morone, or
Celestine
V.

---

* The idea was not original. Instructions to the same effect were given to the
Minorites by Alexander IV. in 1258. It was then provided that the money so
raised should be employed in the prosecution of heretics.

VIII.) sarcastically smiled and said, " It is brother Pietro di Morone, to whom that revelation has been vouchsafed?" Latino answered, " The same; he has written to me that, when engaged in his nocturnal devotions before the altar, he had received the command of God to communicate this warning." Then the cardinals began to discourse of what they knew concerning that holy man. One dwelt on the austerity of his life, another on his virtues, another on his miracles. Presently some one proposed *him* as a candidate for the see; and a discussion immediately arose on that question.

The debate was of very short duration, for reason had given place to passionate emotion, and passion was mistaken for inspiration. Cardinal Latino first gave his suffrage for Pietro di Morone; his example was eagerly followed by his colleagues, and the sudden and ardent unanimity of the conclave was attributed to the immediate impulse of the divinity*.

Its choice had fallen upon a weak and aged recluse, whose life had been devoted to the most rigorous observances of superstition, and whose inveterate habits of solitary meditation disqualified him for the commonest offices of society. His very name was derived from the mountain-top where his existence had passed away. The cave in which he dwelt had been the refuge of a dragon, who obsequiously resigned it to his human successor: we are seriously assured, that his infancy had been the object of that miraculous agency which he so profusely exercised in his later years; and that, even at his entrance into this polluted world, he was protected by the semblance, or the reality of the monastic habit†.

The deputies proceeded to announce to him the astounding

* A suspicious historian would perhaps except Benedict Gaietano from the charge of superstitious enthusiasm. Possibly even then he proposed to profit by the weaknesses of Pietro; but he could scarcely have considered them as the object of God's especial interposition, or have believed that an old man, who had not hitherto filled any office in society, had been selected by the especial favour of Providence to occupy the highest.

† All these fables are sedulously and solemnly related by Bzovius. " Manebat matri fixum quod nascenti olim filio contigerat, ac tanquam magnum aliquod divinumque portendebat. Ex utero siquidem materno exieat circumamictus indumento quodam, quod nihil ab his, quibus religiosi homines vestiuntur, differebat." Ad ann. 1294.

change in his fortune. They arrived at the city of Sulmone, and having received permission to present themselves, ascended with toil and sweat the narrow and rugged path which led through a desolate wilderness to the cell they sought. The cell was closed against them, and they were compelled to make their communication through a small grated window. Through the interstices they beheld a pale old man, attenuated with fasting and macerations, with a beard dishevelled and eyes inflamed with tears, trembling with the agitation into which the awful announcement had thrown him. The Archbishop of Lyons then assured him of the enthusiasm which had united the cardinals in his favour; and pressed him, by accepting the dignity, to compose the troubles of the Church. Pietro answered, "I must consult God—go and pray likewise." He then prostrated himself on the earth, and after remaining some time in supplication, he rose and said, " I accept the pontificate, I consent to the election—I dare not resist the will of God—I will not be wanting to the Church in her necessity." No sooner was the result of this interview bruited abroad, than the sides of Mount Morone were frequented by assiduous visitants, whom piety, or interest, or curiosity conducted to the cavern of the hermit-pope. Churchmen and laymen of every rank hastened to pay homage to his virtues, or his dignity ; and his earliest levee was adorned by the presence of two kings*.

His character.

It was immediately discovered that the qualifications of Celestine V. (Pietro assumed that name) fell far short even of the ordinary limits of monastic capacity. He was entirely ignorant of all science and all literature ; even the Latin language was nearly strange to him ; against the comprehension of worldly matters his eyes were closed by perpetual seclusion, and his blindness was confirmed by old age; his simplicity tempted and rewarded deception, and he was guilty of the most

* Charles le Boiteux of Sicily, and his son Charles Martel, titular prince of Hungary. The pope elect descended to Aquila to assume his pontificals, on an ass, and the two princes held the bridle.

Intumidus vilem Murro conscendit asellum,
Regum fræna manu dextra lævaque regente
Pontificis...

Might there not in this act be some of that "Humility which apes the Divinity ?"

extraordinary errors in the discharge of his easiest duties. Besides this, he brought with him from his cell and his convent (for he had been the founder of a new Order of Monks, distinguished for their illiterate vulgarity) a disaffection towards the higher ranks of the secular clergy, which was not perhaps without reason; and a contempt for their luxuries and abhorrence for their vices, which formed the holiest feature in his character. It was probably this disposition which endeared him to the laity, as well as to many among the regular clergy; and no doubt it was the alienation from his own official counsellors, which subjected him too obsequiously to the influence of the king of Sicily. For under this influence he was assuredly acting, when, without any foresight of the inevitable consequences of the measure, he added to the college of cardinals seven natives of France.

These were circumstances sufficient to excite the dissatisfaction of that body, and their suspicions respecting the nature of the spirit which had decided their choice. They professed apprehensions, which were not wholly unreasonable, lest, by some new imprudence, the pope should compromise or concede the inviolable rights of the Church.—They disliked the frugal severity of his court; they complained, with justice, that he preferred an obscure residence in the kingdom of Naples to the Holy and Imperial City; and the bitterness of their displeasure was completed, when he revived in all its rigour the obnoxious constitution of Gregory X. respecting the manner of papal election.

In the mean time, Celestine had discovered his own disqualifications and his inability to correct them. Amidst the incessant toil of occupations which he disliked and dignities which he despised, he sighed for the tranquillity of his former solitude; and then, that his pious meditations might not wholly be discontinued, he caused a cell to be constructed in the centre of his palace, whither he frequently retired to prayer. On such occasions, he sometimes gave vent to his deep disquietude. " I am told that I possess all power over souls in this world—why is it then that I cannot assure myself of the safety of mine own? that I cannot rid myself of all these anxieties, and impart to my own breast that repose which I can dispense so easily to others? Does God require from me that which is impossible; or has he only raised me in order to cast me down more terribly? I observe the cardinals divided; and I hear from every side complaints against me. Is it not better to burst my chains, and resign the Holy See to some one who can rule it in peace?—if only I could be permitted to quit this place and return to my solitude!"

His resignation.

Several of the cardinals having observed that disposition, were sedulous to encourage it. It was entirely in accordance with their general wishes, with that most especially of Benedict Gaietano; since he designed himself for the successor. Those, on the other hand, who profited by Celestine's simplicity, or reverenced his piety, or admired his popular austerities, dissuaded him from so unprecedented a project. But the good man was sincere and inflexible*; and after tasting for only five months of the bitterness of power, he pronounced his solemn resignation † of the pontificate.

Thus far his vows were accomplished without any obstruction. But the last aspirations of his prayer were not accorded, nor was it given him again to breathe the peaceful breezes of Mt. Morone. The shadow of his dignity continued to haunt him after he had cast away the substance; the man who had possessed the chair of St. Peter, and abdicated it, could not possibly

* Bzovius describes his ardour for abdication, by the strong expression "that no one ever accepted office so eagerly as he resigned it." That writer (if we could forget the miraculous absurdities which overload his narrative) has described this curious episode in papal history more fairly than Mosheim; for the latter overlooks the old hermit's absolute incapacity, in a partial eagerness to attribute the discontent of his clergy to the consciousness of their own vices, and the fear of a rigorous reformation—though that may unquestionably have been one of their motives.

† "I, Celestine V., moved by sufficient causes—by humility, by the desire of a better life, by respect for my conscience, by the feebleness of my body, by my deficiency in knowledge, by the evil disposition of the people, and to the end that I may be restored to the repose and consolation of my past life—resign the papacy freely and voluntarily, and renounce that office and that dignity," &c.... Such was the form of his resignation, as given by Fleury (l. 89, s. 34) on the authority of Wadingus, 1294, n. 6. As his power to resign was by some held doubtful, the cardinals suggested to him first to publish a general constitution, authorizing a pope to abdicate his office. He did so.

descend to insignificance, or rise to independence. The merit
of resigning a throne was insufficient to atone for the imprudence of accepting it; and Celestine was condemned for the
remainder of his days to strict confinement by the jealousy of
Boniface*.

As the pontificate of Boniface VIII. is the hinge on which Boniface
the subsequent history of papacy almost entirely turns, we VIII.
must follow its particulars with more than usual attention.
Whatsoever flexibility or show of moderation Benedict Gaietano
may have exhibited before his advancement, he threw off all
disguise and all restraint as soon as he had attained the object
of his ambition. His pride seemed to acknowledge no limit,
and no considerations of religion, or policy, or decency could
repress his violence. In 1298, Albert of Austria caused himself
to be saluted king of the Romans; and having slain his competitor in battle, made the usual overture to the pope for confirmation. But this favour Boniface was so far from according,
that he placed the crown † upon his own head, and seizing a
sword, exclaimed, "It is I who am Cæsar; it is I who am emperor; it is I who will defend the rights of the empire!" There
is a solemn and affecting function in the Roman Church (celebrated on the first day of Lent), in which ashes are thrown on
the heads of the proud and great, to remind them of their
insignificance and mortality. While the pope was performing
this ceremony, one Spinola, archbishop of Genoa, a political
adversary, presented himself in his turn to receive the lesson of
humiliation. Boniface beheld him, and dashing the ashes in

---

* Soon after his resignation, he escaped from some attendants whom Boniface
had placed over him, with the view of returning to his ancient cell; but finding
himself pursued, he turned towards the eastern coast, in the hope of finding a
refuge in Greece. He was speedily overtaken; but in the mean time he had
materially swelled the catalogue of his miracles, and established that sort of
reputation by which he merited his canonization.

‡ We may here observe that, in consistency with his principles, Boniface VIII.
introduced the regular use of the *double* crown, which before had been assumed
only on occasions. It appears from the images of the popes, as well as from historical evidence, that from St. Sylvester to Boniface VIII., they were contented
with a single crown. From Boniface to Urban V., they doubled the symbol of
royalty, as its substance was really falling from under them. From Urban down-
wards, throughout the decline and overthrow of their authority, they have fondly
clung to the majesty of the triple crown.

his face, said to him, "Gibelline! remember that thou art dust, and that with thy brother Gibellines thou wilt return to dust*." As the kingdoms of Europe were then situated, not only in political reference to papal usurpation and predominance, but also in respect to the revival of learning, the progress of civilization, the change of principles, and the decay even of some inveterate prejudices, there only wanted an intemperate defender, such as Boniface, to decide the wavering balance and precipitate before its time the baseless despotism of Rome.

Those historians are, notwithstanding, in error, who date the decline of the papal supremacy from the reign of Innocent III. On the contrary, the system had not then quite attained the fulness of its force; it had not then achieved its greatest triumph, which, without question, was the deposition of Frederic II. And if it is true, that, from Innocent IV. to Boniface VIII., no additional ground was gained, that no fresh claims were asserted, even that some former claims were less effectually enforced, it is certain, on the other hand, that not one iota of the papal pretensions had been resigned; and that they had met for the most part with ready, or at least undisputed, acquiescence. But in the mean time the understanding of mankind had been no longer stationary; knowledge and genius and reason had revived and taken courage, and were advancing to the assertion of their eternal rights; and in the eye of the philosopher, it was a circumstance of evil omen to the projects of Boniface, that they were urged by the contemporary of Dante. Nevertheless, whether insensible to the weakness of his own cause, or to the progress of the principles opposed to it, or imagining by violence to supply the want of strength, he resolved to push the temporal pretensions of the See to their most extravagant limits†.

* These anecdotes are related by Sismondi (Rep. Ital. chap. xxiv.) without suspicion, on the authority of Pipini and Muratori.

† Ruggiero di Loria having conquered Gerba, and some other islands, till then nearly unknown, near the coast of Africa, was contented to receive them in fief and on condition of tribute, from Boniface, who vouchsafed him a Bull of Investiture, in 1295. ("Insulas objacentes Africæ, Gerbam nimirum et Cherchinas, quas Loria barbaris eripuerat, jure fiduciario, sedis Apostolicæ liberalitate Bonifacius ei possidendas attribuit." Raynaldus. Ann. 1295, s. xxxvi.) It was on the ground of this precedent, that two centuries afterwards, Alexander VI. assumed

His first measures wore, indeed, a specious appearance, since His tempo-
ral preten-
he presented himself as the advocate of peace. He endeavoured sions.
to reconcile Charles of Sicily, and James of Arragon; and
more than once obtruded his mediation upon the Kings of
England and France; these attempts seem to have had no other
fruit, than a considerable contribution levied upon the English
clergy. He then turned his attention in other directions. In
1297, he gave the kingdom of Sardinia and Corsica in fief to
James of Arragon and his posterity, on certain conditions of
aid and subsidy to Rome. In 1300 he laid claim to the kingdom
of Scotland, and directed Edward I. to withdraw his soldiers
from that country; and in the correspondence thus occasioned
between those two great usurpers, each party might have found
it easier to invalidate the claims of the other, than to establish
his own—this burst of empty arrogance passed of course without effect. He pretended to the disposal of the crown of Hungary, and gave it to a grandson of Charles le Boiteux; and
when some of the nobles (in 1302) ventured to support a rival
prince, he addressed his legate there established in the following
terms :—"The Roman pontiff established by God over kings
and their kingdoms, sovereign chief of the hierarchy in the
church militant, and holding the first rank above all mortals,
sitteth in tranquillity in the throne of judgment and scattereth
away all evil with his eyes* . . . . You have yet to learn that
St. Stephen, the first Christian King of Hungary, offered and
gave that kingdom to the Roman Church, not willing to assume
the crown on his own authority, but rather to receive it from
the vicar of Jesus Christ; since he knew, that no man taketh
this honour on himself, but he that is called of God†." In
1303 Boniface found it expedient to acknowledge as king of
the Romans the same Albert whom he had formerly reviled;
this concession was attended by a recognition of his own authority, by that prince, to the following effect. "I acknowledge

---

the right to dispose of all undiscovered tracts, continental or insular; and to concede the whole extent of terra incognita to Ferdinand and Isabella, by drawing a
line on the map from pole to pole. Giannone, lib. xix. cap. 5.

* Prov. xx. 8.   † Heb. v. 4.

that the Roman empire has been transferred by the Holy See, from the Greeks to the Germans in the person of Charlemagne; that the right to elect a king of the Romans, destined to be emperor, has been accorded by the holy see to certain princes ecclesiastical and secular; and that the kings and emperors receive from the holy see the power of the sword." He concluded that act of subservience by an unconditional promise of military aid, if it should be required by the Pope. His sincerity was never put to trial, and when we consider for how long a period, and with what general success, the dependence of the empire had been asserted by the Popes, and recollect the peculiar foundation on which that claim rested, we shall scarcely wonder at its unequivocal acknowledgment by Albert. From these facts, we may at least observe the assiduity with which Boniface pressed his temporal pretensions in every quarter of Europe. We shall now proceed to the principal theatre of his exertions, and watch the accumulation of the tempest which followed them.

Philip the Fair of France. The throne of France was then occupied by Philip the Fair —a man as arrogant, as jealous, as violent as Boniface, and perhaps even surpassing him in audacity. The clergy of France, though very faithfully attached to the Catholic Church and respecting the Pope as its head, had on various occasions, from the earliest period of papal usurpation, displayed an independent spirit of which we find no trace in other countries—yet not such as to give the slightest indications of schism, or even to prevent the holy see from making some successful inroads. The first* mention that we find of the liberties of the Gallican (as distinguished from the Roman) Church is in the year 1229, and on an occasion of which it has no reason to be proud. A very rigorous Ordonnance was then published in the king's name for the extinction of Heresy—enjoining the immediate punishment of offenders, commanding the strictest search to be made for them, and offering a reward on conviction—and the object of this was "to establish the liberties and immunities of the Gallican Church." But the act, from which those liberties

* Fleury, liv. lxxix. sect. 1.

really date their origin, is the celebrated Pragmatic Sanction
of St. Louis, published in 1269, on his departure against the
Saracens.   Its constitutions will be recorded in the next chapter.   Their leading purpose was to protect episcopal election
and preferment to benefices, the privileges granted to monasteries and ecclesiastical persons, and the property of the church
generally, from the intrusions and exactions of Rome.   Thus
this matter rested till the reign of Boniface VIII.   The fixed
and distinct principle on which the Gallican liberties were
finally placed (the inferiority of the Pope to a General Council)
was not yet established, not perhaps even broached; but enough
had been done to prove to a moderate Pope, that neither the
king nor the clergy of France were prepared to acknowledge
an implicit obedience.

The first difference between Boniface and Philip was merely
sufficient to discover the disposition, and inflame the animosity
of both.   The Pope had learnt, that the kings both of France
and England had levied contributions on their clerical, as well
as their lay, subjects for purposes of state.   In consequence, he
published, in 1296, his celebrated Bull, beginning *Clericis* Bull Cleri-
Laicos, of which the substance was this: "Antiquity relates to cis Laicos.
us the inveterate hostility* of the laity to the clergy, and the
experience of the present age confirms it manifestly—since,
without consideration that they have no power over ecclesiastical persons or property, they load with impositions both prelates
and clergy, regular and secular ; and also, to our deep affliction,
prelates and other ecclesiastics are found, who, from their
greater dread of temporal than eternal majesty, acquiesce in
this abuse."   He then proceeds to pronounce sentence of excommunication against all who shall hereafter exact such
impositions, whether kings, princes, or magistrates, and against
all who shall pay them.

* On this sentence, Fleury, the most candid of Catholics, very simply remarks,
"That aversion of laymen for the clergy, which the Pope mentions, ascended
not to a very high antiquity ; since *for the five or six first ages* the clergy secured
the respect and affections of all men, by their charitable and disinterested conduct." (Liv. lxxxix. s. xliii.)   No clergy, which shapes its conduct by any other
principle, ever will secure, or ever ought to secure, either affection or respect.

Very soon afterwards, Philip published, in retort, an edict, forbidding the export of money, jewels, and other articles specified, out of his dominions. The Pope, who was thereby deprived of his ecclesiastical contributions, presently put forth a long reply and remonstrance, in which he explained his preceding Bull to mean, that the consent of the Pope is necessary for the levying of the aforesaid contributions; that, in circumstances of great national exigency, even that might be dispensed with; and that the prohibition did not extend to donations strictly voluntary*. At the same time he enlarged on the liberty of the Church—the ark of Noah—the spouse of Jesus Christ—to which He had given power over all the body of the faithful, and over every individual member of it. By these general expressions he intended to insinuate, not only that princes had no power over the Church, but that the Church possessed unlimited control over princes. The rejoinder on the part of the king had more reason in its theology, and more piety in its reason. It professed a holy fear of God, and respectful reverence for the ministers of the Church; but, in the full consciousness of justice, it repelled with disdain the senseless menaces of man. In the following year, the Pope had the prudence to address to the archbishop of Rheims such an interpretation of the Bull as left to Philip no reasonable ground of complaint. And French historians, with great probability, attribute the rare moderation of Boniface to his necessities or his avarice†.

The truce thus tacitly established between the parties was of very short duration. Indeed, where there were so many undefined and disputable rights, it was not possible that peace could long subsist between two rivals equally disposed to encroachment and usurpation. In the year 1301, Philip arrested (and seemingly with justice) Bernard de Saisset, bishop of Pamiers, a creature of the Pope, on the charge of sedition and treasonable language, and caused him to be confined until the sentence of

* Pagi, Vit. Bonif. VIII., sect. xxviii.

† To the same cause we may probably ascribe the proclamation of the first Jubilee, in the year 1300, by Boniface,—an institution to which we shall recur in a future chapter.

degradation should be passed on him, previous to the infliction
of legal punishment.   At the same time he wrote a respectful
letter to Boniface, praying him to deprive the culprit of his
clerical privileges, or at least to take measures for his conviction.   But Boniface, having learnt that a bishop had been
placed in confinement, addressed his answer (which he sent by
a special legate) to that point only; and denying that laymen
had received any power over the clergy, he enjoined the king
to dismiss the prisoner freely to the pontifical presence, with full
restitution of all his property, at the same time reminding him
that he had himself incurred canonical punishment for having
rashly laid his hand on the person of a bishop.   On the same
day, or very soon afterwards, he published a Bull, addressed
also to Philip, in which, after exhorting his son to listen* with
docility to his instructions, he proceeded in the following terms:
—" God has set me over the nations and over the kingdoms, to
root out and to pull down, and to destroy and to throw down,
to build and to plant†, in his name, and by his doctrine.   Let
no one persuade you, then, that you have no superior, or that
you are not subject to the chief of the ecclesiastical hierarchy.
He that holds that opinion is senseless, and he that obstinately
maintains it, is an infidel, separate from the flock of the good
Shepherd." . . He then continued, still out of his affec-
tion‡ for Philip, to charge him with many general violations
of the ecclesiastical privileges, or, as they were then more commonly called, liberties; and concluded by informing him, that
he had summoned all the superior clergy of France to an assem-

* *Ausculta, fili*—the two first words of this Bull—have affixed to it its historical
name. It was published in December, 1301, and was preceded only two days by
another constitution of Boniface, called *Salvator Mundi*, by which he suspended
all favours and privileges which had been accorded by his predecessors to the kings
of France, and to all their subjects, whether lay or clerical, who abetted Philip.
Pagi, Bonif. VIII., sec. lvii.

† Jerem. i. 10.   The words are addressed to Jeremiah, in respect to his prophetic mission; but they had been perverted to the support of the papal pretensions long before the time of Boniface.   See, for instance, the letter of Honorius
III., written in 1225, to Louis of France.   The " plenitude of power which the
Holy See has received from God" is there placed chiefly on that foundation.

‡ Another reason by which he justified his interference, was his own responsibility to God for the soul of King Philip.

bly at Rome, on the 1st of the November following (1302), in order to deliberate on the remedies for such abuses.

Philip burns the Pope's Bull.
Philip was astonished by this measure, but not so confounded as to deviate either into timidity, or rashness. He convoked a full and early assembly or parliament of his nobles and clergy. In the meantime, he burnt the Bull of the Pope as publicly as possible, and caused that act to be proclaimed with trumpets throughout the whole of Paris. In his subsequent address to his parliament, he mentioned the proceedings of Boniface, disclaimed with scorn any temporal allegiance to him, retorted the charges of corruption and mal-administration, declared his readiness to risk any loss or suffering in defence of the common interests, and referred the decision of the question to the assembly. The barons and lay members pronounced their opinions loudly and unhesitatingly in favour of the king. With them the question was, in a great degree, national. They were jealous of the honour of the crown, and eager to protect it from any foreign insult. And though a calmer judgment would, perhaps, have taught them, that such a restraint upon the monarchy might, in its effects, be beneficial to all classes of the people, they sacrificed every consideration of policy to the passion of the moment. The situation of the clergy was exceedingly difficult, since they had two duties to reconcile, which, even in ordinary times, were not always in strict accordance, and which were then in direct opposition. Their first attempt was to explain and justify the *intentions* of the Pope; but that was repelled with general contempt and indignation. Then they expressed a dutiful anxiety to assist the king, and maintain the liberties of the kingdom; but at the same time they pleaded the obedience due from them to the pope, and prayed for permission to attend his summons to Rome. This permission was clamorously refused by the king and his barons.

The clergy then addressed a letter to the pope, in which they expressed an apprehension lest the violent and universal hostility*, not of the king and his barons only, but of the body

* " The laity absolutely fly from our society, and repel us from their conferences and councils, as if we were guilty of treason against them. They de-

of the laity, should lead to an entire rupture between France and Rome, and even between the clergy and the people; and they prayed that he would release them from the summons to Rome. At the same time the barons also wrote—not, indeed, to the pope, but to the college of cardinals—in severe censure of the new and senseless pretensions of Boniface, on whom personally they cast the entire blame of the difference. In reply, the cardinals disavowed, on the part of Boniface, any assertion that the king of France held his temporalities of the pope; while, in defence of his ghostly authority, they maintained, " that no man in his senses can doubt, that the pope, as chief of the spiritual hierarchy, can dispense with the sin of every man living." In his reply to the dutiful supplication of the prelates, the pope rebuked them for their want of courage and attachment, enforced on them the indisputable subjection of things temporal to things spiritual, and persisted in commanding their attendance at Rome.

The great majority disregarded the summons; but some few were found who considered their first obedience as due to their ecclesiastical sovereign. These proceeded to Rome; and, in spite of their small number, Boniface availed himself of the name of this council to publish the Decretal, commonly known as the Bull *Unam Sanctam*. The propositions asserted in this celebrated constitution are, first, the Unity of the Holy Catholic Church, without which there is no salvation; wherein is one Lord, one faith, one baptism. Hence it follows, that of this one and only Church there is one body and one head, (not two heads, which would be monstrous,) namely, Christ, and Christ's vicar, St. Peter, and the successor of St. Peter. The second position is, that in the power of this chief are two swords, the one spiritual, and the other material; but that the former of these is to be used by the Church, the latter for the Church; the former is in the hand of the priest, the latter in the hand of

Bull Unam Sanctam.

spise ecclesiastic censures, from whatsoever quarter they may come, and are preparing and taking precautions to render them useless. In this extremity (they added) we appeal to your prudence, and we supplicate you, with tears in our eyes, to preserve the antient union between church and state, and to provide for our safety by revoking the summons you have sent us." Fleury, xc., sec. ix.

kings and soldiers, but at the nod and sufferance of the priest.
It is next asserted, that one of these swords must be subject to
the other sword, otherwise we must suppose two opposite principles, which would be Manichæan and heretical. Thence it is
an easy inference, that the spiritual is that which has rule over
the other, while itself is liable to no other judgment or authority than that of God. The general conclusion is contained in
one short sentence,—" Wherefore we declare, define, and pronounce, that it is absolutely essential to the salvation of every
human being, that he be subject unto the Roman pontiff*."

But Boniface did not content himself with mere assertions.
On the very same day he also published a Bull of excommunication against all persons, of whatsoever rank, even kings or emperors, who should interfere in any way to prevent or impede those
who might desire to present themselves before the Roman See.
This edict was, of course, understood to be directly levelled
against Philip. Soon afterwards he sent a legate into France,
the bearer of twelve articles, which boldly expressed such papal
pretensions as were in opposition to those of the king; and
concluded with a menace of temporal as well as spiritual proceedings. The claims contained in these articles have been
already mentioned, and do not require enumeration. But what
may raise our surprise is, that the answer of Philip was extremely moderate; that he condescended to explain away much
that seemed objectionable in his conduct; that he promised to
remedy any abuses which his officers might have committed,
and expressed his strong desire for concord with the Roman
Church.

His moderation may have been affected, and his explanations frivolous, and the abuses in question he may not have
seriously intended to alleviate. But at least it is true that he
had never sought the enmity of Rome; and had Boniface
availed himself of that occasion to close the breach, when he
might have closed it with profit and dignity, his last days
might have been passed in lofty tranquillity : he would have

---

* The texts on which these propositions were chiefly founded are John x. 16;
Romans xiii. 1 ; Jeremiah i. 10 ; 1 Corinthians ii. 15.

been respected and feared, even by those who hated him ; and posterity would still have admired the courage and the policy which had contended against the most powerful prince in Europe, in no very blind or superstitious age, without disadvantage or dishonour.   But the pope did not perceive this crisis in his destiny.   He proceeded in his former course—he proclaimed his dissatisfaction at the answers of the king, and repeated and redoubled his menaces.

Philip had then recourse to that public measure which so deeply influenced the future history of papacy—the convocation of a general council, to pronounce on the proceedings of the Pope.   But while he was engaged in preparations for this great contest, and for the establishment of a principle to which his clergy were not yet prepared to listen *, a latent and much shorter path was opened to the termination of his perplexities.

William of Nogaret, a celebrated French civilian, in conjunction with certain Romans of the Colonna family, who had fled for refuge to Paris from the oppression of Boniface, passed secretly into Italy, and tampered successfully with the personal attendants of the pope.   The usual residence of the latter was Anagni, a city some forty or fifty miles to the southeast of Rome, and his birth-place.   There, in the year 1303, he had composed another Bull, in which he maintained, " that, as vicar of Jesus Christ, he had the power to govern kings with a rod of iron, and to dash them in pieces like a potter's vessel † ;" and he had destined the 8th of September, the anniversary of the nativity of the Virgin, for its promulgation.   A rude interruption disturbed his dreams of omnipotence, and discovered the secret of his real weakness.   On the very day preceding the intended publication of the Bull, Nogaret, with Sciarra Colonna, and some other nobles, escorted by about three hundred horsemen, and a larger number of partisans on foot, bearing the banners of France, rushed into Anagni, with

Outrage on Boniface.

* Not only did the bishops and the whole clergy decline any active part in the proceedings against the pope, but they refused any share in them, and only consented to the convocation of the council through the necessity of seeking some remedy for the disorders of the Church.

† Psalm ii. 9.

shouts of " Success to the king of France !—Death to Pope
Boniface !" After a feeble resistance, they became masters of
the pontifical palace. The cardinals dispersed and fled—
through treachery, as some assert, or, more probably, through
mere timidity. The greater part of the pope's personal attendants fled also.

Boniface, when he perceived that he was surprised and abandoned, prepared himself with uncommon resolution for the last
outrage. " Since I am betrayed (he cried) as Jesus Christ
was betrayed, I will at least die like a pope." He then clothed
himself in his official vestments, and placed the crown of Constantine on his head, and grasped the keys and the cross in his
hands, and seated himself in the pontifical chair. He was now
eighty-six years of age. And when Sciarra Colonna, who first
penetrated into his presence, beheld the venerable form and
dignified composure of his enemy, his purpose, which probably
was sanguinary, seemed suddenly to desert him, and his revenge did not proceed beyond verbal insult *. Nogaret followed. He approached the Pope with some respect, but at
the same time imperiously informed him, that he must prepare
to be present at the council forthwith to be assembled on the
subject of his misconduct, and to submit to its decision. The pope
addressed him—" William of Nogaret, descended from a race
of heretics, it is from thee, and such as thee, that I can patiently
endure indignity." The ancestors of Nogaret had atoned for
their errors in the flames. But the expression of the pontiff was
not prompted by any offence he felt at that barbarity ; not by
any consciousness of the iniquity of his own oppression †, or

---

* Some modern French historians assert that Boniface was severely wounded
by the assailants—a story which is idly repeated by Mosheim, and re-echoed even
by Gibbon. It is the *unanimous* affirmation of contemporary writers, that no
hand was raised against him. See Sismondi, chap.xxiv. The words of S. Antoninus (part 3., tit. xx., chap. 8. sec. xxi.) are express. " Domino autem dispo-
nente, ob dignitatem Apostolicæ Sedis, nemo, ex inimicis ejus ausus fuit mittere
in eum manus ; sed indutum sacris vestibus dimiserunt sub honesta custodia, et
ipsi insistebant prædæ, &c." See Pagi, Bonif. VIII., sec. lxx.

† Boniface VIII. was a very faithful patron of the Inquisition ; and if his
name is not distinguished in the list of persecuting popes, it is rather from the
want of opportunity than of inclination. Persecution being now systematized by

any sense of the justice of the retribution ; it proceeded simply from the sectarian hatred which swelled his own breast, which he felt to be implacable, and which he believed to be mutual.

While their leaders were thus employed, the body of the conspirators dispersed themselves throughout the splendid apartments in eager pursuit of plunder. Any deliberate plan which might have been formed against the person of the Pope was disappointed by their avarice. During the day of the attack, and that which followed, the French appear to have been wholly occupied in the ransack. But in the meantime the people of Anagni were recovered from their panic ; and perhaps they were more easily awakened to the shame of deserting their pope and their citizen, when they discovered the weakness of the aggressors, and the snare into which their license had led them. They took up arms, assaulted the French, and having expelled or massacred them, restored to the pontiff his freedom and authority.

But they were unable to restore his insulted honour and the spirit which had been broken by indignity. Infuriated by the disgrace of his captivity, he hurried from Anagni to Rome, burning for revenge. But the violence of his passion presently overpowered his reason, and his death immediately fol- His Death. lowed. He was attended by an ancient servant, who exhorted him to confide himself in his calamity to the Consoler of the afflicted. But Boniface made no reply. His eyes were haggard, his mouth white with foam, and he gnashed his teeth in silence. He passed the day without nourishment, the night without repose ; and when he found that his strength began to fail, and that his end was not far distant, he removed all his attendants, that there might be no witness to his final feebleness and his parting struggle. After some interval, his domestics burst into the room, and beheld his body stretched on the bed, stiff and cold. The staff which he carried bore the mark of his teeth, and was covered with foam ; his white locks were

the regular machinery of the Inquisition, there were fewer occasions for individual distinction. See Whately on "The Errors of Romanism," ch. v., sec. iii., vi., p. 241—244.

320 A HISTORY OF THE CHURCH. [CH. XX.

stained with blood ; and his head was so closely wrapped in
the counterpane, that he was believed to have anticipated his
impending death by violence and suffocation *.

This took place on the 10th of October; and precisely on
the same day, after an interval of 303 years, his body was dug
up and transferred to another place of sepulture. Spondanus†,
the Catholic historian, was at Rome at the moment. He
relates the circumstances, and mentions the eagerness with
which the whole city rushed to the spectacle. His body was
found, covered with the pontifical vestments, still fresh and
uncorrupted. His hands, which his enemies had asserted to
have been bitten away in his rage, were so free from decay and
mutilation, with every finger entire, that even the veins and
nerves appeared to be swelling with flesh and life.

After the death of Boniface, the French interest presently
prevailed in the college; and in the year 1305 the archbishop
of Bourdeaux, a native of France, was elected to the chair. He
took the title of Clement V., and presently transferred the papal
residence from Rome to Avignon.

* Sismondi, Rep. Ital., end of chap. xxiv. " Concerning which Boniface (says
Matthew of Westminster) a certain versifier wrote as follows :—
Ingreditur Vulpes, regnat Leo, sed Canis exit ;
Re tandem vera si sic fuit, ecce Chimæra !"—
Flores Histor. ad ann. 1303.
Others give the same in the form of a prophecy, delivered by Marone, during
his imprisonment. " Ascendisti ut Vulpes, regnabis ut Leo, et morieris ut
Canis." Antiq. Eccles. Britann. ad ann. 1295.
† Spondanus continued the History of Baronius from the year 1198, in which
it concludes, to 1646. See also Bzovius on this same occurrence, ann. 1303.

CHAPTER XXI.

(I.) *On Louis IX. of France*—His public motives—contrasted with those of Constantine and Charlemagne—His virtues, piety, and charity—Particulars of his civil legislation—His superstition—The original Crown of Thorns—its removal to Paris—its reception by the king—his death—His miracles and canonization—The Bull of Boniface VIII.—(II.) *On the Inquisition.*—Whether St. Louis contributed to its establishment—Origin of the Inquisition—Office of St. Dominic and his contemporaries—Erection of a separate tribunal at Toulouse—by Gregory IX.—The authority then vested in the Mendicants—its unpopularity in France—Co-operation of St. Louis—Conduct of Frederic II.—of Innocent IV.—Limits to the prevalence of the Inquisition.—(III.) *On the Gallican Liberties.*—Remonstrance of the Prelates of France respecting excommunications—firmness of Louis—his visit to the Cistercian chapter—The supplication of the monks, and the reply of the King—Early spirit and sense of independence in the French clergy—the Pragmatic Sanction of St. Louis—its principle—The six articles which constitute it—Consequences of the policy of Innocent III.—(IV.) *On the Crusades.*—Remarks on the character and circumstances of the first Crusade—Exertions of St. Bernard for the second Crusade—its fatal result—Excuse of that abbot—Causes of the fall of the Latin kingdom of Jerusalem—Third, fourth, fifth, sixth, and seventh Crusades—The eighth and ninth—St. Louis—Termination of the Crusades, and final loss of Palestine—General remarks—(1.) On the *Origin* and first motives of religious pilgrimage—Treatment of first pilgrims by the Saracens—Pilgrimage during the tenth and eleventh centuries—Conquest of Palestine by the Turks—Practice of private feuds and warfare in Europe—prevalent in the tenth century—The superstitious spirit of the same age—associated with the military—General predisposition in favour of a Crusade—Failure of Sylvester II. and Gregory VII.—(2.) On the *Objects* of the Crusades—what they were—what they were not—The object of the first distinguished from that of following Crusades—Conduct and policy of the sovereigns of Europe—of the Vatican—Gradual change in its objects.—(3.) On the *Results* of the Crusades—Advantages produced by them—Few and partial—on government—on commerce—on general civilization—Evils occasioned—Religious wars—Immoral influence—Corruption of church discipline—Canonical penance—Introduction of the Plenary Indulgence—its abuses—The Jubilee—Interests of the clergy. *Note* (A.) On the collections of Papal Decretals—That of Gratian—the Liber Sextus—Clementines, &c.—*Note* (B.) On the University of Paris—The Four Faculties—Foundation of the Sorbonne. *Note* (C.) On certain theological writers—Rise and progress of the scholastic system of theology—Peter the Lombard—His " Book of the Sentences"—St. Thomas Aquinas—His history and productions—St. Bonaventura—the character of his theology—The Realists and Nominalists, or Thomists and Scotists—The Immaculate Conception.

IT is seldom that the stream of ecclesiastical history receives any important contribution from the biography of kings. Our

more peaceful course is indeed perpetually troubled by the
eddies of secular polity, and most so in the most superstitious
ages.   The names of Constantine and Charlemagne have, it is
also true, deserved an eminent rank among the heroes of the
Church.   But if we pass over the legendary tales of the
monarch-monks of the darkest days, we shall scarcely discover
any other powerful prince whose policy was formed either on
an ardent sense of religion or an attachment to ecclesiastical
interests, until we arrive at the reign of Louis IX.   And here
we must at once distinguish the principles of that prince from
those either of Constantine or of Charlemagne.   By whatsoever motives of genuine piety those two sovereigns may really
have been influenced, it is certain that their ecclesiastical institutions were chiefly regulated for political ends.   It was their
object—an object worthy of their royal rank and virtues—to
improve the moral and religious condition of their subjects
through the instrumentality of Christ's ministers, and at the
same time to raise the dignity and character of those whose
sacred office, when they are not the worst of men, is calculated
to make them the best.   But the actions of Louis were not
guided by any such considerations.   They proceeded from
that which it was the purpose of the others' policy to create—
an absorbing Christian piety, with its train of concomitant ex-
cellencies.   On this subject there is no difference among historians, except in as far as some are more disposed to ridicule
the superstitious excesses into which he fell, through the practice of his age, than to do justice to the lofty motives whence
his virtues proceeded.

Section I.

On Louis IX.

Character
of Louis
IX.
LOUIS IX. was born about the year 1215, and came to the
throne at a very early age.   He was educated by a mother
named Blanche, who was eminent for her devotion to God and
the Church; and we should here remark, that he drew his
first breath, and received his earliest notions of ecclesiastical

polity, among the groans of the suffering Albigeois. The sanctity of his private life was not sullied by any stain, nor was it clouded by any austerity. " Never since I was born," (says Joinville,) " did I hear him speak ill of any one." He loved his subjects; and had his lot been cast in happier days, he would have loved mankind. But the principles of his Church so contracted those of his religion, that his benevolence could never expand itself into philanthropy.

He was devout in private prayer, as well as a constant attendant on the offices of the Church. On the one hand, his submission to the admonitions, and even to the personal corrections, of his confessor is diligently recorded; and on the other, his adoration of the holy cross * is recounted with no less admiration. He would descend from his seat, and, advancing in a homely garment, with his head, neck, and feet bare, and his children behind him, bend with such profound humility before the emblems of his salvation, that the spectators were moved to tears of affection and piety. He appears, too, from the same accounts, to have washed the feet of monks and of mendicants by a very common exercise of self-abasement. And we may overlook this foolish affectation in that substantial excellence which distributed his charitable benefactions without thrift or partiality, through every class of those who needed them. The foundation of many churches and monasteries secured at the same time the gratitude and fidelity of his spiritual subjects.

Hume has ascribed to Louis IX., together with " the mean *His policy.* and abject superstition of a monk, the magnanimity of a hero, the integrity of a patriot, the humanity of a philosopher." That insatiable zeal for Crusades, which neither his reason, which

---

* See the book " De Vita et Actibus Ludovici," &c. by his chaplain, William (Carnotensis) of Chartres; and his "Vita, Conversatio et Miracula," by F. Gaufridus, his confessor. One object of the latter is to point out the exact correspondence of the character of Louis with that of Josiah. The particular description and changes of his coarse raiment, the days of his fasting, of his abstinence from meat, or from fruit and fish, or from every kind of fish except one, or from every thing except bread and water, and such like details of his devotional observances, are related by both writers; especially by the confessor, and in his 17th chapter. The king's eleemosynary liberality forms the worthier subject of that which follows. Both his biographers were Dominicans.

was powerful, nor his humanity, nor his philosophy, nor all
united, were even in later life sufficient to allay, afforded at the
same time the most pernicious proofs of his superstition and
his heroism. But his patriotism was more honourably displayed in the internal regulation of his kingdom, in the removal of abuses, in the advancement of civilization; and in
this office (as his domestic biographer observes), he so combined the secular with the spiritual interests of his subjects,
that he seemed to discharge by the same acts the double office
of priest and king*. He detested the practice of usury; and
to that motive we may perhaps attribute his hatred for the Jews,
who exercised the trade exclusively. Still we must doubt the
wisdom, while we censure the cruelty, of the edict, by which
he expelled them from the country. He enacted a very severe
(according to our notions, a barbarous †) law against blasphemy. While we praise his bold, though seemingly ineffectual, attempts to restrain the moral profligacy of his nobles,
we shall scarcely less applaud the vigour with which he exerted
against that body the power of royalty in a cause almost equally
sacred. It was a leading object of his policy to protect the
lower classes of his subjects against the brutal ‡ oppression of
the aristocracy, and to unite the interests of the crown and the
people against that privileged order, which was equally hostile
to the independence of both. Justice he commonly administered in person §, and tempered it with his natural clemency.

---

* " Quod etiam quodammodo regale sacerdotium, aut sacerdotale regimen
videretur pariter exercere."—Gulielm. Carnotensis.

† He caused the lips (or, as some say, the forehead) of those convicted to be
seared with a hot iron.

‡ Having learnt, on one occasion, that a nobleman had hanged three children
for the offence of hunting rabbits, Louis condemned him to capital punishment.
But the rest of the nobility united with so much determination to preserve the
life of their fellow-tyrant and the prerogatives of their order, that the king was
obliged to commute the punishment for deprivation of property.

§ " I have often seen the saint," (says Joinville,) " after he had heard mass
in summer, come out to the Forest of Vincennes, and seat himself at the foot of
an oak, and make us sit all round him. And those who had any business came
and spoke to him without any officer giving them hinderance. And sometimes
he would come to the Garden of Paris, and have carpets spread for us to sit near
him; and then he administered justice to his people, as he did at Vincennes."—
Histoire du Roy St. Louis, p. 23. Edit. Paris, 1617. This history, which is the

At the same time, he endeavoured to purify its sources by permanent alterations, and to secure at least for future ages the blessings which he might despair effectually to impart to his own.   Accordingly, he struck at the root of the evil, and made it the grand object of his efforts to substitute trial by evidence for the " judgments of God," and most especially for the most sanguinary among them, the decision by duel.   His ordinances on those subjects were obeyed within the boundaries of his own domains; but he had not the power to enforce them universally. The barons, who were severally the legislators in their own estates, adhered to the venerable establishments of former days; and a more general diffusion of knowledge was required before the plainest reason, aided even by royal authority, could prevail against the inveterate sanctity of instituted absurdities.

It was the same with those humane endeavours to arrest the private warfare, in which he anticipated the course of civilization by more than two centuries*. But when he despaired of effecting this object at once, he attempted at least to mitigate the mischief by a judicious prohibition—that neither party should commence hostilities till forty days after the offence had been offered †. Thus was he compelled to temporize with a great national evil, of which he felt at the same time the whole extent, as well as his own incapacity to correct it. From these instances we may observe, that the civil legislation of St. Louis was generally founded on wise policy, and that it always sprang from benevolent motives. We shall presently notice some of his ecclesiastical enactments; but at the same time it must be admitted, that the charge of " abject superstition," alleged

life of an admirable king and Christian by a candid, loyal, unaffected soldier, is a beautiful specimen of inartificial biography. But, unhappily, the most beneficial, and, therefore, the noblest acts of the monarch, are not those which have most attracted the attention of the soldier. The details of his campaigns and many anecdotes of his private life are related with minuteness and seeming accuracy; but his great legislative enactments are slightly, or not at all noticed.

* The right of private feud cannot be considered as abolished until nearly the end of the 15th century. In collecting a large and, for those days, a valuable library, and in encouraging the progress of knowledge among his subjects, St. Louis opened the only certain path to their civilization.

† Some attribute this regulation to Philippe Auguste.

against him by the philosophical historian, is not less just than the merits also ascribed to him; nor will it here be out of place to recount one celebrated incident in support of this imputation.

His reception of the crown of thorns.

The History of the Church comprises the records of superstition, which in those corrupt ages was indeed so interwoven with piety, that it is rare to find them separate. The character of St. Louis particularly exemplified their combination; it may be perpetually detected in his warlike enterprises; but there is not one among his spiritual adventures which better illustrates himself and his age than the following:—The original Crown of Thorns had been long preserved at Constantinople as the most precious and venerable among the relics of Christ; yet such were at this time the necessities of the government, that the holy treasure was consigned in pawn to the government of Venice. It was delivered over to the commissioners of the republic, who immediately set sail, in a wintry and inclement season, full of religious confidence, and were preserved (as it was thought) through a perilous voyage by the holiness of their charge. The pledge, which the Greeks were too poor or too wise to redeem, was eagerly purchased by Louis, and the relic, after a few months of repose and adoration at Venice, continued its pilgrimage to the west. During the course of an overland journey it was again distinguished by the favour of the elements; and though the rain fell abundantly during the nights, not a drop descended by day to interrupt its progress. At length when it arrived at Troyes in Champagne, the event was notified to the king at Paris, and he instantly set off to welcome it, accompanied by the Queen Blanche his mother, by his brothers, by some prelates, and other nobles.

The royal company met their holy acquisition in the neighbourhood of Sens, and after they had uncovered the case and beheld the object, and moistened it with pious tears, they assembled the clergy of the diocese and formed a solemn procession towards the city. As they approached the gates, the king and his eldest brother, the Count d'Artois, received the venerated burden on their shoulders; and in this manner, with naked feet, and no other covering than a shirt *, they carried it, in the midst of the adoring crowd, into the cathedral. Thence it proceeded to Paris, and there its arrival was hailed with a repetition of the same degrading solemnities. The whole clergy and the whole people were in motion, and again the two illustrious brothers, barefoot and naked as before, supported and deposited it in the destined sanctuary. An annual festival was instituted to commemorate an event of such national importance—the introduction of this new palladium. But its value was soon afterwards diminished by the importation of a formidable rival for the popular adoration. It was not long before the royal enthusiast succeeded in procuring some substantial fragments of the real cross; and this acquisition again furnished him with another pretext to multiply to his lively subjects the occasions of religious festivity.

In the year 1270, St. Louis died before Tunis, while in the His death, prosecution of his second crusade. His last words are said to have been these†—" Lord, I will enter into thine house ; I will worship in thy holy temple, and give glory to thy name. Into thy hands I commend my spirit." From the beginning of his life to its latest breath the same principle predominated, the same religious fervour (however it may sometimes have been perverted) influenced all his actions ; and perhaps, in the interminable catalogue of her saints, the Church of Rome cannot number a name more worthy of that celestial dignity than Louis IX. But the merit to which that pious monarch was chiefly indebted for his heavenly office, was not that to which he had ever particularly pretended. His eminent virtues, his religious life and death, even his services to the Catholic Church, might seem to have entitled him to that high reward. But those claims had been wholly insufficient, had it not also been conclusively attested that he had performed many manifest and astonishing miracles.

The canonization of Louis took place twenty-seven years and canonization.

* Vita et Convers. S. Ludovici, &c., per F. Gaufridum. Aug. 11, 1239, was the day consecrated by this exploit.

† So says William of Chartres, and Boniface VIII., in his Bull of Canonization, confirms it.

after his death, and almost the whole of that time was employed
in collecting the necessary documents *. The rapid succession
of the popes was the cause which retarded it; and it may seem
as if in mockery of his holy character, that the performance of
this office did at last devolve upon Boniface VIII. It was
Boniface who preached the panegyrical sermon, and enlarged
on those various virtues, which had no counterpart in his own
bosom. It was the genius of arrogance which paid homage
to the spirit of humility, and exalted it even to the thrones of
heaven. " Let the hosts of heaven rejoice at the arrival of so
noble and glorious an inhabitant—an approved and eminent
husbandman of the Christian faith is added to their multitudes.
Let the glorious nobility of the celestial citizens sound the
jubilee of joy, for an honoured stranger is adscribed to their
ranks. Let the venerable assembly of the saints arise with
gladness and exultation to receive a compeer who well deserves
such dignity. Arise, thou innumerable council of faith ; zealots
of the faith arise, and sing the hymn of praise in concert with
the Church which is your own. . . . He offered offence to no
one, to no one violence or injury. He carefully observed the
boundaries of justice, without deserting the path of equity. He
punished with the sword the daring and lawless enterprises of
the wicked. An ardent lover of peace and concord—an anxious
promoter of unity—hostile to scandals and dissensions †," &c.
&c. We may remark that this last topic, in the mouth of
Boniface VIII., was at best an equivocal eulogy. A zeal for
" unity," and an abhorrence of " scandals and dissensions," is

* In the first of the two sermons delivered by Boniface on that occasion, he
expressly asserts, that after the fullest examination into the evidence for the
miracles, he has ascertained that sixty-three miracles were assuredly performed,
besides others which God evidently vouchsafed to him—(sexaginta tria, inter
cætera quæ Dominus evidenter ostendit, certitudinaliter facta cognovimus.) Respecting the tedious duration of the investigation Boniface remarks, in the same
discourse, with great simplicity—"Et ita per tot et toties examinatum est, rubri-
catum et discussum negotium, quod de hoc plus facta est descriptura, quam unus
asinus posset portare."

† It is difficult to conceive a more turgid and tautologous composition than
this celebrated bull. The merits which Louis really possessed are enumerated
without taste or feeling; and the author of the panegyric seems to have been
wholly incapable of estimating the character which he pretended to eulogize.

a praise which, when proceeding from pontifical lips, conveys the necessary suspicion of intolerance. Louis has been accused of that crime—the ruling iniquity of his age—and we shall now examine on what facts that charge is really founded.

SECTION II.

On the Inquisition.

IT is asserted, and with truth, that the Inquisition was permanently established in France during the reign of St. Louis; that he never ceased to manifest great partiality for the Dominicans and Franciscans *, and all invested with the inquisitorial office ; and that it was even at the particular solicitation of the king † that Alexander IV. confirmed, in 1255, the institution of that tribunal, and appointed the prior of the Dominican Convent at Paris to be Inquisitor-general in France. That we may be able to estimate the real weight of these assertions, and (what is more important than the reputation of any individual) that we may understand on what ground that frightful structure was erected, we must trace as shortly as possible the causes which led to its foundation.

The itinerant emissaries of Innocent III., among whom Dominic is the name most celebrated, first obtained the title of Inquisitors—that is to say, they were invested by the pope with authority to discover, to convert, or to arraign before the ecclesiastical courts all guilty or suspected of heresy. But this was the limit of their commission. They did not constitute an independent tribunal, nor were they clothed with any judicial

Its original form,

---

* It appears that he intended to educate two of his sons for the monasteries, and that by his testament he consigned one to Dominican, the other to Franciscan tuition.—Gaufridus, Vita et Conversat. chap. 14.

† See Limborch, Hist. Inquisit., lib. i. cap. 16. The annalist Raynaldus has expressed his pious regret, that the admirable institution of the Saint was feebly supported, and even entirely overthrown by his degenerate successors ! We should observe that the domains of the Count of Poitiers and Toulouse, who was then Alphonso, brother of the king, were excepted from the jurisdiction of the prior, as being already subject to a special commission on matters of faith. The act of St. Louis was to establish that generally throughout his kingdom, which had hitherto been confined to the most infected province.

power. The process was still carried on, according to the practice then prevailing, before the bishop of the diocese; and the secular arm was invited, when necessary, to enforce his sentence. But this form of proceeding was not found sufficiently rapid to satisfy the eagerness of the pope and his missionaries. The work of extirpation was sometimes retarded by the compunctions of a merciful prelate, sometimes by the reluctance of the civil authorities to execute a barbarous or unpopular sentence*. And to remove these impediments to the course of destruction, there was no resource, except to institute in the infected provinces, with the direct co-operation of the ruling powers, a separate tribunal for causes of heresy. This object was not immediately accomplished. In the meantime the Dominicans and Franciscans were spreading their numbers and influence in every country. And as they were the faithful myrmidons of the Roman See, and more devoted in their allegiance than either the secular or the regular clergy, thus arose an additional reason for investing them with a distinct jurisdiction. By the council held at Toulouse in 1229 (of which the decrees have been noticed in a former chapter), a canon was published which united "one priest with three laymen," in a sort of council of inquisition. It is this regulation which is reasonably considered as the foundation of the *Court of Inquisition*†.

and complete establishment.　To Pope Gregory IX. be ascribed the honour of this success! Still the court thus established continued subject to the bishops. Its *object* was indeed exclusively such as the most zealous pontiff could have desired; but it was composed of materials

---

* It should be remarked on the other hand, that it was sometimes (especially in the beginning of the persecutions) precipitated by the agency of popular fury, excited by the preachers *against* the heretics. Their favourite text is said to have been (Psalm xciv. v. 16) " Who will rise up for me against the evil-doers? Who will stand up for me against the workers of iniquity?" Many of them were eloquent—the people were superstitious—the preachers were fanatics. In fact, when the ecclesiastical censures were despised, and the secular power refused its aid, popular madness was their only remaining instrument.

† By the Council of Narbonne, held two years before, it was enacted, " that the bishops should establish in each parish synodal witnesses to inquire into heresy, and other notorious crimes, and to make their report." These were truly established inquisitors; still their office was to report, not to judge.

neither wholly destitute of human feeling, nor blindly subservient to the papal will. A further change was therefore
necessary ; and, accordingly, about three years afterwards,
Gregory found means to transfer the authority in the new
court to the Dominican order. It was thus that the Inquisition,
properly so called—that is, a court for the trial of heretics,
erected by papal authority, and administered by papal dependents—was indeed instituted. . . .   Some popular commotions
followed its first proceedings ; besides the indignation excited
by the object of this institution, there was a general objection
among laymen to the establishment of *any* new ecclesiastical
tribunal, to which all classes were alike amenable * ;—the persons of the judges were exposed to insult, and the whole body
was, for a short time, expelled from the city. But the spirit of
Rome was yet too powerful, — the fugitives were presently
restored. And though the inquisitorial system never reached in
France those refinements in barbarity which some other countries
have endured—though it obtained, in truth, no very permanent
footing among a humane and generous people—it continued to
subsist there for several years; and if there was any sceptre
under which it can be said to have flourished, it was assuredly
the sceptre of St. Louis. Still we must not forget that it was
established in his boyhood; so that the guilt of *that* † act is
unjustly cast upon him. He perpetuated the evil which he
found ; and in the religious code of those days, the "unity of
the Church " was so carefully identified with the glory of
Christ, that an ardent desire for the one might easily degenerate

---

* This was not diminished when, to the original offences of heresy, those of
Judaism, Mahometanism, sodomy, sacrilege, and even polygamy, were added.
But we have not observed that this wide extension of the objects of that court
was ever made in France.

† We must notice the injustice which has hastily been offered to the character
of Louis IX. by Mosheim. That writer having asserted (on the authority of the
Benedictine compilers of the history of Languedoc) that Louis published a barbarous edict against heretics, in the year 1229, proceeds thus :—"A great part of
the sanctity of good King Louis consisted in his furious and implacable aversion
to heretics." Now, that this aversion formed, at any age, a prominent part of his
character, will be asserted by no one who has studied the *whole* of his life. But
in respect to this particular edict, was Mosheim ignorant that it was published
under the regency of Queen Blanche, when the prince was not yet fifteen years
old ?

into a misguided zeal for the other. And thus, without intending to exculpate the royal persecutor, we are bound to distinguish between the crime of those who created that ecclesiastical system, and of him who blindly supported it; of the churchmen* who artfully confounded the essence of religion with the maintenance of their own power, and of the pious laymen, who adopted with reverence the undisputed and consecrated maxims.

Progress of the Inquisition. The brutal edicts † of Frederic II., published about 1244, and not exceeded by the most barbarous emanations of the Vatican, were not palliated by any motive of misdirected piety: yet were they much more effectual than the encouragement of Louis in arming the fury of the Dominicans, at least within the limits of his empire. But the intolerant zeal of Frederic neither softened the hostility of Innocent IV., nor preserved himself from the anathemas of the Church. After his triumph, Innocent pursued and exceeded the footsteps of his predecessors. He established the tribunal‡ of the Inquisition in the north of Italy, and in that form which made it most effectually the engine of the Vatican. It is true that in this court the bishop was nominally appointed as coadjutor to the papal inquisitor; but all substantial judicial authority was placed in the hands of the latter§. The civil magistrate was likewise

---

* In 1239, one hundred and eighty heretics were burnt in Champagne, in the same flames, and in the presence of eighteen bishops. " It is a holocaust agreeable to God ! " exclaimed a monk who witnessed the execution. Was it to be expected that a woman and a child should rise up against an ecclesiastical practice which was sanctioned by the concurrent zeal of monks, of prelates, of popes, and of councils ?

† Four of them are cited by Limborch, Hist. of Inquisit., lib. i., cap. 12. He was accused, nevertheless, of having favoured and fostered heresies. His edicts *may* have had that tendency, but he was assuredly innocent of the intention.

‡ Giannone (lib. xix., chap. v., sec. iv.) seems to ascribe the *establishment* of the courts virtually administered by the Mendicants to Innocent IV., and with truth, so far as Italy was concerned. Two circumstances (he remarks) were opposed to it. (1.) The judicial rights of the episcopal courts. (2.) The executive rights of the secular magistrates. The first was obviated by the *nominal* association of bishops in the inquisitorial office. The second, by permitting the magistrate to have his minister in the court, though at the appointment of the grand inquisitor. There was much art in this concession; for thus, while the ecclesiastics really held the whole power, the secular authorities, by being united with them in name, were associated in hatred. They were tools—they were mistaken for accomplices.

§ We learn from Bzovius at a later period, (ann. 1302, sect. x.,) that Boni-

admitted to a seat among the members of the court; but in reality his power was ministerial only. The whole effective power, both judicial and executive, was vested in the Dominicans and Franciscans. . . . From Italy, the pestilence rapidly spread to the island of Sardinia, to Syria, and to Servia *. On the other hand into Spain, the field of its most destructive ravages, it was introduced so late as the reign of Ferdinand and Isabella—a reign more renowned, more panegyrized, than any other in the history of that country. But from Spain even the despotism of Charles V. was insufficient to communicate it to the rest of his subjects; the natural humanity of the Germans perseveringly repelled that pestilence; and the inhabitants of Naples on one side, and of the Low Countries on the other, resisted and rejected it with equal constancy.

We shall not enter more deeply into the records of the Inquisition, nor particularize the combinations of its machinery and the exquisite harmony of its movements, because it did not reach that fatal perfection until a time posterior to the conclusion of this History. It is with no trifling satisfaction that we dispense with this labour; for the details of ingenious barbarity, though they may awaken a transient attention, convey little that is instructive to a reasonable mind; and the feelings of horror and indignation which they excite, do they not sometimes miss their true object, and exceed their just limits ?—do they not sometimes rise into a detestation too general and too unqualified against the Church which permitted such iniquities?

face VIII. confined the inquisitorial office to the Dominicans, publishing at the same time some severe constitutions against heretics. There is one feature in them which we have not remarked in the earliest edicts. Not only were their defensores, receptatores, &c., included in the penalties, but also their *filii et nepotes* —children and grandchildren. The bishop of the diocese was *permitted* to act in concert with the inquisitors; and the investigation was ordered to proceed " simpliciter et de plano, absque advocatorum et judiciorum strepitu et figura !" The accusers were allowed to give evidence secretly, if there should seem to be any danger to them from the publication of their names.

* Limborch, lib. i., cap. xvi. The " Liber Sententiarum Inquisitionis Tholosanæ," published at the end of his work, is of great value, not only as it faithfully represents the spirit of the ruling party in the Church at that time, (there were no doubt many *individuals* of greater moderation and humanity,) but also as the best storehouse of the opinions with which the heretics were charged, and for which they suffered.

—do they not sometimes close our charities against fellow-
Christians and fellow-Catholics, who perhaps abominate, as
intensely as we do, the crimes of their ancestors? To expose
the deviations from the precepts of the Gospel and the principles of philanthropy, into which the Church of Rome, in
different ages, has fallen, is a painful task so commonly obtruded upon the historian, that he may well be spared the
gratuitous denunciation of those, which do not lie within the
boundaries prescribed to his work.

SECTION III.

On the Gallican Liberties.

St. Louis
and his
clergy.

A DIFFERENCE which took place between St. Louis and his
clergy, in the year 1263, throws some light both on his own
character and on the ecclesiastical history of the age. The
bishops were desirous to make to the king a remonstrance
from their whole body; and when they were admitted into his
presence, the bishop of Auxerre spoke in their name as follows:
—" Sire, all these prelates here assembled desire me to say,
that you are permitting the Christian religion to fall to ruins,
and to crumble in your hands." On which the good king*
made the sign of the cross, and said, " Now tell me, bishop,
how that is, and for what reason?" " Sire," continued the
bishop, " the evil is, that no regard is any longer paid to excommunication. In these days, a man would rather die under
the sentence than obtain absolution by making the necessary
satisfaction to the Church. Wherefore, Sire, all these here
present request, with one voice, that, for the honour of God
and in the discharge of your own duty †, it may please you to

---

* Joinville, who tells the story, was present. Prem. Partie Vie de St. Louis,
p. 24.

† " Pour Dieu, et pour ce qu' ainsi le devez faire." We should observe that
the demand on the part of the prelates was not new, and that it had even been
granted by the predecessor of Louis. The first canon of the Council of Narbonne,
held in 1227, mentions, as the law then in force, that whoever remained under
the sentence after three admonitions should pay a fine of nine livres and a denier;
but that whoever remained so for a whole year should suffer the confiscation of
all his property. Fleury, liv. lxxix., sec. xxxii.

command all your bailiffs, provosts, and other administrators of justice, as follows :—That, if any one be found in your kingdom who shall have lain under a sentence of excommunication for a year and a day continuous, he be compelled, by seizure of his goods, to reconcile himself to the Church." The holy man (le saint homme) answered, that he would issue such order in respect to those who should be *proved* guilty of injustice either to the Church or to their neighbour. The bishop pressed, in reply, the exclusive privileges of ecclesiastical jurisdiction; but the king firmly refused the secular aid, unless the nature of the offence and the justice of the censure should be such as required its interference. This was the endeavour of a wise prince to distinguish the boundaries of ecclesiastical and civil jurisdiction, and to restrain the former within its just limits; and it shows at least, that on matters which were still left open to the exercise of reason, Louis, how much soever he might love the religion, was not at all disposed to be overreached or overawed by its ministers.

We may relate another anecdote of the same monarch, which will suggest one or two instructive reflexions to the intelligent reader. St. Louis had promised to be present at a chapter-general of the Cistercian order, to be held in the year 1244 with unusual solemnity. Innocent IV. received information of his intention; and as the contest with Frederic involved him at that moment in some difficulties, he took measures to profit by the pious disposition of the king of France. The monarch arrived, attended by his mother, his brothers, and some nobles; and all the abbots and the monks of the community, consisting of 500, went forth in procession to meet and welcome the royal visitor. Immediately, while he was seated in the chapter, surrounded by his court, the abbots and the monks fell on their knees before him, with their hands in the attitude of prayer, and their eyes suffused with tears—for such had been the instructions of Innocent. Their prayer was this :—" That, according to the ancient custom and liberty of France, he would protect their father and pastor, the holy pontiff, against the insults of the emperor; that he would receive him, if necessary, into the bosom of his kingdom, as Alexander had formerly

been received, while flying before the emperor Frederic and
Thomas of Canterbury, in his persecution by Henry of England." St. Louis descended from his seat, and placed himself
in like manner upon his knees before the holy suppliants. But
his reply was dictated by the calmest prudence and policy—
" that he would defend the Church, as his honour required,
from the insults of the emperor, and no less willingly would he
receive the exiled pope into his kingdom, if his barons should
so counsel him; but that a king of France could on no occasion dispense with the counsels of his nobles *." It was no
secret from the king, nor, perhaps, even from his monastic
petitioners, that the barons of France would never consent to
open their rich domains as a refuge for the rapacious court of
Innocent IV.

If St. Louis, on the one hand, protected the liberties of his
lay subjects from the usurpations of the clergy, he was no less
vigilant on the other in shielding all parties from the increasing
exactions of Rome. Even from very early ages, the Church of
France had exhibited on some important occasions marks both
of independence and good sense above the level of other nations.
The oriental absurdity of the Stylites was rejected by that more
rational people. The rising authority of St. Leo was unable to
silence the refractory bishops of France. The use of images
was for some time discountenanced in that country. The Augustinian doctrine of predestination found, perhaps, its warmest
adversaries among the divines of France. But most especially
in the contest of Hincmar with pope Nicholas, and some other
occurrences of the ninth century, we detect the spirit of a clergy
not prepared to pay implicit obedience to the *foreign* autocrat
of the Church. Nevertheless, no formal declaration of resistance—no national attempt to emancipate the Gallican Church
from any of its fetters, or give it security by a separate constitution against further aggressions—had hitherto been made by
any king of France.

It was the last among the legislative acts of St. Louis to

* See Matthew Paris, ann. 1244. We must not confound this affair with a
conference which did actually take place two years afterwards between the king
and the pope within the walls of Cluni. See Pagi, Vit. Innoc. IV., sec. xxxiii.

publish those institutions which formed the basis of the boasted The Prag-
matic
Sanction. " Liberties of the Gallican Church." Just before his departure for Tunis, he issued his Pragmatic Sanction. It was founded on the necessity of distinguishing temporal from spiritual authority, and became, in after times, the foundation of a more extensive emancipation. Like those, however, which were built upon it, it was peculiarly directed against the pecuniary usurpations of Rome and her claims to the patronage of the Church. The latter subject had indeed occasioned the earliest contentions between the empire and the Vatican at a time when the rights of the dispute were on the side of the latter. But since the days of Innocent II., the usurpations, whether in the imposition of taxes or the distribution of benefices, had proceeded from the court of Rome; and Louis IX. having acquired by his personal character, as well as his wise " Establishments *," the affection and fidelity of his subjects, felt strong enough to repress them.

Accordingly, in the year 1269, that he might ensure the tranquillity of his Church and kingdom during his absence, and also secure for his enterprise the protection of God, he promulgated his celebrated Ordinance. It is comprised in six articles. (1.) The churches, the prelates, the patrons, and the ordinary collators of benefices, shall enjoy their rights to their full extent, and each shall be sustained in his jurisdiction. (2.) The cathedral and other churches shall possess the liberties of elections, which shall be carried into complete effect. (3.) We will, that simony, the pest of the Church, be wholly banished from our kingdom. (4.) Promotions, collations, provisions and dispositions of prelatures, dignities, and other ecclesiastical benefices and offices, whatsoever they may be, shall be made according to the institutions of common law, of the councils, and of our ancient Fathers. (5.) We renew and approve of the liberties, franchises, prerogatives, and privileges granted by

---

* The " Establishments of St. Louis" belong, for the most part, to civil history It is only necessary to observe, that though many particular enactments were severe, and even barbarous, according to the estimation of a civilized age, they were founded upon principles of policy, and even humanity, far above those of the times in which they were promulgated. Le Roi (says Millot) devint législateur : l'anarchie féodale devoit finir. Another half century, and it did so.

the kings our predecessors and by ourselves to churches, monasteries and other places of piety, as well as to ecclesiastical persons. (6.) We prohibit any one from, in any manner, levying and collecting the pecuniary exactions and heavy charges which the court of Rome has imposed, or may hereafter impose, upon the Church of our kingdom, and by which our kingdom has been miserably impoverished—unless it be for a reasonable and very urgent cause, or by inevitable necessity, and with the free and express consent of the king and of the Church*.

Contribution on the clergy.

Six years earlier, when the archbishop of Tyre arrived in France, as the legate of the Holy See, to impose a contribution on the clergy for the cost of a holy war, an assembly of bishops† referred his bull to the king, and ordained that, if any chose to accede to the claim, they would do so by their own free will, not through any legal compulsion from Rome. It is obvious from these occasional ebullitions to observe, that the sordid policy of Innocent IV. was already producing its effect, in disposing the secular clergy to resist the despotism of Rome. Fifty years had not yet elapsed from the death of that pontiff, when we find the prelacy of France placed in direct opposition‡

* "Item exactiones et onera gravissima pecuniarum per Curiam Romanam Ecclesiæ regni nostri impositas vel imposita, quibus regnum nostrum miserabiliter depauperatum extitit, sive etiam imponendas vel imponenda, levari aut colligi nullatenus volumus, nisi duntaxat pro rationabili, pia et urgentissima causa, vel inevitabili necessitate, ac de spontaneo ac expresso consensu nostro et ipsius Ecclesiæ regni nostri." There are some copies in which the last article does not appear. But there is more reason for the opinion, that it was curtailed in those, than interpolated in the rest. Though the other articles do not make express mention of the court of Rome, yet it seems clear that the second, third, fourth, and a part of the first, are levelled against it. See Fleury, liv. lxxxvi. sec. i. Dupin, Nouv. Biblioth., sec. xiii. chap. vii. The act was cited, as here given, by the parliament to Louis XI., in 1483, and in the Act of Appeal of the university of Paris, in 1495.

† The Declaration of the bishops is given by Menard in his notes on Joinville, p. 287.

‡ The same spirit, of course, extended itself to the lower clergy. It was during this reign that a curé at Paris thus addressed his congregation:—"You know, my brethren, that I am ordered to publish an excommunication against Frederic (II.) I am ignorant of the motive. I am only certain that there has been a quarrel between that prince and the pope—God alone knows which is right. I excommunicate him who has injured the other, and absolve him who has suffered the injury." The congregation were amused with the sally. The emperor is said to have sent a present to the preacher; but the pope condemned him to canonical penance; and he performed it accordingly.

to the Vatican, and a politic prince availing himself of that spirit to the disadvantage of the Holy See. As long as the popes were contented to make common cause with their clergy against the secular authorities, they were indeed strong and formidable. But when they openly distinguished between the interests of the court of Rome and of the rest of the hierarchy —when they proceeded to supply the luxuries, or forward the ambitious projects of the one by invading the revenues of the other—from that moment the despotism of the apostolical chair, notwithstanding the swarm of mendicants which it created for its defence, had parted with its only ground or hope of permanence.

Section IV.

On the Crusades.

"The report of the Council of Clermont wafted a cheering gale over the minds of Christians. There was no nation so remote, no people so retired, as did not respond to the papal wishes. This ardent wish not only inspired the continental provinces, but the most distant islands and savage countries *." Accordingly a mighty mass of fanaticism put itself in motion towards the East. The frame of society was convulsed, and seemingly dissolved; and as the will of Heaven is not uncommonly pleaded to justify the extravagance of man, the phenomena of the physical world were pressed into the same adventure : meteors and exhalations pointed out the road to Jerusalem, and the most ordinary signs of nature became portents and prodigies. The first burst of the storm fell upon some miserable Jews, who were living in peace under Christian protection, and many were massacred. It then rolled onwards; and the follies, the sufferings, and the crimes, which marked the progress of the first crusade, have never been equalled in the history of human madness. Nevertheless, as a military enterprise, it was

Exploits and barbarities of the First Crusade.

* Malmsbury, p. 416. He continues: "The Welshman left his hunting; the Scotch his fellowship with vermin ; the Dane his drinking party; the Norwegian his raw fish."

successful. Some exploits were performed of extraordinary daring. The same agency which had lighted the flame was at hand to nourish it on every occasion of disaster; and the spirit that was chilled by famine or by fear, was immediately revived and inflamed by some new and stupendous miracle. Men who could be brought really to believe, while under the endurance of the most frightful reverses, that the favour of God was especially extended and continually manifested to them, were capable of more than human exertion; the entire abandonment of reason left space for the operation of energies which do not properly belong to man.

The victory of Doryleum was followed by the siege of Antioch; the capture of that city led the way to the investment of Jerusalem itself; and the banner of the cross was finally planted on Mount Sion, amidst horrors, which probably had not been paralleled since the triumph of Titus over the same devoted city. Respecting the double massacre inflicted upon the infidels, we shall merely remark, that it had not the excuse of hasty, uncontrollable passion, but that it was designed and deliberate. A deeply-settled resolution of revenge may have had some share in the deed, but the policy of extermination had probably more; and the spirit of religious persecution certainly directed the weapons and poisoned the wounds. In the mean time, *Deux el volt*—it is the will of God—was the watchword and the battle-shout of the Christians; it overpowered the prayers of the women and the screams of their dying children[*]; and was then loudest upon Sion and Calvary when the commandments of God and Christ were most insultingly violated.

St. Bernard preaches the Second Crusade. The loss of the Crusaders, in this first enterprise, is calculated with probability at about 1,200,000 lives!—but the Holy Sepulchre was freed from the pollution of the infidel; and, what perhaps was of more consequence, as respects the continuance of similar expeditions, a Latin kingdom was established

---

[*] "Christiani sic neci totum laxaverant animum, ut nec sugens masculus, aut fœmina, nedum infans unius anni vivens manum percussoris evaderet."—Albert, p. 283, cited by Mills, Hist. Crusades, chap. vi.

in Jerusalem. It is remarkable, that not one of the sovereigns
of Europe adventured his person, or even deeply risked his
reputation, in the unknown perils of the first Crusade. But,
nearly fifty years afterwards, the loss of Edessa, and some other
reverses in the East, awakened the sympathy of Louis VII. of
France and Conrad III. of Germany, and they determined to
aid an afflicted Christian and a brother king. For this purpose
it was necessary to rouse the fury of Europe a second time ;
and the eager co-operation of St. Bernard secured success. A
less powerful instrument might have answered the object. Any
intemperate enthusiast * can excite his fellow-mortals to deeds
of wickedness : the genius of St. Bernard was given him to do
good to mankind—but it was contracted by the severity of
monastic discipline; it was stained with the prejudices of an
ignorant age ; it was distorted by the very austerity of his
virtues ; it was misdirected even by his piety. He entered
with ardour upon his mission of evil. He traversed fruitful
provinces and populous cities. Vast multitudes everywhere
assembled to applaud and to listen; and the energy of his
delivery and the vehemence of his tones and action roused the
feelings of many, who were even ignorant of the language in
which he addressed them †. Such excitement, in a matter
where passion and not reason was engaged, produced every
effect of persuasion ; and if, besides, there were any so torpid
as to resist the natural eloquence of the holy man, he enjoyed
that other resource, so potent in its influence where all the
ordinary operations of the mind are suspended—he possessed
the gift of miracles, and proved his heavenly mission (so his
credulous panegyrists assert) by many preternatural signs. At
the same time he affected, by a more dangerous assumption,

* It is amusing to observe the contempt with which the Abbot of Clairvaux
speaks of the hermit-preacher of the first crusade : " Fuit in priori expeditione,
antequam Hierosolyma caperetur, vir quidam, Petrus nomine, cujus et vos (ni
fallor) sæpe mentionem audistis," &c.—Bernard. Epist. 363, p. 328, vol. i. ed.
Mabil. The reference is made by Mills, Hist. Crusades, chap. ix.

† Latin was the language which he indiscriminately addressed to the vulgar
in all the provinces in which he preached. Since preternatural powers have been
ascribed to him, it has been thought remarkable that the gift, of which he seemed
to stand most in need, was perversely withheld.

the prophetic character; and, on the faith of Him who can neither err nor deceive, he foretold and promised a splendid career of triumphs. Armed with so full and various a quiver against the feeble reason of a superstitious generation—with high personal celebrity and eloquence; with the support of powerful princes; with pontifical approbation; with the repute of supernatural aid, and pretensions to heavenly inspiration— what wonder was it that St. Bernard confounded the sense and broke up the repose of Europe; that he depopulated cities and provinces (such was his own rash boast), and sent forth the whole flower and vigour of Christendom on the holy enterprise!

The history of religious war has not recorded any expedition at the same time more fatal and more fruitless than the crusade of St. Bernard. After two or three years of suffering and disaster almost uninterrupted, a miserable remnant of survivors returned to relate their misfortunes and marvel at their discomfiture. A general outcry was raised against the author of those calamities; innumerable widows and orphans demanded of the prophet their husbands and their sires; or at least they claimed the sacred laurels which he had promised—the triumphs which he had vouchsafed, in his dispensation of the boons of heaven, to the soldiers of the cross. The detected impostor was not ashamed to take shelter under the usual pretext of religious hypocrites. He asserted that his prophecies (the prophecies of God) were only conditional; that in foretelling the success of the crusaders, he had *assumed* their righteousness and the purity of their lives; that their own enormous crimes had diverted or suspended the designs of Providence, just as in ancient days the sins of the Jews in the wilderness had foiled the policy and foresight of Moses *. If at any time we can

---

* This celebrated passage is in the beginning of the second book of his Treatise, " De Consideratione," addressed to Pope Eugenius III., and should be cited :— " Moyses educturus populum de terra Ægypti meliorem illis pollicitus est terram. Nam quando ipsum aliter sequeretur populus, solam sapiens terram? Eduxit ; eductos tamen in terram quam promiserat non introduxit. Nec est quod ducis temeritati imputari queat tristis et inopinatus eventus. Omnia faciebat Domino imperante. Domino cooperante, et opus confirmante sequentibus signis. Sed populus ille, inquis, duræ cervicis fuit, semper contentiosè agens contra Dominum et contra Moysem servum ejus. Bene illi creduli et rebelles—Hi autem quid?

regard with levity any pious artifice of the meanest ecclesiastic for the most innocent purpose, still our smile is not unmixed with melancholy or contempt. But the crime of St. Bernard, the most enlightened prelate of his time, who usurped the attributes and forged the seal of God, in order to launch some hundreds of thousands of confiding Christians into probable destruction, or at best into successful massacre, excites a serious indignation which it would be partial to suppress, and which neither his talents, nor his virtues, nor his piety, nor the vicious principles of his age are sufficient to remove.

Forty years after the departure of this expedition, in the year 1187, Saladin gained the battle of Tiberias, and soon afterwards recovered from the Christians the possession of the Holy City. The Latin kingdom of Jerusalem had struggled through eighty-eight years of precarious existence against internal dissension and tumult and the perpetual aggressions of the infidel Perhaps it must have yielded under any circumstances to the genius of Saladin; but its fate was precipitated by the feudal divisions of its defenders, the jealousy subsisting between the Knights of the Temple and those of the Hospital, and the violent quarrels in which the latter were engaged, through the effect of their papal immunities, with the avaricious hierarchy of Palestine. Subsequent crusades.

The Third Crusade (1189-92) was distinguished by the adventures of the lion-hearted Richard. The Fourth followed only three years afterwards, under the auspices of Pope Celestine III., and terminated in inglorious failure. The Germans, by whom it was chiefly conducted, accused the faint co-operation of the barons resident in the Holy Land. The Fifth and Sixth were protected and fostered, if not created, by Innocent III. The former of these may possibly be ascribed to the still surviving spirit of popular superstition, lashed into fanaticism by

Ipsos interroga. Quid me dicere opus est quod fatentur ipsi ? Dico ergo unum —Quid poterant conficere, qui semper revertebantur, cum ambularent? Quando et isti per totam viam non redierunt corde in Ægyptum? Quod si illi ceciderunt et perierunt propter iniquitatem suam, miramur istos, eadem facientes, eadem passos! Sed numquid illorum casus adversus promissa Dei ? Ergo, nec istorum. Neque enim aliquando promissiones Dei justitiæ Dei prejudicant."

the preaching, or at least by the miraculous pretensions, of an enthusiast named Fulk.   But whatever may have been its origin, its termination—the capture of Constantinople—was certainly neither foreseen nor designed by its advocates.   The warriors of the Sixth Crusade likewise declined from the original object of these military pilgrimages, and deviated, with greater promise of profit if not of glory, into the wealthy plains of Egypt.   Their courage was repaid by the conquest of Damietta; but the advantage thus obtained was neither great nor permanent.   The force of the Christians in the East was weakened by division, and they were contented to despoil what they could not hope to possess.   Still, if we are to assign to this expedition the concluding exertions of Frederic II., it terminated with more honour to the Christian name, and with a nearer approach to the liberation of the Holy Sepulchre, than any which had been undertaken since the first.   And that its results were not more lasting, is to be ascribed, not to the insincerity of the emperor, but to the narrow jealousy of a passionate pope *, who roused all his military and monastic myrmidons in opposition to that very cause which he, as well as his faithless predecessor, had dared to designate the cause of God.

Those of St. Louis.   The chivalrous enterprise of the Count of Champagne and Richard, Earl of Cornwall, followed the council of Spoleto in 1234; and the imperfect success which attended it was rather occasioned by the dissensions of the Mussulman princes than by the cordial co-operation of the Christians.   It added one to the list of the Crusades, and was presently succeeded by two others, the eighth and ninth, with which the melancholy catalogue at length concluded.   Both of these may probably be attributed to the religious fervour of St. Louis.   In the access of a dangerous sickness, in the year 1244, that prince vowed the sacrifice of his personal service to God, should his health providentially be restored.   It was so.   In the following year,

* Gregory IX. Innocent III. died before the departure of the expedition, which he had been particularly and personally diligent in promoting. See the preceding chapter. Not professing to give a regular history of these various expeditions, nor to mention more facts than are necessary for our inferences, we have not noticed the celebrated Crusade of Children under this pope; yet it may fairly be considered as the consummation of the work of fanaticism.

the numerous host of prelates assembled at the council of Lyons, proclaimed the crusade and enjoined four preparatory years of peace and seriousness throughout the Western nations. During this interval, large contributions were levied both on the clergy and laity, and other effectual means adopted to secure success; and at its expiration the pious monarch spread his sails for the East. His immediate object, however, was not the liberation of the Sepulchre, but the conquest of Egypt; and in the conduct of this campaign, he closely imitated both the gallantry and the errors of his predecessors, who had triumphed and perished in the same field. The misfortunes of the sixth Crusade, though still fresh in the memory of mankind, taught as usual no lesson and conveyed no warning to the generation which followed; and the repetition of similar blunders only led to a more disastrous result. The army was defeated, and Louis himself fell a captive into the power of the infidel. But his follies were redeemed by the gold of his subjects; and he returned to expiate his fatal enthusiasm by the exercise of peaceful virtues, and to repair, by useful and humane institutions, the wrongs which he had done to his people.

But the spark of superstition was neither extinguished by the discharge of his best duties, nor chilled by the advance of age. After an interval of twenty years of wisdom, he relapsed into the old infatuation, and unfurled, for the last time, the consecrated banner of fanaticism. His second expedition consisted, for the most part, as the first had done, of French and English; and, like the first, it was again directed against the Moslems of Africa, not against the usurpers of the Holy Land. The heroic plains of Carthage were occupied by the Christian force, and the tombs of Tertullian, Cyprian, and Augustin may perhaps have been rescued from the pollutions of the unbeliever; but the army was still encamped, without any decisive success, before the walls of Tunis, when St. Louis was called His death. away for ever from the sanguinary scene.

His death was immediately followed by the romantic adventures of the English Edward, which closed the long succession of fruitless efforts for a worthless object. The power of the Infidel presently increased in might and boldness; and in the year 1291 the last fragments of Christian rule were swept away from the surface of Palestine. Acre, the conquest of the English hero, was the last possession of the cross: it had long been the only strong bulwark against the Moslem force. It was important, through its situation at the end of that large and fertile plain which extends to the Jordan eastward, and which has been the field of decisive conflicts in every age of the history of Palestine; it was important, as the centre of commercial intercourse between the East and the West, the resort of all nations and all languages. But the universal profligacy which prevailed within its walls and the crimes with which it was stained, beyond the shame of any other Christian city, were thought to justify the judgment of God, when at length he delivered it over to a Mahometan conqueror*.

To this hasty, but necessary, outline of the history of the Crusades, we are called upon to subjoin some general observations on their causes, their objects, and their results: not aspiring to emulate the eloquence with which this subject has been so commonly treated, nor affecting to add anything original in thought or expression to the successful labours of our predecessors, but simply to justify the pretensions of this work, which would vainly assume the title of an ecclesiastical history if it should pass in entire silence over the most amazing phenomena which ever proceeded from the abuse of religion. And if, indeed, it be a true reflection that the only enterprise in which the nations of Europe have at any time engaged with a single arm and a common soul—and that, too, no vague and transient adventure, but the passion or policy of 200 years—stands singularly marked in the historic temple as a monument of human absurdity: if this be true, is it possible to search too frequently for the sources of such unanimous infatuation, or to ascertain too minutely what passions, or what prejudices, or what interests those were which availed to dispossess and enchain for so long a period the reason of mankind? More-

---

* " E questo pericolo non fù senza grande e giusto giudizio di Dio, che quella città era piena di più peccatori uomini e femine d'ogni dissoluto peccato, che terra chi fosse tra' Christiani." Giovanni Villani, lib. vii., c. 144, as cited by Mills, Hist. Crusades.

over, as we have found occasion to observe that an indulgent
Providence will sometimes extract blessings from man's blindest
follies, it becomes us also to inquire whether the fruits of those
wild enterprises were any other than shame, degradation, and
misery. Though, indeed, in this case it might seem presumptuous to look for any manifestation of divine compassion where
impiety called itself religious devotion, and massacre pleaded
for reward, and pleaded in the blessed name of Christ.

To visit the spots which have been consecrated by immortal   Pilgrim-
deeds—to tread in the footsteps which those have traced whose   age.
memory we love and revere—is the suggestion of natural piety,
not the maxim or observance of religion. Nevertheless, such
practice is easily associated with any religion whenever the
qualities of its founder have been such as to excite the enthusiasm of its votaries; and thus the performance of holy pilgrimage became an early, a frequent, and almost a peculiar
usage of the Christians. From an innocent, perhaps useful
custom, it was gradually exalted into a spiritual duty; and the
journey to the sepulchre of the Saviour was encouraged and
enjoined by some of the oldest fathers of the established Church.
The pure principle of pilgrimage was presently mixed and al-
loyed by vulgar motives: a faint shade of superstition was insensibly heightened into a darker; and the traveller returned
from the holy places, no longer satisfied with the consciousness
of pious intent and sincere devotion, but also charged with
relics of departed saints, or fragments of the holy crown or
cross. This degenerate passion was nourished by the rulers
of the Church; multitudes thirsted for those vain possessions
whom a mere ardour to worship at the tomb of Christ would
scarcely have fortified against the toils of the journey; the
Syrian dispensers of the profitable patrimony unceasingly discovered new treasures by revelation, or multiplied the original
by miracles: so that the crowds who thronged the sanctuary
perpetually increased, and the sources which fed their credulity
were never closed nor lessened.

It was natural to expect that the conquest of Palestine by
the unbelieving Saracens would have abolished the means, if
it did not desecrate the objects, of pilgrimage. But it proved

otherwise. The enlightened Caliphs immediately perceived
the policy of toleration; they saw the direct advantages which
flowed into Syria through the superstition and commerce of
the West; they may even have learned from their own practice to respect the motives of the travellers and the kindred
passion which occasioned an annual visit to the Christian
Mecca. Certainly they received the visitors without insult,
and dismissed them without injury.

During the concluding part of the tenth century, a strange
impulse was given to the spirit of pilgrimage by an accidental
cause, which, as it was sown in delusion, produced the customary harvest of wickedness. The belief prevailed of the
approaching dissolution of the world and the termination of
earthly things; Mount Sion was to become the judgment-seat
of the Most High, and the Christian nations were taught to
depart and humble themselves before his throne. Those interested exhortations were too obsequiously obeyed; and though
the notion which created them was after a few years falsified
and exploded, yet the habit of journeying to the Holy Land
had in the meantime gained great prevalence, and the idea of
an expiatory obligation became commonly attached to it. In
the century following, the journey assumed not unfrequently
the form of an expedition, and was sometimes undertaken by
considerable bodies of associated and even armed devotees.
We still peruse, in the narrative of Ingulphus, a native and
historian of England, the adventures of 7000 holy Germans,
who engaged in the enterprise under the direction of the archbishop of Mayence, and in the society of thirty Norman horsemen. They encountered many dangers and suffered many
losses; but they attained their object, and worshipped at the
fountain of their religion. And when they recounted, in
domestic security, their various fortunes, their listeners were
more likely to be inflamed by the admiration of their success
than deterred by sufferings or perils, which greater foresight or
felicity might easily ward off from themselves.

Towards the close of the eleventh age, about the year 1076,
the dominion of Palestine was torn from the Arabian dynasty
by the wilder hands of the Turks. The pure fanaticism of that

rude people was not yet softened by friendly intercourse with
the followers of the adverse faith, nor would it stoop to yield
even to the obvious dictates of interest. Many outrages were
at this time unquestionably perpetrated upon the strangers who
visited the sepulchre, and upon the Christian natives and sojourners in Syria.   Those who returned from the East were
clamorous in their descriptions and their complaints ; and tales
of suffering and of sacrilege, of the prostration of Christ's followers, the profanation of his name, the pollution of his holy
places, tales of Moslem oppression and impiety, were diffused
and exaggerated and believed, with fierce and revengeful indignation, from one end of Europe to the other.

Whatsoever may have been the merits of the feudal principles
in earlier times, they had degenerated, in the eleventh century,
into a mere code of military service and subordination.   The
whole business, the pleasure, the passion of that age was war.
It animated alike the cities and the villages; it presided over
the domestic regulations of every family ;   it was familiar with
the thoughts, where it did not constitute the habits, of every
individual. Even the higher orders of the clergy forgot their
spiritual in their secular obligations, and very commonly engaged in the same pursuits from a common necessity*.   It
was in vain that Charlemagne had restrained by his Capitularies that preposterous practice. The policy of Charlemagne
was too wise for the times in which he lived : he attempted to
anticipate the operation of progressive ages ; he enacted some
useful laws ; but he was unable to perpetuate a premature, and
therefore transient, civilization.   No sooner was he removed
by death than inveterate barbarism resumed its sway, and the
bulwark which his single hand had raised against the principles, customs, and prejudices of ancestral ignorance, was hastily
swept away.   During the two centuries which followed, in

marginal note: Warlike spirit of the age.

* " Olim" (says Guido, abbot of Clairville) " non habebant castella et arces
ecclesiæ cathedrales, nec incedebant pontifices loricati. Sed nunc, propter abun-
dantiam temporalium rerum, flamma, ferro, cæde possessiones ecclesiarum prælati
defendunt, quas deberent pauperibus erogare." Du Cange, Gloss. Lat., art. Ad-
vocatus. The abbot's *olim* extended through the first five centuries, and not
much later.

spite of the general exertions of the clergy, as a body, to arrest
the desolating spirit, in spite of canonical legislation and ecclesiastical censure, the practice of private warfare continued
with no mitigation. Early in the eleventh age, the Treuga
Dei (the Truce of God) was solemnly enjoined, with the purpose of enforcing a suspension of hostilities during certain days
in every week. But though this humane ordinance was frequently confirmed and reiterated, there was no age in which
the military frenzy had such general prevalence throughout
Europe, none in which the exercise of arms and the effusion of
blood were so completely the habit, the motive, almost the
morality, of the western nations.

Supersti-
tious zeal.
At a period when religious notions or observances were
mingled with all customs and all institutions, and thus interwoven
with the whole texture of private as well as public life,—and
when, besides, the corruptions of Christianity had so superseded
its genuine spirit, that the notions which we have called religious should rather have been designated superstitious,—the
ruling passion of the age was easily associated with its ruling
weakness. Martial enterprise went hand in hand with enthusiasm, misnamed pious; the exploits of the one were consecrated
by the expressions, sometimes by the feelings, of the other;
and the words of the priest were repeated, or the image of the
Saviour embraced, even in the fiercest moments of the strife.
Abject ignorance, followed by credulity, held dominion almost
undisputed; and the minds of men were destitute of any moral
principles to restrain, or any moral knowledge to direct, the
course of their passions. The faculties which distinguish sense
from absurdity, piety from fanaticism, truth from falsehood and
imposture, were extinct or dormant; and a restless and irrational generation lay exposed to the impulse of any rising
tempest.

On such an age and race,—so inured to the use of arms, so
alive to the emotions of religion, so familiar with the practice
of holy pilgrimage,—the indignity of Turkish oppression, the
outrages on the name and sepulchre of Christ, fell with an
electric efficacy. At another time, under other circumstances,
the bolt might have passed by unfelt and almost unheeded;

but at that moment it was no premature nor unseasonable visitation : it found men prepared, and intensely sensible to its operation; and the flash which attended it descended on materials ready for explosion.

It argues a superficial knowledge both of nature and of history to suppose that a phenomenon, so astounding as the first crusade, could have been produced in any condition of society without strong predetermining causes; and that the preaching of the Hermit or even the indulgences of the Pope could have excited to that enterprise minds that were not deeply disposed to receive the impulse.   There are some, indeed, who consider the increase of pontifical power during the eleventh age, under the auspices of Hildebrand, to have been a leading cause in producing the Crusades.   It is true that, a century earlier, the aspirations of Sylvester II. were without effect : it is more remarkable that even Gregory himself, though professing an ardent and even personal eagerness for the enterprise, carried his project to no result ; while Urban, with much less individual influence, accomplished the work with great facility.

Gradual growth of the crusading spirit.

But in the time of Sylvester, some of the popular motives for the crusade did not yet exist, others had not attained sufficient prevalence and maturity; and Gregory was diverted from his scheme by the more pressing solicitations of domestic ambition. But when Urban threw the torch among the multitudes of Placentia and Clermont, their hands were prepared and eager to seize it, and extinguish it in Moslem blood.   A pilgrimage to the sepulchre of Christ was then a common and almost customary act of devotion; a pilgrimage in arms was congenial with the spirit of a warlike race; to liberate the holy places and to chastise the usurpers were objects consistent with each other, and with the ruling principles of the age.

And such were the *objects* of the first crusade—to deliver the Holy Land from a state of imaginary pollution, and to take vengeance on the infidel possessor.   No consideration of distant consequences, nor even of immediate utility, entered into them.   Reason was not consulted, nor were her precincts approached : of the passions themselves, those most akin to reason had no share in the adventure.   Ambition was silent in the

Objects of the first crusade.

uproar*.   Policy might, indeed, have offered plausible justification, by suggesting that the hurricane which had wasted Asia
might presently break over Europe; but the *argumenta justi
metus,* if they have satisfied some writers on this subject, entered not in any degree into the motives of the Crusaders.
They were not men to calculate remote dangers; still less did
they perplex themselves with any theoretical speculation as to
the right of hostility, or seek their excuse in the antichristian
principles of their enemy.   From the rule and practice of Mahometan aggression, they might almost have inferred the right
of reciprocal invasion : but they looked for immortality, not for
justification; it never occurred to them to doubt the justice, or
rather the holiness, of their cause; they sought no plea or pretext, except in the passion of their religious frenzy and in the
sharpness of their sword.

There was still another motive which might have seemed
substantial to the warriors of those days, and which they might
equally have borrowed from the Infidel—a design to convert
the miscreants by force, and to drag them in chains to the
waters of baptism; but even this project held no place among
the incentives to the *first* crusade. In later times, indeed, when
in the vicissitudes of military adventure the arms of the Mahometan were found to preponderate, some faint attempts were
made, or meditated†, to convince those, whom it proved impossible to subdue; but the earliest soldiers of the Cross were
moved by no such design : they rushed with thoughtless pre-
cipitation to an unprofitable end, and they believed that a
Power irresistibly impelled them, and that that Power was—
the Will of God.

---

  * The success which had attended the Asiatic, and even Syrian, campaigns of
Nicephorus, Phocas, and John Zimisces (963—975) might have offered reasonable hopes to the ambition of the Crusaders, and almost justified the military
policy of the expedition—if ambition or policy had ever entered into their consideration.

  † In 1285, Honorius IV., in order to convert the Saracens, strove to establish
at Paris schools for Arabic and other Oriental languages. The Council of Vienna
in 1312 recommended the same method; and Oxford, Salamanca, Bologna, as
well as Paris, were places selected for the establishment of the Professorships.
But the decree appears to have remained without effect, until Francis I. called it
into life.

These remarks are properly confined to the origin of the Of those which fol-lowed. first crusade—to that burst of pure fanaticism which was itself unmixed with worldly incentives, though it opened the field for other enterprises, proceeding from the usual motives of human action. An inattention to this distinction has misled some writers, who, failing to discriminate between the circumstances which produced, and those which nourished, the crusades, have not taken an accurate view of either. A multitude of causes combined to impel the machine when it was once in motion, though the agency which launched it was simple and uniform. In the first place, by the success of the first expedition, an important kingdom was established in the East. Immediately measures were taken to provide for its protection, and secure its stability. Natives of most of the western states settled in Palestine. The *Latin* colony adopted the feudal discipline, and the common constitution of Europe. Hence a thousand links were extended of sympathy and of interest; and together they formed an entirely new ground for exertion, and gave a different character to the movement which agitated the West. Henceforward, reciprocal relations existed; the honour of Christendom was now engaged to maintain its conquests over the unbeliever; it was held base to relinquish a possession, acquired through so many losses, even by those who might not think the losses counterbalanced by the possession. It is one thing to rush into a desperate enterprise, and another to encounter some additional risk in defence of that, which by much previous risk has been achieved.

Not one of the sovereigns of Europe was either personally engaged in the first crusades, or very zealous in promoting it : it proceeded from sources wholly distinct from the policy of courts and the springs of civil government. But the second, and most of the following expeditions, were undertaken, some with the aid and countenance, others under the very authority and direction, of the leading monarchs. It is unnecessary to observe how many different ingredients were thrown into the cup of fanaticism by such co-operation,—obedience to the command, affection for the person, gratitude for the favour, hope from the generosity, of the prince—and, what was scarcely less potent than these, the seal of approbation which stamped the practice, which gave it prevalence and fashion, which placed it among the ordinary means of distinction, among the legitimate duties of military service. Again, the policy, which mixed itself almost necessarily with the royal motives, entirely lost sight in some cases of the original object. The pollution of the holy places was forgotten in the fruitful prospect of the plains of Egypt, or of the commerce which thronged the African ports; in such manner, as to make it very questionable whether plunder, rather than conquest, was not the principal motive of three, at least, among the latest crusades. St. Louis himself was, perhaps, as politic as he was pious ; and it is not easy to perceive how the sufferings of the Holy Land could have been much alleviated by any advantages which he might have achieved before the walls of Tunis. At any rate, though the same vows and intentions might still be professed, very different incentives were certainly proposed, and very different methods adopted, to accomplish them.

The policy of the Popes. The principles and motives of the Vatican, which are generally found so consistent, were subject to some fluctuation in the encouragement which it extended to the crusades. The feeling of Sylvester appears to have been the anticipation of that, which animated the first adventurers a century afterwards. Gregory VII. had more specific and tangible objects. His practical mind was not perhaps much moved by the tears of Palestine and the tales of her pollution ; but he considered the union of the rival churches, and the general triumph of the Christian over the Moslem cause, as projects not unworthy of the confederacy of the West, and of his own superintendence.

The popes of the 12th century followed, where they did not direct or inflame the passion of their age; and the successive armaments of martyrs were launched with the apostolical benediction on their holy destination. But the designs of Innocent III. were of a different and more selfish description ; and he did not fear to pervert to their accomplishment the machine intrusted to him for other purposes. The arms which had been consecrated to the service of Christ, against the blasphemers of his name, were now turned against the domestic adversaries of the See of Rome. The views and policy of Innocent were purely ecclesiastical; they did not extend in any direction beyond the interests of the Church over which he presided; and it was the impulse of the moment to crush the foe in his bosom, before he sought for a remote and defensive enemy.

When the precedent of converting the banner of the Cross into a badge of papal subservience was once established, the name and object of a holy war passed through different methods of profanation; and the sword of the Crusader, after being steeped in heretical blood, was drawn, in the same hateful service, against a Catholic adversary. The popes had thus accomplished their final object in substituting the defence of the Church—which really meant the temporal interests of the See of Rome—as a recognized object for arming the subjects of all governments, in the name of Christ; and to this purpose the plenary indulgence, still the great lever of popular fanaticism, was commonly and not vainly applied.

From that time forward it does not appear that the Vatican pursued any fixed policy respecting the expeditions really undertaken for the chastisement of the Infidel. Its general voice was indeed loud in their favour; and bulls and exhortations were perpetually promulgated to quicken or revive the ardour of the Faithful. Notwithstanding, there were particular occasions—such as the attempts of Frederic II. and the Seventh Crusade—on which the pontifical power was employed to thwart, or even to prevent, the enterprise. But the secret of this fluctuation was too often and too openly betrayed. The advantage and aggrandizement of Rome were now become in papal eyes the only legitimate object of the religious spirit; and, according to the more modern and favourite method, she now turned that spirit into the channel of her avarice. The indulgence, which in the first instance was only granted as the reward of actual service in the holy cause, was, in process of time, publicly exchanged for gold; and the timid or indolent devotee was first permitted, and afterwards encouraged, to redeem by his wealth the toils and dangers of a military penance. Again: Innocent III. had taxed the clergy of Europe for the benefit of the Holy Land; but presently we find complaints, that the tax was become the object, instead of the means, and the Crusade only the pretext. And thus the treasury of Rome was filled, amidst the disappointment of all honest enthusiasts and the murmurs of a defrauded priesthood. The memory of Gregory VII., and the fame of his spiritual triumph and lofty ambition, were put to shame by the sordid cupidity of his degenerate successors.

Decline of the Crusading spirit.

The above observations are sufficient to show how widely both the causes and objects of the Crusades varied during the long period of their continuance, and how far they sometimes deviated from the pure martial fanaticism of their origin. As they were thus mixed up with the ordinary motives of policy, and were degraded to the selfish service of Rome, so the fuel by which they were nourished gradually disappeared, and the flame insensibly burnt out; and in this circumstance we observe the limits to which the influence of the Vatican itself was confined. When popular spirit was kindled by other causes, the pope was abundantly powerful to fan and excite it; when it had risen to the height of its fury, he had control sufficient to misdirect it; but when it began to sink and die away, his utmost efforts were unable to sustain or revive it. As long as the Vatican was contented to feed and minister to the universal passion, its influence, which was really great, appeared to have no bounds; but when that passion had once subsided, the Pontiffs lost their hold on human weakness; and neither the increase of exemptions * or indemnities, nor the multipli-

* The Crusaders, besides their plenary indulgences, had several alluring temporal privileges, which are perhaps correctly reduced under the following heads:—1. They were exempted from prosecution for debt during the time of their service. 2. From paying interest for the money which they had borrowed for the outfit. 3. For a certain time, if not entirely, from the payment of taxes. 4. They might alienate their lands without the consent of the superior lord. 5. Their persons and effects were taken under the protection of St. Peter, and anathemas denounced against all who should molest them. 6. They enjoyed all the privileges of ecclesiastics; such as not being bound to plead in civil courts, &c.—(See Robertson's Proofs and Illustrations.) It remained, of course, very uncertain how far these privileges would be acknowledged by the secular authorities, and to what extent those civil courts would consent to forego their jurisdiction over so large a multitude; and thus the real value of these papal immunities depended on the pope's influence and various other causes. The serfs, who exchanged their agricultural service for that of the Cross, appear by that act to have obtained their freedom: at least, that which was conferred by common military service would scarcely be withheld from the Crusader,

cation of indulgences, availed to inflame the descendants of those spontaneous enthusiasts, who, in obedience to the preaching of the Hermit, had rushed forth to restore the honour of Christ, and avenge the wrongs of his worshippers.

As the causes, from which the crusading frenzy at first broke out, were of long and regular growth, so likewise was the process of its extinction slow and gradual. Throughout the space of two hundred years, the original flame, though continually sinking, was not wholly lost;—it was still mingled, though in smaller proportions and fainter colours, with the various mass of new motives, which ineffectually endeavoured to supply its place, and which really derived their brightness from it. But when at length it disappeared, what were the traces of evil or of good which were left upon the face of the earth? What permanent effects were engraven upon the destinies of Europe by the violent hand which had so long directed them? From a system of military aggression, which had no foundation in reason, or even in those passions which are nearest to reason, few indeed were the fruits which could be expected for the benefit o society ; and if any such did in fact proceed from the crusades, it was through circumstances wholly independent of their design. It appears to us, that these fortuitous advantages were both few in number and extremely partial. Perhaps it would be unreasonable to dispute that the decline of the baronial despotism, with the birth of municipal rights on the one hand, and the just extension of royal authority on the other, was accelerated by the violent alienations of property which the Crusades occasioned; but those salutary changes would have been produced, and perhaps at no later period, by the sure agency of wiser principles, advancing with the advancement of knowledge. We may indeed hail the accident which hastened (if it hastened) their appearance; but we should err were we to ascribe to it their existence. The commercial benefits which historians too generally connect with the expeditions to the East were principally confined to three cities of Italy—Venice, Genoa, and Pisa*; and if they were thence partially reflected to some

Effects of the Crusades.

Political.

Commercial.

* The results were probably unfavourable to Hamburgh, Lubeck, and the other towns forming the Hanseatic League, by draining the capital south-

other parts of the Peninsula, that was a poor compensation to the commonwealth of Europe for the violent extortions which exhausted its more powerful members—France, Germany, and England. Their treasuries were drained, and the mighty sources of their national industry dried up, that the sails of two or three small republics might overspread the Mediterranean, and receive the first fruits of the contributions so painfully levied for the chastisement of the Infidel.

The loss of Christian life occasioned by the Crusades is fairly calculated at more than two millions. But if the mutual animosities of princes, or, what was even more destructive, the rage of private warfare, had been suspended during their continuance, some consolation for the sacrifice would have been offered to humanity by the repose and concord of the survivors. The fact, however, was otherwise : for a very few years after the departure of the first Crusaders, the Truce of God was indeed observed; but immediately the tide of feudal barbarism returned into its former channel, and proved that the passion for international or domestic broils was neither consumed in foreign adventure, nor superseded by the thirst for it. It is even probable that the nature of such contests was still further embittered by the introduction of those habits of unrelenting ferocity, which are invariably generated by religious warfare.

On Civilization.

It is, again, at least questionable, whether the arts of peace and civilization acknowledge any obligation to the influence of the Crusades. The barbarians gazed in ignorant admiration at the splendid magnificence of Constantinople—" How great is this city! how noble and beautiful! What a multitude of monasteries and palaces it contains of exquisite and wondrous fabric! How many structures are scattered even in the streets and alleys, which are marvellous to behold! It were tedious to recount what an abundance of all good things is found there, of gold and of silver, of every form of vestment, and of *the relics of the saints**." The records of the time are filled with

---

ward. Besides the aristocratic military spirit, which was nourished by the Crusades, is essentially anti-commercial.

* Fulcher. ap. Bongars. vol. i. p. 386. Fulcherius Carnotensis was chaplain to the Count of Chartres. The original passage is cited by Mills, Hist. Crus. chap. iii. It is certain that the collecting of relics was a very favourite occupation with the

similar expressions of wild astonishment. But have we any
proof that these enthusiasts profited by what they beheld?—
that they imitated what they admired?—that they strove to
transplant to their own soil that exotic genius and taste of which
they felt the excellence? Or were they merely ruffled by a
transient inconsequential emotion, unconnected with any principle of action, or intelligence of observation? It is asserted,
that if the Greeks were far superior to the western nations in
the culture of humanity, the Saracens were scarcely less so;
and the strangers had thus a double opportunity of discovering
and correcting their deficiencies. But it is forgotten that the
soldier of the Cross was no enlightened and leisurely traveller,
searching to instruct himself and his generation; but a fierce,
unlettered fanatic, proceeding on a purpose of bloodshed. In
his prejudiced eyes, the civilization of the Greeks was inseparably associated with luxurious indolence and effeminate
timidity; that of the Saracens with an impious faith and
blaspheming tongue; and the disdain with which he regarded
the one, and the detestation with which he approached the
other, repelled him equally from the imitation of either. And
if it be true, that, during the long period of two hundred years,
some trifling advancement in the arts of civilization did in fact
take place, it would still be difficult to specify a single invention as the indisputable effect of the Crusades. Chronological
coincidences are sometimes mistaken for moral connexions; and
the changes which distinguish any age are thus too commonly
ascribed to the passion or principle which may have predominated at the time. But in the present case, when we reflect
that during the eleventh century—before the commencement of
the Crusades—the human mind had already revived and entered
upon its certain career of improvement, we may indeed wonder
that its progress was so slow, and its exertions so barren, during

Crusaders, who thus enriched with many remarkable treasures the sanctuaries of
the West. But to this pursuit their curious industry seems to have been confined. We do not learn that they brought back any other contributions to the
store of European piety, or any to the store of its learning. On the other hand,
many monks took up arms, who would have been more innocently and more profitably employed at home.

the two which followed; but it would be preposterous to attribute the few advantages, which may really have been introduced, to a cause which was in itself decidedly hostile to every moral melioration.

For, since knowledge is the only sure instrument for the elevation of man, can we imagine a condition of society more fatal to its progress than that which was regulated by the co-operation of superstitious zeal with military turbulence?—wherein two principles, separately so fruitful of mischief and misery, were leagued together against the virtue and happiness of mankind? What need we to pursue the inevitable consequences? War assumed a more frightful character by the impulse of fanaticism; and the ordinary barbarities of European strife were multiplied in the conflicts of the East. This necessarily grew out of the very nature of the contest. When the authority of Heaven is pleaded for the infliction of punishment, it creates an implacable and remorseless spirit, since it supersedes, by a stern necessity, all ordinary motives, and stifles the natural pleadings of humanity. The crusaders exclaimed, " It is the will of God!" and in that fancied behest the fiercest brutalities which the world had ever beheld sought not palliation, but honour, and the crown of eternal reward.

The spirit of religious persecution appears to have borrowed the peculiar * features which afterwards distinguished it, from the practice, and even from the principles, of the Crusades. To destroy the votaries of a different faith was esteemed an act of religion; and that, too, not so much because they were dangerous, as *because they differed.* The principle, which was originally intended against Mahometans only, took root generally. The rude understandings of a superstitious race were perplexed. One sort of difference might be as offensive

---

* We more particularly mean the practice of assaulting whole sects and districts of heretics, as such, by authorized military force. The religious wars between the Catholics and the Arians were of a very different character from those between the Church and the Albigeois, &c.; and from the Arian controversy to the time of the Crusades, persecution in the West had never the opportunity, whether it had the will or not, of destroying by wholesale. The existence of the heresy of the Vaudois during that period, though not improbable, is not historically certain.

to Heaven as another. The word heresy was not less diligently and deeply stigmatized in the tablets of the Church
than infidelity. To the pope, the infallible interpreter of the
spiritual oracles, the former was at least as formidable and as
hateful as the latter. And thus the weapon which had been
applied with so much praise of piety to chastise the one, might
be turned, with the same salutary efficacy, to the extirpation
of the other. Through such an inference, which then appeared
not unreasonable, urged by the authority of a powerful pontiff,
the practice of religious massacre was introduced into the
Church of Christ; and when the ministers of bigotry had
once revelled in blood, they were not soon or easily compelled
to relinquish the cup. Among the many evil consequences of
the Crusades, we may account this, perhaps, as the worst—
that they put arms into the hands of intolerance, and finally
kindled in the bosom of Europe the same fanatical passions
with which they had desolated the East.

If we are to believe the contemporary historians, the heroes
of the cross were remarkable for their contempt of every moral
principle; and the cities of Palestine were peculiarly polluted
by the prevalence of vice. If those who resorted to the birth-
place of their religion were not touched even on that holy spot
by its plainest precepts—if the women were involved with the
men, the priest with the warrior, in equal and indiscriminate
profligacy—there can be no doubt in which direction the moral
system of Europe was influenced by the Crusades; nor can we
suppose that the habits acquired in Syria were forgotten or
abjured by the returning pilgrim.

Ecclesiastical writers are equally loud in their complaints The
respecting the corruption sustained through the same means plenary
by the discipline of the Church. The final cessation of gence.
canonical penance is ascribed to the introduction of the plenary
indulgence. In uncivilized ages, the moderate use of the
spiritual authority was unquestionably attended with advantage. The practice of prayer, of fasting, of alms-giving, under
the superintendence of a pious confessor, was salutary to the
offending individual and useful to society. It taught humiliation to the proud spirit; it taught the exercise of charity; and

it may often have produced the genuine fruits of repentance. It is true that, in early times, some discretion had commonly been intrusted to the bishop to mitigate and even, within certain limits, to commute the ordinary penalties; and it was not later than the eighth century that even pilgrimages to certain specified places were substituted for the appointed penance. But before the times of the Crusades there was no mention of plenary indulgence. It had not hitherto been held out to the sinner that, by a *single act*, he might be discharged from all the temporal penalties imposed on him by the Divine Justice. This was an innovation exceeding the boldness of all former changes, and suited to the extraordinary occasion which called for it. But it is properly observed, that those who introduced it had forgotten the legitimate object of canonical penance; that it was enjoined to the sinner, not so much for his chastisement as for the discipline and purification* of his soul. But what, after all, were the religious duties or merits which took the place of the original system, and through which this full indulgence was acquired? To wear those arms of which it had been penance indeed to be deprived; to turn them against a foreign, instead of a domestic foe; to engage in a mighty and soul-inspiring enterprise, instead of contesting the boundaries of a manor, or the fosse of a fortress. Such were the previous habits of the crusaders; and a system which offered pardon on such easy terms, must have acted with many as a positive encouragement to sin.

As the process of canonical penance was commuted for the plenary indulgence, so was the indulgence itself directly and unreservedly† commuted for money. On the consequences of this second corruption we shall not further dwell than to men-

---

* Such was the original design of penance; but it is also true, that the idea of expiation, or an atonement for sin by suffering, very soon entered into the consideration, and very commonly took place of the first motive. That idea is at variance with the first principles of Christianity; and so far as it was prevalent, the penitential system was founded on a false principle, and its abolition can be no matter of regret to any true Christian.

† Penances, as we have mentioned, had been previously commuted, and commuted for money too, when they were commuted for alms; only that which had hitherto been sparingly and decently and indirectly practised, grew into an avowed, authorized, habitual abuse.

tion it among the causes which finally operated to quench the crusading ardour. So soon as absolutions were made matters of open traffic, the motive became too manifest; and thus at length the preachers of Crusades attracted so few listeners, that it became necessary to promise temporary indulgences— of days or even years—to any who would consent to attend their sermons *.

The evil did not expire with its occasion; and after the Crusades were at an end, the popes discovered for it a new, an easier, and perhaps a more profitable object. By the institution of the Jubilee (in the year 1300), the place of pilgrimage was skilfully changed from Jerusalem to Rome; and the tombs of the apostles supplied, in the popular infatuation, the Cross and the Sepulchre of the Saviour. A consoling compensation was thus made both to the avarice of the Vatican and the superstition of the people; and the indulgence was not abandoned, nor its venality at all restrained, until the insulted sense and piety of mankind at length revolted against the enormous abuse.

If, then, we are obliged to admit that the effects of the Crusades were generally pernicious; if it is true that they caused an useless waste of human life, that they increased the ferocity of war, that they gave a deadlier form to religious persecution, that they depressed the level of morality, that they introduced into the discipline of the Church its mortal corruption, their good effects will be found insignificant in the comparison, even though we should account among them the aggrandizement of the sacred order; for one of their effects certainly was the immediate increase of the ecclesiastical revenues. The property of the crusaders was commonly placed, during the expedition, under the bishop's protection; and in case of his death, it often fell, without supposing any direct fraud, into the possession of the Church. Again, though there were wanting neither priests nor monks who assumed the cross in person, yet the number of those was by no means proportionate to the wealth and multitude of the holy community; so that they suffered less severely than any other class the immediate evils of the con-

Aggrandizement of the clergy.

* See Fleury's Discourse on the Crusades.

flict. But the tax which was imposed on them by Innocent did in effect much more than counterbalance those temporary gains; and even in the most sordid calculation of the sacerdotal interests, we may safely pronounce that they did not permanently profit by that commotion which overthrew for a season the general welfare of society.

NOTE (A) ON PAPAL DECRETALS.

In the first ages of Christianity, the letters written by the leading fathers of the Church for the regulation of doctrine and discipline were called decretals (Epistolæ Decretales). As the authority of the bishop of Rome gradually rose above that of other bishops and patriarchs, he likewise claimed an especial deference for his epistles; and in a synod held at Rome in 494, under Pope Gelasius, the decretals of the Roman prelate were invested with the same authority as the canons of councils.

Collection of Gratian. After the time of Charlemagne, the popes, as they felt their growing power, proceeded not only to deny the necessity of any confirmation of their decretals, but to distinguish and exalt them so as to supersede the canons of the Church. As they increased in weight, they multiplied in number. Gratian, a native of Chiusi in Tuscany, and a monk of St. Felix of Bologna, published his celebrated collection in 1151. Many had been previously put forth, but without obtaining any public authority. But that of Gratian was more favourably received, and was made the subject of the public lectures of the canonists. It was entitled the Book of Decrees, or simply *The Decretal*—Decretum *, and was divided into three parts. The first of these, called *The Distinction,* comprised 101 articles, regarding chiefly the different descriptions of laws, ecclesiastical and civil; the authority of the canons and decretals; the ceremonies of ordination; the duties of the clergy; the power of the

---

* The author admitted the object and difficulty of his work, when he called it " Concordia Discordantium Canonum,"

pope. The second—*The Causes*—contained thirty-six sections relating to various matters of Church discipline and jurisdiction—simony, appeals, evidence, elections, censures, testaments, sepultures, usury; of the rights of monks and abbots; of commendams, oaths, war, heresies, sorcery, &c. The third part— *On the Consecration*—treated of the consecration of churches; of the celebration of mass and the divine offices; of the eucharist and other sacraments; of fasts and festivals, and some other subjects. The work abounded in errors, not only as it attributed to the false decretals and other fabrications the authority of genuine compositions, but also as it falsified many of the passages cited from unsuspected monuments. Nevertheless, it was received without hesitation; and after furnishing alone the materials of canonical learning to the schools of Europe, it became a sort of basis on which new and additional decrees and commentaries were fixed and long supported. Another collection was made by Bernardo Circa, bishop of Faenza, in the year 1191. This work was intended as a supplement to the Decretals of Gratian, and was therefore called the Book of *Extravagants, i. e.,* of matters not comprised in the Decretals. But as this was a private compilation, it obtained no force; and accordingly, about the year 1210, Innocent III. caused a more perfect collection to be made, and gave it the seal of public authority. This was called the *Roman* collection.

The Roman Collection.

As circumstances changed, and edicts increased in multitude, fresh compilations were thought necessary; and Gregory IX.*

---

* It is usual to reckon five different compilations of Decretals between Gratian and Gregory IX.—that of the bishop of Faenza, three during the pontificate of Innocent III., and a fifth containing the Letters of Honorius III.—Dupin, Bibl. Nouv., S. XII, ch. iii. and x. Raimond de Pennafort was the person to whom Gregory committed the labour of his compilation. The effect of these successive collections (as even the moderate Roman Catholic historians avow) was to complete the overthrow of the ancient law, to establish the absolute and unbounded power of the pope, and to create an infinity of suits and processes to be decided by the venal justice of the court of Rome. They were extensions of the principles of Gratian, as Gratian had enlarged upon those of the false decretals, in at least two important points—in exempting the pope from the authority of the canons, and the clergy universally from every sort of lay jurisdiction. See Fleury's Seventh Discourse.

That of
Gregory
IX.

availed himself of so favourable an occasion for establishing and extending the monarchy of his see. In that which was published under his auspices, and which affected to be modelled on the code of Justinian*, such former constitutions as seemed to him unsuitable to the character of his own times, were fearlessly cut away, and others inserted on the plenitude of his own authority, which were more congenial to the age and more favourable to pontifical usurpation. As the compilation of Tribonianus had been divided into five books, so was that of Gregory. This work was immediately published throughout all the schools and universities of Europe; and as it was composed with great diligence and enforced by the highest authority, it was very generally and even eagerly received.

Liber
Sextus.

To this collection Boniface VIII. added, about the year 1299, an additional book, commonly known as the *Sixth* (Liber Sextus), and containing all the constitutions posterior to the pontificate of Gregory IX. This too was universally acknowledged, excepting, perhaps, in France. It was further aug-

Clementines.
Extravagants.

mented, in the following age, by the *Clementines* †; and they were succeeded by the *Extravagants*—a name adopted, probably, from the work of the bishop of Faenza. These were the labours of the popes of Avignon; and as the Decretum was intended to correspond with the Pandects, and the Decretals with the Code, so the Extravagants had their model in the Novellæ of the imperial legislator. Under these heads the different branches of pontifical jurisprudence were, for a long period, comprised‡, until they were further augmented by the much more modern addition of the institutions.

NOTE (B) ON THE UNIVERSITY OF PARIS.

The numerous public schools or academies which had previously been formed in various parts of Italy and France, at

---

* The MS. of the Pandect was discovered among the ruins of Amalfi in 1137.

† John XXII. published, in 1317, the constitutions of his predecessor, Clement V. They were divided, as was the Liber Sextus, into five books, and recommended by a bull to the most eminent universities.

‡ In this short account we have chiefly followed Giannone, Stor. di Nap., lib. xix., cap. v., s. 1. See also Dupin, Nouv. Biblioth., Siècle XII., chap. 17.

Salamanca, at Cologne, and elsewhere, assumed the form by which they were afterwards characterized during the thirteenth century. The most celebrated was that of Paris. It was adorned more than any other by the multitude, the rank, and the diligence of its students, and by the abilities and various acquirements of its professors; and while other academies confined their instructions to particular branches of science, that of Paris alone pretended to embrace the entire range. In its origin*, in the century preceding, it had been composed of two Classes —of artists, who gave instructions in the arts and philosophy; and of theologians, who delivered expositions and commentaries, some of them on the Holy Scriptures (they were afterwards called Biblici); others (denominated Sententiarii) on Peter the Lombard's Book of the Sentences. These two appear to have been the earliest *Faculties ;* nor is mention made of any others † in the Constitutions delivered in 1215 by the legate of Innocent III. But the other two—law and medicine—were founded immediately afterwards; and in a letter addressed by the university, in 1253, to all the prelates of the kingdom, the four faculties are boldly compared to the four rivers of the terrestrial paradise. Over each of these societies a doctor was chosen to preside, during a fixed period, by the suffrages of his colleagues, under the title of doyen, or dean. *The four Faculties.*

In the first instance, the members of the academy were divided into two classes only—masters and scholars. There were no distinctions in grade or title; no previous ceremonies were necessary for advancement to any office. But the introduction of various degrees, to be conferred after certain fixed periods of study, followed very soon; and four were expressly specified—those of bachelor, licentiate, master, and doctor—in *Degrees.*

* We refer not to its antiquity,—since it boasts to have been founded by Charlemagne, and augmented by Louis the Meek and Charles the Bald. Its completion it certainly owed to the kings of the third race, especially Louis the Young and his son Philippe Auguste. It had some celebrity at the end of the tenth century; but before that epoch, the academy at Rheims seems to have been in greater repute.

† Dupin, Nouv. Biblioth., Sièc. XIII., chap. x. Mosheim, Cent. XIII. p. ii. chap. i.

the reform by which Gregory IX. gave a permanent character to the university. While some of the Italian academies may have been more eminent for a peculiar proficiency in the science of law or of medicine*, the palm of theological superiority was conceded, without any dispute, to Paris. To afford still greater
The Sor-
bonne. facilities and encouragement to this study, Robert de Sorbonne, a man abounding both in wealth and in piety, the chaplain and friend of St. Louis, founded, about the year 1250, that very renowned institution, which has associated his name for so many centuries with the theological labours, glories, and controversies of his countrymen.

These few sentences may be sufficient to call the reader's attention to an important and attractive subject, and even to render intelligible such passing mention, as will be made hereafter, of the university of Paris. But as the particulars of its origin, its construction, its growth, and its prosperity, do not strictly belong to ecclesiastical history, we must not permit them to usurp those pages, which may be more appropriately, if not more instructively, occupied.

NOTE (C) ON CERTAIN THEOLOGICAL WRITERS.

The fathers of the early Church were cautious in provoking subtile speculations on the holy mysteries, and seldom engaged in that field of theology, unless to repel the invasion of some popular error. And even then they were usually contented to arm themselves with scripture and tradition, as the principles of their defence, reserving the resources of reason for what they considered its legitimate object in theological controversies, the interpretation of the sacred writings. When philosophy was at length admitted to partake in these debates, the method first adopted, as most congenial to the sublime truths of religion,

---

* As was Bologna, for instance, for the former, and Salerno for the latter. Gratian published his Decretal at Bologna; and the stimulus thus given to the study of canon law continued long to produce its effect. The study of civil law in the same school is dated from about twenty years earlier—*i. e*, from the discovery of the Pandect. The medical precepts, which issued from Salerno, are said to have been derived from the books of the Arabians, or the schools of the Saracens in Spain and Africa.

was that of Plato; and if they were sometimes exalted by this Early pre-
alliance into fantastical mysticism, they at least escaped the valence of
the Plato-
degrading torture of minute and pugnacious sophistry. But nic method.
the rival system also found some early advocates *, though insufficient to give it general prevalence. Boëthius applied the
principles of Aristotle to the mysteries of the Trinity and the
Incarnation, thus moving many abstruse and inexplicable
questions; and John Damascenus afterwards published a me-
thodical exposition of all the questions or difficulties of theology.
In the West, in the ninth century, John Scotus Erigena fell
into the same snare : but his method of subtilizing was not
suited to the genius of his age; and during that which followed,
every operation of the human mind was suspended.

But when reason again awoke, she was straightway delivered Succeeded
into the fetters of Aristotle. Towards the middle of the eleventh by that of
Aristotle.
century, his philosophy was taught after the Arabian method,
in the public schools ; and though, in the first instance, it was
confined to the illustration of profane subjects, yet as men
became commonly imbued with its principles, and as the whole
system, political and moral, in those days was interwoven with
religious, or at least with ecclesiastical considerations, it was
not long before the prevalent method passed obsequiously into
the service of theology†.   John the Sophist, Rocellinus, Be-

---

* To such, and to the errors occasioned by them, is the allusion of Prudentius.
Pref. secunda in Apotheosim.

> Statum lacessunt omnipollentis Dei
>   Calumniosis litibus :
> Fidem minutis dissecant ambagibus,
>   Ut quisque lingua nequior :
> Solvunt ligantque quæstionum vincula
>   Per syllogismos plectiles.
> Væ captiosis sycophantarum strophis,
>   Væ versipelli astutiæ !
> Nodos tenaces recta rumpit regula,
>   Infesta dissertantibus.

Prudentius flourished at the end of the fourth century.

† " Fatendum simul est (says Brucker, Historia Critica Philosophiæ), ex quo
Philosophia Saracenica seculi xii Occidentis Christianis innotuit, plenis eos am-
plexibus inconditum philosophiæ genus recepisse, et insanientium more in Dia-
lecticam debacchatos, malum malo augendo ad Theologiam eam transtulisse."
(See Per. ii., par. ii., lib. ii., cap. ii. and iii.)   That author shows, that, from the
seventh until nearly the twelfth age, philosophy was confined to the possession of

renger, Lanfranc, Anselm, introduced that method : it was
improved by Abelard ; it was rapidly propagated in all the
schools of Europe * ; and its immediate and necessary effect
was to multiply, without any limit, the difficulties which it
affected to resolve. The objects of the investigation were too
immense for human comprehension, yet they were sought by
the meanest exercise of human ratiocination. The end was
unattainable; and, had it not been so, the means were those
least likely to have attained it. Nevertheless, the disputants
proceeded with eagerness and confidence ; and thus it proved
that, in this boundless field, the most different conclusions were
reached by paths nearly similar; and that out of every question
which it was proposed to resolve, a thousand other questions
started forth, more abstruse, more absurd, more immeasurably
remote from the precincts of reason and of sense † than the
original.

Peter the Lombard.

To impose some restraint on this great intellectual licentiousness,—to revive some respect for ancient authorities,—to erect

ecclesiastics, and to the limits of the Trivium and Quadrivium. The system
which succeeded was called scholastic, as emerging from the schools of the monasteries. After the time of Gratian, the study of canon law was very commonly mixed up with it ; and the combination of the three incongruities, Canon
Law, Scholastic Philosophy, and Theology, formed what Brucker aptly denomi-
nates a *Triplex Monstrum.*

* Otho Frisingensis introduced the scholastic system into Germany. That
prelate, the son of Leopold, marquis of Austria, and Agnes, daughter of Henry IV.,
was made bishop of Frisingen, in Bavaria, in the year 1138. He attended Conrad
to the Holy Land in 1147, and died nine years afterwards. He wrote (in seven
books) a Chronological History of the World, from the Creation to his own time,
which is frequently cited by the ecclesiastical annalists.

† Among the multitude of these questions, there were some which ended, and
after no very long investigation, in absolute infidelity. The Latin writers of the
thirteenth age abound with complaints (exaggerated, no doubt, but not unfounded)
of the progress of unchristian opinions, directly deduced from Aristotelian principles,—that the soul perished with the body—that the world had had no beginning, and would have no end—that there was only one intellect among all the
human race—that all things were subject to absolute fate or necessity—that the
universe was not governed by Divine Providence, &c. &c. We should observe,
that the Aristotelians declined what might have been the *personal* consequences
of these opinions by a subtile distinction. These matters (they said) are philo-
sophically true—but they are theologically false—Vera sunt secundum Philo-
sophiam, non secundum Fidem Catholicam. See Mosheim, Cent. XIII. p. i.
chap. ii., and p. ii. chap. v.

some barrier, or at least some landmark, for the guidance of
his contemporaries, Peter the Lombard published, about the
middle of the twelfth century, his celebrated " Book of the
Sentences." Born in the country whence he derived his surname, and educated at Bologna, then more famous as a school
for law than divinity, he proceeded to Paris for the prosecution
of the latter study. He was recommended to the patronage
of St. Bernard ; and presently attained such eminence in
academical erudition, that he was raised, in the year 1150, to
the see of Paris. The Book of the Sentences is a collection of
passages of the Fathers, especially of St. Hilary, St. Ambrose,
St. Jerome, and St. Augustine, explaining and illustrating the
principal questions, which then so violently agitated the scholastic doctors. The author was cautious in intermixing original
observation with the venerable oracles of the early Church;
and he trusted, by the ancient simplicity of his work, and his
contempt of the fashionable subtleties, to restore some respect
for the less vicious system of older times. The intrinsic merit
of this production, the talents and extensive learning which it
exhibited, recommended it to universal attention; and the
" Master of the Sentences " long retained an undisputed supremacy in the theological schools. But the effect of his work
was not that which he had warmly and, perhaps, reasonably
anticipated. The schoolmen made use of his text, principally
that they might hang on it their futile disceptations and commentaries ; and so fruitful was that elaborate book in matter
for ingenious disputation, that Peter the Lombard, so far from
having arrested the current, is usually ranked among the chiefs
or fathers of the scholastic* theology.

> The Book of Sentences.

If the dominion of Aristotle was for a moment suspended by
the decree of the council of Paris† (in 1209), which condemned

---

* See Dupin, Nouv. Biblioth., Cent. XII. chap. xv. " Néanmoins on peut le
considérer comme le chef de tous les scholastiques ; car quoiqu'il ait suivi dans
son ouvrage une méthode bien différente des autres, quant à la manière de traiter
les questions de Théologie ; son livre leur a toutefois servi de fondement et de base,
et ils n'ont fait en apparence que le commenter."

† The reason assigned for the condemnation of Aristotle on this celebrated
occasion was, that his works had given occasion to the errors of Amalric, and
might probably do so to many others. (See Brucker, loc. cit.) And they did so ;

to the flames his metaphysical works, it was effectually restored by the patronage of Frederic II. That emperor caused numerous translations to be made from his most celebrated compositions, and diffused through Italy, and especially at Bologna, the genius which had hitherto ruled with peculiar prevalence in France. At the same time, a new description of disputants had grown up, for whose character and offices the scholastic method was admirably calculated, and who carried it to its most pernicious perfection *. The Mendicants now gave laws to the academies of Europe; and the rules which they imposed were drawn from the code of Aristotle. At this time arose Thomas Aquinas, the "Angelic doctor," the Coryphæus of the disciples of the Stagyrite. He was descended from an illustrious family, and born in the neighbourhood of Naples, in the year 1224. He entered very young into the Dominican Order, and studied at Paris and at Cologne, under Albert the Great, a German scholastic, the dictator of his day†.

St. Thomas Aquinas.

but the errors which scholastic subtlety raised were as easily laid by a different formula of the same incantation—they appeared and disappeared, fleeting, impalpable, unsubstantial. The permanent heresies of the age stood on firmer ground. The grievances of the Waldenses and the Wicliffites were not the creations of sophistry; so neither could sophistry, though backed by persecution, silence the murmurs which they caused.

* We should here observe that the popes, however they profited by the influence of the mendicants, were by no means decided advocates of the scholastic theology. The celebrated Epistle of Gregory IX. to the doctors of Paris, contains (for instance) these words—"Mandamus et strictè præcipimus, quatenus, sine fermento mundanæ scientiæ, doceatis theologicam puritatem, non adulterantes verbum Dei philosophorum figmentis.....sed contenti terminis a patribus institutis, mentes auditorum vestrorum fructu cœlestis eloquii saginetis, ut hauriant a fontibus Salvatoris." The passage is cited by Mosheim. Cent. XIII. p. ii. chap. iii. Brucker (Hist. Crit. Philosoph. p. ii. Pars ii. lib. ii. c. iii.) cites the following passage from a bull of the same pope, published in 1231,—" Magistri vero et Scholares Theologiæ....nec philosophos se ostentent, sed satagant fieri Theodidacti—nec loquantur in lingua populi linguam Hebræam cum asotica confundentes, sed de illis tantum in scholis quæstionibus disputent, quæ per libros theologicos et sanctorum patrum tractatus valeant terminari." But the system was extremely popular with the *students;* their ardour was aided by the edicts of Frederic II.; and the system of Aristotle, superior to all edicts, was destined to yield only to the predominance of another system, that of polite literature and natural reason. See Petrarch's complaints of the dishonour brought on theology, by "the profane and loquacious dialecticians" of his day. De Remed. Utriusq. Fortun., and Tiraboschi, vol. v. p. i. lib. ii.

† This honour was, however, contested by our countryman, Alexander Hales, a

St. Thomas (he was in due season canonized by John XXII.) died at the early age of fifty; but the writings which he has left behind him compose seventeen folio volumes. The most important among them are his Commentaries on Aristotle, and his Sum of Theology. But they likewise contain most voluminous observations on various books of the Old and New Testament, and investigations of many theological, metaphysical, and moral questions. They were studied in those days with insatiable avidity. They are now confined to the shelves of a few profound students, whence they will never again descend. It might seem harsh indeed to say of them, "that they are of less account in the eyes of a sage, than the toil of a single husbandman, who multiplies the gifts of the Creator and supplies the food of his brethren *." But there is room for doubt whether any important practical benefits were ever derived from them; whether the reflections which they awakened were generally profitable either to the present condition of man, or to his future prospects. And we certainly cannot question, that the spirit of contentious disceptation, which some of them nourished and propagated, was injurious to one of the best principles of religion—religious forbearance and universal charity†.

Contemporary with St. Thomas Aquinas was another celebrated ornament of the Church, St. Bonaventura. He was a native of Tuscany ‡, and entered in the year 1243 into the

St. Bonaventura.

Franciscan, who taught philosophy at Paris, and acquired the formidable title of "The Irrefragable Doctor." Another and more attractive appellation was "The Fountain of Life." He entered into the Franciscan Order in 1222, and died at Paris twenty-three years afterwards. His most important work was a Commentary on the "Book of the Sentences," composed by the order of Innocent IV.

* The words are Gibbon's—applied to a different subject.

† Fontenelle, we believe, (see Tiraboschi, Stor. Lett. Ital., vol. iv. p. i. lib. ii.) has somewhere said of St. Thomas Aquinas, "that in another age and under other circumstances he would have been Des Cartes." No one ever questioned his genius and immense erudition; or that he has intermixed many sensible remarks with the fashionable sophistry,—only we should not value him too highly for this. A great mind should oppose the evil principles of the time—at least it should lend no aid to them. Roger Bacon in the same age acted a nobler part.

‡ The Italians are justly proud of the success of their countrymen in the schools of Paris. Besides the three eminent ecclesiastics mentioned in the text, they enumerate, among the Parisian Professors of the same age, John of Parma, a

Order of the Franciscans. He likewise completed his studies at Paris, and with such success, as to acquire the title of the "Seraphic Doctor." In the year 1256 he was appointed General of his Order, and died at no very advanced age. His works are less voluminous than those of Aquinas, and bear the stamp of a very different character*. The tendency of his mind was rather towards the extreme of mysticism, than that of minute disputation. It rose into the regions of spiritual aspiration; it courted no intellectual triumphs and despised the abuse of reason. By this quality he has obtained, and in a great degree merited, the eulogies of Gerson†; who has pronounced (and the authority is respectable) that his works surpass in usefulness all those of his age, in regard to the spirit of the love of God and Christian devotion which speaks in him; that he is profound without being prolix, subtle without being curious, eloquent without vanity, ardent without inflation. There are many (says the critic) who teach the accuracy of doctrine; there are others who preach devotion; there are few who in their writings combine both these objects. But they are united by St. Bonaventura, whose devotion is instructive, and whose doctrine inspires devotion.

The Realists and Nominalists. The celebrated controversy between the Realists and the Nominalists ‡, of which the origin was not long posterior to the general study of Aristotle, was continued with no great intermission till the days of Luther. The fourteenth century was particularly disturbed by its violence. Two of the leading

Franciscan; Egidio da Roma, an Augustinian; Agostino Trionfo of Ancona; and Jacopo da Viterbo. Through the following century the series continued, though with diminished brilliancy—and then it ceased.

* Both these doctors are praised for professional disinterestedness. Bonaventura is related to have refused the archbishopric of York; Aquinas that of Naples, as well as other dignities.

† See Dupin. Nouv. Biblioth. Cent. XIII., chap. iv.

‡ Roscellinus, a native of Brittany, has the repute of having invented these opinions. He was opposed by Anselm, and compelled to abjure before a Council at Soissons, in 1092. He seems also to have incurred some danger from a popular tumult. He was exiled from France, and then passed a short time in England, where he gave great offence by censuring the concubinage of the clergy, attested by their numerous illegitimate children, and by calumniating (as is said) Archbishop Anselm. The authors of the Hist. Litt. de la France treat him throughout as a heretic—but none of his writings (if any ever existed) now remain.

champions of that age were John Duns Scotus *, and his disciple William of Occam.   The former had ventured boldly to impugn some of the positions and conclusions of St. Thomas Aquinas, and his opinions found many advocates.   These formed the party of the Nominalists; and since, in the political disputes of the day, they favoured the cause of the emperor, they fell under the spiritual denunciations of the Vatican. Again, the Dominicans for the most part rallied round the banners of Aquinas and the Pope, while the Franciscans commonly defended the tenets of Scotus, a member of their own order.   Thus the controversy assumed a new name, as its character became more rancorous; and the ambitious polemics of that and of succeeding ages severally enlisted among the conflicting ranks of the *Thomists* and *Scotists*.   The principal points † of theological difference between these renowned adversaries were " the nature of the divine co-operation with the human will," and " the measure of divine grace" necessary for salvation.   These were subjects which have employed the devout in every age, and provoked the perpetual exercise of reason.   But the production which was more effectual, perhaps, than any other in exalting the reputation of Scotus was his demonstration of the Immaculate Conception of the Virgin Mary.   The Dominicans maintained that the holy Virgin was not exempt from the stain of original sin; the deeper devotion, or the bolder hypocrisy of the Franciscan supported the contrary opinion.   That either party was right it is beyond the capacity of man to ascertain; and it is clear that both were equally absurd, in as far as both were equally positive.   Yet, will it be believed that this inscrutable and most frivolous question formed an important subject of difference in the Roman Catholic Church—a subject deemed not unworthy of the cognizance of popes and of councils—for the space of more than two hundred years ?

Controversy on the Immaculate Conception.

---

* This—the subtle—doctor died in the year 1308.   He was a native of Dunse in Scotland, and a Franciscan.

† See Mosheim, Cent. XIV., p. ii., chap. iii.

END OF PART IV.

ANALYTICAL TABLE OF CONTENTS.

VOLUME II.

PART III.

CHAPTER XIV.—*The Government and Projects of the Church during the Ninth and Tenth Centuries.*

A.D.   PAGE

The contents of this Chapter are divided under three separate heads :—

I. The original law of Papal election continued to the time of Charlemagne, and was not disturbed by him. It became, in two respects, offensive to the Popes ; they began to dispense with the Imperial confirmation under the Carlovingian princes, and Charles the Bald (875) resigned his right   .   .   2

960 Otho the Great, after a long prevalence of disorder in the Pontifical elections, resumed the privilege of the empire, and extended it so far as to appoint Popes by his own authority   .   .   3

1047—59 The liberty of the See was gradually recovered, and the appointment vested in the College of Cardinals by Nicholas II.   4

Remarks on the fluctuations of the contest, and the causes which produced them   4

II. The encroachments of ecclesiastical on civil authority were of various descriptions   .   .   .   5

Evils proceeding from the indistinct limits of spiritual and secular jurisdiction ; yet these were not very perceptible till after the death of Charlemagne   .   .   .   6

On the increase of power and privilege conferred on the higher clergy, by the establishment of the feudal system. They became an Order in the State, &c.   .   .   .   7-8

They gradually assumed the military character   .   .   8

The superstitious method of trials was useful to priestly authority, yet, on many occasions, it was opposed by the clergy   .   9

The intellectual superiority of the clergy naturally and necessarily enlarged their influence and power   .   .   10

The property of the Church was liable to perpetual spoliation   .   11

833 *et seq.* On the deposition, penance, and temporary humiliation of Louis the Meek, by the episcopal authority. This act had a precedent in the deposition of Wamba, King of the Visigoths, in Spain, at the twelfth council at Toledo (1682)   .   .   12

These were episcopal, not papal, usurpations   .   .   —

842—859 Other instances of the power of the Bishops and the weakness and dependence of the Crown, in the reign of Charles the Bald   14

Pope Nicholas I. interfered respecting the marriage (870) of

A.D.   PAGE

Lothaire, King of Lorraine, and Adrain II. in the succession to
  that throne   16-17
880 Hincmar, of Rheims, employed strong expressions and a fortunate
  prophecy against Louis III.   18
Charles the Bald accepted the vacant empire as the donation of John
  VIII. This precedent was of great value to the Popes in after
  ages   19
Further progress of ecclesiastical usurpation   .   .   20
687 Robert of France put away his wife and performed penance in obedience to the interdict of Gregory V.   .   .   21
III. The progress of Papal authority was not rapid until the forgery of the False Decretals; and even these were not brought into
  full operation before the time of Gregory VII.   .   .   22
Some French Prelates retorted the threat of excommunication
  against Pope Gregory IV.   23
862, &c. Pope Nicholas I. resorted to his See, by his own authority, a
  Bishop who had been deposed by Hincmar of Rheims, and had
  appealed to Rome   24
Five years afterwards the Pope gained another triumph over the
  Archbishop   25
845—882 Hincmar occupied the See of Rheims—the great Churchman
  of the ninth century   26
A vague notion of the Pope's omnipotence was gaining ground
  among the laity in this age   28
876 John VIII. appointed the Archbishop of Sens his permanent vicar
  and legate in France, in spite of Hincmar and the clergy. The
  pontifical power was further advanced by exemptions of monasteries, by the principle that Bishops derived their power from the
  Pope, by the exclusive convocation of councils   .   .   29
855 Fable of the female Pope (Note)   .   .   .   31

CHAPTER XV.—On the Opinions, Literature, Discipline, and external
Fortunes of the Church.

The vicissitudes of religion, during these ages, in the different
  countries of the West, generally corresponded with their literary
  revolutions   32
A half-enlightened age is more fertile in controversies than one of
  perfect darkness   33
It is a question whether the bodily presence was universally received in the beginning of the ninth age   .   .   34
831—846 Paschasius Radbertus originated the controversy concerning
  the body and blood of Christ   .   .   .   34
His doctrine is expressed in two propositions. Ratramn and John
  Scotus were ordered by Charles the Bald to write on the same subject. The controversy died away before the end of this century,
  without any result, and reposed during the tenth   .   35
848 Gotteschalcus advanced predestinarian opinions, which were condemned by the council of Mayence, convoked by Rabanus Maurus.
  Next year he was again condemned by Hincmar, deposed, flagel-
  lated, imprisoned for life, and deprived of Christian sepulture   36-40
960—1000 Bernard, a Thuringian hermit preached the approaching end
  of the world; the opinion generally spread and produced great
  commotion and mischief to society   .   .   .   40

A.D.   PAGE

800—999 Letters, somewhat revived by Charlemagne, partially flourished
   during the ninth century ; they then expired. In the mean time,
   the Arabians diffused them in Spain ; thence they passed into
   France, and ascended, with Sylvester II., into the Papal Chair   42

The prostrate discipline of the Church, raised by Charlemagne, was
   supported by numerous councils during the ninth age, especially
   in France, and through Hincmar. In the mean time, the False
   Decretals were making silent progress   .   .   .   42-8

817 Benedict of Aniane reformed the monastic order   .   .   48

The election of bishops was nominally restored to the chapters, and
   their translations vainly prohibited   .   .   .   48

896 A posthumous insult was offered to Pope Formosus, who had been
   promoted from the See of Porto to that of Rome   .   .   50

956 John XII. introduced the custom of assuming a new name on elevation to the Papal Chair   50

On the discipline of the inferior clergy and the Synodal Statutes
   of Hincmar   51

830 Claudius, Bishop of Turin, the Protestant of the ninth century,
   opposed the use of relics and other corruptions   .   .   52

Christianity was generally introduced into the north of Europe
   before the middle of the eleventh age   .   .   .   54

830—854 Ansgarius attempted the conversion of Sweden ; that of Russia
   may be assigned to the end of the tenth century ; that of Poland
   was somewhat earlier; that of Hungary somewhat later   .   55

On the contemporaneous progress of the Normans and the Turks   .   57

CHAPTER XVI.—*The Life of Gregory VII.*

SECTION I.

1049 Leo IX., appointed to the see by the Emperor, is recorded to have
   taken Hildebrand with him to Rome, from his monastery at
   Cluni   59

1054 Victor II. succeeded, on the recommendation of Hildebrand   60

1059 Papal election was confided to the Cardinals by Nicholas II. Of
   whom that body then consisted   61

The consent of the rest of the clergy and people was required; but
   Alexander III. afterwards removed that restraint   .   .   62

The original method of popular election had gradually fallen everywhere into disuse   62

The necessity of imperial confirmation was virtually abolished by
   Nicholas II. at the same time   63

The Norman Duke of Apulia received his territories as a fief of
   the Roman See   64

1061 Hildebrand succeeded in placing Alexander II. in the Chair, ruled
   the Church under his name, and developed, during this Pontificate, the leading schemes of his own ambition   .   .   64

1073 Himself was raised to the See, and took the name of Gregory VII.   65

SECTION II.—*Pontificate of Gregory.*

1074 The Pope assembled a council against the concubinage of the
   clergy and simony   67

A.D.   PAGE

A great relaxation in the morals of the clergy during the tenth century ; the Popes, from Leo IX., had attempted to correct it, but
with no effect   68
Gregory endeavoured to enforce his decree, and great confusion
ensued   69
The princess, long before Charlemagne, had gradually usurped the
most valuable Church patronage, and frequently abused it   70
It was Gregory's object to recover it from them ; the question
about investitures was only the means to do so   .   .   —
From the time of Otho I. the sovereigns had performed the office
of investiture with the ring and crosier, symbols of a spiritual
office ; this was the point ostensibly disputed   .   .   71
Henry IV. resisted Gregory's demands, and the Pope deposed some
German prelates, and menaced anathemas   .   .   72
Gregory summoned Henry to Rome, to clear himself from certain
charges alleged by his subjects   .   .   .   72
Henry assembled a Synod at Worms to depose the Pope   .   73
The Pope excommunicated and deposed Henry   .   .   —
A civil war in Germany followed, and a council was appointed, in
which the claims of both parties were to be referred to the deci-
sion of the Pope   74
Henry crossed the Alps, and made submission to the Pope at
Canossa, and was restored to communion   .   .   74-5
The civil wars were then renewed, and three years afterwards
(1080) Gregory bestowed the crown on Rodolphus   .   .   76
Gregory extended his claims of temporal supremacy to the crowns
of France, England, Naples, and many inferior dukedoms and
principalities   77
He designed to regulate the affairs of Christendom by a council
of bishops periodically assembled at Rome.   Some circumstances
which ought to be considered in passing an opinion on that
project   78
What were the grounds on which Gregory founded his pretensions
to his universal dominion   .   .   .   .   —
The power ' to bind and to loose' extended to the oath of allegiance   80
Matilda, Countess of Tuscany, consented to hold her domains on
feudal tenure from the Pope   81
It was the object of Gregory to destroy the independence of the
national churches, and lead the whole hierarchy to look to Rome
only as its head   .   .   .   .   .   —
The objects and some of the contents of the False Decretals   82
1082 Henry advanced to Rome, and after two repulses, in two successive
years, obtained possession of the city.   Gregory retired to the
Castle of St. Angelo, and was relieved by the Normans, under
Robert Guiscard   84
1085 Gregory, having retired with the Normans, died at Salerno.   An
examination of his character as a churchman and as a Christian   86
His private morality was marked by the austerity of the cloister .   90

Section III.

1045 Berenger, Scholastic at Tours, published his opposition to the doctrine afterwards called Transubstantiation ; he was condemned at
Rome five years afterwards, and again by some French councils,

A.D.   PAGE

especially that of Tours ; he retracted, and immediately returned
to his opinion   91
He was summoned to Rome by Nicholas II., when he again retracted, and again abjured his retraction   .   .   93
1078 Gregory VII. required his subscription to a profession, admitting
the real presence, without mention of the change of substance,
and he subscribed. In the year following he subscribed to the
whole doctrine, without any reservation ; and then, returning to
France, taught as before   95
1088 He died in peace, at an advanced age   .   .
Gregory's moderation has occasioned a suspicion that he shared
his opinions   96
The use of the Latin Liturgy was imposed generally upon the Church
by Gregory VII. In a letter to Vratislaus, Duke of Bohemia, he
declared the policy of closing the Scriptures against the people.   —
Both were contrary to the practice of the early Church   96-9
Circumstances of the introduction of the Roman Ritual into
Spain   97

PART IV.

FROM GREGORY VII. TO BONIFACE VIII.

CHAPTER XVII.—*From Gregory VII. to Innocent III.*

1087—99 Urban II. pursued the schemes of Gregory, and in 1095 he
held the councils of Placentia and Clermont, and set on foot the
first crusade   101
The notion of a crusade was first started by Sylvester II., and
taken up by Gregory VII.   103
1099—1118 Pascal II. (like Gregory and Urban, a monk of Cluni) revived the contest with the empire   .   .   .   104
Henry died under the sentence of excommunication, with his son in
arms against him, and his body was kept for five years in unhallowed ground   105
The contest continued with Henry V.   .   .   .   106
The regalia were grants conferred on the bishops by Charlemagne,
partaking of the privileges of royalty, and the emperors claimed
the right of confirming them   107
Pascal II. agreed to cede them, on the Emperor's ceding the right
1110   of investiture. The ceremony of coronation was to follow ; but
a dispute arose in St. Peter's, and the Pope was carried away prisoner to Viterbo, where he made every concession   .   108
A Lateran council was assembled, and cancelled the treaty   .   108
A disputed succession was still usual at the death of almost every
Pope   109
1122 The investiture question was reasonably arranged in a council or
diet held at Worms, under Calixtus II., a relative of the Emperor   109
Some remarks on the arrangement thus adopted   .   .   110
1123 The first Lateran (ninth Latin General) was held for the general
regulation of ecclesiastical matters   .   .   .   112
1124—1154 Rome was disturbed by uninterrupted discord and convulsion. Arnold of Brescia was distinguished during this period
and condemned by the Second Lateran Council   .   .   112

A.D.   PAGE
1155 Adrian IV. placed the city under an interdict, and so effected the
        expulsion of Arnold, who was presently delivered up to him by
        Frederic Barbarossa, and burnt alive. The probable character
        of Arnold   115
     Barbarossa held the stirrup of Adrian   .   .   .   116
     Alexander III., after a long conflict, reduced Frederic Barbarossa
        to terms favourable to the Church. In 1179, he held the third
        Lateran Council, and enacted the final regulations respecting
        Papal election. He was a zealous patron of letters   116-120
     Three descriptions of disputes distracted this period: those be-
        tween the Popedom and the empire; those between rivals for the
        See; those in various states between the ecclesiastical and civil
        authorities   120
     The general correspondence between religion and literature, in their
        progress and decay admits of many particular exceptions   122
     After the first barbarian conquests, the whole office of public instruc-
        tion fell into the hands of the clergy; and no subjects were
        treated, or lessons delivered, except with a view to theology. The
        invasion of the Lombards was destructive to all learning in Italy   124
     The exertions of Charlemagne had much more fruit in France
        than in Italy during the ninth age   .   .   .   125
     In the tenth, everything degenerated in both countries; literature
        and morality; laity and clergy. Yet the literary condition of
        France was not lower at the accession of Sylvester II., than at
        that of Charlemagne   126-9
     On the other hand, the ecclesiastical compositions of those ages
        had commonly a practical tendency, and were directed to moral
        improvement   129
     From the Saracenic conquest of Egypt, papyrus began to be dis-
        used in Europe, and parchment was the substitute; so that MSS.
        could not multiply or spread with any rapidity. An instance of
        their scarcity   131
     This evil was removed in the eleventh century by the invention of
        paper   132
     About eighty councils were held in France during that age. On the
        three characters of æras of theological literature: that of the
        ecclesiastical Fathers; that of the collectors and compilers; that
        of the Schoolmen   133
     On the Trivium and Quadrivium   .   .   .   135
1091-1153 Note on St. Bernard. He founded Clairval, and, in the
        course of his life, about a hundred and sixty other monasteries   137
     He was very influential in establishing Innocent II. in the disputed
        See; and through his numerous ecclesiastical merits, he is deno-
        minated the last of the fathers   .   .   .   138
     In his opinion respecting grace he followed St. Augustin   .   139
1140 He entered the lists in public disputation against Abelard, at Sens;
        but the latter declined the controversy, and appealed to the Pope   140
     He was a zealous supporter of Papal authority and adversary of
        heresy. Various expressions from his writings on both these sub-
        jects   143-4
     He likewise denounced, with great indignation, the numerous
        abuses prevalent in the church at that period   .   .   146
     On his mingled good and dangerous qualities, and the wide extent
        of his personal influence   151

A.D. PAGE

CHAPTER XVIII.—*The Pontificate of Innocent III.* (1198-1216.)

1083-1198 Considerable improvement had been effected in the Church system between Gregory VII. and Innocent. Three Lateran councils assembled in the twelfth century . . 152
1131 Gratian published his famous collection of canon law . . 153
The possessions of the clergy were greatly increased during the same period; and the ecclesiastical jurisdiction had made wide encroachments on the secular . . . 154
Various instances of the persons and causes which had been insensibly drawn into the former courts . . . 155
Thus the clergy exercised, at Innocent's accession, a greater control over society than at any former period . . 157
His designs may be classed under four heads . . 157
I. The character of the Roman people, according to the expressions of Luitprand, a Lombard of the tenth age . . 158
According to those of St. Bernard, addressed to Eugenius III. . 158
The turbulence of the Romans was excused by the weakness, capriciousness, and uncertain character of their government. Some vicissitudes in its form, from Charlemagne to Innocent. The latter at length entirely shook off the imperial claims, and deprived the Prefect of his power . . . 160
Yet other changes and tumults succeeded, and were not appeased till the middle of the fifteenth century . . . 161-2
The circumstances of the empire were favourable to the project of Innocent. He obtained from Frederic a confirmation of the donation of Matilda 162
II. Innocent exercised his temporal authority in the disposal of the empire. Through what causes that authority ever acquired any strength, or received any obedience . . . 164
Many imagined that the ceremony of coronation by the Pope was necessary for the legitimacy of the emperor . . 165
In a contest with Philippe Auguste of France, Innocent threw an interdict over the whole country, and the king made his submission 166
He published some general assertions of his power over thrones; and interfered in Arragon, Navarre, Bohemia, Wallachia, Bulgaria, and Armenia 167
The resistance and final humiliation of John of England . 168-70
III. It was necessary for the success of Innocent to hold the hierarchy in subservience. He endeavoured to usurp all important patronage 170
He imposed a regular tax (the Saladin tax) on ecclesiastical property. The power which the Bishops, as a collective body, had lost, passed into the possession of the Pope . . . 171
1215 The fourth Lateran Council met for the recovery of the Holy Land and the reformation of the Church . . 172
The name of transubstantiation was introduced into the vocabulary of the Church 173
Sacramental confession generally imposed . . . 173
Reformation in the faith of the Church only meant extirpation of heresy. The substance of the third canon of this council on that subject 174

A.D.   PAGE

IV. From the controversy about images, till the twelfth century, the Church had not been stained by any rigorous persecution .   175

1110 Pierre de Bruys originated the sect of Petrobrussians, who rejected some superstitions, and advanced some errors. He was burnt in a popular tumult   176

1148 Henry, from whom the Henricians were named, was opposed by St. Bernard, and died in prison   177

Both these heresies prevailed chiefly in the south of France, as well some others of no name, and perhaps of no very definite tenets, but professing an apostolic character and origin   .   .   178

The Cathari, or Gazari, &c., may probably have descended from the Paulicians of the East, and may thus have been Semi-Manichæans; but it would be absurd to charge this error upon all the heretics of the twelfth century   .   .   .   179

1160 Peter Waldus commenced his preaching, and caused some part of the Scriptures to be translated into the vulgar tongue; but the Vaudois, or Waldenses, were of earlier and immemorial origin, though it is impossible to trace them to the apostolical times. The opinions ascribed to them   181-4

Albigeois, or Albigenses, was the common name for the various heretics of the south of France at the end of the twelfth century   184

1017 Some persons of good condition, charged with Manicheism, and probably guilty of mysticism, were condemned by a synod at Orleans, and burnt to death   .   .   .   185

1163 Alexander III. published, in a council at Tours, an edict against the heretics of Toulouse and Gascony, and afterwards attacked the Cathari in his Lateran Council   .   .   186

1198-1207 Innocent III. attempted to reduce the Albigeois, first by legates, and then by missionary preachers, under the name of Inquisitors, of whom Dominic was one: but failing, he appealed to the sword of Louis Philippe .   .   .   187

Simon de Montfort then led the crusade against them with barbarous success   188

1229 A system of inquisition was permanently established at Toulouse, by a council there assembled. The Scriptures were strictly prohibited to all laymen   .   .   .   190

1216 The circumstances of the death of Innocent are variously recounted. His private character should be distinguished from his ecclesiastical; the former had many good qualities, the latter abounded with crimes   191

His policy was strictly temporal. The taxation of the clergy was the principal change which he introduced into the economy of the Church   193

A comparison drawn between his public character and that of Gregory VII. is to the advantage of the latter .   .   .   194

CHAPTER XIX.—*The History of Monachism.*

For what reasons any general notice of the Monastic Orders has been deferred till this period of the history   .   .   196

SECTION I.

250 The practice of seclusion was indigenous in the East; the testimony of Pliny the philosopher   197

A.D.   PAGE

The original Therapeutæ or Essenes were probably Jews : but in assuming Christianity they may have retained their eremitical habits   198

The Ascetics were Christians ; they were the most rigid among the converts, but were not recluses. Their origin ascribed by Mosheim to the double doctrine of morals . . .   198

250 *et seq.* Many flying from the persecutions of Decius and Diocletian adopted the anchoretical life . . .   199

The first institution of Cœnobites is attributed to St. Anthony, the contemporary of Athanasius ; and Egypt was the country wherein it rose   200

395 Cassian made his visit to the monks of Egypt. They were divided into Anchorets, Cœnobites, and Sarabaites. A passage respecting the first of these . . .   201

The numerous establishments and moderate discipline of the Cœnobites. The times and manner of their devotion. The four objects comprehended by their profession. A great portion of their time was devoted to manual labour   202

The Sarabaites are probably calumniated both by Cassian and Jerome ; what they seem really to have been . .   204

360 *et seq.* Basil, the patriarch of Monachism, is believed to have delivered a Rule, and established the obligation of a vow ; yet this is not certain   205

All the Fathers of that age encouraged the growth of Monachism ; yet their motives were not selfish nor sordid, nor such as are commonly ascribed to them . . .   206

The earliest form of Monachism was subject to many wholesome restraints, which were first weakened by Justinian . .   208

The original Monks were laymen   209

Monastic austerity was not carried to greater excess in the East than in the West, since a variety of motives, derived from papal principles, gained influence in the latter, which had no existence in the former   210

The institution of Nunneries is also attributed to St. Anthony ; but it never attained such prosperity in the East as in the West   211

SECTION II.

341-430 Monachism, said to have been introduced into Rome by Athanasius, was diffused through the north of Italy and the south of France   212

The love for insular retirement, which prevailed among the recluses of the East, was imitated in the Adriatic, and on the western coasts of Italy   213

The general spreading of Monachism was contemporaneous with the barbarian conquests ; and those establishments were of use in preserving religion, and relieving individual misery .   214

The Rule of St. Basil was that first professed in the West .   215

529 Benedict of Nursia instituted a new order . . .   215

His object was excellent, and the principle of his establishment beneficial in those ages . . .   215

Some account of the "Rule of St. Benedict ;" the times of public worship ; duty of mental prayer ; of manual labour ; of reading ; of rigid temperance, rather than abstinence ; of silence, serious-

A.D.   PAGE

ness, and obedience; difficulties offered to the introduction of novices 216-9

The Monastery of Monte Cassino was founded by Benedict, and his Rule spread into France, and elsewhere, though it may not have been universally received in the West before the ninth century . 219

817 Benedict of Aniane reformed the Benedictine Order, and his regulations were confirmed by the Council of Aix-la-Chapelle . 221

900 &c. The order of Cluni, in Burgundy, was established, and was very celebrated for about two centuries. It then became wealthy and corrupt. Gregory VII., Urban II., and Pascal II. were educated there 223

1098 The Cistertian Order was founded in its neighbourhood, and honoured and advanced by St. Bernard . . 224

1178 The Order of the Chartreuse, which had been founded by St. Bruno in 1084, was sanctioned by Alexander III. . . 226

The rivalry among these and other orders, all Benedictines, was of advantage to the discipline of them all . . 227

1040 The distinction between monks and lay brethren was first introduced at Vallambrosa; and it secured the corruption of the former 227

The Abbot was originally subject to the Bishop of the Diocese; the practice of papal exemption occasioned extreme relaxation of discipline 228

The prevalence of monastic corruption was acknowledged by councils held early in the thirteenth century . . . 229

SECTION III.

The order of Canons Regular, professing the institution of St. Augustin, is of uncertain origin. A general rule was imposed on them by the Councils of Mayence and Aix-la-Chapelle, early in the ninth age . . . 229

1059 They were subsequently reformed by Nicholas II., and were first subjected to a vow by Innocent II. . . . 231

SECTION IV.

The Monastic Orders were powerful instruments of pontifical ambition, through their wealth, their obedience, and their popular influence 232

The confusion of the military and ecclesiastical characters had preceded the foundation of the Military Orders . . 233

1050 Four merchants erected a hospital at Jerusalem, which was endowed by Godfrey of Bouillon; and then rose the Knights of the Hospital, afterwards known as the Knights of Rhodes and Malta 233

1118 The Knights Templars were founded. Their Rule was written by St. Bernard; their office and corruption . . 234

1192 The Teutonic Order received its Rule from Celestine III. Afterwards (1230) those knights converted Prussia by the sword; and joined the Reformers in the sixteenth age . . 235

SECTION V.

1217 &c. The number and variety of Heresies made a new order neces-

A.D.   PAGE

sary for their extirpation. St. Dominic instituted that of the
Preachers, and it was sanctioned by the bull of Honorius III. . 236
1210 Innocent III. established the order of St. Francis, which was
originally founded in poverty only   .   .   . 237
The Testament of St. Francis did not enjoin mendicity .   . 238
These two orders adopted each other's characteristics, and presently
became both Preachers and both Mendicants   .   . 239
The severity of the Rule of St. Francis occasioned many dis-
sensions among his disciples, and great insubordination in the
Church   240
The Dominicans were more orderly and obedient   .   . 241
St. Dominic was not the founder of the Inquisition   .   . 241
1228-1259 The Dominicans became learned Scholastics, and contested
the theological chairs with the University of Paris   .   . 242
The good proceeding from this struggle. The prophecy concerning
the " perils of the latter times " was applied to the Mendicants
by a doctor at Paris.   A general remark on Millenarians   . 243
1274 Gregory X. suppressed several Mendicants, and distributed the sect
into four societies : Dominicans, Franciscans, Carmelites, and
Hermits of St. Augustin   244
1209 Albert, Patriarch of Jerusalem, gave a Rule to the Carmelites,
confirmed in 1226 by Honorius III., and afterwards interpreted
by Innocent IV.   245
Alexander IV. collected various Hermits into one order, called the
"Hermits of St. Augustin"   245
The earliest Dominicans were distinguished by great talents and
merits, and professional zeal   246
Great jealousy was occasioned among the Ancient Orders and
Secular Clergy, and violent disputes followed   .   . 247
The influence of the Mendicants depended almost entirely on their
merits and activity 248
Yet they soon became liable to many reproaches   .   . 249

SECTION VI.

On the " Holy Virgins " who existed in the Antenicene Church . 250
350 St. Syncletica is said to have founded the first nunnery   . 251
In Egypt, Marcella, a Roman lady, introduced the institution into
the West, and it spread rapidly   251
The Rule of the Nuns was formed upon those of the Monasteries 252
The necessity of a " Vow of Chastity " strongly urged by St. Basil 253
The Canon of Chalcedon was moderate in the penalty denounced
against its violation ; but Innocent I. increased its severity, and
subsequent ages still more so   253
The assumption of the Veil was earlier than St. Ambrose   . 254
The age of taking it varied at different times and places   . 254
The order of the Nuns of St. Benedict was instituted at the same
time with his first monasteries, and rose in importance and
pride   254
There were also Canonesses, Nuns of the Hospital, Nuns of St. Dominic, following the various monastic denominations .   . 255-6
1537 The Ursulines were a truly ascetic and charitable institution ; indeed
the Nuns were generally free from many of the vices charged
against their monastic brethren. The Protestants have imitated
those virtues   257-9

A.D.   PAGE

The Benedictine, the Military, and the Mendicant orders were all
    peculiarly adapted to the age and circumstances in which they
    flourished, and the qualities required for the support of Papacy;
    as were the Jesuits at a later period   .   .   . 259-62
The Monastic system was only perpetuated by a succession of re-
    formations and regenerations   262-4
Such was the history of every order, and none could have long
    subsisted otherwise   264
Many advantages were conferred on society by Monachism. Tracts
    of land were brought into cultivation; hospitality and refuge
    afforded to the wretched; charity largely distributed; spiritual
    consolation commonly administered to the lower orders; and an
    example set of piety and humanity. Education was intrusted to
    the Monks; and manuscripts, profane and sacred, were pre-
    served and multiplied by them; so that, if they were only useful
    in bad ages, then at least they were seemingly the best mem-
    bers of society   264-72
Yet they were the steady defenders of every superstitious abuse,
    and the sworn enemies of all general reform. The system of
    exemption made them firm supporters of the Papal system; and
    in recompense, indulgences, private masses, and many of the
    worst abuses of the Church were sustained, chiefly for their
    profit, by pontifical authority   272-7

CHAPTER XX.—*From the Death of Innocent to that of Boniface VIII.*

The interests of the Church of Rome were becoming at variance
    with the peace of Christendom .   .   .   278
Frederic II. long deferred his promised departure to the Holy
    Land   279
1227 Gregory IX. was elected; the ceremony of his coronation   .   280
He excommunicated the Emperor. Frederic wrote to the King of
    England in reprobation of the Church   .   .   281
He proceeded to Palestine; he made an advantageous treaty with
    the infidels, in spite of the Pope's persecutions, and returned to
    repel an invasion of his territories   .   .   282
1243—45 Innocent IV. continued the quarrel with Frederic, and as-
    sembled the first Council of Lyons. It professed three objects.
    The Emperor was summoned before it, and on his non-appear-
    ance, deprived of his crown   284-5
Innocent vainly attempted to seduce the Emperor's son into an
    alliance against his father   .   .   .   286
The three professed objects of the Council of Lyons   .   286
1250 Frederic died in adversity, having been virtually deposed by the
    sentence of Innocent   287
The real merits of this quarrel: in what respects Frederic justly
    offended the Church; the fierce edicts against heresy, by which
    he aimed to support it, and by which he deserved his future mis-
    fortunes   288
Some points by which this dispute between the Church and the
    Empire is distinguished from that commenced by Gregory VII.   290
Taxes were rigidly levied by the Pope upon the clergy, and a cru-
    sade was preached against the Emperor   .   .   291
Innocent returned to Italy, and after some successes against the
    kingdom of Naples, died in 1254   .   .   292

A.D. PAGE

His temporal ambition and policy, and triumphant pontificate . 293
Alexander IV. continued the struggle for Naples . . 294
1261-1268 Urban IV. and Clement IV., two Frenchmen, introduced the
French into that kingdom 295
1273 Gregory X., a pious enthusiast, was raised to the See ; and laboured earnestly, and with promise of success, to excite a grand
crusade 296
1274 He convoked the second Council of Lyons for that purpose, and for
the reformation of the Church. The canon was then enacted
which imposed severe restraints upon the conclave . . 298
The Pope died before the expedition set sail, and it immediately
dispersed 299
Martin IV., a Frenchman, accepted the office of senator, and held
it for life 300
1294 The circumstances of the election of Pietro Morone, Celestine V. ;
his utter incapacity ; his simplicity, piety, humility, and good intentions ; his resignation and the pontificate ; and imprisonment
by his successor Boniface VIII. . . . 302-7
The lofty and various pretensions of Boniface ; in whose reign the
Papal supremacy probably attained its highest elevation. His
authority recognized by Albert of Austria . . . 307
The condition of the Gallican Church at that moment . . 310
1296 Boniface published the bull *Clericis Laicos,* against all who should
exact contributions from the clergy . . . 311
It was chiefly levelled against Philip of France. A dispute was
the consequence, but it was soon suspended . . 312
1301 Philip arrested the Bishop of Pamiers. Boniface published the
bull *Ausculta, Fili,* demanding his liberation, &c. ; and it was
publicly burnt by the king 312
Philip was supported by his barons. Some of the Clergy attended
the Pope's summons to assemble at Rome ; and under the name
of this council, he published the bull *Unam Sanctam,* asserting
the unity of the Church, and the use of the double sword . 314-6
1303 William of Nogaret and Sciarra Colonna surprised the Pope at
Anagni ; but offered him no bodily injury. He returned to
Rome and died. The circumstances of his intrepidity, and of
his death 317-20

CHAPTER XXI.—*The age of Louis IX. of France.*

SECTION I.

1215-1270 Louis IX. of France was one of the few monarchs who
founded his policy on religious considerations, and whose life is
thus closely connected with ecclesiastical history. The excellence of his private morality 322
In what language he is characterized by Hume . . 323
His various legislative attempts to extend the civilization of his
subjects 324
Much superstition was mixed with his piety ; exemplified in his acquisition and reception of the Crown of Thorns. He instituted
festivals in its honour, &c. 326
He died before Tunis, and was canonized twenty-seven years afterwards by Boniface VIII. The Bull of Canonization . . 327

Section II.

St. Louis confirmed the institution of the Inquisition in his dominions 329
What was the extent of the commission of the first Inquisitors ; all
trials were still conducted in the Episcopal Courts . . 329
1229 The council of Toulouse established a sort of committee of Inquisition, the foundation of the Court . . 330
The court was still episcopal; but Gregory XI. transferred the
power to the Dominicans, who acted more immediately under
Papal authority 330
1244 The edicts of Frederic II. assisted the progress of the Inquisition.
Innocent IV. established it in the north of Italy, and it spread to
some other countries 332-4

Section III.

1263 The general contempt of excommunication then prevalent is in-
stanced in a conference between Louis and his prelates . 334
1244 Innocent IV. requested a refuge in France, and Louis eluded his
solicitation 335
Before he set off on his last crusade, Louis published his Pragmatic Sanction. It consisted of six articles, which were chiefly
directed against the usurpations of patronage by Rome and its
pecuniary exactions 337
A spirit of opposition to the See was occasionally exhibited by the
French clergy 338

Section IV.

The character of the first crusade ; the battle of Doryleum ; the
capture of Antioch ; and cruelties committed at the storming of
Jerusalem 339
St. Bernard preached the second crusade with success ; his prophecy ; its falsification ; and the authority which he pleaded in
his defence 340
1189-1291 The third crusade was that of Richard of England ; the fifth
and sixth were projected by Innocent III. ; the disastrous expedition and captivity of Louis in Egypt : his second against Tunis
may be considered as concluding the history of the crusades . 343-6
Among the causes of the crusades, the earliest was the practice of
pilgrimage ; the Saracens tolerated the visits of the Christians to
the Holy Sepulchre, and they were multiplied by the fanaticism
of the tenth century ; but towards the close of the eleventh, the
Turks got possession of Jerusalem, and persecuted the pilgrims . 346
Warlike spirit and superstitious zeal were characteristics of the
same ages, and co-operated to the same end, so that the minds
of men were prepared for the preaching of Peter the Hermit . 349
The object of the first crusade was wholly unconnected with reason,
ambition, or policy 350-2
The objects of those which followed became diversified by new circumstances : the Latin kingdom was then to be defended ; the
interest of princes became engaged ; and general views of conquest were formed 353
Innocent III. preached a crusade against Heretics ; Innocent IV.
against the Emperor of Germany . . . 354

A.D.   PAGE

It does not seem that the crusades produced any one general advantage to Europe or to Christendom, either in promoting commerce or advancing the arts   351-9
But they introduced new barbarities into war, and inflamed the
character of religious persecution   .   .   360
They ruined the discipline of the Church by the introduction of the
plenary indulgence, and the subsequent sale of it   .   . 361
The possessions of the clergy may have been augmented, but the
imposition of a tax more than counterbalanced that gain   . 363
Note A. On the first Decretals of the Pope .   .   364
1151 The collection of Gratian was published; divided into three parts;
abounding in errors 364
1210 The Roman collection was published under Innocent III.; the
Liber Sextus under Boniface VIII.; the Clementines under
John XXII.; and the Extravagants presently followed   . 365
Note B. The Academy of Paris first took the name of University;
its classes and lectures: the four faculties   .   . 366
The institution of four degrees   .   .   . 367
Paris was chiefly eminent for its theological proficiency, while law
and medicine were more successfully cultivated in Italy   . 368
1250 Robert of Sorbonne founded the college known by his name . 368
Note C. On the Character of the Philosophy adopted by the early
Theologians; in the eleventh century Aristotle took possession
of the Western Schools, and introduced endless perplexity and
absurdity 368
1150 Peter the Lombard was raised to the See of Paris—the object of
his Book of the Sentences, and the end to which it was turned . 370
1224-1274 Thomas Aquinas, a Dominican, carried the system to its
utmost perfection   372
Contempory was Bonaventura, a Franciscan, a man of great piety
as well as learning, and more inclined to Mysticism than Scholastic subtlety   373
1320 &c. John Duns Scotus and William of Occam were Franciscans,
and headed the faction of the Nominalists or Scotists; the
Realists, the supporters of Aquinas, were called Thomists. Some
points on which they differed, the Immaculate Conception, &c. . 374-5

APPENDIX I.

A CHRONOLOGICAL TABLE AND ACCOUNT OF MOST OF THE PRINCIPAL COUNCILS HELD BETWEEN THE THIRD AND FOURTEENTH CENTURIES OF THE CHURCH.

DATE   PLACE   OBJECT, ETC.

305. ELIBERIS. (See Vol. i. p. 105.) *Can.* xxxiii. Placuit in totum prohiberi Epps. Presbyteris et Diaconibus vel omnibus clericis positis in ministerio, abstinere se a conjugibus suis et non generare filios : quicunque vero fecerit ab honore clericatus exterminetur.

    Can. xxxvi. Placuit picturas in Ecclesia esse non debere, ne quod colitur aut adoratur in parietibus pingatur.

314. ANCYRA. Many canons regard the lapsed. The *tenth* permits deacons to marry, when on the point of ordination; provided they shall then announce their intentions to do so, not otherwise. The *thirteenth* refuses the power of ordination to the Chorepiscopi; others impose penance for various acts of immorality.

314. ARLES. Convoked by Constantine, on the subject of the Donatists, and of Cæcilian, Bishop of Carthage. It consisted of 33 bishops, 14 priests, 25 deacons, 8 clerks. It decreed—That every priest remain in the place to which he has been ordained ; that the priests or deacons, quitting the places assigned them, be deposed; that Christians, on becoming governors of provinces, receive letters of communion ; that the Bishop of the diocese may superintend and excommunicate them, if they commit any breach of discipline; that Easter be everywhere celebrated on the same day ; that clerks, who are usurers and calumniators, be excommunicated ; that deacons do not administer the sacrament ; that absolution be received in the same place whence the excommunication issued ; that bishops do not encroach on each other's rights ; that deacons, in the large towns, do nothing without the consent of the presbyters ; that no bishop be ordained, except by three other bishops.

314. NEOCÆSAREA. The first Canon is, that a Presbyter, who marries, shall lose his rank (τάξιν), or order. The others are not important. The Chorepiscopi are declared to be instituted— εἰς τύπον τῶν ἑβδομήκοντα—a notion not unfrequently repeated in the councils of later ages.

320. LAODICEA. See year 370. The date is uncertain. Labbe places it at 320; Semler at 370. (See Vol. I. Ch. VII.)

325. NICE. *First General.*

DATE   PLACE   OBJECT, ETC.

341. **ANTIOCH.** That Councils be held twice a-year; one, three weeks after Easter; the other in the middle of October. That no bishop appoint his own successor; nor alienate the property of the Church to his domestics, brothers, or *children*.

346. **COLOGNE.** For the condemnation and deposition of Euphrates, Bishop of Cologne, who had denied the divinity of Christ.

347. **SARDICA.** This Council consisted of a majority of Western Bishops and defended against the Orientals the Athanasian doctrine. It besides published some Canons (v. vi.), which laid the foundation of *appeal* to the See of Rome. The privilege was, however, here confined to deposed bishops, and the right of Rome to a revision of the sentence. In *Canon* vii. is the following expression:—Quod si is, quis rogat causam suam iterum audiri, deprecatione sua moverit Episcopum Romanum, ut *de latere suo* Presbyterum mittat, &c. (Hence Legates a latere.) The *first* Canon prohibits the translation of Bishops in these words:—Non minus mala consuetudo, quam perniciosa corruptela funditus eradicanda est: ne cui liceat Episcopo de civitate sua in aliam transire civitatem. Manifesta est enim causa qua hoc facere tentant; cum nullus in hac re inventus sit Episcopus, qui de majore civitate in minorem transiret. Unde apparet avaritiæ ardore eos inflammari et ambitioni servire, et ut dominationem agant. By the 15*th Canon*, bishops are allowed a three weeks' absence from their dioceses, on their private affairs. It is the object of some other canons to prevent the inferior clergy from changing their dioceses, and to attach them to their proper bishops.

359. **RIMINI.** Against the Arians. This and similar Councils are mentioned in Chapter VII.

370. **LAODICEA.** This Council published 60 Canons. Among other things it prohibits the reception of the Novatians, Photinians, and other heretics, till they have abjured their heresy: it forbids churchmen to enter their *Martyria* for purposes of worship, or to give them their children in marriage. Aged women (πρεσβύτιδες ήτοι προκαθήμεναι, Presbyteræ) are not to receive ordination. The multitude is not to appoint to the priesthood. The Sabbath (Jewish) is not to be Judaistically observed; but the faithful may rest on the Lord's day, if they can do so like Christians. Ointment to be used after baptism. Severe fasting to be practised during Lent. After the Bishop's address, prayers are to be said for the Catechumens. When these shall have departed, others for the penitents; when they shall have withdrawn, three prayers are to be made for the faithful—the first in silence, the second and third audibly. Only the ιερατικοι may approach the altar and communicate. (*Can.* xix. The term includes all connected with the Church, even to the θυρωροί.) The deacon is not to sit in the presence of the presbyter, unless by his permission; nor the subdeacon in the presence of the deacon.

DATE   PLACE   OBJECT, ETC.

381. CONSTANTINOPLE. *Second General.*

385. BORDEAUX. Held against the Priscillianists. It led to the death of Priscillian.

395. TURIN. For the arrangement of some affairs of discipline and epis-copal differences. It decreed—That no bishop receive the clerk of another bishop, nor ordain him for himself; that those who, after ordination, shall have children, be excluded from higher orders.

397. CARTHAGE (III). Clerks are prohibited from defending themselves in civil courts, on pain of deposition. They are not to be merchants, or usurers. They are forbidden to make any donations to any who are not Catholic Christians. All about them must be Catholics. Their children are not to attend public spectacles. The Eucharist to be celebrated fasting. Readers, psalmists, door keepers, to have the name of clerks. That the sick, even though speechless, may be baptized, on the responsibility of their friends. Bishops are not to be translated, and the clergy to remain in their own dioceses. It published a list of the Canonical Scriptures, in which the Apo-calypse is included, "such as they had been handed down from anti-quity." (*Semler*, sec. iv. *De Conciliis. Labb. Concil.* t. iii. p. 875.)

398. CARTHAGE (IV). This Council regulates the ordination of bishops, priests, and deacons. The subdeacon is not to receive the imposition of hands; nor the acolyth, the exorcist, or the door keeper. " Exor-cista cum ordinatur, accipit de manu Episcopi libellum, in quo scripti sunt exorcismi; discente Episcopo—Accipe et commenda me-moriæ et habeto potestatem imponendi manus super energume-num, sive baptizatum, sive catechumenum." Widows or nuns, who are elected to the office of baptizing women, are to be capable of instructing the ignorant in the nature and objects of that sacra-ment. " *Ut Episcopus gentilium libros non legat;* hæreticorum autem pro necessitate temporis." (See Vol. i. p. 260.) (22.) Ut Epis-copus sine concilio clericorum suorum clericos non ordinet, ita ut civium conniventiam et testimonium quærat. (23.) Ut Episcopus nullius causam audiat absque præsentia clericorum suorum. (34.) Ut Episcopus quolibet loco sedens stare Presbyterum non pa-tiatur. (37.) Diaconus ita se Presbyteri, ut Episcopi, ministrum noverit. (38.) Ut diaconus, præsente Presbytero, Eucharistiam cor-poris Christi populo, si necessitas cogat, jussus eroget. (66.) Cleri-cus, qui Episcopi injustam circa se districtionem putat, recurrat ad synodum. A bishop, in public, is to sit on a higher seat than a presbyter; but in private he is to consider himself as the colleague of the presbyters. A clerk is permitted to earn his living by trade or agriculture. (Clericus victum et vestimentum sibi artificiolo vel agricultura, absque officii sui detrimento, paret. (*Can.* lii.) There are some severe canons for the excommunication of heretics. A penitent, on the point of death, is to be reconciled by imposition of

hands, and the Eucharist is to be poured into his mouth. Penitents are to carry out and bury the dead. Pagans, Heretics, and Jews may all remain in the church till the *Missa Catechumenorum.* He who withholds from the Church the oblations of the dead is to be excommunicated. This Council published 104 Canons, of which many were very important in that age.

401 (about). TOLEDO (1). It gives to clerks the power of confining, in their houses and in bonds, their wives, if they should have sinned. (Si clericorum uxores peccaverint, accipiant mariti earum hanc potestatem, præter necem, custodiendi et ligandi in domo sua, ad jejunia salutaria, non mortifera, cogentes. *Can.* vii.) The acts at this Council conclude with an attack on the Priscillianists. It also legislates about the widows of bishops, priests, and deacons.

411. CARTHAGE. Conference with the Donatists. We here omit all mention of the numerous councils assembled in Africa about this time against the Donatists and Pelagians. (See Chap. XI.) The various synods, which met in other provinces during this period, were for the most part assembled for the extirpation of some heresy.

429. *In* GAUL. (Place uncertain.) Against the heresy of the Pelagians.

431. EPHESUS. *Third General.* Against Nestorius. (See Chap. XI.) The greater part of the 4th and 5th vols. of Labbe is occupied by the records of this Council.

439. RIEZ. (Regense.) On matters of discipline. It decreed—That *two* bishops, who shall pretend to consecrate a bishop, be henceforth excluded from ordinations and councils ; that on the death of a bishop, the nearest bishop take charge of his diocese; that the rural priests (*the Chorepiscopi*) may give the benediction, consecrate virgins, confirm neophytes ; and that their rank is superior to that of priests, and inferior to that of bishops (this is indirectly and somewhat obscurely expressed) ; that councils be held twice a-year.

441. ORANGE. On matters of discipline. It decreed—That no one reduce to slavery those who belong to the Church ; that no council be dissolved without notice being given of another ; that the functions of an infirm bishop be discharged by some other bishop, and not by priests. This Council prohibits the repetition of confirmation, the delivery of persons taking refuge in a church, the ordination of deaconesses ; and enjoins that catechumens be admitted to the reading of the Gospel.

444. VIENNA. Chelidonius, Bishop of Besançon, was deposed for having married a widow.

449. EPHESUS. *False* General.

451. CHALCEDON. *Fourth General.* Against Eutyches. The objects of general Canons of this Council are, for the most part, to separate a l

DATE	PLACE	OBJECT, ETC.

ranks of the clergy from secular affairs—to secure the periodical celebration of provincial councils—to preserve the subordination of and discipline of the clergy—and to subject the inferior orders exclusively to episcopal jurisdiction.

452 (about). ARLES. This Council was held against the Novatians, the Photinians or Paulianists, the Bonosians, the Arians, and the Eutycheans. It also legislated respecting the *Lapsed*, and on matters of discipline. It decreed—That no one be consecrated bishop without a letter from the metropolitan, or three bishops of the province. That, in a contested election, the metropolitan follow the majority. That the ordination of a clerk out of his diocese, or without the knowledge of his bishop, is null. (*Can.* xiii.) Nullus cujuscunque ordinis clericus, non diaconus, non presbyter, non episcopus, quacunque occasione faciente, propriam relinquat ecclesiam : sed omnimodis aut excommunicatur, aut redire cogatur. The Council directs the convocation of future councils at Arles, and provides for the attendance of the clergy : That a bishop who does not come to the Council, or leaves it before the end, be excommunicated ; that a bishop who has neglected to extirpate the custom of worshipping fountains, trees, stones, is guilty of sacrilege ; that actors be excommunicated ; that penance be not imposed on married persons, except by their common consent ; that the suits of clerks be carried before the bishop ; that a bishop, building a church in the diocese of another bishop, may consecrate, but not present to it ; that to avoid Simony in the election of bishops, the bishops choose three candidates, among whom the clergy and the people decide. The Council forbids the clergy to practise usury, or to busy themselves in the affairs of others ; and restricts the females who may dwell in their houses. It also protects the serfs of the Church from reprisals.

461. TOURS. On discipline. It repeats a former decree, that a clerk may not travel without letters from his bishop. That he may not marry a widow ; nor be guilty of drunkenness.

465 (about). VANNES. On discipline. It confined an abbot to the possession of one monastery. It prohibited divinations (by the *sortes* of the saints, or of holy Scripture) to clerks ; and convivial indulgencies.

475. ARLES and LYONS. Against the Predestinarians.

484. ROME. On receiving the Lapsed of the African (now an Arian) Church.

494. ROME. Held by Pope Gelasius, for the distinction of the canonical from the apocryphal books of the Old and New Testament. It published, at the same time, an index of approved works, especially those of the fathers who had clung closest to the Church of Rome.

DATE   PLACE   OBJECT, ETC.

It also published a prohibitory index of apocryphal and otherwise objectionable works; such as the Acts of the Council of Rimini. Among the denounced were the eight books of Clement; the Acts of Andrew, Thomas, Peter, Philip; the book concerning the infancy of the Saviour, and a multitude of other forgeries; as well as the works of a vast number of heretics. (*Semler*, sec. v. Cap. v. *Labb. Concil.* tom. viii. p. 146.)

502. ROME (III.)   For the abrogation of a law of Odoacer, which made the authority of the King of Italy necessary for the election of the Bishop of Rome.   (*Labb.* tom. viii. p. 265.)   It published regulations against the alienation of Church property, &c.   It was assembled by Symmachus, who held other councils; by one of which a clerk was forbidden to appropriate monies which might have been given him for the remission of sins, or the repose and salvation of souls. In another (*Labb.* tom. viii. p. 230), we read a canon to the effect, that, if the Pope, by the suddenness of his death, should be prevented from *decreeing* (decernere) *concerning the election of his successor*, that person shall be ordained Pontiff whom the majority of the clergy shall elect.

506. AGDE (*Agathense*).   On discipline.   It decrees—That a person unjustly excommunicated should be received to communion by the neighbouring bishops ;   that everything given to a bishop becomes the property of the Church ; that a bishop may not alienate any article of Church property without the consent of two or three comprovincial or neighbouring bishops.   (Yet *Can.* 45, of the same council, allows the bishop terrulas et vineolas exiguas et ecclesiæ minus utiles sine concilio fratrum .... distrahere.)   The same *Canon* (7) regulates respecting the manumission of the serfs of the Church.   In penance the hair is to be cut off, and the garments changed.   That if a clerk be drunk, he be deprived of communion for thirty days, and subjected to corporal punishment.   This Council prescribes the tonsure of clerks, the fast of Lent, and communion at the three grand festivals.   (Sæculares, qui natale Domini, Pascha, et Pentecosten non communicaverint, Catholici non credantur, nec inter Catholicos habeantur. *Can.* 18.)   *Can.* 27. Si necesse fuerit clericum de monachis ordinari, cum consensu et voluntate abbatis præsumat sacerdos.   *Canon* 30 regulates the order of worship; that matins and vespers be sung every day, and chapters from the Psalms read after the conclusion of the morning and evening masses ; and the people dismissed with the blessing by the bishop.   *Can.* 55. Episcopis, presbyteris, diaconibus canes ad venandum aut accipitres habere non liceat.   *Can.* 57. Unum abbatem duobus monasteriis in terdicimus præsidere.   *Can.* 68. Non oportet ministros altaris aut clericos magos et incantatores esse.   It fixes the age, at which a virgin may take the veil, at forty; that of the diaconate at twenty-five; that of the priesthood and episcopate at thirty.   It prohibits

the ordination of married men without the consent of their wives; the building of nunneries near to monasteries; and commands, among many other regulations (*Can.* 36), that the salaries of priests be regulated according to their merits. (Many are mere repetitions of the canons of former councils).

511. ORLEANS. Convoked by Clovis. It regulates the rights of asylum, according to the rule of the *Roman* Church. It places the children and grand-children of clerks under the care of the bishop. It subjects abbots to bishops, monks to abbots : and regulates some other particulars of monastic discipline. It forbids the ordination of a serf, without the consent of his master. (Ante Pascha Quadragesima teneatur, non Quinquagesima. *Can.* 24.) It places all fixed property given to churches under the power of the bishops, and gives them a third part of the offerings ; at the same time enjoining them to provide food and raiment for the poor and infirm. (The frequent mention of the children of clerks, the Canons " De Clericis Bigamis," so commonly found, sufficiently show what was the practice of the clergy of this age).

516. TARRACONA. *Can.* 6. If a bishop, summoned to a synod by his metropolitan, does not attend, that he be deprived of the communion of his brother bishops till the synod following. Bishops are to visit their dioceses every year. Monachis a monasteriis foras egredientibus ne aliquod ministerium ecclesiasticum præsumant agere prohibemus, nisi forte cum abbatis imperio. *Can.* xi.

517. EPAONE (*now Jena, in Savoy*). On discipline. That neither bishops, priests, nor deacons, keep sporting dogs or falcons. Against the alienation of Church property by abbots or bishops. Penance for two years is imposed on a master who has murdered his serf, and on a Catholic who has fallen into heresy. It divides the oblations equally between the bishop and his clergy ; but leaves all the fixed property to the bishop, (unless this be the Canon of a somewhat earlier Council). It enacts some regulations for the discipline of all ranks of the clergy ; forbids clerks to attend to magic ; it prohibits clerks, who are usurious, or quarrelsome, from being ordained ; and clerks not ordained, from entering the sacristy, or touching the holy vessels. (Several Canons are borrowed from earlier Councils).

524. ARLES (IV). It relaxes the severity of ordination, owing to the increasing number of churches, but still prohibits the metropolitan from ordaining a layman to an episcopal see; and bishops from ordaining a layman, priest, or deacon, in less than a year from his conversion.

524. VALENCIA (*Spain*). The clergy are prohibited from plundering the possessions of a bishop, on his death.

527. CARPENTRAS. It decreed, that if a bishop have less money than he

DATE   PLACE   OBJECT, ETC.

wants, and there be any parishes in his diocese which have more, he may apply the superfluity to his own purposes—(*Guizot*, Tableau des Conciles, &c.)

529.   ORANGE and VALENCE.   Defined the Augustinian doctrine, and condemned the Seinipelagians.

529.   VAISON.   *Can.* 1.   That young readers in divinity be instructed in the houses of parochial priests, as is the wholesome custom throughout all Italy—psalmos parare, divinis lectionibus insistere.   *Can.* 3. Et hoc nobis justum visum est, ut *nomen Domini Papæ*, quicunque sedi apostolicæ præfuerit, in nostris ecclesiis *recitetur*. That all priests be permitted to preach.

533.   ORLEANS.   That the metropolitans convoke provincial Councils every year, and the bishops be obliged to attend ; that the bishop receive no fees for ordination ; that no man be ordained deacon or priest, who is illiterate, and ignorant of the form of baptism; that the metropolitan be elected by the provincial bishops, the clergy, and the people, and then consecrated by the provincial bishops. Marriages between Christians and Jews are prohibited.

     Can. 9. Nullus presbyterorum, sine permissione Episcopi sui, cum sæcularibus habitare presumat. *Can.* 17 et 18. Fœminæ quæ benedictionem diaconatus hactenus, contra interdicta canonum, acceperunt, si ad conjugium probantur iterum devolutæ, a communione pellantur. Placuit etiam ut nulli postmodum fœminæ diaconalis benedictio pro conditionis hujus fragilitate credatur.

535.   CLERMONT.   This Council published Canons against clerks who were disobedient to their bishops through secular protection ;* against persons seeking the episcopate by importunity rather than by merit ; against invaders of the Church property. That the bishop who will not constrain his priests and deacons from any commerce, of any description, with women, be himself excommunicated. That a bishop be permitted, with the consent of his clergy, to aid his family from the revenues of the Church. (*Guizot*, Tabl. des Concils de.)

536.   JERUSALEM.   Against the heretics Severus, Petrus, and Zoaras.

538.   ORLEANS.   That no serf, or agricultural labourer, be admitted to ecclesiastical distinctions ; that no one assist at the sacred offices in arms ; that a judge who knows that a heretic is rebaptizing a Catholic, and does not seize that heretic, and send him to the king, be excommunicated for a year. The Council allows new converts to remain in their former marriages, though they be uncanonical. It complains that the people have been taught that they may neither travel, nor cook, nor clean their houses, or persons, on a

---

* The Council of Orleans, three years afterwards, and another in 541, noticed the same offence.

DATE   PLACE   OBJECT; ETC.

Sunday—which observances are Judaic rather than Christian; it limits the restriction from work to agricultural labourers. It likewise contains a very severe interdict against the Jews—"for, by the grace of God, we live under Catholic kings."

541. ORLEANS. This Council commands to celebrate Easter after the fashion of *Rome;* and decides, that on any doubt as to the epoch of any solemnity, the *apostolical* usage is to be followed. It contains Canons, exempting the clergy from the office of guardian, seeing that Pagan priests were exempt from it : restraining the abuse of asylum; the license of the serfs of the Church; permitting persons to found and endow chapels; and excluding from ordinations the descendants of serfs who had not been emancipated.

549. ORLEANS. This Council consisted of 50 bishops, and 21 priests, archdeacons, or abbots, each the representative of a bishop; and such was the constitution of other councils at this period. It condemned the errors of the Eutycheans, Nestorians, and Arians. It enacted that persons afflicted with leprosy were to be fed and clothed *de domo ecclesiæ.* It decreed, in imitation of a former Council, that no one be appointed a bishop in less than a year after his conversion. The close connexion between the Bishop and his *own* clergy was encouraged—(nullus alienum clericum recipere vel promovere sine epistola pontificis sui præsumat); and *Can.* 15 was on the subject of a *Xenodochium* which King Childebert had founded at Lyons.

550. CLERMONT. The Councils of this period have usually some Canons as to the relations of serfs to their masters, in respect to ecclesiastical matters. That no one be permitted to acquire the Episcopate by money; but that (with the consent of the king*), he that is chosen pontiff by the clergy and people, be consecrated, according to ancient Canons, by the metropolitan and the provincial bishops ; that no one be imposed as bishop upon those who are unwilling to receive him; and that, if oppression has been used to obtain the consent of the clergy and people, the bishop so chosen be deposed for ever from the Episcopate.†

553. CONSTANTINOPLE. *The fifth General.* (See Vol. I. p. 354). *Semler*, sec. vi. cap. 4.

554. ARLES. It published some Canons for the better subjection of monasteries and convents to episcopal authority. Abbots not permitted to travel without the permission of the bishop.

* This parenthesis is not found in several MSS.
† Notwithstanding this edict, St. Gall, the Bishop of Clermont, dying about this time, and the bishops, with the consent of the people, wishing to consecrate one Cato for his successor, the king succeeded in forcing his own creature into the see. A Council was held at Metz on the subject.

DATE   PLACE   OBJECT, ETC.

557. **PARIS.** To prevent the spoliation of the Church property (in which is included expressly the private property of the bishops) by the King of the Franks. It likewise declares null the ordination of a bishop who has been named by the king—in spite of clergy and people— non *principis imperio*, neque per quamlibet conditionem, contra metropolis voluntatem vel episcoporum comprovincialium ingeratur. *Can.* 8. This is enforced at some length.

561. **BRACCARA.** Against the Priscillianists; anathema against all who believed (like Priscillian) that the Devil had had any share in the creation of the world, or any part of it. It insisted on uniformity in the order of the ceremonies, and the services of the Church.

567. **LYONS** (II). This Council deposed Salone, Bishop of Embrun, and Sagitaire, Bishop of Gap, for sufficient reason. They appealed to Pope John, and he restored them to their sees. (Two years afterwards, a second Council, on the same subject, was convoked by Gontran, at Chalons, where the two bishops were condemned as traitors). This Council also enacted, that the wills of clerks, of any rank, who bequeathed anything to the Church, were valid, even though they might seem to be, in some respects, at variance with secular law.

567. **TOURS.** Episcopus conjugem ut sororem habeat. Episcopum episcopam non habentem nulla sequatur turba mulierum. There are some Canons for the regulation of monastic discipline, as well as of that of the clergy; against the offerings made by the vulgar, on stated occasions, to the dead, or to stones, trees, or fountains.

572. **BRACCARA.** Twenty days before baptism, the Catechumens must undergo the purgation of exorcism. In these days they are to learn the Creed; they are to be warned against idolatry, homicide, adultery, and the other mortal sins—not to do to others what they would not have done to themselves—to believe in the Resurrection, and the Day of Judgment. It published Canons against the exactions of the clergy; against the practice of building new churches, for the sake of sharing with the clergy the oblations made there; against the Sortes Sanctorum, and other grosser Pagan superstitions. The Eucharist not to be given to the dead.

581. **MACON.** This Council also convoked by Gontran. It decreed, that no clerk should wear silk, or other secular vestments, unbecoming his profession; that a judge who arrests a clerk, except for homicide, theft, or witchcraft, be excommunicated; that a Jew may not be a judge of Christians, nor a receiver of taxes; Christians forbidden to serve Jews.

585. **MACON.** Also convoked by Gontran; consisted of 43 bishops, 15 representatives, and 16 other bishops, whom the Goths had deprived of their sees. It enacted, that Sunday be more regularly observed; that every Christian present his offerings; *that tithes be regularly paid;*

that baptism be not celebrated except at the prescribed times; that the Eucharist be administered fasting; that judges decide nothing on the affairs of widows and orphans, except after notice to the bishop, their natural protector, and in deliberation with him. It regulates the respect to be paid, on accidental meetings, by the layman to the ecclesiastic. It likewise complains of the miseries of the poor, and the general demoralization of the great.

585. TOLEDO (III). On the extirpation of Arianism, under King Recared. It commands some bishops, priests, and deacons, who, after their conversion from Arianism, still retained their wives, to put them away on pain of degradation. Women found in the cells of the aforesaid to be sold by the bishops, and the price given to the poor. Against the practice of idolatry.

590. NARBONNE. This Council forbids clerks to wear purple, and to enter into the conversations held in public places. It prohibits the ordination of priests or deacons who cannot read; also certain Pagan superstitions; and interferes to prevent singing at the funerals of Jews. It subjects offenders (clericos aut honoratos de civitate) confined in monasteries to such penance as the *bishop* may impose on them. There is, also, a strict prohibition against any sort of work on the Lord's Day.

600. ROME. " Quod *imaginem* illius quem colis tibi dirigendam rogasti, valde nobis placuit—nos quidem non quasi ante divinitatem prosternimur ante illam; sed Eum adoramus, quem *per imaginem* aut natum, aut passum, aut in throno sedentem recordamur. Ideoque direximus tibi, imaginem Dei Salvatoris, et S. Mariæ Dei genitricis; beatorum Apostolorum Petri et Pauli; et unam Crucem; *clavem* autem pro benedictione, a S. corpore Petri, ut per ipsum a Maligno defensus permaneas." (Ap. *Semler*. Secul. vi. cap. iv.) Held under Gregory the Great.

601. ROME. Also under Gregory—publishes a decree favourable to the monastic orders—(See *Labbe Concil.* tom. x. p. 486.)—and nine years afterwards, Boniface IV. follows this up by a synodal decree, *permitting monks to assume the priesthood* with all its privileges, and clothing them, like the cherubim, with *six wings.* (Both Gregory, and Augustine, the Apostle of England, had been monks.)

610. TOLEDO. That the metropolitan see of Toledo possessed authority over the other churches of Spain.

615. PARIS. That no bishop choose a coadjutor. That no judge arrest a clerk without the knowledge of the bishop. This Council published decrees respecting the property of the clergy and the Church, and fresh denunciations against the Jews. A Council held very soon afterwards in Gaul, probably at Paris, prohibits the celebration of baptisms, masses for the dead, or the sepulture of laymen, *in*

monasteries, without the permission of the bishop. "Presbyteri aut Diaconi se nulla ratione nubere præsumant."

625. RHEIMS. This Council renews former Canons against the insubordination of priests, and their conspiracies against their bishops. It commands the bishops to seek out and convert any heretics which may be found in Gaul. It enacts other regulations on the privileges of asylum ; on the slaves of Christians ; and of Jews. And it confirms the original law of episcopal election, in strong terms, (as do many of the preceding Councils,) with the addition, that the bishop must necessarily be *indigena loci*. It prohibits the alienation of the sacred utensils, except for the redemption of captives. Its Canons are followed by 21 capitula : "Sine Fide nemo potest Deo placere ; ideo mandamus, ut juxta verbum Dei et S. Eccles. *Romanæ* traditionem teneant." "Eucharistia feratur ægrotis vase honesto, et *lumine antecedente* et præurente." The feasts enjoined are the Nativity, Circumcision, Epiphany, Annunciation, Resurrection, Ascension, Whitsunday ; the Nativity of John the Baptist ; of Peter and Paul ; of the Virgin and her Assumption ; of St. Andrew. (These statutes may be of a somewhat later date).

633. TOLEDO (IV). This important Council published 75 Canons. It enjoins uniformity in rites and ceremonies between Spain and Gaul, or Gallicia—(Galliam. al. Galliciam). A Council, at least, once a year —either general of all Spain and Gaul (or Gallicia*), or special in every province. It commands single, in preference to trine immersion, in baptism. It recommends the benediction of the lamp and taper before the celebration of Easter. It restrains the avarice of the clergy, in the appropriation of oblations, &c. It commands the reception of the Apocalypse, which some churches still rejected. It enjoins the tonsure of *all* the upper part of the head, to all clerks. "Monachum aut *paterna* devotio, aut propria devotio facit." It prohibits from converting the Jews by violence, but decrees to separate their children from them, and save them from error. It regulates (*Can.* 5) that Easter be celebrated throughout all Spain on the same day. Hitherto there had been a variety.

636. TOLEDO (V). Appoints solemn litanies thrice a-year, for the indulgence of sins—nova consuetudo ab nova facinora. It forbids the elevation of any prince, except by the choice of all the people. Of its nine Canons, seven are of a political nature.

638. TOLEDO (VI). The King allows no one to live in his dominions who is not a Catholic. This, and some others, are directed against the Jews. There are 19 Canons, of which 11 regard ecclesiastical matters.

645. ORLEANS. This Council is only remarkable as having been convoked against a Greek, who was preaching Monothelitism in Gaul, and who was expelled from the country in consequence.

* We are disposed to think Gallicia the right reading ; and would accordingly modify a statement made in Vol. I., p. 310.

646. TOLEDO (VII). Against clerks who may assist in choosing another king. Against the rapacity of the bishops of *Gallicia*—(here there is no various reading of Gallia). And against certain itinerant monks, who went about preaching, without knowledge or morality.

649. ROME. *Lateran.* Under Pope Martin—for the condemnation of the Monothelites. A letter is sent to John, Bishop of Philadelphia, commanding him to supply the place of Pope in those regions—to appoint, through all the countries which are under the Sees of Jerusalem and Antioch, orthodox bishops, priests, and deacons, by the *apostolical authority.*

650. CHALONS. This Council shows a jealousy of lay influence, in regard to the invasion of Church property by laymen ; to the intrusion of secular magistrates into parishes and monasteries under episcopal jurisdiction ; and to the seeking after lay patronage by abbots and monks—all these are prohibited ; as also for men to wear arms, or women to sing indecent songs, in churches.

653. TOLEDO (VIII). The first Canon—on faith—admits the *double procession.* Against Simony (this prohibition is frequent in all Councils). Against the impurities of the bishops ; and the marriage of the clergy, even of subdeacons ; some political edicts of former Councils, and some against the Jews are repeated with no great variation. (*Labb. Concil.* tom. x. p. 1210.)

655. TOLEDO (IX). That the founders of churches during their own lives present the incumbent to the Bishop for ordination ; that the sons of clerks be the slaves of the Church of which the clerk was member.

656. TOLEDO (X). *The nativity of the Mother of Christ* is to be kept henceforward as well as that of Christ. That children of either sex, who have assumed the tonsure or religious dress with the consent of either of their parents, may not return to a secular life.

670. AUTUN (*Augustodunense*). That the priest, deacon, subdeacon, or clerk, who does not know perfectly by heart the Apostles' Creed, and the *Athanasian Creed,* be condemned by his bishop. That those laymen, who do not take the communion at Christmas, Easter, and Whitsuntide, be not accounted Catholics.

675. TOLEDO (XI). Forbids the payment of fees for baptism, as well as some other ceremonies. There was a Council at *Braccara* the same year, which published no important enactment : one Canon was, that the bishops, in the Festivals of the Martyrs, do not carry their relics upon their shoulders, &c. &c.

681. TOLEDO (XII). Renews the severe enactments against the Jews, forbidding them to read any books contrary to Christianity, &c. " We admonish the worshippers of idols, stones, fountains, trees, &c., that

the authority of the priest or judge may be employed for the prevention of such offences, and restrain their servants with chains and stripes." Five other Councils of Toledo follow in this century, but they enacted nothing new or important, unless the 5th Canon of the 17th Council be so considered—"that no *mass for the repose of the dead* be celebrated for the living."

692. CONSTANTINOPLE in TRULLO. This Council, called Quinisextum (πενθεκτης), was supplementary to the two preceding (the fifth and sixth General) as they had published no Canons for the general discipline of the Church. This published 102; but as some few of them were never accepted by the Church of Rome, the Council is not by it acknowledged as general. The objectionable Canons were those which (c. 13.) permitted the marriage of the clergy (before ordination, and once only) and even prohibited them from putting away their wives on ordination, under pretence of piety,—προφάσει εὐλαβείας; (c. 67) which commanded both clerks and laymen to abstain from blood and things suffocated; (c. 82) which forbade Christ to be painted in the image of a lamb, rather than in the form of man ;— and (c. 36) declared the See of Constantinople to be equal in authority with that of Rome.

Besides the above, this Council adopted the Apostolical Canons and Constitutions—rejected the Armenian custom of mixing no water in the Eucharistical cup—allowed no one to become a monk younger than *ten* years—prohibited marriage within certain degrees of consanguinity—annulled marriages between Catholics and Heretics—forbade the celebration of Agapæ in churches—besides many other regulations of little interest.

721. ROME. Under Gregory II. who published some Canons in reply to Boniface. A priest, accused by the people, if the evidence was not certain, might clear himself by oath. Those, whose parents had placed them in a monastery, even in infancy, might never quit it. The sacrament might be administered to lepers. (Fourteen presbyters, and five deacons of the Roman Church, afterwards called *Cardinals*, were present at this Council.) A letter written two years afterwards by Gregory III. to the same Boniface, regulates his conduct towards Pagans, besides other matters of general morality.

742. AUGSBURG or RATISBON. This Council was held by Carloman, at the instance of Pope Zachary, and was attended by several lay grandees. It appointed bishops to the cities (of Germany), and placed Boniface at their head. It ordered Councils to be held every year. It prohibited priests from carrying arms, except those who were required in armies to say mass, to carry the relics of the Saints and hear confessions. It enacted several regulations respecting the morals of the priesthood.

743. LEPTINES. This was held by Pepin, in confirmation of the Council

of Carloman. The professed object was to reform the clergy; and they all, of every rank, promised to change their morals, and obey the ancient Canons. We ordain (says Pepin) that every house-holder contribute one *sous* to the Church or Monastery ; that he, who shall be convicted of any Pagan observance, be fined fifteen *sous* ; that the Metropolitan hold a Council every year ; that every bishop, on his return from the Council, assemble his priests and abbots, and enforce the decrees on their obedience ; that every bishop visit his diocese once a year ; that every priest render an account to his bishop at Lent ; that if a priest be found incorrigible, the bishop bring the affair before the archbishop—just as the Roman Church has exacted an oath of me to submit to its correction the priests whom I shall be unable to correct by my own authority.

These Canons begin and end by a profession of obedience to the Pope, who is to be consulted and obeyed in everything. A promise is also given to request the *Pallium* at his hands.

747. **CLOVESHO** (*in Kent*). Boniface addresses Cuthbert Archbishop of Canterbury, and enumerates the Synodical decrees published in Germany. *Obedience to St. Peter* and his vicar. To prevent English women from journeying so frequently to Rome—seeing that few pre-serve their chastity—perpaucæ enim sunt civitates in Longobardia, Francia, aut Gallia, in qua non sit adultera vel meretrix Anglorum. Then follow some of the capitularies of Pope Zachary ; that boys be brought up in the love and study of sacred learning ; that the seven canonical hours of day and night be observed with due psalmody and song ; that the priests learn both to interpret the Creed, the Lord's Prayer, the words of the mass in the office of baptism, and to expound them in the vulgar tongue ; for the serious occupation of monks and nuns; that public prayers be offered for kings and grandees.

748. **VERNE, and 752 VERMERIE.** Councils held by Pepin for the repairs of the churches and the affairs of the poor, of widows and orphans. Also, for regulating the marriages and divorces of serfs ; to prevent the veil from being imposed by force—and to prevent the man, who permits his wife to take the veil, from marrying again.

755. **VERNES.** This consisted of almost all the bishops of Gaul, and was held by order and in presence of Pepin. That there be two Synods every year ; the one at the calends of March in the presence of the king and in the place appointed by him ; the other in October, at a place appointed by the bishops assembled in March ; that all ecclesi-astics, whom the metropolitans shall send, attend that second Synod ; that the bishop have full power to correct his clergy and his monks ; that those who say that they have taken the tonsure for the love of God, and live on their property and as they like, be shut up in a mo-nastery, or lead a canonical life under the hand of the bishop ; that the very rigid observance of the Sabbath, which some have imposed

upon the people, (so as neither to ride, travel, cook, nor attend to their houses or persons,) be discontinued, as Judaical rather than Christian; except in respect to agricultural labours, which tend to keep people away from church. (This is little more than the republication of a Canon of the Council of Orleans in 538.) That all laymen, whether noble or not, celebrate their marriages in public; that royal monasteries give account of their revenues to the king; episcopal to the bishop.

756. LEPTINES. This Council, also under Pepin, attempted to enforce the restoration of property plundered from the Church, but not successfully. The other Canons concerned marriages.

765. ATTIGNY. Nothing remains of this Council, except the measures taken by its members to secure a number of masses and prayers of themselves after their death.

767. GENTILLY. In this, as in some former Councils, there was a discussion between the Greeks and the Latins, touching the Trinity, the procession of the Holy Spirit, and Images.

777. PADERBORN. This Council refuses the right of asylum to persons guilty of capital offences. Its Canons are directed to civil rather than ecclesiastical affairs. (Several Councils about this period legislated respecting the conversion of Saxony).

787. CALCHUTHA (*England*). Pope Hadrian addresses a Canonical letter containing Statutes, which the king, and all the bishops, abbots, and nobles present vow obedience. To hold the Nicene faith, and receive the Six General Councils like the Roman Church, and the *Decretals of the Roman Pontiffs*; to assemble two Councils a year; let the bishops see that the monks and canons live canonically after the fashion of the Orientals. On the seven canonical hours. On the payment of tithes; against usury. That they should cast off the relics of Paganism.

787. NICE (II). *The Seventh General* Council.

789. AIX-LA-CHAPELLE. Charlemagne published a number of Capitularies on ecclesiastical discipline, drawn in a great measure from the Oriental Canons, and the Decrees of the Popes.

794. FRANCFORT. This Council rejected, with anathema, the doctrine of the Council of Constantinople on the *worship of images*, and regarded it as idolatrous. It likewise prohibited the worship of any new Saints It published several Canons for the regulation of monastic discipline—enacting that an abbot could not be chosen without the consent of the bishop; that recluses were not to be made without the approbation of the bishop and the abbot; that the bishop was to be acquainted with the Rule and the Canons. There is a *Canon* (xxii.) against the ordination of rural bishops (Chorepiscopi). That

(*Canon* xxv.) the *tenths and the ninths* be paid to the Church by all from whom they are due—and that the tenth of their estates be paid by all for the residence of the bishops and clergy.   For the destruction of idolatrous trees and groves.   That the worship of God is not confined to three languages only, but that He hears the prayers addressed to Him in *every tongue*.   We likewise observe several Canons of former Councils repeated by this.   The whole number is 56.

799.   RATISBON. The only traces of this Council are in the Capitularies of Charlemagne.   It treated of the Chorepiscopi, among other matters.

802.   AIX-LA-CHAPELLE. On ecclesiastical reform. All present took the oath of allegiance to the Emperor.   There is one, among various constitutions of Charlemagne, published about this time, which permits sinners to *redeem by alms* the sins which they have been unable to expiate by fasting.

803   AIX-LA-CHAPELLE. Charlemagne commanded all the services of the Church to be chaunted throughout his empire after the *Roman fashion*.

809.   AIX-LA-CHAPELLE. This Council treated on the procession of the Holy Ghost, and sent an embassy to the Pope to request his decision on the subject.   Soon afterwards (811) Charlemagne published his Capitulary of Interrogations (*Labbe Concil.* tom. xiii. p. 1070,) conveying a severe censure upon the morals of the clergy.   Among his " Selecta Capitula Ecclesiastica," (apud *Labbe Concil.* tom. xiii. p. 1050,) is that which prohibits bishops and priests from going to the wars—and another *abolishing* the (usurped) privileges of the *Chorepiscopi*, and forbidding their future appointment. Charlemagne had likewise earlier issued a commission, (the members were called *Missi*,) for the inspection of monasteries, convents, and churches, both as to the fabrics, and for the improvement of ecclesiastical and moral discipline.   The following expressions are from these interrogations:—Inquirendum est, si ille seculum dimissum habeat, qui quotidie possessiones suas augere quolibet modo, qualibet arte, non cessat ; suadendo de cœlestis regni beatitudine, comminando de æterno supplicio inferni, et sub nomine Dei, aut *cujuslibet sancti*, tam divitem quam pauperem, qui simpliciores naturæ sunt, si rebus suis exspoliant, et legitimos hæredes eorum exheredant, &c.

813.   ARLES. Five Councils were held this year by order of Charlemagne, for the reform of ecclesiastical discipline.   Their Canons contain, of course, much repetition ; but their general object is both to protect and improve the clergy.   Nearly all of them recommend to bishops and priests gravity of morals, indifference to secular matters, modesty, diligence in study, &c. ; and prohibit oppression, ignorance avarice, and every sort of immorality.   Much is likewise enacted

about *tithes;* about the observance of the Sabbath, and monastic discipline. These Councils recommend great preparations as necessary for taking the communion, and do not seem anxious for the very frequent communication of the laity. *Can.* 2. Ut pro excellentissimo atque gloriosissimo Domino nostro Carolo Rege seu liberis ejus omnes Episcopi, &c. &c. psalmodiam missarum solemnia atque litaniarum officia omnipotenti Deo exsolvant. *Can.* 9. Ut unusquisque *de propriis laboribus decimas* et primitias Deo offerat, sicut scriptum est. (Exod. 22.) *Can.* 17. Ut unusquisque episcopus semel in anno circumeat parochiam suam. Noverint sibi *curam* populorum et *pauperum* in protegendis et defendendis impositam. They are then directed to rebuke the oppressors of the poor, and if this should fail, to give information to the king. *Can.* 19. Ut parentes filios suos et *patrini* eos, quos de fonte lavacri suscipiunt, erudire summopere studeant: illi, quia eos genuerant, isti, quia pro iis fidejussores existunt.

813. MAYENCE. Prohibits any sale of the *goods of the poor* except in public. It recommends the priests to teach the people the Creed and the Lord's Prayer, at least in the vulgar tongue, when they cannot learn it otherwise. It directs bishops and abbots to provide themselves with good stewards (vicedominos) for advocates. Prohibits the transfer of relics from place to place, except by consent of the prince or bishops. Besides various Canons against Sortilegi, observer of omens, wearers of charms and phylacteries, &c.

813. RHEIMS. Prohibits monks from pleading before laymen. *Can.* 14. Ut episcopi diligentius operam dent, lectionique divinæ incumbant, i. e. canonicis libris et opusculis patrum ... et verbum Dei omnibus prædicent. *Can.* 15. Ut episcopi sermones et homilias SS. patrum, prout omnes intelligere possint, secundum proprietatem linguæ prædicare studeant. *Can.* 19. Ut episcopi et judices judicia discernant; quia sunt quædam judicanda modo, quædam Dei judicio reservanda. *Can.* 22. Ut de sacerdotibus omnis suspicio mulierum funditus eradicetur.

813. TOURS. That the bishops read, and, if possible, learn by heart the Gospel and Epistles of St. Paul. That they be not given to excess at table, histrionic amusements, or those of the chase. The priests are not to administer the sacrament indiscriminately to all who come to mass. Universal obedience to be paid to the bishops. *Can* 16. Ut decimæ, quæ singulis dabuntur ecclesiis, per consulta Episcoporum a Presbyteris ad usum Ecclesiæ et pauperum summa diligentia dispensentur. *Can.* 28. Virginibus sacrum velamem accipiendum decreta patrum interdicunt ante 25 annos, nisi forte aliqua cogente necessitate.

813. CHALONS (*Cabilonense*). *Can.* 3. Oportet Episcopi scholas constituant (sicut Dominus Imp. Carolus ... præcepit) in quibus et literas

DATE   PLACE   OBJECT, ETC.

solertia disciplinæ et Sacræ Scripturæ documenta discantur, &c. *Can.* 8. prohibits a monopoly of corn by priests ; others prohibit certain payments which some bishops and archdeacons had exacted from the priests. *Can.* 39. Ut in omnibus missarum solemnitatibus pro *defunctorum spiritibus* loco competenti Dominus deprecetur. Antiquitus hunc morem sancta ecclesia tenet . . . . dicente B. Augustino ; " non sunt prætermittendæ supplicationes pro spiritu mortuorum, quas faciendas pro omnibus in Christiana et Catholica societate defunctis . . . . sub generali commemoratione suscepit ecclesia," &c. It was enacted in one of these councils, that neither bishops nor abbots should prevent their tenants from paying tithes to the churches. This Council attended much to the administration of penance, and repudiated the penitential books then in vogue, " of which the errors are certain, the authors uncertain." (*Can.* 23). *Can.* 33. Some think that they ought to confess their sins to God alone ; others that they should confess them to the priests ; both the one and the other are useful in the Church of God. The confession made to God purges away their sins ; that to the priests teaches how to purge them away. For God is the author and distributor of salvation and health, and he grants much through his own invisible power, much through the influence of his physicians.

816.   AIX-LA-CHAPELLE. This Council, convoked by Louis the Meek, published two sets of enactments—the one for the Canons, containing likewise some general statutes—145 in all,—the other for the nuns, of 28 canons. They were derived from the fathers and the councils ; and prove nothing so much as the growing tendency to extend the monastic profession among all ranks of religious persons. The rules for the canons do not differ greatly from those usually imposed on monks. Those for the nuns prove the difficulty of keeping them in subjection to episcopal authority. They abound with such orders as these :— That abbesses be subject to the bishops : that they do not quit their convents without permission of the bishops : that they presume not to give the veil ; nor to usurp any sacerdotal functions. There are also frequent prohibitions in the councils of these ages against the reception of any males into nunneries, even monks and priests, at forbidden hours. We observe several Capitularies about this time against the too early and hasty assumption of the veil.

These various councils of Aix-la-Chapelle had the effect of creating uniformity between the Gallic and German churches, and of uniting both to Rome.

818.   AIX-LA-CHAPELLE. Some bishops having been condemned for conspiracy by a synodal decree, one of them, Theodulphus, disputed (in poetry) the legitimacy of the tribunal on the ground of the Pallium (Lib. iv. Carm. v.)

> Solius illud opus Romani Præsulis extat,
> Cujus ego accepi *pallia* sancta manu.

Hatto, bishop of Basle, published a capitulary about this time, of which one resolution was this :—the third part of the tithes properly belongs to the bishop ; but I shall content myself with the fourth, after the usage of the Roman Church.

822. **ATTIGNY.** It was in obedience to this Council that Louis the Meek submitted to penance. A matron on this occasion brought a complaint against her husband before the emperor. He referred it to the Council of Bishops, and they again, with rare moderation, left it to the determination of the lay tribunals. The churchmen of this age make considerable exertions against the " Judgments of God."

824. **PARIS.** This Council deliberated on image-worship. The following are published (though with considerable suspicion) as some of its principal enactments :—It established the distinction of the two powers, and placed the sacerdotal far above the regal; it announced to the clergy the necessity of self-correction ; it insisted on the proper administration and explanation of Baptism ; it attacked Simony, the avarice of the bishops, and other immoralities ; it compared the Choepiscopi to the seventy disciples, and complained of their encroachment on episcopal prerogatives ; it commanded the bishops to superintend the schools ; forbade farming to priests and monks, and enjoined residence to bishops and priests ; it forbade women to give themselves the veil, and asserted that there were women who served at the altar and administered the body and blood of Christ ; it restricted the private celebration of the mass ; it declared that no king ought to maintain that he holds his kingdom from his ancestors, but from God. Other canons for the conduct of the kings are found in the third book of the Acts, in the form of a letter to the king ; especially that he should establish schools in various parts of the empire ; that he should dismiss from his court a number of idle monks and priests who haunted it ; and other admonitions in a different tone from that in which Charlemagne was addressed by his bishops. The first book contains 54 canons ; the second 13 ; the third 27.

826. **ROME.** It published 38 canons, some of which strongly enjoin the education of the clergy and the people.

829. **PARIS, MAYENCE, LYONS, TOULOUSE.** They were convoked by Louis the Meek; he named the bishops who were to form them, and prescribed the capitularies that they were to publish.

833. **COMPIEGNE.** This Council deprived Louis of the Crown, which the Council of St. Denis in the following year restored.

836. **AIX-LA-CHAPELLE.** Convoked by Louis the Meek to deliberate on three subjects ;—1. the lives of the bishops; 2. the doctrine of the bishops, together with the lives and doctrine of the inferior clergy ; 3. the person of the king, his children and servants. The canons are for the most part repetitions of those of former councils; they reiterate

DATE   PLACE   OBJECT, ETC.

the observance of the sacerdotal duties, and lay restraints on monastic immorality. It is prohibited to fast, to marry, or to go to law, on a Sunday ; complaints are made of the mutual encroachments of the ecclesiastical and secular tribunals. *Lib.* III. *Can.* 9. Monendo Magnitudini vestræ suggerimus, ut deinceps in bonis pastoribus rectoribusque in ecclesiis Dei *constituendis* magnum studium, solertissmamque habeatis curam. *Can.* 10. Similiter poscimus, ut in abbatissis constituendis et rectoribus monasteriorum, vestrum specialiter caveatis periculum, &c. (Thus they seem to concede the king's right to the entire patronage of the Church). *Labb. Concil.* lib. xiv. p. 690. &c.

843. TOULOUSE. There remain only some capitularies of Charles the Bald, for the protection of the priests from episcopal oppression and exaction.

844. THIONVILLE, VERNE. On ecclesiastical and monastic discipline. That bishops who are released from going in person to war either through infirmity, or by indulgence of the king, entrust their men to some person of confidence to lead in their places. That no novelty be adopted in the explanation of the Scriptures; that laymen do not employ the priests of their churches in attendance on their farms ; that the king take no Canons into his service without the consent of the bishop. The Councils of *Beauvais* and *Meaux* in the following year published similar enactments on the subject of ecclesiastical discipline.

847. PARIS. That the king give the bishops power signed with his seal, that when they may stand in want of the civil authority, they may receive its aid. (*Guizot*, Tableau des Conciles, &c.)

848. MAYENCE. Rabanus condemns Gotteschalcus, and consigns him to the authority of Hincmar.

850. TICIN. The Emperor Louis was present, and 25 canons were published for the improvement of ecclesiastical discipline. For public offences, the penance to be public. Offences not public, to be confessed to persons appointed by the bishop or *archipresbyter* (the priest who presided over the Baptismal Church). *Can.* 13. Propter assiduam erga populum Dei curam singulis plebibus Archipresbyteros præesse volumus ; qui non solum imperiti vulgi solicitudinem gerant, verum etiam eorum Presbyterorum, qui per minores titulos habitant, vitam custodiant. . . et sicut Episcopus matrici præest ita Archipresbyteri præsint plebeis. *Can.* 17. Omnes Christianos scire oportet, quia omnium rerum suarum decimationem Deo fideliter reddere debent ; et secundum Episcoporum dispositionem, sacerdotum et reliquorum clericorum usibus, cæterisque Ecclesiis utilitatibus distribuendæ sunt.

851. SOISSONS. Pepin, King of Aquitaine, deprived of his Crown, and subjected to the tonsure.

853. ROME. On general matters of ecclesiastical discipline. Its 38 canons

contain nothing very new or important. Some of them enforce the necessity of instruction for the clergy, and of the establishment of schools. *Can.* 34. In universis episcopiis subjectisque plebibus, et aliis locis in quibus necessitas occurrerit.

855. VALENCE. This Council published six canons on the subject of pre-destination, and rather in favour of the opinions of Gotteschalcus. It blamed the custom of conflicting oaths in trials, as one which neces-sarily, on the one side or the other, leads to perjury ; it also cen-sured judicial combat, and refused Christian sepulture to him who should fall in it ; it recommended the erection of schools for the divine and human sciences and the chants of the Church, " since the long interruption of studies, the ignorance of the faith, and the failure of all the sciences, have overrun many of the churches of God." Some councils held in 855 and 859, were occupied by the war between Charles the Bald and Louis of Germany.

860. AIX-LA-CHAPELLE. Two Councils held the same year on the sub-ject of the divorce between Lothaire and Teutberge.

863. IN AQUITAINE. This Council was held by the command of Pope Nicholas, and his legates were present ; as was another at Soissons in 866 on the affair of Hincmar and Rothadus.

866. TROYES. Pope Adrian wrote to this council to recommend that those only should be consecrated bishops whom the Emperor should ap-point : the bishops refused their consent. There was a dispute be-tween Hincmar and a part of the bishops, in which Hincmar tri-umphed.

868. ROME. This council approves the restoration of Ignatius to the See of Constantinople, and rescinds all the Acts of Photius.

868. WORMS. On ecclesiastical discipline. Baptism only to be adminis-tered at Easter and Whitsuntide ; the Bishop alone to confer the Chrism. In respect to Trine and Single immersion, Trine represents the Trinity and Single the Unity of the Godhead ; therefore either may be practised—and on the authority of Gregory. *Can.* 7. De redditu ecclesiæ et de oblatione fidelium quatuor fiant portiones ; quarum unam sibi retineat Episcopus, alteram clericus pro officiorum suorum sedulitate distribuat, tertiam pauperibus et peregrinis, quartam eccle-siasticis fabricis noverit reservandam. *Can.* 59. Ut decimæ in potes-tate Episcopi sint, qualiter a presbyteris dispensentur.

869. CONSTANTINOPLE. *The Eighth Latin General*—for the condem-nation of Photius ; one was held ten years afterwards by Photius, which the Latins call the False Eighth. The Greeks acknowledge the latter.

869. METZ. This Council gave to Charles the Bald the kingdom of his ne-phew Lothaire who died in Italy.

869. **VERMERIES.** Hincmar, Bishop of Laon, nephew of the Archbishop of Rheims, accused before this Council by his uncle and Charles the Bald, of issuing unjust excommunications, breach of faith to the king, and other offences, appealed from the Council to the Pope.

876. **TICIN.** This Council, of which canons differ very little from those of Pontion, (which follows), was assembled soon after the assumption of the Imperial title, on Papal authority, by Charles the Bald, and thus addressed him:—Divina vos pietas, Beatorum Principum Apostolorum Petri et Pauli interventione, per Vicarium *ipsorum* summum pontificem et universalem Papam (or Patrem) vestrum, ad profectum sanctæ Ecclesiæ ad imperiale culmen S. Spiritus judicio provexit. (*Semler* Sec. IX., c. II., Labb. *Concil.* t. xvii., p. 323). The Pope next year confirmed the appointment in a synod at Rome. The expressions in this age of the Church are important:—Et quia pridem Apostolicæ memoriæ decessori nostro Papæ Nicolao id ipsum jam inspiratione cœlesti revelatum fuisse comperimus, *elegimus hunc* merito et approbavimus, una cum annisu et voto omnium fratrum et coepp. nostrorum, atque *aliorum* sanctæ Romanæ ecclesiæ ministrorum, amplique *Senatus*, totiusque Romani *populi* gentisque togatæ, et secundum priscam consuetudinem solemniter ad imperii Romani sceptra proveximus, et augustali nomine decoravimus, unguentes eum Deo extrinsecus, &c., &c. (See Vol. II., p. 20.) Nosque quod jam in Romana ecclesia, quæ est *magistra*, mater et caput ecclesiarum, &c. In the 'Reply of the Bishops' we read—Sedet nos o domine et *evangelice* (*coangelice*) Papa, vestigia vestra sectantes, &c. (Append. tom. xvii., *Labb. Concil.*, p. 172.) A synod at Ravenna presently followed, by which every metropolitan was commanded to apply for the Pallium at Rome within three months from his appointment, and to perform no duty in the interval. After a synod at Ravenna in 882, Charles the Fat published a "Decretum Immunitatis," to protect ecclesiastical persons and property from the invasion of the secular and public authorities.

876. **PONTION.** This Council was held just after Charles the Bald was crowned Emperor. It enacted that the holy Roman Church be venerated by all as the mother of all the churches; and that no one presume to do anything unjustly against its right and its power; that respect be shown by all towards the Lord John, (John VIII.) our spiritual Father, Sovereign Pontiff, and universal Pope; that all observe with great veneration the things which he has decided by his apostolic authority; and that he receive in everything the obedience which is his due; that honour be paid to all ecclesiastics; that the imperial dignity be universally respected, &c.; that tithes be paid without fraud, and be dispensed by the presbyters, at the discretion of the bishop.

878. **TROYES.** Pope John presided; published some edicts, and crowned Louis the Stammerer.

DATE   PLACE   OBJECT, ETC.

879. **CONSTANTINOPLE.** *The Eighth General of the Greek Church.* In favour of Photius.

888. **MAYENCE.** This Council was held to repair the disorders occasioned by the Norman invasion. It prohibited a priest from lodging any female, even his sister, in his house ; it prohibited a clerk of an inferior order from accusing one of a superior ; it regulated the number of witnesses necessary for a sentence of judgment—for a bishop, seventy-two ; for a *cardinal priest* (presbyter in cardine constitutus) forty-two ; for a *diaconus cardinarius* constitutus urbis Romæ, twenty-six ; for a sub-deacon, acolyth, exorcist, lector, or door-keeper, seven. (This canon is taken from some Roman Council). Two others enforce the payment of tithes.

888. **METZ.** That no lay lord receive any portion of the tithes of his church, but that the priest who serves it have the whole ; that no priest have more than one church.

892. **VIENNE.** To protect the clergy against the violence and avarice of the lay-aristocracy.

895. **TRIBUR** *(near Mayence).* This Council was entirely composed of German bishops. It enacted, that the *wehrgeld,* paid for the death of a priest, be divided into three portions—one for the Church—another for his bishop—the third for his relatives. That it is a sacrilege deserving penance, to enter a church with a drawn sword. That nothing be paid for the place of sepulture. That no layman be buried in the churches. *Can.* 30. " In memory of the Apostle St. Peter, we honour the holy Apostolical See of Rome, in such manner, that that Church, Mother of the Sacerdotal Dignity, is to us the mistress of ecclesiastical law. Wherefore, with mildness let us preserve humility, and though a yoke scarcely tolerable should be imposed on us by that see, let us endure it in piety and devotion." The bishops then express their intention of sending, under certain circumstances, for instructions to Rome. There are likewise many regulations, more of a civil than ecclesiastical nature ; many Canons on forbidden marriages, and on penance.

Uncertain. **NANTES.** Let the priests know that tithes and offerings are the revenue of the poor and stranger, and that they are not given, but entrusted to them, as a deposit of which they will render account to God. Their distribution, according to the holy Canons, is to be after this fashion—one portion for the fabric ; a second for the poor ; a third for the parish priest ; and a fourth for the bishop. (*Can.* 10.) A strict inquiry is ordered into the moral and literary character of the candidate for ordination. A prohibition to women, especially nuns and widows, to appear and speak in public assemblies, without the permission of the bishop. An injunction to bishops and priests to abolish Pagan superstitions.

DATE   PLACE   OBJECT, ETC.

909. TROSLI (*near Soissons*). This Council complains of the condition of the monastic order ; that many monasteries have been destroyed by the Pagans ; that others are places of prostitution ; that others are the residences of lay-abbots, with their wives and children, soldiers and dogs, who cannot even *read* the Rule of their House. It further extends the obligation of tithe to all productions. "One will say, perhaps, I am no farmer—I have neither land nor flocks of which I can pay the tithe. Let every one know—be he soldier, merchant, or citizen, that the talent by which he makes his bread comes to him from God, and that he owes to God the tithe of it." It is to the non-payment of tithe, that the Council ascribes the devastations of the Pagans, and the infelicity of the seasons. (*Can.* 6.) The priest is directed to interrogate the congregation, before he performs the marriage ceremony, whether there be any just cause or impediment. (*Can.* 8.) The publicity of the marriage ceremony is frequently enjoined by early councils.

922. COBLENTZ. *Can.* 5. Si Laici capellas proprias habuerint, a ratione et auctoritate alienum habetur ut ipsi decimas accipiant—sed potius presbyteri ecclesiarum istas accipiant—et inde restaurationem ecclesiarum, et luminaria, et hospitum et pauperum receptionem exhibeant, ac pro sancta ecclesia et pro statu regni Dei misericordiam studiose implorent.

932. ERFURT. There is a Canon against any who may impose on themselves extraordinary fasts, without the permission of the bishop, or his *missus.*

952. AUGSBOURG. This Council was composed of French, Italian, and German bishops, and published some Canons of discipline, containing no new regulations, unless the following be one :—Episcopus, presbyter, diaconus, subdiaconus, ut multis conciliis firmatum est, ab uxoribus abstineant. *Cæteri* autem clerici, quando ad maturiorem ætatem pervenerint, licet nolentes ad continentiam cogantur. Almost all the other Councils held in this age (and there were above thirty held in France alone) concern private disputes, or other matters of no general importance to ecclesiastical history.

963. ROME. John XII. is deposed, and a successor appointed under the immediate authority of Otho the Great. Thence the controversy, whether Leo VIII., the Emperor's nominee, or Benedict V., subsequently chosen by the Romans, was the legitimate Pope. Otho afterwards held two or three other unimportant Councils at Rome and Ravenna.

971. LONDON. To decide the limits of regal and monastic privileges.

1016 (about). TICIN. Under Benedict VIII. It published some severe edicts against the marriage of the clergy.

1017. ORLEANS. Against a sect of heretics, usually accused of Mani-

DATE   PLACE   OBJECT, ETC.

cheism, existing at Orleans, as well as at Toulouse. Some were burnt. (*Labb. Concil.* tom. xix. p. 373).

1022. SALEGENSTADT. Held by the Archishop of Mayence. Two of its Canons (15 and 16) were directed *against pilgrimages or appeals* to Rome ; that no one should go to Rome without the permission of his bishop; that those on whom penance is imposed should not go to Rome to seek an indulgence. The expressions deserve to be cited :— Quia multi tanta mentis suæ falluntur stultitia, ut in aliquo capitali crimine inculpati pœnitentiam a sacerdotibus suis accipere nolint, in hoc maxime confisi, ut Romam euntibus Apostolicus omnia sibi dimittat peccata, sancto visum est concilio ut talis eis indulgentia non prosit, &c. That all slaves pay tithes, like other people.

1025. ARRAS (*Atrebatensis*). Against certain heretics who had come from the confines of Italy.

Some Councils are held in Gaul about this time, denouncing, in various ways, the marriage of the clergy—(*e. g.* that no one shall marry the daughter or widow of a clerk, &c.) And there were still some edicts issued against the worship of the sun, moon, fountains, &c., and witchcraft. Another object of their meeting was to obviate the civil anarchy prevalent, and its attendant evils. It was in 1041, that the *Treuga Dei*—the Truce of God—was generally established, by numerous Councils.

1051. RATISBON. Leo IX. suspended a deacon of Mayence, because he had not chaunted the service after the Roman manner. The Bishop of Mayence refused to administer the Sacrament unless the deacon were restored : the Pope yielded.

About the same time, Alfrick published some constitutions in England. He described the offices of the seven orders of clerks, (ostiary, reader, exorcist, sub-deacon, deacon, priest, bishop), and affirmed the two last, to be of equal rank, though the bishop's was the more honourable office. Haud pluris interest inter missalem presbyterum et episcopum, quam quod episcopus constitutus sit ad ordinationes conferendas et ad visitandum curandumque quæ ad Deum pertinent. Ambo si quidem unum tenent eundemque ordinem, quamvis dignior sit illa pars episcopi. It was the office of the acolyth to bear the candle, or lighted taper, during the reading of the Gospel, and the consecrating of the Lord's body in the Eucharist—" for the honour of Christ, who is our light." The sub-deacon is he who presents the holy vessels to the deacon, and ministers to him, with all humility, at the holy altar. The deacon is in the ministry of the presbyter; he places the oblations on the altar, and reads the Gospel. He may also baptize, and exhibit the Lord's Supper to the people. Presbyter est sacerdos missalis, aut senior—non a senectute, sed quia senili gaudet prudentia. Illius est corpus Domini in sacramento consecrare, &c. (*Labb. Concil.* tom. xix. p. 699.) The priest

DATE   PLACE   OBJECT, ETC.

was to explain the meaning of the Gospel, Lord's Prayer, and Creed, to the people—and it seems that the *vulgar tongue* was then used—on Sundays and holidays. (*Semler.* Secul. xi. c. ii.)

1059. ROME. The Council of Nicholas II. for the regulation of papal elections. (See Chap. XVI.)

1063. ROME. Let no one hear mass from a priest, whom he knows to have a concubine. That no *layman* be admitted to communion, who has at the same time a wife and a concubine. There are likewise some statutes against Simony.

Councils are held (under papal authority) in Spain, for the introduction of the Roman Liturgy, in the place of the Gothic, or Mosarabic.

1074. ROME. Gregory VII. holds his first Council, for the prevention of Simony, the celibacy of the clergy, and the extension of papal power. By one Canon it was enacted, that the parochial clergy were bound to obey the Pope, in preference to their own bishop. In *Capit.* 2. Gregory acknowledges the authority of *four* Councils, as of four Gospels—Nice, Constantinople, (I.) Ephesus and Chalcedon. In *Cap.* 3, the Council says—Decreta vero SS. Roman. Pontificum, si possemus, etiam studiosius quam illa quattuor concilia venerari et observare debemus, &c. .. And in *Cap.* 4, it proceeds to determine what authority attaches to the other Councils. In *Statut.* 23, the following passage of Pope Gelasius is cited :—Cuncta per mundum novit ecclesia quod SS. Rom. ecclesia de omni ecclesia fas habeat judicare ; nec cuiquam de ejus liceat judicare judicio ; siquidem ad illam de qualibet mundi parte appellandum est, ab illa autem nemini appellare licitum. And then *Statut.* 24. Et hoc declaratur, quod cujusvis episcopi parochianus *potius Domino apostolico quam proprio episcopo* obedire debet. ... Attendat sane cujus vis episcopi subditus ne vel proprio episcopo contra apostolica præcepta obediat in aliquo, &c. Gregory ends his decree against the incontinency of the clergy, by declaring, that all who shall attend the ministry of an incontinent priest, are guilty of idolatry—Samuele teste, et Beato Gregorio instruente ! *Peccatum ariolandi est non obedientia, et scelus idololatriæ nolle acquiescere.* Peccatum igitur Paganitatis incurrit quisquis, dum Christianum se asserit, sedi apostolicæ obedire contemnit.

In the 5th Roman Council of Gregory (held 1078), is the following decree against lay investures :—Quoniam investituras ecclesiarum contra statuta sanctorum patrum a laicis personis in multis partibus cognovimus fieri, et ex ea plurimas perturbationes in ecclesia oriri. ... decernimus ut nullus clericorum investituram episcopatus, vel abbatiæ, vel ecelesiæ de manu imperatoris, vel regis, vel alicujus laicæ personæ, viri vel fœminæ, suscipiat.

Several Councils followed, especially in Germany, (at Poitou,

Utrecht, Mayence, Brixen, Worms, and Erfurt,) in opposition to the edicts, and legitimacy of Gregory. At the first of these (See *Semler*, Sec. xi. *De Conciliis*,) the bishops at once asserted, that they would not and could not abandon a custom (that of matrimony) which they had enjoyed from ancient times, under all preceding bishops. And this appears, in despite of Canons, to have been the truth.

Gregory held several (ten) other Councils at Rome for the improvement of ecclesiastical discipline, the advancement of letters, and of the interests of the See. The acknowledgment of lay investiture was about this time designated the *Simoniacal heresy*, and the marriage of the clergy the *Nicolaitan heresy*. Those which were held on the heresy of Berenger, both by Gregory and before his time, are mentioned in Chap. xvi. sec. 3.

1095 PLACENTIA. Several Canons against Simony. The 14th ordains the observance of four general fasts (more solito), at Lent, Whitsuntide, in September, and December.

1095. CLERMONT. It set on foot the first Crusade. *Can.* 2. Quicunque pro sola devotione, non pro honoris vel pecuniæ adeptione, ad liberandam ecclesiam Dei Jerusalem profectus fuerit, iter illud *pro omni pœnitentia* reputetur. *Can.* 12. Ut nulli clericorum liceat in duabus civitatibus duas præbendas obtinere. *Can.* 14. Ut nullus in una ecclesia geminos honores habeat. *Can.* 17. Ne episcopus vel sacerdos regi vel alicui laico in manibus ligiam fidelitatem faciat. *Can.* 19. Ne laici decimam partem de laboribus suis retineant; et sicut nec debent retinere, ita nec accipere. *Can.* 28. Ne quis communicet de altari, nisi *corpus separatim* et *sanguinem similiter* sumat, nisi per necessitatem et cautelam—that no one communicate at the altar who does not take the body and the blood separately, unless it be through necessity or caution.

1100. POITOU. Regular clerks may perform the ecclesiastical offices *jussu episcopi*. But no monk may presume to perform the parochial office of the presbyter.

1102—1108. LONDON. Against the letting out of archdeaconries and churches to the highest bidder, and other matters of ecclesiastical discipline. The celibacy of the clergy and the question of investitures were treated in these and other Councils, under the authority of Anselm, according to the principle of the Roman See. One Canon of the Council of 1102, prohibits monasteries from giving a scanty salary to the presbyters, who minister in their churches, and appropriating the revenue themselves.

1110. COLOGNE. In this, a provincial Council, the founder of a monastery, named Guibertus, was *canonized*. (This rite had not yet been appropriated by the Pope. When Alexander III., some sixty years afterwards, canonized Edward the Confessor, he used these expressions: negotium canonizationis arduum et sublime non frequenter nisi in solemnibus conciliis de more, concedi .... tamen juxta votum et desiderium regis .. *corpus* ipsius confessoris ita glorificandum censuimus, et debitis præconiis *adorandum* in terris, sicut eum Dominus glorificavit in cœlis . . . ut ipsius *intercessionibus* apud districtum, judicem mereamin veniam obtinere. (*Semler*, secul. xii. cap. 3.) See Vol. III., p. 267.

1112. ROME. *Lateran.* To cancel the compulsory treaty made by Pascal with Henry.

1119. TOULOUSE. *Can.* 3. We condemn as heretics those who, under pretext of religion, reject the sacrament of the body and blood, infant baptism, the priesthood and other ecclesiastical orders, and lawful marriage: et per *potestates exteras* coerceri præcipimus.

1122. WORMS. A Concordat was passed for the final settlement of the question of investitures.

1123. ROME. *Lateran I. Gen.* This was the first General Council of the Latin Church. It confirmed the Concordat of Worms. (See Chap. XVII. p. 112.) *Can.* 11 takes under the protection of St. Peter, the houses, families, and property of all crusaders. *Can.* 16 prescribes that no one molest pilgrims to Rome (Romipetæ) on their journey to the Apostolical City. *Can.* 17 prohibits Abbots and monks from imposing public penance. *Can.* 19. Servitium quod monasteria aut eorum ecclesiæ a tempore Gregorii Papæ VII. usque ad hoc tempus episcopis fecere et nos concedimus. *Can.* 21. Presbyteris, diaconibus, subdiaconibus, et monachis concubinas habere, seu matrimonia contrahere penitus interdicimus: contracta quoque matrimonia ab hujusmodi personis disjungi et personas ad pœnitentium debere redigi . . . . judicamus.

1128. TROYES. A Rule is given to the Templars—nine years after the institution of the order—Divina Providentia sumpsit exordium hoc novum genus religionis, ut religioni militiam admisceretis, et sic religio per militiam armata procedat—therefore, it allowed them fixed property, lands, serfs, &c.

1131. RHEIMS. Monks and canons regular are prohibited from the practice of law and medicine. It is called a prava et detestabilis consuetudo. *Can.* 9. Placuit etiam ne conductitiis presbyteris ecclesiæ committantur, et unaquæque ecclesia, cui facultas suppetit, habeat sacerdotem. *Can.* 10. Præcipimus etiam, ut presbyteri, clerici, monachi, et mercatores, rustici euntes et redeuntes, et in agricultura persistentes, et animalia cum quibus arant, et oves, omni tempore sint securi. The 11th regulates the *Treuga Dei;* and the 12th prohibits tournaments—detestabiles illas Nundinas vel Ferias, in quibus milites ex condicto convenire solent, ad ostentationem virium suarum et audaciæ, unde mortes hominum et animarum pericula sæpe proveniunt &c. . . and refuses ecclesiastical sepulture to the slain. *Can.* 14. extends the right of asylum to cemeteries.

DATE   PLACE   OBJECT, ETC.

1134. PISA. Its deliberations were conducted by St. Bernard, who was Pope's legate in Italy. It renewed some former Canons.

1139. ROME. *Lateran II. Gen.* Under Innocent II. for the extirpation of heresy, and the general reformation of the Church. It condemned Arnold of Brescia, and caused his exile from Italy. Its 32 Canons repeat a number of former enactments against Simony, the incontinence of the clergy, usury, uncanonical marriages, the accepting benefices from lay patronage, &c. The following Canon (the twentieth) we have not observed to have been published before : Sanè *regibus* et principibus *facultatem faciendæ justitiæ*, consultis archiepiscopis et episcopis, *non negamus.*

1146. COLOGNE. Against some heretics, who thought themselves to be the true Church, as following the spirituality and poverty and wandering life of Christ : they baptized with fire and the spirit, as well as water. Of these men all retracted except two—their bishop and another—and these were seized by the people and burnt—nobis sedentibus (says the narrator) et invitis ; et *quod magis mirabile est*, ipsi tormentum ignis non solum cum patientia, sed et cum lætitia introierunt et pertulerunt. Several other heretics are related to have suffered the same fate under the Bishop of Cologne in 1163. (*Semler*, Secul. xii. cap. iii.)

1163. TOURS. *Can.* 4 is very severe against the damnable and very general heresy of the Albigenses prevalent at Toulouse, which had diffused itself through Gascony and other provinces—it enacts, that there be no commerce with those heretics in buying or selling—that having lost the solace of humanity, they may learn to recover from their error. *Can.* 5. Quoniam enormis quædam consuetudo in quibusdam locis contra sanctorum patrum constitutiones invaluit, ut sub annuo pretio sacerdotes ad ecclesiarum regimen constituantur—id ne fiat modis omnibus prohibemus. Quia dum sacerdotium sub hujusmodi mercede venale disponitur, ad æternæ retributionis præmium consideratio non habetur. *Can.* 10 endeavours, at great length, to protect ecclesiastical property from lay invasion.

1164. CLARENDON. (See below.)

1175. LONDON. Against many who refused to pay tithes—a variety of objects, of which the tithe is due, is specified. That the Eucharist be only consecrated in a golden or silver cup.

1179. ROME. *Lateran III. G.* Under Alexander III. (See Chap. XVII. p. 118.) The first Canons regulate the election of the Pope. In limiting the expenses of visitations and the pomp of the hierarchy, we observe that archbishops are allowed a suite (evectionis numerum) of 40 or 50 persons ; cardinals only of 25 ; bishops of 20 or 30 ; archdeacons of 5 or 7 ; deans, who are placed under them, of 2. The prohibition of tournaments was in imitation of the humane edicts of Innocent II. and Eugenius III. *Can.* 13 and 14 prohibit pluralities, and exact residence in the strongest terms. *Can.* 18. Quoniam ecclesia Dei . . . . indigentibus, sicut pia mater, providere tenetur, ne pauperibus, qui parentum opibus juvari non possunt, legendi et proficiendi opportunitas subtrahatur, per unamquamque ecclesiam cathedralem magistro, qui clericus ejusdem ecclesiæ et *scholares pauperes gratis* doceat, competens aliquod beneficium assignetur. The rest of the Canon is levelled against those who have oppressed such masters by arbitrary exactions. *Can.* 23 confines lepers to a separate church and cemetery. The *last* is the celebrated Canon against heretics—in which the secular man is invoked (on the authority of St. Leo), and also a crusade proclaimed as follows :—nos autem, de misericordia Dei et beatorum App. Petri et Pauli auctoritate confisi, fidelibus christianis, qui contra eos arma susceperint . . . ad eos decertando expugnandos, biennium de pœnitentia injuncta relaxamus. They are likewise placed, in some other respects, on a footing with the crusaders. A multitude of other enactments follow in the form of an appendix. (*Labb. Concil.* tom. xxi. p. 209.)

1209 PARIS. In condemnation of Aristotle. See Vol. II., p. 371.

1212. PARIS. There are no important edicts, except one against the monstrous abuse of masses then prevalent—their sale for immediate payment or legacy, and the bargains and exactions which they occasioned. There are 27 statutes for the regulation of monastic discipline.

1215. ROME. *Lateran IV. Gen. Can.* 11 confirms that of Lateran III., and adds, that in every cathedral or *other important* church, there be a master to teach grammar to the clergy and the poor; and in every metropolitan church, a professor of theology (theologus) besides. *Can.* 10 establishes preachers, to be chosen by the bishop, and sent out into his diocese. These men the bishops are to consider as " coadjutors and co-operators," not only in preaching, but in hearing confessions, imposing penance, and all else pertaining to the cure of souls. *Can.* 13 prohibits the foundation of new orders. *Can.* 21, on penance, strictly enjoins secrecy to the confessor. *Can.* 29. after admitting that little or no fruit has been derived from the *repeated statutes against pluralities*, proceeds to enact, that whoever shall accept a benefice, with cure of souls, vacates any that he may already possess. It adds, that none may hold more dignities than one in the same church, even without cure of souls. Circa *sublimes* tamen et litteratas *personas*, quæ majoribus sunt beneficiis honorandæ, cum ratio postulaverit, per *Sedem Apostolicam* poterit dispensari. *Can.* 32 repeats former enactments against patrons of churches, who appropriate the revenues and appoint a minister to perform the duties at a miserable salary. *Can.* 43. That a clerk, holding no temporalities from a layman, be not bound to do any homage to him. *Can.* 46. That no taxes to be imposed on clerks, except by ecclesiastical authority. *Can.* 54. *That tithes be paid before rent.* *Can.* 60. To

DATE   PLACE   OBJECT, ETC.

abbots from usurping any episcopal prerogative. *Can.* 62. Against the adoption of new relics.

1229. TOULOUSE. For the inquisition of heresy. (See Vol. II. p. 190, where the most important enactments are mentioned.) Besides, *Can.* 12 obliges all persons, male and female, to be registered; and to swear, the males at fourteen, the females at twelve years of age, that they reject every heresy against the Holy Catholic Roman Church; that they will preserve the faith which the Roman Church preaches, and will persecute heretics with all their strength, and faithfully denounce them. The oath to be renewed every two years. He who does not take it to be held *suspectus de hæresi*. *Can.* 13. That those who do not confess and communicate twice a-year be held suspected of heresy. *Can.* 14. Prohibemus etiam *ne libros* Veteris *Testamenti* aut Novi *Laici permittentur habere :* nisi forte Psalterium, vel breviarium pro divinis officiis, aut horas Beatæ Mariæ aliquis ex devotione habere velit. Sed *ne præmissos libros habeant in vulgari translatos* arctissime inhibemus. *Can.* 15. Those suspected of heresy are not permitted to act as physicians, or to approach the sick : neither (*Can.* 17) to hold any office, public or private. The other canons, for the most part, respect civil matters. (It is a singular error that Semler places this Council at 1129.) Several Councils were frequently held in various places to further the objects of this.

1231 and 1233. TREVES, MAYENCE, FRANCFORT. On the subject of the chastisement of heresy.

The *first* of these complains that there were three schools and many sects of heretics ; that there were many instructed in holy Scripture, of which they possessed a German translation ; that they did not believe in the *body* of the Lord ; and rejected confirmation, unction, prayers for the dead, the Pope, the clergy, and the monastic system (religionem), &c.

It appears from the acts of the *second*, that many heretics suffered by fire in Germany at that time, and many unjustly. The law was, that the accusation was assumed to be true ; and that, therefore, the accused had only the alternative—to confess and live—or to assert his innocence and be burnt. These accusations gradually reached the higher classes, and then it was thought expedient to examine the principle.

At that of Francfort, the Emperor Henry reproved the intemperate zeal of Conrad, formerly professor at Paris, a Dominican, who had preached a crusade against the Albigenses. (*Semler*, Secul. viii. cap. ii.)

1234. ARLES. *Can.* 11. If any one be discovered to be a heretic, after his death, that his body or bones be dug up and subjected to the secular tribunal.

DATE   PLACE   OBJECT, ETC.

1245. **LYONS.** *I. Gen.* Held by Innocent IV., for the deposition of Frederic. It published 17 Canons, which, for the most part, concern the administration of justice. The four last exhort the faithful to the "liberation" of Constantinople and the Holy Land, and to taking measures of defence against the expected invasion of the Tartars.

1260. **ARLES.** *Can.* 4. That those laymen who have presumed to join their sons and daughters in marriage, without the authority of the Church, be excommunicated. (Canons to this effect are very frequently repeated.) *Can.* 5. Since most of the churches in this province belong to monasteries or convents, which have now ceased to maintain any resident minister there, that henceforward there be at least a perpetual vicar, sufficiently paid, resident in every parish, presented by the patron, and instituted by the bishop.

1261. **MAYENCE.** Against quæstuarii prædicatores, and vagabond clergy whose life was a scandal to the laity. Prayers were ordered against the approaching invasion of the Tartars: and indulgences for ten days. The avarice of the monks was especially denounced, who were not contented with the stream of wealth which they had swallowed, ut si in os eorum totus Jordanus influat; and that henceforward no churches should be conferred on any monastic establishment whatsoever. There are many other expressions indicating the abuses prevalent in the ecclesiastical system.

    The hasty and intemperate use of excommunication is commonly prohibited by the Councils of this age. *Can.* 11. Ne quis excommunicationis sententiam in aliquem nisi competenti admonitione præmissa et præsentibus idoneis personis, per quas, si necesse fuerit, possit approbari ammonitio. The Council likewise severely condemns any priests who shall usurp this strictly episcopal privilege—immemores quod episcopis et prælatis clavium sit collata potestas. In the same manner we find numerous complaints against contumacious persons who disregarded the sentence, and refused to perform the penance necessary to reconcile them to the Church. The 37th and 38th Canons of the Council of Cologne (held 1266) invoke the secular arm to enforce the execution of the sentence. There are fifty-four Canons, which begin with excommunicating all heretics, &c.

1274. **LYONS.** *II. Gen.* See Vol. II. p. 298. Besides the particulars mentioned in the text, it was enacted in the same Canon (2), that the cardinals present at the death of the Pope were to proceed to election, on the spot, within ten days from his death, whether the other cardinals should have joined them or not. *Can.* 23 does not, in fact, permit the office of preaching, hearing confession, or sepulture, to any order of mendicants, except the Dominicans and Franciscans—quos evidens ex iis utilitas Ecclesiæ Universali proveniens perhibet approbatos.

1279.   MONASTERIENSE. (*Westphalia.*) Chiefly to add sanctity to the offices of the Church and the sacraments of the eucharist and confession. *Can.* 12. Si evomuerit, partes colligantur; contritæ cum vino ab aliquo fideli sumantur, residuum coimburatur et ponatur in terra juxta altare. Sacerdotes ne respiciant vultum confitentis, maximè mulieris. Distinctè mortalia peccata confitenda quemadmodum notatur in hoc versu—*quis, quid, ubi, cum quo, quoties, cur, quomodo, quando.* Venialia sufficit generaliter confiteri. *Can.* 15.

1281.   COLOGNE. This Council had the same object as the preceding, and repeated many of its expressions. Among its regulations it is enacted, that infants, in danger, be baptized before their birth, if any part of them be visible. Si prægnans moriatur, teneatur os ejus apertum, et uterus ejus æperiatur; si vivus sit infans educatur et baptizetur—si mortuus, tumuletur extra cœmeterium. Et ista forma et modus frequentius parochianis imprimatur, &c. &c.

In the Canons of other Councils of this age there is enough to show that the marriage or concubinage of the clergy, howsoever prohibited, was still very common in practice: *e. g.* Ne sacerdotes secum habeant prolem, quem in ordinibus genuerint, ob scandalum. Si quis presbyter de suis filiis et filiabus solemnes nuptias presumpterit celebrare suspendatur. One Council (in Germany) expressly prescribes to the rulers and presbyters, that the Lord's Prayer, and the Creed, be intelligibly expounded to the people *in the vulgar tongue* every Sunday; and the Ten Commandments once a month, or at least three or four times a year. Five of the sacraments are *necessary*, and without them no man can be saved. The other two (Orders and Matrimony) *voluntary*. A Council at Avignon (1282) commands the restoration of "an ancient and salutary practice"— that no one make his will without the aid of his parish priest.

The *Missi*, or Commissioners, mentioned in some of the above Canons, were nobles, spiritual or temporal, sent about the provinces by ancient Christian kings, for various public purposes. The practice seems to have originated with Clovis, or about his time. The Missi were of three descriptions,—(1) directed the administration of justice—(2) the advancement of public discipline—(3) the regulation of certain matters of finance. The *first* (called in England, barons-errant, or itinerant justices) had cognizance of ecclesiastical as well as civil affairs; of the causes of clerks; patrons and patronage; the repairs of churches; the complaints of bishops against clerks, and of clerks against bishops; and various offences of the clergy. The authority of the *second* extended to the morals and canonical discipline of clerks; to the internal condition of monasteries and convents; and to all the details of monastic observances, even to the food and clothing. They were present at the principal councils, and at the elections of bishops, and they had the care of public education—besides various sorts of civil superintendence, as of roads,

DATE   PLACE   OBJECT, ETC.

bridges, ships, meadows, woods, and the currency. The *third* looked
after the *beneficia* and *regalia* of churches, bishops, abbots, &c. . . .
Besides these, who were the Missi Dominici, or King's Commissioners, we read of Missi Apostolici, Missi Ecclesiæ, Missi Episcopi,
—ecclesiastical Commissioners. For all bishops and abbots had
Missi (laymen)—called Advocates or Vice-masters—by whose means
they exercised much of their temporal jurisdiction. This subject is
treated at great length at the end of vol. xxvii. *Labb. Concil.*

II. ENGLAND.

The Church of England presents itself to the attention of the ecclesiastical
historian much less frequently than those of the East, of France and Germany,
and is less prominent as a member of the general system. Not that it was
slow to submit to the spiritual authority of Rome, or to follow the changes
in her character and her fortunes—but, partly, because it was farther
removed from the influence of pontifical intrigue—partly, because a succession of vigorous monarchs exercised so strong a control over ecclesiastical
matters, as to involve them very closely in the civil politics of the nation.
Thus it is that there are only a few great occasions—such as the affair of
Thomas à Becket, the humiliation of King John, and others—on which the
mention of England is forced upon the annalist of the Church of Rome. We
have, therefore, thought it expedient, in this place, to separate for the most
part the Councils held in Britain from those of the Continent, and to present
an undivided, though, of course, a very imperfect, view of their objects and
regulations, and of the history of the Church, as it is reflected from them.

668. HERTFORD. *Theodore*, a native, like St. Paul, of Tarsus, in Cilicia, was
       raised to the See of Canterbury, on the recommendation, rather than
       by the authority, of the Pope. He succeeded in establishing an unifor-
       mity on two points, on which there had hitherto been differences—the
       time of the celebration of Easter, and the form of the tonsure admi-
       nistered to clerks. His Council published nine other regulations.
       Of these, the *first, third,* and *fourth,* respectively ordained—that no
       bishop should quit his own diocese; no monk his monastery ; no
       priest the diocese in which he was ordained. The *second* provided,
       that no bishop should, in any way, molest such monasteries as were
       consecrated to God, nor violently take from them aught that was
       theirs. The *sixth,* that a Synod be assembled once a year, on
       August 1, at a place called Clovesho (probably Cloveshaw, Cliff'sho,
       or Cliff, near Gravesend). The *eighth,* that the number of bishops
       be increased, owing to the daily increase of converts.
            This is commonly considered the first Council of the English
       nation.

735. CLOVESHO. Held under *Cuthbert*, Archbishop of Canterbury, at the
       instance of Boniface, Archbishop of Mayence. It published thirty-

one Canons, of which the greater part resembled those published by the French and Spanish Councils of the same period. One of them commanded all priests to be acquainted with, and teach the people, the Creed, the Lord's Prayer, and the words of consecration in the Mass, in the English tongue. Another enjoined, that prayers be publicly offered for kings and princes.

Egbert, Archbishop of York, published his " Canons for the Remedie of Sin," about ten years afterwards.

803. CLOVESHO. The Archiepiscopal See is fixed at Canterbury (whence it had been removed to Lichfield), under the authority of Leo IV. This Council was attended by 13 bishops, 26 abbots, 39 presbyters, and 4 deacons.

816. CALICHYTH. Held under Wolfred, Archbishop of Canterbury. It was decreed, among other matters, that new churches be consecrated with holy water by the bishops, and the *saint*, to whom the church is dedicated, somewhere *painted* therein; that abbots and abbesses be appointed by the bishop, with the consent of the monastery or convent; that no Scotsmen baptize, or administer the eucharist, in England—it being uncertain whether, or by whom, they may have been ordained; that water be not poured on the heads of infants, but that they be immersed in the font, in imitation of Christ.

848 or 855. WINCHESTER. Held under Ethelwolf, King of the West Saxons. It was on this occasion that the kingdom was first formally subjected to the payment of tithes.

974 and 977. WINCHESTER, KIRKLINGTON, CALNE. This was the period of the reformation of the discipline of the Church, by King Edgar—especially in respect to the celibacy of the clergy; and of the restoration of the monastic order, through the exertions of *Dunstan;* the Danish invasion had caused the destruction of many monasteries, the occupation of others by the secular priesthood, and a general relaxation of discipline. These Councils legislated for the remedy of those evils.

Edward the Confessor (about 1060) published some statutes—one of which exacted the tithe of sheep, pigs, bees, and the like; and another ordered Peter's-pence, or Romescot, to be faithfully paid to the Pope.

Fuller mentions some points on which the doctrine of the church was still uncorrupted at the Norman conquest—(1) the books of holy scripture were still open to the people; (2) the prayers offered for the dead were commemorative only, not yet propitiatory; (3) " Purgatory, though newly hatched, was not yet fledged;" (4) the communion was administered under both kinds.

1102. WESTMINSTER. Summoned by Anselm. William II. had usurped the revenues of sees during their vacancy, which he prolonged for that purpose, and frequently sold those to which he did at length appoint. Hence the exertions of Anselm, in co-operation with the Pope. At this Council the chief lay-lords were present, at Anselm's request. It published 29 Canons, the principal of which were levelled against simony, and the marriage of the clergy; others were borrowed from former Continental Councils. *Can.* vii. provided, that none be admitted to the order of sub-deacon, or any higher order, without the profession of chastity. *Can.* xiv. That tithe be paid to none, except the churches. *Can.* xviii. That abbots may not invest with the order of knighthood. *Can.* xix.-xxi. That monks do not enjoin penance, without permission of their abbot; neither take any lands in farm. *Can.* xxviii. That none presume, hereafter, to sell men, like brute beasts. This humane attempt at civil legislation did not meet, of course, with very successful acceptance from the laity.

Four years afterwards, the investiture dispute between the Pope and Henry I. was brought, still under the primacy of Anselm, to very nearly the same conclusion with that which was afterwards agreed on at Worms between Calixtus and the Emperor.

1138. WESTMINSTER. Under the legate of Innocent II. Many of the Canons, usual in that age, were here enacted—that none shall accept a benefice from a layman, and such like. It was provided, besides, —that priests do no bodily labour; that the host remain only eight days in the box, for fear of corruption.

1139. WINCHESTER. Held under the Bishop of Winchester, who was Pope's legate, and brother of King Stephen. The Council summoned the King into its presence. Its object was to oblige him to restore certain castles which he had taken away from some of the bishops. One of his pleas was, that bishops could not canonically possess castles. William of Malmsbury was present at this Council.

1164. CLARENDON. The rivalry of the lay and ecclesiastical tribunals had now risen to a great height; and the spiritual, through their superiority in talents and learning, had gained the ascendency. These claimed, of course, the exclusive right of judging clerks—a term including all who had taken the tonsure—and exercised it with too great leniency towards clerical transgressors. Henry II. determined to destroy, or, at least, to diminish this prerogative, and with this view convoked the Council of Clarendon, under the pretext of restoring the ancient usage in this, as well as in some other matters. On this occasion, it was enacted—that all vacant dignities, whether sees, abbeys, or priories, of royal foundation, be left in the King's hands, and their revenues paid to the King; that when it is his pleasure to provide for the vacancy, a new election be made, in consequence of his writ, by the chief clergy of the church, assembled in the King's chapel, with the assent of the King, and the advice of such prelates as the King may call to his assistance; that almost every suit, civil or criminal, in which each or either of the parties was a clerk, should commence before the King's justice, who should decide whether the cause ought to be tried in the secular, or in the bishop's courts, and that, in the *latter*, the defendant, if convicted in a criminal action, should lose his benefit of clergy; that all causes, not ecclesiastical, be finally determined in the King's courts; that all clerks tenants-in-chief of the crown follow the King's custom, and sue or be sued as to their fiefs in his courts, like other barons; that no tenant-in-chief of the King, or officer of his household, be excommunicated, or his lands laid under interdict, without application to the King, or grand justiciary; that no dignitary go beyond the sea without the King's permission; that no ecclesiastical appeals proceed beyond the archbishop's court, without the King's consent.

Thomas à Becket revoked the consent which he had given at Clarendon to these Constitutions; and hence arose the dispute, which ended in his murder.

1176. WESTMINSTER. A Pope's Legate held a Council to decide the disputed claims to precedency between the Sees of Canterbury and York.

The dispute between King John and Innocent IV., in the beginning of the following age, involved the question, whether the monks of Christchurch should appoint to the See of Canterbury, on ancient prescription antecedent to the Norman conquest,—or the King, with the advice of the prelates, according to more modern usage. Innocent decided in favour of the monks; but, in this instance, made the appointment himself.

In 1215, John conceded to the clergy perfect freedom of election of bishops and other dignitaries; and this concession was confirmed by the first article of Magna Charta.

1222 OXFORD. Archbishop Langton published a code of discipline of 42 Canons.

1279-1285. WESTMINSTER. In these (Parliaments rather than) Councils, Edward published the Statute of Mortmain, and endeavoured to fix the limits between the spiritual and temporal jurisdictions.

1343. ———— The Statute of Provisors. There had been complaints, for the last ninety years, of the Pope's *Provisions*, which filled the sees with foreign bishops, many of whom never resided, and so drained the kingdom of their revenues; and Edward I. had made some attempts to check the abuse: but in the time of Edward III. the Pope had extended his provisions to the inferior benefices, and so increased the disorder. This led to the Statute of Provisors, prohibiting any person to bring into the realm, receive, or execute provisions, reservations, or letters of any other description, contrary to the rights of the King, or his subjects.

In 1351, a new Statute provided—that ecclesiastical elections should be free, and the rights of patrons preserved; and if the Pope, by provision or reservation, should disturb such rights, the collation should, in certain cases, fall to the King; and, again, in 1353 and 1364, other Statutes passed, to the same effect, with certain additions and extensions.

1393. ———— The Statute of Præmunire provided—that if any one pursue or obtain in the Court of Rome, or elsewhere, translations, excommunications, bulls, instruments, or other things against the King's crown or regality, for appointment to benefices, or the translation of bishops out of the country, or bring such things into the realm, or notify, or execute them, &c.—such persons, their notaries, procurators, &c., shall be out of the King's protection, their goods, chattels, lands, &c., forfeited,. and their persons attached wherever they may be found.

Immediately, Pope Martin published his Bull—*Quamvis dudum in regno Angliæ Jurisdictio R. Ecclesiæ et libertas ecclesiastica fuerit oppressa, vigore illius execrabilis statuti quod omni divinæ et humanæ rationi contrarium est*; tamen adhuc non fuit ad tantam violentiam prolapsum, ut in Sedis Apostolicæ Nuncios et Legatos manus temere mitterentur, sicut novissime factum est, &c. . . . The remainder of the Bull is feeble and querulous, indicating the consciousness of a weak, if not of a bad, cause.

A sort of compromise followed between the Pope and the King (Richard II.), by which provisions in favour of aliens, unless cardinals, were wholly abolished; and those in favour of natives generally granted to persons who had previously obtained the royal license.

1399 ———— The Statute De Hæretico comburendo consigned the contumacious heretic to be burnt to death by the civil authorities.

III. SPAIN.

At the end of the Eighth Volume of Labbe's Councils is collected " An Index of the Holy Canons by which the Church, especially the Church of Spain, was governed, from the beginning of the sixth to that of the eighth age." It is divided into ten books, each of which is subdivided into a number of heads or *tituli*. The Canons were for the most part enacted by the Councils of Africa and Spain; and though the greater part of them was equally acknowledged by the rest of the Christian world, and several have been already cited in the preceding pages, yet it may be worth while to present to the reader some of the most important among them, according to the arrangement adopted in the document from which we extract them,

Book I. On the Institutions of Clerks. Tit. 1 and 2. Disqualifications for the ministry : to be in any respect maimed ; to be ignorant of letters ; to be the husband of an adulteress ; of a widow ; of a woman divorced, or of a different sect ; to be guilty of incontinency ; to have been twice married ; to have done penance (ex pœnitentibus ordinatus clericus deponatur. *Carthag. IV. Tit.* 68 *et alibi.*) Freedmen, whose patrons are laymen, may not be promoted to the ministry ; no slave may be ordained, without the consent of his master ; nor causidici, curiales, sæculari militiæ dediti ; nor any one who has been guilty of a mortal sin ; neither persons who have been very lately baptized ; nor energumeni, or men possessed of devils. *Tit.* 4. The sons of clerks may not go to plays ; nor intermarry with gentiles, heretics, or schismatics ; nor reside among heretics. *Tit.* 5. Clerks may bequeath nothing to unbelievers, however near akin they may be. *Tit.* 8. That if there be any clerks slaves, the bishop ought to give them their freedom. *Tit.* 9. That clerks, how learned soever, ought to seek their bread by manual industry (artificiolo) ; and that the stipends of clerks should be distributed according to their merits. *Tit.* 10. That every clerk be ordained to some cure ; and that he remain where he has been ordained (ubi quis ordinatur, ibi permaneat). *Tit.* 11. That clerks be not ordained without the testimony and concurrence of the clergy and people (civium). *Tit.* 12 concerns those whose parents have engaged them from their infancy in the office of the ministry (in clericatus officio manciparunt) ; and enacts besides—that, if there be any want of clerks, they be chosen from among the monks. *Tit.* 13, *et seq.* : clerici non comam nutriant, nec barbam radant ; Junior seniori non præponatur ; that clerks do not frequent the streets and public assemblies ; nor attend the markets or forum without necessity ; nor enter taverns ; nor exact usury ; nor undertake secular farms ; nor be stewards or agents. (We should observe that, while the whole of this discipline was binding upon the three orders of the priesthood, a great part of it extended to subdeacons, acolyths, exorcists and readers, if not to ostiarii et psalmistæ.) *Tit.* 28. That clerks be not made in the presence of the catechumens. *Tit.* 29. That persons baptized in sickness be not ordained presbyters, nisi fide et caritate cogente. *Tit.* 30. It is not within the office of a presbyter to give the benediction ; to impose penance ; to make the chrism (conficere chrisma) ; to consecrate churches or altars ; to give the veil ; to reconcile penitents ; nor, of course, to ordain. *Tit.* 31. The age of ordination for a deacon is fixed at twenty-five ; for a presbyter or bishop, at thirty. *Tit.* 36. That monks or laymen be not made bishops till they have passed through the inferior grades of the ministry. *Tit.* 39, *et seq.* That no one be ordained bishop, except by the metropolitan, and in the presence of three other bishops, and with the consent of all the absent bishops of the province. *Tit.* 48. That a bishop protect the poor and infirm ; that he exercise the control over widows and wards, not in person, but by agents ; and do not undertake the execution of wills. *Tit.* 58. That no clerk leave his own bishop, and pass over to another ; nor serve two churches.

Book II. On the Institutions of the Monks. This Book contains little of importance, which has not already been mentioned ; and nothing, as far as we can observe, peculiar to the Church of Spain. It is remarkable that (Tit. 4) two Councils (of Carthage) fix the earliest age for taking the veil at twenty-five; two others (held in France) at forty.

Book III. De Institutionibus Judiciorum, &c. It contains the often repeated provisions: that Councils be assembled twice a-year; that they be convoked by the metropolitan; that every bishop attend, on pain of excommunication; or send a substitute; that certain presbyters, and some of the laity be likewise summoned to attend. *Tit.* 39 respects the freedmen of the Church; they were still bound by professions of obedience to the Church; their children were not allowed to leave the precincts, even for their food, and were subject to subordination and discipline; they were not permitted to alienate their property under any other lordship.

Book IV. On the Institutions of the Offices, &c. Tit. 5. That the faith of the three hundred and ten fathers, and of the eight Councils, be observed. *Tit. 7. Ne picturæ in ecclesia fiant.* De basilicis, quæ sine Martyrum reliquiis dedicatæ sunt, ut destruantur. *Tit.* 11. That those who come to Church without taking the sacrament be excommunicated. *Tit.* 18. That those who deliberately fast on the Lord's Day be not held Catholic. (*Carthag. IV. Tit.* 64.) That every Saturday be observed as a fast. (Ut omni sabbato jejunetur. *ibid. Tit.* 26.) *Tit.* 21. Catechumens may hear the gospel; but not approach the baptistery; nor receive the benediction with the faithful. *Tit.* 26. That baptism be only conferred at Easter and Christmas Day, (other Canons say Easter and Whitsunday,) except in case of sickness. *Tit.* 35. Those who have been baptized by heretics need only to be confirmed by the invocation of the Holy Spirit, with imposition of hands. *Tit.* 36. The ceremony of the chrism which follows baptism may only be performed by the bishop.

Book V. Concerning Marriages and other matters. Tit. 15 contains several statutes against vain observances, such as auguries, auspices, dreams, incantations, &c.

Book VI. (De generalibus Regulis Clericorum, &c.) contains nothing remarkable. *Tit.* 1. Docendus est populus, non sequendus.

Book VII. (De Honestate et Negotiis Principum) entirely concerns secular matters.

Book VIII. (De Deo et de iis quæ sunt credenda de eo) contains the condemnation of several heresies, and the affirmation of many truths, but inculcates no peculiar article of faith.

Book IX. (De Abdicatione Hæreticorum,) declares: *Tit.* 1, that the very blessing of a heretic is a curse to him that receives it; that no one may pray in their society; nor feast in common with them; nor marry them; with other similar enactments.

Book X. (De Idololatria) contains nothing new or very important.

Till nearly the end of the sixth century, Spain was overrun by the heresies of Priscillian and Arius, and its ecclesiastical exertions were paralyzed by the differences thus occasioned. The age which followed was distinguished by a series of Councils and much useful legislation ; which was again arrested, in the beginning of the succeeding century, by the Mahometan conquest. As late, at least, as the year 800, there is every reason to believe that the Church of Spain acknowledged no dependence on that of Rome, but rather sought the sources of its polity in Africa. (Concil. Toled. II. Can. 5.) We observe in both the same jealousy of any foreign interference. A Council of Milevi in Africa (in 416) permitted a clerk, in dispute with his bishop, to bring the matter before the neighbouring bishops, and even before an African Council ; but it expressly prohibited any appeal beyond Africa. So the Ninth Council of Toledo (in 655) declared, that appeals should lie from the bishop to the metropolitan, from the metropolitan to the hearing of the king—but that that should be final. In like manner the 15th of Toledo, in dealing with the heresy of the Monothelites, disclaims in strong expressions any subserviency to the Roman See. From some of the Canons cited in the preceding pages, we learn at least one point of difference—that the celibacy of the clergy, so strenuously enjoined by Rome, was not yet a part of the discipline of the Spanish Church.

Again : in the year 623, the Fourth Council of Toledo ordained one uniform order in all the churches; which led to the universal establishment of the Gothic or Mosarabic Liturgy.* This differed in some essential respects from the Roman or Gregorian. And the first mass, according to the latter form, was celebrated in Arragon, in the Monastery of San Juan de la Pena, on the 21st of March, 1071 ; and in Castille, in the Grand Church of Toledo, on October 25, 1086. And Gregory VII., who had been the instrument of bringing about this change, commemorates it as "the deliverance of Spain from the illusion of the Toledan superstition." The circumstance has been mentioned in the 16th Chapter; presently the whole kingdom acknowledged the authority of Rome ; and in 1204, Pedro II. of Arragon went to Rome to receive his crown from Innocent III., did homage to him, and engaged to pay an annual tribute as a mark of fealty.

Soon afterwards, when the Albigenses were persecuted in France, they fled in great numbers into the North of Spain. Thither they were followed by the Dominicans ; who presently multiplied in every part of the country, and secured to the Apostolical See its spiritual conquest.

* Also called the Isidorian or Ildefonsian—from the two great Archbishops of Seville who corrected it. See Dr. M'Crie's excellent History of the Reformation in Spain.

END OF THE SECOND VOLUME.

LONDON :
Printed by WILLIAM CLOWES and SONS,
Stamford Street.

14